D1446888

THE EARLY AMERICAN NOVEL

The Early American Novel

BY HENRI PETTER

OHIO STATE UNIVERSITY PRESS

Contents

TO MY WIFE

Preface

THIS is a descriptive and critical survey of the American novel up to the year 1820. The achievements of the major American novelists of our century sent me back to reading their immediate and more remote forerunners. I then discovered how unevenly the work of Cooper's predecessors had been studied and made accessible to us. There has been no comprehensive study of the period in question since Lillie Deming Loshe's *The Early American Novel* (1907). Individual writers have been dealt with—some of them repeatedly—in full-length studies and doctoral dissertations, and many varied aspects have received attention in dissertations and contributions to scholarly journals. Histories of American fiction have devoted to the beginnings of the novel the limited number of pages that could be spared in an extensive survey, and the student gratefully turns to the opening chapters of Quinn, Cowie, Van Doren, Wagenknecht, to mention only a few names. Among scholars who have treated the subject at some length within the specific context of their work, Herbert Ross Brown, Teut Riese, and Terence Martin should particularly be mentioned.

Many findings in Dr. Loshe's doctoral dissertation at Columbia University are sound and stand in no need of correction. But we do know more today about the early American novel than was known at the beginning of this century; the results of research done in the past sixty years have been incorporated in the present study. Some of the data, such as the synopses of the novels discussed, may make this survey useful as a handbook. Dr. Loshe's book covered the years from 1789 to 1830; mine ends earlier but includes some works of fiction written before

1789, among them three novels published (or prepared for publication) in London. *The Power of Sympathy* (1789) must still be considered the first American novel written by an American author and published in the United States, but perhaps *Adventures of Alonso* (1775) and *Mr. Penrose: The Journal of Penrose, Seaman* (completed ca. 1780), and certainly *Adventures of Jonathan Corncob* (1787), have a claim to be considered in a study of the early American novel. So do the novels of Helena Wells as well as Imlay's *The Emigrants.* Nor is there any reason why we should depart from the custom of including Mrs. Rowson, and John Davis deserves at least a passing mention.

I have thought it advisable to cut off the last decade treated by Dr. Loshe. It seems to me that the more sophisticated climate of the first decade of the Cooper era is more profitably considered as a new beginning. Whereas in each of the three decades preceding the year 1821 thirty-odd works of fiction appeared in America, more than four times that number were published from 1821 to 1830. Magazine fiction is not studied here, though it might confirm the findings gained by the examination of the novels; it must be remembered, however, that many of the magazine stories were translated or adapted from European sources, usually without acknowledgment. On the other hand, certain essay-series which first appeared in newspapers and periodicals and were later published in book form are treated in their appropriate contexts. Proceeding on the assumption that the American novelists were following current English and Continental models, I have made no further attempt to define the kind and extent of individual influences on authors or single works. The comparative approach might be rewarding both with avowed and unconscious imitations; but it would have overburdened the expository structure of this study while remaining precariously conjectural more often than not.

It is hoped that the reader will be led to see, beyond the information on the nature of the contemporary novel, some characteristic features of the age. A number of current assumptions and concerns may emerge, more particularly with respect to the possibilities and limitations of fiction and the genre of the novel, its moral soundness and its role within literary and national traditions. I might echo the observations made by a number of scholars over the past thirty years or so: Stanley T. Williams and William L. Hedges, for example, in their studies of Irving; or Richard Beale Davis in his *Intellectual Life in Jefferson's Virginia,* from whose introduction I may quote three sentences easily applicable, *mutatis mutandis,* to the present study: "This work is in large part an assemblage of evidence. It includes minutiæ and details, many of them of little intrinsic separate value, which add up to what it is hoped is at least the broad outline of an image. The majority of the belletristic writers here discussed, for example, have left no great impression in the history of American literature. But they do offer through their work clues to an understanding of Virginia interests and tastes in a significant period, and a few of them deserve more attention generally than they have received."

Parts I and II of this study take stock of the views, materials, and resources of the readers, novelists, and critics; Parts III and IV focus on the novels that grew out of these views, materials, and resources. In trying to recapture the expectations and misgivings of the people concerned with and about fiction, evaluation has been made only incidentally. I have followed the example of J. M. S. Tompkins, who stated in the preface to *The Popular Novel in England, 1770-1800* that she had treated this fiction "with perhaps over-scrupulous gentleness," since nothing was to be gained from exposing it "on the gibbet of scorn." In the dedicatory epistle prefixed to *The Polite Marriage* Dr. Tompkins also anticipated some of the results of the present study of minor American authors, when she said that such authors need not have any clear conception of "the nature of literature or of literary forms. They have taste, not passion. They accept the literary fashions of their day and shape their materials contentedly to them; or they please themselves by mild reforms and small adjustments."

Most of the early American novelists, who usually wrote only one or two books, tamely and unimaginatively employed just such themes and materials as will be isolated in the first chapters of this survey, but in a few cases the conventional brick and mortar of the novel-builder were used with a certain degree of independent artistic consciousness. No doubt the study of the more skillful writers is easier to justify and much more attractive than that of the mass of imitators. I definitely prefer Henry James to Mrs. Rowson, and Faulkner to Brockden Brown, but I do not wish to sound too apologetic about the time and effort devoted to the poor ancestors of the masters. Nearly a century ago Edwin P. Whipple stressed, in his contribution to *The First Century of the Republic* and with reference to Brockden Brown, that no writer should be the victim of "the bitterest irony of criticism, that, namely, of not being considered worth the trouble of a critical examination." More recently, an exchange of views in *American Literature* (1961) about Emmons's *The Fredoniad* raised this question again. We must attempt a balanced view of the individual significance and the historical importance of any work of literature: neither must be emphasized at the cost of the other. It is undesirable—and indeed, impossible—to conceal the fact that most of the early American novels are failures; but it is possible to say in what sense and for what reason they failed. By answering such questions, we pay a tribute to the pioneer efforts made to keep the novel alive, and prepare the ground for an adequate appreciation of the comparative achievements among the contemporary and the later fiction in America.

Since the fiction treated here must have its significance supported by a close interrelation with its background, footnotes and references have multiplied rather formidably. To forestall a further proliferation, I have included in the text volume and page references to the novels and tales individually discussed. I have also preferred not to burden the quotations with too frequent a use of "[sic]"; the vagaries of eighteenth-century spelling and typesetting are not too distracting, nor is the erratic punctuation an obstacle to the understanding of the texts.

It is a pleasant task to acknowledge here the generous grants of the *Schweizerische Nationalfonds* and of the *Janggen-Pöhn-Stiftung* in St. Gallen, Switzerland, which enabled me to spend nearly one full year in the United States in 1961-62. I collected my source material chiefly at the Houghton and Widener Libraries

of the Harvard College Library and at the seat of the American
Antiquarian Society in Worcester, Massachusetts. I also had
access to rare books at the Boston Athenaeum and the Boston
and New York public libraries. I have obtained microfilmed
material from the Alderman Library (University of Virginia,
Charlottesville); the Beinecke Library (Yale University, New
Haven, Conn.); the Howard Tilton Memorial Library (Tulane
University, New Orleans, La.); and the Library of Congress
(Washington, D.C.). Previous to my stay in America and since
my return to Switzerland, the services of the Stadtbibliothek Biel
and the Zentralbibliothek Zürich have helped me in many ways.
The staffs of all these libraries invariably proved friendly and
resourceful, and I gladly take this opportunity to extend my
warmest thanks to them. I am also very grateful to Mrs. Jeannette
Zehnder, Miss Karin Wogatzky, and Mr. Walter Naef for their
painstaking proofreading and indexing, and to Mrs. Susan Col-
lins, of the Ohio State University Press, for her efficient and
sympathetic editorial advice.

  Professor Heinrich Straumann, of the University of Zürich,
Switzerland, who was the first to hear of and respond to my
interest in early American fiction, has lent a patient ear to my
discussions of the topic ever since. Other colleagues and students
of mine, too, have had to listen to them; and I can only express
my gratitude for their courtesy, from which I have derived much
encouragement and stimulation.

H. P.

July, 1970

List of Abbreviations

The following abbreviations have been adopted in the footnotes and bibliography for frequently cited periodicals.

AL	*American Literature*
AQ	*American Quarterly*
CAAS Bul.	*Canadian Association of American Studies Bulletin*
CE	*College English*
EALN	*Early American Literature Newsletter*
HLB	*Harvard Library Bulletin*
HLQ	*Huntington Library Quarterly*
JA	*Jahrbuch für Amerikastudien*
JEGP	*Journal of English and Germanic Philology*
MLN	*Modern Language Notes*
MLQ	*Modern Language Quarterly*
NAR	*North-American Review*
NEQ	*New England Quarterly*
PAAS	*Proceedings of the American Antiquarian Society*
PBSA	*Papers of the Bibliographical Society of America*
PMHB	*Pennsylvania Magazine of History and Biography*
PMLA	*Publications of the Modern Language Association of America*
SP	*Studies in Philology*
SR	*Sewanee Review*
Trans. Wisc.	*Transactions of the Wisconsin Academy of Science, Arts and Letters*
VMHB	*Virginia Magazine of History and Biography*
WMQ	*William and Mary Quarterly*

I. THE MORAL AND CRITICAL DISCUSSION

THE THREE DECADES ending in 1820 are not considered a distinguished epoch either in the history of American writing or, more specifically, in the development of the American novel.[1] Indeed, the student of the period is likely to be struck not with many individual achievements but with widespread mediocrity. In the contemporary judgments on the writers of the age he will find little praise that is reasonably well deserved and generally agreed to; but he will frequently hear complaints, and among them two which turn up regularly in prefaces, in book reviews, and in essays. Neither went uncontradicted; yet in spite of the counterarguments, the complaints did not cease, and to us they still express a feeling of dissatisfaction.

One of them concerns the lack of distinction, originality, and productivity which many thought characteristic of the American literature[2] of the day. The other is the criticism aimed at the contemporary novel generally, partly because of the faults attributed to the genre and partly because of the lack of skill or the idiosyncrasies of the individual writers. The evidence of this mood of dissatisfaction is considered in the first part of the present study, for it provides a relevant background to the manner in which writers of fiction in the United States went about creating and defending their work in those days; the views referred to are often those of writers who at one time or another wrote fiction themselves. Not all the comments are American: usually the severe tone of English observations and the apologetic remarks made by Americans reveal an equal dissatisfaction with the literature of the United States.[3] This chapter deals with views on that literature; the second offers a sample of a novel of the age; and the third discusses then current opinions about that form of fiction.

[3]

Chapter One

AMERICAN LITERATURE?

I N 1789 *The Power of Sympathy* was proudly announced as the first American novel. It was about that time that the fictitious Updike Underhill, the hero of Royall Tyler's *The Algerine Captive* (1797), left America. When he came back after seven years, he noticed at least one remarkable change:

> When he left New England, books of Biography, Travels, Novels, and modern Romances, were confined to our sea ports; or, if known in the country, were read only in the families of Clergymen, Physicians, and Lawyers: while certain funeral discourses, the last words and dying speeches of Bryan Shaheen, and Levi Ames, and some dreary somebody's Day of Doom, formed the most diverting part of the farmer's library. On his return from captivity, he found a surprising alteration in the public taste. In our inland towns of consequence, social libraries had been instituted, composed of books, designed to amuse rather than to instruct; and country booksellers, fostering the new born taste of the people, had filled the whole land with modern Travels, and Novels almost as incredible.[4]

This development, Underhill said, was of course "pleasing to the man of letters" but not entirely satisfactory: the American authors did not profit from it. Underhill was right. Had *The Power of Sympathy,* for example, been the herald of a large crop of American novels? Apparently not. In fact, in 1820, more than twenty years after the publication of *The Algerine Captive,* a notorious verdict did not even acknowledge the existence of any American work of fiction. The judgment was that of a British commentator, Sydney Smith, writing in the *Edinburgh Review.* His sweeping attack on chauvinistic estimates by Americans of their literary achievements was adequately summed up in the famous words, "In the four quarters of the world, who reads an American book? or goes to an American

play?"[5]   A slightly earlier list of deprecatory remarks about
American literature concluded: "Prairies, steam-boats, grist-mills,
are their natural objects for centuries to come.   Then, when
they have got to the Pacific Ocean—epic poems, plays, pleasures
of memory, and all the elegant gratifications of an antient people
who have tamed the wild earth, and set down to amuse themselves.—This is the natural march of human affairs."[6] Far from
being an ancient nation, the readers were given to understand,
the Americans were still immature—only four decades old, as
compared to the centuries of other peoples.   Nor could they be
expected to grow in literary stature, it was generally assumed,
as long as practical concerns were predominant and urgent with
them and their life remained "a round of practical duties."[7] This
phrase ends an enumeration of factors that were thought to slow
down the development of American writing.   There were many
inquiries into the puzzling problem of the "literary delinquency"[8]
of America.   The British-American observer John Bristed presented a comprehensive account of the question in 1818.   Referring to the United States, he spoke of "the infancy of its national
independence" and concurred with others in the opinion that
the American was simply too busy to devote much time and
application to literature.   First, he had to find a way of earning
a livelihood; and there obviously were easier ways than the
pursuit of literature to keep body and soul together, especially
in a land of opportunities where "the means of subsistence are
so abundant and so easy of attainment, and the sources of
personal revenue so numerous, that nearly all the active talent
in the nation is employed in prosecuting some commercial, or
agricultural, or professional pursuit, instead of being devoted
to the quieter and less lucrative labours of literature."[9] Second,
for those who had any ambitions left after their struggle for existence, there were various possibilities more immediately rewarding than literature.   Samuel Lorenzo Knapp named one of the
callings that deprived the country of the poets it should have:
". . . The popular form of our government—by taking out of the
market a large proportion of the best talents—has had its effect
in prolonging our literary minority."[10] The point had already
been made by George Watterston, who spoke of "the general

[5]

privilege of politics."[11] The elder Dana said much the same thing when he emphasized how much Brockden Brown's decision to become a writer was at odds with the common active interest in the "hot and noisy contest of party politics."[12]

Politics was, or could be, an honorable career; the "universal rage for riches"[13] which passed for typically American seemed less commendable. If a man "scarcely hesitates, whether to prefer a habitation on the fertile banks of the Mississippi, to a more elevated seat on Parnassus,"[14] this is sensible and appears harmless enough. But what is one to think of the "business-doing, money-making"[15] American, absorbed by wage-earning, who lets his intellectual potential be "forced into some professional refrigeratory, where it undergoes the process of condensation, and is then turned out for ordinary use, as a common preparation of the shops?"[16] It was argued that some of the best talents of America were wasted simply because the political and professional careers promised quick returns, whereas that of the writer definitely did not; therefore, America had no writers.

Evidently the situation was not quite so simple as that, and there were other elements to be considered. If there were to be writers and material rewards for them, there had to be a reading public as well: "Authors will, in fact, be always found, and books be written, where there is a pecuniary recompence for authors, and a ready sale for books. . . ." Engrossed with pursuing his career or amassing wealth, the American apparently not only left his literary gifts untended but also neglected the attempts of fellow countrymen braver than himself. This attitude in turn raised a further obstacle to the spread of American literature: it was a very difficult undertaking indeed for the writer to find a publisher willing to issue his books.

When the American student has completed a laborious work, he carries it to the bookseller, and offers it for sale. . . . But the offer is very properly and prudently rejected by the bookseller, for, says he, here have I a choice of books from England, the popularity and sale of which is fixed and certain, and which will cost me nothing but the mere expences of the publication; whereas, from you I must purchase the privilege of printing

[6]

what I may, after all, be unable to dispose of, and which therefore may saddle me with the double loss of the original price and
the subsequent expences.[17]

The immaturity of the country and the interests of career and
business that interfered with the literary development of America
were held responsible, too, for the unformed taste and the lack
of receptivity noticed by witnesses of the American literary scene,
especially in the second decade of the nineteenth century. The
hope for a spontaneous and rapid growth of an indigenous literature in the independent United States had by then yielded to
anxiety about its retarded development. The blame could be
laid on "what is termed a liberal education"[18] and the failure to
interest the students in "Classical Literature and Belles-Lettres."[19]
Only a small elite knew "the standard works in modern literature,
the ancient classics."[20] To James Kirke Paulding and William
Tudor, who spoke in such terms, it seemed clear that the country
did not lack, as Bristed thought, a social class of wealth and
cultured leisure which could encourage literature and provide
for competition among native writers;[21] what the American
writers and public badly needed was a vigorous sense of the
artistic, and the conviction that the literature of a nation played
an important part in its life. The more talented men followed a
career in politics or business; meanwhile, Knapp complained,
"the field of literature is abandoned to empiricks and pretenders
whose jejune productions gain some notoriety because our
national vanity has nothing better to feed upon."[22] As for the
readers, it could only be their crude taste that made them
applaud worthless books, perhaps of the kind that George Tucker
had in mind when he wrote: "Here you may see novels that had
dropped dead-born from the press revived by the smiles of the
ladies, and fairly besprinkled again with their tears."[23] On the
other hand, the public could also be carried away by a tendency
to faultfinding. This seems to have led Paulding to assert in 1817:
"...The want of a greater number of good models in our literature is not owing so much to a want of genius as to a taste
radically bad. This taste is the product of criticism, which of
late years has almost devoured and superceded every other
species of literature."[24]

[7]

Both Tucker and Paulding were professedly exposing southern foibles; but their statements, and Paulding's especially, were probably meant for the whole country. The overeagerness to criticize harshly, which is blamed by Paulding, may be attributed to a basic lack of assurance in the critics; if so, there is here a connection with a contemporary attempt at explaining such diffidence: "This continued dependence upon England has not only turned us away from the observation of what is well done here, but has begotten a distrust of our own judgment and taste. We hesitate at pronouncing an opinion on what has not received judgment there; and dare not confess where we have been offended or pleased, lest her tribunals of criticism should, by and by, come down upon us and tell us we were wrong."[25]

Dependence upon others was considered worse than merely to ignore or despise the native writers, an attitude common in the days "when to make literature one's main employment was held little better than being a drone."[26] Walter Channing meant to make this clear when he wrote in 1815: "The truth is, we have wanted literary enterprise, and been sadly deficient in genuine intellectual courage.... The literary dependence to which we have been long reconciled, has become so much a part of our character, that the individual who ventures to talk about surmounting it, is thought the wildest of schemers."[27] Yet there had been some who talked "about surmounting it." Mrs. Sarah Wood, for instance, had done so in 1801.[28] In 1810 Watterston obliquely made the same point when he complained that in order to be successful in America, a novel had to use foreign scenes and characters.[29] In 1818 Knapp blamed foreign models for the unsatisfactory development of native literature.[30] In the same year Solyman Brown exhorted the American critics to patriotic courage and fairness, at least toward their fellow citizens; referring to the example of Addison and Dr. Johnson, he wrote:

> Oh, that some other such may rise to save
> A Payne, a Dwight, a Barlow, from the grave!
> Let critics here, from foreign critics learn,
> And proud contempt for proud contempt return;
> Their chosen weapons to their rage oppose,
> And make them love as friends, or fear as foes.

[8]

A critic's fame should not from *this* arise,
To find where fault of foreign author lies;
But home-born Wit should share his honest praise,
And find, in him, the patron of her lays.
To wield the pen in modest Merit's cause,
And justly execute the critic's laws;
Disclose the Patriot in every line,—
Is great, is gen'rous, noble, and divine.
Be this the pride of those, whom Heav'n design'd
To form, instruct, and mould the public mind.[31]

All those champions of the American cause clearly felt that it was England, rather than Europe as a whole, upon which American literature had remained dependent for such a long time. This became increasingly galling to many Americans as the years went by. Whereas in 1797 it was chiefly the fanciful and possibly immoral character of British writings which worried Tyler, George Fowler, in 1810, was indignant about the respect accorded as a matter of course to all British books and its reflection on those written by American authors: "It is truly amusing to listen to the pompous boast of these people, respecting their 'superior illumination,' when, in the most slavish manner, they look up to England for every production, both of amusement and instruction, and seem to think it impossible that an American can write a book. They are freed from the political dominion of Britain, but in respect of literature they are still only her satellite and thence receive all their brightness."[32] Walter Channing, too, pointed out in 1815 that to prolong the dependence on English literature was making things unnecessarily difficult for the native writer; it might even discredit the idea that America could have a literature of its own.[33] As if to confirm his misgivings, the *Edinburgh Review* wrote three years later: "But why should the Americans write books, when a six weeks' passage brings them, in their own tongue, our sense, science, and genius, in bales and hogsheads?"[34]

The uneasy sense among Americans that they were tied to Great Britain by the links of a common language and literary tradition was the more irritating because the decades between 1780 and 1820 were a time of acute sensitivity to any form of

competition between the two countries.[35] If some British judgments on the literary activity of the new nation sounded rather
condescending, Americans were all too inclined to magnify such
"slights."[36] At the same time, they could not think of repudiating
the heritage of English literature as a means to complete their
independence. Nor, accepting the standards of that literature,
could they deny that the British writers of those days were better
than their own.

Furthermore, what the new country inherited or borrowed
from the older one could make up for the lack in America of
features considered essential to a national literature. The
romantic movement then beginning was characterized in America by a reliance on old forms to express what was new.[37] More
specifically, it was held, for example, that the United States was
sociologically so uniform as to lack that variety of materials
which would make for fruitful contrasts and tensions in literary
treatment.[38] But this deficiency, which was thought to handicap
chiefly the development of the novel, weighed less with the men
concerned about the future of American writing than another
consideration. The United States was a country with a history
limited in time and scope, and what history it did have did not
seem suitable literary material. *Blackwood's* stated the contemporary view on America's historical resources only a shade
more discouragingly than others: "...It contains no objects
that carry back the mind to the contemplation of early antiquity;
no mouldering ruins to excite curiosity in the history of past
ages; no memorials, commemorative of glorious deeds, to call
forth patriotic enthusiasm and reverence; it has no traditions and
legends and fables to afford materials for romance and poetry;
no peasantry of original and various costume and character for
the sketches of the pencil and the subjects of song; it has gone
through no period of infancy. . . ."[39] With regard to the recent
past and its figures, Sarah Wood wrote in defense of the French
setting of her novel *Julia*: "It may perhaps be objected, that the
annals of our own country display a vast field for the imagination. . . . But an aversion to introduce living characters, or those
recently dead, rendered Europe a safer, though not a more
agreeable theatre."[40]

It may be indicated to sum up, here, the failings and handicaps with which American literature was afflicted in the opinion of such judges as seriously thought about it at all. The country was too young to have a literature of its own. Its inhabitants were too much preoccupied with questions of survival or with ambitious political careers or with trying to get rich quickly to write themselves or to support the efforts of the few that wrote. They had no standards and no ability to recognize good writing, nor did they understand the value of a national literature. Therefore they accepted what the booksellers offered them; and that, whether good or bad, was mostly of foreign origin. The large majority of the imported and reprinted books, in fact, were by British authors. In spite of the calls for complete independence, America might well remain for some time to come provincially subordinate to Britain. It could no more renounce its literary heritage than it could give up its language, nor could it match the art of Britain's contemporary writers.[41] Small wonder, then, that Dana, looking back in 1827, saw the turn of the century as a time "when a man might look over our wide and busy territory, and see only here and there some self-deluded creature seated, harping, on some weedy knoll, and fancying it the efflorescent mound of all the Muses."[42]

The numerous statements on the poverty of the American literary achievement elicited voices of disagreement in various quarters. But even those very dissenting opinions tended rather to confirm the majority view than to constitute convincing counterarguments, for either they were not based on serious foundations or they represented views qualified in such a way as to prevent any generalized application. Take, for example, the one American writer who was unanimously respected on both sides of the Atlantic, Benjamin Franklin. It was Franklin to whom Noah Webster dedicated his *Dissertations on the English Language*;[43] whom Mrs. Lydia Huntley Sigourney held in high esteem;[44] and to whom the *Edinburgh Review*, after stating that American literature was "all imported," grudgingly allowed some claim to recognition.[45] Nevertheless, it is undoubtedly true that Franklin's fame as a patriot and scientist, and his eminence in "literature," not "belles lettres," qualified him as a great writer.

As for other instances of praise for American authors, we find Dana restricting his to political writers.[46] In listing American models of good writing, Mrs. Sigourney betrayed a Federalist bias.[47] In Benjamin Silliman's eulogy of President Dwight there is evidence of another partiality, not political or patriotic so much as personal and local; this led Silliman to speak very grandiloquently indeed of the reverence to be experienced by future visitors to Dwight's Greenfield Hill.[48] Figures such as Dwight certainly deserved respect, to say the least; in their case admiration was better founded than where a "Philenia" or "Constantia"[49] or the author of *Laura*[50] was made the object of exaggerated praise. The fact that Isaac Mitchell included Miss Warren, the author of *The Gamesters,* among the noteworthy American novelists[51] must be looked upon as just one more instance of respect accorded to undeserving subjects merely because there were no others.

The achievements of individual writers were evidently liable to overestimation. Perhaps less so was the rise of conditions generally favoring the creation and spread of literature. But while the observations made on that count were mildly encouraging, by their very nature they referred to the future rather than the present and to hopes perhaps to be fulfilled rather than to what was accomplished. They could not, therefore, be made into any clear case for actually improved standards in American literature. Significantly, Tyler sounded a note of irony when he wrote about the growing popularity of entertaining literature in 1797. For a number of years William Bentley's diary recorded indications of the spread of books, but nothing beyond that.[52] Paulding's remarks on the stifling nature of criticism implied that there was some response to literature and to judgments passed on literature, but no more. From the East, William Tudor reported simply the general ability to read, describing the various reading matter consumed according to the kinds of readers.[53]

In this climate of only moderate receptivity and promise it remained difficult to subsist as "a man of letters by profession"; and "perseverance in literary labour [was] very rarely witnessed."[54] It was the novelist who stood the best chance of success, yet even the novelist felt that he had to offer certain extra inducements if he wished to improve his prospects. It was clearly not enough to state that his novel provided a useful lesson in entertaining form,[55] for that was, in a way, a mere convention, accepted tongue in cheek by readers and writers. The author who appealed to the patriotic spirit of the public indulged in a necessary piece of sales promotion. Mrs. Wood, for one, did so repeatedly; John Neal dedicated his first novel to his countrywomen; and Samuel Woodworth declared that *The Champions of Freedom* was meant to become "a monument of American patriotism and bravery" that could not fail "being patronised by Americans."[56] A friend of Neal's, reviewing *Keep Cool*, recommended the novel to the public on the ground that it painted native ways: "The most useful lessons of wisdom are those which are derived from the most natural and most common occurrences. The conversations at the family fire-side of an American farmer, may supply as many subjects to the moralist, as those in the drawing-room of a noble lord."[57] The reviewer further stressed Neal's use of American scenery, a device which, according to many, in the future would contribute powerfully to the development of American writing. A brilliant future for American literature was, if not fervently believed in, at least unconsciously taken for granted. In fact, in some places so much was *said* about that future that it is difficult not to suspect a feeling of embarrassment disguised in the prolix expression of hopefulness.

The promise of American literature is obliquely implied, too, in the reasons advanced to account for the poverty of that writing in the late eighteenth and early nineteenth centuries. These explanations seem to say that an improvement must needs follow. Given time, American authors, who cannot help rising above the woeful level of their national literature, will soar to heights comparable to those reached by other writers. In 1804 William Austin introduced an analysis of the state of American writing with the following statement: "Literature cannot be expected, at present, to flourish in the United States, so luxuriantly, as it will in a few years."[58] Hope was the keynote of many other passages on the subject. Bristed was, like Austin, implicitly looking forward to the days when practical concerns would lose some of their urgency, and Americans would then turn their creative energies to fresh fields. No one could have been more thoroughly convinced than Paulding that the literary independence of America, once secured, would produce outstanding results: "The time will assuredly come," he said, "when that same freedom of thought and action which has given such a spur to our genius in other respects, will achieve similar wonders in literature."[59] But not before 1829 did a writer state with any conviction that the necessary liberation of the country's intellectual energies had at last been accomplished.[60] No doubt America's peculiar advantage of being "less liable to be interrupted by revolution and war"[61] would soon make itself felt. At least the proof could be given that there was some truth in the *Port-Folio's* assertion that there were "no physical causes to prevent the American genius from reaching the highest eminence in the arts and sciences." It would no longer be necessary to add cautiously, "In proportion to its opportunities, it has already exhibited as much talent and intellectual energy, as the more highly cultivated genius of Europe."[62]

It is rather remarkable that American optimism managed to keep going in a climate of lamentations about its literature merely on the strength of such promises as were contained in the various passages quoted. To be sure, some more positive credos were also expressed. The most forceful was probably that of Noah Webster, who as early as 1789 praised the American variety of the English language. Judging in the main by his knowledge of conditions in New England, Webster asserted that American English, in practical use among a population that would number a hundred million "within a century and a half," was "the most *pure English* now known in the world," and could thus well dispense with the unreliable and incomplete dictionaries published in London.[63] Voices as confident as Webster's were heard only rarely, but promises of a more general kind could be liberally made. In 1820 the London *New Monthly Magazine* listed a number of elements which seemed to ensure a rewarding development of American literature:

The elements of noble material are certainly at hand. The

division of the country into separate states, and the consequent variety of individual character—the emigrations to the back-settlements—the rencontres with the savage tribes—the collisions between the habits and sentiments of the remoter and more central districts—the multiplicity of religious sects—the developments of the republican character in its progressive stages of refinement—all this, and much more, added to the magnificent aspect of the country, with its gigantic mountains and primeval forests, and wide savannas and majestic rivers, must furnish such stores for romantic, pathetic, comic, and descriptive representations, as it would be vain to look for in the now-exhausted resources of the parent country.[64]

If the reader disregarded the fact that several of the elements named had also, at various times, been thought a handicap rather than a potential advantage to American writing, a list of this kind seemed comprehensive enough to strengthen the American hopes. Moreover, it received support from the recollection of similar ideas expressed by Paulding, Watterston, and others.[65]

Still the glowing pictures of the future could not make the actual accomplishment any more impressive. There can hardly have been many Americans who responded to Paulding's vision of a time when they would take pride in the humble and laborious start of American literature during the first years of the independence of the United States: "It is then that our early specimens will be sought after with avidity, and that those who led the way in the rugged discouraging path will be honoured, as we begin to honour the adventurous spirits who first sought, explored, and cleared this western wilderness."[66] In retrospect, George Tucker, who had witnessed the slow beginnings of some American writers, was inclined to see that period in a mellow light. He wrote about the American literature of the first fifteen years of the nineteenth century:

It assumed now a higher stand, and took a nobler aim. The more gifted of its votaries escaped from the smoky atmosphere of politics for the loftier regions and brighter skies of wit, humor, and fancy. They were no longer content to speak to the *understandings* of their countrymen, but they also addressed themselves to their imaginations, and to their tastes for the refined, the fanciful, the beautiful, and the ludicrous. The American public, for the first time, was presented with original pictures of native manners and scenery, copied from the life, instead of being compelled to look for this species of literary gratification to what was imported from abroad, or what was yet worse, to feeble and servile copies of European productions. Then broke forth somewhat of the same spirit of independence in letters, which thirty years before had showed itself in government.[67]

In so writing, Tucker was obviously influenced by the general recognition of Irving and Cooper after 1820, in the wake of which Brockden Brown, too, enjoyed a renaissance. He was forgetting his earlier observations and projecting back across three decades the growing self-assurance of Americans with regard to their literature in the year of Emerson's *American Scholar*.

1. Charles Angoff is particularly severe toward the American writers of the period; see *A Literary History of the American People* (1931), Preface, Vol. 2 (hereafter cited as Angoff, *A Literary History*). There are sobering short verdicts on the fiction of the day in Grant C. Knight, *The Novel in English* (1931), p. 107; and Jacques Cabau, *La Prairie perdue* (Paris: Eds. du Seuil, 1966), p. 12. Arthur Hobson Quinn's *American Fiction* (1936) (hereafter cited as Quinn, *Fiction*), reaches Cooper on p. 53 of its 725 pages, while Edward Wagenknecht devotes Chapter 1, pp. 1-13, of his *Cavalcade of the American Novel* (1952), 575 pages (hereafter cited as Wagenknecht, *Cavalcade*), to "Charles Brockden Brown and the Pioneers." The fiction in question was poor literature and yet hugely popular, and therefore influential in forming the tastes of the reading public; this has been pointed out by Lyle H. Wright, "A Statistical Survey of American Fiction, 1774-1850," *HLQ* 2(1939): 309-18; and Herbert Ross Brown, *The Sentimental Novel in America, 1789-1860* (1940), p. vii.

2. "Literature" was generally understood in the comprehensive sense of "learning" and "culture"; the modern editors of S. L. Knapp's *Lectures on American Literature* (1829), have appropriately changed the title of the book to *American Cultural History*. For the purposes of this chapter it is accurate enough to consider literature (in the sense of *belles lettres*) covered by the wider meaning then current.

3. Cf. William Ellery Channing on the effect of apologies made on behalf of American literature, "Remarks on National Literature" (1830), in *The Roots of National Culture*, eds. Robert E. Spiller and Harold Blodgett (1949), pp. 726-38, especially p. 730.

4. This passage and some others to which reference is made in the present chapter are included in the excellent collection edited by Robert E. Spiller, *The American Literary Revolution, 1783-1837* (1967) (hereafter cited as Spiller, *Literary Revolution*). For the first part of the Tyler quotation, see the corroboration in Samuel Woodworth, "The Influence of Juvenile Reading," which refers to the early 1790s, in Kendall B. Taft, ed., *Minor Knickerbockers* (1947), p. 62. New England was better equipped than other parts

of the country to diffuse reading matter equally; see the figures for the editions of *Charlotte Temple* between 1794 and 1840, in William Charvat, *Literary Publishing in America, 1790-1850* (1959), p. 32.

5. *Edinburgh Review* 33(1820):79. See Robert E. Spiller's analysis of Smith's opinions about America, "The Verdict of Sydney Smith," *AL* 1 (1929): 3-13. One of Cooper's characters states that the progress of American literature "is really astonishing the four quarters of the world" (*Home as Found*, 1838 [Capricorn Books, 1961], p. 373. See also the contrasting sketch, p. 371, of the American who unreservedly accepts the British judgment of American writings).

6. *Edinburgh Rev.* 31(1818):144.

7. *Blackwood's Magazine* 4(1819):647.

8. *North-American Review* 2(1815):34.

9. *The Resources of the United States of America* (1818), p. 310 (hereafter cited at Bristed, *Resources*).

10. *Extracts from a Journal of Travels in North America* (1818), p. 101 (hereafter cited as Knapp, *Travels*).

11. *Glencarn,* (1810), p. 189.

12. Richard Henry Dana, *Poems and Prose Writings* (1851), 2:327 (hereafter cited as Dana, *Writings*). Dana's remark was written on the occasion of the reissue of Brown's novels (1827).

13. Watterston, *Glencarn*, p. 189; cf. Dana, *Writings*, 2:327.

14. William Austin, *Letters from London* (1804), pp. 97-98 (hereafter cited as Austin, *Letters*).

15. Sarah Hall, *Selections from the Writings of Mrs. Sarah Hall* (1833), p. xxix. The phrase is used in a letter written in 1821, which also states, "literature has no career in America."

16. *Blackwood's* 4(1819):647.

17. *American Register* 1(1807):184, 185. Related ideas were expressed by Philip Freneau, "The Pilgrim, ix" (1782), in *The Prose of Philip Freneau*, ed. Philip M. Marsh (1955), p. 55; Hugh Henry Brackenridge, *Gazette Publications* (1806), pp. 347-48; George Fowler, *The Wandering Philanthropist* (1810), pp. 116-17; Irving, in a letter of August 12, 1819, *Letters of Washington Irving to Henry Brevoort*, ed. George S. Hellman (1918), p. 319. A famous later corroboration of this point as well as many others is that of J. F. Cooper, *Notions of the Americans* (1828), letters 23 and 24; Achille Murat, *Esquisse morale et politique des Etats-Unis de l'Amérique du Nord* (Paris, 1832), p. 379, uses equivalent terms.

18. Knapp, *Travels*, p. 101.

19. James Kirke Paulding, *Letters from the South* (1817), 1:64; cf. Henry C. Knight's unflattering remarks about William and Mary College, *Letters from the South and West* (Boston, 1818), reprinted in *A Mirror for Americans*, Warren S. Tryon, ed. (1952), vol. 2, sec. 18.

20. William Tudor, *Letters from the Eastern States* (1820), p. 122 (hereafter cited as Tudor, *Letters*).

21. Bristed, *Resources*, pp. 310 ff.

22. *Travels*, p. 101. Knapp praised Dennie and his influence through the *Port-Folio* because Dennie set up a firm standard of taste; see *Cultural History*, p. 137.

23. *Letters from Virginia* (1816), p. 213.

24. *Letters from the South*, 1:251. Cf. Charles Jared Ingersoll's phrase, "a

usurpation of hypercriticism is subsisting on the excoriation of literature" (*Inchiquin, the Jesuit's Letters* [1810], p. 97). The preface of Eliza Pope's *Henry and Julietta* (1818), protests against "the severe criticism that frequently flows from the press of our native country, and which falls most heavily upon the productions of American writers" (p. iv).

25. Dana, *Writings*, 2:102 (from Dana's review of Allston's poem, *The Sylphs of the Seasons*, in *NAR* [1817]). In his poem "To a New England Poet," 1823, Freneau complained about the American indifference to the arts, and the passive acceptance of what English fashions sanctioned; he was contemptuous of Washington Irving, who submitted to English practices, literary and social. See *The Last Poems of Philip Freneau*, ed. Lewis Leary (1945), p. 112-13.

26. Dana, *Writings*, 2:327.

27. *NAR* 2(1815):37. A reviewer grumbled that poets like Joseph Brown Ladd, "Croaker," and Ray were neglected while British writers sold well; see William Ray, *Poems* (1821), p. 35. Quantitatively speaking, at least, things were soon to improve; compare the twenty-eight titles written by Americans, out of a total of 1200 titles in Caritat's circulating library in 1804 (see George R. Raddin, *An Early New York Library of Fiction* [1940] [hereafter cited as Raddin, *Library*]), with Goodrich's figures for 1820, 1830, and 1840 (see Taft, *Minor Knickerbockers*, p. xxxvi). On American literary nationalism see Benjamin T. Spencer's informative *The Quest for Nationality* (1957).

28. *Dorval* (1801), p. iii.

29. *Glencarn*, p. 207. Cf. Tucker, *Letters from Virginia*, p. 147. In the novel *Rosa* (1810), there is an American writer who achieves success by publishing his novels under the guise of translations from wellknown English and French authors (chap. 5).

30. *Travels*, p. 100.

31. *An Essay on American Poetry* (1818), pp. 32-33. "Payne" is Robert Treat Paine.

32. *The Wandering Philanthropist*, p. 116. See also James E. Cronin, "Elihu Hubbard Smith and the New York Friendly Club, 1795-1798," *PMLA* 64(1949):471-79; there was a gap between Smith's postulates in his diary and the disappointing reality of the club meetings, at which the American writers were tacitly ignored (p. 478). Smith contributed articles on American poets to an English magazine as early as 1798; see Marcia Edgerton Baily, *A Lesser Hartford Wit, Dr. Elihu Hubbard Smith, 1771-1798* (1928), p. 129.

33. *NAR* 2(November, 1815):35-36. Cooper's account of his literary beginnings, as given in *Letter to His Countrymen* (1834), may be recollected in this context.

34. *Edinburgh Review* 31(1818):144. The items of this list remind us that influence and imitation were not restricted to works of poetry or fiction. Such a treatise as Blair's *Lectures on Rhetoric*, for example, was reprinted in America; see the references to Blair in William Hill Brown, *Ira and Isabella* (1807), title-page, and George Watterston, *Glencarn*, Preface.

35. See, e.g., Tucker, "On American Literature" (1813), in *Essays on Various Subjects* (1822), pp. 41-66, esp. pp. 51-52; *NAR* 1(September, 1815):307-8; Dana, *Writings*, 2:101-2 (the Allston review of 1817). Moreau de Saint-Méry gave his impression of the mixed feelings of the Americans toward the English in *Voyage aux Etats-Unis de l'Amérique, 1793-1798*, ed. Stewart L. Mims (New Haven, Yale UP, 1913), p. 288.

36. See Noah Webster's angry protest, "A Defence of American Letters" (1788), reprinted in E. H. Cady, ed., *Literature of the Early Republic* (1950), pp. 467-73. The publication of *Inchiquin's Letters* (1810) triggered chauvinistic outbursts on either side of the Atlantic; see Chapter 5, note 23. Thomas Moore made himself rather unpopular in America by making of his praise of Dennie an effective denigration of the American literary scene as a whole; see Jay B. Hubbell, ed., *American Life in Literature* (1949), 1:916 n. These aspects of Anglo-American relations are studied in William B. Cairns, *British Criticisms of American Writings, 1783-1833* (1918 and 1922). See also Spencer, *The Quest for Nationality*; H. H. Clark, "Nationalism in American Literature," *University of Toronto Quarterly* 2(1933):492-519; and Charles W. Cole, "Jeremy Belknap: Pioneer Nationalist," *NEQ* 10(1937):743-51."

37. See Rob. E. Spiller, "Critical Standards in the American Romantic Movement," *CE* 8(1947):344-52.

38. See, e.g., Bristed, *Resources*, p. 355, and *NAR* 15(1822):251.

39. *Blackwood's* 4(1819):647; cf. Bristed, *Resources*, p. 355.

40. *Julia* (1800), p. v. See also *NAR* 2(July, 1815):39-40. Echoes of this attitude led, for example, to statements on historical subject matter in John Pendleton Kennedy's preface to his *Horse-Shoe Robinson* (1835), and Simms's "History for the Purposes of Art" (1842-45), an article included in *Views and Reviews in American Literature, History and Fiction* (1845) (edited by C. Hugh Holman [1962]); this collection also contains the illuminating review article "Americanism in Literature." Kennedy's nationalism was more militant in the 1810s; see William S. Osborne, "The 'Swiss Traveller' Essays: Earliest Literary Writings of John Pendleton Kennedy," *AL* 30(1958):228-33.

41. Neal, introducing the "American Writers" papers which he wrote for *Blackwood's* (Sept., 1824), warned against any overpraising of American writing; according to him no national American literature, distinct from English literature, had yet appeared. See *American Writers*, ed. F. L. Pattee (1937), pp. 29-30.

42. Dana, *Writings*, 2:327.

43. Boston, 1789, pp. iv-v.

44. *Moral Pieces in Prose and Verse* (1815), p. 80 (hereafter cited as Sigourney, *Moral Pieces*).

45. *Edinburgh Rev.* 31(1818):144.

46. Dana, *Writings*, 2:327.

47. *Moral Pieces*, p. 80.

48. *A Sketch of the Life and Character of President Dwight* (1817), p. 13. Silliman has this compliment to make: "Never, probably, did a single individual, and especially, one, in an inconsiderable village, both concentrate and diffuse a greater flood of light." The remarks suggest a (relevant) comparison which Silliman and Dwight would have been horrified to hear: with Voltaire at Ferney, spreading his own brand of enlightenment.

49. "Philenia" (Mrs. Sarah Wentworth Morton) was praised in Mrs. Wood's *Julia*, p. 81, and, together with Tyler, in the *Farmer's Museum;* see *The Spirit of the Farmer's Museum*, p. 76. Mrs. Wood expressed even more unqualified praise of "Constantia" (Mrs. Judith Sargent Murray); see *Julia*, pp. 81-82, and *Dorval*, p. 78. A panegyric of "Constantia" forms part of the first chapter of Henry Sherburne's *The Oriental Philanthropist* (1800).

50. See the *Port-Folio*, [3rd] New Ser., 1(1809):68-70, 274-75.

51. *The Asylum* (1811), p. xix. See also this early piece of general praise

for American literature: "...I view the surprising advancement that has been made in literature and politeness, and see the justness of sentiment, the elegance of style, and force of expression, which adorn the manly productions of some American geniuses..." (*The American Bee* [1797], pp. 99-100).

52. *The Diary of William Bentley* (1905), 1:415 (December 7 and 11, 1792); 3:73 and 77 (January 7 and March 2, 1804); 3:166 (June 16, 1805).

53. Tudor, *Letters*, p. 121. Halleck's Fanny "Had skimmed the latest novels, good and bad,/And read the Croakers when they were in fashion;/And Dr. Chalmers' sermons of a Sunday;/And Woodworth's Cabinet, and the new Salmagundi" (*Fanny* [New York, 1819], stanza cxviii).

54. *Port-Folio*, [3d] New Ser., 1(1809):21, and 5(1805):125. The remarks refer to Brockden Brown's career.

55. See, e.g., *Glencarn*, p. 3, and Samuel Relf, *Infidelity* (1797), p. 11.

56. Mrs. Wood. *Julia*, pp. iii, v: *Dorval*, pp. iii, v, 78; *Ferdinand and Elmira* (1804), Publisher's Advertisement; Neal, *Keep Cool* (1817); *The Champions of Freedom*, 2 vols. (New York, 1816), iv, iii.

57. *The Portico* 4(1817):162.

58. Austin, *Letters*, p. 97.

59. *Salmagundi, Second Series* (1819-20), in Spiller, *Literary Revolution*, p. 385.

60. Knapp, *Lectures on American Literature*. In 1829, too, Samuel Kettell's *Specimens of American Poetry* were published. A year earlier George B. Cheever had written in the preface to *The American Common Place Book of Prose* (Boston, 1828): "It is hoped that it may not be found inferior in excellence or interest to any of those compilations which have hitherto embraced only the 'morceaux delicieuse' [sic] of English genius."

61. Samuel Austin, *An Inaugural Address* (Burlington, Vt., 1815), p. 10.

62. *Port-Folio* 1, no. 48(1801):378. Two years before, Dennie, who was to be the first editor of the *Port-Folio*, had rather forcibly expressed different views. See Harold Milton Ellis, *Joseph Dennie and his Circle* (1915), pp. 100-101. "Robert Slender" thought in 1788 that the literary independence of the United States was not likely to be accomplished within 700 years; see *The Prose of Freneau*, p. 95. Cf. Félix de Beaujour's pessimistic prophecy concerning the development of a national literature in America (1814), quoted in Durand Echeverria, *Mirage in the West* (Princeton UP, 1957), p. 251.

63. *Dissertations on the English Language*, pp. 21, 290-92, and cf. Preface, *An American Dictionary of the English Language* (New York, 1828). See also Benjamin Rush's remarks on "Philology" in his plan for a federal university (1788), in L. H. Butterfield, ed., *Letters of Benjamin Rush*, 2 vols. (Princeton UP, 1951), 1:491-95. In *Modern Chivalry* (1792) (edited by Claude M. Newlin) we read that some Americans write better English than the English themselves (1:78).

64. *The New Monthly Magazine and Universal Register* 14(1820):617.

65 Paulding, *Salmagundi, 2d Ser.*, in Spiller, *Literary Revolution*, pp. 384 ff.; Watterston, *Glencarn*, pp. 207-8, and *Letters from Washington* (1818): "The eye of an American is perpetually presented with an outline of wonderful magnificense and grandeur; every thing of nature is here on a vast and expansive scale, the mountains and lakes and rivers and forests appear in all the wild sublimity of nature, and render the mountains, lakes and rivers of Europe, mere pigmies in comparison. While the political and religious freedom they experience, removes all shackles and gives an elasticity, a loftness and

impetus to the mind that cannot but propel it to greatness. Thus operated upon by moral and physical causes, what must be the ultimate destiny of the people of this country and the range and expansion of intellect they will possess?" (pp. 133-34).

66. *Salmagundi, 2d Ser.,* in Spiller, *Literary Revolution,* p. 385.

67. "Discourse on American Literature," Charlottesville Lyceum, December 19, 1837, printed in the *Southern Literary Messenger* 4(1838):81-88, esp. p. 84.

Chapter Two

A NOVELIST'S PRACTICES: MRS. ROWSON

AMERICANS, then, had high ambitions for their national literature and were therefore either too eager to claim distinction for individual works and writers, or more frequently, too prone to despair of seeing American writing rise to the level of English and European literature. Before turning to their concern over the moral problems raised by prose fiction and by the practices of contemporary novelists, it may be useful to have a look at the work of an average writer of the age. For this purpose Mrs. Rowson's fiction has been selected; it may illustrate the characteristic quality of the mass of late eighteenth-century novels and show what were the stock devices employed by their authors in their effort to satisfy their readers' appetites.

The choice of the person of Susanna Haswell Rowson (c.1762-1824) appears propitious for various reasons. Mrs. Rowson herself was a representative of the westward migration of people, ideas, and fashions at the end of the eighteenth century. Born in England of British-born parents, she came to America when still a child and spent some ten years or so in Massachusetts.[1] At the end of this period her father returned to England with his second, American-born wife and his family. But in 1793 Mrs. Rowson settled permanently in America.[2] In the same year she began republishing some of the books that had appeared under her name in London.[3] This reissuing of her works illustrates the usual way in which the Americans were then furnished with fiction: England was their main source, and the American book-sellers were the mediators who either imported British editions or published one of their own that was generally unauthorized.

Mrs. Rowson's tales and sketches, apart from being an individual author's work, are also an index to the fiction then popular in America. Her work can be looked upon as a deliberate collection of the ingredients that went into the making of an average novel designed to be fashionably successful and derived from earlier successes. The patterns of Mrs. Rowson's stories owe much to popular models, just as the manner used in *The Inquisitor* is borrowed from Sterne and the character named Mentoria from Fénelon's widely read *Télémaque*. From *Charlotte* to its sequel, *Charlotte's Daughter,* Mrs. Rowson adopted with more or less discretion and skill the conventional plot elements of contemporary fiction, both English and American.[4] That fiction was largely imitative, harking back to the examples of Richardson, Fielding, Goldsmith, and Sterne. But it was not just in her novels that Mrs. Rowson made use of the situations and characters that the writers of the time so glibly manipulated. *The Inquisitor* and *Mentoria,* which cannot be termed novels, are themselves marked more distinctly by such interchangeable elements than by the manner or plan adopted. Plainly the conventional elements of plot and characterization exercised an irresistible attraction upon a host of minor writers, including Mrs. Rowson, who lacked the imagination and inventiveness needed to inform other material. There is a simple reason why *Charlotte* was so much more successful and still reads better than the rest of Mrs. Rowson's work: in writing that book she was using material which could to some extent be called her own,[5] and she withstood the temptation of elaborating it with borrowed additions. This is a commendable restraint considering how easily available were a large number of predictable events or clichés of behavior.

Two further contributions of Mrs. Rowson are revealing to the student of the novel: her explicit remarks on some aspects of the writing of fiction and her definitions of, and distinction between, two kinds of novels. Her views of the novel as a genre and of some of its practical problems can be briefly outlined.

Mrs. Rowson insisted on the moral purpose prompting her to write. Thus she justified a three-page digression addressed to the "flutterers in the fantastic round of dissipation"[6] by saying: "I confess I have rambled strangely from my story: but what of that? if I have been so lucky as to find the road to happiness, why should I be such a niggard as to omit so good an opportunity of pointing out the way to others."[7] A solemn apostrophe identified Mrs. Rowson's audience: "My dear girls—for to such only am I writing."[8] She felt she could defy any criticism for indulging in novel-writing, since she made it an instrument of conscientious teaching and praised "meek-eyed virtue," "that all may behold her transcendent beauties, and, with a degree of glorious enthusiasm, follow her faithful votaries."[9] She watchfully distributed rewards and punishments, explaining that her heroine Sarah, who suffered in life, would be amply compensated after death, and offering a sort of epitaph on the treacherous Mademoiselle La Rue: "...She died, a striking example that vice, however prosperous in the beginning, in the end leads only to misery and shame."[10] Mrs. Rowson seemed certain, too, that her lessons would be all the more attended to as she related facts; thus she gave a distressful tale of filial disobedience the following conclusion: "The author cannot help here remarking, that as this story is authentic and not the offspring of fancy, she hopes it will make a lasting impression on the minds of her fair readers."[11] Fiction, she said on another occasion, entered only slightly into her books, as a "slight veil" and in the substitution of places and names.[12]

When she named a few lady writers who would "snatch the British novel from oblivion,"[13] she implied that there were not many novels worth reading. Mrs. Rowson consequently deplored the popularity of the novel: in the mass of them that were consumed, the good novels were liable to pass unnoticed, whereas, on the other hand, there was sure to be an audience for

> ...The pen whose baneful influence
> Could to the youthful docile mind convey
> Pernicious precepts, tell loose tales,
> And paint illicit passion in such colours,
> As might mislead the unsuspecting heart,
> And vitiate the young unsettled judgment.[14]

Mrs. Rowson especially regretted the appeal exercised on inexperienced and "volatile"[15] young girls by the romantically colored love stories so much in vogue. A girl who had been led by novel-reading into imagining herself in love made this point when she thought of the affected love letters she had composed:

[24]

Wrote, as they were, at a time when my imagination was so strongly tinctured with the style of the books I had been reading, that I almost involuntarily wrote the very sentiments which I had just embibed with all the enthusiasm of romantic affection. Ah! Celia, those books drew very deceitful pictures of human life, their false colouring had raised my expectations and exalted my ideas of love and friendship, far above any thing I can find in the little circle of acquaintance I have formed. Perhaps those elevated sentiments and actions may be confined to people of an elevated sphere of life, for I never remember meeting with any hero or heroine of a story, but either were at first, or afterwards proved to be persons of rank and fortune.[16]

The statement made above concerning Mrs. Rowson's didactic motive seems to require qualifying, for in her preface to *The Inquisitor* the author asserted that she was writing for fun, and even went so far as to pretend being indifferent about her success: while amusing herself she could not help it if others were not amused.[17] Yet, in a more careful appraisal, this very book is found to be, like *Mentoria*, mainly a didactic appeal, whereas Mrs. Rowson's novels are stories first and lessons last. The novels rely less on the writer's moral commitment than on her sense of narrative control; but *Mentoria* and *The Inquisitor* depend on the didactic continuity underlying and linking up the various episodes that constitute their story content.[18] Though there is this difference in degree, Mrs. Rowson's didactic bent is genuinely at work in all her books. From *Victoria*[19] to *Charlotte's Daughter* she seemed to increase her enjoyment of storytelling by the satisfaction of carrying a lesson to her readers. Significantly the ring which renders the Inquisitor invisible first permits him to witness events and instances of human behavior—that is, it functions as an element in the service of the narrative—and furthermore allows him to use this sort of omniscience to give moral rewards and retributions.[20] We are inclined to believe Mrs. Rowson when she writes about her aim to instruct, which is not the case with many other contemporary writers. Considering her inclination, it is quite possible that she meant all her tales to turn out somewhat like *Mentoria*, with its character sketches and fable-like stories and their moral, but she was carried away while writing them. What ran away with her pen was not an exceptional narrative talent but rather the sheer pervading mass influence of the fashions of novel-writing. Only in *Charlotte* does Mrs. Rowson seem to have hit upon a subject matter particularly appealing to her and, at the same time, congenial to the contemporary conceptions of the novel.

Mentoria is a collection of variations on the theme of filial obedience and dutifulness; the majority of the stories gathered in it are about victims of disobedience to the wishes of parents in matters of love and marriage. In the context of a discussion of novel material the stories are more important and relevant than the book as a whole,[21] for they belong to the moralizing narrative tradition exploited by novelists, who knew only too well what was popular with the middle-class majority of their readers. Something similar can be said of the plot material used in *The Inquisitor;* yet it has a higher degree of independent narrative relevance. If *Mentoria* teaches the necessity of submissive behavior in young people and of respect for their parents' superior experience and wisdom, *The Inquisitor* is an advocate of sensibility or, to speak more specifically, of the practical applications of that sensibility, an advocate of compassion, pity, understanding, toleration, and forgiveness.[22]

To call forth the reader's sensitive reaction, Mrs. Rowson used in *The Inquisitor* three chief narrative means: the motifs of (1) actual or attempted seduction and adultery, (2) social prejudice and oppression, and (3) cupidity.[23] Whether introduced separately or in conjunction, these three motifs form the main pegs upon which the novelists of Mrs. Rowson's day hung their plots. The three motifs of *The Inquisitor* and the central topic of *Mentoria* could conveniently be combined: obedient or disobedient children often had an important role to play in stories of seduction, social prejudice, and cupidity. Mrs. Rowson's novels give several instances in which girls disregard their parents' wishes and become the victims of seducers, and young men and girls brave their parents' wrath by defying the barriers between the noble and the humble, the rich and the poor.[24]

One other point may yet be made by going back to Mrs. Rowson's theorizing about the novel. In *The Inquisitor* an author outlines one of his works of fiction:

It is called 'Annabella'; or 'Suffering Innocence'—my heroine is beautiful, accomplished and rich; an only child, and
surrounded by admirers—she contracts an attachment for a man,
her inferior in point of birth and fortune; but honourable, handsome, &c.—She has a female friend, to whom she relates all that
passes in her breast—her hopes, fears, meetings, partings, &c.—
She is treated hardly by her friends—combats innumerable difficulties in the sentimental way, but at last overcomes them all,
and is made the bride of the man of her heart.[25]

At this point the novelist is ridiculed and offered a "Sketch of a
Modern Novel," which presumably embodies, in ironically exaggerated form, the demands made upon the writer by the tyranny
of fashion:

In the first place, your heroine must fall violently in love with
an all-accomplished youth at a very early age—keep her passion
concealed from her parents or guardians; but bind herself in
her own mind to wed no other than this dear, first conqueror of
her heart—ill-natured, proud, ambitious fathers are very necessary to be introduced—kind, affectionate, amiable mothers. The
superlative beauty and accomplishments of your heroine, or
perhaps the splendor of her fortune, must attract the attention
of a man diametrically opposite in person and disposition to her
first lover—the father must threaten—the mother entreat—and
the lover be very urgent for the completion of his felicity—remember to mix a sufficient quantity of sighs, tears, swooning,
hysterics, and all the moving expressions of heart-rending woe—
her filial duty must triumph over inclination; and she must be
led like a victim to the altar.—
So much for the first part.
The second volume displays her angelic, her exemplary conduct in the character of a wife—the husband must be jealous,
brutal, fond of gaming, keep a mistress, lavish all his fortune on
sharpers and lewd women—the wife pious, obedient and resigned—
Be sure you contrive a duel; and, if convenient, a suicide
might not be amiss—lead your heroine through wonderful trials
—let her have the fortitude of an anchorite; the patience of an
angel—but in the end, send her first husband to the other world,
and unite her to the first possessor of her heart—join a few other
incidents; such as the history of her bosom friend, and a confidant—Manage your plot in such a manner as to have some
surprising discovery made—wind up with two or three marriages; and the superlative felicity of all the 'dramatis personae'.[26]

The two synopses are apparently juxtaposed to reveal that the fashionable modern novel is more complex in plot and relies much more than the "Annabella" type on conventional devices meant to heighten the interest of the story. The first story is about a girl who fashions as best she can an existence according to her legitimate wishes; the second is that of mishaps, coincidences, retarding events, misunderstandings, hardships, and a host of vices opposed to lonely and single-minded virtue. Mrs. Rowson's diagnosis of the average novel of her time is shrewd and to the point; she might have profitably applied it to her own fiction. Her analysis does not probe deeply enough, though. The root of the trouble was that a great many writers who evidently subordinated characterization to plot, were in fact unable to create convincing characters. They would, for example, have found it difficult to conceive an Annabella strong enough to sustain the role assigned to her in Mrs. Rowson's outline.

This does not mean that the novelists were really much better at fashioning plausible plots; but at least they had some variety of materials at hand, thanks to the efforts of their forerunners. Therefore they concentrated on the machinery of the events to be used, giving only little thought to the intimate relation between character and behavior—and ultimately action—in a novel. They found it sufficient to hint at the acknowledged respective attributes of a villain and of a hero or heroine. Instead of imagining human beings derived from their own experience and observation, they resorted to secondhand stereotypes. Consequently, human motives were replaced by literary motifs.

Mrs. Rowson herself usually submitted to the dictates of fashion and followed the line of least resistance, choosing to put her novels together out of the parts provided ready-made for the novelist. Compare *Charlotte*, her best work, to *Trial of the Human Heart* and *Sarah*. The first is a simple and straightforward tale, with some sentimental ballast, about a young girl and her seducer, and is moving in a way because the protagonists achieve a measure of plausibility and consistency.[27] The second has as its heroine a girl whose extreme naïveté is made the cause of, or rather the pretext for, humiliating experiences repeated again and again in constantly changing forms. The last of these books begins with a situation that, even within the limits of eighteenth-century fiction, might have been treated as adequately as the theme of *Charlotte;* but the girl who marries not for love but protection becomes simply another victim of combined wickedness, malevolence, and thoughtless victimizing, just as do many of her long-suffering contemporaries. Both the four-volume *Trials* and the comparatively short *Sarah* depend for their interest chiefly on the cumulation of adverse experiences, with rare intervals of more pleasant meetings and adventures for their heroines. Like Sarah, Meriel Howard is hardly ever in a position to act instead of merely reacting or truly to be herself instead of thinking and existing mainly in terms of flight and sacrifice.[28] She belongs to a tradition of novel-writing whose heroines were just feeble echoes of Richardson's Pamela or Fielding's Amelia, far too retiring and resigned to assume the individual character of an Elizabeth Bennet or even Miss Burney's Evelina. They were in fact not characters but stereotypes, whose few facets could be seen only in stock situations.

The novel as exercised by Mrs. Rowson might be called the novel of victimization. It is a novel that relies for its success on the contrast betweeen the readers' cozy comfort and the heroine's sorrows and insecurity.[29] The reader of the tale of "doleful disasters" and "interesting intricacies"[30] is at home, as it were, enjoying the cheering warmth of the fire, while outside, in the sleet and cold blasts of winter, the heroine is looking for some hovel as a temporary shelter. Whether the reader truly sympathizes with the heroine's plight or not depends not only on the writer's skill but also to a considerable extent upon the reader's familiarity with situations similar to hers—perhaps through his own experience, but more probably because of their current use in fiction. One source of the reader's gratification may well be his resentment at the heroine's humiliations, for such indignation gives him the assurance that he knows right from wrong and stands uncompromisingly on the side of what is right. In this sense the happy endings, though they grant a relief long yearned for, frequently are an anticlimax: confirming the reader's self-righteous verdict, they also put an end to a situation in which he was called upon to take sides.

[29]

Within the group of the novels of victimization, a distinction can be made between the novel of personal struggles and suffering on the one hand and the novel of impersonal vicissitudes on the other. *Charlotte* belongs to the first class; so does its sequel, *Charlotte's Daughter,* though it does not lend itself to classification so easily.[31] The other class includes *The Fille de Chambre, Trials of the Human Heart, Reuben and Rachel,* and *Sarah.* This group may be dealt with collectively, for their chief interest here is the way in which the plot elements are made to function.

The heroines of these books must generally fend for themselves,[32] since they are deprived at a comparatively early age and at critical moments of their life, of whatever protection they relied upon. In *The Fille de Chambre,* Rebecca, living in poverty and with a mother inimical to her, loses first her father and then her benefactress Lady Mary, and finds herself at the mercy of proud Lady Ossiter and her concupiscent husband.[33] Before becoming an orphan the heroine of *Trials* has long been estranged from her parents, and at their death is no longer in possession of her inheritance; later in her life, such assistance as she receives is suddenly discontinued because of her protector's illness.[34] In the case of Rebecca it is a misunderstanding that precipitates a similar crisis.[35] Sarah, motherless at an early age, marries for the very reason that she wants a sheltering home, but finds her husband Darnley to be as improvident as her own father, as well as incorrigibly flighty and irresponsible. During her brother Reuben's absence, Rachel loses her last near relation, her aunt. Entirely destitute, she finds happiness in the love of Hamden only to have it withheld again when circumstances mislead her husband.[36]

Once a Rowson heroine is left without the support of parents or benefactors and the means to keep body and soul together, anything can happen to her.[37] She finds herself, like Rebecca in the Ossiter household, an object of envy and contempt, and therefore humiliated.[38] Inexperienced and naïve, she attributes to others only her own engaging qualities and lays herself open to such cruel deceptions as Meriel suffers through Clara's duplicity.[39] She is often obliged to consort with people like Mrs. Littleton or the Mossops, who are capable only of the basest interpretation of her actions. The faults she is accused of may be assigned to her because of the limited understanding of human nature among her acquaintances; more frequently and sinisterly, she is malignantly slandered, as Meriel and Rebecca are slandered by jealous Hester and wicked Mrs. Varnice. And since the friends and lovers of the late eighteenth-century novels are inclined to be taken in by the slightest appearance of faithlessness and hypocrisy, the effect of such calumny can be catastrophic; witness Kingly and Hamden. The heroine is often made the scapegoat for someone else's misbehavior, such as Lady Winterton's affair with Mr. Savage in *The Fille de Chambre*.[40] She finds help and pity only among those as poor and lonely as herself, like the old woman in Dublin who spends the night on the floor so that the homeless Sarah can sleep in her bed.[41] As often as not the heroine shares other people's misfortunes, as does Rebecca in America. She sacrifices her chances for improvement and gives up her hopes of personal fulfillment in order to undertake the salvation of others; thus Meriel marries Rooksby to please his mother and rescue him from the evil influence of his mistress. She falls seriously ill when she has no money left; or she is thrown into the debtors' prison, without hope of communicating with anyone she knows (except possibly those she has pledged herself not to trouble under any circumstances) or securing the means of release.

Having sunk to the bottom of human misery, the heroine may find some measure of tranquillity in resignation and in the expectation of death; she may depart this life like Sarah, leaving it to a faithful and admiring friend to extol "her angelic, her exemplary conduct."[42] She may, however, fare quite differently. In the preface to *Sarah*, Mrs. Rowson asked, "Who of common reflection but would prefer the death of Sarah, resigned as she was, and upheld by faith and hope, to all the splendors, wealth and honors that were ever heaped upon the heroine in the last pages of a novel?"[43] The answer is that many readers are all in favor of the "splendors, wealth and honors"; this was so when Mrs. Rowson was writing, and she knew it as well as her fellow novelists. Meriel is therefore finally transformed into the Harcourt heiress and marries Frederic Kingly; Rebecca's Sir George turns out to be her still unmarried and loving cousin; and Reuben and Rachel, though showing a republican contempt of titles, do not complain about the fortune they inherit from their English relatives.

The reversal of the heroine's fate is a near miraculous achievement. It depends in the main on (1) the villains running out of luck and being finally unmasked as the deceivers, embezzlers, forgers, and the like (which the reader has known them to be all along); and (2) "some surprising discovery,"[44] such as that of a case of mistaken identity. As the result of the ubiquitous gypsies' having exchanged the babies, it is Rebecca's cousin who is brought up as Sir George Worthy; the real Sir George is found under an oak (and therefore named Oakley) by his own uncle. The proverbial birthmark eventually makes it possible to identify him:

> "...Should he ever be found, he has on his right arm, just below the shoulder, the mark of a mulberry."
> "Saddle my horses—send off all my servants....Rejoice, rejoice, my girl, for upon my soul the young dog had that mark on his arm when I found him sprawling under the oak."[45]

The set of coincidences operating in the case of Sir George is one instance among many of the ways in which the novelists contrived their solutions. To begin with, Sir George's mother agrees to her brother's proposal that their two children, Lady Eleanor and Sir George, should marry. By the time the wedding is being discussed, however, Lady Eleanor finds herself in love with Oakley, and Sir George loves Rebecca. At that critical moment, when the parental planning threatens to cause unhappiness one way or another—through either the children's obedience or disobedience—the convenient discoveries of Oakley's and Sir George's true identity are made. Oakley, being the real Sir George, must marry Lady Eleanor, a necessity that could not be more pleasing to either of them. In addition, Rebecca becomes free to marry "Sir" George without breaking what she considers a promise to her former mistress.

Meriel is as lucky as Rebecca when she is suddenly turned from a miserable orphan into the child of loving and wealthy parents, and then becomes Kingsley's wife after his first wife conveniently dies. No wonder she writes on her wedding day,

"Where! where! is there a human being as superlatively happy as myself? happier they cannot be."[46] In assuming her real parents' name, Meriel is relieved of a particularly distressing burden. Twice when she was living with the Howards (who she thought were her parents), Mr. Howard had come to her bedroom at night, and only with difficulty had the poor girl managed to resist him. Meriel is now no longer haunted by the idea of having been the object of an incestuous passion, "one thought . . . too dreadful, too shocking to human nature, to wear even the face of probability."[47] Yet this horrible idea is mentioned a second time in *Trials*: only a timely revelation prevents Richard Howard from marrying his half-sister.[48] In *Charlotte's Daughter* Lucy's prospects of happiness are shattered when Franklin turns out to be the son of Montraville, whose illegitimate daughter she is. In *Mentoria* there is a similar instance: Marian nearly becomes the mistress of her own father, Major Renfew.[49]

The near-incest, one of the more sensational elements occurring in the fiction of Mrs. Rowson's day, seems to attest the force of fashions in storytelling rather than a writer's didactic dispositions.[50] Another indication of that force is to be seen in the very accumulation of sufferings undergone by the heroines. Miss Loshe was undoubtedly right when she said that the very number of Meriel's vicissitudes made them incredible.[51] Coincidences and retarding elements also belong to the arsenal of devices handed down and copied by the novelists. Though Mrs. Rowson refrained from having her heroine's life saved by the opportune appearance of the stranger who is to become her husband, she contrived, for example, the meeting of Rebecca and Lady Eleanor at the jeweler's. The birthday charity drive leads Lady Eleanor to Rebecca, who has been overlooked by the chaplain in charge, only because the designated recipient of her bounty points the girl out as a more deserving object. Then there are the discoveries made by jealous wives and husbands. Mr. Lacour is found at Meriel's feet, Mr. Penure is seen slipping Rebecca some money, and Jenny's husband enters a room just in time to witness a scene definitely not played for his sake: "She sunk on a seat beside him, her head fell on his shoulder, and they both wept.—What a moment was this for the husband to enter,—he did enter."[52] If the jeweler's story had not been interrupted by the arrival of new customers, Rebecca would have learned that she could honorably apply for help to Sir George, and thus be spared some further worries.[53] Retardation is also achieved through the various narrative digressions in Mrs. Rowson's books. Though these digressions tend to have a more legitimate connection with the main plot than is the case with many other novels, the temptation to make them too long frequently proved irresistible to Mrs. Rowson, and thus the tying together of main plot and subsidiary episodes leaves much to be desired. In *The Fille de Chambre* Uncle Littleton's story is to some extent relevant to the central action, but the one about Jenny has a merely sentimental connection with Rebecca's experiences. The story of Harriet Venables in *Trials* contributes to exposing Rooksby's villainy. The story invented by Clara is taken for a true confession (in spite of some reservations) by Meriel, who has been prone to overestimate fiction. She is to learn at the end of her trials that Clara's tale was entirely fabricated: like the sketches included in *The Inquisitor* but contrary to Mrs. Rowson's intention, Clara's story functions as a burlesque of the novel of victimization, more particularly of Mrs. Rowson's novels and quite specifically of Meriel's own vicissitudes. It might also have served as an example of irresponsible fiction, passing off as truth the mere product of the imagination, which critics of the novel frequently attacked. And, of course, it also shows how easy it was to amalgamate the prefabricated parts of romantic fiction into a narrative of some consistency.

Mrs. Rowson's two epistolary novels *Trials of the Human Heart* and *Sarah* handle the form too clumsily to gain anything from it. The former book is a diary rather than an exchange of letters; significantly, some of the few letters not written by Meriel can be laid before the reader only by being included in one of Meriel's. Occasionally the author tried to make the epistolary form serve the creation of suspense by ending a letter at a critical point; in one case Meriel apologizes because her story must be delayed by other duties, in another she cannot stand recollecting a harrowing experience: ". . . I found myself alone on the wreck, slightly fastened to it by a small cord, that was passed round my waist and tied to a ring on the remaining part of the deck. The terrors which at that moment took possession of my mind, are still too fresh in my memory to suffer me to proceed."[54] The various correspondents of *Trials* hardly ever refer to the same incident from their different points of view, so as to heighten its importance or bring out its diverse meanings. In *Sarah* the different letter-writers are given still less of a chance to offer their own interpretation of some occurrence. Their letters do not convey additional information and become tediously repetitive.

Whatever Mrs. Rowson was trying to do when she wrote *Reuben and Rachel,* the result is not brilliant.[55] Nevertheless the book must be briefly considered here, for it is not *only* a novel of victimization. It deserves notice because of its attempt at including historical and American material. Reuben and Rachel are its heroes, but they appear only at the end of the first volume. Rachel's adventures are very much those of the victimized young lady unable to vindicate herself in the face of the impersonal evils that beset her. Her happiness is restored when she goes to America.[56]

The New World plays an important part in this book of Mrs. Rowson. Much of the first volume describes the settlement of some parts of South and North America. Reuben's adventures take him to Philadelphia first, and later into a campaign against the Indians. When he succeeds in regaining the family fortune, he can use it to establish himself permanently in the New World with his wife, as well as Rachel and her husband. The Indian background used by Mrs. Rowson is in itself almost an innovation in American fiction.[57] Mrs. Bleecker's *History of Maria Kittle* was the only earlier work of fiction that employed Indians. Unlike Mrs. Bleecker, who used some autobiographical material in *Maria Kittle,* Mrs. Rowson had to rely on secondhand knowledge exclusively. She may have acquired it from the "captivities," from which, of course, Mrs. Bleecker also profited.[58] The Pocahontas legend, too, seems to have influenced Mrs. Rowson. Her Indian chapters are insufficiently coordinated with the more usual parts of her novel; they read like an element deliberately introduced to give the story a dash of the uncommon and are not so much part of the narrative as a picturesque feature, rather like the Columbus material in the opening chapters. *Reuben and Rachel* is clearly not a historical novel but a poorly organized book, setting fashionable plots against a sketchy background of historical fact. Yet it may have contributed to awaken a sense of the American past and its various ante-national roots: Italian, Spanish, English; Catholic, Protestant, Quaker; native, colonial, immigrant.

Mrs. Rowson adopted one pattern to begin her novels. *The Fille de Chambre* may serve as an example. It opens with a short dialogue, pathetically intimating the situation of the Littletons;[59] this is followed by some explanation concerning their past, their individual characters, and their mutual relations, after which the story is carried on to its completion in short chapters. The comparative freshness of the story of Rebecca owes much to its incorporating Mrs. Rowson's autobiographical relation of her first voyage across the Atlantic and stay in America, though that passage, too, is tinged with pathetic and moralizing tones. Yet if *The Fille de Chambre* is a better book than either *Trials* or *Sarah,* it cannot compare with *Charlotte;* in its latter part it becomes increasingly flat.

Like the rest of Mrs. Rowson's novels, both *Charlotte* and *Charlotte's Daughter* go back, after an opening scene, to earlier events, and then recount the stories of two young girls, Charlotte and Lucy. Charlotte is made to pay for her own transgression; Lucy, her daughter, suffers as a result of her parents' sin. Since *Charlotte's Daughter* is designated as a sequel to *Charlotte,* it is difficult to ignore either of the novels when speaking of the other. In the moral sense, indeed, they complement each other, but as stories they adopt different plans. *Charlotte* has something tragic about it, whereas *Charlotte's Daughter* begins as a kind of fable, only to have the balance between its three main figures upset by an extraneous element. *Charlotte's Daughter* cannot stand by itself either as a narrative or as a didactic entity, *Charlotte* definitely can—the popularity which it enjoyed is sufficient proof of it.[60]

Unlike Mrs. Rowson's other novels, *Charlotte* is, or just fails to be, a unified entity. This coherence expresses itself in the simplicity of its plot, which is especially striking to the reader who turns to *Charlotte* after reading Mrs. Rowson's other novels. In writing it Mrs. Rowson found herself treating a tale that was moving enough and had just the right attributes to be successfully turned into a novel of victimization and sentiment. She felt no need, however, to introduce into the book and the heroine's life a spectacular variety of events and characters. Charlotte is seduced, Montraville begins to tire of her, and Belcour uses his influence to separate them completely: there is a fair degree of plausibility and consistency both in the way in which the characters act and in the linking up of their actions. Granted that the note of sentiment and pathos is forced, especially in the over-proportioned story of the Temples and in the account of the heroine's final hours,[61] yet thanks to Charlotte and Montraville the novel has more to recommend it than the average fiction of the time. The girl, who is otherwise perfect, commits one serious error, which is accounted for by her lack of experience and proper guidance. She becomes pitiable and at times almost moving as she gradually realizes Montraville's disengagement during the successive stages of his desertion. The concessions which she makes to her passion and her lover begin early, so that she cannot strike us as a "faultless monster"[62] before she falls; nor does she become one in her long-suffering readiness to atone for her error. She retains to the end enough humanity not to tire the reader following the account of her trials. Judged by the standards of the age, Mrs. Rowson was rather reticent in her use of sentimental appeals during much of that account.

Part of our patience with the seduced heroine is due to Mrs. Rowson's treatment of Montraville. Her refusal to paint him as an out-and-out villain does much to encourage in the reader a sane approach to Charlotte. In the case of the ordinary seducer in fiction, the act of seduction is frequently the mere confirmation of his villainous nature; or it starts him for good on a career of crime because he becomes the victim of his own action, unable to free himself of its influence on his character and behavior. But Montraville is shown as a young man temporarily stifling his scruples, the better to obey an impulse dictated by his senses and vanity, yet without losing his conscience and his sensibility.

[37]

He therefore shares many of the sorrows which he causes Charlotte and suffers his own as well in the dilemma of his relations with Julia. This girl is herself a useful figure in the conflict and an index to Montraville's standards. The young officer does not give up Charlotte for an unworthy rival, mean of character and desirable only for her fortune; on the contrary, Julia is a competitor whom Charlotte might have had to acknowledge under any circumstances.

If Mrs. Rowson avoided the cruder temptations of the stereotype in the central couple of *Charlotte,* she was not so fortunate with her two villains. Both Mademoiselle La Rue and Montraville's false friend Belcour perform as all seducers and calculating, immoral females should in the climate of the novel of seduction, yet neither achieves any degree of lifelike credibility. As do other female characters of Mrs. Rowson, Mademoiselle La Rue incurs the author's particular blame for assisting in the corruption of young girls.

The characters of *Charlotte's Daughter,*[63] the heroine included, are fragmentary and sketchy. Franklin in particular suffers from not being a more conspicuous personage than the two orphans with whom Lucy is contrasted. As to Lucy and her companions, they remain remote because of what they were designed to be: three different types of girls facing the same situation at the beginning of their adult life. Lady Mary's fate is that of the heroine of *Female Quixotism,*[64] transposed from the satirical to the tragic, to show the possible serious consequences of immoderate novel-reading. Aura Melville is the lucky one to whom happiness comes as a matter of course—almost, because after all she appears to deserve her happiness by living up to the high principles of the Reverend Mr. Matthews. Lucy is reserved for a fate more cruel than Lady Mary's, since the frustration of her legitimate hopes is caused by no fault of her own. After her separation from Franklin she dedicates herself to making up for her parents' error; the self-denial of her charitable and public-spirited activities is matched by Franklin's death during the wars in Spain, a death worthy of an officer and gentleman.

The best that can be said of Mrs. Rowson's style is that it is generally free of the self-conscious over-writing which many contemporary novelists indulged in. In occasional scenes of dramatic revelations and confrontations, though, she did use pathetic and melodramatic tricks of emphasis, and in some rare instances she introduced touches of the Gothic.[65] Otherwise, she wrote rather straightforwardly. At the same time, her reticence in embellishing her pages appears to be not so much a quality as a defect, inasmuch as it prevented her writing from achieving anything like a recognizable individuality. Take, for example, this description of a heroine: ". . . She is rather below the middle size, and inclined to 'en bon point'; her face is not regularly pretty, but she has a lovely pair of hazel eyes, through which you may read every emotion of her soul. She is fair, a fine glow of health animates her face, and a smile of good humour plays about her mouth; a luxuriant quantity of chestnut hair hangs in ringlets down her neck and shades a forehead that is orna-mented with the most beautiful eye-brows I ever beheld."[66] Some of the elements of the heroine's physical appearance studi-ously stress that she is far from being a great beauty, which is not unoriginal; yet the diction is so much the customary one that the reader must make an effort to realize he is not being intro-duced to another girl of superlative charms. This sort of stylistic conformism is at its most exasperating in the presentation of a villain:

> Perfect master of the art of deception; he conceals under the mask of integrity and honour every vice which can disgrace human nature: With that versatility of temper which makes him appear every thing to every body; with the religious he is grave and solemn; with the gay cheerful and affable, with the splenetic he can rail at the vices and follies of mankind, and with the libertine practice those vices himself: though where it is his inter-est he can appear devout, yet no man ever conceived a more contemptuous opinion of religion, or strove with more diabolical earnestness to corrupt the young and inexperienced heart.[67]

The limited range of Mrs. Rowson's art is also clearly evidenced by a passage like the following description of a landscape:

> It was a charming evening in the beginning of June; the ruddy streaks of the parting sun-beams had given place to sober grey;

the moon with silver crescent shed a feeble light, and the stars, by imperceptible degrees, appeared in the blue expance of heaven, till all was one continued scene of radiant glory. A nightingale perched on a thorn, was tuning her melancholy pipe, and the zephyrs passed gently over a long canal wafting on their wings the distant sound of the tinkling sheep bell, and the rustic shepherd's whistle.[68]

Here are all the hackneyed properties of such a setting, and the appropriate diction, affixing some epithet to almost every noun without even attempting to avoid the threadbare associations of "nightingale" and "melancholy," "crescent" and "silver." Just as obvious are the phrases "the zephyrs passed gently" and "wafting on their wings."

This, then, may be concluded from reading a conventional late eighteenth-century novelist. Plot elements were found readymade and in profusion, and offered a starting point as well as the main substance of the narrative. The novelist tended to prefer stereotypes to characters because they fitted the existing plot elements.[69] Together, the situations and personages, as well as the devices of digression and embellishment, strongly suggested to the writer the structural pattern and fashionable style which could conveniently be adopted. Except in the cases of *Charlotte* and *Reuben and Rachel,* Mrs. Rowson remained strictly within the limits of such novel-writing. In *Charlotte* she managed to infuse into a stock situation an ingredient of personal and moral vitality, giving her tale a degree of human warmth which saved it from the obvious literariness of the rest of her work. In *Reuben and Rachel* she drew attention to historical and Indian material, though her experiment did not result in an improved form of the novel.

1. Mrs. Rowson herself furnished some data concerning her life, but left the year of her birth unmentioned; her introduction to *Trials of the Human Heart* and her obituary of her father contain contradictory information. She was perhaps trying to make herself appear a few years younger than she was, and she may well have been eight years old when she came to America in 1767, like Mariana in *The Inquisitor* (p. 113), whose story is perhaps the story which Susanna Haswell told the Duchess of Devonshire when applying for a post in her household. If she was born in 1759, Mrs. Rowson would have been sixteen in 1775; the heroine of *The Fille de Chambre* is about that age when she experiences difficulties which obviously reflect the Loyalist Has-

wells' troubles in Massachusetts. It may be significant that the novels *Trials* and *Sarah* both start off in the spring of 1775, as if the agitated years then beginning for their heroines were a parallel to the American war years (which in *The Fille de Chambre* end an era of happiness). Incidentally, Charlotte, too, was born in 1759, since she is 15 in the year 1774.

2. To Kendall B. Taft, Mrs. Rowson is "an Englishwoman who spent most of her life in America" (*Minor Knickerbockers*, p. xxxvii n.). A letter of Mrs. Rowson to a former pupil (1808) reveals her divided loyalties and her awareness of the problems of America; see Elias Nason, *A Memoir of Mrs. Susanna Rowson* (Albany, N.Y., 1870), pp. 151-52.

3. The following books by Mrs. Rowson were reprinted and are going to be referred to in the following pages: *The Inquisitor* (1788); *Mentoria* (1791); *Charlotte* (1791), entitled *Charlotte Temple* with the appearance of Matthew Carey's edition of 1797; *The Fille de Chambre* (called *Rebecca, or the Fille de Chambre*) (1792); Mrs. Rowson first published in America *Trials of the Human Heart* (1795) (the last of her books to be published in Philadelphia in their first American editions; later titles bear Boston imprints); *Reuben and Rachel* (1798); and *Sarah* (1813) (serialized in the *Boston Weekly Magazine*, 1802-3). *Charlotte's Daughter* appeared posthumously in 1828. Mrs. Rowson's first novel, *Victoria* (London, 1786), not reissued in the United States, is not considered here; it may have been available to American readers (see R. W. G. Vail, *Susanna Haswell Rowson, the Author of "Charlotte Temple": A Bibliographical Study*. Reprinted from *PAAS* [Worcester, Mass., 1933]).

4. Gothic devices are, however, almost totally absent from her pages.

5. The Colonel Montrésor (*DAB* 13:101-2) who is supposed to have been the model for Montraville was a cousin of Mrs. Rowson. If the events related in *Charlotte* took place in 1774, they happened during Mrs. Rowson's first stay in America, and she may have first heard about them at that time, perhaps through some gossip among the military circles to which both her father and Montrésor belonged.

6. *Charlotte*, 1:46.

7. *Charlotte*, 1:47-48.

8. *Charlotte*, 1:38.

9. *The Fille de Chambre*, p. vi.

10. *Charlotte*, 2:83.

11. *Mentoria*, p. 75. Cf. *The Fille de Chambre*, pp. 155 n., 134 n.

12. *Charlotte*, 1:v-vi.

13. In *Trials of the Human Heart*, 4:74, Mrs. Rowson praises Mrs. Bennet, Miss Sophia Lee, and Miss Burney. The author of *Evelina* is named again, together with Miss More and Mrs. Inchbald, and included among the Muses' favorites, in *The Inquisitor*, p. 89.

14. *Mentoria*, motto on title page. Cf. *The Inquisitor*, p. 139.

15. *Charlotte*, 2:52.

16. *Trials*, 1:118. Cf. the fate of Lady Mary in *Charlotte's Daughter*.

17. *The Inquisitor*, pp. vi, 88.

18. Charles Angoff deplores the didactic restriction imposed on Mrs. Rowson's and other writers' works, "mainly sermons in fiction form addressed to virgins, drunkards, and wife-beaters" (*A Literary History*, 2:315). Terence Martin takes a more positive view of the didactic spirit of Mrs. Rowson's novels, pronouncing it a novelist's method of self-discipline ("The Emergence of the Novel in America. A Study in the Cultural History of an Art Form,"

DA 20:3299-301); his judgment seems fair, especially if we compare Mrs Rowson's work to that of her didactic contemporaries Angoff mentions by name: Miss Warren and Miss Wells.

19. *Victoria.* "A novel. In two volumes. The characters taken from real life, and calculated to improve the morals of the female sex, by impressing them with a just sense of the merits of filial piety."

20. *The Inquisitor*, p. 10.

21. *Mentoria* and *The Inquisitor* are also briefly discussed below, in the context of "Didactic Fiction," Chapter 4.

22. Mrs. Rowson's plea for forgiveness, in particular toward the girl who has been seduced, has been praised by Alexander Cowie, *The Rise of the American Novel* (1948), p. 13 (hereafter cited as Cowie, *Novel*), and Edward Wagenknecht, *Cavalcade,* pp. 4-5. See also Margaret Wyman, "The Rise of the Fallen Woman," *AQ* 3(1951):161-77. It is, however, difficult to see Mrs. Rowson's attitude as that of a satirist, as does Ernest Jackson Hall, *The Satirical Element in the American Novel* (Philadelphia, 1922), p. 63.

23. The two hundred pages of *The Inquisitor* tell a dozen tales with some sort of coherence and conclusiveness (apart from merely anecdotal episodes). In these tales there occur eleven instances of seduction, elopement, and adultery, accomplished in most cases, proposed and prevented *in extremis* in four of them. Cupidity is a motivating factor in seven, social prejudice in five, of these stories.

24. Charlotte acts against the principles taught by her parents, Lady Mary in *Charlotte's Daughter,* against the advice of her former guardian. Charlotte's father refuses the wealthy girl chosen for him by his father (who thereupon marries her himself), preferring love in a cottage with Lucy Eldridge. Hamden in *Reuben and Rachel* marries the heroine secretly: he does not want to lose either the girl or the favor of an aunt who disapproves of marriages with poor girls.

25. *The Inquisitor*, p. 152.

26. *The Inquisitor*, pp. 152-54.

27. In a review of *Charlotte's Daughter* Whittier applied what is more strictly true of *Charlotte* to the whole of Mrs. Rowson's fiction: "She has indeed little to do with the imagination. Her pictures, simple and unadorned as they really are, doubtless appear tame and spiritless to those who are satisfied with nothing which approaches the bounds of probability. But there is a truth—a moral truth in her writings,...a language which appeals to the heart, not in the studied pomp of affectation, but in the simple eloquence of Nature" (*The Uncollected Critical Writings of John Greenleaf Whittier,* ed. E. H. Cady and H. H. Clark [1950], p. 17).

28. The resourcefulness of Meriel Howard and Rebecca Littleton, which is commended by Quinn, *Fiction* (p. 19), is mostly a gratuitous exercise of the girls' spirits, for they depend after all on the intervention of some *deus ex machina* device to achieve happiness. Their resilience is nonetheless striking and exemplary, and Constance Rourke's calling the Rowson novels "feminist" is understandable (*The Roots of American Culture* [1942], p. 79). Although the feminist tendency is discernible in other novels beside Mrs. Rowson's, the personal experience of the author of *Charlotte* may have given her an extra right to speak out.

29. Quinn attributed the vogue of *Charlotte* "to that quality which delights in reading of the misery of others which by contrast makes us satisfied with our own lot" (*Fiction*, p. 15).

[42]

30. *Monthly Anthology and Boston Review* 5(1808):499.

31. *Charlotte's Daughter* has an essentially didactic, contrast-built, structure, within which different elements of the novel of victimization play a part.

32. The novel of victimization is essentially the story of a heroine, for the world as depicted in eighteenth-century fiction is a man's world in which the active roles are assigned to male heroes and villains. Thus Reuben, who nominally should play a part parallel to his twin sister's, starts out with all the advantages of his sex: fending for himself means for him to assert his rights. But a girl like Rachel must first submit to the existing rights: she can discover what her own claims are only because they are restricted on all sides through prerogatives and customs.

33. *The Fille de Chambre,* chaps. 1, 10-12, 17-20.

34. *Trials of the Human Heart,* letters 27, 30.

35. *The Fille de Chambre,* chap. 31.

36. *Reuben and Rachel,* 2:chaps. 6, 14-15.

37. Herbert Ross Brown speaks of Mrs. Rowson's "deft manipulation of the might-have-beens" (*The Sentimental Novel,* p. 173). With Mrs. Rowson and other authors, such might-have-beens result from mere coincidences, or from some villain's evil influence, or the heroine's change of mind (owing, for example, to some fresh moral scruple).

38. The first part of Rebecca's adventures is reminiscent of *Pamela*: the humble heroine is unexpectedly befriended by a lady, then loses her protectress and is humiliated by her proud daughter, who quarrels with her brother when he defends the girl. In *Trials* Clara's faked confession derives inspiration from Pamela's account of her temptation to commit suicide (3:99).

39. Cf. also: "Humane, generous, and credulous in the extreme, she felt that every human being had a claim upon her affection; and willingly allowing that claim to others, she readily believed every profession of friendship made to herself" (*Reuben and Rachel,* 2:230).

40. *The Fille de Chambre,* chap. 30.

41. *Sarah,* letter 30.

42. *The Inquisitor,* p. 153.

43. *Sarah,* p. iii.

44. *The Inquisitor,* p. 153.

45. *The Fille de Chambre,* p. 187.

46. *Trials,* 4:171.

47. *Trials,* 1:66.

48. She is the daughter of Richard's father and the Mrs. Talbot who stayed under the Howards' roof under the guise of a distant relative.

49. "Marian and Lydia, Part V," *Mentoria,* 2:19-27. Since *Mentoria* was written previous to Mrs. Rowson's settling in the United States it is unnecessary to assume that Mrs. Rowson was influenced by the example of *The Power of Sympathy* in her use of the near-incest motif (*DAB* 16:204).

50. Fashion could make its influence felt in two ways: (1) either a popular device was taken over from other writers, or (2) in order to escape using the same elements as a host of fellow novelists, the writer could rack his brain to devise some spectacularly unheard-of feature.

51. *The Early American Novel* (1907), p. 13.

52. *The Fille de Chambre,* p. 95.

53. In *Charlotte's Daughter* the old sergeant's story (chap. 7), if concluded, would not of course have materially altered the fate of Lucy and her half-brother, but it might have spared Montraville his agonizing confession. This, however, would have robbed the story of a didactic climax, too.

54. *Trials*, 3:154. Pity the reader who could not immediately procure volume 4 for the passage occurs at the very end of volume 3!

55. Contrary to most critical estimates of Mrs. Rowson's fiction, the *Boston Weekly Magazine* ranked *Reuben and Rachel* above *Charlotte* (1, no. 13 [1803]: 53; Mrs. Rowson was then editor of the magazine, so the opinion might be her own).

56. Mrs. Rowson seems to have been happiest during the years which she spent in America, both before the Revolution and from 1793 to her death in 1824.

57. Mrs. Rowson has been praised for her handling of the Indian material by Pattee, *The First Century of American Literature* (1935), p. 90, and Cowie, *Novel*, p. 19.

58. As a narrative exercise and popular tradition, the captivities certainly deserve attention. See below, in the chapter entitled "Strands of History."

59. " 'But who knows, my dear father,' cried Rebecca Littleton, laying her hand on that of her father, 'who knows something yet may be done to reward a veteran grown grey in his country's service' " (p. 7).

60. Charles F. Richardson (*American Literature*, 1886-88 [Reprinted ed., New York, 1896], 2:285) and Leslie Fiedler (*Love and Death in the American Novel* [1960], pp. 68-69) have spoken scathingly of *Charlotte*. At least they have taken the book seriously long enough to do so, which Charles Angoff thought only Rowson's nineteenth-century biographer Elias Nason could do. *Charlotte* was, however, taken seriously in another sense, which Angoff readily admits: it was a bestseller, and influenced the reading habits of generations of Americans (*A Literary History*, 2:204-6). Mathew Carey wrote to Mrs. Rowson in 1812: "Charlotte Temple is by far the most popular and in my opinion the most useful novel ever published in this country and probably not inferior to any published in England....It may afford you great gratification to know that the sales of Charlotte Temple exceed those of any of the most celebrated novels that ever appeared in England. I think the number disposed of must far exceed 50'000 copies; and the sale still continues..." (quoted in Earl Bradsher, *Mathew Carey* [1912], p. 50). William Charvat suggested that Carey's publishing of the "misery novel of the *Charlotte Temple* type" prepared a market that responded to Scott and later to Cooper (*Literary Publishing*, p. 24). Leslie Fiedler tries to account for the success of *Charlotte* by making it "the myth or archetype of seduction as adapted to the needs of the American female audience," and its message "a ritual assurance that Good (the simple, the female, the American) triumphs, while Evil (the sophisticated, the male, the European) goes down in defeat"; it is not quite clear why the English girl whose story was written for an English-reading public should have been thus identified in the United States. The latest editors of *Charlotte Temple*, Clara M. and Rudolf Kirk (1964), think that the book "is still interesting to American readers," suggesting that its survival may derive from its "air of truth," Mrs. Rowson's "ardent temperament," or from her training as an actress with an eye on the immediately effective; they have also traced Mrs. Rowson's first use of the *Charlotte* material in a poem of hers, "Maria, Not a Fiction" (Introd., esp. pp. 12, 22, 16 f.).

61. The remark that "the distance impedes rescue and thus facilitates Mrs. Rowson's reaching a lachrymose ending" (R. B. Heilman, *America in English*

Fiction, 1760-1800 [1937], p. 76) must be qualified by remembering the factual source of the story.

62. *Sarah*, p. iii.

63. The manuscript title was, "Lucy Temple, or the Three Orphans. A Sequel to Charlotte Temple."

64. See the following chapter of this study.

65. There is, for example, the following Gothic description in *Reuben and Rachel*: "It was now near midnight. The moon, which had shone so bright on the beginning of the evening, was now enveloped in black clouds. The wind whistled hollow through the branches of the half-naked trees, and the turrets of the old Castle echoed its melancholy notes. A cold rain beat against the casements, that shook in their frames from the violence of the rising tempest, and every thing wore a dreary, sombre appearance" (1:74).

66. *Trials*, 1:13-14.

67. *Trials*, 1:25-26.

68. *The Fille de Chambre*, p. 160.

69. The stock characters and stock situations, of course, implied certain moral standards which the writer could easily choose to emphasize, according to the bent of his nature, or merely his ostensible purpose.

Chapter Three

THE PERNICIOUS NOVELS EXPOSED:
"FEMALE QUIXOTISM"

M RS. TABITHA TENNEY (1762-1837) published in
1801 a novel modeled after *Don Quixote* and meant
to be a warning against romantic fiction: *Female
Quixotism: Exhibited in the Romantic Opinions and Extravagant
Adventures of Dorcasina Sheldon*. Dorcasina has been reading
too many novels ever since she was a young girl; as a result she
has imbibed notions difficult to conciliate with the demands made
on her by a normal existence among people not similarly influenced by novel-reading.[1]

From the outset Mrs. Tenney's heroine is predisposed to
respond to all the dangerous influences that may be conveyed
by fiction. Her romantic turn of mind[2] conditions her attitude
toward novels and, through them, toward sober life. This peculiar receptivity of Dorcasina was of course purposely invented and
exploited by Mrs. Tenney to achieve her didactic aim. It is this
intention of hers, to expose the dangers of novel-reading, that
is first to be considered.[3] Her purpose is very much a reality
throughout the book, however rewarding and enjoyable writing
the burlesque may have turned out to be.[4] Mrs. Tenney's message
may therefore be dissociated from its comic literary form, as
indeed it must have been by the contemporary readers who
welcomed her indictment of the modern novel.[5] Her lustily
exaggerated attack on fiction can easily be corroborated and
supplemented by references to the writings and opinions of
others more directly and sternly hostile to the novel.[6]

Mrs. Tenney dedicated her book "To all Columbian Young
Ladies, who Read Novels and Romances" (1:iii).[7] Her heroine
is, at the beginning of the novel, just such a young lady: the
dedication, and the choice of the heroine, are not accidental or

[46]

mere matters of convention. It was the ladies who were commonly held to constitute the body of novel-readers,[8] and especially the *young* ladies who had leisure and opportunity to read much fiction. Moreover, being young, they were liable to be strongly impressed and possibly lastingly influenced by their reading.[9] Being ladies, they were *per definitionem* romantically inclined, that is, open to suggestions and appeals to the imagination, the fancy, the feelings.[10] Being young ladies, finally, they were thought to respond with particular warmth to the subject of love, so much in the foreground of novels and romances.[11]

Novels and romances were lumped together by Mrs. Tenney, as they were by most opponents of fiction among her contemporaries.[12] There is no need for a detailed discussion of the terms here; it may be stated generally that the criticism of the novel took mainly the form of an attack against the romantic and sensational treatment of the theme of love in the fiction of the day,[13] and that other strictures were subordinate to, and a consequence of, that fundamental objection. Mrs. Tenney's *Female Quixotism* clearly illustrates this attitude of disapproval.

The novels of the day were often declared by their authors to be based on truth.[14] Mrs. Tenney did not miss her opportunity of making fun of the pretense. The story of Dorcasina is "a true picture of real life," "a true uncoloured history" (1:iii); at the same time Mrs. Tenney testified to the authenticity of her tale only by referring to a fictional precedent, the authority of *Don Quixote*. In other words, her book is as little a report from life as the writings of other authors who rely patently on literary models or on pure invention.

Just as Don Quixote set out to realize ideas and ideals fashioned out of the romances he had made himself so thoroughly familiar with, Dorcasina expects to find life a counterpart of the versions of it offered by the novelists. For her head "had been turned by the unrestrained perusal of Novels and Romances" (1:iv),[15] and she is governed by the "Romantic Opinions" so acquired. How has this come about? Handicapped by the romantic inclination already referred to, Dorcasina is also the victim of circumstances beyond her power to control. She early loses her mother and is then brought up by her father in a remote

[47]

Pennsylvania village. Her mother's death is a crucial calamity: "At the age of three years, this child had the misfortune to lose an excellent mother, whose advice would have pointed out to her the plain rational path of life; and prevented her imagination from being filled with the airy delusions and visionary dreams ...with which the indiscreet writers of that fascinating kind of books, denominated Novels, fill the heads of artless young girls, to their great injury, and sometimes to their utter ruin" (1:5).[16] Since Mrs. Tenney was speaking to young ladies and future mothers, her stress on a mother's educational role was an absolute necessity. It is also clear that Mr. Sheldon is found not to have attended to his duties properly.[17] He has failed to make up for the maternal advice Dorcasina did not receive; he should have pointed out to his daughter not just her everyday duties but the part that novels are allowed to play in a girl's life. This specific error of Sheldon is accounted for, though it cannot be excused: a great reader himself, Sheldon reads novels as a relaxation from studying history. When his daughter follows his example, he does not make sure that she observes like himself the relative importance of the departments of instruction and entertainment. Dorcasina is quickly fascinated[18] by novels and, as she later confesses, becomes quite incapable of more serious and informative reading.[19]

Her reading shapes her imagination according to definite patterns that are basic to romantic fiction but, from the point of plain common sense, mere "airy delusions and visionary dreams." Dorcasina's other faults combine with her romantic inclinations to render her particularly vulnerable: she is vain of her appearance and sensibility, and she is stubborn. It is due to her vanity that she likens her position and appeal to that of many heroines of romances (with whom she may well have in common the pathetic attribute of being motherless); her principal vision is that of being swept off her feet by a perfect lover. It is owing to her obstinacy that, when convinced of having met that ideal lover, no reasoning, and not even the evidence of her senses, can make her realize that she may, after all, be terribly wrong.

Having once envisioned herself as a young lady compelling love[20] and merely waiting for the all-accomplished lover to turn

[48]

up, Dorcasina no longer heeds her very real qualities. Yet they are by no means negligible: "She had received from nature a good understanding, a lively fancy, an amiable cheerful temper, and a kind and affectionate heart" (1:6). This is confirmed by Mrs. Stanly, a neighbor and faithful friend, long after Dorcasina has started making a fool of herself by trying to translate her romance-formed notions of love into principles of practicable social behavior: "Miss Sheldon is possessed of an amiable disposition, and an excellent heart; and, on every other subject but one, her understanding is strong, and her judgment good; and in her youth her person was tolerably pleasing" (2:37).

Dorcasina's appearance is pleasing enough, though Mrs. Tenney could not keep from poking fun at the superlative beauties of the conventional novel-heroine:

> Now I suppose it will be expected that, in imitation of sister novel writers (for the ladies of late seem to have almost appropriated this department of writing) I should describe her as distinguished by the elegant form, delicately turned limbs, auburn hair, alabaster skin, heavenly languishing eyes, silken eyelashes, rosy cheeks, aquiline nose, ruby lips, dimpled chin, and azure veins, with which almost all our heroines of romance are indiscriminately decorated. In truth she possessed few of those beauties, in any great degree. She was of a middling stature, a little embonpoint, but neither elegant nor clumsy. Her complexion was rather dark; her skin somewhat rough; and features remarkable neither for beauty nor deformity. Her eyes were grey and full of expression, and her whole countenance rather pleasing than otherwise. In short, she was a middling kind of person, like the greater part of her countrywomen; such as no man would be smitten with at first sight, but such as any man might love upon intimate acquaintance. (1:6-7)

The first part of this passage contains something like Dorcasina's own estimate of herself. But when her first lover comes, he sees her as she is in reality and conforms to the pattern of behavior predicted by Mrs. Tenney—which is to say, too, that he disappoints Dorcasina.

The poor girl feels all the more painfully let down as she has experienced contrasting emotions since she first heard of Lysander's coming. At first she was rather chilled at the businesslike

[49]

way in which their meeting was arranged for by their fathers: "She would, to be sure, have been better pleased, had their acquaintance commenced in a more romantic manner" (1:8). The reader, who does not know what the "more romantic manner" may be, will learn by reading on: he will then see Dorcasina respond most warmly to a handsome stranger playing the flute all by himself in Dorcasina's favorite grove; he will find her moved and interested when discovering in the wood a letter addressed to her by an adorer she has not yet met; and he will see her fall in love at merely hearing that a gentleman has arrived at her father's house, an officer wounded while fighting the Indians and unable to pursue his journey home.

There is, in addition to the initial disappointment just mentioned, another feature about her designated fiancé that is unpleasant to Dorcasina's sensitive nature: she surmises that, coming from Virginia, Lysander must be a slave-holder, and her humanitarian notions revolt at the very idea of the sufferings he must cause and tolerate. The idea of a young girl compassionately suffering with the slaves is not necessarily to be ridiculed; it soon becomes plain that Mrs. Tenney is not criticizing that particular emotional reaction but rather Dorcasina's tendency to sentimentalize all subjects and to take herself too seriously in the role of the sorrowing sympathizer. The consequence of feeling in extremes is naturally a blunting and leveling of the emotions.[21] When a clandestine suitor of Dorcasina is described as looking very much the worse for wear because of a drubbing he has received, the girl's grief is therefore described as follows: "Dorcasina had taken to her bed, with marks of as great sorrow as ever was experienced for the death of a lap-dog, or favourite parrot" (1:67). Dorcasina's maid Betty, a commonsensical creature who knows her lady quite well, is shrewdly aware of the heroine's tendency to play her emotional roles. She quickly transforms Dorcasina's misgivings at the prospect of marrying a withholder of freedom into the anticipation of turning into a giver of freedom herself: why shouldn't she emancipate the slaves, once she has become Lysander's wife?

So it is with high expectations restored that Dorcasina meets Lysander. Her hopes seem about to be fulfilled, for this is what meets her eye: "His person was noble and commanding; his countenance open and liberal; and his address manly and pleasing" (1:8). What with her opinion of her charms, she now fully counts upon love taking its course, a course that she will outline on a later occasion: ". . . The man to whom I unite myself in marriage, must first behold me, and at a glance be transfixed to the heart, and I too sir, must conceive at the same time a violent passion for him. In short, our love must be sudden, ardent, violent, and mutual. Matches made upon this foundation can alone be productive of lasting felicity" (2:66). Events do not conform to this pattern, however. Lysander is formal and respectful but not ardent, and Dorcasina is at first so taken aback that she appears unduly reticent and laconic. Yet all is not lost. Dorcasina regrets her coolness, and in the course of his stay with the Sheldons, Lysander evidently falls in love with the girl. Dorcasina, an obedient daughter who loves her father truly, might now reasonably be expected to accept the offer of a young man who has much to recommend him. She is very eager to have his first letter, in which Lysander is sure to ask for permission to write to her as her accepted suitor. But the letter is another blow to Dorcasina's image-making. It is true to the young man's qualities: "His understanding was rather solid than brilliant, and much improved by education and travel. His ideas of domestic happiness were just and rational; and he judged from what he had observed, that an agreeable matrimonial connexion was much the happiest state in life" (1:8).

Dorcasina, who has been seeing and talking to Lysander for weeks, should by now know what he is like, but she does not because she relies only in part upon her observation and much more on the rules of behavior as taught by the romantic novelists. This reliance explains Dorcasina's reaction to Lysander's letter:

Upon the perusal of this letter, Dorcasina experienced but one sentiment, and that was mortification. She read it over and over again; and was, to the last degree, chagrined at its coldness. She compared it with various letters in her favourite authors; and found it so widely different in style and sentiment, that she abhorred the idea of a connexion with a person who could be the author of it. What added greatly to her disgust was, that

[51]

he said not a word of her personal charms, upon which she so much valued herself. Not even the slightest compliment to her person; nothing of angel or goddess, raptures or flames, in the whole letter. (1:15)

The girl clearly sets great store by the forms of courtship. Conventional clichés, expressions, and ideas are to her the sum of an emotion, and the closer they approximate the precedents of romance, the more genuine she judges them to be. The protestations of love have an absolute value; if those addressed to her are very much below par, that is an offense against love and an indication of inadequacy in her lover. Moreover, Lysander insults her personally by neglecting to flatter her.

The Lysander episode is dealt with in the first two chapters and sixteen pages of *Female Quixotism,* which runs to twenty-six chapters and nearly four hundred pages. The twenty-year-old Dorcasina is there shown renouncing common sense with regard to love and marriage. We are to understand that she could, by marrying Lysander, easily have overcome her passion for novel-reading, though at a later age than most.[22] Instead, she appears to have confirmed her belief in her attractiveness and in her role as a novel-heroine in the walks of ordinary life. Her whole life from now on is governed by reliance on the etiquette and ritual of the romantic novel. The flute-playing Irish adventurer O'Connor, the schoolmaster and practical jokester who calls himself Philander, and the wounded officer Barry successively win her favor, each one merely on the grounds of the circumstances of their first meeting. Other phases of romantic love-making play a part in the deceptions to which Dorcasina submits, among them actions which a sensible girl like Harriet Stanly would easily recognize and consequently reject as morally wrong.[23] The girl "whose head had been turned," however, takes them in her stride, maybe with emotions flattering to her vanity, but with little show of surprise.

One plan for an elopement she almost assents to (1:69); another is carried out but fortunately breaks down (2: chap. 5). Twice carried off by force (1:chap. 17, and 2:chap. 15), she is hardly less thrilled the second time than the first. If she is not ruffled by such intended or actual happenings, no wonder that she considers jealous lovers or an irate rival normal, if somewhat exhilarating, concomitants of a love-suit—particularly when the rival is considerate enough to use the style sanctioned by fashionable novels: "...You shall not go on thus practising your devilish arts, with impunity. Your basilisk glance shall not thus rob every man of his heart, and every woman of her lover or husband. Those bewitching eyes, that cause mischief, wherever they are seen, I will tear them from their orbits" (1:136). To be expected, too, in a lover's career, are misunderstandings and difficulties of all sorts. When Dorcasina is completely taken in by O'Connor, she is all too ready to explain away circumstances unfavorable to him as the result of slander and envy. Nor is it impossible for her to console herself when her father is against the match, however grieved she may be at his attitude: "...Dorcasina retired to her closet; and turning over her favourite authors, she found numerous instances of persecuted lovers, cruel parents, and tyrannical guardians. To find herself precisely in the situation of many sister heroines afforded her more consolation than, in the present juncture, she could have derived from any other source" (1:94). She is blind to the evidence of O'Connor's crooked nature because in novels it is a customary thing to see the hero-lover temporarily suspected of the greatest villainies, only to be spectacularly exonerated in the end. O'Connor's leaving the inn without paying his bill cannot be interpreted by Dorcasina in any other way than as a result of distraction by grief. So obsessed is the heroine with her view of things that even the public whipping of O'Connor, which she is made to witness, does not undeceive her completely. It is only after she has shamefully been ridiculed by the schoolmaster and the barber that she is quite sobered.

Even as an old maid, Dorcasina does not give up the hope of romantic bliss she has been cherishing since her youth. Captain Barry, who was hoping to meet a pretty young girl, recoils at the sight of her; this she construes to be a symptom of bashfulness and thus lays herself open to another victimization. The ignorant John Brown in her household must needs be a gentleman in disguise secretly in love with her because Roderick Random furnished a precedent when serving in Narcissa's house

[53]

as John Brown. Finally, when her friends have her taken to Stanly's farm to keep her out of mischief, she cannot help being pleased at what to her is just another proof of her charms. Her claim of having been abducted by a passionate admirer, however, meets with skepticism among her new acquaintances, for Dorcasina is by now a white-haired, wrinkled, toothless old maid. One of them says, "I thought. . . that the poor lady talked wildly, when she told about her sweet-hearts, and her being carried off for love" (2:171). Everything about Dorcasina's deportment proves that Mrs. Stanly was right: "Dorcasina certainly labours under a species of derangement, which renders her incapable of listening to reason" (2:155).

It is on the assumption that she is insane that the scoundrel Seymore plans to marry her: once in possession of her fortune, he will have her locked up in an asylum (2:chap. 17). His plans are frustrated, and he spitefully tells Dorcasina the truth about herself. His words sink in, and as if by magic, the spell worked by the "fascinating" novels is broken. Dorcasina comes to her senses again, realizing at last what she has so long allowed herself to do, to feel, and to think, and (more cruelly) what she has failed to be and to achieve. She knows now that she has crimes more serious to repent of than occasional cases of disobedience to her father or impatience with well-meaning friends: ". . .Instead of being a matron, rendering a worthy man happy, surrounded by a train of amiable children, educated in virtuous principles, and formed by our mutual cares and examples to virtuous habits, and of promoting and participating the happiness of the social circle, in which we might be placed, I am now, in the midst of the wide world, solitary, neglected, and despised" (2:211).[24] Truly repentant, Dorcasina considers ways of atoning for her wasted life. She can devote part of her time to charitable activities; she can offer her own story as a warning, for there are others that run the same risks she thought she could defy: "My fate is singular; and I sincerely wish it may serve as a beacon to assist others, of similar dispositions, to avoid the rock on which I have been wrecked" (2:210).

One thing, however, Dorcasina is not willing to do: she is not going to give up novel-reading. Why should she? She has learned what she did not know when she first read fiction. Life, fact, and reality which we experience are one thing, but life, fact, and reality as presented in the pages of novels are quite another thing. Knowing this, she can no longer be harmed by novels and romances: "I read them with the same relish, the same enthusiasm as ever; but, instead of expecting to realize scenes and situations so charmingly pourtrayed, I only regret that such unallayed felicity is, in this life, unattainable" (2:212).[25] Mrs. Tenney's contemporaries, who were suspicious of the common novel, perhaps found her oblique way of pointing out a path to a usable fiction rather unsatisfactory. In an age of uncertainty as to the true function and possible misapplication of fiction, they may have preferred direct denunciation to satire.[26] Undoubtedly, however, they understood what Mrs. Tenney's novel demonstrated: that fiction could be put to didactic uses and that a satirical treatment could possibly succeed with some subjects.

1. The distrust of novel-reading is of course just one manifestation of the distrust of imaginative literature. Josiah Quincy, looking back upon his student days at Andover about 1815, remembered that *The Pilgrim's Progress* was the only "work of imagination" that could be read (see Jay B. Hubbell, ed., *American Life in Literature* [1949], 1:221 [hereafter cited as Hubbell, *American Life*]). Novels being so much in the ascendant in the late eighteenth and early nineteenth centuries in America, they were assailed with particular venom.

2. *Female Quixotism,* 1:6 and 2:210. All page references are to the first edition; they will hereafter be included in the text.

3. For a discussion of *Female Quixotism* as a work of fiction rather than a lesson, see below, in the chapter entitled "Fortune's Football."

4. It is plausible that Mrs. Tenney at first did wish to teach a lesson and did not know how enjoyable the writing of Dorcasina's story might be. In this sense she appears related to Mrs. Rowson, in whose work, incidentally, there are a few minor Dorcasinas (Meriel, Lady Mary). It is perhaps significant that Mrs. Tenney's first publication was an anthology, *The Pleasing Instructor,* containing "pieces which...tend either to inform the mind, correct the manners, or to regulate the conduct" and selected with the aim "to blend instruction with rational amusement" (*DAB* 18:374). Other writers who profess to illustrate a moral through an entertaining tale seem, above all, to be apologizing in anticipation of any criticism of their use of fiction and their literary talents. Thus Mrs. Wood had the message of *Julia* spelled out on the title page; and the title page of her *Dorval* pleads for leniency, since her "intention is good, though the performance be deficient." Cf. Mrs. Read, *Monima,* title page and preface.

5. Mary S. Benson mentions a reader who approved of Mrs. Tenney's model *The Female Quixote,* by Charlotte Lennox, because it could teach one

to avoid excessive reading of romances; see *Women in Eighteenth-Century America* (1935), p. 45 (hereafter cited as Benson, *Women*).

6. Two names may be singled out to represent the opponents of the novel. Samuel Miller's chapter "Romances and Novels" in *A Brief Retrospect of the Eighteenth Century* (1803), 2:370-99, accuses fiction of all possible offenses against common sense, morals, and social institutions. Miller judged that less than one novel out of a thousand could be considered *"innocent* and *amusing"* and therefore be allowed to be read (2:395). Timothy Dwight's condemnation of modern fiction, in *Travels in New-England and New-York* (1821-22) (hereafter cited as Dwight, *Travels*), may have been written only a few years after Miller's. In a few pages (1:474-77) Dwight sketched the frustrations of a girl not unlike Dorcasina, stressing in particular the tendency to religious indifference resulting from too much novel-reading. Miller and Dwight both zealously opposed the theater on the grounds of its immoral and irreligious foundations and effects. Their authority may be tacitly assumed to support all the individual criticisms of the novel mentioned in this chapter; many of their views are echoed as late as 1887 in Howells's essay "Pernicious Fiction." For criticism of prose fiction in England, see, e.g., Joyce M. Horner, *The English Women Novelists and their Connection with the Feminist Movement* (1688-1797) (1929-30) (hereafter cited as Horner, *English Women*); and John Tinnon Taylor, *Early Opposition to the English Novel: The Popular Reaction from 1760 to 1830* (1943). Walter Francis Wright, *Sensibility in English Prose Fiction, 1760-1814* (1937), quotes a revealing passage from Charlotte Smith's *Desmond* (p. 77).

7. As exemplified earlier by the "first" American novel, *The Power of Sympathy,* the young ladies of America are addressed as the natural and immediate audience of any American novel-writer, with the additional implication that they must be kept free from the vices that might be spread by foreign authors. In this context a passage from Mrs. Foster's *The Boarding School* is relevant; it is often quoted to belittle the early American fiction, but the speaker being a rather light-headed young thing, the irony of her statement is really aimed at herself and her enjoyment of foreign novels: "They have attained to a far greater degree of refinement in the old world, than we have in the new; and are so perfectly acquainted with the passions, that there is something extremely amusing and interesting in their plots and counter-plots, operating in various ways, till the dear creatures are jumbled into matrimony in the prettiest manner that can be conceived! *We,* in this country, are too much in a state of nature to write good novels yet. An American novel is such a moral, sentimental thing, that it is enough to give any body the vapours to read one" (pp. 156-57).

8. John Neal dedicated his first novel to them (*Keep Cool* [1817]). John Davis spoke of the obvious design of Caritat's library to meet the wishes of his lady readers (*Travels of Four Years and a Half in the USA* [1803], pp. 186-87 n.); cf. also Raddin, *Library,* which studies the 1804 stock offered by Caritat. Paul Kaufman, commenting on English circulating libraries, has questioned the idea of an almost exclusively female clientele ("In Defense of Fair Readers," *A Review of English Literature* 8, no. 2 (1967):68-75.

9. "The free access which many young people have to romances, novels, and plays, has poisoned the mind and corrupted the morals of many a promising youth..." (Enos Hitchcock, *Memoirs of the Bloomsgrove Family* [1790], 2:186-87 [hereafter cited as Hitchcock, *Bloomsgrove Family*]).

10. "Nothing can have a worse effect on the mind of our sex, than the free use of those writings which are the offspring of modern novelists. Their only

te**n**dency is to excite romantic notions..." (Mrs. Bloomsgrove to some girls, Hitchcock, *Bloomsgrove Family*, 2:82).

11. "...The omnipotence of *love* over all obligations and all duties is continually maintained" in the novel, according to Miller (*A Brief Retrospect*, 2:393). Cf. Neal, *Keep Cool*, p. 20.

12. There are occasional attempts at distinguishing between the romance and the novel. Mrs. Foster, Miller, and Isaac Mitchell restrict the former to the Scudéry-type of fiction; they consider it inferior to the novel, in the age of enlightenment, as well as morally harmless. See *The Boarding School*, p. 17; *A Brief Retrospect*, 2:373; *The Asylum*, pp. xi-xii. The *Port-Folio* (2, no. 18[1802]:141-42), humorously establishes a line of descent from the romance to the novel and seriously judges the novel to be too realistic and coarse in some ways.

13. The attack on the novel superimposed itself upon the basic distrust of fancy and fiction, resulting from both Calvinistic and Common Sense School conceptions; see Terence J. Martin, *The Instructed Vision* (1961). Since the sentimental love story relied heavily upon the responses of a romantic imagination, it was sharply censured as a threat to the rule of reason and, in addition, to morals. Mitchell's view was that "in most of our modern novels, seduction forms the prominent feature. . . . The language glows with the 'sorcery of sentiment,' the scenery with meretricious voluptuousness..." (*The Asylum*, pp. xiv-xv); see also the *Port-Folio* 2, no. 14(1802):106, and Alexander Cowie, "John Trumbull Glances at Fiction," *AL* 12(1940):69-73, which examines a very conservative statement of Trumbull (1779). The modern novel is also singled out for reproof by Noah Webster, *A Collection of Essays* (1790), esp. p. 29, and Hitchcock, *Bloomsgrove Family*, 2:82, 88. In a number of instances fiction is simply lumped together with all reading "for mere amusement" (Mrs. Foster, *The Boarding School*, p. 26) and as such frowned upon more or less in earnest; see, e.g., Tyler, *The Algerine Captive*, quoted above (p. 4), and Hitchcock, who opposes the profitable reading of "history, biography, travels, voyages, memoirs" to "romances, novels, and plays" (*The Bloomsgrove Family*, 2:89, 186-87). Cf. also *Polyanthos* 9(1813):72-73.

14. Mitchell prefaced *The Asylum* with the remark, "If any should object to it as a work of fancy, the author informs them that this is not, exclusively, the case,...the principal characters...are still living,...witnesses yet remain" (p. xxiii). In this study 34 titles are included under the heading of "The Love-Story" and 29 under "The Novel of Adventure." Of these, 17 and 20, respectively, state or imply on their title pages and in their prefaces, that they are largely based on fact. Such designations as "novel," "tale," and "romance" occur in 15 and 11 cases, respectively. Only nine out of the 63 titles use both the term "novel" and the guarantee of authenticity: it was obviously held unwise to mix up fact and fiction. The conventional claim of authenticity was sarcastically commented upon by a reviewer of Mrs. Read's *Monima*: "To increase the interest which the writer has endeavoured to excite, the reader is informed that the story is founded on fact. Under this impression we must be careful not to impute the numerous absurdities and improbabilities connected with the tale, to the want of judgment or ingenuity in our fair author ...." (*American Review and Literary Journal* 2, no. 2[1802]:164-65). Another dig at the convention of the true tale is found in William Ray, *The American Tars in Tripolitan Slavery*. Into his autobiographical narrative Ray introduced a story neither wonderful nor English but "very nearly" true (p. 47).

15. "Unrestrained" reflects both upon the quantity and varying quality of novels. The figures and catalogues of booksellers and libraries prove that the

number of novels and novel-readers was considerable. This quantity was deplored explicitly; this is implied in the seriousness of tone and in the frequent
repetition of the warnings against fiction. It can also be read out of the concession made by some novelists that there were indeed objectionable novels, a
concession that would hardly have been made if the genre as such had not been
firmly established. (Naturally such admissions also served as puffs for the
particular novelists' work, saying in effect, "Be sure to read only good novels
such as mine.") The critics of fiction were willing to concede that there were
harmless and even commendable works of fiction, but they insisted that it was
necessary to prevent uncontrolled "free access" to fiction because its addicts
"devoured" it (*Bloomsgrove Family*, 2:186) "promiscuously" (*A Brief Retrospect*, 2:397) and "indiscriminately" (*Boston Weekly Magazine* 1, no.
13[1803]:53. Timothy Flint's statement about the Mississippi region in the
1820's seems to prove that the warnings were ineffectual (quoted in Harvey
Wish, *Society and Thought in Early America* [1962], p. 239).

16. In *Female Quixotism* "indiscreet" refers mainly to Dorcasina's romance-
inspired love code. An association with "Jacobinism, atheism, and illuminatism" (2:202) does not seem too farfetched, since this love code and the new-
fangled notions of "French philosophy" might have the same effects upon
"that much-suffering, and insulted sex, *all* of whom the *morals,* and the
manners, and the *pursuits* of the atheists, and the jacobin-spoilers of the
present day, are incessantly labouring...to turn over, as poor, wretched,
forlorn victims,—to shame, and remorse, and anguish, and tribulation, and
barren sorrow, and irretrievable destitution" (*Monthly Register* 2[1807]:263).
Writers such as Sterne, Godwin, Rousseau, and Goethe were thought to spread
various kinds of "indiscreet" notions: see, e.g., *The Boarding School,* p. 205;
A Brief Retrospect, 2:382; *Port-Folio* 1, no. 17(1801):134; Dwight, *Travels,*
3:21-23; Mrs. Rowson, *The Inquisitor,* 3:172; Mrs. Read, *Monima,* p. 368;
Benjamin Rush, *Essays* (1798), p. 82; *Literary Magazine* 6(1806):451. *Werther*
in particular is connected with the suicides in William Hill Brown, *The
Power of Sympathy* (1789); *The Hapless Orphan* (1793); Relf, *Infidelity;* and
also John Davis, *Letters of Ferdinand and Elizabeth* (New York, 1798). See
O. W. Long, "English and American Imitations of Goethe's *Werter*," *MP*
14(1916):193-213, and *George Ticknor's 'The Sorrows of Young Werter,'* ed.
Frank G. Ryder (1952).

17. "...He who regards the welfare of a child will be as anxious to withhold from him the view of many natural and lively descriptions of vice, as to
keep him from the company of those who are really vicious" (Miller, *A Brief
Retrospect,* 2:396). Samuel Woodworth stated that the reading of *Peregrine
Pickle* at the age of fourteen (about 1798) at once threatened "all the lessons
of morality and religion" he had been taught. ("The Influence of Juvenile
Reading," in Taft, *Minor Knickerbockers,* p. 63.)

18. Cf. the statement of "Betsey Thoughtless": "I have Novels on my toilet,
Novels on the table, Novels on my chimney place, Novels in my chairs, Novels
all over my chamber. I would prefer a new Novel to a new gown, and had
rather lose my dinner than break off from a tender love-scene. In Novels I
find all the nourishment of food, all the refreshment of sleep:—with my Novels
I am most happy; without them I should be miserable" (*Boston Weekly
Magazine* 1, no. 23[1803]:94).

19. According to *The Boarding School* "reading what can yield no instruction" is a waste of time, while novel-reading "dissipates the ideas, relaxes the
mind, and renders it inattentive to the more solid and useful branches of
literature" (pp. 26, 161). Cf. Benjamin Silliman's remarks about novels in

his comments on John Trumbull's *Autobiography,* quoted in Theodore Sizer's edition of that work (New Haven: Yale University Press, 1953), pp. xiii-xiv.

20. Both Mrs. Foster (*The Boarding School,* p. 17) and Dwight (*Travels,* 1:474-77) condemned novel-reading as encouraging vanity. Of the addict he was depicting, Dwight said: "If her imagination is to be trusted, she is to be romantically rich, and romantically happy" (475). Dorcasina is however very much aware that final happiness is attained only after many ups and downs (2:86).

21. Rush, Miller, Dwight, and others distrusted fiction because they thought it liable to direct compassion toward imaginary instead of real objects.

22. "At best novels may be considered as the toys of youth; the rattle boxes of sixteen" (Webster, *A Collection of Essays,* p. 29). Cf. *Monthly Anthology and Boston Review* 5(1808):499. It is not irrelevant to recall that many novel-heroines of the age are about sixteen and get married or seduced at that age. Dorcasina appears retarded, for it is only at eighteen that she feels she must adopt a romance-like name, and changes plain Dorcas to Dorcasina.

23. Mitchell said of novels, "The most important objection to these productions, is their immoral tendency" (*The Asylum,* p. xiii), and Miller pronounced them either "contemptibly frivolous" or "positively seductive and corrupting in their tendency" (*A Brief Retrospect,* 2:393). Cf. *The Boarding School,* p. 17.

24. A novel addict who was cured at an earlier age and could readjust herself to a normal existence is described in William Wirt's *The Old Bachelor,* pp. 24-25.

25. Dorcasina might have agreed with a "lady in Jamaica" who wrote in the *Columbian Magazine:* "I am now sixty-three, yet I can enjoy a good novel, as I never exclude any species of reading that I can comprehend, and which has a moral tendency" (5[1791]:142). Less favorable opinions on novel-reading in the same magazine appeared in the issue of October, 1792 (6:225-26, 262).

26. Perhaps some such regret that *Female Quixotism* could not be taken quite seriously was expressed in the *Monthly Anthology:* "Many of us have doubtless dwelt with great sympathy on the pathetick story of the unfortunate Dorcasina Sheldon, and have been inclined to believe that the ingenious author had almost out-quixoted Don Quixote" (5[1808]:499).

II. USABLE FICTION

MRS. TENNEY'S burlesque of the sentimental novel of her day is an instance of "usable fiction." This term is intended to cover books which combined an unobjectionable subject matter with the guise of fictional reports, correspondences, and narratives, and therefore can be said to have encouraged a more tolerant acceptance of imaginative writing; it is comparatively unimportant whether their authors meant to palm off on fiction addicts what merely looked like fiction or rather to demonstrate the validity and adaptability of the fictional prose narrative as a form. Some writers obviously exploited the popularity of the novel: they gave their didactic theories the air of novel-like tales.[1] A number of books, including partisan and sectional propaganda, are at least by implication expressions of nationalism,[2] and their literary identity is subordinated to their purpose. To various authors the existing forms of satirical prose fiction, classical and modern, whether limited to strictly topical and local issues or suitable for a comprehensive picture of human foibles, provided helpful and widely accepted models; these satirists have been grouped according to the literary precedent which they followed, but also according to their themes.

The writings assembled under the heading of "usable fiction" are studied with three aims in view: (1) to establish their significance and literary character, (2) to illustrate, as a further elaboration of the two preceding chapters, the writers' material resources and technical devices, and (3) to point out certain of the topical issues and views of the age. On the one hand the examples of usable fiction inform us of attitudes and subjects that were controversial or in particular vogue and which may be expected to appear in, or to influence, the work of the novelists. On the other hand, they may themselves profit from the treatment of these subjects in the novels. Thus, for example, opinions on

[63]

the aims of female education or the rights of woman may contribute to our understanding of an individual novelist's conception of his heroine; at the same time, to illustrate such opinions by, say, a young girl's story, a writer is likely to borrow narrative means employed by the novelists or attributes of novel-characters.[3]

Chapter Four

DIDACTIC FICTION

PROTESTING against the abuses of the modern novel, Mrs. Tenney herself employed the form of the novel. She not only found it the weapon best suited to fight the enemy on his own ground, but she probably also counted on the popularity of the genre as a powerful help.[4] She referred to the authority of an instance of useful fiction, *Don Quixote*. Others who also wished to point out that fiction was not without its merits brought forwards the example of the New Testament parables.[5]

1. The Pilgrim's Progress

It is therefore hardly surprising to find a religious allegory among the earliest works of fiction written in America, if indeed it is not the very first: *The History of the Kingdom of Basaruah* (1715), by Joseph Morgan (1671-post 1745).[6] Labored yet consistent, this abstract book makes for reading far more demanding than Bunyan's *The Pilgrim's Progress*. Bunyan's faith and message were based on, and addressed to, common sense and religious feeling, whereas Morgan's book is an intellectual exercise, an exposition of various points of doctrine.[7] Here, in a passage typical of Morgan's allegorical interpretation, the author describes election by predestination among one class of men:

14. As to the County of *Morality,* one of the *Finest* Places in the Wilderness, on this side, from hence his Lordship called some, but not very many; for they living so *near* the Water, would not be perswaded that they had any need to go over; and seeing their Country was so much better then the rest of the Wilderness, and a place where there grew but few wild fruits,

and their County being a Neck in the River, and they seeing some part of the River behind them, *viz.* the Gulph of *Amendment of Life,* they would not be perswaded but that they lived in the Borders of the *Happy Land.*

15. So the Publishers could do no more with these then with those farther off; The Fruits of *Self-Dependence* grew exceeding plenty here, which the people of *Basaruah* love greatly; So they mostly abode here, till Mr. *Maveth* came and carried them to the *Lake,* to a very *bitter Slavery,* yet *not so bitter* as the Slavery of those in the Counties of *Prophaneness, Unjust Dealing,* &c. (p. 140)

The journey allegory, which operates intermittently in *The Kingdom of Basaruah,* has appealed to man's mythological imagination at all times. Undoubtedly the tradition lived on in America in some of the numberless sermons preached there. A related instance of religious testimony, which might conceivably have served as a sermon, is *The Spiritual Voyage* (1819). The full title of this allegory by the Baptist preacher Edmund Botsford (1745-1819) reads, "The Spiritual Voyage, performed in the ship Convert, under the command of Captain Godly-Fear, to the haven of Felicity, on the continent of Glory." The thirty-two pages of Botsford's work are closer to *The Pilgrim's Progress* than *The Kingdom of Basaruah*; the very shortness of the allegory gives it an effect of directness on the whole adequately supported by Botsford's style: "Not long after a fog arose, which soon became so thick that we could scarcely see each other on deck, and when night came on it was dreadful; the darkness was like the Egyptian darkness, it might be felt; we hoped it would soon be over, but it continued many days, and with the best light we could possibly make, we could not see a yard before us: and at the same time a very great heaviness or drowsiness seized the whole crew; which was succeeded by a horror and dread on our spirits, which terrified us to a very great degree."[8]

2. *Mentoria*

It was however not in an age of meditation, congenial to the elaboration and interpretation of religious allegories, that American fiction took its first steps. The secular bent of the eighteenth-century mind, when it was brought to bear on the possible uses of fiction, conceived practical applications, such as the propagation of educational, social, and humanitarian notions.

The Reverend Enos Hitchcock (1744-1803), described as a liberal-minded and public-spirited gentleman,[9] set forth in *Memoirs of the Bloomsgrove Family* (1790) the possibility of grounding the children's education at home. By example and precept parents should teach their children to realize the ideals of behavior which perfectible man may attempt. Hitchcock particularly stressed two aspects: the need for an education appropriate to time and place, with special reference to the United States, now emancipated from Great Britain; and for women, educational opportunities as adequate and liberal as those for men. Hitchcock's argument is that women have been deliberately handicapped and at best "have been taught a graceful deportment, some of the fine arts, and the less useful parts of needle work";[10] insufficient education has made many a woman vulnerable, and her vulnerability has been exploited. As one of them writes to a male correspondent, ". . . Are not your sex, in a great measure, the cause of our frailty; by first denying us the advantages of education, which you take care to appropriate to yourselves; and then flatter and admire us for adventitious powers, and shadowy accomplishments" (2:20).

The ninety-three letters which make up the two volumes of *The Bloomsgrove Family* consist of the direct statement of the elder Bloomsgroves' precepts and, either as confirmation or foil, of illustrating anecdotes.[11] By the end of the book the Bloomsgrove children, Osander and Rozella, have become fit to marry, the young man having escaped, among other dangers, contamination through the bad company he was tempted to keep while at the university.[12] They will continue with their own children what their parents have begun with them. Hitchcock's educational report frequently suffers from repetitiousness and the obviousness of some of its illustrating material. The book displays many of the marks of the fiction of the age. There is, for example, the tendency to mobilize the sensibility, as in a conversation about filial ingratitude, at the end of which "the old

[67]

gentleman dropt a tear" (2:146). There are, too, the affected diction and conventional clichés clearly transposed from poetry into prose, as in the following description: "On a day, when the declining sun had tinged the mountain tops with its milder rays, and reddening skies invited the tuneful choir to serenade the groves, with the faint lays of their evening song; these happy parents were invited, by the serenity that followed the shower, to the gravel walk" (1:91).

A book in many ways similar to Hitchcock's, *The Boarding School; or, Lessons of a Preceptress to her Pupils* (1798), by Mrs. Hannah Webster Foster (1759-1840), sketches how girls equipped with elementary knowledge and some sense of their family membership might be further prepared to fulfill their civilizing roles as well-bred ladies, wives, and mothers. Mrs. Foster wrote, "I trust that our improved countrywomen...are able to convince the world, that the American fair are enlightened, generous, and liberal. The false notions of sexual disparity, in point of understanding and capacity, are justly exploded; and each branch of society is uniting to raise the virtues and polish the manners of the whole."[13] Like Hitchcock, Mrs. Foster did not mean that her countrywomen should become learned ladies; it was enough if they knew how "to taste the delights of literature, and be qualified to bear a part in rational and improving conversation" (p. 182).[14] She spoke at some length of her conventional views about the caution to be exercised in the choice of novels—there were so few that deserved being read. She shared with Mrs. Rowson the opinion that a girl seduced need not be a girl irremediably fallen; on the other hand she warned, as did others, against the hasty acceptance of the maxim, "That reformed rakes make the best husbands" (p. 103).[15] She thought society much too lenient toward the seducer and commented bitterly on the effrontery of the seducer who would not marry the girl he had led astray because only a chaste bride was good enough for him (p. 189).[16] She resented the dissipations of the town and praised, in a style meant to be elevated, the beauties of the country and (like Hitchcock) the serenity of an evening which must incline the sensitive to gratitude: "The sun had nearly finished his diurnal course, and was leaving our hemisphere to

[68]

illuminate the other with his cheering rays. The sprightly song-sters had retired to their bowers, and were distending their little throats, with a tribute of instinctive gratitude and praise" (p. 138). In the *American Review* Mrs. Foster was reproached for having failed to at least establish a good model of letter-writing; since she could lay no claim to originality in the matters she expounded, the reviewer felt that she ought to have called herself the editor, not the author, of the book.[17]

Alcuin, by Charles Brockden Brown (1771-1810), also pub-lished in 1798, could hardly have been called the work of a mere compiler. Though Brown's feminist radicalism was not so violent[18] or consistent as might appear from isolated quotations, his plea for improved educational facilities for women and a true acknowledgment of woman's individual social value as op-posed to her mere social duties sounds nevertheless more original and convinced than Mrs. Foster's mild injunctions. The reader of *Alcuin* may conjecture that if Mary Wollstonecraft's *A Vin-dication of the Rights of Woman* (1792) was read in the United States,[19] it received from Brown support more impressive than, for example, from *The Emigrants*.[20] Alcuin's assertion that woman is equal to man in point of intellect and superior to him as to beauty and sensibility (p. 75) reflects an attitude that de-termined the parts to be played in Brown's novels by his male and female protagonists. Mrs. Carter, Alcuin's antagonist, is a lady gifted with intellectual vigor who despises fashionable "senti-ment," a lady after the heart of the Mary Wollstonecraft of the *Rights of Women*. Brown's idea of marriage as outlined in the later fragment of *Alcuin*[21] is strictly institutional—that of Con-stantia, not Martinette, if we think of the views expressed in *Ormond*.

Whereas Hitchcock and Mrs. Foster wrote somewhat compre-hensive educational treatises, *Alcuin* focused on the one ques-tion of the rights of woman. Mrs. Rowson's *Mentoria*[22] also has one main theme, that of obedience and dutifulness in children, specifically respecting their parents' and elders' decisions in questions of marriage. Mentoria, who has acted wisely in this as in everything, writes her young charges letter after letter ex-emplifying the woeful consequences of marriages entered upon without parental approval; she recommends submission to the superior experience and wisdom of the older generation. Each of her stories might be elaborated into a full-scale novel.[23] Belinda Dormer is another Dorcasina Sheldon.[24] The longest of Mentoria's tales, which in some sixty pages extends over two generations, uses the themes of seduction, a fake marriage, and near-incest.[25] There is also an "Essay on Female Education,"[26] the basic ideas of which sound like Hitchcock's and Mrs. Foster's; it emphasizes in particular woman's domestic duties and her role as an educator.

The style of *Mentoria* is generally conventional, as is usual with Mrs. Rowson—more than in the narratives themselves, it is rather painfully predictable in descriptions and pathetic uses: "I am a mother. I hear the darling of my heart, the child of my bosom asking for food, and have it not to give him. I am a wife, and see my adored, my almost idolized husband, sinking under the complicated evils of famine, grief and sickness, yet have neither comfort or consolations to offer..." (1:74-75). When Mrs. Rowson's aim and style are not directed at her readers' emotional response, she occasionally attempts caricature, in spite of her lack of a sense of humor: "Prudelia is a woman who pays the nicest regard to propriety and decorum, she is ever prying into her neighbour's conduct, and if their actions do not exactly agree with her scrupulous notions of rectitude, she hesitates not to conclude them abandoned and lost to every sense of virtue" (2:106).

The need for circumspection not merely in young persons but in anyone thinking, or forgetting to think, of marriage is the main subject of *The Art of Courting* (1795), by the Reverend Ebenezer Bradford (c. 1746-1801). The writer meant to sound a warning against too firm reliance on various preconceived ideas about marriage: it is difficult to say beforehand whether a match is practicable or whether some partners are incompatible. Bradford insisted on the authenticity of his examples, like Mrs. Rowson, saying, "The principal scenes of courtship, here displayed, are taken from actual life; and consequently must be more interesting to the reader, than if they were merely fictitious."[27] He wanted to be quite sure, that much is clear, that *The Art of*

Courting should be considered instructive literature, as opposed to "novels and plays" read by young ladies wishing to be fashionable, "accomplished," and "to form themselves companions agreeable to gentlemen who are determined to live a vicious and irreligious life" (p. 76). However, the ideas and the style of the popular fiction of the age were catching: the conception of a perfect wife outlined by one of Bradford's lovers would not have been out of place in one of those much-despised novels:

> I wish her to be the favourite child of respectable parents, educated in the Christian religion. With respect to her person, I should wish she might be above the common size of women, well proportioned in body and limbs; her skin white and ruddy; her eyes black and sparkling; her hair brown and flowing, and her features well proportioned one with the other: But what I should prize above all the rest, is a dignified mind, full of activity, generosity and meekness—unless it be some peculiar qualifications of heart, such as benevolence and patience, with a soul turned for love. (p. 39)

Most of Bradford's energy went into relating the serious and successful campaign conducted by Harriot to reform Damon. That young man has become a deist while at the university. The girl is fortunately well read in the deistical writers, having enjoyed a liberal education such as even Mrs. Foster and Hitchcock might have been alarmed at, whereas it would doubtless have pleased Brown's Ormond. Harriot refutes the deistical arguments and convinces Damon of their weakness before undertaking his conversion to a true Christian faith.

It is interesting that *The Art of Courting* should have been criticized for its lack of "tender sensibilities."[28] Whether consciously or not, Bradford apparently tried to make his guidebook for marriage candidates commonsensical and to steer clear of sentimentality by using what Tremaine McDowell called "broad jocularity." But Bradford's clumsy humor has no more appeal to the modern reader than the appallingly humorless productions of those fellow writers of his who were not afraid of using fiction and addressing their readers' sensibility quite openly.

Questions of practical behavior were also discussed by the

"Gleaner," a Mentor-figure created for the *Massachusetts Magazine* by Mrs. Judith Sargent Murray (1751-1820) in the early 1790s. The Gleaner enjoyed playing hide-and-seek with his readers and inserted into his essays and stories their supposed conjectures about his identity; he also weighed with them the significance of his opinions or commented upon his manner.[29] The obvious self-consciousness of Mrs. Murray reveals how seriously she took her role; she was a monitor and arbiter demonstrating the "necessity of religion, especially in adversity" (chap. 31) or exposing her "sentiments on education" (chaps. 35-36). She also offered her readers a "Panegyric of the American Constitution" (chap. 27), praised Washington's military and civic firmness (chaps. 76-78), and recommended "a spirit of national independence" (chap. 96). Mrs. Murray shared Mrs. Foster's hope that the education newly available to woman would do her abilities justice (chaps. 63, 88-91). She stated her suspicions and reservations with regard to novel-reading (chap. 40). According to her, it could best profit girls between eight and fourteen, for whom it might serve as a pleasant training in reading; once used to books, they would have no trouble in choosing serious reading matter more appropriate to a later stage of their mental development. Even so, it was necessary to protect them from unsuitable novels. Mrs. Murray praised *Clarissa* but blamed *Evelina,* especially because of the uncharitable and unladylike nature of the remarks passed on Madame Duval and the practical jokes played on her (chap. 43). Her own novel-like "Story of Margaretta," which occupies a large part of the first volume of *The Gleaner,* includes a warning against fiction, since novel-reading may well render a girl in love impervious to sound advice, such as Margaretta's guardian can give her.[30] Even without guidance, the girl realizes that Sinisterus Courtland is not a husband for her: she comes to her senses by being allowed to make her own observations and reasonably assessing his qualities and faults. She does so even before finding out that he seduced Frances Wellwood and deserted her and their three children. The reader is encouraged to believe that, whatever crises are in store for her, Margaretta will be a good wife to Edward Hamil-

ton; her education, of which Mr. Vigillius (the "Gleaner") gives
an outline, has been thorough:

> Of needle work, in its varieties, my wife pronounced her a
> perfect mistress; her knowledge of the English, and French
> tongues, was fully adequate to her years, and her manner of
> reading had, for me, peculiar charms; her hand writing was neat
> and easy; she was a good accomptant, a tolerable geographer
> and chronologist; she had skimmed the surface of astronomy and
> natural philosophy; had made good proficiency in her study
> of history and the poets; could sketch a landscape; could furnish,
> from her own fancy, patterns for the muslins which she wrought;
> could bear her part in a minuet and a cotillion, and was allowed
> to have an excellent hand upon the piano forte. We once
> entertained a design of debarring her the indulgence of novels;
> but these books, being in the hands of every one, we conceived
> the accomplishment of our wishes in this respect, except we had
> bred her an absolute recluse, almost impracticable; and Mrs.
> Vigillius, therefore, thought it best to permit the use of every
> decent work, causing them to be read in her presence, hoping
> that she might, by her suggestions and observations, present an
> antidote to the poison, with which the pen of the novelist is too
> often fraught....in the receipts of cookery, she is thoroughly
> versed; she is in every respect the complete housewife; and our
> linen never received so fine a gloss as when it was ironed and
> laid in order by Margaretta. (1:70-71)

There is nothing very original either in the conception or the
execution of *The Gleaner*. Mrs. Murray appears to have been
an energetic sort of person, and yet of a moderate and conservative temper. This had the merit of launching her in her literary
enterprise, but of keeping her from overdoing the appeal to the
"tender sensibilities" or indulging in elaborate stylistic embellishments. From a literary point of view her production seems rather
pedestrian; but since *The Gleaner* first appeared in serialized
form, it may well have had a more varied and lively effect than
the collected edition.

Compared to the books so far treated in the present chapter,
Mrs. Rowson's *The Inquisitor*[31] has a larger number of the surface attributes of entertaining fiction and also seems to indulge
more freely in sensibility for its own sake. Yet it is not out of

place among didactic writings in which a central figure, through superior knowledge and by manipulation, draws lessons from his or her observation and makes these lessons available to an audience within the book and to the reading public. *The Inquisitor,* an exercise in Sternean sensibility,[32] uses in fragmented form the plot elements typical of the fashionable novel of Mrs. Rowson's times; but what emerges in the end as its most memorable feature is the author's plea in favor of all that have a claim on our understanding and compassion. Mrs. Rowson attempted to persuade her readers to try to overcome the alienation that results from moral wrongdoing or from the pride of rank and riches. She apparently enjoyed varying her tone and approach; her familiarity with the stage shows in the ease with which she occasionally slipped into the stylistic personality of some of her personages.[33]

Among those to be treated with sympathy are the debtors, whose plight is often desperate because of the existing laws and the literal interpretation and application of them.[34] With Mrs. Rowson as with others, the theme of the debtors' prison may be used as a rebuke addressed to the father and husband who has dissipated the family wealth, as in *Trials of the Human Heart* or *Sarah.* More often, it functions as one appeal among many stressing some unfortunate heroine's helplessness in the face of impersonal forces of victimization, as in *The Fille de Chambre.* Stories as pathetic as any similar novel scene were contributed by Joseph Dewey Fay (1779-1825) to the New York *Columbian,* to campaign for humane consideration of the debtors' jail legislation. When these *Essays of Howard* were reprinted in book form in 1811, the publisher included a (possibly fictitious) reply called forth by the original publication, reproaching Fay with passing off fiction as truth.[35] Fay, however, meant to expose the truth, not to write fiction; if his book was looked upon as such, that was simply because the public were used to just that note of didactic pathos in novels which was sounded in his essays.

The anonymous author of *Rosa; or, American Genius and Education* (1810) rather recklessly employed a mixture of fictional elements; yet for all its narrative variety, the novel is above all concerned with aspects of education. Its heroine is mainly passive; both to her father and to Mrs. Charmion she is a means of illustrating and embodying the advantages of a sound upbringing. The book offers a contribution to the noble savage theory and the concept of civilization. According to its author, the American native and European civilization are quite compatible; there is no hopeless struggle of the pure, natural instincts against restraining and atrophying institutions. Rosa indeed fulfills her Incan father's expectations: she extracts all the benefits from an enlightened eighteenth-century education and thus fully develops her innate gifts. But not only can the New World compete with the Old with respect to the individual's potentialities; *Rosa* also sets forth the superiority of the New World, deriving from the democratic encouragement given the individual in America.[36]

In one sense only are the Old World critics proved right: America is as yet an uncivilized country (p. 145). This state of affairs is responsible for the unsavory experiences which Richard Orvaine must undergo. This young man subjects himself to an educational process rather unlike that of Rosa, his future wife. Having yielded to the temptation of gambling, Orvaine decides to make a fresh beginning in new surroundings, a resolution which starts him on a short picaresque progress from Maryland to Boston (chap. 5). He is thrown into the company of drinkers, confidence men, and forgers; yet in the end he can be reinstated in the good graces of his former employer and protector. Practically, by trial and error, he has thus come to know and avoid the pitfalls of his future career. The overall balance is in favor of trust and honor, and Orvaine is clearly considered worthy of becoming Rosa's husband.

The author's underlying view is that chance education such as Orvaine's will soon be a thing of the past, and America will produce more and more Rosas. The strict and purposeful guidance on the part of Mrs. Charmion (pp. 53-54) demonstrates that systematic education is practicable, and the product of her supervision indicates that confidence may safely be placed in models like herself or Derwent. If much civilizing work remains to be done, especially by the ladies (pp. 27-28), people from

[75]

over-civilized countries may already profit from the American environment: "In time, by associating in rational company, Mr. Longpee and his spouse lost their English and French oddities, ...the uncorrupted manners of America are more favourable to happiness than the frivolities of Europe, which are the spume of luxurious indolence" (pp. 262-63).

Such is the reassuring message of *Rosa*. Against its background it was permissible and advisable to single out for ridicule some aspects offending against a rational and urbane pattern of social life. A journalist and an illiterate justice of the peace come in for their share of satire (chaps. 2 and 3); so do a group of gossips (chaps. 2), who belong—with the diffident lover (pp. 225-26) and the hypocritical enthusiast of love and the softer sex, cruelly venting his anger on a lapdog (pp. 32-33)—to a species not restricted to the young American republic. The justice of the peace is assigned a role in a comedy that is less satirical than it is robustly crude (pp. 67-68), and of a temper relating it to Richard Orvaine's picaresque encounters. The author of *Rosa* was here perhaps trying to counterbalance the essential seriousness, if not solemnity, of his concern over the American practice of education.[37] Some unintentional humor derives in part from the complexity of certain plot devices, patently so in the final chapter: there the true identity and relationship of several characters must be unfolded together with the Gothic mysteries of Rosa's desertion by her father, deliberately engineered to place Rosa under Mrs. Charmion's protection.

The implausible plot of *Rosa* is structurally very awkward; it loosely links up the clusters of events related in the six chapters. The characters are introduced in varying scenes of social comedy and a Gothic event; the retrospect of Mrs. Charmion's life then jumbles together many favorite elements of the novel of adventure. The following chapter, comprising one-fourth of the entire book, unfolds the panorama of Orvaine's experiences. Finally, after the young man's ousting of the other rivals for Rosa's love, the motives of the characters are hastily revealed. The connection of the main theme of education with the multiple events and characters is only intermittently realized; though the author's message is clear, the reader frequently wonders why it had to be conveyed in such a questionable shape.

3. "Bildungsromane"

In the *Mentoria* type of didactic fiction, the criteria of right behavior are preached and taught by the author, sometimes through a mediating speaker; the narrative element of these books is concentrated in the stories exemplifying models of good conduct or deviations from the right path. Some books are now to be introduced which, in a rather special sense, could be called "Bildungsromane"; they have at their center not the teacher, but one who learns by experience.

Enos Hitchcock outlined his program of experiences in 1793 on the title page of his tale *The Farmer's Friend, or the History of Mr. Charles Worthy*. "Who, from being a poor orphan, rose, through various scenes of distress and misfortune, to wealth and eminence, by industry, economy and good conduct." Throughout this farmer's progress, the career of Worthy is contrasted with the faults and errors of others. They lack his strength of faith, sound morals, common sense, and his ability to work hard. He is very much a subject fit for a writer like Hitchcock, whose aim is "to write of worth, to detail transactions, and unfold virtues which dignify human nature, and extend the blessings of society."[38] Novel-like, the story ends with two marriages; but this is a mere outward element of conclusion because the book is what it was meant to be; the relation of a Franklinesque career from rags to riches. Only rarely is Hitchcock's prose colloquial;[39] he seems at ease only when he feels he can call upon sensibility and pathos—his reader's and his own: "Here they wallowed about half buried in the snow banks, exerting their weary and enfeebled limbs, to reach the wished for home, while the anxious wife prepares the best repast the humble room afforded, to warm and refresh them at their return. But alas, how vain is all her care! While she is thus employed for their comfort, the blood chills and grows stagnant in their veins!" (p. 248).

Charles Worthy's common sense and his openness to what is

[77]

good and useful are paralleled in the main character of *The Life and Reflections of Charles Observator* (1816), by the Reverend Elijah R. Sabin (1776-1818), again combined with a fashionable dash of sensibility.[40] In this book, too, seducers are branded with infamy and their victims interceded for; the reading of the Bible is recommended, and sermons are shown to move the hero deeply. Washington is praised, and so is the American political system, which "lies exactly between" the extremes of British and French politics (p. 179). The end of this book "of experience" (p. 36) reads like a fairy tale: "Charles returned, was married to Prudelia and entered on the oversight of her father's affairs; and they now live the pattern of conjugal affection, as well as of Christian duties" (p. 271). Other parts of *Charles Observator* benefit from elements successfully used in the novel, such as a richly varied description of nature (pp. 51-52) or a grotesquely repulsive character whose appearance, of course, serves the ends of our didactic author: "His face was bloated, his nose of a double size, and somewhat resembling a piece of red hot iron. He presented an unwieldy carcase, and was groaning under a fit of the gout. One could see BRANDY written in livid capitals on his lips" (p. 74). A facile comic effect is obtained through the spelling of an illiterate would-be teacher (p. 25), but otherwise the tone of this book is as solemn as that of very nearly all didactic fiction.

The Soldier's Orphan (1812), attributed to John Finch,[41] is termed a novel, we are told, because its publishers "cannot assert that it is anything else" (p. iv). Their embarrassment is probably owing to the didactic nature and consequent episodic structure of the book. Its heroine, Emily Thompson, is an interested onlooker before whose eyes there unrolls a panorama of the problems, the vicissitudes and compensations that are part of man's life. Her education is not a process she actively shares in; it seems instead to be dissociated from her, to be constantly analyzed and commented upon for her benefit. Her outward life, punctuated by the departures and returns of her seafaring uncle, is exceptional only in the fact that she was orphaned on the day of her birth. In a late chapter she assumes the charge of her cousins after the death of their mother. Between these two points,

Emily's existence is marked emotionally and morally by the brief appearance for the duration of a visit or a conversation of people familiar with distressful maladjustments or comforting arguments. When troubles close in, the reader feels he need not be alarmed, so clearly can Emily be trusted with doing what is required of her. Fittingly, when her cousin Robert Center comes home, a word of advice from her uncle and a brief conversation with Center are all it takes to make her accept the young man for her husband. This is so sensible a decision that it reduces to near-irrelevance the fact of the couple's mutual love. In such a climate of placidity Morris's violent outburst of grief on learning that his wife has died[42] must quickly yield to a rational concern—the very suggestion that Emily and Center should marry.

The stress in this narrative, which ends with the heroine's wedding, is on conjugal love, not romantic passion. The theme is introduced through the examples of Emily's parents and the Morrises, brought into relief by a miserable tale of seduction (chap. 5), given substance in a clergyman's chapter-long apology of marriage in reply to a question from Center (chap. 7), again approached through the story of thoughtless Sally (chap. 8), and finally glorified when Emily and her husband erect a monument to the girl's parents, "those godlike beings" (p. 179). Next to married love, the subject of death ranks second in importance: general reflections and memories of dead relatives and friends are used insistently and, at times, gratuitously.[43] These topics, as well as some others, are familiar features of the contemporary didactic and sentimental fiction; so is the author's stress on the heroine's perfections (pp. 24-25, 48) and his "style of sensibility."[44]

The sensibility so much in demand with the heroes and heroines of the fiction of the age turns into grievously didactic sentimentalism in the stories of Miss Sarah Savage (1785-1837). *The Factory Girl* (1814), which might have furnished the writer with fresh subject matter, becomes the dreary relation of the self-effacement of a humble girl, "always accustomed to trace her misfortunes to her own faults, rather than to those of others."[45] When Captain Holden, whose children she has been looking after for many months, wishes to thank her, the conversation takes an expected turn: " '. . . I wish I could thank you, but I can't do it just now; there is such a high swell of my heart, that my gratitude is raised aloft to Him who made you so excellent, so benevolent.' 'God is the proper object of your gratitude, my dear cousin, you owe me nothing,' said Mary, who felt, in witnessing such a scene of parental joy, fully compensated for all the sacrifices she had made" (p. 103). In the end Mary is found ready to be rewarded with happiness: she marries a widower and becomes a perfect stepmother to his children.[46]

The heroine of Miss Savage's *Filial Affection, or the Clergyman's Granddaughter* (1820) loses successively her father, lover, mother, grandmother, and grandfather. At no time does she allow herself to forget her duties to parents and neighbors, surrendering even her chance of becoming a clergyman's wife. This is the end of the book:

> The death of Dr. Unwin was the last severe calamity Phebe ever suffered; her time, divided between religious, social, and domestic duties, passed on in an even tenour. The remembrance of those she loved was sweet, for it was unimbittered by the recollection of neglected duties. The present was cheerful, because she constantly occupied herself in acts of benevolence, the cultivation of her mind, or the necessary cares of life, and the future, seen with the eye of faith, opened scenes which reflected back upon her mind a cheerful serenity, that excited and secured the love of all who had the happiness to know her. Even to the young and frivolous the epithet "old maid" lost its opprobrious sound, when connected with the name of the "Clergyman's Grand-Daughter."[47]

Though intent upon the perfection of their heroines, Miss Savage and the author of *The Soldier's Orphan* could not quite conceal the imperfection of some of their sisters. *The Vain Cottager: or, The History of Lucy Franklin* (1807) is an anonymous tale about a girl who becomes the victim of her own vanity. Too often praised for her pretty face, Lucy starts wearing clothes "beyond" her humble social rank and suffers the shame of seduction. Finally given a chance to repent and reform, she cannot, however, achieve the simple domestic happiness that might have been hers; that her former suitor should marry her own sister serves to emphasize the bitterness of Lucy's punishment. *The Vain Cottager* is no more than a literary exercise in didacticism, designed to justify the strict sumptuary laws of old: it is introduced and spiced with remarks on the necessity of dressing according to one's rank and occupation.[48]

Our specimens of didactic fiction rarely sink to the dismal level of Miss Savage's tales or *The Vain Cottager,* but they do not offer much literary excitement either. The two that might have benefited from their traditional form, the allegories of Morgan and Botsford, are at best competent and yet, more generally, plodding attempts. The other books are marred by downright bad writing, their author's didacticism having proved stronger than their creative impulse, which may only intermittently be guessed at. There are thus evidences in *Mentoria* and *The Inquisitor* of Mrs. Rowson's skill, and *The Art of Courting* has a basic diversity that occasionally enlivens its author's style.

Generally, however, it is the revealing use of the stock situations of fiction and the corresponding manner that appear most striking to the student of this didactic storytelling. This is especially pronounced in the tales meant as warnings, not models: in such narrative illustrations the necessity of making a forceful impression led the authors to borrow from the novelists' arsenal suitable material and, particularly, rhetorical stresses. The unfortunate result of applying borrowed resources may be exemplified by the portrait of the foil meant to enhance the merits of Osander Bloomsgrove:

> He never stopped in his fatal career, till he had reduced himself to beggary, and broken the hearts of his parents. His vices at length undermined his constitution—a threatening disorder seized him—Emaciated by sickness and worn out with pain, he gave up the ghost, amidst the horrors of an awakened conscience, and the tremendous apprehensions of his future condition; and, what rendered the scene most distressful, was, that reflecting upon the neglect and indulgence of his parents, as the cause of all his miseries, he cursed them with his dying breath.[49]

1. Novelists who humbly pretended to a didactic purpose first and a literary one last, and appeared to consider the novel a simple vehicle for their views, could appeal to Blair's "Fictitious histories might be employed for very

useful purposes." See William Hill Brown, *Ira and Isabella*, motto; Watterston, *Glencarn*, p. 3; and cf. *Fidelity Rewarded*, p. iii; Relf, *Infidelity*, p. 11.

2. One derivation from this nationalism is the patriotism that was to find expression in the historical novel; and the historical novel in turn helped to render prose fiction respectable, since its patriotic subject matter was eminently instructive. See John Pendleton Kennedy, *Horse-Shoe Robinson*, ed. Ernest E. Leisy (New York and London: Hafner, 1962), p. xvi.

3. There is in Benjamin Silliman's *Letters of Shahcoolen* (1802), just after a denunciation of Mary Wollstonecraft, a long passage offering an ideal picture of the majority of American women, which seems to sum up contemporary conceptions. It may serve as a standard relevant to a proper valuation of the role and behavior of heroines and female villains in fiction. It is also a good instance of the stylistic tradition linking up the pietism and sensibility of a declining age with the genteel outlook of later generations: "They are placed above the miseries and meanness of poverty; and below the vices and vanity of wealth.

"Early imbued with virtue and modesty, they are rational, domestic and industrious. Their life is divided between useful employment, cheerful society, and virtuous and moderate amusements. Rarely at the theatre and assembly room, and *never* at the circus and card-table, their pleasures give a zest to life, and render welcome the return of the fire-side happiness, and the family society. Business is with them the pleasure, not pleasure the business, of life. They rise to breathe the sweet incense of the morning, which the joyful earth offers to the great Creator; they listen to the matin song of the lark, while she mounts into the clouds that are gilded with the first effusions of light.

"The volumes which contain the precepts of religion and morals; those which unfold the springs of human action, and delineate the thousand shades of human character; the clear page of history; the books of the fine arts, and the treasures of poetical lore, all lie open to their perusal, and occupy a portion of each passing day.

"The domestic offices, and the household good, are not forgotten. Conscious that the family is the great scene of female action, and of female pleasure, here they concentrate their most serious thoughts, and make their most serious exertions.

"Despising, alike, that contemptible servility, which would ascribe to them the perfections of angels, and offer them the adoration of Gods; and that unnatural system of false philosophy, which would harden them into masculine beings, too proud to be women, too weak to be men, they cultivate the feminine virtues, sweeten every action by tenderness, and grace every sentiment by love" (pp. 60-62).

4. Miss Helena Wells wrote in this sense in the preface to her *Constantia Neville* (1800): "While the younger part of the fair sex continue to devote so large a portion of their time to the light reading which circulating libraries furnish, it is incumbent on those who employ the pen with a view to their edification, to avail themselves of the same channels for conveying useful lessons; which might not be perused under any other form" (p. iii). Cf. also the prefaces to Gilbert Imlay, *The Emigrants* (1793), and Sukey Vickery, *Emily Hamilton* (1803).

5. Samuel Miller deplored that "depraved man" had been unable to maintain fiction at the level of religious prophecies and parables; see *A Brief Retrospect*, 2:370.

6. "If *Pilgrim's Progress* is to be reckoned as one of the early examples of the English novel, then *The History of the Kingdom of Basaruah* may well

be called the first American novel" (Richard Schlatter, ed., *The History of the Kingdom of Basaruah* [Cambridge, Mass.: Harvard University Press, 1946], Introduction, p. 3).

7. In this context it may be recollected that, of the first twenty bestsellers of Colonial times, twelve were written to teach lessons of piety and doctrine; see F. L. Mott, *Multitudes*, p. 12.

8. *The Spiritual Voyage*, p. 16.

9. See *DAB* 9:72-73. Hitchcock consulted Benjamin Rush, "a respectable citizen of Philadelphia," on the plan of *The Bloomsgrove Family*, but did not adopt Rush's view that the family should have half a dozen children instead of just two. See Benson, *Women*, p. 155. One other publication of Hitchcock is *A Discourse on Education*, "delivered...in Providence, November 16, 1785."

10. *Bloomsgrove Family*, 2:24. Richardson's views on female education, as exemplified through his novels, were conservative in the sense Hitchcock meant; Latin and Greek, for example, Richardson feared were apt to overtax women's minds (see Benson, *Women*, pp. 49-50). At the school of Nancy Maria Hyde (1792-1816), a friend of Mrs. Sigourney, practical usefulness was stressed rather than ornament and fashionable accomplishments (*The Writings of Nancy Maria Hyde*, pp. 156-57).

11. The existence of evil cannot be ignored; but since Hitchcock shared with others the view that its manifestations should not be described in a novel, vice is only allowed to hover on either side of the narrow path of virtue.

12. Various heroes have contacts with wicked people and pernicious ideas while at the university and beyond parental control; see, e.g., Bradford, *The Art of Courting* (1795), chap. 8; Watterston, *Glencarn*, chaps. 9-11; Woodworth, *The Champions of Freedom* (1816), chaps. 11-12. Such heroes are men of sensibility (see Tremaine McDowell, "The Big Three in Yankee Fiction," *SR* 36[1928]:157-63). But unfeeling villains also attend the universities and frequently develop a vindictive inferiority complex there when competing with others superior to them in intelligence, industry, and morals.

13. *The Boarding School*, p. 151.

14. Cf. *The Bloomsgrove Family*, 2:25.

15. Eliza Wharton, the heroine of Mrs. Foster's novel *The Coquette* (1797) thought that she could rely on the truth of this adage (p. 76). The maxim is referred to in several other novels, for example, Miss Vickery's *Emily Hamilton*, p. 108.

16. Cf. Miss Caroline Matilda Warren, *The Gamesters* (1805), p. 80; *Emily Hamilton*, p. 123.

17. *American Review and Literary Journal* 1, no. 1(1801):85-86. The reviewer concluded: "In these days, when so many books of questionable utility are published, it may be thought some commendation to say of the present volume, that if it is not calculated to do much good, it will do little harm, unless to the bookseller."

18. *Alcuin* perhaps did sound deliberately provoking; but so do all revolutionaries, and Mary Wollstonecraft's attack itself had its conscious exaggerations. See Horner, *English Women*, p. 79.

19. A reviewer of *Letters of Shahcoolen*, which contained an attack on Mary Wollstonecraft's doctrines, thought that in Boston no one bothered with them (see *Monthly Anthology* 2[1805]:85-88). A contemporary testimony does not quite support this dismissal: "It does not follow...that every female who

indicates the capacity of the sex is a disciple of Mary Wollstonecraft. Though I allow her to have said many things which I cannot but approve, yet the very foundation on which she builds her work will be apt to prejudice us so against her that we will not allow her the merit she really deserves,—yet, prejudice set aside, I confess I admire many of her sentiments..." (written in 1801; see *A Girl's Life Eighty Years Ago: Selections from the Letters of Eliza Southgate Bowne*. With an Introduction by Clarence Cook [1887], pp. 61-62).

20. *Alcuin* was offered to the public as a book in 1798 and in a shortened version, bearing the title "The Rights of Women," in the Philadelphia *Weekly Magazine*, March 17-April 7, 1798. For Imlay and his novel (ostensibly elaborating on Mary Wollstonecraft's theories), see below, pp. 216-21.

21. See William Dunlap, *The Life of Charles Brockden Brown* (1815), 1:91-92. Cf. Benson, *Women*, pp. 173-75.

22. *Mentoria* was published in London in 1791, in Philadelphia in 1794 in two volumes. References are to this American edition.

23. Mentoria's own story (1:15-20) reminds the reader of Mrs. Rowson's novels and of Miss Helena Wells, *The Step-Mother* (1799). Mrs. Rowson was to have a successful career as a teacher conducting her own "academy." Among her pupils was Eliza Southgate, quoted above (note 19) on Mary Wollstonecraft, clearly very properly educated to refuse to love "unsolicited" and encourage a suitor too much before he had presented his aspirations to her parents (*A Girl's Life*, pp. 40-41, 139-41). Susan Warner's best-selling novel *The Wide, Wide World* was recommended for publication to Putnam by his mother, who had been educated at Mrs. Rowson's school (see Helen W. Papashvily, *All the Happy Endings* [1956], p. 8).

24. Belinda disregards her father's advice and elopes with Horton, an officer. She later regrets having given up Lord Gaymore, whom her father had selected for her, for Gaymore actually possesses the qualities that Horton has only in appearance (1:38-48).

25. This is the story of Marian and Lydia. They are the daughters of Dorcas who had been tricked into marrying Melfont, and later betrayed and deserted. Marian is seduced, then abandoned, and reforms just in time to escape becoming her father's mistress; she dies repentant. Lydia, who has led a blameless life, marries an earl; and Dorcas is rehabilitated (1:76-106; 2:3-37). Unlike the other stories in *Mentoria*, that of Marian and Lydia is embarked upon without preamble, as if Mrs. Rowson, in her hurry to get on with her narrative, had forgotten to state once more her didactic motivation.

26. There were to be many more pleas for an improvement of female education. A late one summing up many of the points raised during that period is Emma Willard's *An Address...to the Legislation of New York...* (Albany, 1819). Another book that might be treated in this context is William Wirt's *The Old Bachelor* (1814); see below in the next chapter, under the sub-heading "American Spectators."

27. Bradford added: "Several of the parties are now alive, and the original letters in the hands of the writer" (*The Art of Courting* pp. vii-viii). An extreme example of a guarantee of authenticity is that of Mrs. Manvill, *Lucinda, or the Mountain Mourner* (1807).

28. See the evidence in Tremaine McDowell, "Sensibility in the 18th-Century American Novel," *SP* 24(1927):383-402, especially p. 396.

29. Mrs. Murray presumably adopted a male disguise because her age preferred Mentors to Mentorias (see Benson, *Women*, p. 176). The "Gleaner"

contributions, after being first published in the *Massachusetts Magazine* chiefly from 1792 to 1794, were reissued in three volumes "by Constantia," Boston, 1798. References are to this edition, which also contains two comedies, "Virtue Triumphant" and "The Traveller Returned."

30. "...I was aware that, manured by the prejudices prepared in the hot-bed of novel reading, the impressions made upon young minds, with the passions implanted in the tender soil, were not easily erased, or up-rooted..." (1:82).

31. First published in London in 1788, reissued in Philadelphia in 1793. References are to the later edition.

32. Mrs. Rowson, who announced that she meant to imitate Sterne, was deliberately "sentimental," as an example may show. The Inquisitor has begun reading some verse printed on a scrap of wrapping-paper: "I turned the paper, but there was no more—There are times when the mind is affected by mere trifles; such was now my case—I was vexed at not finding the continuation of the story, and determined to go back to the fruiterer's, and inquire if they had the remainder" (1:15). He is, however, distracted from this intention by overhearing a tale of distress, and charitably offers help; thus the trifling vexation leads to an opportunity to do good. Cf. also the Inquisitor's return to his anxious wife (2:62).

33. The Inquisitor himself generally sounds either sententious or sentimental. Mariana tells her story straightforwardly and rather breathlessly, while the East Indian embellishes his tale with biblical turns (see 2:112-14, 102-3).

34. Heartfree is in debt because he has been too generous in helping others (1:16-19). The East Indian, a slave given his freedom without the possibility of earning a living, must wait in jail till his creditor dies (2:102-6).

35. "The introduction of a pathetic story—of a prisoner starving in confinement—his wife clinging round his neck—his children at his feet petitioning for bread—bereft of his liberty, and encountering all the horrors of his situation, without one gleam of hope, one glimmering ray of comfort to support him in this adversity—these are pretty stories for the entertainment of children by the winter's fire-side, but they lose their effect on a moment's reflection, with the conviction that incidents of that nature are never to be met with among us" (*Essays of Howard* [1811], p. 49; cf. also p. 95).

36. *Rosa*, p. 256.

37. Only the praise of Baltimore (p. 24) sounds as earnest as the discussion of education!

38. *The Farmer's Friend*, p. 14. Another farmer's friend is speaking in parts of Crèvecoeur's *Letters from an American Farmer* (1782), e.g., in chapter 2, "On the Situation, Feelings, and Pleasures, of an American Farmer," or in the "History of Andrew, the Hebridean." Novels like Imlay's *The Emigrants* (1793), Mrs. Rowson's *Reuben and Rachel* (1798), and Mitchell's *The Asylum* (1804-11) continue the tradition that combines the fresh start in emigration with the return to the soil.

39. "Her personal appearance was a true picture of the house within. Here every thing was at sixes and sevens" (p. 87).

40. "...He took his leave. The scene was truly affecting. The father was first seen embracing and kissing the son; his last words were, farewell, my son—follow the advice I have given you. The mother took him by the hand, but uttered not a word—her tears spoke for her. The younger children wept. —It was too much for Charles—he hasted away" (*The Life and Reflections of Charles Observator*, p. 51).

41. See *The Soldier's Orphan* copyright notice, and Wright, *American Fiction,* item 267.

42. "With frenzied strides he paced the room—His glaring eye-balls seemed started from their sockets—...The distended fibres of his crazed brain must soon have cracked, and death relieved his distress. But...kind tears gave vent to that excess of woe which nature could not bear; and reason resumed her empire in the breast" (p. 158).

43. The dead are either closely related to Emily (her parents, her aunt) or hardly connected with the plot at all (though possibly close to the author: the clergyman's friend, chap. 6; Harriet, chap. 8).

44. See the characterization of a clergyman (p. 36), the Thompsons' parting (p. 11), and the quotation in note 42, above. Among topics not immediately linked up with the educational trend, there are some comments on the French Revolution (chaps. 9, 11) and on slavery (chaps. 12, 13).

45. *The Factory-Girl,* p. 67.

46. In due time the children buy her a Bible, with a rose "fastened to the following passage; 'Her children rise up and call her blessed'" (p. 112).

47. *Filial Affection,* p. 162.

48. See the "Address to Young Women in Humble Life," pp. 3-14, and Mr. Nelson's remarks to Lucy as she is recovering from the shock of her fall, pp. 62-63. The edition referred to appeared in New Haven in 1807.

49. *The Bloomsgrove Family,* 2:148. Cf. also, in *The Inquisitor,* the cumulation of vice in Cogdie—seducer, embezzler, gambler, procurer—a typical example of the "complicated" villain.

Chapter Five

SATIRICAL AND POLEMICAL FICTION

THE TENSIONS which precipitated and accompanied the establishment of the independent United States, the growth of its political parties, and the awakening of national and regional feelings produced at one level the Declaration of Independence and the *Federalist* papers, and at another a flow of oratory and a mass of satirical and polemical writings. Although most of the oratory evaporated, the writings remain.[1] Most of them, violently partisan pamphlets and broadsides or abusive newspaper contributions, merely testify to the heat which the debated issues generated. But a few of the satirists and polemicists used literary means and achieved literary effects not irrelevant to a discussion of the contemporary American novel.

1. John Bull and Brother Jonathan

Francis Hopkinson, Jeremy Belknap, and James Kirke Paulding, three American authors who expressed their opinions of Anglo-American relations, used "the pleasing and popular form of an allegory"[2] and followed one and the same model, Arbuthnot's *John Bull*. Of these writers, Belknap (1744-98) was the most moderate. Though in *The Foresters*[3] he adopted the Arbuthnot personifications consistently and borrowed various other details from his model,[4] his satire is only in appearance a "sequel to the history of John Bull the Clothier," as its title page has it. Belknap's view of the conduct of the British and the Americans (the "foresters") was very much conditioned by the historian's approach; and as a result, *The Foresters* strikes the reader less as a satire than as allegorical history with an American bias.[5] Thirteen of the eighteen letters contained in the final edition of

1796 deal with the development of the British colonies in North America, letter 14 introducing the national phase. The last letters added in 1796 abandon the major issues and the consistent forward sweep of the narration to hint at less inspiring aspects: the Genet affair and the Georgia speculations.

That Belknap owed much to Arbuthnot is obvious:

> ...The foresters had a respect for their old master and landlord, and when they had anything to sell, they always let him have the refusal of it, and bought all their goods of him. But though he called himself their father, and his wife their mother, yet he began to abate of his parental affection for them; and rather looked on them with a jealous eye, as if they were aiming to deprive him of his claim and set up for independence. Had he been contented with the profits of their trade, as was certainly his interest, they might have remained his tenants to this day; but ambition, avarice, jealousy and choler, inflamed by bad counsellors, have wrought such a separation, that it is thought Mr. Bull will go mourning all the remainder of his days, and his grey hairs will be brought down with sorrow to the grave.
> (pp. 99-100)

The one quality, however, which above all made Arbuthnot's *John Bull* successful—its caustic vividness in the treatment of a controversial subject—is replaced in Belknap's allegory by a far milder tone.[6] There is less originality in Belknap's handling of the dispute between Britain and America than in his manner of humorously characterizing the various colonies, but this remains a subordinate feature within his historical presentation.

The Arbuthnot asperity was adequately caught and disciplined to a lesser robustness and bitterness by Francis Hopkinson (1737-91) in *A Pretty Story* (1774).[7] This short pamphlet devotes two chapters to the Magna Charta and the settlement of North America before detailing, in five more chapters, the various measures which, from the late 1760s onward, step by step increased the distrust and antagonism between Britain and the colonies. *A Pretty Story* was written in time to be read by the colonial delegates assembled in Philadelphia to discuss their grievances against the English Parliament. Hopkinson concluded his pamphlet with a reference to the measures taken against

Massachusetts after the Boston Tea Party in a sentence left meaningfully incomplete: "These harsh and unconstitutional Proceedings irritated *Jack* and the other inhabitants of the new Farm to such a Degree that *************** *Caetera desunt"* (p. 197). The thirteen asterisks evidently called on the colonies to provide a continuation. Hopkinson's point was more than merely opportune and highly topical: by going back in his first chapter to the old British rights of the individual, the author added to the significance of the immediate issue that was in everyone's mind, raising it above the level of political bargaining. This effect was helped, too, by leaving the parties without proper names (except for "Jack" or Massachusetts): there are on the one hand the nobleman,[8] his wife and the steward, and on the other the noblemen's sons. The combination of the general with the precise and topical, a feature of all allegorical presentation, is ingeniously and thoroughly realized in *A Pretty Story*.[9] The title itself expresses an irony which in the pamphlet is sensed in the shifts from the general to the particular, for they emphasize the shortsightedness and final insignificance of the temporary rationalizations behind which essential values are being betrayed. Political hypocrisy is thus revealed by the account of the situation after the French and Indian Wars:

> But now the Nobleman's Wife began to cast an avaricious Eye upon the new Settlers; saying to herself, if by the natural Consequence of their Intercourse with us my Wealth and Power are so much increased, how much more would they accumulate if I can persuade them that all they have belonged to us, and therefore I may at any Time demand from them such Part of their Earnings as I please. At the same Time she was fully sensible of the Promises and agreements her Husband had made when they left the old Farm, and of the Tenor and Purport of the *Great Paper*. She therefore thought it necessary to proceed with great Caution and Art, and endeavoured to gain her Point by imperceptible Steps. (pp. 187-88)

Hopkinson's last chapter naturally showed the colonies united. Having shared the troubles of settling the country, the colonists sympathize with the people of Massachusetts, "assuring them that they looked on the Punishments and Insults laid upon them

[89]

with the same Indignation as if they had been inflicted on themselves, and that they would stand by and support them to the
last" (p. 196). At a later period Belknap presented the United
States as evolved out of individual settlements and therefore
varied: symptoms of dissension were to be expected.

Nor do the regions and interests of the United States appear
unanimous in *The Diverting History of John Bull and Brother
Jonathan* (1812), by James Kirke Paulding (1778-1860). Congress is described on one occasion as being "almost always of at
least *seventeen* different opinions";[10] later "Mrs. Jonathan" de-
bates without achieving anything: "So she went on for a whole
six months at least, chattering away every day to a different tune.
Sometimes she talked like a farmer, at others like a tobacco
planter, anon like a boatman, or a distiller of whiskey..."
(pp. 81-82). On the eve of a new war the New England states
scorn Jonathan's appeal to assist him as seconds against Squire
Bull (chap. 15). One party supports Bull, another is in favor
of Beau Napperty, whose portrait is drawn as follows:

> He wore...a three coloured cockade, as large as an ordinary
> target, and a three coloured plume higher than all the rest of
> him put together, so that when the wind blew he was so top
> heavy he could not stand without some ballast in his pockets.
> ...His sword [was] of such immeasurable size that every body
> wondered how he could drag it along. In fact it was the general
> opinion that he would in time exhaust himself in the trailing of
> this unwieldy toasting iron. (pp. 22-23)

The first of the sixteen chapters sketches the history of the
settling of the colonies and the winning of their independence;
the rest of the book presents the three main aspects of the contemporary situation: (1) Squire Bull's proud and proprietary
attitude concerning the sea-trade and the impressment of Jonathan's rowing crews, which he justifies with his fight with Beau
Napperty; (2) the latter's cunning and ambitious nature; and
(3) the regional diversity and political discord of the farmers on
Jonathan's "Bullock's Island," with a special dig at the shrewdly
acquisitive and restless tenants of Yankeeland. Bonaparte and
Congress notwithstanding, it is Squire Bull who is the chief target of Paulding's characteristic barbs.[11] The book ends aptly on

the hopeful suggestion that Bull may yet revise his attitude toward Jonathan. Although his immediate purpose was as limited
and urgent as Hopkinson's had been forty years earlier, Paulding
failed to achieve his precursor's concentration and economy.
His tone, to be sure, is nearer even than Hopkinson's to that of
the original *John Bull*, humorously rough and hard-hitting; yet
Paulding did not succeed in channeling his powers[12] so consistently as Arbuthnot had done, or as had Hopkinson within
the tighter framework of his witty summing-up.

The form of the allegory imposes upon the writer using it a
fair measure of control; indeed only a skillful practitioner can
preserve some liberty of movement within its limits. A writer is
therefore likely to refuse to submit to such formal restraint if he
feels that it may hinder him from saying what he has to say with
all the force he thinks appropriate. The indignation given vent
to in *A Journal of a Young Man of Massachusetts* (1816) is not
unlike Paulding's resentment of things British. The *Journal* does
not adopt the guise of an allegorical satire: it is a straightforward
narrative, with perhaps a hint of fiction in its outward aspect.
The work is attributed to, or at least assigned to the editorship
of, Benjamin Waterhouse, the physician (1754-1826); it has been
described as "so vivid and lifelike that it must have been written
or dictated by a participant in the events described."[13] It seems
probable that the basis of the *Journal* is hard fact, colored not
by deliberate fictitious borrowings and elaborations but rather
by the resentment which the original narrator felt: "I have made
it a point of honor, a matter of conscience, and a rule of justice,
to adhere to the truth; and am contented the British reader
should say all that fairness admits to soften down the coloring
of some pictures of British barbarity, provided he does not attempt to impeach my veracity" (p. 227).

The contents of the *Journal* are summarized on its title page,
where the "young man of Massachusetts" is described as "late a
surgeon on board an American privateer, who was captured at
sea by the British, in May, eighteen hundred and thirteen, and
was confined first, at Melville Island, Halifax, then at Chatham,
in England, and last, at Dartmoor prison." The indignant accounts of ill-treatment suffered by the American prisoners[14] and

of attempted escapes betrayed by "secret informers among our crew, perhaps some Irish, Dane, or Dutchman" (p. 106), are "interspersed with observations, anecdotes and remarks, tending to illustrate the moral and political characters of three nations," that is to extol the American virtues and expose the vices of Britain and France. Not surprisingly, considering the character of the *Journal,* its merits as literature and fiction are slight.[15] One point must be made here, however: part of the author's reaction against his idea and experience of the British is also aimed at what he has come to consider the Federalist delusions of his native New England concerning Britain.[16] The pro-British prejudice which he acquired there is just what Paulding criticized in *John Bull and Brother Jonathan.* Ironically, the author, so contemptuous of British chauvinism, filled his own book with American claims to superiority over the English. He so zealously expressed his resentment at the British and pro-British that he made of his *Journal* a document not unlike those travel books by English tourists whose hasty and unflattering conclusions angered many touchy Americans in the first decades of the nineteenth century.[17] From the general education provided in New England to that region's splendid autumn (pp. 39-41, 139), and from the wealth and freedom enjoyed by the Americans to the chastity of their womenfolk (pp. 16, 142),[18] the author praised the advantages of his nation over others and found nothing to criticize at home.

Waterhouse, or whoever wrote the *Journal,* might be called an (involuntary) American traveler in England, whose report is a retaliation upon the work of some British travelers in America. Royall Tyler (1757-1826), who in 1809 published *The Yankey in London,* was only an imaginary tourist. The fourteen letters that make up his book are allegedly chosen from the correspondence of an American with his Boston friends.[19] They good-humoredly make fun of some of the political, social, and literary aspects of English life. The author visits the House of Commons and the House of Lords and has a word or two to say about the English weather. Women's fashions are ridiculed and warned against, and so are "medical, mechanical, and culinary quacks."[20] The writer voices his concern over linguistic affectation and the decadence in literary taste (p. 179). He rejects the Boswellian type of biography and its inclusion of irrelevant anecdotic material; he deplores the fuss made over the mystification in the cases of Macpherson and Chatterton, obscuring as it does the genuine literary merit of their work. The author, who evidently ridicules American foibles, too, indicates his general attitude in a chapter on "Prominent traits in the English character" (letter 43, pp. 145-65). He pronounces the English vain, conceited, and convinced of the unparalleled excellence of their government, army, liberty, and climate, and then abruptly confesses that his estimate was meant as a joke: "...If I could in serious mood asperse a great people in this manner, I should abhor myself, and feel degraded from the rank of intelligent beings, and reduced to a level with *English travellers*....Amid all their weaknesses, and all their follies, they have many men, and *very many* women, many achievements and many virtues, of which they may justly be proud without the imputation of *vanity*" (p. 165).

Adopting the convention of the *Lettres persanes* and similar models, Tyler vividly created the impression of having witnessed the scenes he described. His sound reflections on various literary subjects gave additional plausibility to his sketches—for example, of the House of Commons and the House of Lords—even though his mask of seriousness could be seen through. The author's very first letter gives an inkling of his mood; it contains an account of his conversation with a lady novelist whose only novel "had passed the ordeal of taste in all the circulating libraries, and was actually the last book the great Burke ever read, indeed, some said he expired with it in his hand" (p. 15).[21] In view of this lightness of manner, it is not to be supposed that *The Yankee in London* was looked upon as an authentic report.[22]

Charles Jared Ingersoll (1782-1862) committed himself more seriously than Tyler to the defense of some aspects of American life, against British as well as Continental judgments. *Inchiquin, the Jesuit's Letters* (1810) would not have aroused such heated discussions across the Atlantic[23] if the author's views had not been supported by an earnest sound of conviction and had not appeared to be well substantiated. The tone of the pamphlet is not objective throughout, though: at times Ingersoll uses superlatives and high praise, for instance, concerning American oratory or the religious sense and the morals of the Americans. The last of Inchiquin's five letters from Washington states that "setting aside two, or perhaps three, of the most enlightened empires of Europe, the literature, arts and sciences of the people of the United States of America, are equal, and their general information and intelligence superior, to those of any other nation."[24] This assertiveness, however, is at odds with the general sense of proportion and moderation displayed in the book as a whole. Concerning American literature, the author made no exaggerated claims, pronouncing it to be "rather solid than shining" (p. 126); he found Barlow's *Columbiad* distinguished for its conception and acceptable as to its technical qualities, but definitely lacking in poetic originality and greatness. Ingersoll maintained that what some foreign observers called faults were rather assets at the present stage of America's development (pp. 112-13).

Prefixed to the supposed Jesuit traveler's account, there were three letters addressed to Inchiquin by three different correspondents, each of them expressing prejudiced opinions on the unenviable state of America. These letters, which echo and exaggerate the condescending views of the United States held in Europe, contain in themselves enough contradictions to undercut the scornful treatment of America very ironically. Thus, the Belgian who writes the first letter finds himself caught by the French conscription, symptomatic of an unenviable state of affairs. The second letter comes from a Frenchman, who lists the brilliant achievements of France; his burst of nationalistic praise leads him unguardedly to propose effecting American unity by means of the French language and (French) Roman Catholicism. Inchiquin's brother-in-law, the Irishman Clanrickard, who lives in London, laments his relative's fate: Inchiquin has first been sent to France and must now go to America, while he, Clanrickard, is allowed to enjoy the benefits of England— that is, poverty, the fear of being robbed, and the need for protection. And he concludes:

The American federation, I suppose, cannot maintain itself

much longer. According to the best judgment I can form of the prospects of that distracted country, the crisis is not very distant, when it will implore once more the protection of a parent state, which it has ever studied to outrage. Notwithstanding all the injuries that have been received from those despicable freebooters by this magnanimous nation, I believe the cup of reconciliation is not yet exhausted. (pp. 28-29)

Ingersoll's point was just that "the best judgment" formed at a distance was not good enough. But the man advising his friend about to leave for America was unfortunately typical of the European attitude and even of the books about America by men who had been there but were blinded by "the operation of national prejudice" (p. 138 n.).[25] Ingersoll singled out "Anacreon" Moore among the vilifiers of America, but he was thinking of the various nations that at one time or another had judged his country unfairly. His counterattack is strengthened by Caravan's letter (pp. 33-50), included in Inchiquin's first letter from Washington. The Jesuit himself states that the aspect of the federal city is America at its worst (p. 31)[26] and may well give the uneducated and the rash a poor impression of the United States; one must achieve detachment in order not to be over-impressed by Washington as described by Caravan. To generalize from these observations reveals more about the observer than about the country observed; only in the observer's imagination, Inchiquin added, was it barely settled and civilized, furnished with inadequate housing and roads, and peopled mostly with hunters and duelists for whose taste horse races and camp meetings have been designed as exciting spectacles.

2. Federalist New England versus Jeffersonian Republicanism

Among the satirical fiction employed in the warfare between Federalists and Republicans, a large majority speaks on behalf of New England Federalism against the Republicans. It is not difficult to understand why there should be such a one-sided body of partisan satire. New England was far more of a unity than the other regions, not only politically speaking (in that respect

Virginia had equal strength) but also owing to a literary tradition which was there to support the political stand. Since Federalism was the political line of gentlemen,[27] and since gentlemen were literate and articulate, the New England Federalists knew how to speak their views forcefully and skillfully.[28] In addition, the person of Washington may have acted as a restraining influence on the Republican satirists during the era in which the predominance of the Federalists made them objects of satire *par excellence*. Washington perhaps called Freneau a rascal because attacks against his person as pointed as Freneau's were comparatively rare.

Freneau's *Letters on Various Interesting and Important Subjects* (1799)[29] express the Republican point of view. These twenty-four letters by "Robert Slender, O.S.M.," that is, "One of the Swinish Multitude," were dedicated to "the Freemen, the Lovers of Liberty, the Asserters, the Maintainers and Supporters of Independence throughout the United States," the "true republicans" (p. vii) of his country—meaning, of course, the Republicans of Jefferson. We must suppose these readers to be as naïve in ways worldly and political as Slender himself, who cannot conceive that Christian rulers ever abuse their power and is baffled by the long and glorious words bandied about by politicians. Though unsophisticated and inclined to shrink from loud arguments, the "true republicans" hold their own. Their convictions help them to resist even "a deep laid, well concerted and organized plan, to influence the people into federal ideas at the next *election*" (p. 21). In Pennsylvania they saw through the propaganda against the Republican Thomas McKean which accused him of being a "democrat" and "an enemy to our mother country, Great Britain," and of having "as president of Congress, signed the instrument of all our woes, the Declaration of Independence!" (p. 28). Freneau's trenchant style and occasional use of the colloquial phrase undoubtedly rendered his Robert Slender a lovable or hateful figure. But Freneau, convinced though he was of the rightness of his cause, was not supported by an assent so active as that of the New England Federalists. No one thought of him as the "first American master of belletristic prose" in an age when to be "the leading journalist...of Jeffersonian and

French democracy"[30] could easily be interpreted as a serious offense, if not downright treason, by the eloquent speakers of the opposing party.

Freneau was described as "a poet remarkable only for the quantity of verse which he has written" by Benjamin Silliman, the author of *Letters of Shahcoolen* (1802),[31] who on the other hand praised the Connecticut Wits for their efforts to raise American literature to the level of English writing.[32] The summary dismissal of Freneau is one of the clues to the Federalist outlook of Shahcoolen which also colors his denunciation of Mary Wollstonecraft (letters 2 to 4), who is described as a revolutionary monster of viciousness, hostile to all traditions of religion and morals. Silliman thought he could detect symptoms of her demoralizing influence in the fashions adopted by American women, and in their tendency to play cards, swear, and take up skating. He then sketched a prototype of the virtuous American woman.[33] To Silliman the "false philosophy" of Mary Wollstonecraft was merely one aspect of the "philosophical reveries of the present day." Shahcoolen's last letters therefore contain a "Dialogue with a modern Philosopher" (pp. 138-52), intended to expose the foolishness of a man to whom "republicanism" and "modern philosophy" (pp. 138-39) mean the same thing; a misguided person who can think that the advent of Jefferson's first administration is a step forward toward securing the democratic liberties, "while the minions of monarchy and aristocracy are skulking into private life" (p. 139). This modern philosopher is allowed freely to expound his views, for, of course, any sane (that is, Federalist) reader will reject them, together with the related ideas of Rousseau and Mary Wollstonecraft.[34] The zeal of Silliman's satire of the "Rights of Woman" and "Back to Nature" programs completely overshadows his discussions of poetry in general and American and Indian poetry, and the Song of Solomon in particular. The reader puts down *Letters of Shahcoolen* with a distinct impression of some of the notions—political, social, and moral—which Federalist New England attributed to Jefferson and his Republican supporters.

Fragments of the History of Bawlfredonia (1819)[35] represents the views of those New Englanders who could not forgive Madison for "his" war and thought of him as a plague divinely appointed:

> When Heaven, in vengeance for our sins, permitted this little
> man to ascend the throne, and plunge our country, unprepared,
> into a most bloody war, he withdrew the national troops from
> the defence of Asylumonia. When the prowess of our citizens
> had convinced our enemy, "that we could conquer though our
> king should fly," Pigman patched up a treaty of peace, in which
> he "remembered to forget" to secure to the fishermen of
> Asylumonia, the privileges which had been guaranteed to them
> by all former treaties. (p. 134 n.)[36]

The complicated apparatus of mystification which obliquely
ensures that the *History of Bawlfredonia* should be recognized
as a satire of American Republicanism states that its subject is
a country discovered about 1789, not far from Botany Bay.
Accidentally sailing into Asylum Harbour, some surviving members of a French crew settle there among the inquisitive inhabitants of Asylumonia. One of them, M. Traducteur, later trans-
lates the *History*. His manuscript makes its way to Baltimore,
where the editor gets possession of it. The seven fragments
which he publishes contain so many similarities to American
history, the editor says in his introduction, that people will think
it is a mere satire of the United States and its leaders, but such
an idea must be dismissed as ridiculous because "the immaculate
purity of the characters, the transcendent intellectual powers
which all our great men have possessed, both for civil and
martial government, and the unparalleled prosperity to which
they have, especially of late years, raised this flourishing commonwealth; all these, I say, set them far above the loftiest flights
of the shafts of satire" (p. 13). Bawlfredonia is a name derived
not from the original discoverer but from one who bawled loud
enough to appear capable of such a discovery. Having given an
account of the discovery, the author in the next two sections
relates how Blackmoreland and Asylumonia were settled and
then broke with their mother country. Fragments 4 to 7 are
devoted to Tom Anguish, Thomas Tammany Bawlfredonius,
and Pigman Puff, and their efforts to discredit religion and
undermine the Federal authority. The author speaks chiefly

in tones of either offended and offensive anger or pronouncedly ironical praise. Now and again he refers sarcastically to the Republican way of interpreting the separation of church and state: to him this interpretation appears as a Macchiavellian distinction between the commercially or politically expedient and the morally justifiable, and also as an excuse to abolish the Christian religion altogether. He comments on the Republican reaction to the Sedition Act of 1798, remarking that when in power the Republicans arbitrarily used some of its provisions, even after it was invalidated. There are allusions to Jefferson's Illuminatism, to Paine's influence among the Republicans, to the Virginian aristocracy and dynasty of national leaders, and to slavery, upheld by Jefferson contrary to his own obviously hypocritical statements.

To his satire of the Jeffersonians the author added some ironical remarks concerning man generally. The Republicans are not alone in failing to apply the moral test to some of their decisions; long before they existed questionable arguments were used—for example, to justify the importation of slaves: "Even if they are men, our business is not to consider the sin, or the duty of the matter, but the policy. If that can be settled, we have no more to do. The church may think of the rest" (p. 63).[37] Referring to the presidential candidates of 1797, Adams and Jefferson, the author wrote that "the better informed and more discerning men of the nation, weighed both these great men in the balance, and pronounced them wanting" (p. 148).

Some of the anti-Republican points made in the *History of Bawlfredonia* within the perspective of American history and human nature[38] occurred a few years earlier in *The Adventures of Uncle Sam, in Search after his Lost Honor* (1816), by the pseudonymous Frederick Augustus Fidfaddy, Esq. To heighten his effect, the author made some use of the nomenclature of Arbuthnot, Belknap, and Paulding, speaking of the American presidents as chief stewards, of Congress as Uncle Sam's wife, and mentioning Bull; Napoleon becomes a Bunyanesque Appolyon. His own inventions are not too witty: General Hull, for example, is "Count Scratch-us-off," and General Smyth, "Count Smite-us-off." The United States is turned into an allegorical table whose thirteen legs have been increased by five apparently unequal ones, so that it now stands rather insecurely. In some chapters the writer chose to use a biblical style; in the one presenting Jefferson, called "Thomas, the Magician," one passage refers to the Sedition Act and the *Notes on Virginia*:

> 53. And it fell out in the Stewardship of John, that he made a decree saying thou shalt not speak evil of the rulers of thy people; thou shalt not lie. And the thing displeased Thomas and he said the decree is not good, So he destroyed the decree and said thou mayst lie; but thou shalt not speak the truth against the rulers of thy people....
> 57. And he wrote a book containing many wise sayings and much wisdom; for he spake of mountains and rivers and fishes; and of trees from the Oak that maketh the beams of ships, to the Tobacco plant that burneth before the nostrils.[39]

The main object of Fidfaddy's attack, however, was the War of 1812, into which the United States had been rushed. He devoted ten of his twelve chapters to it, lamenting Madison's ambition, and the ineptitude of the army leaders, and deploring that none of the issues advanced to justify the war were settled by the Treaty of Ghent. The ignominy of the American flight from Washington moved him to elevated strains:

> Is there an American heart unwounded at the recollection! Or have we lost all distinction between virtue and vice....Has a repetition of the act of bowing our necks, with a sinic servility, to the burden of shame, neutralized our feelings and blunted our perceptions! Why did not the verdant sod that covers the ashes of Washington burst asunder. But no! Had his pale ghost met the shameless fugitives with the stern upbraidings of a seraph, they would have dodged regardless along, "let us live to enjoy our offices" would have been the answer. (pp. 123-24)

An issue which angered the Federalists particularly was the naval disarmament ordered during Jefferson's administration. Fidfaddy did not fail to stress that whereas the armies frequently proved incapable of enforcing their generals' "proclamations,"[40] the American warships obtained many victories: the "genius of Columbia presided over the destinies of our little Navy...scattering laurels with the discriminating wisdom of a sage" (p. 63).

Meanwhile, the Quixotic campaigns on land only caused disputes among the commanding officers: "...They threw the charges of 'incapacity' and 'cowardice,' with such rapidity to each other, that our Uncle sat, rolling his huge eyes, first at one, then at the other, like a kitten, watching the pendulous motion of a ball of yarn..." (p. 74).[41]

The War of the Gulls; an Historical Romance (1812), by Jacob Bigelow (1786-1879) and Nathan Hale (1784-1863), also ridiculed General William Hull's efforts on land and praised Isaac Hull's successful action at sea. A pamphlet of thirty-six pages, it meant to show that the Americans had gullibly allowed themselves to be misled by the shortsighted naval and foreign policy of the Republicans. It made a point of stressing that General Hull was a Republican—so why expect victories on land? But on the Atlantic,

> The federal Hull
> Gave chase to John Bull,
> And was soon along side of the thundering Guerrier;
> With his balls and his powder
> So thickly he plough'd her
> She sunk a mere wreck, and the Gulls ne'er sung merrier.

This is the second of four stanzas which conclude the pamphlet[42] and offer as parting advice:

> . . . if we must be gulls
> O let us be sea-gulls,
> And give up our conquests to Bidwell and Gannett.

In some quarters there was an acute consciousness of the divergence of views separating the various subdivisions of the country, and it was feared that the forces of dissension might eventually disrupt the unity of the new country. The Reverend William Jenks (1778-1866) imagined in 1808 what the situation might be like seventy years later. His *Memoir of the Northern Kingdom,* allegedly " written A.D. 1872" and published at "Quebeck, A.D. 1901," saw the United States split into three regions. Looking back from an imaginary future, the author of the

[101]

Memoir remembers how the Southern States, under the leadership of Virginia, seceded from the United States. They had leaned more and more toward France, whence came many immigrants, chiefly officers. Among these was Napoleon's brother Jerome, who married a young lady from Baltimore[43] and whose son was designated to rule the Southern kingdom. In the face of Southern dissidence, New York and New England formed a union with closer ties and a more centralized administration, choosing a President elected for life. But the royal government of Canada turned against the Northern States; at length the Canadian king married the daughter of the Northern States' president and effected a personal union between their countries. Meanwhile, only the Middle States remained true to the republican idea, but their center of gravity shifted toward the interior of the country. The *Memoir* begins by advising the "Illinois Republicans," those descendants of the truly democratic Americans of the late eighteenth century, to reestablish a monarchy or to accept annexion to the Northern Kingdom. A monarchy, after all, is a natural form of government—thus runs the argument of the sceptic in matters of democratic self-government and mutual concessions:

> ...The truth is, no man is indifferent to personal honours, however he may for the present, and most probably for the sake of obtaining a more abundant share in future, affect to despise them.
> In principle then, by far the greater part of the United Americans were republican. In manners the most influential among them were generally aristocratick. But I do not impute this circumstance to them as Americans, or as republicans, but as men. It is human nature, and we cannot expect to change that nature merely by the form of government.[44]

Jenks's point was not, it may be assumed, that the American experiment in republicanism was absolutely doomed to fail; but he wanted to make clear that the United States could not stand a further weakening of its interior ties. The Southern States', and especially Virginia's, Gallophilia, as well as the individual Republican leaders' ambitions, threatened to destroy the nation and to render the very idea of the democratic state suspect. In this sense the *Memoir* is really "an anti-Jeffersonian tract of considerable felicity."[45] Yet although Jenks's preferences were Federalist,[46] his work reveals a rather moderately partisan attitude. It is the more regrettable that the author did not make a more skillful use of the device of historical anticipation.

A further example of the anti-Republican fictional writings of New England attracts attention by means of features other than partisan satire. This is the anonymous *The Yankee Traveller, or the Adventures of Hector Wigler* (1817). The book attacks Jefferson too, but not, however, the political figure so much as the "philosopher" and "Illuminatus."[47] Jefferson is mocked for his scientific pretensions and his rejection of the Christian faith, the result of his reading of Rousseau, Shaftesbury, Hobbes, Condorcet, Godwin, and Paine, all of them the villains of the New England Federalists. Among those who, like the narrator, visit "Thomas Conundrum" at "M—o," we find a philosopher of the New French School, called Nihil, and a fat doctor from New York, Van Stufflefunk.[48] Nihil, a fervent supporter of Mary Wollstonecraft's ideas, woos a Mrs. Wimble who poses as Miss Wimble. Another assembly of "Conundrumites" gathers at an inn, a locale indicative of their moral character, apparently, just as much as their various callings[49] or the name of one among them, the Hon. Judge Bubble.

The inn provides the storyteller with a helpful way of naturally introducing a group of characters; the same function can be assigned to the coach which in *The Yankee Traveller* takes the party of pilgrims to Monticello. The storyteller rather than the satirist is also in evidence in several elements of episodic action. The hero has been staying with his Jeffersonian uncle Humbug, whom he suspects of really being his father. He finds himself prompted to leave Humbug's farm when his uncle marries again and begins fathering children upon his young Dutch bride.[50] He leaves in the company of the pedantic schoolmaster Whack when the latter is involved in a case of doubtful paternity and assists him in outwitting and knocking out Squat, the true father of the child laid at Whack's door. When the policy of "Mundungus," or Madison, plunges the country into the War of 1812, Hector becomes a soldier; he is disappointed at not being made a sergeant, and must suffer for expressing his disappointment too rebelliously. The treatment of such adventurous passages is more to the author's credit than his handling of the satirical situations; he writes at times with the zest of Smollett. His book unfortunately breaks off very abruptly with Hector's discomfiture in the army, and *The Yankee Traveller* remains a mere hint of the possibilities of blending satire and the novel.[51]

There is little fiction and not much genuine satire in *The Life and Travels of Father Quipes, otherwise Dominick O'Blarney* (1820), a pamphlet attributed to John MacFarland.[52] This scurrilous piece of writing was aimed by a politician at a local rival. Two equally unattractive pictures—of the attacker and of his victim—emerge from its pages. The former was apparently fond of political invective and was generally quarrelsome, attributes which would seem to provide adequate equipment for penning a *Father Quipes*. Quipes, who might be a relative of Freneau's Father Bombo and Brackenridge's Teague O'Regan, candidly describes himself as an illiterate Irish upstart, given to exploiting and mocking those who have helped him. He has come to America as the victim of a press-gang. The account of his rise through imposture and slander is occasionally interrupted by episodes illustrating his naïve ignorance of the polite ways of the world. The oblique undermining of the character is very clumsily done; it is nevertheless recognizably akin to the *Jonathan Wild* type of biography and to the sketches of charters like Simon Suggs, Senior and Junior, or Ovid Bolus.

Of the satires that have been discussed in this chapter, it is clearly Freneau's that most successfully combines an original conception with good writing. Each of the other works is decidedly inferior to Robert Slender's *Letters*; the *History of Bawlfredonia* is perhaps more unified and more truly humorous than the others.

3. Letters from America

Many writers of the eighteenth century used the concept of the foreign observer whose testimony has a corrective function: it should open the eyes of the inhabitants of the country he visits to errors and affectations to which they have grown accustomed. The *Letters of Shahcoolen* were introduced by their publisher with a reference to Montesquieu's and Goldsmith's imaginary travelers. The *Lettres persanes* and *The Citizen of the World,* however, have a vaster scope than Silliman's *Letters* and point out a greater variety of national foibles. Shahcoolen limited his view to two subjects: American literature and, more importantly, a combination of political radicalism and religious anti-traditionalism; his personal outlook branded the work, making it a partisan satire of Jeffersonian Republicanism.

Samuel Lorenzo Knapp (1783-1838)[53] published in 1817 *Extracts from the Journals of Marshal Soult.* The pretended French marshal, now living in the United States, claims that he has always taken a great interest in America and promises to be an impartial observer and thus more reliable than most travelers from Britain and France.[54] He starts out from Boston, visits Massachusetts, Vermont, and New Hampshire, and concludes that the American republic will prove more durable than others: the resources of the country are immense, and its democratic structure is the natural outcome of organic conditions. The diarist sketches various eminent New Englanders as well as his idea of the North American Indians: "The native savages were of gigantic stature, fleet in motion, capable of sustaining incredible hardships of cold, fatigue and famine, accustomed to war, glorying in blood and death, and fearlessly bidding defiance, and breathing vengeance for their real or imagined wrongs."[55] In his account of the career of a local politician, the author uses the manner of a novelist describing the sad fate of one of his heroes: ". . . Misfortune followed misfortune, until 1784, found him involved beyond the hope of redemption, and he retired to a country seat, avoided the world, and in a few years fell a victim to sensibility" (p. 94).

In the following year Knapp dropped the disguise of the Frenchman to adopt that of "Ali Bey," but *Extracts from a Journal of Travels in North America* (1818) covers very much the same ground again. A "Translator's Advertisement" promises another description fairer to America than the travel books written by Frenchmen or Englishmen. Ali Bey's second letter, or extract, takes up a point of the former series, the discussion between "Calvinists" and "Latitudinarians":

The Calvinists are led by their peculiar temperament to draw mankind in dark colours. They would make us believe that we are a very wicked and worthless race of beings, deserving of all manner of punishment—which it would seem we are now undergoing, for they insist upon it that there is nothing in this world but sorrow, misery and sin.

The other party are less saturnine—they look upon man to be a pretty clever sort of a being naturally, with many good and some bad principles in his nature, either of which he is at liberty to cultivate, and which he does cultivate according to the force of temptations, and the predominance of a good or a bad education. As to the world, although disfigured with much misery and vice, they still think that the balance is in favor of happiness and virtue. And they do not see the advantage or propriety in painting the world or its inhabitants in darker colours than truth requires. Much less allowable do they deem to draw the character of the Almighty according to the gloomy imaginations of men, without regard to revelation.[56]

Ali Bey goes on to criticize manners and fashions, the education of young girls and the corruption of civil servants, hypocrisy in matters of church attendance and humanitarian activities. After giving his American friend an opportunity to air his grievances about the American "literary inferiority" (p. 100), the visitor concludes, in his most successful satirical passage, that the Bostonians might be won over to Islam if certain conditions were respected:

The Imaums and Fakirs selected for the high trust of sowing the seed of truth in this benighted land, must be men of talents, education and address. They should be invested with all the splendor that money can command. Their mosques should be magnificent and richly endowed. With these prerequisites a few able Imaums would find no difficulty in attracting, first to their drawing rooms and then to their mosques, all the fashionables and literati of the city. The example of these, always contagious, would soon influence the middle and lower classes. With a good voice and commanding manners, with funds sufficient to appear men of the world, to give dinners and routs, frequent the theatre, &c. our teachers would be certain of success. (pp. 114-15)

Neither of the series of *Extracts* has uncommon merits, though perhaps a livelier fancy animates the second. A better book than either had used four decades earlier the idea of establishing a bridgehead for a foreign power in some part of the United States. Knapp was possibly inspired by Mehemet, the central figure of *The Algerine Spy in Pennsylvania* (1787), but his books do not reflect the high spirits of Peter Markoe (ca. 1752-92).[57] A slight yet entertaining production, *The Algerine Spy* was written at a time nearly as critical as the year 1774, when Hopkinson's *A Pretty Story* appeared. Markoe's aim, too, was similar to Hopkinson's: he meant to underscore the necessity of a radical change in the system of government in America. If the Federal powers were increased, defections like that of Rhode Island or troubles like Shays's Rebellion would hardly occur any more, and certainly would no longer mean any real danger to the country. Mehemet suggests offering the protection of Algiers to Rhode Island, but speedily drops this plan when he becomes aware of the unity of purpose manifested by the other states, as well as the endless resources, physical and governmental, of the United States.

Mehemet finds little to blame in the republican spirit and democratic provisions of the country. He is puzzled by the Quaker meeting he attends, though he does not fall asleep as Franklin had done. He hopes that the American universities will not ossify like their European models. Mehemet trusts that no nationalistic considerations may lead the Americans to abandon their neutrality, for it is plain to him that "they are too strong to be conquered, and too weak to think of conquering others."[58] When he is struck with the businesslike air of many Americans or the manner in which fashions establish their rule, his reflections are much like those he made during his stops at Gibraltar and Lisbon—on Occidentals generally, not on different nationals. At times he shows hostility to the French, whom he describes as objects of "hatred and contempt" (p. 13), as vain, chauvinistic, and exaggeratedly fond of dancing. A ball, though, presents

him with the delightful opportunity of watching Western dancing for the first time:

> ...In the course of their fooleries, I thought I perceived a
> degree of mystic morality. The lady at times fled from the
> gentleman, as if she was offended; whilst he, from the hope of
> appeasing her anger, followed her with becoming tenderness;
> but deeming her implacable, and conscious of his own dignity,
> gives over the pursuit and flies from her. She, justly apprehen-
> sive of losing him entirely, follows him in turn; a reconciliation
> ensues, and their hands are reunited. (pp. 48-49)

Everything considered, human weaknesses such as fashions and
social affectations do not count so much as the aggregate of
good will which operates, for example, in the American "popular
assemblies, who are more studious to increase the happiness of
the people than to create enemies" (p. 114). Mehemet, therefore, is not at all unhappy when he is told that he is in disgrace
at the court of Algiers, that his estate has been confiscated, and
that his wife has eloped with his chief gardener, a slave. "No
longer either a slave or a tyrant," he is now "at once a christian
and a Pennsylvanian,...doubly an advocate for the rights of
mankind" (p. 126). On a note of strained rhetoric, he finally
addresses Pennsylvania: "...Open thy arms to receive Mehemet,
the Algerine, who...hopes, protected by thy laws, to enjoy, in
the evening of his days, the united blessings of FREEDOM and
CHRISTIANITY" (p. 129).

The virtues of the American—or at least, the Pennsylvanian—
republic, to which Mehemet so heartily subscribed, escaped the
notice of an alleged Frenchman whose observations reached the
public in *The Hermit in America on a Visit to Philadelphia*
(1819). Robert Waln, Jr. (1794-1825), who invented the Hermit,
made him speak instead of "beaux and belles, dandies and coquettes, cotillion parties, supper parties, tea parties."[59] This one-
sided preoccupation seems understandable to some extent, since
the Hermit is about to leave on a voyage into the interior of the
world from which he might conceivably not return.[60] The Hermit's
peevish remarks tire the reader the more quickly because they
are helped by neither originality nor wit.

Hardly more original than Waln's Hermit, but at least less cantankerous, the Chinese traveler employed by George Fowler in *The Wandering Philanthropist* (1810) speaks as a serious and well-meaning prophet warning a people against the possible serious consequences of what to them are mere foibles and trifles. Occasionally he also praises some of the institutions and achievements that come under his observation. He deplores extremes of partisan spirit but notes the advantages of a two-party system. The treatment of the natives of the New World appears appallingly cruel and brutal to him; however, he finds their status and opportunities in the United States not unsatisfactory. He has no sympathy whatever with the slaveholders of the South and does not understand how their protestations of natural rights can be reconciled with the treatment they often give their slaves. Hypocrisy and hollow phrases strike him when he visits Congress and attends a Fourth of July celebration. He finds, like Brackenridge's Farrago, that "the loudest professions" are considered the mark of "the best patriot"[61] and derives from his observation another conclusion Farrago would have agreed with: "The great defect of an hereditary government is the despotick power which rulers exercise over the people; the great defect of an elective government is the despotick power which the people exercise over rulers" (p. 193). He particularly resents "the invincible prejudices that have existed in this country against original productions" (p. v). He comments on this in an indignant passage that is all the more striking because it follows words of praise for the rise of science and general education in the country, and a panegyric of George Washington bristling with the superlatives so readily applied to the first president in Fowler's days (pp. 110-11).[62] The author drops his usual moderation in one more case: when he paints a picture of the sublimity and variety of the American landscape. Here Fowler's language, which is otherwise adequate to his purpose, fails him, and his attempt to render the grandeur he has experienced only results in an amateurish pseudo-Radcliffean accumulation:

In other places I found myself enclosed in long and deep vallies where the awful heights which surrounded me almost obscured the light of day. Here towering trees of every description grow in crouds, and spreading out in their wild and natural magnificence, their limbs are so thickly entwined as almost to defy the approach of light, and in the midst of day to enshroud the darkness of night. The awful cliffs looked down upon me and seemed to threaten to crush me to pieces. The craggy rocks rose one above another, and hung over the dreadful precipice. Here immense trees have been torn up by the roots, and falling spread devastation among others, plough up the ground and are dashed into a thousand pieces. (pp. 133-34)

In his preface Fowler states that fancy must play a part "in so diversified a subject" (p. iv) as he is attempting, but there is little sign of its influence in *The Wandering Philanthropist*. James Kirke Paulding[63] knew how to use fancy more freely, just as he commanded the wit and originality so sadly lacking in *The Hermit in America;* he also assisted them with comic vigor. At the beginning of his *Letters from the South,* in a "historical" chapter inspired by the same spirit of burlesque that sparked off the *History of New York,* Paulding demonstrated why the American Indians must be considered the ancestors of the Europeans:

The Indians are much given to high play; so are the fashionable people abroad. The Indians neglect their wives; so do the fashionable people abroad. The Indians are mightily given to long pompous harangues; so are the fashionable orators abroad. The Indians are great smokers; so are the Dutch and Germans. The Indians are fond of high sounding titles, such as Iron Cloud, Negro Legs, Jumping Sturgeon, Big-eared Dog, Shifting Shadow, &c; so are the fashionable people abroad. The Indians are great beggars; so are the Italians. They are deep drinkers, like the Germans and English; they are smoky and dirty, like the Russians; great dancers, like the French; proud and lazy, as the Spaniards; and as vain as all these put together. Certainly all this shows a common origin; and the logical conclusion to be drawn, is, that a people like the Indians, uniting in themselves the various and distinguishing characteristics of the principal nations of the earth, *must* be the great common ancestor of all.[64]

Again and again Paulding repeats the need for more intellectual independence on the part of the Americans. His *Letters,* though ostensibly from the South, urge the people of all the different states and counties, and of town and country, to overcome their mutual prejudices. He voices, too, the concern expressed earlier by Markoe over the neglect of agriculture now that commerce and industry are encouraged everywhere. Here and there he allows himself to pause for the description of some historic site or a striking view, modestly attempting, perhaps, to supply a picture of one of those many beauties of America that, according to him, had not yet found their poet:

> In descending the mountain, we...saw, what seemed a vast and interminable waste of waters, spreading far and wide, and covering the whole face of the lower world. The vapours of the night had settled in the wide valley, at the foot of the hill, and enveloped it in one unbroken sheet of mist, that in the grey obscurity of the morning looked like a boundless ocean. But as the sun rose, a gentle breeze sprung up, and the vapours began to be in motion. As they lifted themselves lazily from the ground, and rolled in closer masses towards the mountains, the face of nature gradually disclosed itself in all its varied and enchanting beauty. The imaginary sea became a fertile valley, extending up and down, as far as the eye could reach. In the midst of the green foliage of oaks and solemn pines, were seen rich culti- vated lands, and comfortable farm-houses, surrounded by ruddy fields of clover, speckled with groups of cattle grazing in its luxuriant pastures, or reposing quietly among its blossoms. Still, as the mists passed silently away, new objects disclosed them- selves, with a sweet delay, that enhanced their beauty. Here was seen a little town, and near it a field, animated with sturdy labourers. (1:107-8)

Whereas Fowler, in the passage quoted before, composed a pic- ture out of "sublime" materials which remained intractable to his powers of description, Paulding's imaginative grasp produced a more harmonious result, both with the unusual spectacle in the first part of his landscape and the more familiar one, rather like a genre painting, which follows and forms a contrast to it. Paulding, however, refused to take himself too seriously in the role of the painter in words; and therefore, in another context of lyrical admiration, we find him pricking the balloon of his mood by introducing in the same scene the preoccupation of his geology-minded companion, who "had somehow or other heard of a parcel of oyster or muscle shells, bedded in a rock some-where in this neighborhood, which made his hobby-horse to caper and curvet, and kick at such a rate, that he could attend to nothing else" (1:177). Such touches, which transform the literary notion of a traveler into the feeling that he exists or the wish that he should exist, were beyond the other authors of "letters from America." Paulding, without being a great writer, at least knew and used his craft. He could convey his ideas and impressions to his pages, and was able to keep his subject alive and to avoid pretentious writing.

Paulding also refrained from inventing mysterious and elab-orate circumstances "explaining" the genesis of the work he published. His title page simply stated that the *Letters from the South* had been "written during an excursion in the summer of 1816." George Tucker (1775-1861),[65] in the manner of the other writers discussed in this chapter, added to the title of his *Letters from Virginia* (1816) "translated from the French," and prefixed a "Translator's Preface" to the *Letters,* saying among other things: "It is unnecessary, I suppose, to explain by what accident they came into my possession, because all will see that I have just as good a right to be lucky as another man" (p. v). In spite of the irony obviously aimed at a current convention, Tucker maintained the pretense which that convention implied by having the writer address his letters to different correspondents: those dealing with love to his girl friend, the descriptive and gossipy ones to her brother, and the reflective letters to their father.[66] With these correspondents the writer of the letters, supposedly an opponent of Napoleon like them, has spent the first years of his exile from France. He deplores the existence of slavery in Virginia[67] and comments on the indifference of the public toward native poets such as Richard Dabney. In a dream the times when marriageable young girls had to be imported are recollected: he sees them offered for sale on some market, like any other merchandise, and occasionally causing disappointment and dis-satisfaction to those who have acquired them. A Virginian friend of his disapproves of the Yankees because "they love money a little better than their own lives" (p. 38). But the visitor thinks this charge not much more serious than the Virginians' "gluttony," which influences even their judgment of people, as a gentleman's praise of Washington shows: "I knew the General mighty well. That was a fine man indeed. It would have done you good to see him eat a sheepshead!" (p. 117).

That the *Letters from Virginia* should have been attributed to Paulding is understandable, for their banter is not unlike that of the *Letters from the South;* moreover the remarks on the English travelers also suggest the possibility of Paulding's authorship (pp. 46-51, 147). There are in the two series of letters similar opinions on Yankee shrewdness, too, and the tone of Tucker's reflections about Fourth of July orators recalls Paulding's satirical voice: "These are men who set up once a year, (generally in very hot weather), to proclaim their independence with a loud voice, and abuse the British 'con amore'. In fact they sometimes carry their malice so far, as to vent their spite upon the very language they speak in, its unoffending parts of speech, and innocent rules of syntax, only because they are English" (p. 207).

The question of American standards of oratory also occupies some space in *The Letters of the British Spy* (1803), by William Wirt (1772-1834). With him, the subject obviously had a particular importance. When he speaks of "divine eloquence,"[68] he appears to be thinking of an ideal of complete communication between any artist and his public. The passage, famous in Wirt's days, about the blind preacher is a revealing illustration of Wirt's conception:

> But when he came to touch the patience, the forgiving meekness of our Saviour, when he drew, to the life, his blessed eyes streaming in tears to heaven—his voice breathing to God, a soft and gentle prayer of pardon on his enemies, "Father, forgive them, for they know not what they do"—the voice of the preacher, which had, all along, faltered, grew fainter and fainter, until his utterance being entirely obstructed by the force of his feelings, he raised his handkerchief to his eyes, and burst into a loud and irrepressible flood of grief. The effect is inconceivable. The whole house resounded with the mingled groans, and sobs, and shrieks of the congregation. (p. 56)

The sympathetic harmony of the preacher and his flock is accomplished through a forceful appeal to, and play on, the listeners' emotions or "sensibility." This is something which Wirt himself repeatedly attempts. He does so when drawing attention to the wrongs the Indians have suffered at the hands of the invaders and conquerors of Virginia, and again in his rhapsodizing over the broken steeple among the ruins of Jamestown, so suggestive of the past and of the march of time: "...As I look at it, I feel my soul drawn forward, as by the cords of gentlest sympathy, and involuntarily open my lips to offer consolation to the drooping pile" (p. 51).

The writer acknowledged that he was a disciple of Sterne (p. 50), but the author of *Tristram Shandy* was not his only model: the British Spy also expresses the wish that every family should read a few numbers of the *Spectator* daily, for "what person, of any age, sex, temper, calling, or pursuit, can possibly converse with the Spectator, without being conscious of immediate improvement?" (p. 79). The combination of Sterne's sensitive whimsicality with Addison's urbane soundness of mind and soul, which Wirt had in mind and attempted to realize in the *British Spy,* may have been an example that many of his contemporaries tried to follow. Unfortunately, neither were the two individual models easy to imitate, nor was the combination easily achieved. The Addisonian essay could become drab and dull, and the Sternean manner turn into mere mannerism. It was due in part to mistaken efforts at equaling Sterne and others that the very "style of modern productions" which Wirt objected to came into fashion:

> The writer who contends for fame, or even for truth, is obliged to consult the reigning taste of the day. Hence, too often, in opposition to his own judgment, he is led to incumber his ideas with a gorgeous load of ornaments; and when he would present to the public a body of pure, substantial and useful thought, he finds himself constrained to encrust and bury its utility within a dazzling case, to convert a feast of reason into a concert of sounds; a rich intellectual boon into a mere bouquet of variegated pinks and blushing roses. (p. 81)[69]

In addition—and Wirt knew this when he wrote of *Tristram Shandy* that it was a book "which every body justly censures and admires alternately" (p. 50)—Sterne's style could be felt to express a moral attitude vaguely related to the deistic and radical notions exposed by the British Spy and potentially no less harmful than them: "...The noxious weed of infidelity, has struck a deep, a fatal root and spread its pestilential branches far around. I fear that our eccentric and fanciful countryman, Godwin, has contributed not a little, to water and cherish this pernicious exotic. There is a novelty, a splendor, a boldness in his scheme of morals, peculiarly fitted to captivate a youthful and an ardent mind" (p. 59).[70]

A biographer of Wirt wrote of the *Letters* in 1832: "They were composed in a great degree for diversion of mind, with little care, and with still less expectation of the favourable reception they met at the time, or of the popularity they retained afterward."[71] Popular and widely read they were, though some critics praised them only cautiously,[72] and it is difficult to understand today why they should have been so successful.

4. American Spectators

William Wirt's delight in the humorous responsiveness of Yorick to his environment was shared by Joseph Dennie (1768-1812). One of Dennie's "Lay Preacher" essays admonished his readers to believe, with his "predecessor Sterne, that comfortable assertion, worth a million of cold homilies, that every time we smile, and still more every time we laugh, it adds something to the fragment of life."[73] The "Advertisement" prefacing the 1796 edition of *The Lay Preacher* mentioned the author's models, stating that "the familiarity of Franklin's Manner, & the simplicity of Sterne's proved most auxiliary to his design. He, therefore, adventured their union" (p. iv). Certainly an American could consider Poor Richard as honorable and helpful a precedent as Sir Roger de Coverley; Sterne's "simplicity," not so obvious a model, was presumably derived from the informality of Yorick's sermons. In his own sermons the Lay Preacher treated a variety of subjects, recommending to his readers the virtues of a simple and industrious life in the seclusion of the country and warning them to beware the tempting theories of Jefferson and of Paine, "that infidel in religion, and that visionary in politicks" (p. 19); one may easily be taken in:

> Very suddenly have most of our political fashions past away. Britain has been called a mother, a hag, a sister or a fiend. Our rulers are perpetually wrangling concerning the garb of government. Some, from Geneva or Virginia, affect the broad mantle of republicanism, *which covers a multitude of sins.* Others prefer French manufacture of the *Paris cut.* A few, perhaps, wish to import materials from England, but there is a good warm well made, easy garment, made to fit any one, called Federalism, which the Lay Preacher actually prefers to his own canonicals, and prays may be constantly worn, and an unchangeable mode. (pp. 71-72)

Dennie delighted his readers by his pleasant merging of humor and commonsensical preaching, and by his style, easy and figuratively sententious.[74] In 1801, when Dennie had left New Hampshire to settle in Philadelphia, some of the work which he had done in Walpole, N. H., was included in the miscellany called *The Spirit of the Farmer's Museum, and Lay Preacher's Gazette.* Apart from anti-Jacobin denunciations and satires, the American material included some humorous pieces.[75] There is in the collection a fair proportion of literary criticism which tends to be conservative but testifies to taste and solid standards. *Ossian* is censured, but so is Pope; Addison's prose is praised, and so are American writers like Mrs. Morton ("Philenia"), Robert Treat Paine, and Dennie's collaborator and friend Royall Tyler. There are parodies of Mrs. Radcliffe and Della Crusca, and one of Charlotte Smith as a representative of the European writers distinguished for "the judicious use of epithets": the fashion of regularly decorating each noun with an adjective disfigured the page of many writers of verse or prose, in England as well as in America.[76]

A series of essays with a more limited scope and little distinctive merit appeared anonymously in the New York *Morning Chronicle* in 1802 and 1803: *Letters of Jonathan Oldstyle,* by Washington Irving (1783-1859).[77] This juvenile production begins on an Addisonian note, introducing an old gentleman who deplores certain fashions adopted by the ladies of the day and regrets the passing away of familiar customs, especially with respect to engagements and weddings. Oldstyle disapproves of the freedom accorded to married ladies: "...What husband is there but will look back with regret to the happy days of female subjection" (p. 10). His last letter contains remarks on the ungentlemanlike fashion of the pistol duel. The majority of Oldstyle's letters discuss the shortcomings of the New York theater —the playhouses, the choice and quality of the plays, the merits of productions and performances, performers, playgoers, and critics. It is a very vague and shadowy, slightly cranky, character that emerges through the Oldstyle *Letters,* an affectedly stylish old gentleman.[78]

His pale identity is effectively shown up by the better-profiled actors playing a part in *Salmagundi; or, The Whim-Whams and Opinions of Launcelot Langstaff, Esq. and Others* (1807-8). This series is the joint work of Washington Irving, his elder brother William (1766-1821), and James Kirke Paulding, their brother-in-law. The authors introduced themselves to their contemporaries as monitors and critics of manners; at the same time they intimated that theirs were only facetious roles.[79] The fact may have required stressing in view of the morally apologetic tone of much fiction by American writers, who wanted to be taken seriously. True to their pose, the authors later complain that their strictures are not attended to (2:275); but they evidently enjoyed themselves enormously during the best part of the year of the life of *Salmagundi.*[80] In the very first number they created the three "columnists" and "gossip writers" called Launcelot Langstaff, Esq.,[81] William Wizard, Esq., and Anthony Evergreen, Gent. Langstaff, reporting from his "Elbow-Chair," introduces collaborators and individual objects of satirical comment. Wizard, an old bachelor remarkable for his confirmed oddities and perhaps a direct descendant of Jonathan Oldstyle, offers criticism on theatrical productions, poems, and style. Evergreen attends social functions and gives forth his views on the fashions and follies to be observed there. In addition the trio mobilizes informants with different viewpoints. Pindar Cockloft, of Cockloft Hall, represents with his family the habits and ways

of thinking of a country squire's household. Mustapha Rub-a-
Dub Keli Khan, a successor to Markoe's Algerine Spy, reports
on those aspects of the political and public life which strike a
foreigner. Jeremy Cockloft, Jr., goes traveling and offers observations on New Jersey or Philadelphia.

The variety of contributors, however, is a mere external effect
of *Salmagundi,* for they all display or imply a common denominator: a mellow and by no means doctrinaire conservatism in
manners and ideas which finds plenty to ridicule in the changing
features of the local scene. The mockery is perhaps least gentle
and tolerant in some passages of the political satire conveyed
by the Mustapha letters. These speak in a Federalist idiom, as,
for example, when the American system of government is being
discussed:

> ...Some have insisted that it savors of an aristocracy; others
> maintain that it is a *pure* democracy; and a third set of theorists
> declare absolutely that it is nothing more nor less than a
> mobocracy. The latter, I must confess, though still wide in
> error, have come nearest to the truth. To let thee at once into a
> secret, which is unknown to these people themselves, their gov-
> ernment is a pure unadulterated LOGOCRACY or *'government of
> words'.* (1:126-27)

Mustapha compares Jefferson's proclamations to a cock's crow-
ing on discovering a worm and concludes: "Oh, Asem, Asem!
on what a prodigious great scale is every thing in this country!"
(1:135). This last sentence, a burden to many of Mustapha's
communications, expresses the spirit that also informs the sketch
of a politician rewarded for his cringing party loyalty with a
suitable post, a sketch entitled "the rise, progress and completion
of a LITTLE GREAT MAN" (2:324). Generally, however, a tone
of kindliness is more in evidence than such wry severity. The
treatment of the Cockloft material is typical of the good-humored
manner of *Salmagundi.* The "propensity to save every thing that
bears the stamp of family antiquity" (1:111) is mentioned; there
is a passage warmly praising bachelordom (1:115) and a deli-
cately ironical portraiture of Barbara and Margery Cockloft,
the latter of whom "seemed disposed to maintain her post as a

belle, until a few months since; when accidentally hearing a gentleman observe that she broke very fast, she suddenly left off going to the assembly, took a cat into high favor, and began to rail at the forward pertness of young misses" (1:117). We cannot be quite sure who wrote the various contributions of *Salmagundi*. William Irving is generally supposed to have written the verse; and it seems probable that Paulding wrote the Mustapha correspondence, and Washington Irving, the Wizard pieces. The authors naturally collaborated on many parts of the work, maybe exchanging suggestions or proposing changes here and there. On the evidence of what was to follow from the pen of Washington Irving and Paulding, the sketch of Pindar Cockloft—"of the true gun-powder temper; one flash, and all is over" (1:33)—might be an exercise anticipating William the Testy in *A History of New York* or Peter Piper in *Koningsmarke*. One is readier to assign to Irving the "Chronicles of the Renowned and Ancient City of Gotham" (2:354-60) and "The Little Man in Black" (2:361-70), who in a few strokes becomes a living presence in the reader's imagination:

> ...The busy community of our little village was thrown into a grand turmoil of curiosity and conjecture—a situation very common to little gossiping villages—by the sudden and unaccountable appearance of a mysterious individual.
>   The object of this solicitude was a little black-looking man, of a foreign aspect, who took possession of an old building, which having long had the reputation of being haunted, was in a state of ruinous desolation, and an object of fear to all true believers in ghosts. He usually wore a high sugar-loaf hat with a narrow brim; and a little black coat, which, short as he was, scarcely reached below his knees. He sought no intimacy or acquaintance with any one; appeared to take no interest in the pleasures or the little broils of the village; nor ever talked, except sometimes to himself in an outlandish tongue. He commonly carried a large book, covered with sheepskin, under his arm; appeared always to be lost in meditation; and was often met by the peasantry, sometimes watching the dawning of day, sometimes at noon seated under a tree, poring over his volume; and sometimes at evening gazing with a look of sober tranquillity at the sun as it gradually sunk below the horizon. (2:361-62)[82]

[119]

On the whole, *Salmagundi* is remarkably sophisticated when compared with other American writings of that early period.[83] The three authors' fair and easy talent combined with their lively spirits and buoyant inventiveness. The three gentleman-writers also seem to have taken the responsiveness of the public for granted; if for one whole year they found enough encouragement to maintain their roles as well-bred entertainers, their readers must be assumed to have been numerous.

At any rate, more than ten years later the memory of the enjoyable achievement of *Salmagundi* encouraged Paulding to attempt on his own a continuation of it.[84] But he was not well-advised in this undertaking. Instead of recapturing the former success, he only managed to produce a diminished echo of the earlier series. He should have learned from his own observation that, since it is the same subjects that return in satires of manners and society,[85] a change of form and tone was all the more necessary. Paulding's tone in the second *Salmagundi,* however, recalls precisely that of the first. The sparkling inventiveness which made for sufficient variety in the earlier series had deserted Paulding; and the imaginary new collaborators, providing information on New England and Virginia and suggesting further contrasts, do not sufficiently alter the scope and style of the miscellany. A few touches are entertaining enough, as, for example, the neglected Muses' letter which bears only seven signatures because "their sister Melpomene disappeared from the world about the time Otway died, and their sister Thalia has never been heard of since the news of poor Mr. Sheridan's death" (1:135). The modern reader is likely to find Paulding's essay on "National Literature" at the end of the second volume of more interest than the rest. For it expresses, on the eve of the international recognition of Irving and Cooper, a writer's personal view of the literary situation in the United States, a situation marked by the uninspiring dictates of fashion and by indifference to some individual efforts that were worthy of attention and support because they at least potentially offered encouragement for the generations to come.

Another collection of essays that probably owes something to the first series of *Salmagundi,* and certainly much to Addison and Goldsmith, is William Wirt's *The Old Bachelor*.[86] Here we find again the nostalgic and romantic features of the same author's *Letters of the British Spy*. The Old Bachelor comments on the happiness of Switzerland forty years earlier, which derived from the simplicity and serious hard work of its inhabitants as well as from their sound education. His moralizing views are expressed through the picture of a novel-addicted girl, brought to her senses by regular duties in the household; he also paints the consequences of gambling, which include the temptation of suicide. His gentle irony lights on the professions, then shifts to narrow-mindedness in religious matters; and the occasional use of some imaginary correspondent's indignant or approving comment serves to stress several of the remarks made by the Old Bachelor. The latter, characterizing himself, writes: "I am a bachelor, as Molière's Mock Doctor was a physician; 'in spite of myself'. For the last five and twenty years of my life, I have not failed to dispute this point of dying a bachelor, once a year, with some charming woman or other; but as in every case the lady was both judge and party, I fared as it might have been expected; I lost my suit" (p. 1). Later he draws a picture of his gaunt appearance and of his nose and chin that "have sallied out, like two doughty champions, to meet in mortal combat" (p. 46). Having pointed out some deficiencies in the educational practices of Virginia, he quotes his adopted son's view concerning women, "perfect by nature" but "crippled by education" (p. 186). Occasionally Wirt reverted to the emotional tone characteristic of some of the most popular passages of the *British Spy*; thus, when watching and listening to a young girl playing the harp, the Old Bachelor is deeply touched "to mark the fine contour of her figure, her striking attitude, her eye of heavenly blue, raised to the cornice and rapt in all the sublimity of inspiration, while her 'eloquent blood' undulating over 'her cheek of doubtful die' speaks to the heart with more emphasis than even the melody of her lips!" (p. 8). Generally, however, there is more detachment in his attitude, in spite of his longing for the good old times; and he impresses the reader as a likeable person living in the present with definite convictions and a pleasing manner.

There appears to be a continuity from *Jonathan Oldstyle* via *Salmagundi* and *The Old Bachelor* to Irving's *Sketch-Book of Geoffrey Crayon, Gent.* (1819-20).[87] At first sight, the more or less serious spirit of conservatism and, to a lesser extent, the ways of the satirist appear to give these various collections of essayistic opinions a marked affinity. Bracebridge, Senior, and the country squire in his pew, of *The Sketch-Book*, are cousins of Launcelot Langstaff and Pindar Cockloft; and the author who, in *Salmagundi*, introduces "a Poem with Notes, or rather Notes with a Poem" (1:70) must be related to that other writer, in "The Boar's Head Tavern, Eastcheap," who conceives of the Shakespeare scholar producing volumes of commentary (3:221). Yet the old-time observer, wryly expressing his bafflement at new-fangled notions, may become more than a convenient literary device in the hands of the satirical writer. The reader of *The Sketch-Book* quickly senses the sincerity of Crayon's nostalgia and also detects a peculiar sense of the past and the transience of men and things, a sense which causes the writer to look for modes of living with, and assimilating, the fact and the external manifestations of the passing of time.

Crayon, realizing that "Europe held forth all the charms of storied and poetical association" (1:7), turns his back on America and travels across the distance in time and space in order to look at the real face of the Old World. The voyage itself to the other side of the Atlantic loosens his native country's hold on him, and he enters a condition of altered sensitivity. His is from the first a "sentimental journey" in which he may allow his attention to be captured by mere incidents and its energy to be transmuted into forces of the imagination and sympathy. Beyond the physical dangers of the storm, he shares with voyagers less lucky than he the terrors of a shipwreck and the grief of losing, with their life, the love of others. In England he enjoys a spirit of companionship with nature and with the essential features of the people that inhabit the country, a spirit kindled by "rural life" and still at times inadequate, as in his encounter with the widow who mourns her son.

Such sorrow is rendered less heart-rending and easier to sympathize with by customs and traditions like those painted and referred to in "Rural Funerals," for they establish a community across the ages that transcends the mere rites to become a community of feeling. Both joyful celebrations and commemorations of sorrow, in themselves transitory, also counteract the passing of time, rendering the past tangible and visible and making it possible to return to it. Thus the travelers aboard the stagecoach enter, each in his own way, into a festive mood which is the continuance of the festive spirit of Christmas, as it has been experienced by countless others before them. To some it will be a season of cheerfulness qualified by earnestness, to others it will carry all the joys of what was soon to be Dickensian jollity, joys which are sensed in the excitement of the schoolboys on their way home and will be realized in the convivial gathering at Bracebridge Hall.

Geoffrey Crayon, the voyager and foreigner hospitably received, shares man's past by reliving it in the imagination and by readily going along with others who make a point of keeping it alive. He reveals a particular sensitiveness to efforts to verbally record the memories and to give a narrative body to what is remembered. Then he steps forward to repeat and to mediate. Thus he becomes the narrator of Rip Van Winkle's story when it has "settled down precisely to the tale" (1:93) which he offers to his readers, or he invites them to join him in listening to "The Spectre Bridegroom: A Traveller's Tale" (4:303). Before beginning to narrate "The Legend of Sleepy Hollow," Crayon remarks that visitors to Sleepy Hollow soon imbibe the "visionary propensity" (6:55) of its inhabitants, thus preparing his readers for the suspension of disbelief that they will have to practice if they are to follow his account of Ichabod's experiences.

"The Spectre Bridegroom" requires the American reader to follow the narrator far back into the past of a distant country;[88] but in "Rip Van Winkle" and "The Legend of Sleepy Hollow" he remains on his side of the Atlantic and within one generation. The relative remoteness in time and space does not matter so much; what is important is an imaginative response to the interaction of the transient and the durable in order to come to terms with the past. It is not just formal customs and traditions that survive but their very spirit too, for our fundamental values are durable and live on from the past into the present. Roscoe, in this view of things, illustrates the permanence of the cultivated mind which expresses itself through his stoical fortitude and his disregard of personal misfortunes, as well as his belief in human prevailing. Woman's fine nature provides a counterpart to his manliness: she who inspired *The Kingis Quair* is not really different from Leslie's wife, and their integrity and wholehearted devotion are found again in "The Broken Heart" and "The Pride of the Village," determining the fate of their heroines.[89]

Living with, and assimilating, the past, then, does not mean withdrawing from the present and becoming absorbed in the contemplation of what was; but neither must the past be totally ignored. Imaginatively speaking, the past may be richer; so it proved for Irving and, in another sense, for Ichabod Crane. The present engages our attention practically, as a matter to be attended to; and so Katrina Van Tassel engages the rival attention of Brom Bones and Ichabod Crane. The girl is, like Brom Bones, the product of a rich past; but they are both of them so saturated with its spirit as to be no longer conscious of it or aware that it must soon end. For Ichabod Crane, to whom the past is all too powerfully suggestive, transforms the defeat at the hands of his rival into a successful adjustment to different conditions. It is *his* future, as *A History of New York* had stated and "Rip Van Winkle" repeats, that is to be the future of the country: the Yankees are to have their way, not the Dutch.[90] Irving, conscious of man's past, which informed the narrative traditions he rendered so successfully, remained an American, a citizen of a country where "a remote period" meant "thirty years since" (6:55). His "Prospectus" and "Author's Account" make plain his attachment to his native country and "the dearest wish of his heart to have a secure and cherished, though humble, corner in the good opinions and kind feelings of his countrymen" (1:iv).[91] In "English Writers," and also in "The Angler" (7:41), he asked for fairness toward America. His portrait of John Bull at times comes dangerously near to betraying signs of that very condescension his compatriots were inclined to detect in British judgments on the United States.

His commitment to the country of promise imposed upon the

gentleman given to adventurous excursions into the past a certain restraint. Indulging in daydreaming, he had to be sure of remaining aware, as it were, of the border line separating actual concerns from imaginary experiences. Some reservations are seen to operate against the fascinations of the past. One, which is employed only occasionally, is the writer's fancy, rather freely playful in "The Art of Bookmaking" or "The Mutability of Literature." Another check is his absorption in the contemplation of a peaceful landscape, such as the following description from "Rural Life in England":

> Nothing can be more imposing than the magnificence of English park scenery. Vast lawns that extend like sheets of vivid green, with here and there clumps of gigantic trees, heaping up rich piles of foliage. The solemn pomp of groves and woodland glades, with the deer trooping in silent herds across them; the hare, bounding away to the covert; or the pheasant, suddenly bursting upon the wing. The brook, taught to wind in natural meanderings or expand into a glassy lake—the sequestered pool, reflecting the quivering trees, with the yellow leaf sleeping on its bosom, and the trout roaming fearlessly about its limpid waters: while some rustic temple, or sylvan statue, grown green and dank with age, gives an air of classic sanctity to the seclusion. (2:128)

There is, however, one guard keeping the past within its bounds which is entirely characteristic of Irving and his literary attitude: his irony. Irving's humor is throughout tinged with an element of defensiveness which, however nearly imperceptible it may become, gives it an ironic twist. Whether directed at himself or at others, it is seen from the beginning to the end of *The Sketch-Book*. It operates in "The Author's Account of Himself" (1:5-10), whose opening paragraphs carry implications of the relative importance of things and events to different individuals, and it is manifest in Crayon's report on his uneasy role as leveler of differences between the factions of "Little Britain" (7:93-123). It is present, too, in the warning which concludes Knickerbocker's manuscript of "The Legend of Sleepy Hollow," the tale that in later editions stood at the end of *The Sketch-Book:* a "cautious old gentleman" having expressed his scepticism concerning some points of the tale, the storyteller replied, "Faith, sir, as to that matter I don't believe one-half of it myself" (6: 120).

In spite of the irony, there remained for Irving and his readers the important willingness to half-believe. How important that was is shown in the unsympathetic question of the listener who, having heard the story, wanted to know, "What was the moral of the story, and what it went to prove" (6:119). Most of the writers of fiction since Irving's birth had asserted—and often meant to show through their work—that there must be a moral to every story. That the moral could be a thing of only relative merit and reliability, the American spectators smilingly demonstrated. It was Irving who, as a graceful entertainer and excellent craftsman, began to encourage through his art a belief not in the story's moral or its usefulness but in the importance of using the past and the imagination.[92]

5. Quixotic Travelers and Fabulous Voyagers

In the writings discussed in the two preceding chapters, some traditions or conditions furnish material for personal observations, often ironically suggestive and satirical in method; these fictional writings are nonetheless sober in conception and execution. The present chapter is devoted to books of a more subjective and distinctive charater that derived from their authors' pronounced views on specific subjects and the imaginative freedom and skill with which they approached their subject matter.

Modern Chivalry, the unwieldy book modeled on *Don Quixote* which Hugh Henry Brackenridge (1748-1816) worked upon for nearly thirty years, appeared in various installments between 1792 and 1815.[93] To say that Cervantes's work was the model for *Modern Chivalry* requires some qualifying.[94] At first Brackenridge intended to write a verse satire aimed at a political opponent, and drew on the Hudibrastic model and the conception of the knight-errant at odds with his surroundings. The misunderstandings between his knight, Captain Farrago, and Farrago's fellow citizens derive from the erring practices of the latter, not from any mistaken notions of the captain. It is he who is essentially sane, and the world in which he lives that has become crazy, as he says himself: "...I hope I shall not be considered as resembling that Spaniard in taking a wind-mill for a giant. ...It is you that are the Don Quixottes in this respect, madcaps..." (p. 783).

Now it is true that Farrago's sanity is that of an idealist: being quite clear in his mind about his country's constitution and institutions, he wants them to be applied with optimal thoroughness and effectiveness. In this sense he is indeed a cousin of Don Quixote, who came to pursue not one ideal of romantic and chivalric purity but simply *the* ideal. Farrago's servant, the Irishman Teague Oregan, is a parallel to Sancho, and reminds the captain again and again of the sober realities of life and human frailty. Teague, however, never assumes the function of the guardian at times attributed to Sancho or to such an American counterpart as Betty, Dorcasina's maid in Mrs. Tenney's *Female Quixotism*. It is always Farrago who is master, while his servant is not a mediator between his standards of consistency and the public level of erratic impulsiveness, but rather a representative of that impulsiveness—often at its most amoral and irresponsible. Teague is, of course, the narrative hero of the book, particularly in its first part, when the possession of him, as it were, makes him an object of dispute between Farrago's wisdom and the people's will. As long as the concerns of the people and of the captain converge in his person, it is he who ensures *Modern Chivalry* its liveliness and three-dimensional effect of comedy. Later Teague becomes increasingly a mere representative of the irrational masses, and Farrago is faced less and less with the Irishman's individual pranks, resulting from his appetites or the malleability of his ambitions. If in the earlier stages of the novel Farrago is a fatherly guide and guardian who can efficiently help Teague to overcome his weaknesses and temptations, he is afterward pushed into the role of a doctor who rightly diagnoses the anonymous cancers of demagogy and anarchy, yet is not allowed freely to administer his remedies.

If the second part of *Modern Chivalry* is less interesting than the first, the fault lies both with Brackenridge's management of it and with the subject that forms its substance. Starting from his own partly emotional experience of political life, the author succeeded in the first part of his book in transcending its personal significance and in embodying antagonistic forces in individual figures which he related to the nature of man. But he failed in a far more difficult task in the latter part of *Modern Chivalry*. He was incapable of expressing, in the terms of a narrative, his political and civic concern over a crucial issue: the discrepancy between the high aim of the democratic experiment and the demands made on man by the means of its realization, on the one hand, and the cumulative inadequacies of a body of men, on the other. He failed because to him there were two tasks to be undertaken at the same time, each of them really depending upon the completion of the other: the promises of democracy and the Constitution had to be fulfilled, and the people had to be made conscious of these promises and of the fact that they would not be realized spontaneously. Since in *Modern Chivalry* the captain maintains his efforts to enlighten his fellow citizens, and they just as stubbornly remain unappreciative, the overall structure of the book—a record of the apparent alienation of the people and its leaders—might be interpreted as expressing the author's aristocratic prejudices. If he had any, he probably shared the suspicions of Virginia leaders like Jefferson,[95] but not the more reactionary views held by many Federalists, particularly in the last decade of the eighteenth century.

A glance at the parts employed in the composition of *Modern Chivalry* shows that, even more than *Don Quixote,* Brackenridge's book is made up of individual episodes and lacks a proper plot. These episodes expose one main theme and incidentally a few subsidiary ones: the main theme is democracy in theory and practice; various human foibles, which also condition the abuses of democracy, form the subsidiary themes. *Modern Chivalry* was written during a period which was widely believed to herald a decisive improvement of the human condition, moral, social, and intellectual. That improvement was to be accomplished through secular and social, not religious and individual, means. In the light of such views *Modern Chivalry,* a commentary on one experiment in secular and social reorganization, was also an illustration of perfectible human standards and attributes.

It was that second aspect that lent itself to treatment in the form of a fictional narrative, and therefore the subsidiary themes, embodied chiefly in the personage of the ever-tempted and readily relapsing Teague Oregan, became the most lively individual ingredients of *Modern Chivalry*. At the end of his first paragraph, the author suggestively refrains from sketching Teague: "I shall say nothing of the character of this man, because the very name imports what he was" (p. 6), that is, an Irishman and, considering his station in life, an illiterate one. He proves serviceable in the very manner of Sancho, though, when his master is attacked by a racetrack mob; but from chapter 2 on, it is Farrago's duty to look after his servant. He finds Teague in danger of becoming some party's candidate for a seat in the state legislature and in consternation attempts to make the people see how utterly unfit the Irishman is for such a trust:

> This young man, whose family name is Oregan, has been my servant for several years. And, except a too great fondness for women, which now and then brings him into scrapes, he has demeaned himself in a manner tolerable enough. But he is totally ignorant of the great principles of legislation; and more especially, the particular interests of the government.... You are surely carrying the matter too far, in thinking of making a senator of this hostler; to take him away from an employment to which he has been bred, and put him to another, to which he has served no apprenticeship: to set those hands which have been lately employed in currying my horse, to the draughting bills, and preparing business for the house. (pp. 15-16)

The basic situation in which Teague is to be found again and again has thus been sketched: it is that of a man impelled by interest and ambition to aspire after positions for which he is not qualified, with the aggravating circumstance that his candidacy may not have been his idea in the first place. Such an inclination is a dangerous liability, as Brackenridge may have observed himself. But people may well disagree with Farrago and hold that "it is better to trust a plain man like him [Teague], than one of your high flyers, that will make laws to suit their own purposes" (p. 16). In the context of politics and administration, Teague and the imaginary opponent which Farrago's interlocutor sees as an alternative (implying that someone very much like the captain might be that rival) conjure up an early instance of the distrust of the "egghead."

Finding that he cannot change the voters' minds, the captain addresses himself directly to Teague. Because he knows him well, he paints a disturbing picture of a politician's duties and of the attacks from various quarters which he must expect, and concludes with an appeal not to reason but to sentiment, for Teague's sense of honor is a sentimental affair and not a matter of integrity:

> ...I would not for a thousand guineas, though I have not the half of it to spare, that the breed of the Oregans should come to this; bringing on them a worse stain than stealing sheep; to which they are addicted. You have nothing but your character, Teague, in a new country to depend upon. Let it never be said, that you quitted an honest livelihood, the taking care of my horse, to follow the new fangled whims of the times, and to be a statesman. (p. 17)

The pattern of the mutual relationships between Farrago, Teague, and various bodies once established, Brackenridge's inventiveness[96] does the rest. The unfortunate servant becomes eligible for membership in a philosophical society and is seriously considered for posts as different as those of a preacher and a fake Indian chief negotiating a new treaty. After a couple of abortive affairs and an attempt at becoming a lawyer, Teague accompanies his master to Washington. There he is popular at the alehouse and among the ladies, who "thought him a plain, frank, blunt spoken Irish gentleman; not harrassing them with deep observations, drawn from books, or an ostentation of learning; but always saying something gallant, and complimentary of their persons, or accomplishments" (p. 228). Appointed a federal excise officer, Teague is tarred and feathered by the irate inhabitants of a western district and in this strange condition again attracts the attention of the philosophical society. He is sent to France, nearly executed under Robespierre, and then encouraged to write his autobiography. He temporarily assumes

diabolical appearances as little in keeping with his amoral naïveté as the various posts suggested for him, and later is quite
undeservedly considered a hero too:

> ...The declivity of the hill was such that he found it impossible
> to arrest himself, being under the impetus of the projectile mo-
> tion which he had acquired; and seeing nothing before him but
> death from the tomahawk of at least sixty Indians, and neverthe-
> less being unable to stop his career, no more than could a stone
> projected from the precipice, he raised the tremendous shout of
> desperation; which the savages mistaking for the outcry of onset,
> as it is customary with them when they are sure of victory, to
> raise the war-whoop; magnifying the shout, by their imagina-
> tions into that of a large party overtaking them, they threw
> away their packs and scalps, and made their way towards the
> Indian country.... (p. 596)

Teague basks in the sunshine of popular favor and, because he
has allegedly taught a cat to speak, becomes the principal of a
newly established academy of animals. When he is dissatisfied
with the job, the people suddenly lose their interest in him; but
they just as abruptly support him again as soon as it is rumored
that he has found the philosophers' stone and that Farrago (by
then governor of a settlement in the West) opposes the plan of
using it to produce gold and silver. In the end, while Farrago
is tolerated in his office by the people, Teague returns to his
master and the position that was his at the beginning of the
story. Back in the governor's house, he also shares Farrago's
bachelorhood: "Teague, as we have seen, had been heretofore
much in request with the ladies; and still more so from the late
reputation of his generalship, and the display of his tumbling
at the camp-meetings. But the circumstance of his having taught
a cat to speak, was against him; for no woman would like to
have a tell-tale of such domestic animal. *It would render it
unsafe to have a cat about the house*" (p. 800). Teague himself
emerges essentially unchanged from the trials he has suffered
and from the catalyst's role which he has been playing unin-
tentionally. Very much in the foreground in the first part of
Modern Chivalry, especially until his exile in France, he constantly precipitates the events that cause Farrago to alter his

[131]

estimate of the democratic system and its sovereign. Teague provides the narrator with the very stuff out of which grow the preposterous incidents he gets involved in; it is rich material, for Teague is the embodiment of typical human conduct and not an individual character.[97] Teague's adventures in turn require the author to use a style and language of comic vigor and sarcastic asperity.[98]

Teague's experiences reflect back upon the measures and manner adopted by Farrago to restrain both his servant and those that use and influence the person of the Irishman. The captain's principles are too firmly anchored to be swayed by what happens to his servant and his surroundings; he only learns to be more and more tolerant. As opposed to the range of Teague's serio-comic impersonations and the contrasts revealed by his quick changes of mind, Farrago's attitude therefore appears as stability itself. His is the firmness of conviction that seeks through action to realize the promises and possibilities of his beliefs. On the contrary, Teague's entertaining variety is a passive thing, the result of animal impulses and extraneous influences. A motley figure, the victim of circumstances and environment, Teague often appears designed for the stage rather than the novel. His Irish brogue is an eminently stageable feature, apart from being an instance of his imperviousness to any educating influence.

Teague's vitality, embroiling him in improbable adventures, prevents his master from undue theorizing and helps the reader over dull stretches of *Modern Chivalry*. If Teague can be called the narrative hero of Brackenridge's novel, it is obviously Farrago that is its intellectual hero. He is introduced as "a good honest man; and means what is benevolent and useful; though his ideas may not comport with the ordinary manner of thinking, in every particular" (p. 22). He dissents from the established opinion of dueling and of a duelist's honor. Common sense conditions his view, and even Teague, who is not the brightest lad, can be convinced by the captain that the custom of the duel is nonsense. Admittedly Farrago paints its dangers in rather strong colors, but his servant would probably also have agreed with his sober answer to a challenger:

[132]

Sir, I have two objections to this duel matter. The one is, lest I should hurt you; and the other is, lest you should hurt me. I do not see any good it would do me to put a bullet through any part of your body. I could make no use of you when dead, for any culinary purpose, as I would a rabbit or a turkey.... As to myself, I do not much like to stand in the way of any thing that is harmful. I am under apprehensions you might hit me. That being the case, I think it most adviseable to stay at a distance. If you want to try your pistols, take some object, a tree or a barn door about my dimensions. If you hit that, send me word, and I shall acknowledge that if I had been in the same place, you might also have hit me. (p. 52)[99]

Farrago's various attempts at courtship testify both to his modesty and to his unfamiliarity with the uses of the day. In the question of slavery, he uses some heavy irony to explain that there cannot be anything morally wrong with it, since "humane and just persons...promote and support the evil" (p. 138).

It is, however, on matters of government and politics that Farrago is heard most frequently. He once states that "power is the great law of nature; and nothing but the pacts or conventions of society can contravene it" (p. 135). Such pacts and conventions are continually liable to be circumvented in the universal attempt at securing and accumulating power. The individual candidates as well as the parties are after power, and an observer can easily see through their maneuvers. Why, for example, should a candidate offer whiskey to those who will support him? In Congress, listening to opposing votes on a bill, Farrago is dismayed at the facility with which obviously biased views are uttered to ensure the success of one party: one representative denounces a bill as contrary to nature, causing snow "in the heat of harvest, and dog days in winter"; he is answered that on the contrary, its effects will be to "moderate the sun's heat, and the winter's cold" (pp. 123, 124). The whiskey candidate's honesty is as little to be trusted as the congressmen's, whose position is determined by the observation that "in a deliberative assembly, it is difficult to be honest. *Party will not suffer it*" (p. 436).

In a democracy power should lie with the people and not with individuals or any section of the country; but how is this to be safeguarded if the people are not sufficiently informed of their rights and of the ways to secure them, and if an *"uninformed spirit of reform"* (p. 416) prevails among them because politicians and parties promise improvements but forget to mention that they can be realized only at the cost of unreasonable sacrifices? A specific instance of the appeal to the masses is mentioned significantly at the very beginning of Farrago's journey through the country: a conjurer explains to the bewildered captain the principle that favors the inferior rival of a deserving candidate: "...There is a certain pride in man, which leads him to elevate the low, and pull down the high" (p. 19). As though consoling himself, the author adds: "...Let no man who means well to the commonwealth, and offers to serve it, be hurt in his mind when some one of meaner talents is preferred. The people are a sovereign, and greatly despotic; but, in the main, just" (p. 21). That sovereign, "as liable to the impulse of passion, and as open to the insinuations of flatterers as an individual tyrant" (p. 382), whose "power unbalanced, is but the despotism of many instead of one" (p. 740), has less and less to recommend it in the eyes of Farrago. The people even discuss including the animals among the citizens and giving them the right to vote: "...A man with a strong voice in particular called out that it should be so. A bull happening to roar, and a horse neigh at the same time, it was called out that it was the voice of the people" (p. 712). They consider the necessity of electing some of the animals as their representatives, for "it did not occur to them until suggested, that the representative is chosen, or in contemplation of the constitution, supposed to be chosen for his superior knowledge and information over that of the constituent" (p. 665); the suggestion of course must have come from someone like Farrago, or Brackenridge.

As Brackenridge thought that he had himself been vanquished by an adversary who did not possess the required superiority, he returned to this point repeatedly in relating Teague's adventures. At the same time he continually stressed through Farrago the demands which democracy made, with the electorate and the legislators, not only upon the understanding of the principles of government but also upon every individual's integrity. He believed in American democracy, but he was also aware of man's fallibility; though he thought that a true democracy was possible, he never lost sight of the dangerous tendencies, latent or visible, in the American experiment. His civic and legal mind was constantly at work, planning and weighing, but it did not function separately or abstractly: it joined forces with an imaginative and artistic talent aroused by the observation of the human shortcomings which could endanger the realization of the democratic plan.

In an early chapter Brackenridge wrote: "We have seen here, a weaver a favoured candidate, and in the next instance, a bog-trotter superseding him. Now it may be said, that this is fiction; but fiction, or no fiction, the nature of the thing will make it a reality" (p. 22). In a page that was not published until 1815, more than twenty years after the first volume of *Modern Chivalry*, there occurs a related passage which illustrates the disillusioned, though not bitter, tone of the author, even while he is defending himself against charges of undue severity and implausible exaggeration:

> ...It has been thought by some, that the incidents have been all common and natural, that there is nothing improbable in them; and that the triteness of occurrence, rather than the unusual, and extravagant, ought to be the objection. What extraordinary can there be, say some, in such a creature as Teague O'Regan receiving appointments to office, or being thought qualified for the discharge of the highest trusts? Do we not see instances every day of the like? Is it possible to say how low the grade of human intellect that may be thought capable of transacting public business?...Some have been forward enough to tell me, that, so far from my bog-trotter being a burlesque upon human credulity, and pretension to office, that the bulk of men in office are below even his qualifications; and that if I were to go into any deliberative body, and pull out the first man that occurred to me, nine times out of ten I would find that I had a Teague O'Regan by the tail. I have no idea that things are just brought to this pass, notwithstanding there may be colour for the allegation. (p. 674)

The passage suggests that Brackenridge had been conversing with some of his readers and profiting from their remarks. If such was the case it must have been gratifying to an author who wanted his book to be read by *"the people.* It is for them my book is intended. Not for the *representatives* of a year or four years, but *for themselves.* It is Tom, Dick, and Harry, in the woods, that I want to read my book" (p. 471). What inducements did Brackenridge offer to Tom, Dick, and Harry, in order that they should read his *Modern Chivalry?* The comedy of Teague's adventures doubtlessly amused many readers, and it still is one of the truly enjoyable achievements of early American fiction. Others may have relished the opposition between the West and the cities of the East which is implied in the confrontation of Teague and Farrago, or the burlesque of the American experiment that may have been aimed at in the description of the new settlement under the captain.[100] What is certainly very attractive about *Modern Chivalry* is the feeling of being in touch with its author. His presence is, of course, felt in the sincerity and seriousness of his opinions and the plan of the entire book. Brackenridge also appears as a cultured gentleman, well read and in general very much at ease with his material and resources,[101] who frequently steps forward to address his readers after the manner of Fielding, pleasantly offsetting whatever impression of forbidding severity or even pompousness some of his reflective pages may have caused. Though in the days of Brackenridge many reviewers spoke out only when they wished to damn a book and left their judgments rather vague where there was something to be said in favor of some writer, the conclusions of the *Monthly Anthology* seem sound enough a century and a half after they were written: rather unsatisfactory as a formal narrative, *Modern Chivalry* (whose author wished "to regulate the inordinate spirit of ambition") "may be read without disappointment, and even with much satisfaction, by those, who would beguile a vacant hour with amusement, and he that reflects on the argumentative parts, may draw from them no small improvement."[102]

In England, but in the United States as well, there were many readers in the 1820s who discovered Irving's *A History of New York* (1809) only by way of the later *Sketch-Book;*[103] if to them Irving was identified with Geoffrey Crayon, they may well have been surprised at meeting him again in the shape and spirit of Knickerbocker. But though there were some striking differences between the two, the attentive reader could not fail also to detect features common to their books. To be sure, Crayon is milder and displays more urbanity than his predecessor, both in the choice of his subjects and in the treatment which he gives them. Yet the very view of things that is implied in Knickerbocker's title draws attention to the historical sense informing or influencing Crayon's approach to his subject matter in *The Sketch-Book*. The roots of Irving's humor are the same in the two books, and if it seems more vigorous in the *History,* this is largely due to the cumulating effect of the author's concentration on one group of related subjects.

The reading public probably did not know, but may have guessed, what Peter and Washington Irving originally meant to achieve in *A History of New York,* for its first book still testifies to their burlesquing intent.[104] When Washington Irving carried on alone the task of writing, he did not simply grow tired of, and therefore abandon, his first motive. What is far more important, he discovered a new interest—or rediscovered an old one—in going back to the times of New Amsterdam. His appreciation of it was such as to keep him going even through the times of grief after the death of Mathilda Hoffman.[105] It was, however, not just the cozy quaintness of the Dutch forebears of New York that appealed to him but the more generally suggestive material which they provided for his imagination: intimations of the nature of the Dutch as well as the Yankees, of features of the contemporary political scene, and, beyond that, of the erratic behavior of man, acting upon momentary impulses and explaining them away by rationalization.

In such a perspective the strictly historical background had merely a relative importance, and its parts could be manipulated by the author to enhance the dramatic and comic function of other elements entering into his pseudo-chronicle. The three Dutch governors of New Amsterdam, therefore, turn out not as portrayals of their actual prototypes but as "humours"; they are tested on circumstances of their terms of office that are particularly appropriate to demonstrate their main feature or are

[137]

somehow relevant to a further significance with which the author wishes to invest them. Thus William the Testy, while retaining all the marks of his fiery nature, also functions as a caricature of some conceptions and attitudes of Jefferson.[106] His predecessor, Walter the Doubter, is seen as a representative of that Dutch deliberating procrastination which finally, under the last governor, is to prove fatal to New Amsterdam. That last ruler, Peter Stuyvesant, the Headstrong, may be said to enjoy more of his creator's sympathies than do his two forerunners. In the end, though it is plain that his arbitrariness and stubbornness have not contributed to preparing the town for resistance, the reader feels that Peter stands for more than the prerogatives of the original settlers and the force of historical inertia. The country gentleman he becomes after the disappearance of the Dutch colony is in the line of the conservative Cocklofts and Bracebridges, whose very oddities increase their likableness as human beings.[107]

It is plain, too, that certain of Peter the Headstrong's idiosyncrasies must be ascribed to his gubernatorial experience with subjects not always amenable to common sense or certain weighty decisions. The mob (viewed with intense suspicion by the Federalists of Irving's day) has been in existence since the times of William the Testy, and the expression of its will has been encouraged by William's frequent changes of opinion.[108] Under Peter the mob becomes a positive nuisance not so much because of what it wants for the good of the *res publica* but because it can be influenced very easily:

The patriotic address of Burgomaster Roerback had a wonderful effect upon the populace, who, though a race of sober phlegmatic Dutchmen, were amazingly quick at discerning insults; for your ragged rabble, though it may bear injuries without a murmur, yet is always marvellously jealous of its sovereign dignity. They immediately fell into the pangs of tumultuous labour, and brought forth, not only a string of right wise and valiant resolutions, but likewise a most resolute memorial, addressed to the governor, remonstrating at his conduct. (2:222)

As Peter gains by being contrasted with his subjects, the Dutch themselves fare quite well when compared with the Yankees.

[138]

True, the people of New Amsterdam have their weaknesses, but these have been rendered endearing by the patina of age. And since the New Englanders are judged from the vantage point of Dutch habits, they appear as grasping upstarts, as squatters with no respect whatever for the rights of others. Their interpretation of the liberty of conscience is characteristically narrow-minded: "...'Liberty of conscience'...they now clearly proved to imply nothing more, than that every man should think as he pleased in matters of religion—*provided* he thought *right*" (p. 170). The Yankees therefore proceed with severity to suppress the dissenters, that is, all those who do not think right. At this point Knickerbocker himself defends the Yankees' attitude, stating that it very much resembles the behavior of all groups of people toward rebellious individuals and has the merit of being an unambiguous statement of belief.

The successive cancellation of charges against individuals or groups serves less to moderate Irving's censure than to reestablish a sense of balance and proportion in the self-righteous reader.[109] The same effect is also achieved when Irving directs his satirical darts alternately at rather sinister or at innocuous objects, as when he shifts from the subjects of bigotry and witch-hunting to that of the New England custom of bundling. The leveling of all mankind to the same common denominator is clearly hinted at when the *History* relates how that Yankee usage, hitherto unknown and therefore considered strange by the Dutch, fails to become naturalized among them: "Among other hideous customs they attempted to introduce among them that of *bundling,* which the dutch lasses of the Netherlandts, with that eager passion for novelty and foreign fashion, natural to their sex, seemed very well inclined to follow..." (1:105). If Irving's contemporaries enjoyed his ridicule of the phlegmatic Dutch colonists (or felt called upon to protest against it) and recognized all the details of the satire on Jefferson and the "mobocracy," the modern reader is likely to relish other features more than the topical ones. The demeanor of the three governors of New Amsterdam really depends little on their being Dutch, but much on the fact that they are actuated by individual traits of character. The Dutch dismay at the encroachments of the

Yankees, the Swedes, and the English results from the human love of property; it reminds the reader of a parallel situation, that of the natives at the time of the Spanish, and also Dutch, intrusion into their territory. The invaders formulate spurious theories in order to justify their claim to the lands they conquer, such as those of "the right of discovery," "the right of cultivation," and "the right acquired by civilization" (Book I, chap. 5). This last privilege is declared particularly important, because it signifies that the natives are to profit from, and be improved by, the coming of more enlightened people; these, the historian however records, "introduced among them the comforts of life, consisting of rum, gin and brandy," and "used every method, to induce them to embrace and practice the true religion—except that of setting them the example." Indeed, "the cause of Christian love and charity were so rapidly advanced, that in a very few years, not one fifth of the number of unbelievers existed in South America, that were found there at the time of its discovery" (1:52-53, 54).

Judgments and practices cut either way then. In the case of the proprietary rights and the brutality of some acts of colonization, Irving made his point with an almost Swiftian acerbity. He supposes that explorers from the moon, who have discovered the earth, report to their ruler; the sequel must be imagined as follows:

> At these words, the great man in the moon (being a very profound philosopher) shall fall into a terrible passion, and possessing equal authority over things that do not belong to him, as did whilome his holiness the Pope, shall forthwith issue a formidable bull,—specifying, "That—whereas a certain crew of Lunatics have lately discovered and taken possession of that little dirty planet called 'the earth'—and that whereas it is inhabited by none but a race of two legged animals, that carry their heads on their shoulders instead of under their arms; cannot talk the lunatic language; have two eyes instead of one; are destitute of tails, and of a horrible whiteness, instead of pea green—therefore and for a variety of other excellent reasons— they are considered incapable of possessing any property in the planet they infest, and the right and title to it are confirmed to its original discoverers.—And furthermore, the colonists who

are now about to depart to the aforesaid planet, are authorized and commanded to use every means to convert these infidel savages from the darkness of Christianity, and make them thorough and absolute lunatics. (1:62-63)[110]

From the moment Irving concentrates on his Dutch subject matter and deals with individual figures like the three governors —or with Hudson himself, the *miles gloriosus* Van Poffenburgh, and Antony Van Corlear, the trumpeter so much admired by the ladies—he sticks to a tone of genial mockery and tolerant humor (which he is not averse to using on himself and his techniques). Like Fielding and Brackenridge, the author of *A History of New York* enjoys explaining to his readers the possibilities and advantages of his craft. A virtuoso and complete master of his material and means, he points out the functions that may be assigned to a thunderstorm he has been describing:

> ...The storm was played off, partly to give a little bustle and life to this tranquil part of my work, and to keep my drowsy readers from falling asleep—and partly to serve as a preparation, or rather an overture, to the tempestuous times that are about to assail the pacific province of Nieuw Nederlandt—and that overhang the slumbrous administration of the renowned Wouter Van Twiller. It is thus the experienced play-wright puts all the fiddles, the french horns, the kettle drums and trumpets of his orchestra in requisition to usher in one of those horrible and brimstone uproars, called Melodrames—and it is thus he discharges his thunder, his lightning, his rosin and salpetre, preparatory to the raising of a ghost, or the murdering of a hero. (1:165)

The mock-heroic battle between Peter the Headstrong and Jan Risingh, during which "the rocks burrowed in the ground like rabbits, and even Christina creek turned from its course, and ran up a mountain in breathless terror" (2:143), is bracketed by remarks of the narrator: he must not change the course of the historical events in his pages, but he can allow the defeated party to hit their adversaries a few good blows before they are overtaken by their fate. The narrator's role is more important than often realized, for it is for the sake of his record that the great of this world attempt to distinguish themselves. At one time Irving pictures his readers at his mercy:

If ever I had my readers completely by the button, it is at this moment. Here is a redoubtable fortress, reduced to the greatest extremity; a valiant commander in a state of the most imminent jeopardy—and a legion of implacable foes thronging upon every side. The sentimental reader is preparing to indulge his sympathies, and bewail the sufferings of the brave. The philosophic reader, to come with his first principles, and coolly take the dimensions and ascertain the proportions of great actions, like an antiquary, measuring a pyramid with a two-foot rule—while the mere reader, for amusement, promises to regale himself after the monotonous pages through which he has dozed, with murders, rapes, ravages, conflagrations, and all the other glorious incidents, that give eclat to history, and grace the triumph of the conqueror. (1:191-92)

Irving not only re-created the individual figures and events of his history but also lovingly stopped to paint features of its background. He praised the Hudson landscape as it appeared to Peter the Headstrong. When he conjured up the romantic first sight which Hudson had of Manhattan, he relied on the contrast between his picture and the one his readers could be expected to be familiar with, and described as a striking addition to the peaceful scene the appearance of a savage before the eyes of the startled sailors:

The island of Manna-hata, spread wide before them, like some sweet vision of fancy, or some fair creation of industrious magic. Its hills of smiling green swelled gently one above another, crowned with lofty trees of luxuriant growth; some pointing their tapering foliage towards the clouds, which were gloriously transparent; and others, loaded with a verdant burthen of clambering vines, bowing their branches to the earth, that was covered with flowers. On the gentle declivities of the hills were scattered in gay profusion, the dog wood, the sumach and the wild briar, whose scarlet berries and white blossoms glowed brightly among the deep green of the surrounding foliage; and here and there, a curling column of smoke rising from the little glens that opened along the shore, seemed to promise the weary voyagers, a welcome at the hand of their fellow creatures. As they stood gazing with entranced attention on the scene before them, a red man crowned with feathers issued from one of these glens, and after contemplating in silent wonder the gallant ship, as she sat like a stately swan swimming on a silver lake, sounded the war-whoop, and bounded into the woods, like a wild deer, to the utter astonishment of the phlegmatic Dutch-men, who had never heard such a noise, or witnessed such a caper in their whole lives. (1:72)

Another passage, descriptive of "the fairy hour of twilight" which allows the fancy to work upon objects indistinctly seen, thus "producing with industrious craft a fairy creation of her own" (2:96-97), suggests to the reader an analogy with the results of Irving's own fancy, busy in the twilight of the traditions of New Amsterdam. In *A History of New York* as in *The Sketch-Book*, Irving responds gratefully to the spell of the past; yet there is a difference between the two books. In the *History* the author's humorous attitude was spontaneous, called forth by a subject to which he responded with youthful buoyancy and whose main features at the same time made for a proper distance between the writer and his work. In *The Sketch-Book*, however, the sympathetic nostalgia which Geoffrey Crayon experiences requires him to be on his guard so as not to be too much affected by it, to temper his reaction with a measure of coolness. In spite of the fanciful tone of parts of the later book, some products of Irving's exuberance, which fit so well in Knickerbocker's *History*, would have been foreign to Crayon's record: the treatment of the Yan-kees, for example, or that passage rendering the heroic mood on the eve of the war between the Dutch and the Swedes, in which Irving's prose turns into blank verse and sounds like an epic of chivalry:

The gallant warrior starts from soft repose, from golden visions and voluptuous ease; where in the dulcet, "piping time of peace," he sought sweet solace, after all his toils. No more in beauty's syren lap reclined, he weaves fair garlands for his lady's brows; no more entwines with flowers his shining sword, nor through the live-long lazy summer's day, chaunts forth his love-sick soul in madrigals. To manhood roused, he spurns the amorous flute; doffs from his brawny back the robe of peace, and clothes his

[143]

pampered limbs in panoply of steel. O'er his dark brow, where late the myrtle waved; where wanton roses breathed enervate love, he rears the beaming casque, and nodding plume; grasps the bright shield and shakes the pondrous lance; or mounts with eager pride his fiery steed; and burns for deeds of glorious chivalry.

But soft, worthy reader! I would not have you go about to imagine, that any *preux chevalier* thus hideously begirt with iron existed in the city of New Amsterdam—This is but a lofty and gigantic mode in which we heroic writers always talk of war, thereby to give it a noble and imposing aspect.... (2:68-69)

If later Irving felt inclined to apologize for his disrespect of history, and his particular subject in *A History of New York,* what he offered his readers in 1809 was nonetheless a very enjoyable book,[111] at least to lovers of lively, imaginative, and humorous writing.

Later readers of this type who took the Duyckincks's advice and read *A General History of Connecticut* (1781) by Samuel Peters (1735-1826), may well have found it rewarding too.[112] Of course Peters meant a large part of his *History* to be taken seriously, whereas Irving's was only a pretended chronicle; but once this has been established, there appear to be quite a few similarities between the two books. There is a first slight resemblance in the discussion of the proprietary rights (with due allowance for the difference of tone). A number of Yankee features are prominent among the themes of the two histories, the custom of bundling being singled out for special consideration in each case. The criticism of Puritan fanaticism by the Loyalist clergyman, angrily denouncing the Connecticut blue laws, has its counterpart in the ridicule of Dutch conservatism and slowness in Irving's *History.* It becomes difficult to push the analogy between the two books any further, however, except in one important point: they share a tradition of humor that is not unrelated to the tall tales of the frontier. The explanation offered by Irving of the name "Antony's Nose," which designates a cliff on the Hudson,[113] is fantastic enough to be placed next to Peters's anecdote of the frogs of Windham, Connecticut, which terrified the town one night in 1758, as they traveled from their dried-out pond to the nearest river: "The consternation was universal. Old and young, male and female, fled naked from their beds with worse shriekings than those of the frogs. The event was fatal to several women. The men, after a flight of half a mile, in which they met with many broken shins, finding no enemies in pursuit of them, made a halt, and summoned resolution enough to venture back to their wives and children...."[114] A similar flavor is found in several other passages of *A General History of Connecticut*. There is one that recounts how a caterpillar invasion laid waste the country but was succeeded immediately by a providential abundance in pigeons, which allowed thirty thousand people to subsist for three weeks (pp. 154-55). In describing a particularly narrow spot the Connecticut River has to pass, Peters reports, "Here water is consolidated, without frost, by pressure, by swiftness, between the pinching, sturdy rocks, to such a degree of induration, that no iron crow can be forced into it" (p. 127). A further instance of fiction that is not out of context in an account of Calvinist intolerance presents the exotic whip-poor-will to Peters's English-reading public:

The Whipperwill has so named itself by its nocturnal songs. It is also called the pope, by reason of its darting with great swiftness, from the clouds almost to the ground, and bawling out 'Pope!' which alarms young people and the fanatics very much, especially as they know it to be an ominous bird. However, it has hitherto proved friendly, always giving travellers and others notice of an approaching storm, by saluting them every minute with 'Pope! Pope!'....The superstitious inhabitants would have exorcised this harmless bird long ago, as an emissary from Rome, and an enemy to the American vine, had they not found out that it frequents New-England only in the summer, and prefers the wilderness to a palace. Nevertheless, they cannot but believe it to be a spy from some foreign court, an agent of antichrist, a lover of persecution, and an enemy of protestants, because it sings of 'whipping', and of the 'pope', which they think portends misery and a change of religion. (pp. 257-58)

Brackenridge, Irving, and even Peters retained their distinctive allegiances to America in spite of the disillusionments, minor or major, which they experienced; but their tempered attachment could not engender any glowing vision of the future of America such as is embodied in the pseudonymous Celadon's *The Golden Age: or, Future Glory of North-America* (1785). The early date of its publication perhaps in part accounts for its utopian zeal, which may also owe something to the spirit of the visionary allegories that influenced its form. *The Golden Age* borrows conventional features from the fictional style of the age to set forth a number of ideas characteristic of the revolutionary and constitutional climate of the late eighteenth century. It praises the "matchless sagacity" of the United States and the role the country is to play as a refuge when "the poor, the oppressed, and the persecuted will fly to America, as doves to their windows" (p. 9). More soberly, it assesses the physical advantages of the country and the benefits that may derive from a democratic confederation. Celadon maps out the states one day to be occupied in the southwest by the Negroes and the Indians, respectively called Nigrania and Savagenia, and foresees the establishment in the West of "a French, a Spanish, a Dutch, an Irish, &c. yea, a Jewish State" (p. 12). The original assertion of the providential guidance granted the United States, and revealed to Celadon because of his devoutness as well as patriotism, is restated in the outline of New Canaan, "populated with Jews converted to Christianism, more zealous than the lukewarm Christians of the day" (p. 13), and destined to be the wellspring of a general renewal of the Christian faith: from western America it shall spread over the whole continent, and then the entire globe.

The second part of Celadon's vision is given him on a mythical summit "in the centre of North-America," overtopping all the other mountains, "in figure like a broken globe. And for circumference about thirteen geographical miles." The description is further elaborated:

> The trees which adorn its towering summit, are clad with unfading green.—Cedar, pine, laurel, &c. are the principal product of the irriguous soil. It put me in mind of the famous Helicon, so often celebrated by the poets, as the native residence of the muses.—Especially, as I perceived several limpid springs bursting from its sides, and flowing in fertilizing meanders through

the circumjacent plains, and refreshing the vales below. . . .
Then the Angel washed my eyes with a crystaline elixir, which
he carried in a pearly phial. Whereupon I found my visive
faculty amazingly strengthened. So that I could distinctly view
the whole continent from shore to shore. (p. 10)

The final paragraph metaphorically completes Celadon's removal
from worldly experience into a realm of supernatural fantasy.
This is also the world of other dream books whose action is
set in distant lands or planets. One of these is George Fowler's
A Flight to the Moon, or. The Vision of Randalthus (1813).
The inhabitants of the moon, whom Irving called Lunatics, are
named Lunarians by Fowler:

Their complexion is of a beautiful golden cast; their cheeks and
lips are tipped with a lively red; their eyes blue; and their golden
hair oft falls down their shoulders in beautiful ringlets. There
is great symmetry and delicacy in their shapes and features; and
they move with inimitable grace. . . . They are feelingly alive to
all the virtues which we possess; but angry looks never distort
the beauty of their features, nor even passion, pollute the purity
of their hearts. They are extremely quick in their motions, and
equally quick of apprehension. They are fonder of music, painting and poetry, than philosophy and abstract studies, which
they say only tend to bewilder the mind without either amusing
the fancy or adding to the comforts of life.[115]

Randalthus himself is very much in sympathy with these sensitive and artistic beings. This is apparent in what he says, and
especially in the way in which he expresses his opinion. He belongs to the sentimental school of writing. When he speaks of
the emotional harmony between his moon hosts and himself, he
seems to be describing a love feast; and remembering what he
felt at the Lunarians' welcome, he writes: ". . . Let me, through
the ages of eternity, cling to the dear reflection, that the Lord
of the universe then bent from his awful throne, and beheld the
brilliant scene with joy" (p. 38). This is a tone very different
from that of either Brackenridge or Irving, and yet it may have
similar results. Thus it serves to increase the sense of disillusionment which Randalthus experiences as he becomes aware of the
Lunarians' reaction to his account of the earth and its inhabi-

tants. He has first felt superior to his hosts because their scientific knowledge strikes him as primitive, but he reconsiders when he understands that they would think it shameful to be so constantly involved in wars and disputes as the terrestrians (pp. 29, 45). He undergoes a disillusionment similar to Gulliver, who from a giant among the people of Liliput was turned into a diminutive creature in Brobdingnag: mysterious and majestic in appearance, after a while Randalthus stands revealed as a despicable human being. How ridiculous man's pretensions are becomes plainer still after he has been taken on a flight above the moon and into the universe, which leads him into the sun: he discovers that the outer layer of flames can be traversed and that the sun is inhabited by creatures in a number of ways similar to the Lunarians. The latter's sensitive mildness is with them replaced by a more vivacious temper: "They sometimes fall into a momentary passion; but it is soon over" (p. 182). Their main attributes are cheerfulness and a patient acceptance of such evils as must beset them. These evils are balanced by a blessing: "...The gods could not form man from imperfect matter without some alloy to his happiness; but gave him woman to remove the evil, and afford a balm to his every sorrow" (p. 182). The examples of contentment bear fruit with Randalthus, for when he finds his adventures to have been a dream only, he promptly derives a lesson from his experience: "I...thought it my duty to be satisfied on the world on which I was destined to exist" (p. 185).

The banality of Fowler's fantasy is possibly due to the fact that he may originally have planned to write only the first part of his "flight to the moon"; his book is entertaining, but only so long as it relates the shock of Randalthus's disillusionment. The hero's further adventures on and around the moon merely repeat this experience. The only new elements which they introduce are a series of contrasting thumbnail sketches of various countries and an ecstatic description of an ice-scape seen from the top of a moon summit. Even here the author fails: he must confess that the description is beyond his powers to conclude.[116]

Sobering reflections were in store for the pseudonymous Captain Adam Seaborn, too, when he ventured on a voyage into the interior of the world. *Symzonia; a Voyage of Discovery* (1820) combines a satire of John Cleves Symmes's "Theory of Concentric Spheres, demonstrating that the earth is hollow, habitable within, and widely open about the poles"[117] with features strongly reminiscent of *Gulliver's Travels.* Having managed in 1817 to enter the earth at the South Pole, Seaborn lands with his crew in a country which he calls Symzonia, "out of gratitude to Capt. Symmes for his sublime theory."[118] He frequently converses with the ruler of the country, the Best Man, but his gradual revelations about man's nature and the condition of the external world at length determine the Best Man to have nothing whatever to do with Seaborn's fellow beings. Seaborn renders the Best Man's conclusion in the following words:

> ...It appeared that we were of a race who had either wholly fallen from virtue, or were at least very much under the influence of the worst passions of our nature; that a great proportion of the race were governed by an inveterate selfishness, that canker of the soul, which is wholly incompatible with ingenuous and affectionate good-will towards our fellow-beings; that we were given to the practice of injustice, violence, and oppression, even to such a degree as to maintain bodies of armed men, trained to destroy their fellow-creatures; that we were guilty of enslaving our fellow-men for the purpose of procuring the means of gratifying our sensual appetites; that we were inordinately addicted to traffic, and sent out our people to the extreme parts of the external world to procure, by exchange, or fraud, or force, things pernicious to the health and morals of those who receive them, and that this practice was carried so far as to be supported with armed ships. (p. 196)

The Symzonians' opinion of the terrestrians is even more unflattering than that of the Lunarians; but both testify to the high ethical standards of those who hold them. The Symzonians and Lunarians have other things in common: they need less sleep than the humans, they have fewer and less-demanding wants, and they do not place so much faith in knowledge and in scientific and technical attainments. This last point is made clear by the system of government adopted in Symzonia. The Best Man is assisted by a council chosen from among the "worthies," that

is, representatives selected for their goodness, their usefulness, or
their wisdom (or learnedness): among the hundred members of
the council, fifty-five are "Good," forty "Useful" and only five
are "Wise," these five being scholars and learned men. The distrust of the "Wise" is referred to again when the Best Man mentions a war-engine devised by one of them, Fultria,[119] for he
thinks that the dangerous enemies it was designed to fight may
have been simply invented by Fultria to create an opportunity
for showing off his skill. In spite of their neglect of technology,
however, the Symzonians have built an "aerial vessel" that impresses Seaborn very strongly (though he refuses to admit it)
(pp. 113-14). More remarkable than this airship, the war engine
invented by Fultria has attributes that seem to anticipate twentieth-century developments:

> ...It was a vast machine moved upon wheels, and rendered
> of but little specific gravity, by means of the apparatus employed
> in their air vessels, by the help of which it could, in an emer-
> gency, be raised into the air for a short time, to cross rivers or
> broken ground.
>
> It was propelled by means of a great number of tubes, project-
> ing very obliquely through the bottom near the ground, through
> which air was forced with such prodigious violence, that the
> resistance of the earth and atmosphere impelled the machine
> forwards: in this way it was moved with astonishing velocity.
> From all sides of this engine a great number of double tubes
> projected, through which two kinds of gas were caused to issue.
> These gases uniting in the extremities, produced a flame of in-
> tense heat, like that of our compound blow-pipe on a large
> scale, which flame, according to tradition, was ejected with such
> force, as to consume every thing for half a mile in every direc-
> tion. The interior of the machine was sufficiently capacious to
> admit men enough to direct its motions and prepare the gases,
> and also the materials and apparatus necessary to their produc-
> tion. (pp. 168-69)

This invention was intended to scare the inhabitants of Belzubia
at a time when they appeared to threaten Symzonia. When Seaborn tries, in his account of the earth, to establish distinctions
between the various nations, he compares the British to the
Belzubians.[120] Earlier he has proudly shown his hosts the works

of Shakespeare and Milton, but after studying them, the Symzonians have found them to display all the unpleasant attributes characteristic of certain Symzonians that had to be banished from their country. By his behavior, Seaborn only bears out the low opinion which the Symzonians have formed of the externals. The Best Man has asked him not to take back any of the pearls found in the interior of the earth, so as not to arouse the externals' cupidity; but Seaborn smuggles a handful out of Symzonia all the same: "This deviation from what was expected of me, will, I trust, be excused by my external friends, when they remember that I have been much addicted to commerce, and consider the force of habit, and the security with which the operation could be performed" (p. 212).

The author of *Symzonia* skillfully uses the satirist's trick of cutting down to size an overly self-assured and self-righteous person by reversing his imagined superiority into a similar position of inferiority. The author displays only average ability in his writing, but the character of Seaborn himself is cleverly contrived. The captain is not, as often is the case in Swiftian satires, a neutral representative of the body of people to be criticized; on the contrary, his very actions and general shiftiness exemplify the weaknesses which he is trying to pass over in silence.[121] The parts of the story concerned with the voyage to and from Symzonia are conventional features of the tale of adventure.

The clarity of the satirical design of *Symzonia*, the ease of Irving's writing and humor, and the seriousness and comic sense of Brackenridge are all conspicuously absent from *The Oriental Philanthropist, or True Republican* (1800), by Henry Sherburne, unidentified except for his name. The book opens with a defense of the fable-like fictitious tale, which can "rebuke and reform ...adolescence, or even riper years,"[122] and a verbose passage of praise for "Constantia" or Mrs. Judith Sargent Murray. It also contains in its first chapter an address to America: "Happy American States! so richly adorned with sons and daughters of refined genius and exalted virtue! happy in thy illustrious chiefs, statesmen and legislators, whose fame rebounds through every region of the globe!" (pp. 6-7). Since the final chapter prophesies America's future, a time when the country will be a universal model of humanity and virtue, the intervening story of an island where perfection reigns might be thought to be applicable to America. It remains, however, only a vague and rhapsodical fantasy, inspired by some tradition of the Oriental tale and abounding, like the fairy tale, in exemplary beings and supernatural powers. Ostensibly, its hero is Nytan, son of a Chinese emperor, but he depends entirely on a diffuse higher being of unlimited power and benevolence named Ravenzar. Nytan is first the victim of a plot in China which has nothing to do with the utopian fairy tale about Ravenzar's island, the true republic of the future. He is then sent to various countries to spread the gospel of Ravenzar; in one instance, facing a hostile African audience, he wins them over on the spot by a naïve discourse on altruism: "A new light sprang up in each mind. Numbers convinced, (and now angry only with themselves) immediately retired from public business. They retired to reflect, and reform. The sacred influence spread. The flame of celestial love was enkindled. And thousands of bright genius' soon became gloriously active in noblest deeds of fame which Heaven itself records" (pp. 199-200). Eloquence is mentioned but not felt in a passage that describes how Persia is converted to religion, virtue, industry, and happiness, apparently by spreading tracts on these subjects. Apart from using such elements as queens threatened by their enemies and saved through Nytan's or Ravenzar's influence, and lovers separated and unexpectedly reunited,[123] the author also attempted descriptions of factitious Oriental splendor, and finally let one newly arrived on Ravenzar's island prophesy: "Soon shall...bliss and glory universal reign! Pride, lust and jealousy, hatred and dire contests shall then forever cease! Celestial love shall dwell—forever dwell in every breast!" (p. 205)

When Sherburne wrote *The Oriental Philanthropist*, the promise of American fiction was perhaps not much more substantial than this prophecy. Within a few years, however, the efforts of the pioneers Brackenridge and Brockden Brown were to be assisted by Irving; and by 1820 a number of authors, though not outstanding individually, had contributed to strengthen the confidence of American writing. The satirists in particular did their best to keep fiction alive and in touch with the realities of life.

1. For the entire revolutionary period, see Bruce I. Granger, *Political Satire in the American Revolution, 1763-1783*.

2. *Monthly Magazine and American Register* 1(1799):434; from the review of *The Foresters*, pp. 434-38.

3. Serialized in the *Columbian Magazine* (June, 1787-April, 1788), *The Foresters* appeared in Boston as a book in 1792 and with additions, including a *clavis allegorica*, in 1796; references are to the latter edition. Quinn, *Fiction* (p. 5), and H. R. Brown, *The Sentimental Novel* (p. 70), consider Belknap's use of the letter form in the two Boston editions as evidence of the vogue of the epistolary novel.

4. See George E. Hastings, "John Bull and his American Descendants," *AL* 1(1929):40-68. Hastings's conclusion that *"The Foresters* is most decidedly an imitation of *The History of John Bull"* applies to Belknap's use of the ingredients of his model, not to his manner and style.

5. See Charles E. Cole, "Jeremy Belknap: Pioneer Nationalist," *NEQ* 10(1937):743-51.

6. Cf. the review in the *Monthly Magazine:* "If...Dr. Belknap has not displayed as much humour, nor delineated with equal fidelity, the manners of common life; if there is not, in this 'sequel,' the same just observance of allegorical propriety, nor the same colloquial spirit and animation, as may be found in the *original* tale; yet the writer of the former has avoided the low vulgarity and occasional obscenity; faults which, we think, deform the pages of the latter....Dr. Belknap has maintained a style free and familiar, yet chaste and correct, throughout his narrative" (p. 438).

7. The text of the first Philadelphia edition of 1774 (there were three of them) was reprinted with notes by Benson J. Lossing, under the title *The Old Farm and the New Farm* (New York, 1857). References here are to one of the few complete 20th-century reprints of the 1774 text, in Walter C. Bronson, ed., *American Prose* (1916). The *Miscellaneous Essays and Occasional Writings by Francis Hopkinson* (1792), offers a revised and tamer version (1:65-91).

8. As Quinn suggested (*Fiction*, p. 4), the nobleman is a character rather than an allegorical type.

9. Hopkinson's allegory *A New Roof*, in favor of the Constitution of 1787, is another instance of his skill in this manner of treating a controversial subject (*Miscellaneous Essays*, 2:282-319).

10. *The Diverting History of John Bull and Brother Jonathan* (New York, 1812), p. 61. References are to this edition.

11. Paulding certainly laid himself open to censure like that of Bristed (*Resources*, p. 305), who reproached him for blindly attacking and belittling whatever came from England; it was *The United States and England* (1815), that most outspokenly expressed Paulding's Anglophobia.

12. Paulding's works, such as *Sketch of Old England* (1822), *Koningsmarke* (1823), and *John Bull in America* (1825), equally demonstrate that this was an inherent weakness, rather than a result of his Anglophobia. Paulding was easily carried away by his ironical exuberance, whether his subject was British institutions, fashions in literature, or the characteristics of Frenchmen, and British tourists in America.

[153]

13. Wright, *American Fiction*, item 2673; cf. the biographical notice prefixed to the edition of the *Journal* in *Magazine of History* 5:Extra No. 18 (1911). Waterhouse was 59, not a young man, in 1813, but his patriotism seems to warrant that he would have vigorously patronized the *Journal*. There were five issues in 1816; references are to the first edition. A comparable book, with more pronounced but rather unfortunate literary pretensions, is William Ray, *The American Tars in Tripolitan Slavery*, "containing an account of the loss and capture of the U.S. frigate 'Philadelphia'; treatment and sufferings of the prisoners; description of the place; manners, customs, &c. of the Tripolitans; public transactions of the U.S. with that Regency, including Gen. Eaton's expedition, interspersed with interesting remarks, anecdotes, and poetry on various subjects, written during upwards of 19 months' imprisonment and vassalage among the Turks." Reprinted in the same series as the *Journal* (1911).

14. The American prisoners were confined below deck: "All the air and light came through the hatch way, a sort of trap door or cellar way. In this floating dungeon, we miserable young men spent our first night in sleepless anguish, embittered with the apprehension of our suffering a cruel death by suffocation. Here the black hole of Calcutta rose to my view in all its horrors; and the very thought stopped my respiration, and set my brain on fire" (p. 29).

15. Both the *Narrative of Colonel Ethan Allen* (1779) and Freneau's "The British Prison-Ship" (1780) are superior to the *Journal*, from a literary point of view. Freneau's essay "The Philosopher of the Forest," 5(1781), subtitled "Containing some particulars relative to the Island of Snatchaway," lists among characteristic features of England: a captain who rescues shipwrecked people but robs them before setting them ashore; men proud and ambitious, greedy, selfish, contemptuous of "Fickle-land," or France; an aristocratic order; a general lack of liberty; "almost perpetual executions of criminals"; no charity; a large number of eccentrics. See *The Prose of Freneau*, pp. 212-16.

16. "...My family were of that party in Massachusetts called Federal; that is, we voted for Governor Strong, and federal Senators and Representatives; our Clergyman was also federal, and preached and prayed federally, and we read none but federal newspapers, and associated with none but federalists ...We believed entirely that the war was unnecessary and wicked, and declared with no other design but to injure England and gratify France. We believed also that the whole of the administration, and every man of the Republican party, from Jefferson and Madison, down to our——was either a fool or knave. If we did not believe that every republican was a scoundrel, we were sure and certain that every scoundrel was a republican..." (pp. 63-64).

17. The *Journal* is itself an expression of that touchiness, and could not have contributed to alter the English opinion of America.

18. See among the many apologists of the purity of American women: Jacob Duché, *Caspipina's Letters* (Philadelphia, 1774), pp. 48-49; Samuel Peters, *General History of Connecticut* (1781), pp. 327-28; Ingersoll, *Inchiquin's Letters*, p. 136; "Lindor to Caroline," *The American Bee*, p. 120.

19. The principle of selection might have been counted upon to explain the rather haphazard progress of the writer through his topics. Yet, as G. Thomas Tanselle has pointed out, the various opinions gradually combine into a unified view (*Royall Tyler* [1967], pp. 192, 204).

20. *The Yankey in London*, letter 42, pp. 132-43.

21. The novel has all the marks of fashionable fiction, including "an immense black forest of twenty aged trees; two crazy castles; three murderers·

a trap-door with rusty bolts; a bloody key, ditto dagger; two pair of broken stairs; a sheeted ghost; a ghostly monk, and a marriage," as well as "the elegant expressions 'pleasing anguish,' 'delightful despair,' and 'heart-rending felicity,'...the phrase 'subterraneous matter in the clouds,' which she had introduced into a thunderstorm" (p. 15).

22. *Letters,* by William Austin, the creator of "Peter Rugg," was such an authentic commentary on things British, and, by comparison, on things American too.

23. See in the *Quarterly Review* 10(1814):494-539, a review of *Inchiquin's Letters* that was actually a virulent attack, "a compilation, from Cobbett and from various travelers, of the worst charges against American morals and manners, public and private" (W. B. Cairns, *British Criticisms of American Writings, 1783-1815,* p. 87). Two Americans replied anonymously in 1815: Paulding (*The United States and England*) and Timothy Dwight (*Remarks on the Review of Inchiquin's Letters*). The exchange reads like the talk of small boys trying to out-boast each other. It is true that in 1814 and 1815 feelings were embittered by the war. But the review of *Inchiquin's Letters* in the *Port-Folio* shows that in 1811 already this defense of America was received with satisfaction: "A work of this kind has been long wanted—long a desideratum in American Literature," The reviewer found fault only with its comparative shortness, and commended its "argument, style, matter and manner" ([3d] New ser., 5[1811]:300-17, 385-400).

24. *Inchiquin,* p. 133.

25. Watterston was another writer who held an unflattering opinion of the travel books; he put this view into the mouth of an English lord: "We have been deceived, my lord, by the ignorance and misrepresentation of men who called themselves travellers; and who, I find, were totally unacquainted with the American character, and totally ignorant of the American Constitution. On such sources as these you must not depend for correct information;—they are fallacious and deceitful, false and exaggerated. Those who have furnished this information are men, you know, my lord, who have either been bribed to calumniate and detract, for an object with which you cannot now be unacquainted, or the refuse of society, ejected from our prisons, without intellect, without knowledge, and without honor" (*Letters from Washington* [1818], p. 8).

26. English travelers frequently ridiculed the conception of the capital and especially the execution of the ambitious plans. Henry Unwin Addington came to Washington in 1822 with preconceived ideas which he found confirmed by what he saw. See *Youthful America: Selections from Henry Unwin Addington's "Residence in the U.S.A., 1822, 23, 24, 25,"* ed. Bradford Perkins (Berkeley and Los Angeles: University of Calif. Press, 1960), pp. 20-21.

27. "Federalism is the politics of a gentleman, and of a lady, but Republicanism is the low cant of the vulgar." This opinion was attributed by Benjamin Waterhouse to New England Federalists; it concludes the passage quoted in part in note 16, above. Cf. L. P. Simpson, "Federalism and the Crisis of Literary Order," *AL* 32(1960):253-60.

28. They were the more willing to do so because they combined conservative American views of the role of the writer (as a defender of the moral order and rational means of expression and communication) with their distinctive condemnation of writings that could be said to "condone rebellion of any kind against the existing social order" (R. B. Davis, *Jefferson's Virginia,* p. 259).

29. These essays appeared in the *Aurora* from March to October 1799 and were reprinted in book form in 1799; references are to this edition. For a discussion of the Slender *Letters,* see Lewis Leary, *That Rascal Freneau* (1941), pp. 307-11.

30. See H. H. Clark, "What Made Freneau the Father of American Prose?" *Trans. Wisc.* 25(1930):39-50, especially p. 39. Clark's study refers also to other prose writings besides the *Letters,* in particular to the "Philosopher of the Forest" papers. These have not been collected in their entirety, but a number of them are included in *The Prose of Freneau* (1955). Marsh ranks the "Tomo-Cheeki" essays higher than the "Philosopher" (p. 10) among the nonpolitical essays; both of these series are, however, more derivative than the Slender contributions and lack a speaker as distinctive as Robert Slender himself.

31. *Letters of Shahcoolen,* p. 69. The *Letters* originally appeared in the New York *Commercial Advertiser,* but they state the views of a New Englander: Silliman was Connecticut-born and spent all his life in Connecticut. His book was formerly attributed to S. L. Knapp, but see the facsimile reprint edited by Ben Harris McClary for conclusive evidence in favor of Silliman. A fairer view of Freneau, though by no means an indulgent one, was expressed in 1807 by Dennie, a Federalist like Silliman ("Freneau's Poems," reprinted in E. H. Cady, ed., *Literature of the Early Republic,* pp. 481-95).

32. Livingston, Linn, and Hopkinson are mentioned, together with the Hartford Wits.

33. See above, note 3, to chap. 4.

34. "What, but a distempered civilization, has rendered it criminal to obey the dictates of nature in promiscuous concubinage? Why should I be confined to one woman, while the whole animal world beside, obey the impulse of passion, and seek gratification, wherever it may be found? Why should I be compelled to support and educate those beings, whom my physical energies operating according to the established laws of nature, without the assistance of mind, have produced? I am no more accountable for their existence, than the mountains for the cedar, which it bears, or the stream for the wheel, which it turns. As therefore the cedar is cut down, and the mountain does not mourn; the wheel is removed, but the stream continues to flow; so those beings may be born, grow up, and die without any claims to my assistance, and with no title to my love, or my grief" (pp. 141-42).

35. Attributed to an unidentified Jonas Clopper and perhaps printed in Baltimore. See Wright, *Fiction,* 1: item 551.

36. For "Asylumonia" read "Massachusetts, New England"; for "Mr. Pigman Puff" read "Madison"; for "Blackmoreland" read "Virginia"; for "Tom Anguish" and "Thomas Tammany Bawlfredonius," respectively, read "Paine" and "Jefferson."

37. The measures adopted against the natives also must somehow be justified: "...They comforted themselves, and appeased their consciences, (if they had any,) with a declaration, that the people, whose property they destroyed, were savages; and deserved to have their towns burnt, because they had been so untaught as to object to a free intercourse with their females. It was asserted that women ought to be held in common, and that for any one man to appropriate to his sole use a woman, who was capable of making many happy, was an unpardonable sin, inasmuch as it tended to decrease 'the sum of human happiness'" (p. 33-34).

38. V. L. Parrington, Jr., in *American Dreams: A Study of American Uto-*

pias (1947), discusses Clopper's work in the larger framework of utopian writings.

39. *The Adventures of Uncle Sam*, pp. 18-19. Similar biblical echoes occur in a Freneau satire on Adams in 1797 (*The Prose of Freneau*, pp. 380 ff.) and in Gilbert J. Hunt, *The Historical Reader*, "Containing the Late War between the United States and Great Britain" (New York, 1819) (see the extract in Charles L. Sanford, ed., *Quest for America, 1810-1824*, pp. 264-69).

40. General Hull addresses the Canadians, the "People of Snowfields," in vain; thereupon, "finding the stupid inhabitants of the Snowfields, so dilatory about accepting the blessings of Liberty and safety,...with the most nettlesome indignation and precipitate activity he pulled up stakes and recrossed over to the territory of Uncle Sam" (p. 52).

41. The generals accusing one another are Smyth and Dearborn.

42. *The War of the Gulls*, pp. 35-36.

43. Jerome Bonaparte married Elizabeth Patterson in 1803.

44. *Memoir of the Northern Kingdom*, p. 26. The pamphlet was reprinted in the *Magazine of History* 39:no. 2, extra no. 154(1929).

45. *DAB* 10:54.

46. There is a Federalist bias in the author's remarks on American literature; he ranks as its best works John Adams's *Defence of the American Constitution* and the *Discourses on Davila*, and John Marshall's *Life of Washington*.

47. The satires here discussed were written from three to ten years after the end of Jefferson's second administration, and yet their authors still felt obliged to spend quite a bit of energy in bitter comments on his failings.

48. This physician is probably a caricature of Samuel Latham Mitchill, scientist, supporter of Jefferson, and author of *Picture of New York*, which started Peter and Washington Irving on the parody that was finally to turn into Knickerbocker's *History of New York* (see above, under the heading "Quixotic Travelers and Fabulous Voyagers," Chapter 5, part 5.). The same S. L. Mitchill is presumably the "Samuel Ell Centumvir" to whom Clopper dedicated his *History of Bawlfredonia*, listing his achievements and his fame, "dignitas centum societates [sic] sustinens." Mitchill favored the idea of replacing the name "America" with "Fredonia."

49. The Conundrumites include an apothecary, a money-lender, a cobbler, a pettifogger, and a fiddler.

50. As in the fairy tale, the stepmother figure causes many a hero and heroine to leave the paternal home; Brockden Brown's Arthur Mervyn and Watterston's Glencarn are two other examples taken from the American fiction of the age.

51. "It is a cross between a satire upon contemporary scholarship, or rather the American Philosophical Society, and the politics of the period on the one side, and a romance of roguery on the other" (Earl L. Bradsher, "Some Aspects of the Early American Novel," *Texas Review* 3[1918]:255). Bradsher pointed out that *The Yankee Traveller* could be looked upon as "reacting against the pellucid purity of the average woman's novel of the period and the smug virtue-rewarded type such as the popular *Two Shoemakers*." We might add that it has affinities to a book like *The Adventures of Jonathan Corncob* (see below, in "The Novel of Adventure," Section IV). Bradsher's claim that *The Yankee Traveller* is well written seems exaggerated.

52. The only (imperfect) copy of *Father Quipes* is in the Library of Con-

gress. For some comments on the pamphlet and its author, see David Wilson Thompson, *Early Publications of Carlisle, Pa., 1785-1835* (Carlisle: The Sentinel, 1932), pp. 67-69.

53. For information about Knapp see the reprint of Knapp's *Lectures on American Literature* (1829), under the title *American Cultural History*. Silliman's *Letters of Shahcoolen* used to be attributed to Knapp; the copy in the Harvard College Library has on its title page the penciled note, "By Samuel Lorenzo Knapp."

54. The book was published in the "touchy" decade when Americans looked with suspicion on books of "Travels in the United States."

55. *Extracts from the Journals of Marshal Soult,* "addressed to a friend: how obtained, and by whom translated is not a subject of enquiry," p. 38. For the appearance of the Indian in American fiction, see Chapter 16, "Strands of History."

56. *Extracts from a Journal of Travels in North America,* p. 16.

57. See Sr. M. Chrysostom Diebels's *Peter Markoe.* Her brief reference to *The Algerine Spy* places Markoe in the tradition of the apologists of democracy who make fiction the vehicle of their views; as such Markoe is a precursor of Brackenridge.

58. Markoe, *The Algerine Spy in Pennsylvania,* p. 96.

59. Waln, *The Hermit in America on a Visit to Philadelphia,* "edited by Peter Atall, Esq.," title-page. A second series of the *Hermit* appeared in 1821.

60. This is an allusion to Captain Symmes's proposal to prove his own theory that the earth could be entered at the poles. See below, the discussion of *Symzonia,* pp. 148-51.

61. *The Wandering Philanthropist, or Lettres* [sic] *from the Chinese,* p. 37. George Fowler "of Virginia," otherwise unidentified, also wrote *A Flight to the Moon;* see below, pp. 147-48.

62. See the various biographers of Washington and novelists like Mrs. Wood, *Julia,* pp. 131-35; Sabin, *Charles Observator,* p. 82; Woodworth, *The Champions of Freedom,* 2:335-36; Watterston, *Letters from Washington,* pp. 116-17.

63. See above, in "John Bull and Brother Jonathan," for the discussion of another aspect of Paulding's work (Chapter 5, part 1).

64. *Letters from the South,* 1:9-10. In a later letter Paulding pronounces the American, and especially the Yankee, to be a nomad, much like the Indian, an attribute which of course has quickened the settling of the continent (1:83).

65. Jay B. Hubbell, *The South in American Literature,* p. 250, sees no reason to doubt Tucker's authorship of the *Letters;* see also Robert C. McLean, *George Tucker: Moral Philosopher and Man of Letters* (Chapel Hill: Univ. of North Carolina Press, 1961). *Letters from Virginia* (Baltimore, 1816), has also been attributed to Paulding (by Foley), and in the copy in the Harvard College Library there is the penciled note, "The author of this book is Mr. Maxwell of Norfolk. He was educated at Yale College and is well known to Mr. Sherman, Preceptor of Bacon academy at Colchester."

66. Markoe also varied the recipients of his observer's letters.

67. Jay B. Hubbell considers Tucker's remarks on slavery a sufficient reason for the anonymous publication of *Letters from Virginia.*

68. *The Letters of the British Spy,* p. 24. The *British Spy* first appeared in the *Virginia Argus* in August and September, 1803.

69. Cf. Tucker's "Translator's Preface" to the *Letters from Virginia:* "I hope

the reader will believe that I understand how to write long winding sentences of the most fashionable and soporific construction" (p. vi).

70. Tucker was to detect an influence of deism, atheism, Godwin, and Paine on the students at William and Mary College: "The usual consequences soon followed. Idleness, intemperance, profanity, and in short, dissipation of almost every kind and name, leading not unfrequently to duels of death, prevailed and triumphed" (*Letters from Virginia*, p. 130).

71. *The Letters of the British Spy*, 10th ed. (New York, 1832), p. 50. Wirt himself had no high ambitions; see the letter quoted by Hubbell, *The South in American Literature*, p. 237. To Ticknor, Wirt was simply "the author of *The British Spy*, etc.," when he first met him in 1815, and if he was not too favorably impressed, this was no doubt in part due to the expectations fostered by Wirt's literary fame (see George S. Hillard, *Life, Letters, and Journals of George Ticknor*, 9th ed., 2 vols. [Boston, 1878], 1:33). In 1832, too, John Pendleton Kennedy dedicated his *Swallow Barn* to Wirt and, clearly referring to the *British Spy*, marveled how easily success had come to him (ed. W. S. Osborne [New York and London: Hafner, 1962], p. v).

72. "There is some liveliness of fancy, and a sparkling style in the effusions of this writer: there are many marks of a juvenile [Wirt was thirty-one years old when the *British Spy* appeared] and undisciplined pen, and in most of his recitals we have found that degree of interest and amusement which it was probably the whole intention of the writer to afford" (*Literary Magazine, and American Register* 1[1804]:261).

73. *The Lay Preacher; or Short Sermons, for Idle Readers*, p. 40. Dennie published his first "Lay Preacher" essay on October 12, 1795. There were to be 118 of them. A second collection was published five years after Dennie's death by John E. Hall in Philadelphia, 1817; the two volumes, containing 36 and 28 essays respectively, have been edited by Milton Ellis. Before 1795 Dennie wrote another series, begun in 1792; these Farrago essays, 29 in number, have not been collected. For Dennie, see Milton Ellis, *Joseph Dennie and His Circle*.

74. "The essays of the 'Lay-Preacher' were afterwards collected in a volume, which is, I believe, the most popular work on the American continent" (Davis, *Travels*, p. 204). Of course Dennie's audience, as Teut Riese has reminded us (*Das englische Erbe in der amerikanischen Literatur*), differed considerably from that of Addison and Goldsmith, whose readers had at least an upper middle-class sophistication; most of the "Lay Preacher" essays were written for the *Farmer's Museum* of Walpole, N.H., whose title may fail quite to define the public it catered to yet indicates that it was not a London coffee-house audience.

75. *The Spirit of the Farmer's Museum*, p. 155 (a specimen of "Pennsylvania Dutch").

76. The lines from the New England primer, "The cat doth play,/And after slay," allegedly become an entire Smith sonnet, beginning with the following quatrain: "Child of lubricious art! sanguine sport!/Of *pangful mirth!* sweet ermin'd sprite!/Who lov'st, with silent, *velvet step*, to court/The bashful bosom of the night." (pp. 290-91)

77. The nine letters of Oldstyle were published between November 15, 1802, and April 23, 1803. Letters 2 to 9 were republished in New York in 1824; references are to this edition; S. T. Williams edited the New York edition for the Facsimile Text Society in 1941, with the uncollected first letter. John Lambert, *Travels through Lower Canada, and the U.S. of North America*, reprinted

the letter on dueling (2:219-26). According to P.M. Irving, in that "barren period" *Jonathan Oldstyle* attracted attention in New York and led to a visit from Brockden Brown (*The Life and Letters of Washington Irving,* 4 vols. [New York, 1862], 1:47).

78. William L. Hedges thinks that Irving gradually "reduces Oldstyle to utter absurdity" (*Washington Irving: An American Study,* p. 32).

79. "Our intention is simply to instruct the young, reform the old, correct the town and castigate the age....We are all three of us determined beforehand to be pleased with what we write....We are laughing philosophers, and clearly of opinion, that wisdom, true wisdom, is a plump, jolly dame, who sits in her arm-chair, laughs right merrily at the farce of life,—and takes the world as it goes" (*Salmagundi,* 1:4).

80. *Salmagundi* was published in 20 numbers from January 24, 1807, to January 25, 1808. The intervals were of about a fortnight or less in the first half of the year, and after the long summer break (June 27-August 14) tended to become longer, probably because the authors were beginning to tire of their enterprise.

81. The portrait of Langstaff in no. 8, April 18, 1807 (1:145-51), is said to be that of Dennie, whom Washington Irving had visited some time earlier. See Ellis, *Joseph Dennie and His Circle,* chap. 10.

82. It has often been pointed out that *Salmagundi* foreshadows a number of features of *A History of New York* and *The Sketch-Book.*

83. *Salmagundi* was rather well received. One reviewer wrote: "This [satirical] design is executed with so much spirit, wit, genius, elegance, and humour, as to place the Salmagundi on the same height of excellence with the effusions of Rabelais, of Swift, of Addison, and Voltaire" (*Monthly Register,* New York, 3[August, 1807]:150); the reviewer further commended the authors for the variety of their tones. Lambert, who described a New York parade that may have been the very one which Mustapha depicted, praised *Salmagundi* and reprinted a big chunk of it (*Travels,* 2:144, 203, 234-349).

84. *Salmagundi. Second Series.*

85. Langstaff, irritated by certain features of the fashions in vogue, discovers to his surprise, when looking at an old picture, that half a century earlier there existed affectations in dress as ridiculous as the contemporary ones (1:91-103).

86. The "Old Bachelor" essays began appearing in the Richmond *Enquirer* in 1811 and were collected and published in book form in 1814; references are to this edition. They include occasional contributions from others besides Wirt, who however "managed the enterprise and wrote most of the numbers" (Hubbell, *The South,* p. 238). See also Davis, *Jefferson's Virginia,* p. 280.

87. *The Sketch-Book* appeared in seven numbers in New York; in later editions the order of the papers was altered. For the English edition in book form Irving included the two Indian papers, written for the *Analectic Magazine,* and they became a part of *The Sketch-Book* from then on. The pagination is continuous to the end of the four numbers published in 1819, and begins again in V and in VII; quotations are given with the number of the issue and the page.

88. This tale is an instance of "sportive Gothic," to use the term coined by Oral S. Coad, "The Gothic Element."

89. Those tales with the appearance of the fashionable sentimental story may have been based, as is the case with "The Wife," on authentic facts

known to Irving (see Edward Wagenknecht, *Washington Irving*, p. 176). These he preferred to treat in a serious manner, whereas apparently for legendary, less immediate material, he adopted a lighter and more freely imaginative treatment.

90. See also Allen Guttman, "Washington Irving and the Conservative Imagination," *AL* 36(1964):165-73; and Donald A. Ringe, "New York and New England: Irving's Criticism of American Society," *AL* 38(1967):455-67.

91. William L. Hedges rightly insists (*Washington Irving*, p. 128) that there are implicit comments on America in many of Crayon's observations on England, and more generally, that Crayon's "responses to people and places are as important or more important than the people and places are in themselves" (p. 146).

92. Irving's letters show that he had a clear conception of his writing and his career. See, e.g., the letters to Ebenezer Irving, March 3, 1819; Brevoort, July 10, 1819; Scott, September 25, 1819, in all of which he stresses his need for leisure. In his letters to Brevoort, March 3, 1819, and December 11, 1824, he explains his preference for the fanciful and the short tale; there may be a certain amount of retrospective rationalization here, though. Godwin's opinion of *The Sketch-Book*, incidentally, is put in terms that would not have pleased the American Irving: "Everywhere I find in it the marks of a mind of the utmost elegance and refinement, a thing as you know I was not exactly prepared to look for in an American" (letter to James Ogilvie, September 15, 1819, quoted by P. M. Irving, 1:422).

93. Brackenridge probably began writing *Modern Chivalry* in 1788. The first three volumes of Part I were published in 1792-93, Vol. IV followed in 1797. Material then accumulated by fits and starts as circumstances spurred Brackenridge's imagination, and two more volumes came out in 1804-5. The revised version of 1815 contained an additional volume. References are to the 1937 edition by Claude M. Newlin. See Newlin's introduction, and his *The Life and Writings of Hugh Henry Brackenridge*. Daniel Marder's *Hugh Henry Brackenridge* (Twayne, 1967), is a sound brief study. Lewis Leary's edition of *Modern Chivalry* contains the portions published from 1792 to 1797.

94. John R. Hendrickson, "The Influence of *Don Quixote* on *Modern Chivalry*," a Florida State University dissertation (1959), traces many details of Brackenridge's "plan, character portrayals, and situations" to his great model, and concludes on a close kinship in the two writers' purpose. (See *DA* 20[1959]:661.)

95. Farrago himself wishes to appear more sober than Jefferson: "Do you take me for *Jefferson*? You are mistaken if you think I have so good an opinion of you. I would ill deserve your confidence if I made your whims my guide; or regarded popularity obtained in such a way. It never came into my head, because I had got the chair of government, there was a millenium about to come, when all men would do justice, and there would be no occasion for judges and lawyers; nations could be coerced by proclamations; and no war would ensue" (p. 783).

96. The inventiveness was active about 1770 when the undergraduates Freneau and Brackenridge wrote "Father Bombo's Pilgrimage," probably firing one another to think up improbably picaresque adventures. See Newlin's biography of Brackenridge, pp. 15-21, and Lewis Leary, "Father Bombo's Pilgrimage," *PMHB* 66(1942):459-78. In the introduction to his edition of *Modern Chivalry*, Leary rightly ascribes the survival of the novel to its lively episodes, straightforwardly told (p. 18).

97. See Cowie, *Novel*, p. 54.

[161]

98. The *Monthly Anthology* 5(1808):501, reproached Brackenridge for having concentrated on "low and illiterate" characters, but added, "his talent for drawing them is vigorous." Both the fault and the merit are considered by Leary to be part of the American touch operating within the European framework of the picaresque *Modern Chivalry* and linking the novel up with, e.g., *Georgia Scenes*. Leary also more questionably thinks that Brackenridge treated the quixotic journey as a quest, and as such finds it related to *Huckleberry Finn* (Introduction, p. 15).

99. In this passage and in the references to the philosophical society traces of the former collaboration with Freneau might be detected. See some of the "Tomo Cheeki" essays and the "Pilgrim" essay, VII ("A Challenge Received and Rejected"), in *The Prose of Freneau*.

100. See F. L. Pattee, *Literature*, pp. 156-64, and Van Doren, *The American Novel*, p. 7.

101. Brackenridge's pretense of writing only a model of style (that could not be criticized since it created new standards), and treating his subject matter as of secondary importance, was responded to appreciatively by at least one contemporary reader: "There are two particulars in which we cannot agree with Mr. Brackenridge—that his stile is a model of perfection, and that his book consists *entirely* of nonsense" (*Columbian Magazine* 6[1792]:125).

102. *Monthly Anthology* 5(1808):499-508, 554-58, especially p. 558.

103. "A History of New York, from the beginning of the world to the end of the Dutch dynasty. Containing among many surprising and curious matters, the unutterable ponderings of Walter the Doubter, the disastrous projects of William the Testy, and the chivalric achievements of Peter the Headstrong, the three Dutch governors of New Amsterdam, being the only authentic history of the times that ever hath been, or ever will be published. By Diedrich Knickerbocker" (1809). All references are to this edition. A revised version appeared in 1812, and Irving made more considerable changes when preparing the 1848 edition. See *Diedrich Knickerbocker's A History of New York*, ed. Stanley Williams and Tremaine McDowell; and Clarence M. Webster, "Irving's Expurgation of the 1809 *History of New York*," AL 4(1932):293-95. Scott was an early discoverer of *A History of New York;* see his letter to Brevoort (April 23, 1813), in which he warmly praises the book, its Swiftian parts equally with its Sternean touches (quoted in Hubbell, *American Life*, 1:244-45).

104. "Book I. Being, like all introductions to American histories, very learned, sagacious, and nothing at all to the purpose; containing divers profound theories and philosophic speculations, which the idle reader may totally overlook, and begin at the next book." The Irving brothers, who apparently collaborated only on the opening book, were parodying *A Picture of New-York*, by Samuel L. Mitchill (New York, 1807).

105. Charlton G. Laird, "Tragedy and Irony in *Knickerbocker's History*," AL 12(1940):157-72, offers a convincing account of the composition of the book.

106. See Edwin Greenlaw, "Washington Irving's Comedy of Politics," *Texas Review* 1(1916):291-306; and Tremaine McDowell, "Gen. James Wilkinson in the Knickerbocker *History of New York*," MLN 41(1926):353-59, an article in which Irving's Van Poffenburgh is shown to be a caricature of Wilkinson.

107. Laird (see above, n. 105), and Wagenknecht (*Washington Irving*, p. 172) find in Stuyvesant features which they call tragic but which, though serious enough, hardly deserve this appellation.

108. ". . . By incessantly changing his measures, he gave none of them a fair

trial; and by listening to the clamours of the mob and endeavouring to do every thing, he in sober truth did nothing....Lucky was it for him that his power was not dependant upon the greasy multitude, and that as yet the populace did not possess the important privilege of nominating their chief magistrate. They however, like a true mob, did their best to help along public affairs; pestering their governor incessantly..." (1:254-55). Cf. Irving's letter to Mary Fairlie, May 2, 1807, in which he complains of having been dragged into campaigning (for the Federalists) and shaking hands with the mob (quoted in Hubbell, *Literature*, 1:230).

109. William L. Hedges in *Washington Irving*, makes the point that the *History*, like Swift's satire, stresses the relativity of judgment; the point applies to other books treated below, too (e.g., *A Flight to the Moon, Symzonia*).

110. The sense of this passage and related satirical pages certainly connects *A History of New York* with writings such as *The Celestial Railroad, The Monikins, The Confidence-Man* (Hedges, *Irving*, p. 88).

111. The *Monthly Anthology* 8(1810):123-24, called it "the wittiest our press has ever produced" and praised its "lively flow of good natured satire." John Bristed (p. 359) was warmly appreciative of both *Salmagundi* and *A History of New York. An Account of Abimelech Coody* (New York, 1815), though a satire of Verplanck, who had criticized Irving's ridicule of the New York Dutch, disapproved of the *History*, calling it "really intolerable" and protesting against its mixture of history and fiction. F. L. Mott ascribes the great success of the *History* to the pre-publication announcements about the "man in black," but thinks that the book was too expensive (at $3 a copy) to become a bestseller (*Golden Multitudes*, p. 70).

112. Evert A. and George C. Duyckinck, *Cyclopaedia of American Literature*, 2 vols. (New York, 1855), 1:191: "Looked at as history, we may say it is unreliable; but regarded as a squib, which the author almost had the opportunity of writing with quills plucked from his writhing body, and planted there by his over-zealous brethren of Hebron, it is vastly enjoyable and may be forgiven. The General History of Connecticut is as good, in its way, as Knickerbocker's History. The full-mouthed humorous gravity of its style is irresistible. Its narrations are independent of time, place and probability."

113. The trumpeter Antony Corlear's nose, freshly washed, reflects the first ray of the sun "hissing hot" into the Hudson, where it kills a large sturgeon.

114. Peters, *A General History of Connecticut*, pp. 152-53.

115. *A Flight to the Moon*, p. 11. For Fowler's earlier *The Wandering Philanthropist*, see above, in "Letters from America," Chapter 5, part 3.

116. "Ah! why do I attempt to describe my feelings? The copious tears falling on my paper blot out my words, and bid me renounce the fruitless attempt. Surely not more delicious are the emotions of the saint, who, having literally burst the chains of death and escaped the persecutions of a bigoted or blood-thirsty world, beholds the gate of heaven opening to receive him, sees the light of the countenance of the Great Eternal, hears the melting sounds of golden harps, the joyful acclamation of innumerable hosts of angels; and meets all the joys of ever-lasting felicity" (pp. 96-97).

117. This is the title of a book "compiled by Americus Symmes, from the writings of his father, Capt. John Cleves Symmes," Louisville, Ky., 1878.

118. J. O. Bailey suggests that Symmes himself was the author of *Symzonia* and was praising himself in referring to his "sublime theory" (see "An Early American Utopian Fiction," *AL* 14[1942]:285-93; and the introduction to the facsimile ed. of *Symzonia*). But it seems clear that the phrase is used ironi-

cally; it also occurs on pp. vi and 77, and echoes in expressions on pp. 20, 42, 104. The note of irony is sounded from beginning to end. In the very opening paragraph of his narrative, Seaborn announces that he means to discover new worlds, since the known world has had "its every thing investigated and understood"; but how well things are understood is brought home in the statement, "having...*discovered* that air and water are much the same elements, and are governed by much the same laws, at sea as on shore" (p. 22). There is possibly irony, too, in the reference to Fulton (see following note), and certainly in the passages of pseudo-scientific accuracy (pp. 60, 61, 229-30), as well as in the reason given for the publication of *Symzonia*: "...I heard that Capt. Riley had obtained some pecuniary relief, by publishing a book of Travels, containing accounts not much more marvellous than those which I could relate of Symzonia" (p. 246). The reference is to James Riley, *Authentic Narrative of the Loss of the American Brig 'Commerce'* (New York, 1816). In his introduction to *The Narrative of Arthur Gordon Pym* (Hill & Wang, 1960), which establishes Poe's probable debt to *Symzonia*, Sidney Kaplan calls Seaborn "one of the champions of Symmes" (p. xiii). He raises the important point of the white coloring of the Symzonians, as representing perfection; but this is only part of the story, for Seaborn notes the analogical difference "negro : white man" and "white man : Symzonian," that is, the white man may be superior to the negro but he must admit that he is inferior to the Symzonian. This establishes a parallel to the Swiftian pattern of sobering realization, with its analogies "Liliputian : Gulliver" and "Gulliver : Brobdingnagian." We may apply this to the significance of Seaborn's (and Symmes's) scientific ingenuity: it is remarkable enough in the human perspective, but it must not be taken too seriously because in the superior Symzonian view it merely teaches its own questionable value. Contemporary references to Symmes in works of fiction are to be found in Robert Waln, Jr., *The Hermit in America*; and George Watterston, *The L— Family at Washington* (1822), which introduces a wild young man about to join Symmes on a journey into the interior of the earth, "a wild-goose chase" (p. 159). Seaborn himself intimates that this view of things is wide-spread (p. 228). The Symmes theory is still alive: see the advertisement in the *New York Times Book Review* (October 2, 1966) for Dr. Raymond Bernard, *The Hollow Earth*, Fieldcrest Pub. Co.

119. There is probably an allusion to Fulton in this name. In his Advertisement Seaborn acknowledges that his voyage was made possible through the Symmes theory and the "application of steam to the navigation of vessels, for which the world is indebted to Fulton" (p. vi).

120. The British are also accused of having provisionally claimed discoveries in unknown parts of the world, so that any actual discovery will leave them the rights of first claimants.

121. When asked about the system of government in his country, Seaborn is careful "to say nothing about the qualities for office, nor of the means resorted to to obtain preferment" (p. 148); see also his craftiness in resolving to publish his memoirs. Seaborn is consistently vain of his vast knowledge (pp. 105, 180, 224, 247), which in some cases, he implies, is superior to Symmes's; he boasts of being a greater man than Columbus, who discovered only a continent, while he has discovered a whole unknown world (pp. 96-97). He despises his fellow-beings, his crew and the credulous public (pp. 46, 48-49, 51-52, 92-93, 247), and is altogether too unsavory a character for Symmes to have used to propagate his ideas. Seaborn's dishonesty is the more serious as he clearly perceives the moral excellence of the Symzonians (p. 205).

[164]

122. *The Oriental Philanthropist,* p. 3.

123. Contrary to the opinion expressed by Tremaine McDowell in "Sensibility in the Eighteenth-Century American Novel," *SP* 24(1927):383-402, Sherburne relies on sensibility to some extent, both in his manner and in the use of certain plot-elements; see the quotations in the text and such a passage as Selina's joy at not having to part from Amelia, whom she has just met (p. 128).

III. THE LOVE STORY

L OVE has been the main theme of most novels, whatever the time and place of their writing. Predictably, this universal theme also conditions the bulk of the American fiction under discussion. It is fiction written for the most part by inexperienced authors, to whom love was indeed "the meat and drink of fiction," and who related "what the lovers suffered or enjoyed in getting married, or whether they got married at all or not."[1] This romantic love, usually treated in a moralistic spirit and occasionally given a sensational emphasis,[2] tended to assume a guise of sensibility to which the readers of fiction could be expected to respond.[3]

These treatments of the love story will be grouped according to the several plot elements which seem to shape the course of their action, that is, to further or prevent the fulfillment of the central love relationship. Where there is an organic connection between the plot material and the characters, the procedure is evidently likely to yield illuminating results. But such focussing on single plot-elements may be thought arbitrary in the many instances when these elements are by no means clearly more important than other features.[4] Since the first American novels possess little individuality, however, to label them according to thematic categories at least provides a temporary definition of their character; out of this it should be possible to develop a less artificial definition and a more subtle assessment of the various contributions of the novelists. Quite often, parallels and contrasts suggest themselves across the more or less arbitrary limits fixed upon. It is of course essential to establish cross-references of this kind when different works of the same author are treated under separate headings.

Chapter Six

SELF-DENIAL

I N A FIRST GROUP of novels a basic element of plot and
motivation is furnished by a frustrating clash of values in the
main characters: a desirable love match is thwarted, at least
temporarily, by idealistic conceptions. These, commendable
enough *in abstracto,* urge some protagonists to an attitude of self-
denial or impose such an attitude upon others not at all inclined to
it. The self-denial may be encouraged by a more or less conscious
wish for self-punishment; it may be conditioned by a conservative awareness of the social stratification, as in *The Step-Mother*
or *Precaution,* novels with an English setting, or rather by individual views of duty and moral obligation, as in *Clara Howard*
and *Emily Hamilton.*

The Step-Mother (1798) is the first of two novels known to
have been written by Helena Wells (fl. 1798-1809).[5] It is
avowedly didactic fiction:[6] its heroine Caroline Williams should
be a model stepmother to the four daughters of the widower
whom she marries and soon loses. The concept implies devotion and self-effacement. Inevitably the narrative focuses on the
four girls and their suitors and lovers, while the "central" character, though retaining a unifying function, is reduced to a
near-abstraction, something like a morality figure. The total
effect of this part of the narrative is disappointing in at least two
ways. For one thing, Miss Wells yielded to the temptation of
using the mere surface arabesques of romantic storytelling: its
righteousnesses and villainies, the motives of envy and greed
causing treachery or seduction. The very number of personages
introduced and the closeness of their mutual relationships suggest that the author had not planned her book beyond inventing an accumulation of crises and handicaps for the girls and
their stepmother. Another reason for our disappointment with

[169]

the book is the fact that Caroline no longer grows and changes as she devotes herself to keeping her charges happy, or at least out of harm. She has reached a relative perfection of wisdom by the time she takes up her stepmotherly duties, and we cannot really expect her to develop any further so we lose interest in her; and since the alternative appeal of her girls' repetitive adventures is itself limited, the story becomes very dull indeed.

Now, before becoming Mrs. Wentworth, Caroline has shown signs of her willing acceptance of self-sacrifice, but she has also revealed a certain amount of independent thinking and acting.[7] The didactic mission thrust upon her by Miss Wells quite smothers that part of her and the potential tension between the poles of her character. Caroline's businesslike determination to do her duty at the cost of her personal fulfillment is indicated by the fact that she never gives another thought to the crisis which conditioned her entire existence. By refusing Edward in spite of her love for him, she wished to avoid offending the aristocratic prejudices of her protectress, Lady Glanvile, Edward's mother.[8] Her position later is such that marrying Wentworth is a highly prudent step, but then she could have given Edward a different answer, ensuring their mutual happiness, without for all that making Lady Glanvile miserable; this Caroline never chooses to consider, not even when, many years later, she reads Edward's parting letter.

The Step-Mother is a poor book. Its characterization is as unsatisfactory as its author's inventiveness. Its structure is weakened by the shift of focus mentioned before.[9] Miss Wells's style, generally dull, deviates from its mediocrity only to become clumsy, periphrastic, and simply faulty.

Whereas everything about *The Step-Mother* breathes an air of imitation, another, later, novel with a related theme appears to embody some material derived from firsthand experience. *The Mother-in-Law* (1817), by Horatio Gates Spafford (1778-1832),[10] has a stepmother for its title figure. She is named Glorvina, and her experiences derive almost exclusively from the consequences of her husband's unfortunate first marriage: she must repeatedly cope with intrigues involving her stepchildren. In this sense her situation is similar to that of Caroline Williams. But the latter,

being alone, must make her own decisions; she does so consistently and according to her upbringing, and thus emerges as a character more distinct than Glorvina is permitted to become. This
is also due to the permanence of Caroline's involvement in the
destinies of her stepdaughters: she never knows periods of
respite such as Glorvina is favored with, in journeys on the
Continent and through England.

The information and descriptions offered in these travel passages are curiously uneven. The itinerary of the trip from Keswick
to London and York (pp. 165-69) sounds real enough, what
with the stops mentioned and the relatives introduced; but the
Continental scenes read rather like the heightened pictures of a
writer who depends on secondhand sources—maps, literary
models—and an awkward vocabulary of the sublime, to convey
a sense of the unfamiliar (pp. 106-11). Yet Spafford devoted
considerable space to these descriptions; otherwise his episodes
are sketchy, like first notes that have been retouched just enough
to give them a flavor of narrative style. Many places and a
large number of characters are introduced and mentioned by
name, but both the localities and the characters are afflicted with
a painful two-dimensional effect. Since an appreciable slice of
time is consumed within the 180 pages of *The Mother-in-Law*,[11]
the author apparently felt he could not afford to pause; he
hurried on, breathlessly and jerkily, until after listing the names
of the husbands and wives of all of Glorvina's stepchildren and
children, he could report his model heroine's death.

James Fenimore Cooper (1789-1851) called *Precaution*
(1820) a moral tale,[12] a designation with which Miss Wells
would no doubt have agreed. His first novel is also, like *The
Step-Mother*, a book stiffly complex in the interrelatedness of
its characters, especially in that part devoted to unraveling the
mystery of Denbigh's identity. It has a comparable shift of focus
too: where Miss Wells concentrated first on one central personage and then on many subsidiary ones, in Cooper's novel one
setting serves for most of the first half, but there is a restless
change of scene in the second.

George Denbigh, the hero of *Precaution*, may be said to be,
like Caroline Williams, too acutely sensitive to the existence of

social classes. But whereas Caroline refuses a connection that is considered lowering for her lover and thus emphasizes the social barrier, Denbigh tries the experiment of tricking it out of existence—temporarily, that is, and in actual practice only to some slight extent. His Emily is no mere tradesman's or farmer's daughter, after all; nor is there anything about Denbigh to suggest that he does not take the aristocratic hierarchy for granted: he is a creation of the Cooper who thought the British social structure not without its merits. Nevertheless, when it comes to selecting a wife, Denbigh wants to be loved for his own sake, and not for his title, and therefore assumes the guise of an non-aristocratic person. In so doing he runs the risk that his mystification may boomerang on him. And indeed, Mrs. Wilson becomes suspicious of him. Her experience of mankind has taught her to expect duplicity rather than honesty as the motive for assuming a social mask, and she fails to see that Denbigh's motives are different. This is, incidentally, a wry comment on the possibility of confusing appearance and reality; for the reality that is rejected in this case means not only the very suitor to be desired for Emily but also the identical Lord Pendennyss whom Mrs. Wilson so much admires. No wiser than Jane or Lady Moseley in this specific instance, the over-prudent Mrs. Wilson advises her protégée to dismiss Denbigh. It would be easy for the latter to write to Mrs. Wilson in his true identity and explain the apparent contradictions in his statements and half-statements; yet he makes no move to exculpate himself. Denbigh is aware that he has laid himself open to charges of dishonesty and evidently chooses to punish himself more severely than Mrs. Wilson and Emily have done through their implicit rebuke.

At this critical juncture Cooper introduces the confusion with the unfortunate lover's namesake. In order that the reader may be more easily taken in by this trick, Emily's Denbigh drops completely out of sight, the author contriving to keep both George Denbighs away from Bath while Emily meets the Denbigh ladies there. This tangling of identities achieved, mere hints are insufficient to point the way to the solution of the Denbigh mysteries; Cooper had to step forward himself and, probing back into two past generations and introducing characters never heard of before, employ about one fourth of his second volume to account for the confusions puzzling his reader.[13]

Emily, quite a conventional heroine,[14] is throughout the story too much overshadowed by her mentor Mrs. Wilson to become a girl with a mind of her own. She does not seem to have any genuine affection for her family, perhaps because her parents have quite given her up into Mrs. Wilson's hands. This lady is so constantly employed in cautionary and defensive reflections and moves in Emily's behalf that one begins to doubt her capacity for gratitude and admiration, which is the basis of her attitude toward Pendennyss. As for the latter, we may sympathize with the predicament he is in, even when we yet only guess at the nature of that predicament; but the very "split personality" that is his makes it hard to visualize him and to integrate him into the social scene depicted by Cooper.

Surprisingly enough, it is that English world, experienced at secondhand only,[15] which now and again yields some pleasure and amusement to the reader. Witnessing the discomfiture of a Lady Moseley or Lady Chatterton and the deportment of the Jarvises may give the impression of *déjà vu*; but all the same, these characters are entertaining because they truly belong to their setting and at the same time achieve sufficient individuality to be acceptable in their small comic excesses. On the other hand, the villain, Egerton, and a character like Mrs. Fitzgerald have an obviously mechanical plot function; and such oddities as Mr. Benfield and his steward make the reader uncomfortable (they are typical of Cooper's often heavyhanded attempts at humor).[16] Nor are the more explicitly didactic passages any subtler; certain melodramatic or sentimental scenes, too, are handled with an awkward insistence.[17] There is a passage somewhat akin to these on woman, which has the merit of shedding light on Cooper's conception of woman and female characters, and which illustrates his style in *Precaution,* as well:

It is said that women are fertile in inventions to further their schemes of personal gratification, vanity, or even mischief; it may be—it is true—but the writer of these pages is a man—one who has seen much of the sex, and he is happy to have an opportunity of paying a tribute to female purity and female truth; that there are hearts so disinterested as to lose the considerations of self, in advancing the happiness of those they love—that there are minds so pure, as to recoil with disgust from the admission of deception, indelicacy, or management—he knows, for he has seen it from long and close examination; he regrets, that the very artlessness of those who are most pure in the one sex, subjects them to the suspicions of the grosser materials which compose the other. He believes that innocency, singleness of heart, ardency of feeling, and unalloyed shrinking delicacy, sometimes exist in the female bosom, to an extent that but few men are happy enough to discover, and most men believe incompatible with the frailties of human nature. (1: 153-54)

There is enough in Cooper's first book, and above all in its opening chapters, to suggest that he knew *Persuasion* and *Pride and Prejudice* quite well.[18] But he lacked Miss Austen's elegant incisiveness, which worked so effectively both as insight into her characters and as irony in the comments, for instance, on their fellow beings or our fashions that she had them utter.[19] Intentionally or not, Cooper produced a novel reminiscent of models less worthy of imitation than Jane Austen's novels.

Cooper's praise of woman puts the reader in mind of another writer in whose work the peculiar female sensitivity in matters of morality and feeling is frequently asserted: Charles Brockden Brown (1771-1810). His *Alcuin*[20] sounds that note in 1798; it rings on with persistence throughout the author's short period of intense productivity in the field of the novel. But Brown's heroines, with their claim to intellectual equality and their determination, must be taken more seriously than Cooper's, "whose combination of propriety and incapacity places them at the farthest possible remove from the heroic."[21] *Clara Howard* (1801) has for its heroine a young lady of high principles, an enthusiast of love[22] who appears to distinguish between Love, universal and self-sacrificing, and love, personal and selfish. Her conceptions are acted out upon, and through, the person of Philip Stanley.[23] Though she loves him, Clara refuses to accept him as her friend or her husband; according to her, Mary Wilmot, a girl who may with some reason have expected Stanley to propose to her, has claims superior to her own.[24] However impatient Stanley may feel with Clara's principles, and resenting the moral order "which makes our very virtues instrumental to our misery" (p. 28),[25] he starts out in search of Mary, tracks her down, and persists in proposing to her though she wishes him to marry Clara. This he does with such self-willed conviction that Mary's rejection plunges him into a mood of self-pitying renunciation and drives him to impose exile from his true love upon himself; a journey—to quote his melodramatic announcement—"from which I neither wish nor expect to return. I at this moment anticipate the dawn of comfort, from the scenes of the wilderness and of savage life" (p. 208). In her effort to restrain him Clara happily manages to conciliate the demands of Love and love. She reminds Stanley that withdrawing from the world would make him guilty of a comprehensive sin of omission, since he would then fail to support those dependent on him (letter 29);[26] at the same time, his return to Philadelphia would mean coming back to the guidance he needs from her:

> My maturer age, and more cautious judgment, shall be counsellers and guides to thy inexperienced youth. While I love thee and cherish thee as a wife, I shall assume some of the prerogatives of an elder sister, and put my circumspection and forethought in the balance against thy headlong confidence.
>
> I revere thy genius and thy knowledge. With the improvements of time, very far wilt thou surpass the humble Clara; but in moral discernment, much art thou still deficient. Here I claim to be more than equal. . . . (p. 265)[27]

This passage clearly suggests that Clara's is the dominating role given to many heroines in Brown's fiction.[28] *Clara Howard* is the first book that Brown named after its heroine; she is essential to its plot in the way that headquarters are essential to the conduct of a campaign. The English publisher of the book chose to use the hero's name for a title, in the approved Brown manner up to that time, and of course it *is* Stanley who goes through the motions of the campaign. But we are never allowed to forget that the moves are mapped out for him by his high-principled fiancée, and that in all he does or tries to do he is prompted by Clara's conceptions and directions. His one inde-

[175]

pendent move to determine the course of their relationship is to renounce her and prepare for a journey across the American continent, and this move proves abortive. Immature and inclined to act upon impulses, Stanley indulges in self-pity and self-righteousness. His behavior toward Mary may indeed well have failed to be quite honest, in spite of his repeated assertions that he knew all the time he felt respect or pity, but not love, for the girl: "I was bound by every tie of honour, though not of affection, to Mary Wilmot" (p. 96).[29]

Clara insists that (social) reason must at all times keep the (selfish) feelings in check: it always promotes the sum total of happiness within a group of people. She therefore reproaches Stanley in no uncertain terms for his lack of discipline,[30] and is consistently ready to prove her capacity for sacrifice: "I resign you to this good girl, as to one who deserves you more than I; whose happiness is more dependent on the affections of another than mine is" (p. 196). Clara never pretends that such control of the emotions is easy, but she stresses above all that her readiness to give up Stanley to Mary is in the best interests of the three of them. Only if logically convinced that she is wrong will she allow Stanley to return to her as her acknowledged suitor (p. 57); and logically, almost mathematically, convinced she finally is, for it turns out that she has given insufficient consideration to an imponderable quantity, the love of Sedley and Mary. Mary Wilmot's disinterested views are early expounded. She tries to ensure Stanley's happiness both by explicitly renouncing her claims and by taking herself out of his life. Her willingness to give up her lover, however, is matched by Clara's. The ensuing deadlock can be broken only by the introduction of Sedley in the guise of a genuine lover and disinterested human being: Mary falls in love with him, a possibility earlier as little taken into account by herself as by Clara. The reader has been rather unfairly kept in the dark concerning Sedley, who is rumored to be unreliable and disreputable, whereas he proves high-minded and generous, and undoubtedly a fit partner for Mary.

The artificial plot of *Clara Howard* might perhaps have been redeemed by a subtler shading of the psychological portraits[31] and by a writer more skillful than Brockden Brown at establishing a sound structure to support his narrative. Brown's handling of the epistolary device is stiff and ungainly, and the individual letters, stylistically uniform, are no more than surface subdivisions of the tale—or rather debate—in progress. One recipient is obviously introduced merely to give Stanley a chance to tell his own story, in a letter which grows to a full quarter of the entire book.[32] The elements of romantic mysteries and benevolence related there parallel those in the past of Mary's family, and none of them have any bearing on the moral discussion that is central to the novel. This discussion is prevented by its abstractness from achieving real urgency or a sense of fated inevitability such as derives from Wieland's meditations, or, to take the example of another writer, from the train of thought of Melville's Pierre. Brown's intensity in *Clara Howard* quickly lapses into monotony.[33]

Whatever objections may be raised against *Keep Cool* (1817), by John Neal (1793-1876), the book can hardly be called monotonous. It is far more likely to be blamed for its haphazard structure and its incoherence.[34] There is already in Neal's first novel the mixture of heterogeneous elements found in all his fiction.[35] Following Neal as he slips from burlesque and parody into satire and eccentricity, and again into social criticism and romantic characterization,[36] we find him unwilling to commit himself seriously to any one approach or theme. *Keep Cool,* though it does give some indication of its author's talents, above all has all the marks of improvisation about it, suggesting that Neal became interested in, or bored with, his characters as quickly as certain of his figures fall in and out of love.[37] At first a comic novel of manners, with variations on the theme of love —infatuation, flirting, coquetry, vanity—in different settings, the novel later singles out four characters for more detailed treatment: wise Mrs. Granville, the eccentric and contradictory Echo,[38] Laura, and the Byronic Sydney.[39] The issue of dueling[40] has at one time or another played an unpleasant part in their lives, and Sydney and his sister can be eloquently indignant about it. After his sensible refusal to fight Echo, Sydney yet suffers himself to be blackmailed into accepting Percy's challenge by the code of gentlemanly society. The fight itself simply serves as a crisis to effect some dramatic changes in the various relationships; it only obliquely affects what is clearly the main theme of *Keep Cool*, the love of Laura and Sydney.

It may be called the main theme because it provides the nearest thing to a narrative backbone for the novel, yet it is presented sketchily and involves two characters fragmentarily realized, so that it fails to sustain its function quite adequately. Out of mistaken notions of love and the tendency to act the part of a coquette, Laura rejects Sydney's honest proposal; to punish her, Sydney perseveres until he in turn is in a position to jilt the girl.[41] They part, but are doomed to carry the burden of their mutual love and guilt; and when they meet again, they still feel bound to refuse themselves a reconciliation. The meagre facts known about their past intrigue their New York friends; the air of mystery which surrounds them is however chiefly the result of a sense of their uneasy relationship. Seemingly in love with Percy and Louisa, in reality they merely try to escape from their common predicament and to make their self-denial final. Sydney's self-decreed banishment after Percy's death is just another attempt at ending the anguished tension of guilt, love, and scorn, though he conceivably also feels that he deserves punishment for having betrayed his convictions and accepted Percy's challenge; he might indeed even think he has done so in order to get rid of his rival in Laura's affections. The girl stresses her coquettishness on purpose when Sydney returns from his Indian exile; it proves a last effort, and a futile one, to resist the appeal of their love. Whereas Sydney's attitude is compounded of fiction's conventional chivalric heroism and some urge to purify himself by renunciation, Laura appears to have been intended as a more original and a psychologically finer piece of character drawing. Her main faults, a shallow flirtatiousness and sentimentally exaggerated expectations, blind her to Sydney's merits. But once her eyes have been opened, she tries to live up to such standards of excellence as truly exist, that is, the standards exemplified by Sydney before his disillusionment, including the faculty to refuse oneself pleasure and happiness. From then on Laura's coquetry is no longer a playful attitude only but a mask shielding her from too close a contact with the world of admirers and suitors; in the final instance she even uses it to try and protect Sydney from her unworthiness. This, no doubt, is making the workings of Laura's character a good deal more conscious and more precise than we find realized in *Keep Cool.* But there are at least hints of an ability in Neal to feel his way into his heroine's emotional ways which is superior to that of most of his American colleagues. This cannot be entirely obscured by Neal's uneven expression of his insights and conceptions, skirting the trite and the sentimental as it often does.[42] The modern reader is likely to find these attempts at characterization more appealing and suggestive[43] than the story of Elizabeth and Echo alias St. Pierre, lovers driven apart through mere circumstances and not through any effect of their own characters (chap. 21), or the hackneyed comedy of the hunting partners speaking English with their native French, Scotch, and Irish pronunciations. There are more felicitous satirical passages, though, as, for example, one which describes the repercussions of chauvinistic anger at some form of foreign arrogance through the provincial newspapers of America (1:121-22),[44] or that ironical description lavishing praise on Laura and simultaneously mocking the pretty ways of feminine vanity:

Not once, during the whole evening, did she cross the room when all was hush, though she walked like a spirit; not once did she stretch out that lovely arm of hers to play with some distant book, or to hand some trinket to a person who had seen it fifty times before; to point at what nobody wanted to see, or to snuff a candle when a servant was standing by. She knew her voice was melody itself, yet was not once heard to hum an air carelessly to herself—in that genteel forgetfulness, that always betrays a favourite belle, even when she is among strangers; not once did she praise such a lady's voice, who sung such and such a song "so and so;" not once did she stretch out her fine throat to whisper half across the room, about the *"uncommon mildness of the weather,"* or some equally mysterious affair; not once did she attempt the languid loll, though conscious that her form would have furnished a painter with the very image of *Volupté;* not once did she draw off her glove, or fasten her hair, or throw her arms behind her head and lean upon them, though she knew that the snowy whiteness of the one never could be better opposed, than by the dark, glossy luxuriance of the other. She forgot herself, and remembered her visiters. (1:94)

By comparison with Neal's exuberant combination and treatment of various materials, *Emily Hamilton* (1803), by Sukey Vickery,[45] is decidedly moderate, if not tedious; yet on the whole the reader is grateful for the writer's restraint. Although the lack of romantic coloring and a variety of tones may appear as weaknesses, they are more or less compensated by the relative straightforwardness of the plot and the consistency of the admittedly slight characterization of the three girls who function as correspondents and part-narrators. Miss Vickery dispensed with any over-intricate grounding of the action in the past experiences, long kept a secret, of some one or other of her characters; she offered no complex masking of identities, and only discreetly hinted at the many crimes of the blackguardly Lambert. In his case she did resort, however, to a stock-type villain: Lambert the seducer cannot bring himself to marry the girl who is pregnant by him and therefore tainted by scandal;[46] he tries fortune-hunting, is jailed for debt, and is finally sentenced to death for some unspecified atrocity. Apart from this figure, there is another element of conventional fiction in *Emily Hamilton*: the marriage imposed for reasons of wealth upon young people whose affections run to someone other than their parents' choices. Belmont, the young man involved, accepts the parental decree, even though he falls in love with another girl, Emily herself, shortly before marrying Clara. But the latter, prevented from asking Belmont to refuse the match arranged by their parents, resolves upon having her cake and eating it: she marries the rich young man selected for her, but does not give up her lover.[47]

She is evidently no believer in sacrifice or in personal and social discipline. Unlike Lambert's criminal wickedness, her refusal to submit to convention is passed lightly over and, indeed, treated with some measure of sympathy. Clara's behavior nonetheless does serve to set off that of her husband and especially of the heroine. Emily is shocked by the discovery that the unknown gentleman with whom she has fallen in love after he has saved her life, and who has moved into her neighborhood,[48] is a married man. When Mrs. Belmont is seriously ill, the girl is perhaps tempted to wish her rival dead, especially as she knows that Belmont does not love his wife; to keep herself from such thoughts, she turns to the subject of Mrs. Belmont's chances of recovery (letter 57). The latter dies, yet now that there are no legal impediments any more to prevent his proposal, Emily raises moral obstacles and decides beforehand that she will not listen to Belmont. She means instead to keep her engagement to her longtime friend Charles Devas, though she does not love him, and has become engaged very much to protect herself against her passion for Belmont. Providence, grim and kind at the same time, interferes by drowning Devas and forbearing to further test Emily's fidelity and firmness.

The timing of Devas's accidental death is one instance of a happy coincidence; others are Emily's meeting with Belmont and the opportune revelation of Lambert's seduction of Betsey. Such features presumably reflect the author's faith in the welfare of the good and the just meting out of rewards. *Emily Hamilton,* too, is very much a moral tale, like *Precaution.*[49] It also makes deliberate use of the sentimental value of reflections on death, particularly during Sophia's slow decline (in the course of which the girl is grieved chiefly by the sorrow of her relatives and friends over her fate), and again in the letter which Emily writes after Devas's death—a letter that devotes twice as much space to general observations on religion and dying as to her former close friend and intended husband.

The styles of sensibility and sententiousness are frequently favored, though the general tone of the book is gossipy. Whether to recall memories, to provide fresh insights into a character yet hardly known, or to make for a deeper harmony of feelings and possibly encourage sensations of gratitude for the Creator, moonlit evenings are regularly called upon: they seem infallibly to furnish sympathetic settings which should catch the reader's emotions just as they provoke response in the personages:

A walk by moonlight, you are sensible, was always highly grati-fying to me. This evening, I walked for some time, and at my

[181]

return, seated myself a short distance from the house, beneath a venerable elm. The moon shone, with more than usual lustre, all was serene and beautiful, no sound was heard but the cherup of the cricket and the soft sighing of the breeze. The time and place was suited to contemplation, the beauty of the scene diffused a soft calmness over my mind; I retraced all the innocent, sportive scenes of our childhood.... I was seated with you and Eliza Anderson on the sloping bank—I saw the willows waving over the stream which fell dashing from rock to rock with its usual murmuring sound.... (p. 19)[50]

Emily and Belmont appear extremely susceptible to such scenes; yet they fail to suggest the richness of feeling which they so loudly proclaim and seem to detect in others. All the listing of the heroine's qualities of morality and sensibility does less for her than is achieved for others by individual slight touches: one opportunistic gesture of a friend of Emily, or the sprightly refusal of another to be heart-broken over her fickle lover's desertion.[51]

1. The phrases are borrowed from William Dean Howells's "A Possible Difference in English and American Fiction," *NAR* 173(1901):134-44, and apply to minor authors; the love story written by "the best American novelists" attempted to portray "what sort of man and maid their love found them out to be, and how, under its influence, the mutual chemistry of their natures interacted." Among early American novelists, such psychological probing was at best faintly sketched by Brockden Brown in *Ormond* and *Jane Talbot*, or by Mrs. Foster in *The Coquette*.

2. See Charles Edwin Howard, "Romantic Love in Major American Novels, 1789-1860," *DA* 20:2802-3.

3. The tendencies noted by Roy Harvey Pearce, "Sterne and Sensibility in American Diaries," *MLN* 59(1944):403-7, for the period of 1777 to 1783, could certainly be substantiated among later letter-writers and diarists, e.g., Eliza Southgate Bowne, Theodosia Burr, Julia Cowles, and Nancy Maria Hyde.

4. How precarious any attempt at distinguishing between an author's motives and purposes, models and final effects, must be is exemplified by various labelings in Florence May Anna Hilbish, *Charlotte Smith* (Philadelphia: University of Pennsylvania Press, 1941), esp. pp. 330, 337, 345. We might apply to the average author of the fiction of the age a definition of Harold Robbins: "He is not so much a novelist in the traditional sense of the word as what might be called a story engineer" (review of *The Carpetbaggers, Newsweek*, June 5, 1961).

5. See Allibone, *A Critical Dictionary of English Literature*, 3:2642. Cf. the biography of her brother, William C. Wells, *DAB* 19:644-45, and "A Memoir of His Life, Written by Himself," in *Two Essays* (London, 1818), pp. vii-lxi; one episode related there (p. xxii) suggested chapter 20 of *The Step-Mother*. For a discussion of Miss Wells's *Constantia Neville*, see Chapter 10 below.

6. See her prefaces to the first and second editions of *The Step-Mother*; the former also presents the novel as the author's attempt at consoling herself. No copy of the first edition seems to be extant, but its preface is reprinted in *The Step-Mother,...* by Helena Wells of Charles Town, South Carolina (1799).

7. An instance of this independence is her decision to marry Wentworth when she is expected to jump at the chance of marrying Brummell.

8. Unlike Rebecca in Mrs. Rowson's *The Fille de Chambre*, who also refuses the advances of her protectress' son, Caroline thinks her wooer sincere and not merely another upper-class seducer of insufficiently protected girls.

9. This shift of focus is prepared by the deaths, in quick succession, of those closely connected with Caroline: Mrs. Belton, Edward, and Wentworth (chaps. 13-15).

10. See Julian P. Boyd, "Horatio Gates Spafford," *PAAS* 51(1941):279-350. Spafford states that the material for his book was brought over to America by a niece of a protégée of Glorvina, who used the latter's own notes; this might be a thin disguise, adapted from the convention of "novels founded in fact," in order to give a factual narrative the air of fiction. It may even be true. The consistent use of precise dates, as practiced in *The Mother-in-Law*, is rare in fiction. *The Mother-in-Law: or Memoirs of Madam De Morville* was published in Boston in 1817.

11. After a reference to the French emigration of 1685, the narrator makes a quick transition to the third generation of emigrants. In chapter 7 (p. 40), the year 1775 is reached. The following chapters are devoted to the Charlotte-like Nanette, who dies in childbirth in America early in 1777 (35 pp.). Chapter 20 (p. 139) reports De Morville's death, in 1801, and that of Glorvina is the subject of the concluding chapter; it takes place in 1814.

12. See *The Letters and Journals of James Fenimore Cooper*, ed. J. F. Beard, 1:42, 48. Cf. Robert E. Spiller in *J. F. Cooper: A Re-Appraisal*, ed. Mary E. Cunningham (New York State Historical Association, Vol. 35, No. 4, Oct., 1954), p. 544.

13. *Precaution*, Cooper's first novel, which was conceived as a short tale, was written very hastily, and *"no plot* was fix'd on until the first volume was half done" (*Letters and Journals*, 1:42, 66).

14. See Emily's portrait (1:126); the description of Denbigh is quite as conventional (1:102), and so is his moving reading aloud from *Gertrude of Wyoming* (1:172). Another stereotype is the girl (Jane Moseley) who fancies herself adored by a man whose perfections are all her own imagining (1:70, 124-25).

15. Imitation must have been Cooper's first incitement, the aim "to impose on the public" a later rationalization; he may have been aware before starting on *The Spy* that "the task of making American Manners and American scenes interesting to an American reader is an arduous one" (*Letters and Journals*, 1:66, 44). Cf. his preface to the 1839 London edition, and Arvid Shulenberger, *Cooper's Theory of Fiction: His Prefaces and Their Relation to His Novels* (Lawrence: University of Kansas Press, 1955), esp. p. 13. The English reviewers of the anonymous *Precaution* apparently did not doubt that its author was English (W. B. Cairns, *British Criticisms*, p. 112). Simms passed a devastating judgment on Cooper's imitative first novel (*Views and Reviews in American Literature, History and Fiction*, ed. C. Hugh Holman, p. 259). John Macy thought that it was Cooper's secondhand material that prevented *Precaution* from being a success like Cooper's American tales (*The Spirit of American Literature* [Doubleday Page, 1913], p. 35). Warren S. Walker calls

The Spy a countering weapon to objections to the English setting of *Precaution* (J. F. *Cooper* [Barnes & Noble, 1962], p. 12); this is acceptable if the objections came from his wife and the close friends who may have seen portions of the manuscript, for when critics read the published novel, Cooper had long been at work on *The Spy* (*Letters and Journals*, 1:44).

16. See the grotesquely exaggerated picture of old-fashioned Peter Johnson (1:220-21). Later humorous characters (e.g., David Gamut or Dr. Battins) have functions of their own within the new social patterns of America.

17. See Volume 1, chapter 11, on dancing and entertainments, and Volume 1, chapter 22, on reading; the scene of mad Francis Denbigh's death and his one final lucid moment on seeing Marian, the girl who broke his heart many years earlier (Volume 2, chapter 20); a passage on a poor gardener's family (1:159), and the long-delayed revelation of Pendennyss's identity (1:205-6).

18. See Horace H. Scudder, "What Mr. Cooper Read to His Wife," *SR* 36(1928):177-94; Marcel Clavel, *Fenimore Cooper* (Aix-en-Provence, 1938), pp. 251-62; and George E. Hastings, "How Cooper Became a Novelist," *AL* 12(1940):20-51. Cooper must have been familiar with the English fiction of the age, and this comprehensive knowledge influenced him when he began writing in the manner of the lady novelists, perhaps more especially in that of *Persuasion*. In the relevant passages of his letters and journals, only two titles are mentioned: Mrs. Brunton's *Discipline* and Hannah More's *Coelebs*. He ordered a copy of the former on July 17, 1820, and offered to compare *Precaution* with it. He declared *Coelebs* definitely superior to his first novel; but they share the same moral tone, which was also that of Maria Edgeworth and other popular lady novelists (see *Letters and Journals*, 1:49, 66; T.R. Lounsbury, *J. F. Cooper* [Boston, 1882], p. 21; H. W. Boynton, *J. F. Cooper* [Century, 1931], pp. 80-86).

19. But see the sketch of Lady Moseley at church: "...her cambric handkerchief concealed her face as she sunk composedly by the side of Sir Edward, in a style which showed, that while she remembered her Maker, she had not entirely forgotten herself" (1:43); and the picture of John Moseley, torn between love and stubbornness (1:186).

20. *Alcuin* is discussed above, in Chapter 4, section entitled "Mentoria."

21. Lounsbury, *Cooper*, p. 27, with particular reference to Emily and similar figures.

22. In the 1827 edition, *Clara Howard* has for an alternate title "the Enthusiasm of Love." References are to the first edition.

23. The protagonist was originally called Edward Hartley, but became Philip Stanley in the English edition of 1804, called after him. Edward Hartley may have been rejected as unsuitable for a title because of its resemblance to Edgar Huntly.

24. "You know what it is that reason prescribes to you with regard to Miss Wilmot. If you cannot ardently and sincerely seek her presence, and find, in the happiness which she will derive from a union with you, sufficient motives to make you zealously solicit that union, you are unworthy not merely of my love, but of my esteem" (p. 32). Cf. p. 130.

25. Cf. pp. 201-2 for a similar protest of Stanley.

26. For another related rebuke, see pp. 33-34.

27. Stanley owes his intellectual development to Mr. Howard, who has been a father to him (pp. 65, 68). There is a touch of the fairy tale about such protection, and something miraculous about the change in Stanley's situation, summarized in the opening letter (pp. iii-iv).

[184]

28. E.g., Mrs. Fielding, Mrs. Lorimer, Louisa, and Clelia. Other elements of *Clara Howard* are characteristic of Brown's fiction: the mystery of complex antecedents, including the love match and emigration; lofty motivation; argumentation that is involved, broody and repetitive. The narrative has distinct parallels with *Edgar Huntly* and less obviously, with the other novels of Brown.

29. Cf. also pp. 74, 127.

30. "Thou art fiery and impetuous, my friend. Thy spirit is not curbed by reason. There is no outrage on discretion; no crime against thyself, into which thy headlong spirit may not hurry thee" (p. 44).

31. To D. L. Clark, Clara is the realization of Brown's concept of woman, as expounded in *Alcuin:* intellectual and sensitive, determined and sympathetic (*Charles Brockden Brown: Pioneer Voice of America*, p. 182). Yet Clara lacks qualities that render Constantia Dudley and Clara Wieland more memorable and more attractive, while no less admirable, than herself.

32. Letter 13, pp. 63-135 (the book has 264 pages of text).

33. Judgments on *Clara Howard* have tended to be unfavorable; see Dana, 2:327; Martin S. Vilas, *Charles Brockden Brown* (Burlington, Vt.: Free Press Association, 1904), pp. 42-43; W. B. Berthoff, "The Literary Career of Charles Brown" (Ph.D. diss., Harvard University, 1954), p. 221. Harry R. Warfel, in *Charles Brockden Brown, American Gothic Novelist,* concludes that "horror and terror, not love and romance, were Brown's proper precinct" (p. 193). Leslie A. Fiedler states (p. 74) that in *Clara Howard* Brown turned to "sentimental analysis in a domestic setting"; the analysis itself is, however, less apparent than the testing of its results by the discrepancy dividing high principles from human imperfections and unpredictability.

34. O. S. Coad called Neal's stories "the wildest, most incoherent pieces of imagination in American literature" ("The Gothic Element," p. 85).

35. At times Neal appears to write for the medium of the stage. There are theatrical successions of entrances and exits (the very opening scene, and chapter 6), asides (1:118, Harriet and Echo), projections of scenes: "All had expected a 'dénouement', a catastrophe....All were prepared to throw themselves into different 'attitudes,' and form a 'group'..." (1:143). Neal's style of dialogue might have been effective on the stage too. For discussions of Neal's style, see Harold Martin's "The Colloquial Tradition in the Novel: John Neal," *NEQ* 32(1959):455-75 and "The Development of Style in 19th-Century American Fiction," *Style in Prose Fiction,* pp. 114-41; some of the observations made by Harold C. Martin in these essays were anticipated by Whittier's review of *Authorship,* reprinted in *Whittier,* pp. 42-46.

36. Burlesque conditions the "review" in 1:ix-xiv; there are parodies of manner and style (1:50, 131; the mock-serious mottoes), and of syllogisms and spurious causality, expressed through the use of "therefore" (1:146-47, 2:84-85). Satire touches upon novel-writing (chap. 1), a landlady (1:chap. 3, especially p. 36); and Laura's views of her lovers (1:169-70, 2:136). Eccentricity is represented by Echo. Themes for social criticism are furnished above all by dueling (1:209, 222-23, 231), and the fear of public opinion (chaps. 8 and 10). For examples of romantic characterization, see 1:58-59, 148; 2:30, and, with a strong dash of irony, 2:72: "He was so like the heroes of novels and romances, over whose miraculous disinterestedness and eccentricity she had so often wept; before whose fustian grandeur she had so often knelt in mingled admiration and suspicion; but here was *proof*—her suspicions vanished. Here was a mortal, a ready made hero, six foot high and fashioned like

a God; who shoots her own brother, and then blubbers over him; who begs one's pardon, wrings another's nose, kicks a third through a partition, and challenges a whole room full in a breath."

37. The reader had best beware of "precipitate judgments" (1:31), for Neal is inclined to conceive one role and development for some character only to abandon them when struck by a new idea. Since we are not shown the characters' behavior but only offered Neal's analysis of it, it is difficult to be aware, e.g., that Sydney is deceiving himself when he thinks that he loves Louisa (chap. 23), and therefore not to be shocked by a later counterassertion (2:166). Cf. Earnest's infatuation with Laura, Harriot's feigned love for Percy.

38. Echo is perhaps something of a self-justifying portrait of Neal: ". . . He had an unbounded and unlicensed imagination; ungovernable passions; he related a *truth,* as if it were a *falsehood,* and a *falsehood* as if it were a *truth.* He would even confess this propensity; admit that he told a lie like a fact, and a fact like a lie; because he was so accustomed to one, and so little familiar with the other. 'One,' he would say, 'is the language of the poet; the other of a dull, plodding, mechanical matter of fact rehearser.' He would even defend lying, for he could defend any thing." (1:192-93). Cf. I. T. Richards, "The Life and Works of John Neal" (Ph.D. diss., 1932), 1:317, 319. This thesis contains a thorough study of Neal's writings as well as a collection of letters by and to Neal; its bibliography at least was made available in H.-J. Lang, ed., "Critical Essays and Stories by John Neal," *JA* 7(1962):204-319.

39. Without the sinister implications of Brown's hero, Sydney is also reminiscent of Ormond.

40. Neal himself was later to be challenged to a duel; he refused to fight.

41. There is a parallel to this in Harriot's decision to win Percy's love and then to reject him, in order to punish him for his desertion of Elenore (chap. 6).

42. See Laura's second thoughts after she has rejected Sydney's proposal, 2:179; and cf. 1:71; 1:93; 2:135.

43. "Despite the conventional absurdity of hero and heroine, this novel of little plot is probably strongest in its characterization" (Richards, "The Life and Works of John Neal" (Ph.D. diss., 1932), 1:313.

44. The *Portico* reviewer must have had episodes other than this one, or Sydney's various adventures, in mind when he stated, "There is not so much variety of *incident,* as the modern novel-reader would expect to find" (4[1817]: 169). Neal's close association with the *Portico* perhaps explains the friendly tone of the review (he conceivably had a hand in the inspiring if not the writing of it); see Marshall W. Fishwick, *"The Portico* and Literary Nationalism after the War of 1812," *WMQ* 3d. ser., 8(1951):238-45.

45. The reviewer who spoke in cautiously encouraging terms of *Emily Hamilton* stated that the author was born about 1785 and was helping to support her family by her writing; this may have been a welcome publicity item, for it smacks of the romantically fictitious, while the novel is "founded on incidents in real life"; see the *Monthly Anthology,* 2(1805):267-68.

46. When Lambert says, "I am half resolved to have her, yet my pride will not suffer me to stoop so low," Emily replies: "If your pride was not too great to prevent you from committing a crime, I should not think it ought to be too great to prevent you from making atonement for it" (p. 104). Cf. pp. 102, 123; and some remarks on reputation and seduction, pp. 44, 97-98, 107, 108.

The author pleaded for more tolerance for seduced girls (p. 107), as did Mrs. Rowson and Mrs. Foster.

47. This is the reversal of the situation which would-be seducers dream of (as does de Burling in *Margaretta*) and occasionally manage to realize (Sanford does so in *The Coquette*).

48. The situation is similar to Eliza Wharton's, in *The Coquette*, except that Sanford's move is part of a deliberate scheme to seduce her.

49. Selwyn is rewarded for his discretion during Eliza's unfortunate engagement with Cutler: when the latter deserts the girl, Selwyn has tacitly been promoted to the likeliest candidate for her hand. The moral aspect is confirmed by didactic digressions, e.g., general considerations on retirement and social pleasures, a letter (14) about a girl betrayed by her lover, and another (30) about an unfortunate woman married to a drunkard and atheist.

50. See also Belmont's moonlight complaint, p. 64. Another sentimental occasion is Emily's meeting with Belmont at the theater (p. 86). Though no distinctive features can be expected in letters conveying everyday news or extending invitations, the more emphatic passages that might sound personal tend to be tiresomely hackneyed; any genuine lyrical intent is warped into a sentimental effect.

51. See letters 21 and 34; and Quinn, *Fiction*, p. 20.

Chapter Seven

CRUEL PARENTS

P ROVIDENCE deals kindly with some characters, un-
kindly with others: in *Emily Hamilton* it takes no less
than the deaths of Mrs. Belmont and Devas to clear the
heroine's path to happiness. And Clara Belmont might have
thought of herself ill-treated by fate, even before her premature end. Like Mrs. Malcolm in *The Step-Mother,* she has
been forced into a marriage for money; she may not have
committed adultery, as did Mrs. Malcolm, but she considered
holding on to her true love Le Fabre. When their parents try
to marry them against their will, the heroes and heroines of
fiction either submit more or less passively, hoping for some
last-minute reprieve, or they elope and marry against the wishes
of their families. In either case the result is liable to cause much
grief and pain; at best, the lovers may find only a long-delayed
and short-lived happiness.

In *St. Herbert* (1813)[1] the hero runs away with Louisa Howard
because his father and the girl's guardian do not want them to
marry. His triumph is soon followed by sorrow, for his wife's
health breaks down when it is discovered that they have really
been living in sin: theirs was a mock wedding ceremony only.
It is as though their parents' disapproval had beforehand blighted
their chance of happiness. In trying to keep the young lovers
apart, Maurisson and the elder St. Herbert were moved by
revenge and guilt; St. Herbert and Louisa, like Romeo and
Juliet, pit their love against a law of hate. This is a further
claim on our sympathy, in addition to the fact that they are to be
disposed of in marriage against their will; nor is it irrelevant that
they rebel against the matches arranged for them only when
mutually supported by their love.

They seek shelter in a house thought to be haunted. St. Her-

[188]

bert and Louisa brave its Gothic dangers, but their courage is in vain because the building was erected by Maurisson to imprison the lady who preferred the elder St. Herbert to himself. The young couple have thus remained within the reach of his rule of revenge. Briefly their love changes the desolate spot into a bower of pastoral bliss:

> Though unaccustomed to labour, I arose each morning with the sun, either to guide the plough, or press the spade, and when my diurnal task was finished, I would stroll with my happy girl, along the banks of a creek, and amuse myself with catching small fish, which her soft hands would dress for my evening's repast; or we would wander to our neighbour's cot, and there with his little family, and perhaps some passenger who had strayed that way: we would divert ourselves upon the green with songs and innocent chat, or the guileless sports of youth. We knew no anxiety—we were contented: true we were poor, yet poverty did not afflict us, for ambition and envy found not a place in those hearts that were consecrated to pure and lasting affection. (p. 24)

Their daughter Louisa longs to return to this retreat when, years later, she is pining for her lover and the social pleasures of New York no longer distract her from her grief;[2] it is in such seclusion that one may learn to appreciate man's essential values.[3] At a later date still, another lover, Albudor, in search of his Caroline, responds to the Gothic gloominess of the remote district: "The sun was verging towards the empurpled horizon, and the evening winds had already unfolded their dewy wings, when the weary Albudor entered the forest, within whose gloomy confines he hoped to find his solitary Caroline, who fleeing from the rigour of parental authority, had taken up her residence with an aged nun of Montreal in the wilderness" (p. 3). To Albudor the episode is to be a mere passage through a purgatory of anguish, as it were, on his way to nuptial bliss with Caroline; their story treats in a spirit of pleasantry the theme used with somber didactic connotations in the main narrative of *St. Herbert.*[4]

The setting of this tale, upper New York State, is used also in *The Fortunate Discovery. Or, The History of Henry Villars*

(1798), a novel by "a young lady of the State of New-York."[5] Its main protagonist is introduced first as a personage of the subsidiary plot: our attention focuses at the beginning, and again in the last quarter, of *The Fortunate Discovery* on the story of Bellmore and Louisa. Both this episode, set in the present, and the middle sections, glancing back into the past of the Villars and Beauclair families, are in the main sentimental love stories which use or hint at the elopement and the seduction motifs.[6] The concluding pages turn into social comedy; Louisa and Bellmore are spared the cruel sufferings imposed by the Beauclairs upon Villars and Lady Maria and seem to profit by the mood of repentance and rehabilitation that has restored the Villars to love and prosperity.

Henry Villars alias Hargrave serves first as a well-meaning witness to the precarious love of Louisa and the wounded British officer Bellmore; the couple are thrown together in the atmosphere of divided loyalties in the Villars household at the outbreak of the Revolutionary War. Both Hargrave and Bellmore know that the latter's father will inevitably oppose a match with Louisa. There follows Hargrave's successful courting of Eliza, then Mr. Villars relates his adventures; by now the reader has guessed that Hargrave is connected with Louisa's family. Hargrave himself is aware that Lady Maria's claim to the Beauclair fortune is stronger than his own. The revelation that he is the Villars' long-lost son is not much of a surprise any longer. It serves above all to intensify his interest in the Louisa-Bellmore affair, since it is now clear that he has sanctioned his own sister's marriage to his best friend. He therefore busily tries to arrange for the happiness of these two, and he succeeds by combining his general knowledge of man's affectations and his specific knowledge of Miss Lovemore's real affections.

In spite of his importance to the plot, Hargrave is not more than a stereotype novel-hero, accomplished, gentlemanly, resourceful. The other personages, whether in the sentimental or the satirical parts of the book,[7] stand even less of a chance of achieving true and living characters. The stress is on the narrative anyway, not on the protagonists; and that narrative is a concoction of popular plot elements, in style perhaps slightly more sentimental than the average story of this type; its fairy-tale ending is rather characteristic:

> ...Mr. Villars and his family retired to a beautiful little retreat, Lord Beauclair had purchased for them nigh Hampton-Hall [old Lady Beauclair's country-house]. Lord and Lady Beauclair continued with the old Lady, and spent their summers with her in the country.
>
> Captain Bellmore went to live at Union-Park, (a seat which his Father had presented him on his marriage) about five miles from the Hall. He gave up his commission, and resided wholly in the country: blessed with his Louisa, his happiness was complete, and joy beamed around. Lord Bellmore lived to an advanced age, honoured by his children.
>
> Mr. and Mrs. Villars, in their decline of life, enjoyed every felicity. Blessed in seeing their children happy, their every wish was complete. (pp. 178-79)[8]

The most successful of the satirical touches are perhaps to be found in the scene at Miss Lovemore's, when Hargrave ironically belittles Bellmore's genuine qualities and thus reflects on the shallow standards of the fashionable world (pp. 170-71).

Even if compared with a routine tale of sentimental moralism like *The Fortunate Discovery,* Mrs. Patterson's *The Unfortunate Lovers and Cruel Parents* (1797)[9] is an atrocious performance. It tells of another instance of rebellion against parents in the name of love and honor. Gauze breaks an agreement with his former business partner, clearly unimpressed even by the providential encouragement given to their joint plan;[10] but his mercenariness after Beaumont's bankruptcy is followed by his punishment. His daughter's elopement with Samuel Beaumont is doubly justified: it is a form of retribution and also simply the fulfillment of Gauze's own pledge to have Samuel for a son-in-law. The story ends in a style quite indicative of its author's talents, as in evidence in *The Unfortunate Lovers*: "He conveyed her to a Coffee-House, sent for a Justice of the Peace, and they were joined in the bands of wedding, it being on Saturday evening....They crowned the remainder of their days in love and unity; and thus enjoyed all the pleasures which can contribute to the happiness of a rural life" (p. 27).

In Charles Brockden Brown's *Jane Talbot* (1801) the thwarting influence of the elder generation is furthered by the young heroine's self-denying response. In the manner of *Clara Howard*, Jane, too, raises obstacles of her own that delay her happiness. The hero-lover is not *a priori* a blameless character; Jane retrospectively confesses that she had her reservations about him, even at times when she felt inclined to renounce her other ties (p. 344).[11] Colden himself readily admits that he may well be distrusted, though he tends to feel guilty of other errors than those he is charged with. At any rate, in *Jane Talbot* there can be no black-and-white presentation wholeheartedly hostile to the characters assuming parental functions. On the contrary, those who advise Jane obviously have the good of the girl in mind; they are not moved—like St. Herbert, Sr., or Lord Beauclair—above all by revenge, or by material and social assertions.[12] Mrs. Fielder is willing to support Jane after the girl's dismissal of Colden and to forget how harshly she has judged the girl; yet she has nothing to gain when she insists on taking Jane under her protection again. It is simply that she thinks the girl needs help, given her character and weaknesses: "Certain indications, I early saw in you of a sensibility that required strict government; an inattention to any thing but feeling; a proneness to romantic friendship and a pining after good not consistent with our nature" (p. 93).

Jane's world is thus at least more complex, if not necessarily more compelling and plausible, than those of St. Herbert or Beauclair. The protagonists of *Jane Talbot*, in spite of their differences, still find it possible to communicate with one another. They attempt reasoning and persuasion, and it is therefore not necessary for them immediately to resort to force or ruse. Even the villains, Jane's brother Frank (who plays the part of her protector as convincingly as Huck Finn's father does Huck's) and jealous Miss Jessup, can be talked to and at least temporarily swayed. Nor is there a fixed line laid down (as there is in *Clara Howard*) between passion and reason, or between enthusiasm and prudence, or even between radicalism and conservatism. Jane is tolerant of Colden's past, while the young man is capable of changing his position. In so doing he proves less consistent than Jane herself, who may be irresolute outwardly but is firm in her fundamental beliefs; this is the reason why Colden can be overmatched by the girl.[13] He is a volcano of radicalism that is rapidly cooling, and can be compared to the *young* Brockden Brown or the *young* Shelley only.[14]

Jane is to begin with caught between two impulses. She may either obey her powerful feelings—that is, overrule her scruples and conform with her beloved Colden's views—or she may accept Mrs. Fielder's guidance and her idea of the dangerous immoral and irreligious influence exerted by the young man. She is from the first too confused to make up her mind once and for all;[15] she is keenly aware, more poignantly so than the usual novel heroine, not just of the conflict between love and duty but of a clash between positions that cannot be reduced to entire clarity. For evidently she feels there is something to be said for and against both Mrs. Fielder and Colden, neither of whom, to Jane's mind, is doing full justice to the other side. It is this very failure of Jane to subscribe unreservedly to one or the other party that keeps up the contact between them.

Now Jane, widowed after a short marriage to Talbot,[16] should be in a position to disregard opinions hostile to Colden, but she never quite convinces herself that she is right in loving and admiring him. At least she feels she can decide whether she is ready to risk marrying him: at that point, however, Jane is held back and moved to her first formal renunciation of Colden, for she abruptly comes to think her shortcomings more serious than his, and to conceive of herself as a damaging liability: ". . . What shall I bring to thy arms? A blasted reputation, poverty, contempt. The indignation of mine and of *thy* friends. For thou art poor and so am I. Thy kindred have antipathies for me as strong as those that are fostered against thyself" (p. 114). She gradually recovers her self-confidence and her belief that she has something essential to share with, and bestow on, Colden—her religious faith (pp. 190-91). But once more she withdraws when she hears that she has been the cause of a break between Colden and his father; she holds that the claim of kinship takes precedence over even the most intense love between man and woman. This decision is entirely consistent with Jane's experience so far. She accepted without murmur the choice of Risberg for her husband; and after that young man's defection she became Mrs. Talbot, following the advice of her father and Mrs. Fielder. She has at first hesitated at also obeying Mrs. Fielder with regard to Colden because of genuine doubts about the lady's competence in deciding for her in this particular instance, and also, in spite of Jane's usual gentleness, because she has felt pique at Mrs. Fielder's uncharitable hints and accusations.[17]

Brown uncharacteristically, in the case of Jane and Colden, joined more or less equal partners into a couple. While his exchanges with Jane are taking place, Colden is by no means any longer the dynamic figure he seems to have been at an earlier date. He sets great store by his honesty (p. 142),[18] but this proud love of truth makes him seem stubborn and defiant rather than confident. Often self-accusatory and helpless privately,[19] he strikes one as too reticent and secretive to have much to say for himself and those of his convictions so offensive to both Mrs. Fielder and the well-meaning Thompson.[20] Jane indeed reproaches him for his silence (p. 134), though she may be willing to consider it as a refusal to obtrude himself and an instance of his self-discipline, similar to his restraint in the face of temptation (at a time when she might herself have yielded) (p. 83). The presentation of Colden by means of rumors and secondhand accusations is unsatisfactory.[21] This is felt above all when he is finally converted to orthodoxy in matters of morals and religion, for this conversion is important: it is such a comforting fulfillment of Jane's secret hopes (pp. 190-96, 343). Colden has not so much made his way from one well-established position to another that is gradually acknowledged as superior; he seems rather to have passed, almost as a matter of course, from a phase of immaturity to a clearer sense of responsibility. In other words, it is not the man Colden who has gained through his conversion but a mere literary figure that has been changed by having an additional attribute superimposed on its former character.[22] Colden's sincerity seems genuine, but we have been inadequately prepared for his final development.

Still, some provision has been made for the fact that Jane and Colden must secure religious and moral harmony before they can

[194]

find fullfilment in love. When the girl relates how she has been affected by wrestling with Colden's doubts and her own too easy certainties, she brings to light an important and appealing aspect of their relationship:

> Thus I grew up, never beset by any doubts; never venturing on inquiry. My knowledge of you, put an end to this state of super-stitious ignorance. In you I found, not one that disbelieved, but one that doubted. In all your demeanor there was simplicity and frankness. You concealed not your sentiments; you obtruded them not upon my hearing. When called upon to state the his-tory of your opinions, it was candidly detailed; with no view of gaining my concurrence, but merely to gratify my curiosity.
>
> .   .   .   .
>
> In no respect has your company made me a worse, in every respect it has made me a better woman. Not only my piety has become more rational and fervent, but a new spring has been imparted to my languishing curiosity. To find a soul, to whom my improvement will give delight; eager to direct and assist my enquiries; delicately liberal no less of censure when merited, than of praise where praise is due; entering, almost without the help of language from me, into my inmost thoughts; assist-ing me, if I may so speak, to comprehend myself; and raising to a steadfast and bright flame, the spark that my wayward fancy, left to itself, would have instantaneously emitted and lost. (pp. 193, 195-96)[23]

The reader is not likely to lose his interest in the partners of such a confrontation[24] and is more inclined to believe them in earnest than when reading Jane's earlier "heart-dissecting" correspon-dence (pp. 129-30).[25]

Yet, everything considered, only a small proportion of Brown's last novel sustainedly interests us. The colorless to and fro of the tale, which reflects the heroine's refusal to decide rashly in face of complex views and attitudes, strikes the reader as the most characteristic feature of *Jane Talbot*. The detective element concerning Miss Jessup's forgery is all too naïve, and so is this treacherous lady's unexplained retraction of the confession made to Colden. The concluding phases of Jane's apparently hopeless waiting for Colden to return are only perfunctorily tacked on to the narrative. No less than *Clara Howard*, its immediate predecessor, and far more than Brown's earlier fiction, *Jane Talbot* gains from the comparative lack of distinction among the contemporary American novelists.

Mrs. Margaret Botsford (fl. 1812-30)[26] used in *Adelaide* (1816) a heroine who is physically as passive as Jane; and since she has no comparable intellectual gifts, Adelaide is entirely helpless when faced with the problems thrust upon her. She lives in a world marked by violent action, whose pressures are physical rather than moral. Literally as well as figuratively, she is dragged to the altar to be joined to a husband she does not care for. Her father has no consideration whatsoever for her feelings or her true lover's, but much respect for his own wishes and whims and the appearance of his authority. The heroine's apology for resignation is an adequate reflection of her character and, beyond that, of the simplified motivation of the plot: "I must learn to suffer. I have been enviably happy; but felicity, I am conscious, cannot be expected in this imperfect state of existence, and I must be resigned to my destiny..." (2:11). Adelaide's words probably deserve our approval, or at any rate the reader feels that such must have been Mrs. Botsford's opinion. As with the remarks of Mrs. Clifford, however, according to whom Adelaide and her friend Elinda "are possessed of superior minds" and "inspire admiration and command respect" (1:18), we must be content with accepting the author's bare judgment, for Adelaide never steps out of the pages of the novel to vindicate any claim made for her. Yet she is loved by Mandeville Clifford and Montwilbert, she has all the sympathy of Clifford's cousin Morgiana and Caroline Danvers. It is her very passiveness that seems to attract trouble. Significantly, Adelaide never leaves the place to which our author conveyed her at the beginning of the tale; all the other characters must consequently be carried there as well. Morgiana rushes from Barbados to her assistance; Wellingham stops with his companion at V*** on his quest for health; Olivia following her father reaches the place just before Clifford returns from his despairing journey to Europe. Then, at last, the stage is set for disposing of the villains and establishing the prosperous happiness of the virtuous.

Delmont, capable of any villainy and violence with regard to

Adelaide, is simply the personification of parental tyranny: "By G - - I will not thus be trifled with. She shall transfer her affections to a suitable object. She shall, I repeat, love only the man whom I approve. Nor dare to irritate me by practicing more of the d - - n'd arts peculiar to her sex; tears, hysterics, swoonings and supplications, in order to gain her point. . ."(1:248). He may be said to be on the decline already when he tries to make her do his will; the loss of his partner in crime, Vironaldi, together with the reappearance of his son Edgar (who can easily afford to give Adelaide 50,000 pounds), just about finish him off. In former years he possessed dimensions more formidable; the recollections of his sensitive wife reflect his earlier qualities of Radcliffean glamor (1:72). Vironaldi himself is an offspring of Montoni and Schedoni but without their stern impressiveness, so that his effect on the reader is close to that of a caricature.[27] The relation of his misdeeds provides for digressions from the main narrative.[28]

Another way of obtaining relief and an alternation of moods is attempted in the comedy of a *servus gloriosus,* Vironaldi's servant Le Rapiere, whose pride in, and emulation of, the achievements of his master make him an easy victim for a practical joke and a seduced girl's harmless if costly revenge.[29] Morgiana's satirical humor, too, has its uses for the creation of relief. The girl, reproached for her levity by Mrs. Clifford and Adelaide, pokes fun at Clayton because he is so respectfully shy, "a perfect sentimentalist. . .precisely calculated to give one the vapours. . ., a creature who will not quarrel for the pleasure of becoming friends again" (1:8). Used protectively, and without too much insistence when matrimony is really in question, Morgiana's coquetry neither discourages Clayton nor prevents the girl from accepting his proposal with pleasure. We never doubt Morgiana's actual reliability: it is she who supplies an effective spirit of resistance and hurries to Adelaide's side when Delmont's schemes are unfolded.

But Mrs. Botsford's well-meant efforts at varying her tone cannot offset the pervasively pathetic or picturesque features of her novel. They are features which conform with the fashionable tendencies of the contemporary fiction just as much as the plot

[197]

elements or the types used for characters.[30] The emphasis of the following passage from Mrs. Delmont's story, for example, is too marked not to permeate whole sections more neutral in tone:

> The voice of Pembrooke faltered; a convulsive groan impeded further utterance; indescribable agony pervaded my bosom; I suspired convulsively; my whole frame was agitated. Pembrooke caught my hand, and tremulously conveyed it to his quivering lips; he kissed it with impassioned tenderness. His emotion over-powered him; he groaned in anguish of soul, and bathed my trembling hand with copious tears. Mine flowed profusely and in silence; respiration became short; my frame was agitated almost to dissolution, and, in anguish of soul, I exclaimed falteringly, ah! ill-fated Emilia! death, only, can mitigate thy anguish! I sank unconsciously on the shoulder of Ormond. (1:122)[31]

Individual elegant phrasings also contribute to the artificial character of the book,[32] a character further strengthened by the use of elaborate landscape settings which encourage and reflect the sentimental lyricism of certain figures.[33] The writer's inability to choose discerningly from the tempting abundance of popular fiction material results in many passages and details obviously written for effect alone. Here is a literary landscape typical of the stylized manner of the minor novelists of the age; it describes by means of accumulation and heterogeneous variety, instead of by selection and arrangement, and ends on a pious admonition:

> From a thicket composed of venerable oaks, pines, cedars, &c. and which you would suppose impenetrable, you are led by a winding path into a beauteous lawn, nearly encircled by wood, and from thence a serpentine path conducts to an eminence on which the mansion is erected. On approaching it, you pass through an enclosure where a profusion of shrubbery diffuses grateful fragrance and regales the eye with various vivid hues. Passing through an arbour in the centre, which is composed of grape-vines, jasmine, and honey-suckle, you at length arrive at the portico; while the feathered inhabitants of this little paradise salute the ear with various exquisite notes, in which they vie to compensate for their intrusion. The opposite side of the building commands an extensive view of the Delaware, which

is scarcely two hundred yards distant. The adjacent scenery is romantic beyond description. The eminences command extensive and sublime prospects, calculated to elevate the soul. Rocks of immense height, covered with moss of the most vivid green, wild roses and flowers of various hues, contrasted with the laurel, cedar, silver pines, &c. have a pleasing effect. In another direction, the rivulet's serpentine course among the richly embroidered meadows, is scarcely inferior. And can the eye be ever sated with the beauties of nature? How insensate the being who can behold and merely admire. The numerous beauties which are perpetually present should awaken rapturous sensations, on reflecting that the hand which formed them is Divine. (1:150)

Clayton, Colden, Samuel Beaumont—they all undergo various adventures abroad until the obstacles raised by parental prejudices can conveniently be done away with. In *Fidelity Rewarded, or, The History of Polly Granville* (1796)[34] Danford is similarly exiled when the father of his Polly abruptly decrees that the hero is not good enough for the girl. What happens to him on the voyage that is to bring him prosperity remains unknown; only the fact of his prosperity is relevant, since it is part of Polly's reward for her fidelity. The girl makes plain in her very first letter, to her friend Sophia, that she believes in keeping promises. Though the person of Mr. Stapleton, promoted by Mr. Granville, is morally and physically repulsive enough to account for the young lady's refusal, yet it is chiefly the fact that she considers herself engaged to Danford—with her parents' tacit agreement, too—that gives Polly the strength to resist her father's wishes. Hers is not just a struggle between love and duty but between two different orders of duty. On the one hand, there is a temporal one, valid enough in itself but distorted through the conceptions that influence it, especially the materialism that blots out love; on the other hand there is a sort of duty which immediately and unadulteratedly reflects its dependence on transcendent principles.[35] Backed by her love for Danford, Polly maintains her willingness to meet all the legitimate requirements of filial duty, as long as she must not offend against religion and honor. She is very quickly victorious,[36] for Granville underestimates the force that can be derived from convictions such as

[199]

Polly's. He also misunderstands the motives of Danford in leaving Polly and is therefore so much baffled when his daughter persists in rejecting Stapleton even after her lover's seeming desertion that he gives her up as hopeless. The truce achieved when Polly is allowed to go and stay with her uncle paves the way for the girl's triumph. She obviously deserves it, we are given to understand, if only because she has resisted the temptation of eloping with Danford and marrying without her father's consent.[37] Providence steps in as her ally and humbles Mr. Granville into a proper notion of his insignificance. Threatened with bankruptcy and abandoned by those he thought his friends, he cannot help concluding that Polly was right in relying on a transcendent being. One of Polly's rewards, therefore, turns out to be her father's conversion to a moral view of things (p. 71).[38] He becomes fully aware of Danford's merits; and his son-in-law Murfee in turn experiences a similar change from flint-heartedness to Christian disinterestedness, so that Granville can be the first to congratulate him on his reformation (p. 94).

The characters of this novel generally move in pairs, such as Granville-Murfee. Danford, altruistic, generous, and forgiving, has a partner in the person of Polly's uncle (pp. 7, 45). The worldly Stapleton (pp. 16-17), whose very ugliness (p. 5) reflects his inner rottenness, finds himself yoked in marriage to a caricature of a suitable wife.[39] Danford and Polly form one unit rather than a couple; their very letters mutually echo and repeat certain statements and phrases;[40] they are truly "of a consonant turn of mind" (p. 11). Polly carries off the role of the steadfast girl with greater confidence than other heroines and with commendably few tears. For all her confidence, she responds, like Pamela, rather sensitively to her trials; among these we must include the meetings with her unwelcome suitor and her irritated father (pp. 15, 43), as well as her wedding: ". . . Tremble, tremble went my feet all the way! Lay still, said I, you little fool! why should you be so uneasy? For my heart was ready to leave its orbit. After the first flutter was over, I held up better, while the ceremony was performing, than I was afraid I should" (p. 64). Like Richardson's heroine, too, she has her husband set forth explicitly his views on, say, the correct behavior toward guests and the disregard to be shown all foolish affectations and fashions.[41]

The author of *Fidelity Rewarded* remained bogged down in the morass of a naïve fictional moralizing. Rebecca Rush,[42] who wrote *Kelroy,* fashioned within the limitations of the contemporary standards among novelists and their readers a tale more convincing and, in its execution, considerably more careful and finished. With the partial exception of *St. Herbert,* this is the only novel using the "cruel parents" pattern that does not offer a happy ending: it is as if the necessity of rewarding the virtuous and deserving kept the authors stuck with certain materials and compulsive ways of treating them.[43] If Brockden Brown managed to preserve some of his genuine personality and artistry in the face of such pressures, the distinction of his achievement in *Clara Howard* and *Jane Talbot* is very much a relative one only: a comparison of these novels to *Kelroy* shows up their limitations.

Despite its title, the novel of Miss Rush is not so much about Kelroy, in love with Emily Hammond, as it is about Mrs. Hammond, the girl's mother. She is introduced, with praiseworthy economy, as a widow who has been left none too well-off, and is now soberly planning a shrewd investment of her resources. Her purpose is to create an impression of comfortable wealth in order to obtain for her two daughters husbands correspondingly rich. She emerges from years of retirement and a comparatively frugal life which people think she has accepted for the sake of personally supervising her daughters' education. This is true in a sense, and Mrs. Hammond's confidence of having ensured beforehand a complete success for her schemes derives in particular from her faith in the example she has set the two girls, that is, reliance on calculating principles and rational coolness. As if to prove her right, within a short time Lucy wins the admiration and love of a visiting lord, Walsingham.[44]

It appears, however, that Mrs. Hammond's conquest of a first son-in-law may prove a Pyrrhic victory only. Lucy embodies all of her mother's notions of purposeful and ladylike self-possession, and her very appearance bespeaks the fact (pp. 5-6): it is plausible indeed that she should quickly realize her mother's ambitions. But the explicit opposition between Lucy and her younger sister Emily (p. 12)[45] suggests that the latter will not come up so satisfactorily to Mrs. Hammond's expectations. Walsingham has one friend whom he prizes particularly, Kelroy, to whose poetic gifts Emily responds instinctively even before having met him in person. In so doing she forgets her mother's rule to regard rank and wealth before anything else in a potential suitor and husband. Emily and Kelroy soon meet face to face; their attraction is mutual and not long kept secret because the two rely on their innate sense of values and therefore easily see through all that is mere social disguise and restraint.

Mrs. Hammond is anxious to dispose of her daughters favorably before her financial resources are exhausted; failure to achieve this would to her mean losing face and consequently giving up the chance of maintaining the lavish style of living she has had to miss so long. Her flaw becomes visible here: she has planned her campaign with circumspection, but she has neglected properly to assess her resistance to worries and delays. Furthermore she has forgotten to take into account her own liability to enjoy more of the pleasures of society than are strictly necessary to secure her daughters' marriage and consistent with her financial situation. Since Kelroy's position is at best only vaguely promising, Mrs. Hammond must envisage keeping up her rather showy way of life longer than reckoned. Still in possession of her wits, she refrains from asking the lovers not to see each other, but she tries to prevent their meeting privately. In this she fails because her general coldness has generated hostility against her, and a servant who sympathizes with Emily and has penetrated his mistress' motives admits Kelroy into the house during Mrs. Hammond's absence. Emily's mother finds out that the lovers have exchanged confidences and promises; she then unexpectedly encourages an unpleasant newly rich character named Marney, hoping to bring him to the point before Kelroy formally proposes. She is thwarted by the short-range worrying and inward nagging of her current expenses. Realizing that she is in difficulties, Walsingham none too gently blackmails her into agreeing to Emily's engagement. Mrs. Hammond has never liked Kelroy (p. 57) and therefore bitterly resents the engagement forced upon her, the more so as upon second thoughts she feels that she might have bluffed Walsingham. She cannot, however, encourage Marney any longer. But when, during Kelroy's absence, another suitor turns up who is more to Emily's liking than Marney, Mrs. Hammond maneuvers her daughter into his arms by forging "Dear John" letters for Emily as well as Kelroy. This piece of treachery is to haunt her to her dying day: she learns that there is a tremendous difference between looking for the main chance on behalf of one's children and what she has been led to do, separating a pair of lovers by means of vicious slander. Her crime clearly cannot be rationalized into a sensible measure of protection but instead reveals mercilessly an essential and monstrous selfishness. Mrs. Hammond, who has come to adjust to her financial situation and to keep her appetites in check (p. 210), too late pays heed to the moral issue of her ways.

Though intent upon moralizing, Miss Rush succeeded in conveying with some plausibility the two levels of Mrs. Hammond's concern over Emily's fate—the one justifiable if petty, the other criminal. Various characters, in the service respectively of more or less unmitigated materialism or idealism, serve to bring into relief the nature and built-in dangers of Mrs. Hammond's preoccupations. The social criticism of *Kelroy* is harsh, though only once does it sound the depths of disillusionment (in some remarks which Walsingham addresses to Emily):

Experience will teach you the real characters of the beings who chiefly compose your species. You will find them a set of harpies, absurd, treacherous, and deceitful—regardless of strong obligations, and mindful of slight injuries—and when your integrity has been shocked, and every just, and native feeling severely tried, the sensibility which you now so liberally bestow on others, will then be absorbed in lamenting its own cruel disappointments, and inefficacious tenderness; and you will gladly consult the dictates of your understanding, to prevent being preyed on by continual depravity. (p. 129)

Generally it is rather the thoughtless acceptance of shallow social distinctions that is criticized; a small number of persons like Mrs. Cathcart are sufficient to give it currency, and it may then make for the rise of men like Marney, who "spend the latter half of their lives in striving to erase from the minds of the community all remembrance of the former" (p. 99). Moral indifference and intellectual mediocrity, Miss Rush was saying, can easily render themselves acceptable to society, whereas on the other hand the sensitive, reacting strongly on the level of the moral and the aesthetic, cause social discomfort and are treated as freaks.[46]

Kelroy is obviously meant to be an exceptional being. He is very much a romantic conception: gifted with exalted faculties and inclined to sympathetic understanding or arrogant rejection, he is endowed with an aura of melancholy. He curiously combines dependence on his friend with a realistic view of the necessity of independent decisions and of his chances of obtaining Emily (p. 63). Yet he remains a shadowy creation; and we are not given any encouragement to elaborate the author's presentation of him, which consists of direct statements and Emily's thoughts concerning her lover. The girl, who hardly comes to life either, projects all her high hopes of mankind into her view of Kelroy:

> In his character was combined all that appeared to her worthy of estimation, and she contemplated this living image of her own cherished standard of excellence, with indescribable emotions both of pleasure and pain. His learning, genius, temper, and understanding, were such as might silence the most fastidious critic; and she felt soothed by the consciousness that her preference, however misplaced in other respects, could only reflect honour on her judgment.

This is very far indeed from the disillusionment voiced by Walsingham. But Emily's reflections now take another turn:

> But his depressed situation, and her perfect knowledge of her mother's views, convinced her that she ought, if possible, to banish him entirely from her thoughts. She endeavoured to turn her mind from these melancholy ideas to the happier lot of her sister, but the contrast afforded aggravated uneasiness, and she felt tempted, for the first time in her life, to arraign fortune of unkindness. She saw Lucy, cold, and heartless, in possession of the undivided affections of an amiable man, whose worth she

was incapable of appreciating, and mistress of immense wealth which she would never employ to any better purpose than the attainment of luxury or fashion; and whilst Walsingham was thus cheated into a union with one whose deficiencies she feared would be too early displayed to him, Kelroy and herself might waste the bloom of life in pursuing hopes, which if unsuccessful would embitter the remainder of their days. (p. 60)

Emily's fate is to justify her misgivings. Like many heroes and heroines of fiction, Emily betrays herself as much as she is betrayed: by her willingness to accept the forged letter as coming from Kelroy, she proves false to her lofty conceptions. Even the spiritual legacy transmitted to Kelroy through the agency of her faithful friend Helen cannot efface that moment of treason. But Emily's reaction to the fatal letter, on the other hand, may be said to contribute to rendering her more human. The Mr. Dunlevy whom she eventually marries (pp. 223-24) further helps to adjust the heroine to a scale of things not quite so exalted as the one she might wish to be measured by. Comedy is, perhaps surprisingly, also represented in *Kelroy:* there is the inveterate proposer Dr. Blake and the spectacle of the Gurnets, who are coarsely and derisively shown to be incapable of rising to anything like genteel social rank.[47]

Although *Kelroy* is an uneven production, the book nevertheless possesses sound qualities and offers reading both pleasant and interesting enough. The author was especially successful in her creation of Mrs. Hammond, a noteworthy step toward the conception of a fictional character which is both memorable and plausible.[48] Other assets of this novel include a plot which is relatively unencumbered and a style which errs on the side of dryness rather than the elaborate manner favored by minor writers of the age.[49]

1. *St. Herbert* appeared anonymously and was first printed in the New York *Weekly Magazine* in 1796 (see Warren H. Smith, *Architecture in British Fiction* [New Haven: Yale University Press, 1934], p. 195). References are to the edition published at Windsor, Conn. (1813).

2. The passage here referred to shows a sympathy with Roman Catholicism which is exceptional among the American fiction of the age. See also the story of the "nun" from Montreal, a former Mme Dugazon rejected by her family for having married a Catholic Frenchman.

3. St. Herbert is taught stoic acceptance by an Indian who learned to appreciate his blessings only after he had lost them.

4. The reintroduction of Albudor after St. Herbert has completed his tale comes as a surprise: the Albudor episode had seemed a simple pretext for St. Herbert's story. Albudor's tale must be finished, too: it is a sort of comment upon the central narrative, and also provides a compensatory happy ending.

5. References are to the first New York edition of 1798. The same, unidentified, author also wrote *Moreland Vale;* see below, in Chapter 10, "Overwhelming Odds."

6. There are initial resemblances with *Amelia, or the Faithless Briton* (1798). See below in Chapter 12, entitled "Seduction."

7. See e.g., the perfunctory sketches of Bellmore (p. 16), Eliza (p. 27), and Eliza and Hargrave (p. 147). Thoughtless and malicious gossiping is mocked with the help of "humours" given allegorical names (Eliza's letter, pp. 27-37); there is satire of vanity and social affectations typical of a young lady like Miss Lovemore (pp. 170-71).

8. At one point Mr. Villars is so strongly moved that he must interrupt his story (p. 81), and the author once feels she must give up trying to express what passes expression (pp. 101-2).

9. Nothing is known either of Mrs. Patterson or of any of the alleged seventeen editions which preceded that of 1797, printed at Random [?].

10. Gauze and Beaumont plan marrying their children after the birth of Samuel but before that of Nancy; happily it is a girl that is then born to Gauze, and the two children miraculously do fall in love.

11. References are to the first edition, Philadelphia, 1801.

12. Cf. Warner B. Berthoff, "The Literary Career of Charles Brockden Brown," p. 228.

13. See Fiedler, *Novel,* p. 76.

14. See Robert F. Almy, "The Rôle of the Club in American Literary History, 1700-1812," p. 344; and "Charles Brockden Brown," *Atlantic Monthly* 61(1888):710-14.

15. Jane is not a weak character, for all that; obviously warmer and more balanced than Clara Howard, she is less intellectual and domineering. Brown used "psychological analysis" to present her but only "character traits" in his drawing of Clara, who, like Colden, remains in the background (the terms, not their application, are borrowed from Mrs. L. R. Wiley, *The Sources and Influence of the Novels of C.B. Brown* [Vantage Press, 1950]).

16. There are some misleading statements in the summary of *Jane Talbot* in Clark, *Brown,* p. 183. Talbot is not Jane's cousin; but Risberg, her parents' first choice, was. Jane met Colden, and they began their exchange of views, before her marriage with Talbot, though at a time when it was already decided. Talbot was estranged from his wife but did not marry Miss Jessup—he died.

17. Her pique expresses itself in sarcasm (p. 90; cf. p. 84). Jane's gentleness must not be mistaken for feebleness. It is difficult to accept Harry R. Warfel's view that Jane is "born to command" (Warfel, *Brown,* p. 198), yet she does insist "upon an exercise of independent judgment" (Clark, *Charles Brockden Brown,* p. 183). She may show symptoms of sensibility but she is of the type that does not swoon (see Loshe, *Novel,* p. 49). On the other hand she is hardly a "tragic" heroine; but see R. A. Miller, Jr., "Representative Tragic

Heroines in the Work of Brown, Hawthorne, Howells, James, and Dreiser,"
DA 17(1957):2612.

18. Cf. Jane's corroboration, p. 75.

19. "And whence this incurable folly? This rooted incapacity of acting as every motive, generous and selfish, combine to recommend? Constitution; habit; insanity; the dominion of some evil spirit, who insinuates his baneful power between the *will* and the *act*" (p. 287, cf. pp. 142, 75).

20. Thompson acts the part of a genuine friend and guide, though he seems to betray Colden. Mrs. Fielder, partly relying on information received from Thompson, paints Colden as "the advocate of suicide; a scoffer at promises; the despiser of revelation, of providence and a future state; an opponent of marriage, and as one who denied (shocking!) that any thing but mere habit and positive law, stood in the way of marriage; nay, of intercourse without marriage, between brother and sister, parent and child!" This system of morals is attributed to the influence of Godwin's *Political Justice* (pp. 99-100). Colden's guilt is like Hermsprong's, in Bage's novel, who is accused of having read *The Rights of Man* and having lent the book to a friend of his.

21. He resembles the mysterious Colden (with his religious preoccupations) that Brown began sketching in "Jessica"; see Dunlap, *Brown*, 1:108-69.

22. It is he above all who is less a character than a device for clarifying issues; see Cowie, *Novel*, p. 89.

23. Cf. Mrs. Fielder's opinion of Jane's zeal (p. 95) and the remarks addressed to Colden by Thompson's sister (pp. 296-97). The reported speech and the succession of hypothetical clauses in the last-mentioned passage tend to emphasize Colden's detached attitude; the same effect derives from Colden's relation of his meeting with Frank, as if he had been an observer and not a participant (p. 182).

24. This confrontation has been aptly described by Fiedler, *Novel*, p. 76.

25. Like other heroines, Jane is a marathon letter-writer and can "maintain the writing posture, and pursue the writing movement for ten hours together, without benumbed brain or aching fingers" (p. 149).

26. Apart from *Adelaide*, Mrs. Botsford also wrote *The Reign of Reform; or Yankee Doodle Court* (Baltimore, 1830) (Wright, *American Fiction*, p. 341).

27. "You know but little of Vironaldi," returned Le Rapiere, "if you suppose that a few words uttered by a sanctified old priest, can bind him to any woman. He glories in enumerating his conquests, and makes vows merely to impose upon innocent credulity. I have been a witness to half a dozen such ceremonies since I have been in his service, and I have been the confidante of numberless intrigues" (2:8). See also Mandeville's portrait of Vironaldi as a perfect villain (2:6).

28. Among these interpolated stories is that of Cazelli, which Mrs. Botsford tried to introduce naturally: being entreated to flee by a witness of his duel with Vironaldi, Cazelli "returned many acknowledgements for the service he intended, but politely declined it, and presented him a manuscript in Italian, in return for the interest which his misfortune had excited..." (2:148).

29. Olivia's maid Maria, once deserted by Le Rapiere, takes the place of an American farm girl with whom he is planning to elope, and the scoundrel must buy himself off with gold and jewels in order to escape.

30. See, e.g., the stereotype portrait of Clifford (1:50). The *Port-Folio* reviewer may also have been thinking of the conventionality of *Adelaide* when

he described the book as "so insufferably vulgar" that he gave it up after a few pages (5th ser., 2, no. 3, [September, 1816]:259). The same issue of the *Port-Folio* spoke of the forthcoming publication of "The Invisible Monitor; or Memoirs of the D'Alvara Family, by Mrs. Shephard," but no trace of this novel has been found.

31. See also Mrs. Delmont's palpitations (1:78) and the scene of Vironaldi's death (2:206).

32. "She raised her languid blue eyes, and I perceived a tear glittering on their long dark lashes, like a dew-drop, tremulous among violets" (1:217); cf. 1:223, 2:227.

33. See, e.g., 1:20 and 107.

34. The book is further described on the title page: "In a Series of Letters; Giving an account of her sufferings for her stedfast adhering to her promise; and also of her deliverance from her troubles, and her marriage, in consequence of her father's commencing a virtuous and religious course of life." The moral intent of the book is also borne out by the remarks "To the Public," which stress the authenticity of the story, and the "happy family" ending (pp. 98-99).

35. There is duty and Duty for Polly, just as there seemed to be love and Love for Clara Howard.

36. She wins her mother over even faster than her father, yet must overcome her mother's family pride and view of marrying for profit (see pp. 6, 9).

37. She is advised to do so by Sophia; see letters 5, 12, 14.

38. "Your behaviour, Sir, was ever consistent with virtue, and a religious mind—whilst mine was quite the reverse" (p. 57). For the "reverse" see p. 42.

39. "She is of a dark complexion, with coarse black hair, and black eyes; which, at the first sight, show a degree of brilliance; but it needs but a small degree of physiognomy, to discover, that they are filled with malignant spite. She is full faced, and all her features rather coarse; and being pretty tall and bulky, one would be led to think, that none could like her for her person. ...She is of a ludicrous turn of mind, and affects to be a wit; which leads her to very loquacious; though for the most part, her prattle is without connexion or sense. And this she generally makes more contemptible, by setting up a large laugh at the end of every sentence, which I think indicates brutality of manners. She is of a dictatorial temper, and therefore cannot bear to be contradicted" (pp. 86-87).

40. In letters 8 (from Danford) and 9 (to Danford), the following sentence is repeated verbatim: "We ought not to use fraud in any case whatsoever, but trust all our affairs in the hands of a kind Providence" (pp. 29, 31). Letters 1 and 2 similarly express the same thoughts in language identical or closely resembling.

41. See letter 26. Sophia's coy playing with the word "husband" is another borrowing from the Richardsonian school of writing (p. 48).

42. Allibone, *A Critical Dictionary of English Literature*, 3 vols. (Philadelphia, 1858-71), 2:1893, informs us that Miss Rush, the daughter of Judge Jacob Rush and niece of Benjamin Rush, was paid $100 for *Kelroy*. The book appeared in Philadelphia in 1812.

43. In passing, mention may be made here of the twelve page *Eugenius and Selima; or, The Fatal Effects of Parental Tyranny*, which ends on the decline of the broken-hearted lovers; "The Cruel Father," in which Malvolio victimizes his son Adolphus and the latter's young wife, and repents only after

the couple's death (R. Ladd, comp., *The History of Albert and Eliza*, pp. 55-88); "History of Amelia, or Malevolence Defeated," first published in the *Columbian Magazine* (August, 1787) and reprinted with *Amelia, or the Faithless Briton*, where the malice of Mrs. Wormwood is explained by her being the child of a wealthy miser; "Suicide Attempted," chap. 4 of William Ray, *The American Tars in Tripolitan Slavery*, a story which ends happily although the young girl in question is first tricked into marrying a man of her father's choice.

44. Mrs. Hammond's task must not seem too easy; the first candidate for the hand of Lucy proves too prudent to be caught (p. 14).

45. To match Lucy's portrait (pp. 5-6) there is one of Emily (pp. 6-7).

46. Kelroy, though deeply moved by a song, is wounded by the raucous applause of those present and provokes a discussion on the merits of not feeling and imagining too keenly and thus avoiding extremes of grief or joy (chap. 4).

47. Chap. 14, esp. pp. 250-51.

48. Quinn, *American Fiction*, p. 39, pronounces Mrs. Hammond a lifelike character. In the view of Dr. Loshe the whole of *Kelroy* is rather more natural than other works of fiction of the age (p. 15).

49. Neither plot nor style quite escape blame. There are too obvious coincidences, such as the fire which destroys Mrs. Hammond's property, with the exception of a lottery ticket that wins her $50,000, some time later, or the accident which throws Dunlevy and Emily together. There are passages skillfully written, such as the one on Marney, but there are very clumsy ones, too (e.g., pp. 201-2).

Chapter Eight

PERFIDIOUS RIVALRY

IN THE FICTION under discussion, forged letters such as
Mrs. Hammond's are means used by rivals rather than parents; for whereas parents can exert some direct pressure,
rivals are obliged to work in concealment and frequently through
acts of perfidy similar to letter-forging. The instances of treachery are crass enough in the four novels gathered in this chapter.

Rosalvo Delmonmort (1818), by a writer who called himself
"Guy Mannering," makes for needless complexities by introducing a variety of episodes into its main plot[1]—episodes unin-
teresting, in spite of some sensational aspects, and irrelevant,
for they are linked up with the central story by mere names and
not by characters or by a unifying narrative climate. The author
used heterogeneous moods and elements, ranging from satirical
touches and the sentimental seduction motif to Gothic ingredients. Unfortunately his sense of style was as insecure as his grasp
of the rules of storytelling. The ludicrous attempt at the mysterious in the opening pages, which becomes an involuntary parody
of suspense, seems to result from an entirely inadequate linguistic
equipment;[2] this also mars, for example, the satirical character
sketch of a literary seducer: "His mind was richly stored with a
knowledge of books, and those of the most favorite authors in
poetry, and the classics in general. The irresistable temptation
he inspired when reciting some of his favorite poems, and the
elegance of his delivery, could but attract my whole sense of
comprehension, and wound around my feelings, to the highest
pinnacle of adoration" (p. 67).[3] The author's deficiencies are as
painfully evident in numerous other passages marked by incoherence and clumsiness;[4] his book offers many examples of the
turgid and sentimental overwriting developed by novelists whose
only qualification for their craft seems to have been a keen spirit

of competition.[5] The characters of *Rosalvo Delmonmort* stay remote; at best there are indications that they conform to average requirements of heroes and villains. The evil dimensions of a Mandoni, a Radcliffe-inspired protagonist of wickedness, may be said to serve him well, for they remove him beyond the sphere of everyday plausibility to a level of fairy tale or myth to which the reader is likely to respond instinctively. But in the case of a "mere" congenital rake and pursuer of innocence like Fitzalban-Bellerton or an envious and vengeful character such as Mrs. Oldrix, we expect something different, a more suggestive material, embodying traits of the familiar, which can be seized upon by our imagination. Considering that it is the villains' actions (as thwarting rivals) which provide the main climaxes in novels of this type, with the heroes and heroines doomed to simple reaction, the lack of substance and profile in the wicked characters is here particularly felt.

The title of *Henry and Julietta, or Virtue Rewarded* (1818), by Eliza Pope,[6] is already a clue to the structural weakness of the book. This novel consists of two narratives told in alternating installments, at the end of which the brother and sister named in the title are each joined to their partners in love. All too many parallels occur in the two main sections,[7] and this basic defect could not be counterbalanced by Mrs. Pope's meager talents. Her heroine Julietta Granville is a model of meek perfection. Her contribution to the interest of the story is her carelessness: she manages to lose her way within walking distance of the cottage where she has lived for years (chap. 3) and is so imprudent that she ventures out of sight of her dwelling even though she has had ample warning of designs against her person (chaps. 4, 7). Henry, known as Lord Ormond, makes his appearance in the guise of the first rescuer of Julietta from Lord Monmouth; and thus conveniently graced with the manner of the true hero, he cannot be expected to behave otherwise than gallantly toward Rosabella. He completes the conquest of her heart by manifesting his predilection for her own favorite "little alpine spot" in the English Lake District (p. 154).

However clumsily, Mrs. Pope apparently tried to differentiate between her two heroines, making Julietta rather cooler in critical situations than the tremulous Rosabella; but she was unable to make their lovers significantly different. What with their accomplished characters and their record of heroism, Clareville and Ormond are interchangeable, and the latter's portrait may stand as representative of the models of characterization as well as style which our author followed:

> His features were strong without being harsh, his eyes full and black, with a spirit and expression superior to any she [Rosabella] had ever seen: his countenance was interesting, and his form so perfectly answered every idea of a hero, that had her eye only been consulted, it was impossible to deny him the preference to all the men she had ever seen. In addition to these exterior advantages, she beheld the most captivating address, and those manners which are produced only by a liberal education acting on an excellent understanding.... (p. 147)

The villains Monmouth and Monteith are very similar, too, though the latter is less obdurate than Julietta's persecutor.[8] Between these extremes of distinction and evil, there are some mixed characters, as for example some that are too susceptible to fashionable amusements (chap. 6). They prove harmless and are presumably as capable of reforming as Granville, who tries to make up by a frugal life in retirement for his earlier prodigality. Apart from these poor attempts at characterization, Mrs. Pope introduced, by way of variety, comic relief through the contrast between Clareville's romantic idealism and his servant's observance of regular mealtime hours (pp. 8, 21); she further employed a range of mood extending from extreme sentimentality[9] and rapture at romantic landscapes (pp. 179-80) to breathless, nightmarish anxiety (pp. 129-30, 45). There are scenes of pursuit in which hours fly and miles are swallowed up within a few lines (chaps. 4, 6) and visits minutely detailed although their outcome is never doubtful (pp. 164-76). A miniature lost by Ormond while rescuing Julietta is improbably seen and picked up by his pursuer; the proverbial strawberry birthmark that identifies the unknown protector of the girl as her long-lost brother (pp. 75, 77): such features are an index to the qualities of the plot of Mrs. Pope's novel. Her manner is equally hackneyed. Straining for effect in rendering extreme sensations, whether sublime or terrifying, the author frequently sounds awkward and stilted; the relatively numerous errors in the book need not all be attributed to the printer. The apologetic preface proves justified only too soon[10] and too often, and it is not easy "to pass slightly over all the imperfections with which the work may abound."

In the anonymous novel *The Hapless Orphan; or, Innocent Victim of Revenge* (1793), Eliza, though the chief instigator of the heroine's sufferings, remains tantalizingly unreal. She is introduced early, in the third of Caroline Francis's 121 letters, as "the only child of parents who had ruined her in her education."[11] Soon after, Caroline receives from her the letter which provides the decisive motivation of the remaining 425 pages of the book:

> Most detested of your sex,
> How have you involved me in wretchedness by encouraging the private addresses of a man long engaged to another. Pretend not to vindicate yourself. I have been a witness of your treachery. Remember your confusion when we unexpectedly met in the arbour. I then discovered the sentiments of your heart.
> Blinded by attachment for Clarimont, I would not suffer an idea of his duplicity to impress my mind until the night previous to the suicide, when I accidentally discovered your hated picture hanging around his neck. This memento of his baseness I tore from him: It is now in my possession, where it shall for ever remain an indubitable evidence of your treachery and deceit; and you may be assured the vengeance of Eliza shall ever follow Caroline. (1:33)

But only once more can Caroline report having seen Eliza (letter 55); for the rest of the time her implacable pursuer is either uneasily mentioned, or sensed through the attempts at violence against the heroine that punctuate the narrative.[12] Eliza's are the sinister ways of a legally unassailable enemy;[13] these very ways unfortunately are inappropriate for the chief agent of a novel.

Though given a passive role, it is Caroline Francis who is at the center of things. An orphan, she wanders back and forth between two aunts, must throw in her lot with the less helpful and pleasant of the two, and finally feels compelled to leave her. Her refusal to become dependent upon an unreliable relative and her distaste for patient suffering are unusual in a fiction heroine:[14] more often than not, heroines submit to embarrassment by their next of kin and are willing to sacrifice their happiness rather than sever family ties. In a sense Caroline's decision is unfortunate, since many of the acquaintances she is to form later know sorrow more often than joy, and Caroline generally is affected by their experiences. As a kind of compensation she is very popular with men generally;[15] but these successes notwithstanding, her outlook tends to be pessimistic and defensive. Even when she sympathizes with the innocently suffering Lucretia Wilkins and Fanny Gardner, the unfortunate consumptive, she strikes one as rather cool in her attachments; the criticism of a contemporary reviewer, who found little genuine kindness in our heroine, is reasonable.[16] When turning her back on her sour aunt (1:20-21) or commenting on possibly calculating suitors (1:23-24, 65), Caroline already reveals a characteristic coolness, a feature gradually hardened into a pronounced attitude of wariness. Considering her experiences, it is plausible enough that she should move toward a comprehensive distrust and despondency.[17] Caroline combines her coolness with a remarkable resiliency; only rarely do the resources of consolation provided by her creator prove insufficient. She fights off an illness which many another heroine would have been made to bear as another claim on our sympathy (1:88). When she patiently struggles to accept her lot,[18] we find her more appealing than other persecuted girls who readily withdraw into a complacent faith.

Not that Caroline's trust in Providence is quite convincing. The fact that she apparently does not derive any more forceful encouragement from it is part of an inconsistency that affects her character and, hence, the structure of the story built around her. Whereas we are expected to believe in her firmness, both religious and commonsensically worldly, we wonder at her passivity. Caroline clearly refuses to come to terms with the reality of her enemy's hatred, ignoring it at the same time as she is quick to respond to the love of her gentlemen friends and the unhap-

piness of her lady friends. Only verbally does she acknowledge
the potential danger represented by Eliza's threats; actually she
derives a foolish comfort from the long stretches of time when
Eliza's schemes do not manifest themselves.[19] Together with the
use of plot clichés,[20] this inconsistency deprives the narrative of
much of its potential interest. It is also regrettably connected
with another fault in the method of telling Caroline's story. The
autobiographical relation as practiced in *The Hapless Orphan*
levels all individual experiences out to a singular degree of flatness. The letters are in effect a diary, kept for the benefit of
Caroline's friend Maria B——, for no answering letters are included, and replies are hardly ever referred to. There is little
variation of tone between the unfolding of the sentimental main
plot, the quick drawing of satirical character sketches,[21] the episodic didactic tales,[22] or the heroine's sententious moralizing.[23]
The sense of doom that might have been built up beginning with
Eliza's ominous letter turns into mere sinister dullness, with the
villainess increasingly obscured while the heroine naïvely thinks
her other concerns more important than her foe's threats.

If there is little differentiation between the sections of the narrative, there is even less effective characterization, either of the
heroine or of the people she writes about. Caroline expresses
only indignant and satirical disapproval or a gushingly sympathetic admiration of her acquaintances. Thus she is bitterly scornful of the miser (2:41; 1:79) and mechanically registers her fear
of the seducer: "By the death of my uncle and aunt, I was left,
my dear Maria, at an age the most necessary to be protected,
exposed to the attack of every seducer" (2:13). She accuses
Chesterfield (2:38) and especially Goethe (2:195, 205-6, 213)
of having prostituted their gifts and written corrupting books.
On the other hand she is not sparing of superlatives in the style
of fashionable sensibility, as when she speaks of Lucretia
(1:111) and Fanny (2:148), appeals to Maria's compassion
(1:149), or grieves at the loss of the unreconciled Evremont:
"He has left the world alienated from Caroline. I cannot lisp,
but in the most feeble accents, the bitterness I feel. Can my
exhausted nature sustain so severe a stroke! My eyes are dim
with sorrow; a universal langour is diffused throughout my

frame. The tear which often relieves the troubled mind, is congealed; the pearly drop is petrified" (2:121-22).[24]

One of Caroline's minor worries is to keep friendship and love apart. When she is in love with Evremont, she nevertheless highly esteems Clark, who is a pronounced admirer of hers as well as a good friend of Evremont, and she later also encourages Mr. Helen.[25] She feels that, despite generally accepted opinions, there can be such a thing as friendship between the sexes (1:202). This very notion of a platonic relationship proves the downfall of P.P. in *The Emigrants* (1793), by Gilbert Imlay (ca.1754-1828?).[26] A guest at Lord B—'s, P.P. falls in love with his host's wife. His first impulse is to leave, but he stays on because the lady suffers from the patently unfeeling way in which she is treated by her husband, who once complains that it is considered "quite *brutish* for a man to go to bed to his wife in a state of intoxication" (1:203). The ultimate consequence of P.P.'s decision is the ignominious repudiation of Lady B— by her husband. Yet P.P.'s responsibility is slighter than one might think: it turns out that Lord B— has used P.P.'s compassionate nature deliberately in order to be eased out of his marriage. The character of Lord B— is meant to serve as an argument for the necessity of improving the English divorce laws. But this argument is considerably weakened in effect, for the discussion of Lord B—'s behavior is overshadowed by the exchange of views between Caroline T—n and P.P., her uncle, which deals less with Lord B— than with P.P. himself. In an eloquently rational manner the heroine states her objections to her uncle's attitude: he was wrong in staying with the B—s when his love for Lady B— rendered him liable to compromise her. Though Caroline comes to accept the revelation of B—'s baseness as a belated justification of her uncle's behavior, her letter on the virtues of strict divorce laws (letter 27) seems the most convincing part of the otherwise unconservative argument; if a victory is scored for the charges against the existing divorce legislation, it is a sentimental rather than a rational one.[27] Not only the heroine's uncle but her sister, too, Mrs. F—, is involved in a divorce tangle. On the advice of P.P., Mrs. F— is prepared to retaliate upon all such men as Lord B— and her husband by taking the law into her own hands and legally severing a connection which, morally speaking, has already been invalidated by F—'s actions. Though the seriousness of the author's interest in the divorce question need not be doubted,[28] in *The Emigrants* the main emphasis lies on the story of Caroline and Captain Arl—ton rather than on the element of purpose. There are moreover other ingredients that deflect from Imlay's stated purpose: the feminist discussion of education (1:174), the predictable indictment of seducers (1:180-81), the propaganda for the backwoods-settlements of America.[29] This topic stands in the context of the opposition between the corruption of Europe and the simple virtues of the New World. The T—ns have been ruined by the mother's and the son's insistence on maintaining a fashionable style of living quite beyond their means (1:1-4). T—n himself appears to have had some slightly dishonest dealings which alone might have been sufficient cause to send the whole family across the Atlantic. Another emigrant, Mr. S—, is a European confidence man two generations before the Mississippi variety became a byword. The Old World taint is ineradicable in T—n, his wife, and especially their daughter Mary, and in S—. The latter drinks himself to death, but the three T—ns must be shipped back to the social ritual of England. There they can do no harm, nor can they be harmed themselves anymore, since they are inured to that form of society which has absorbed, and come to accept unthinkingly, enslaving compulsions (3:102).

For the other members of the T—n family, there is hope. Given a good start by the European estate inherited by P.P., they will contribute to realizing a society free of the Old World errors. George, the once spendthrift son now determined to mend his ways, finally appears worthy of marrying Mrs. S—, who was formerly courted by that model of manly and gentlemanly perfection, Il—ray (3:190).[30] Caroline and Arl—ton, the lovers, have had to suffer from the jealous and scheming Mary because in their naïveté they cannot discern between the real and the apparent; they have been betrayed in times of emotional crisis by their credulity, their doubts, and their susceptibilty to the sentimental. Fundamentally, they rely on a common intuitive perception of man's innate goodness and sense of values, which

[217]

must, according to them, find expression in a similarity and harmony of individual responses to experience, and therefore encourage uninhibited and undisguised responses.

The effusive description of Caroline in Mrs. W—'s words (1:39-40), and Caroline's sketch of Arl—ton (1:87-88), are typical of the tone employed in portrayals or climactic scenes. The author's style rises enthusiastically to occasions for the picturesque. There are no detailed localized descriptions in *The Emigrants,* only occasional rhapsodies (e.g., 3:51); yet such a novel really calls for vivid and realistic scenery, and its propagandistic aspect would have profited much more by skillful descriptions than by the mere mention of place names and distances, as well as Indian atrocities and one captivity.[31] If there is no visualization, this is likely to be due to our author's lack of talent, which is also illustrated very tangibly by other examples of his style. Imlay at times went to awful lengths to convey the idea of powerful feeling, as in his description of Arl—ton watching over the sleeping Caroline:

When Venus lies sleeping on the couch of night, and one half of the world is cheered by the brilliancy of her charms, so looked my Caroline when Somnus had sealed up her eye-lids; and while Morpheus, his minister of dreams, was agitating her tender heart, her bosom disclosed the temple of bliss, while her lips distilled nectareous sweets. I was already distracted with the potency of the bewitching joys which I had snatched in my embrace upon the river bank; and while I was constrained to watch as she slept, it was impossible for me to withstand the reflection of the taper, that Andrew had lighted, and which cast its rays upon a bosom more transparent than the effulgence of Aurora, when robed in all her charms, and more lovely than a poetical imagination can paint, when influenced by all its enthusiasm;—and which was now half naked. I was obliged to extinguish the light, to preserve my reason. (3:40-41)

The occasional descriptions of a more factual nature, which occur in some of Caroline's letters, and the argumentation of P.P.'s determined rejection of English and Continental customs, are by contrast sobering elements. Yet the total effect is one of overwritten episodes, the more obvious because of the hackneyed plot-machinery put together by Imlay. With its triggering devices deriving from the scheming of the treacherous rivals, this obtrusive machinery neutralizes what might have been more original and significant contributions: on the one hand, the divorce theme, and on the other the American propaganda.[32]

1. The opening pages, which try to interest the reader in a few of the characters, lead up to a surprising announcement: "The reader must not be astonished, when informed we shall here leave them to their fate, and resume our more immediate story" (*Rosalvo Delmonmort*, p. 25).

2. See p. 5 (a patrol at night), p. 11 (a fight).

3. Another satirical passage concerns a young girl spoiled by novel-reading (p. 94).

4. See the hero's comments on the ladies of London (p. 89), the man in black explaining his choice of a place of exile (p. 20), Ceceline's innocence when Fitzalban woos her (p. 28).

5. One example should suffice: "The tear of sensibility sent from her heart by the direction of virtue's guard, forced its way from her eyes of black, and rolled down her vermil cheek. A symbol of the pearls of artless affection, which surrounded her innocent and spotless mind" (p. 78). See also a picturesque scene (p. 23), the heroine's tenderness (p. 27), and Ceceline's epitaph (p. 63).

6. The attribution to Eliza Pope is suggested by the copyright notice. Nothing seems to be known of the author, whose preface has been mentioned above, p. 18 n.24.

7. Both Clareville and Ormond save the life of their beloved one, both interfere with Monmouth's attempts upon Julietta; Clareville and Rosabella respond in similar fashion to their first sight of the Granville cottage; Julietta and Rosabella are each provided with a blameless adorer and a wicked persecutor lusting after them because of their reputation for beauty; the hunting trip of the Granvilles can be compared to the trips to Cumberland of the Wentworth party; twice abducted, Julietta escapes twice and on both flights runs away from a real villain as well as from a protector mistaken for a villain.

8. Monmouth, who in typical seducer fashion offers Julietta luxury and social dissipations, displays "all that ferocity in his countenance, which marks the Englishman" (p. 62), a piece of prejudice rather out of place in a novel set in thirteenth-century England, and with English heroes as well as English villains.

9. See the tears and "pleasing melancholy" of General Dermot, and the "sensibility" of Rosabella (pp. 173, 86, 95-96).

10. There is a very unprepossessing opening sentence to the novel (pp. 5-6).

11. *The Hapless Orphan*, 1:29.

12. Letters 5-7, 12, 16, 18-19, 21, 41, 43, 55, 69, 77, 120.

13. Eliza is not really invulnerable. Her letter and program of revenge is in Caroline's possession, and given the latter's wealth and her ability to make friends, there is no reason why she should not take action against Eliza.

14. Cowie notes Caroline's reasonable self-interest and independent actions (*Novel*, p. 20). Loshe finds that Caroline has the same practical commonsense

as Richardson's Pamela (*Novel*, p. 17). Calling her a "living creation" (Quinn, *Fiction*, p. 14) seems an exaggerated claim.

15. Her conquests include some Princeton students (1:23), Clarimont (1:28), Evremont, into whose arms she faints when Clarimont shoots himself (1:31), Clark (1:161), Mr. Helen (2:105, 107, 108-9, 166, 178) and his unwelcome rival, Trevers (2:175-76).

16. Caroline herself anticipated (1:38) this criticism, which was made in the *Massachusetts Magazine*, 5(1793):367-68, 431-32. This review, of exceptional length and violence, was perhaps aimed less at the specific book discussed than at the genre of the novel quite generally; its style, incidentally, is no better than that of the poorer fictional productions of the age.

17. "I am destined to the severest trials—continually involving my friends in affliction. The idea saps every promised pleasure; and I find their anticipation a chimera" (2:29).

18. Within a few pages the following reflections occur: "Notwithstanding my wish to submit to the dispensations of Providence...I am frequently ready to relinquish every cherished idea of resignation" and "These events, however, although beyond our investigation, could not have taken place, without divine permission" (1:158, 163-64). Similar conflicts are found in 1:191, and 2:29.

19. Caroline characteristically contradicts herself: "I am unwilling to believe Eliza still intends to pursue me. Her disposition will deprive me of the little happiness allotted to human life" (1:119).

20. Among common plot devices we find the function of the miniature, the irruption of a jealous lover upon an innocent couple, and the meeting of Caroline and Eliza at the theater. The heroine ends up on a dissecting table, but this sensational element loses some of its punch when we hear that Caroline has died the death of the true sentimental heroine, caused by "a broken heart" (2:233). The plot has no organic link with the setting which, though ostensibly American, is only accidentally and outwardly so: there is no localization but a mere shifting from one place name to another, to convey the notion of place.

21. See the portraits of her aunt (1:6-7, 8) and the remarks on the latter's "renewed" marriage (1:9, 209).

22. See letters 50-51 (runaway Mr. Little and the consolable worthy wife he leaves behind); 52-54 (Lee's seduction of Harriet); 66 (Henrietta Careless's love affair, and a passage praising American women, 2:69); 100, 104, 107 (the near-incest of Mrs. Leason and King); 47, 63-65, 88, 90, 102, 111 (the match between Laura and Gibbins, the ambitious young girl and the wealthy old man).

23. The topics touched upon include: civilizing or campaigning against the Indians; death, marriage, and especially education. Eliza has been spoiled (1:29), and so have Caroline's cousins (1:14, 16) and Laura; the latter read novels instead of history (1:56-57). Caroline states her ideas of female education only by condemning the views of her aunt, who is convinced that women should be content with the education they have had so far; as long as they are good housekeepers and charming hostesses, "she cannot imagine what business women have with books, unless it is now and then an entertaining novel" (1:45).

24. Cf. Caroline's feelings for Evremont (1:69). Other mannerisms of genteel sentimentality occur, e.g., in 1:122; 2:10, 18, 169.

25. "Mr. Helen has politely called upon me. He increases upon an ac-

quaintance. I dare not say half I really think, of this charming young man. He insensibly engages the heart. Be under no apprehensions respecting Captain Evremont: My affections are not diminished for him" (2:107).

26. See *DAB* 9:461-62; *DNB* 10:417-18; Ralph L. Rusk, "The Adventures of Gilbert Imlay," *Indiana University Studies* 10(March, 1923):1-26; Edith Franklin Wyatt, "The First American Novel," *Atlantic Monthly* 144(October, 1929): 466-75; Oliver Farrar Emerson, "Notes on Gilbert Imlay," *PMLA* 39(June, 1924):406-39; Robert R. Hare, "The Base Indian: A Vindication of the Rights of Mary Wollstonecraft" (Master's thesis, University of Delaware, 1957). Hare edited *The Emigrants* for Scholars' Facsimiles and Reprints from the Dublin edition (1794); my references are to the three-volume London edition of 1793. Hare attributes the novel to the joint authorship of Imlay and Mary Wollstonecraft, considers the latter to have been the really creative partner, and assumes that she could have written *A Topographical Description* too, which also bears Imlay's name on its title page. Considering the close association of Mary Wollstonecraft and Imlay, and the introduction of the divorce issue in *The Emigrants,* the influence of Mary Wollstonecraft can hardly be disputed; but a literary collaboration must remain a mere conjecture. The promotional writing included in the *Description* and partly repeated in *The Emigrants* might easily have been gathered by Imlay when he was trying to secure an immediate source of income in London, and a future one as well, by publicizing the Western lands. The main arguments against Mary Wollstonecraft's active share in the writing of *The Emigrants* are two: for one thing there is too much to distract from the purpose element of the novel, for another the writing is particularly bad.

27. In fact, P.P. does not answer Caroline's main point about the honesty and purity of his supposedly chivalric motives; he bases his entire defensive argument, as far as it applies to his particular situation—much of his letter is of a general character—upon the acknowledged fact of mutual attraction, and concludes: "What, shall two beings who have justly inspired a confidence in each other, who feel an affinity of sentiment, and who perceive that their happiness or misery are so materially connected, that to separate them would prove fatal to both, not to consider themselves superior to prejudices which are founded in error, and which would lead them to ridiculously sacrifice a real and substantial, for an imaginary good; and when too no person can be injured by the unity?" (2:49)

28. See the Preface. Another novel by an American living in London combines the novel of purpose and the love story: Edward Bancroft's *The History of Charles Wentworth* (1770). Bancroft spent only a few years of his childhood in America.

29. One might presumably have said of Imlay what was written about Thomas Cooper: "Cooper wrote in order to sell the better the lands, he and Priestley jun. had purchased..." (penciled note in Cooper's *Some Information Respecting America* [London, 1794], Widener Library, Harvard University).

30. The early George was different: "George...had by this time roused himself from his pillow, and like a torpid beast which takes shelter in some cavern during the inclement season of the year, insensible to every thing passing, which when the genial spring has again warmed into life the vegetable world, saunters out and eagerly devours whatever falls in his way; so came the drone from his lethargic bed" (1:28); the style of this passage is representative, but its intentional humor is not.

31. Caroline's captivity, letters 56-59. Arl—ton is given an opportunity to

[221]

distinguish himself in the rescue of the girl; see especially his fight with two Indians (3:33).

32. For examples of promotional writing, see, e.g., 1:92, 103, and letter 68. One reader saw Crèvecoeur and Imlay as similar writers of "romantic works" who "would seduce us into a belief that innocence, peace and freedom had deserted the rest of the world for Martha's Vineyard and the banks of the Ohio." (Quoted in H. N. Fairchild, *The Noble Savage* [Columbia University Press, 1928], p. 269; there is also a suggestion (p. 241) that *Don Juan* [Canto VIII] has a reference to Daniel Boone possibly derived from *A Topographical Description*.)

Chapter Nine

A RIVAL PASSION

W HETHER using force or ruse to break the stubborn faithfulness of a pair of lovers, the parents and rivals of fiction invariably count on the help of time. Once an initial wedge has been driven in, they seem to assume that the couple may be expected to grow further apart, to become susceptible to new interests, and possibly to submit to the alliance they first resisted. A fault can perhaps be seized upon and turned into a factor of estrangement between the lovers: a case in point is the potential distrust and jealousy of many heroes and heroines, Rebecca Rush's Emily and Kelroy, Cooper's Emily, Evremont in *The Hapless Orphan,* Imlay's Arl—ton. There is in the severity and cunning of baffled authority or thwarted love some residual justification which the reader, as the author must be aware, is willing to make allowance for. This is not the case when sheer envy or malice causes the separation of the lovers: writer and reader must in such cases share the same detestation of the evildoers and think them capable of any crime. These sinister mischief-makers of fiction frequently appeal to the passion for gambling to rival the love and virtue which they resent. Hardly less a threat to domestic happiness than seduction, gambling is often paired with it in fiction, as a sort of personal union in the character of the villain.[1] Three specimens of "gambling fiction" may here be examined. They have many features in common, though they vary in their emphasis on the addiction to gambling, the person of the gambler, or that of the unscrupulous instigator who first led him astray.

The extant second edition of *The Gambler, or Memoirs of a British Officer* (1802), which was published in Washington, might be taken for a reprint from an original English edition were it not for its introduction. In these opening pages the narrator speaks in his own voice, implicitly praising the true hospitality of the democratic Americans, who judge a visitor on the strength of his personal merits and not, as the British are charged with doing, by his letters of introduction. He mentions that England has a strikingly large number of prisons and derives from this observation an unflattering estimate of the state of English society. There follow two confessions, gathered in the King's Bench prison, from a gambler and a "prodigal." The former relates with self-pitying pathos the steps of his fall, the ultimate cause of which, according to him, was the over-indulgence of his mother and the servants in charge of his education. There is little to interest us, with or without such a palliating circumstance, in this character who relapses again and again into ruinous gambling. Although never losing his sense of guilt and remorse, he is unable to change his conduct; and in his confession story he can only sentimentalize, first over his brokenhearted mother and sister, and finally over his wife and children starving in prison with him. A touch of originality, and a welcome relief from this pervasive self-pity, occurs in the interpolated story "The Prodigal"[2] in the person of the hero-victim's guardian. He is an oddity full of contradictions, who shows little leniency even when his spendthrift ward promises to reform: "Have heard of your distresses—must say you deserve it.—A gaol is the proper reward of extravagance.—Believe you are a great scoundrel. . . ." (p. 67).[3] But though the guardian's abruptness is refreshing, there is no indication that he is aware of his share of responsibility for his ward's excesses, by having kept him in the dark concerning his expectations. Possibly, though, the bequest of his fortune to the prodigal and his wife is a gesture of atonement for his former sins of omission.

There are distinct parallels between *The Gambler* and *St. Hubert; or, Mistaken Friendship* (1800). St. Hubert, too, is spoiled by his mother and thus fails to develop at an early age the strength to withstand temptation; he temporarily reforms, but backslides under the auspices of a lady of perfectly good reputation. St. Hubert is as weak as the Gambler; his weakness causes his ruin, which involves those he loves best and whose trust he should be the last to betray. His wife is endowed with the necessary amount of long-suffering patience but cannot help him. Both *The Gambler* and *St. Hubert* are tales of confession and repentance told shortly before the death of their confessors. St. Hubert's experiences, which include the satisfaction of penance, are narrated in a relatively unencumbered style; in this the tale is superior to *The Gambler.* A further quality is to be found in the difference between the hero and other gamblers. St. Hubert's weakness is differentiated into various aspects, one of which is his love of gambling and another his vanity. The latter attribute is exemplified at the same time as we are reminded of the hero's genuine goodness: he feels he cannot openly approve of benevolence because to do so would expose him to his companions' ridicule. Trying to keep pace with his associates' ways leads him into matching Delaserre's costly sprees; he then succumbs easily to the corrupt Delaserre's efforts to drag him down to his own level of shame and dishonesty and progresses further to adultery, bankruptcy, and the desertion of his wife and child.

Whereas the Gambler drifts into error by his own self-indulgence, it takes a malicious influence to lead St. Hubert astray. "Mistaken friendship" similarly causes Leander's downfall in *The Gamesters; or, Ruins of Innocence* (1805), by Caroline Matilda Warren (ca.1787-1844).[4] This novel uses an American setting, unlike the two other tales, and stresses its authenticity: the title page announces, "An original novel, founded in truth." The story is to be a warning, a purpose reiterated in its concluding paragraph. This assertion was presumably indispensable because in *The Gamesters* the element of suicide is dealt with in a way that could appear theologically and morally equivocal. But Miss Warren's villains are quite unambiguous, and by that standard her intent must have been clear. There is Ebbert, really a subordinate troublemaker designed to serve some mastermind's purpose, such as the humiliation of Williamson by means of the seduction of his daughter Celestia[5] or the undermining of Leander's reputation and security. The chief villain, Edward Somerton, is driven to harm Leander very much as Delaserre corrupts St. Hubert, out of envy and a sense of inferiority. But he is given much greater scope than Delaserre to act upon his fiendish conceptions.[6] Under a hypocritical mask of friendship he tests

Leander's steady virtue until he manages to make him "taste" gambling; in this he succeeds only in the last third of the novel when he tempts Leander rather implausibly under a camouflage of crudely sophistical arguments (chap. 22).[7] The hero's yielding ominously suggests the dissolution of the moral order that is soon to become manifest: "The fatal blow was struck. The foundations of his virtue were sapped, and one after another they must moulder away, till the fair fabric of innocence totter on the brink of destruction" (p. 191). Somerton thereafter can devote all his energies to seducing Eliza, while Leander steeply descends into a constant repudiation of all the ways and values he has so far adhered to.

For unlike the Gambler and St. Hubert, Leander starts out under propitious auspices and with all the makings of incorruptible solidity.[8] He has excellent parents; he returns from college with an outstanding record and "uncorrupted in his morals" (p. 3).[9] Yet when tempted, Leander, too, falls, and this just after he has been rehabilitated after a merely supposed offense. As he lives up to the forebodings of our sententious author (p. 250), sinking past hope once his weakness has been made manifest, he illustrates the typical gambler's progress,[10] which resembles the fate of the victim of seduction: if their apparent invulnerability can be violated, they are caught in a sequel of misdeeds, involving also those intimately connected with them. The act of suicide epitomizes the desperateness of their state; Eliza is probably saved from killing herself, as Leander and the seduced Celestia do, only because she goes mad: "Nature struggled, reason tottered, and could not maintain her dominion, and Eliza is a maniac" (p. 288). Both Celestia and Leander succumb to malicious betrayers. But whereas the girl's only crime before her suicide consists in passively yielding to her love, Leander accumulates acts of weakness and is crudely inconsiderate of his family: he obviously attempts to shift on to others the responsibility for his wrongdoings, once even contemplating murder (p. 280). Yet for Leander no less than for Celestia (whose very name suggests salvation), Miss Warren equally claimed God's mercy. The late eighteenth-century clash between orthodox beliefs within the strict Calvinist tradition and liberal views is reflected in the opinions of the author and her critics.[11] Leander benefits from his reliance on a remnant of faith (pp. 277, 294, 297); and, being a victim, he is contrasted with the conventional "pure" villain, one of whose distinctive marks is his rejection of any transcendent belief.[12] The virtuous characters instinctively perceive the divine creative power in the beauty of the creation (p. 24). They are sensitive to religious feelings, which is a specific manifestation of their pure and spontaneous emotional responses; Somerton and Ebbert, for example, have deliberately dulled themselves to displays of genuine feeling. There is a high emotional charge in many passages of grief and joy in Miss Warren's novel. An early instance of it, emphasized by the diction adopted, occurs in connection with the death of Leander's mother:

> The husband of her affection stood in the bending attitude of affectionate solicitude, watching her languid features, her hand clasped affectionately in both of his. He pressed it to his lip; a tear fell on it. Precious drop! it flowed from the chrystal fount of sensibility! Leander gazed in silent grief on her pallid countenance; and his beautifully expressive eyes shone with added lustre through the tears that suffused them. (p. 4)

The comments on seduction (p. 244), as well as the dark predictions about Leander's inevitable doom, furnish other opportunities for sentimental dramatizing. Scenes of love are enhanced by settings with a reflecting mood (pp. 9-10), also serviceable in order to give impressions of "pleasing melancholy" (p. 24).

The entirely conventional manner goes hand in hand with the use of familiar plot devices and characters. There is, for instance, the threadbare plan for a "sham marriage, sham certificate, sham clergyman" (p. 145), whose intended victim conveniently falls into a swoon when she discovers with whom she is running away from home. The pedant Christopher Dilemma appears borrowed from the stage; so does the figure of a maid who describes her meeting with Dilemma and whose speech is meant to indicate ignorance, superstition, and a lack of discrimination between true and affected feelings (p. 117). Comic relief is achieved by means of a type-character of a related sort: Tom

Tarpaulin, whose figurative language is inspired by his calling (p. 159).[13] As Miss Warren's style is imitative, it is perhaps not inappropriate that her characters should be conscious of literary parallels.[14] The sixteen lines which Leander carves, with no apparent trouble, into the bark of a tree, are painfully artificial, in the manner of much minor versifying of the age (p. 71); clichés and well-worn figures of speech abound.[15] So do emphatically expressed states of mind, like Williamson's when he meets Celestia's seducer (p. 240), and self-consciously reticent phrasings, as when Somerton seduces Eliza: "Suffice it to say, the setting sun threw his last rays on the tops of the trees; they shone not on the *virtuous* Eliza" (p. 268).[16] In another sense Miss Warren was explicit when she had better have left certain things unsaid. Thus her early sketch of Somerton's character informs the reader so fully that it nearly robs the plot of any possibility of suspense.

The lack of suspense, however, derives from another flaw of *The Gamesters,* a flaw connected with the didactic zeal of Miss Warren and similar writers and understandably alarming to those who objected to the whole genre of the novel. Amelia, the perfect heroine, has hardly been mentioned in this discussion of Miss Warren's novel. This is no coincidence: it reflects the ineffectual nature of the "good" characters which is felt throughout the book. The plotters' schemes, too early outlined, are assured of a maximum of effectiveness. Celestia, Leander, Eliza must fall, they are so easily isolated from their friends by their antagonists. In the face of such functional neutralizing of the positive forces for the sake of the explicitness of the story and its moral, the apology for suicide is not so much irreverent as distressingly irrelevant; and the reader may well wonder who in such a world is likely to escape its temptations. Nor are we reassured by the reward granted to Amelia's patience[17] or the presumably promising match between Harriot and Lorenzo, since in the world which these survivors inhabit, consistency is apparently to be found only among the villains. None of Miss Warren's methods of elaboration and relief, whether structural,[18] topical,[19] or stylistic,[20] could compensate for the weaknesses of a work of fiction established on such a basis.[21]

A RIVAL PASSION

1. The villain is moreover often addicted to drinking, a failing that was to become a staple topic of fiction later, in the temperance novel.

2. "The Prodigal" occupies pp. 36-74 in the 94-page book.

3. Cf. the guardian's refusal to accept his ward's thanks (p. 70).

4. Allibone has two relevant entries: it lists under Warren not the original Boston edition of *The Gamesters* (here referred to) but an 1806 London edition entitled *Conrade, or The Gamesters* (3:2587), and under Miss Warren's married name, Thayer, her later tract *Religion recommended to Youth* (3:2382).

5. Having seduced Celestia, Ebbert writes her a cynical parting letter: "I shall always remember Celestia with pleasure, but the lady with whom I would unite my future destiny, must possess unconquerable virtue" (p. 80).

6. We are told that "his heart delighted in the ruins of innocence" (p. 16); his envious feelings are "similar to those of the Prince of Pandemonium, when he beheld the first created pair, in the garden of Eden" (p. 99). Cf. Ebbert's admiration of Somerton's remorselessness (p. 131).

7. Somerton is as clumsy in his first attempt to poison Leander's sense of Amelia's purity (chap. 5).

8. The reviewer of the *Boston Magazine* (no. 7 [Dec. 7, 1805], p. 26), thought it highly improbable that the almost perfect Leander could have been corrupted by Somerton.

9. Doubts are voiced in *The Art of Courting, St. Hubert, Glencarn,* and *The Champions of Freedom* about the influence of university contacts on the individual student's moral character.

10. A career similar to Leander's was outlined by Eliphalet Nott: "He commences with play; but it is only for amusement. Next he hazards a trifle to give interest, and is surprized when he finds himself a gainer by the hazard. He then ventures, not without misgivings, on a deeper stake. That stake he loses. The loss and the guilt oppress him. He drinks to revive his spirits. His spirits revived, he stakes to retrieve his fortune. Again, he is unsuccessful, and again his spirits flag, and again the inebriating cup revives them. Ere he is aware of it, he has become a drunkard, he has become a bankrupt. Resource fails him. His fortune is gone; his character is gone; his tenderness of conscience is gone. God has withdrawn his spirit from him. The demon of despair takes possession of his bosom; reason deserts him. He becomes a maniac; the pistol or the poignard close the scene, and with a shriek he plunges, unwept and forgotten, into hell" (*The Addresses delivered...at the Anniversary Commencements in Union College,* pp. 193-94).

11. Having stressed that according to the Bible Leander must be damned, Miss Warren added, "Yet we are assured, that the Author of our existence is 'able to save, even to the uttermost' " (p. 298). The *Monthly Register* credited Miss Warren with good intentions but held her novel to be a plain apology of suicide (Vol. 1, ii, no. 7 [1806]: 190-201). The *Boston Magazine* (no. 8 [Dec. 14, 1805]:30) suggested the book might serve as a deterrent by arousing "fears of being treated as a suicide."

12. "There is no future world! and death—is an *eternal sleep*" (p. 131, Ebbert to Somerton).

13. There are similar sailors in *Margaretta, The Asylum, Adelaide,* and, of course, *The Pathfinder.*

14. See the references to Mackenzie (pp. 54-55), and the stage heroine who reminds Leander of his beloved Amelia (chap. 28).

15. A sonnet of Leander is given on pp. 177-78. Within a few lines Leander says, "I was basking in the sunshine of bliss, and sipped the sweet nectar of love," and "All around me was one gilded scene of innocent enjoyment" (p. 294). Another typical cliché is "to barb the arrows of affliction" (p. 166).

16. See also p. 284, and the reference to the seduction of Celestia (p. 78).

17. What are we to make of the possibly dubious source of the money left to provide for the little Alonzo?

18. The Williamson story (chaps. 8, 10, 29) was praised in the *Boston Magazine* (Dec. 7, 1805, p. 26). Chapter 22 is a chapter of climaxes: the moving visit to the house of Leander's father, the announcement that he is to be his own master, Somerton's appearance and his success in paving the way for Leander's first visit to a gaming house. Chapters 25 and 26 are strongly contrasted: the peaceful evening walk is followed by Leander's first taste of gambling.

19. See the remarks on education (pp. 3, 29, 166, 304); writing as a profession (p. 92); partisan newspaper editing (p. 93); party strife (chap. 9).

20. Her use of the comic, the sentimental, and the melodramatic mood and manner has been variously illustrated in the preceding pages.

21. The *Monthly Anthology* described *The Gamesters* as the "most puny" among the "ephemerae" of fictional writing and wondered at its success (2[December, 1805]:669-70); if the book was really "run after" with "avidity," one is tempted to suppose that it received some publicity independent of its literary merit. The *Boston Magazine* (December 14, 1805, p. 30) raised objections against Miss Warren's style, but was inclined to leniency, on the grounds of the author's youth and good intentions. To Quinn, *Fiction,* the novel represents a climax of absurdity (p. 22). For its topic, cf. also Parson Weems's pamphlet, *God's Revenge Against Gambling,* with its suggestive title page.

Chapter Ten

OVERWHELMING ODDS

I N NOVELS like *The Gamesters* the good characters prove disturbingly powerless against the influences that threaten them, and the forces of darkness correspondingly tend to become absolute. These derive not from one isolated impulse in an individual but from his or her general predisposition to evil, something quite beyond the understanding of the figures that stand for the Christian and humanist beliefs and that are of a trustful, unsuspecting nature. This confidence is an essential attribute of the heroines in another group of novels: girls who suddenly discover that there is no stable balance of good and evil in the world. On the contrary, they feel, it is ruled arbitrarily by the evil-minded, and they are thus surrounded by hostility, which ranges from monstrously outspoken destructiveness to petty and sly scheming.

The most conspicuous qualities of the heroine of *Monima; or, The Beggar Girl* (1802), by Mrs. Martha Read, are her filial devotion, her willingness to do all the honest work necessary to support herself and her father, and her capacity for gratitude in a world prejudiced against poverty. Just as obviously, Monima is quite unable to guess how far her enemies will go in persecuting her.[1] Even after she has realized that she is being victimized, she fails to acquire prudence in dealing with new acquaintances who are potentially as dangerous to her as Madame Sonnetton[2] or Pierre de Noix. These two she comes to consider the personification of a jealousy and lust aimed at her exclusively, as it were; on the other hand, Sonnetton's acts of charity seem impersonal to her, the manifestations of Christian love and no more. Sonnetton does indeed for a long time act in such a spirit of benevolence (chaps. 4, 9, 24, 26), thinking himself guided by pity, not love. In the eyes of de Noix this is downright hypocrisy,[3] but the world at large, too, is likely to view suspiciously the interest of a married man in one particular unprotected girl.

The concentration of Madame Sonnetton's and de Noix's hatred and lust on Monima endows their feelings with a virulence for which temperate compassion is no more a match than Monima's meekness and ingenuousness or Fontanbleu's debility. What preserves a Monima from destruction is the steadfastness of her moral convictions. Monima develops a long-suffering resilience in the face of an antagonism which, by contrast, is constantly driven to renew itself. If Madame Sonnetton's jealousy and its kindred ally, the greed of de Noix, do not quite burn themselves out, they sap the restraints of self-discipline and elementary caution that control them. The villains cause their own defeat by overreaching themselves. Thus Madame Sonnetton, in the paroxysm of her fury at her husband and Monima, blurts out the truth about Monima's trials and even the fact that she has been unfaithful to her husband (chap. 29). And de Noix taunts the heroine, anticipating his rape of her, even though she is armed and capable of defending herself; later he overrates the power his bribe holds over the witness he is using against Fontanbleu (chaps. 34-35).

Monima within a few months suffers enough through the agency of her two enemies to last her a long time.[4] In addition to her individual trials she is of course under a continual stress as soon as she becomes aware of the implacability of her persecutors. There is no one to help her or sympathize with her; this is brought home to the reader from the very first by the fact that it is she who supports her father, and not the other way round. She falls in love with Sonnetton, but the unlikelihood that her love may be fulfilled is only another burden for her to bear. She apparently does not abandon all hope in this respect, however: after Madame Sonnetton's death she refuses to marry Greenaway (chap. 34). Eventually Sonnetton turns up in time to save her from a jail sentence, and they marry: Monima is rewarded. This conclusion, which vindicates disinterested love and irrepressible truth, also emphasizes social values, in particular the institution of the family. Sonnetton and Monima in the end belong to a social unit which also includes Monima's father and her two brothers, lately restored to them. Fontanbleu is more than a father-in-law to Sonnetton: it was his support that earlier helped the young man through a period of dejection (chap. 23). Characters like Madame Sonnetton and de Noix, on the contrary, destroy the social fabric, and the family above all. Madame Sonnetton, whose own upbringing was inadequate (p. 213),[5] perverts conjugal love into jealousy and adultery. De Noix's evil nature is a threat to the whole of the social and moral order. He was directly responsible for the deaths of Julia and Ferdinand in France (chaps. 22, 23); the circumstances of his duel with the latter secured a semblance of honor to his character, however. In America he must at length again face a tribunal; and this time, though he is not prosecuted any further, the verdict against him is plain.[6] He is unmasked as ruthlessly selfish, a relentless plotter against others, and constantly driven by malice and greed.

Yet for all his consistency and resourcefulness, he is not in the least a remarkable villain, such as Brockden Brown's Ormond or Welbeck. Neither could Monima compete with Brown's Constantia: a very mediocre creation, she has no initiative of her own and is therefore doomed to passiveness or mere reaction against villains and circumstances. The reference to Brown is suggested by more than these comparisons. Monima and Fontanbleu together may well owe some of their features to Constantia and Dudley. One is also tempted to trace the plague background to *Ormond* rather than to the more realistic scenes of the epidemic in *Arthur Mervyn* because it serves in the former novel much as in *Monima,* as one of a number of adverse factors that render the heroine's life more insecure.[7] The parallel must not be pursued too far. For all their attributes of the extraordinary, Brown's novels remain fundamentally realistic. But what passes for realism in *Monima* is a technique of exaggeration of a sentimentally functional sort.[8] It must emphasize various melodramatic conflicts: between the isolated conscience and integrity of Monima and Sonnetton and the rather callous expediency which is characteristic of their surroundings; between the courageous individual and the inert mass of his or her fellow beings; between the victim of unthinking prejudice and the shallow adherents to preconceived opinions. Mrs. Read was probably trying to sound lifelike; this might at any rate be concluded from her criticism of current fashions among writers and readers (chap. 26, especially pp. 252-59). She drifted nonetheless into the use of the standard ingredients of contemporary fiction, blending plot elements and introducing characters and states of mind that must have sounded all too familiar to some readers, though many others no doubt welcomed the familiar.[9] This also applies to the characteristic note of pathos sounded in the opening lines: " 'This is a bleak morning,' said Monima's father, as he was covering his silver locks with his white cap; 'how excessively the storm rages. Are you entirely out of work Nima?' 'Yes father.' 'And Madame Sontine cannot supply you with any?' 'No!' 'And that,'—said he, with a piteous look toward heaven, 'is our last morsel!—what Nima is to become of us?' " (p. 13).[10]

We are spared such insistent emotionalism in the anonymous novel in letters entitled *Margaretta; or, the Intricacies of the Heart* (1807), although its heroine undergoes as many hardships as Monima with as little possibility to radically improve her lot. It cultivates variety more vigorously than *Monima*. This is evident already in the change between three main settings—the United States, San Domingo, and England—and also in the relative importance of plots involving the generation of Margaretta's parents.[11] Moreover, the novel, in the beginning and again toward the end, moves more lightly than Mrs. Read's because of its author's use of the epistolary form, with short letters written by a variety of correspondents. These letter-writers are characterized with a somewhat clearer differentiating intent than Mrs. Read's figures; and at first the letters do indicate by their manner who is wielding the pen, though on the whole the circumstances in which new characters are introduced tell us more about them than genuine characterization through their action and style.

Margaretta's first real hour of peril is her meeting with Custon, a selfish, devious schemer then (p. 108) and later. He is moved afterward chiefly by his desire to punish Margaretta for not being swept off her feet at first sight of him. She prefers Will de Burling instead, and Custon wishes to cause trouble for him, too, since de Burling is obviously disinclined to share the girl with him.[12] Custon is instrumental in informing Arabella of de Burling's breach of faith, and he later makes sure that the wounds to her pride and vanity do not heal. Arabella's weaknesses respond to his treatment (p. 107),[13] and so does the naïveté of Margaretta. She mechanically believes from the very first that de Burling must be a personification of the gentleman wolfishly courting a lower-class girl. Vernon, a conquest of hers, is later to fall as easily for the suggestion that Margaretta is no better than she should be; and de Burling himself is susceptible to rumors of the same sort, spread by Custon, Arabella, or someone like them. Since the victimized characters thus contribute themselves to being kept in a state of wretchedness, there is no need in *Margaretta* for such spectacular and unmitigated evildoing as in *Monima*. A varied mixture of features both commendable and unwholesome determines the behavior of Margaretta's supporters. Captain Waller interprets the fact that the girl would not willingly marry him as a decree of Providence; his guilty conscience suggests to him that he must yet atone for his assistance in separating Lady Matilda from Warren, and he vows to become Margaretta's watchful protector. This at the same time makes him the friend and adviser of de Burling. As for the latter, his lapse into distrust—that is, into believing that Margaretta is living in sin with Montanan—must be accompanied by the bitter reflection that he had earlier himself contemplated making the girl his mistress and then rejected the idea for the sake of her love.[14]

De Burling and Margaretta share the responsibility for at least some of the obstacles that rise in the path of their love, but in other respects the girl is to be classed among the unfortunate beings who are at the mercy of circumstances quite dissociated from their disposition and will. The chain of events which have led from the separation of Lady Matilda and Warren to that of Lady Matilda and Margaretta, then to Lady Matilda's second marriage, and on to the meeting and mutual attraction of Warren and the heroine[15] is of course beyond the heroine's control. She is fortune's football, depending entirely on chance to achieve happiness in this world; perhaps the more so as there is definitely a social as well as a moral clause to the definition of happiness implied in the ending of the book. Montanan is turned into Lord Warren, and his daughter's blood is thus ennobled, at about the same time as her love finds fulfillment: here is a confirmation of the social or cultural prejudice referred to by Miss Stewart in her first letter, where Margaretta's refusal to marry Nelson, a young farmer, is connected with the observation that she is "apparently of superior intelligence to the common peasants of her class" (p. 2).[16] The structure of society and the patterns of behavior attaching to its layers (p. 207) are plainly as little to be influenced by the heroine's struggles as the fortuitous operations of fate. When Margaretta is left to the enjoyment of both her true lover's restored faith in her and her newly discovered aristocratic[17] parents and personal status, the reader can only feel that she has been providentially rewarded for her constancy, even though it is a constancy rather too passive and appropriately illustrated by the girl's disposition to swoon at critical moments.

Very much an average production, *Margaretta* offers its readers many varieties of stilted diction.[18] It has additional defects, such as the use of a peculiarly mixed imagery[19] and a tendency to sermonize.[20] It is a pity that the author stopped after the first letters to do much in the way of distinctive individual styles; though this might have produced no more original results than stock speeches such as Waller's sailor idiom (p. 87), it would still have been an improvement over the monotony of Margaretta's manner, which is dominant over long stretches of the narrative (letters 38-59). That something might have been made out of the material of the different correspondents is indicated in the first three letters, in which the fellow travelers forced to stop at E—n, each give their impressions of Margaretta.[21]

Yet there is a relative variety of speakers and writers in the whole of the novel. More importantly perhaps, the preference shown throughout for direct rather than reported speech saves this novel from the tedious uniformity which mars the eleven hundred pages of narrative in *Constantia Neville; or, The West Indian* (1800), by Helena Wells.[22] Its preface states its didactic aim, and later we read that it is intended to expound the merits of "a dutiful, affectionate daughter, a sincere friend, and a professor of the religion of her ancestors" (1:172). These qualities are put to the test in circumstances that really owe nothing to the novel of the supernatural scorned by Miss Wells (1:171); but so mediocre was her talent that the reader soon begins to long even for the dubious entertainment and variety provided by the more extravagant features of other contemporary novels. To prove her heroine's endurance, Miss Wells required three volumes of struggles, but at the end of the second, when there seem to be no valid objections left to a match between Constantia and Marmaduke, their happiness is gratuitously delayed. The plottings of a Madame Sonnetton, or the repercussions (in *Margaretta*) of a former generation's errors, are implausible and farfetched enough; but at any rate, once introduced, they do seriously endanger the heroines, whose occasional discouragement is understandable. Now, Constantia Neville is a decidedly independent and plucky girl when compared with many other heroines; it therefore seems difficult to believe that she is really unable to disregard malicious gossip (chap. 25). Rochford alone is more immediately threatening;[23] yet even his menace remains peripheral, as distant as Montagu's career of dissipation. Such deficiencies are inevitable in fiction that depends almost exclusively on the workings of a plot dissociated from the characters. In addition the dramatic nature of the introductory pages, which tell the story of Constantia's parents and the Haymans, leads the reader to expect adventures as swift and varied for the heroine; but they are not and have the effect of an anticlimax. There is hardly the material here for situations in which Constantia might be reduced to helplessness by the forces opposing her: she is not really challenged. Yet Miss Wells proceeded to round off her narrative only after having "rewarded" her heroine "for all her sufferings" (3:349). The settling of accounts with the remaining characters, some twenty-five of them, is briskly attended to in the final fifteen pages. There is here and there a touch of satire, the only form of humor in *Constantia Neville*. Generally, and more especially with respect to her heroine, Miss Wells struck a note of self-righteousness and sententiousness, which drearily combines with the gloomy tints of Constantia's imagination and apparently affects the very style of the novel.[24]

Like Margaretta and other heroines, Constantia is never quite without a friend or a possible place where to weather out a storm; this only makes the seemingly invincible hostility which she experiences the more exasperating. In *Moreland Vale; or the Fair Fugitive* (1801),[25] too, the villains' sway is long unbroken, even though they are suspected of various wrongs. The main plot is laid in the present when their luck begins to turn: a weak spot in their defenses is detected and made use of, another move of theirs quickly countered,[26] and soon the wicked stepmother and her partner in crime run away, only to be promptly caught up with by providential justice: "They had rushed unprepared on their fate—for they had not been at sea but a few days, when they were overtaken by a violent storm—the ship foundered, and every soul on board was lost" (p. 135). All the mischief done the passive heroine, whose single action consists in flight, turns into benefits. The repentant tool of fraud is given a chance to reform; the lover exiled from the country returns a wealthy man and, having already been instrumental in his uncle's atonement for an earlier error, promotes a match between two discarded lovers before being married to his true love.

This complex case of rights redressed[27] is, to generalize, the reflected picture of the villains' power over their victims. Whereas the latter depend on, and wait for, the assistance of Providence, the former are favored by an active singleness of purpose, gaining strength from the reserve energy of their comprehensive wickedness. They easily outwit their trusting, liberal-minded, improvising opponents. Furthermore, the virtuous characters are by no means perfect; they are weakened by entirely normal human faults. Until the villains overreach themselves and the slow machinery of rehabilitation and retribution is set in motion, the reader must therefore witness a near-frustrating process of unlawful triumphs over helpless innocence.[28]

1. In *The Sentimental Novel,* Herbert Ross Brown offered a summary of *Monima* because "it affords a fair sample of the soul-wringing sufferings to which uncomplaining virtue was often subjected" (p. 172).

2. The name is here uniformly spelled in its Americanized form, Sonnetton, and not in its original French form, Sontine.

3. "...He was bent on revenge against Sonnetton, whom he considered as a fawning hypocrite, in his asseverations of friendship and pity to the beggar.

He judged of others by himself, and hence he concluded, that she was an object of illicit love to him..." (p. 324). For de Noix's technique of insinuation and his "fiend-like purposes," see also p. 266. All references are to the second edition of *Monima* (New York, 1803), which appears to have been a reissue of the first.

4. The more spectacular among her vicissitudes are a stay in a workhouse (chap. 3), weeks of confinement in a lonely country house, ending in near-starvation (chaps. 5-9), some days in a lunatic asylum (chap. 27), and of course her various clashes with de Noix (especially chaps. 32 and 34). A heroine who undergoes a persecution equally unreasonable is Louise Passementier, an orphan girl who eventually marries her protector, too ("The New Pygmalion," *A Collection of Moral and Entertaining Stories*, pp. 35-62).

5. Her husband has a poor opinion of her (p. 42); she is shown in her tantrums: "Raving and frantic with the excess of jealousy, Madame Sontine roved, and roared about the kitchen like a lion" (p. 43).

6. It means the end of his self-assurance and criminal career: "...When his eye caught Sonnetton's, a cannon-ball to his heart, could not have carried more horror with it" (p. 456).

7. There are also instances of stylistic affinity which would seem to point to Brown as a model for Mrs. Read, e.g.: "...It was obvious that some unhappy victims were groaning under the pressure of her direful revenge. In how far they might have made themselves guilty of faults or crimes that could have merited it, was to be decided by personal enquiry" (p. 67).

8. Considering the general character and tone of *Monima*, another possible influence suggests itself, that of Mrs. Sarah Wood. The *American Review and Literary Journal* (2, no. 2[1802]:164-66), criticized the implausibility of the plot and the unconvincing characterization, as well as the affected style of *Monima*, but offered guarded praise in calling the author "a lady of delicacy and sensibility" whose "sentimental observations do no discredit to her heart or understanding" (p. 166).

9. See, e.g., the picture of Monima waiting for an interview with Mme Sonnetton (p. 29); a portrait of Sonnetton, the "youthful sentimentalist" (p. 209); the happy family ending (p. 456); or the following evocation: "...The moon arose from her watery horizon.—To a soul of sensibility, it is ever an interesting sight, and seldom fails of creating sublime sensations; but on the wide-extended prospect of the ocean, nothing can be imagined more magnificent" (p. 209).

10. There is a similar beginning to Mrs. Rowson's *The Fille de Chambre*. For other pathetic passages and expressions, see pp. 14 (Monima wandering through the streets), 80 and 414 (the girl and her father making their escape), 420-21 (the heroine's illness).

11. Their elements include the separation of lovers by force, a case of mistaken identities after a secret exchange of babies, a number of aliases, an instance of bigamy unknowingly committed, and one case of near-incest. References are to the first edition of *Margaretta*.

12. Custon himself intends to lodge Margaretta in a brothel and proposes to his friend Rutter to introduce her to him: "...Should she chance to please your fancy, you may rely on the ready services, of your devoted, Archibald Custon" (p. 70).

13. A lengthy discussion of passions and reason (p. 418) traces the source of all anguish to Arabella's failure to study "the intricacies of her heart" and place her passions under the control of reason.

14. De Burling's change of heart (letters 15, 24, 31, 95, 104) in its first stages resembles that of Harrington, in *The Power of Sympathy*. Still fluctuating in these early statements, his willingness to sacrifice his happiness is later firm: "...From my still dear Margaretta, I had a proof, an exquisite testimony of a remaining tenderness; and yet, I had resolution enough, because my poverty came in competition with my love, to evince by firm intention of quitting England, and leaving Lord Orman in possession of a prize I so long and so vainly sought" (p. 395).

15. It is mutual with a difference, though, as Margaretta's comment shows: "I was in the protection of a stranger, who with all the honor so nobly conspicuous in his character, might, by the influence of passion, become my greatest persecuter" (p. 210).

16. Cf. Margaretta's remark: "I begin to think that I was not destined by nature for an humble cottage" (p. 80). Yet she still feels that she must be doubly watchful because her suitor is a gentleman, socially above her and therefore privileged (pp. 29-30, 66).

17. There is a rather incongruous retreat from the aristocratic position when Margaretta praises her father's decision to emigrate to America (p. 398), though there have been earlier statements favorable to America, e.g., in connection with the abolition of slavery (p. 235). A parallel emigration to America occurs in Mrs. Rowson's *Reuben and Rachel*.

18. See, e.g., the picturesque description on p. 1, Margaretta's portrait (pp. 8-9), the passages of sentiment (pp. 179-80, 305, 349-50), the expressions of rage and revulsion (pp. 182-83, 231).

19. "His eye was caught by the beauty of Margaretta; and bold, as a lion, he seized his prey, and would have at once hurled destruction over her, had I not, by the most fortunate chance, found her, when her danger was at its very crisis, and released her from his ravenous claws!" (de Burling about his rescue of Margaretta from Custon, p. 77).

20. See the reflections on "the purest philosophy" (p. 270), breach of promise (p. 401), reason and passions (p. 418).

21. It is presumably deliberate that Miss Stewart and de Burling use a similar terminology to set forth their very different plans for Margaretta (pp. 8-9, 15).

22. References are to the second edition. For a discussion of Miss Wells's first novel, *The Step-Mother*, see above, Chapter 6.

23. "Such were the sentiments of a modern *philosophist*, who prided himself on being an *illuminé*, and a propagator of those doctrines which were to enlighten Europe, and to free all mankind from the shackles of superstition under which they had for so many ages groaned" (2:242).

24. Here is a passage typical of the accumulation and breathlessness of large portions of the narrative: "The promptitude with which Caroline had yielded to an imperious necessity, had scarcely allowed her time to consider what kind of reception she should meet with from her aunt, or whether the short notice she had given of her coming might not indicate that her motions were as little regulated by propriety, and a sense of justice, as her brother's had been. Left to meditate on the future, the suggestions of hope gave place to a train of gloomy reflections, awakened by recollecting, that, though on the road to a sister of her mother's, that sister had not, in her recollection, proved herself such in affection, the partiality to Montagu being the only instance that her conduct had afforded of her being possessed of any tenderness for objects beyond the pale of her own family circle" (3:119-20).

[240]

25. The novel was published in New York. *The Fortunate Discovery*, by the same anonymous lady, is discussed above in Chapter 7.

26. Quibble's confusion when the matter of the will is brought up, and Lovemore's attempted abduction of Eliza, respectively.

27. A parallel to the main plot is set forth in the interpolated story of Julius and Juliana, with its definitely pastoral note anticipating that of the ending of *Moreland Vale* (pp. 143-64).

28. *The American Review* (1, no. 4[1801]:491) spoke with severity of *Moreland Vale* in order to discourage any housewife tempted "to devote that time to increase the number of useless books on the shelves of our circulating libraries, which might better be employed in *household affairs*"; its verdict was plain: "*Moreland Vale* is a story framed with little art, destitute of incident, and tending to no purpose."

Chapter Eleven

ILLEGITIMATE LOVE

IN NOVELS of the *Monima* type a happy ending is reached after the heroine has undergone many trials, including hairbreadth escapes from one form or another of a fate "worse than death."[1] Margaretta, for one, just barely escapes marrying her own father. Her escape is as narrow as that of the heroine in *The History of Albert and Eliza* (1812):[2] had Eliza's marriage to Blake been consummated, she would have been the wife of a bigamist, and one married to his own half-sister. Eliza, too, after suffering various delays and anxieties, finally marries her true love, a happy ending already in sight when the truth about Blake becomes known. The retrospective horror of hearing about Blake's incest, and also that he unwittingly killed his (admittedly wicked) half-brother, does not quite blot from Eliza's memory her earlier harrowing experiences, but it certainly seems more important than the ordeals of her beloved Albert, who among other things has been a slave in Algiers.

The author of *Albert and Eliza* apparently was not quite sure about the propriety of his use of the incest motif. It is both relevant to the final outcome of the story and yet minimized, since it does not truly affect the main characters. It occurs only on the edge of the sphere of frustrating influences in which Eliza and Albert must move; nor does it really count against the person of Blake. For this young man is very much the victim of circumstances and, at first, unaware of the criminal nature of some of his acts. He is informed that he is related by blood to his wife after they have been married for some time, and learns only long after the encounter that Palmer, whom he killed in a duel,[3] was another illegitimate Blake. His incest and fratricide do not really taint him; he appears distinctly eligible as a husband because he behaves like a gentleman throughout.

[242]

He presumably considers his former marriage annulled. His major failing is his jealousy toward Palmer and Albert, an attribute in keeping with his passionate temperament (p. 10); but the same impulsiveness perhaps also prompts him to do "the right thing" in the end: "He hastily rose from his seat—distraction had seized upon his brain. He cast a wild despairing look around him, and rushed out at the door. In a few minutes the report of a pistol was heard in his chamber, the people ran upstairs; his door was locked; they burst it open; he lay dead upon the floor!" (pp. 51-52). Miss Smith, his half-sister, is more dangerously jealous; it is she who is the real villain of the story, unless we assign the role to the blind fate that causes painfully inopportune meetings, delays, and misunderstandings. She tries to kill Eliza and later divulges the truth about the Blakes, and her own shame at the same time, simply because she cannot bear that another should enjoy her half-brother's love. Yet she is used as an extraneous *diabolus ex machina* device, and plays practically no part in the story to which she provides the startling conclusion. Miss Smith slightly resembles the vengeful Eliza of *The Hapless Orphan*. There are other similarities with contemporary American works of fiction: the use of a namesake to cause confusion and despair, as in *The Asylum*, and the various plot elements that recall *The Unfortunate Lovers and Cruel Parents*.[4]

The incest motif has a far more important function in *The Power of Sympathy: or, The Triumph of Nature* (1789), attributed to William Hill Brown (1765-93).[5] This novel is about lovers who, like Blake, must pay for the wild oats sown by their father. Unlike Blake, Sr., Mr. Harrington himself is also made to suffer by the repercussions of his earlier behavior.[6] His crime has been the seduction of Maria, who died after he had deserted her. Others have been similarly treacherous: two further episodes of seduction are inserted into the main narrative;[7] and a footnote (pp. 50-53) refers to a recent *cause célèbre* of New England, the story of Elizabeth Whitman, which was to be treated in fiction by Mrs. Foster in *The Coquette*. The seduction motif thus appears to dominate *The Power of Sympathy*. There are two reasons for its importance: the popularity of the motif with novel readers since the days of Richardson, and the built-in justification for the writer's professed aim to instruct and warn his female readers. In his dedication and preface, Brown declared that he meant to expose the crime of seduction and propose a way to counteract its dangers.[8] He then introduced Mrs. Holmes, to whom he gave an important speaking part: she holds forth on the necessity of giving young girls an education that will be useful to them when they enter the world and meet potential seducers (letter 29).[9]

Yet in spite of the didactic treatment it is given, the subject of seduction fails to dominate Brown's novel. The figure of Mrs. Holmes provides a clue why this should be so. In offering her opinions on education, she is indeed didactic and explicit; but she also has another, dramatic, function to fulfill, and it is the relative importance of her two roles that appears significant. Brown allowed much of the suspense of the story to derive from Mrs. Holmes's suggestive hesitancy to reveal the truth about Harriot's origin (letters 26-37). She means to spare Mr. Harrington, presumably; but she succeeds above all in directing attention to the notion of incest, which is thus given an entirely superfluous emphasis. The latent incest situation is obviously a consequence of the previous seduction; all the same, Brown's intention to expose the dangers of seduction might have been better served without the introduction of the incest motif. Brown laid himself open in yet another respect to the charge of toying with unsavory topics:[10] in the Ophelia-Martin episode, a transparent disguise only was thrown over the persons involved in the notorious real affair which had involved Mr. Morton and his wife's sister, Frances Apthorpe, an affair of a particularly scandalous, almost incestuous, nature, because of their relationship.[11]

Half a century earlier, Fielding and others had found that Richardson's Pamela seemed less concerned with virtue than with the material reward which virtue preserved might yield. Some readers of *The Power of Sympathy* may have raised similar objections. The lovers do not act as if they were relieved at being spared the crime and shame of an incestuous marriage; but they are deeply grieved by the necessity of renouncing their mutual love. Thus Harriot writes:

I indulge, in idea, the recollection of his caresses—of his protestations, and of his truth and sincerity—I become lost in a wilderness, and still I travel on, and find myself no nearer an escape. I cherish the dear idea of a lover—I see the danger and do not wish to shun it, because, to avoid it, is to forget it—and can I, at one stroke, erase from my mind the remembrance of all in which my heart used to delight? Ah! I have not the fortitude—I have not the virtue, to "forget myself to marble." On the contrary, I strive no longer to remember our present connexion. I endeavour to forget—I curse the idea of a brother—my hand refuses to trace the word. (2:110-11)[12]

Up to this crisis they have obeyed the abstract moral precepts inculcated by their elders. To do this automatically will no longer do when they are faced with the practical, challenging aspects which their life abruptly assumes. As a consequence of their father's conduct, they find themselves in a situation they feel unable to cope with. Their desires have been awakened, yet must remain unsatisfied; their emotional and imaginative life has been stimulated and is now suddenly being thwarted.

To treat such a conflict demanded understanding and artistic skill. Brown either did not possess the required abilities or would not make the effort to summon them. He outlined a cycle running from the violation of the moral order in one generation to the retribution it entails in the next; at its conclusion the lovers are frustrated by issues that seem inescapable, without becoming tragic. Even the evocation of the final hours of Harriot falls flat. The girl appears to be still hoping against hope that the "triumph of nature" might, after all, be the consummation of her love, whereas it cannot of course mean anything except the negative affirmation of the law of blood-relationship. At no time, to be sure, does anything about Harriot imply that she could seriously consider flying in the face of convention. She is no more than a typical novel heroine, pathetic in her helplessness and dependence upon her surroundings, and susceptible to loving without reservations when the right man turns up. Though occasionally she seems endowed with some naïve common sense,[13] her sensibility remains her most important attribute. A similar sensibility is characteristic of Harrington, too, who invokes it in his first letter: "But come thou spirit of celestial

language, that canst communicate by one affectionate look—
one tender glance—more divine information to the soul of sensibility, than can be contained in myriads of volumes!" (1:10).[14]
This sensibility is chiefly responsible for Harrington's quick conversion from a would-be seducer to an enthusiastic admirer of
Harriot's virtues;[15] but this very quality of his worries Harriot
and Myra, who fear that it might make him yield to the temptation of suicide, should Harriot die. The young man's case is
further complicated by his familiarity with *Werther*.[16] Only late
in the novel did Brown add an individual feature to Harrington's
portrait: in a letter to Worthy, the young man admits his need
for help and that something could be done to save him from his
desperately self-centered and obsessive emotions (2:124).

But Worthy is an abstract reasoner, and he cannot respond to
Harrington's appeal. He merely offers him arguments against
suicide that strike one as more likely to render the idea of it more
insistently present in his friend's hypersensitive state of mind
than rationally to dissuade him from committing the act. Worthy's role is similar to that of Mrs. Holmes. They both bear a
heavy didactic burden but also serve to focus the reader's attention on a latent possibility of crisis. At any rate, Worthy immediately guesses what must have happened when he is told
that Harrington is dead: "He has killed himself!" (2:148). Mrs.
Holmes and Worthy differ from the other characters in the novel
through their essentially rational nature. If a balance between
the rational and the emotional is achieved in *The Power of
Sympathy* (something which the tenor of the preface entitles us
to expect), it is found in the sum total of its personnel rather
than in any one of the individual figures. These tend to be "humours" of sensibility or common sense, respectively.[17] The different sensibilities in the aggregate make for a mood of sentimental receptivity, enhancing the various scenes of melancholy,
in particular; didactically speaking, they create pretexts for mes-
sages to the reader. Maria's parting letter to Mr. Harrington
teaches the necessity of forgiveness and compassion (2:44-47);
it is echoed by Holmes in a sterner manner (2:49-56). Mr. Harrington's consciousness of his guilt gives him a foretaste of the
retribution awaiting him: in his infernal habitat he will have no

communication even with other inmates of hell (2:95-106). This is an appropriate punishment, because the victims of seduction on earth are doomed to be alienated from those they love.[18]

Considering the insistence on sensibility and moralizing, it is easy to guess what the style of The Power of Sympathy must be like. Occasions of intense feeling are provided by the falls from virtue and the related deaths of Ophelia, Henry, Maria, Harriot, and Harrington, as well as Elizabeth Whitman. One passage from such a context conveys an impression of the tone prevailing in the novel.

> Is it necessary to depicture the state of this deluded young creature after her fall from virtue? Stung with remorse, and frantick with despair, does she not fly from the face of day, and secrete her conscious head in the bosom of eternal forgetfulness? Melancholy and guilt transfix her heart, and she sighs out her miserable existence—the prey of poverty, ignominy and reproach! Lost to the world, to her friends, and to herself, she blesses the approach of death in whatever shape he may appear, that terminates a life, no longer a blessing to its possessour, or a joy to those around her.
>
> Behold her stretched upon the mournful bier!—Behold her silently descend to the grave!—Soon the wild weeds springs afresh round the *little hillock,* as if to shelter the remains of betrayed innocence—and the friends of her youth shun even the spot which conceals her relicks. (2:54-55)

In other respects, however, Brown attempted variety. His eight correspondents write different kinds of letters. Some of them comment, from different points of view, on the contrast between the bustle of the city and the calm of a country retreat (letters 5, 7, 10). Subsidiary episodes combine with the main narrative and, like the verse with which some letters are sprinkled, touch upon its chief subject.[19] Suspense is attempted, first, after a brisk conversational beginning, in connection with Harrington's campaign against the virtue of Harriot, and afterward, through Mr. Harrington's evasive attitude concerning the marriage of the young couple. But the gradual revelation of Mr. Harrington's paternity and the hints about the young lover's impending suicide are devices of protraction rather than suspense.

Lacking in continuity, inadequate in characterization, hovering between its didactic message and its potential of lurid ingredients,[20] *The Power of Sympathy* blends so many elements of the minor fiction of the age (not unlike Mrs. Rowson's *Charlotte*) that its appearance at the beginning of an era of imitative novel-writing in the United States seems highly appropriate. The only additions made in Brown's first novel to the canon of that type of fiction concern the new nation: there are mentions of democracy and of a new world as yet uncivilized and therefore uncorrupted, where free men may fashion an example for the degenerate Old World; they will free their slaves (letters 17-18), and a moral literature shall be their answer to the decadent writings of Europe (letters 29-30).

The title page of *Ira and Isabella: or the Natural Children* (1807) bears the name of its author, "the Late William H. Brown, of Boston." This piece of information does not, unfortunately, help us to decide whether the same man also wrote *The Power of Sympathy*, which would be reassuring, since Brown's claim as the author of the "first American novel" is none too secure. Thirty-five years ago Milton Ellis suggested the evidence that, according to him, justified the attribution of the two novels to the same author.[21] It is doubtful, however, if the style of the two books is as much of a help as he suggested. In the minor American fiction of the late eighteenth century, stylistic criteria are generally unreliable when it comes to attributing a book to a particular author. The writers of the age had little skill and inventiveness and consequently inclined to imitation; but as the current plot elements suggested at best only few variants in expression, the individual styles tended to become anonymous instead of distinctive. The misspellings listed by Ellis might indeed be thought more idiosyncratic than the stylistic features. It is perhaps the relationship in tone and approach which best supports the theory that *The Power of Sympathy* and *Ira and Isabella* are the work of the same writer; at any rate, a discussion of the author's tone and approach may serve as an introduction to the second novel.

Though *The Power of Sympathy* was advertised in the *Massachusetts Magazine* as the first American novel, the term "novel" itself does not appear on its title page at all, where the book is described as "founded in truth." *Ira and Isabella,* on the other hand, is said to be "a novel," with the additional qualification "founded in fiction." This sounds like a gibe at the many novels that proclaimed their faithful adherence to actual events, perhaps to arouse their readers' curiosity and to anticipate critics who might consider them the fruit of an undisciplined imagination. Of such novels, *The Power of Sympathy* was the very first in America. It would seem that Brown later wanted to make fun of its pretended truthfulness, and he appears to have been ridiculing its pompous didacticism as well. Whereas the introductory pages of *The Power of Sympathy* had gravely asserted the moral and patriotic intent of the book, in the preface to *Ira and Isabella* a lighter tone prevails, even in the comments on the decline of the novel or, in a more caustic spirit, on the large number of novel-readers, especially among the ladies. Brown's manner of addressing the latter is here markedly different from the seriousness displayed in the earlier dedication, and though it might pass for a variant of the style of sensibility, it obviously has its touch of irony (pp. x-xi). Brown appears temporarily serious when he echoes his former statement that the novel should unequivocally teach that vice is to be avoided and virtue emulated,[22] but he quickly returns to the merry mood in which he remarked on the obsolescence of superhuman machinery and deprecated his own lack of inventiveness. In conclusion he gives marks to a number of European writers: Dr. Johnson heads his list, followed by Swift, Cervantes, Voltaire, Sterne, and Richardson.[23]

After reading the preface, we carry into *Ira and Isabella* a feeling that we had better not accept events and reflexions quite at their face value, that we are to attend a comedy performance; and just before the end of the novel there is another piece of ironical de-romanticizing. The story framed by such an introduction and conclusion is likely to be taken with a grain of salt. The de-romanticizing anecdote referred to is significant, especially in the light of a comparison of *Ira and Isabella* with *The Power of Sympathy.* The last-named novel insists on the degrading nature of seduction—degrading because the odds are so clearly against unsuspecting innocence at the mercy of the seducer's villainous cunning. But in *Ira and Isabella* Mr. Savage tells a story apt to shake the accepted view or legend of the ruthless male triumphant over female helplessness:

> Lucinda, lively, affable and simple as she was, had successfully laid a snare for me. She was not won from the way of prudence by my means, but had had the fortune to have been apparently beguiled three or four times....My rural disciple, with the greatest pleasantry imaginable, told me it was her intention to make me the father of a child. It was in vain to remonstrate, for I, like all gentlemen in my honourable situation, had accustomed myself to comply with all the whims of my mistress. (pp. 113-14)[24]

This novelty is refreshing not necessarily because of the case made against a prejudice thoughtlessly renewed and sanctioned but certainly because Savage's irony quite dissolves the mood in which the seduction motif tended to be treated: a morbidly sentimental mood it generally was, though it is possible that the authors meant their work to sound genuinely pathetic and tragic. Although William Hill Brown himself may not have clearly realized what a revealing light he shed on the workings of the plot machinery of *The Power of Sympathy,* it seems conceivable that he deliberately added a measure of burlesque, if not self-parody, to his *Ira and Isabella.*[25]

There is more to support this view than just the relation existing between Maria, who was seduced by Mr. Harrington, and Lucinda, who did the seducing of, among others, Mr. Savage—a relation not unlike that between Richardson's Pamela and Fielding's Lady Booby.[26] The question of responsibility in cases of seduction is also touched upon when Isabella speaks to her old nurse. She blames her for her archetypal notion of man as an unreliable and unfaithful creature, congenitally prone to seducing maidens; if there were no such preconceived idea of man, she argues, he would be less likely to behave according to the pattern (pp. 36-38). Furthermore, some characters and features of *The Power of Sympathy* may be said also to turn up in *Ira and Isabella,* but with inverted signs, as if with a burlesque design. Harrington, rejecting Worthy's counsel, starts out as an apparently unscrupulous man-about-town with black designs on Harriot; Lorenzo is akin to this early Harrington, for he suggests that the love of his companion Ira may not be all that pure (p. 24). It is Lorenzo who represents the frailer part of mankind, and the hero has as much reason to shun him as Harrington has to follow Worthy's advice. Mr. Harrington fails to admit his error until faced with the fact that the secret is out; on the contrary, both Savage and Dr. Joseph come to acknowledge their children, however reluctantly. The allegation of the two lovers' kinship is made after the wedding ceremony and the apparent beginning of an incestuous relationship, whereas in the case of Harrington and Harriot the incest can be prevented through Mrs. Holmes's intervention; yet the event which has the appearance of a gruesome joke played by fate upon two blameless victims is in reality more innocent than the mutual attraction of Harriot and Harrington. For Ira and Isabella are not truly the children of the same father and therefore can be rewarded with a happy ending.[27] Before Savage's confession reassures them, they also prove better able than Harriot and Harrington to stand the shock of mythical horror at their incestuous connection and capable of discussing their plight stoically. Harriot and Harrington, shattered by the blow, are deprived of all the resources of calm reasoning; their story consequently is increasingly permeated with an overpowerful sensibility and self-pity connected with the melancholy indictment of the seducer (in which there is no room for Savage's view of woman as an equal partner in the business of seduction, of course).

Yet it is not tenable to discuss *Ira and Isabella* exclusively as the reworking of material used in the main plot of *The Power of Sympathy,* with some of its features reversed or given an ironical slant. There are also parallels between the books which are presumably independent of any burlesque design and some traits which give *Ira and Isabella* a modest degree of distinctiveness. The similarities in the plot structure have been referred to. Its main stages are the mutual attraction between the lovers, the intimation that they must not marry, and the unsettling revelation of their being closely related; in the second half of each book, the author must of course tell the circumstances to which the illegitimate children owe their birth.

In either couple, the girl seems to have a shrewder grasp of the realities of life and a clear sense of the relative weakness of her partner. Harriot's strength is shown only obliquely, through her resentment at the trick played by fate upon her love; she also perceives that, left alone, Harrington may be unable to deal with his accumulated troubles. In the context of the whole novel, however, Harriot, a conventional sentimental heroine, is reduced to a comparative insignificance by the weight of the words of Mrs. Holmes, Worthy, and Holmes, and further by the mere fact of Harrington's survival. There is considerably more originality in Brown's conception of Isabella and the views which he put into her mouth. He introduced her traits of character and potentialities before sketching a picture of her appearance, an unorthodox procedure.[28] Ira admires her ability to ignore certain patterns of expected behavior in young ladies. Thus Isabella has no patience with the idea of courting according to which the girl must remain passive until she has been proposed to and coyly refuse, after that stage, to commit herself once and for all (p. 30). She therefore does not attempt to disguise her feelings even before she has received a formal declaration, and she responds— Juliet-like—to Ira's outspoken compliments to her as a desirable woman (pp. 32-33). After rebuking her nurse for her prejudices, Isabella proclaims her independence, saying, "Happiness is within ourselves, not in the opinions of others" (p. 40). She does qualify her youthful defiance, though, by expressing her gratitude for the nurse (p. 43). To Ira she is a source of strength. When he plans to go away, she not only shows "evident symptoms of dislike at this resolution" (p. 68) but sets about, and easily succeeds in, dissuading him. Ira indignantly rejects his friend Florio's suggestion that he should seek distraction among prostitutes and, as a natural conclusion to the incident, hurries back to Isabella, "his sister, his wife" (p. 67), and a friend "of decency, of truth, and of sobriety," who will "open the sluices of tranquillity" for him (p. 92). The girl treats him to a number of mottoes couched in Johnsonian periods, at the end of which tuition the qualities of leadership in the girl are acknowledged by Ira more fully than ever: "The unfortunate youth, gazed upon his beautiful monitor with eyes swimming in tears, and with a soul, lost in wonder and ecstacy" (p. 99). This is the only time in *Ira and Isabella* when the sensibility so much in evidence in *The Power of Sympathy* emerges for a number of pages. Generally, Brown's playful approach, and the commonsensical frankness of his (or Isabella's) remarks on certain conventions, prohibited its use. The climax of seriousness apparently rendered him more dependent on stylistic means designed to do justice to exceptional situations; he thus overstressed the emotional significance of some of his statements, as above, or struck a pompous note so much out of tune with the wider context as, once more, to suggest deliberate parody: "As Isabella pronounced these words, her posture was firm, and her eye fixed upon her brother; her right hand placed upon her breast, and her left pointing towards heaven" (p. 101). Everything considered, *Ira and Isabella* is an unsatisfactory medley. Some of its ingredients may be justifiable if we assume that the book was written, among other things, as a wry comment on another individual piece of writing or possibly a whole subgenre: the novel of seduction. But that does not redeem the production as a whole. Nor, of course, is the conceivably burlesque nature of this novel sufficient by itself to determine whether *The Power of Sympathy* must be attributed to William Hill Brown.

1. "...This night shall subdue your pride, and humble you with the dust!" "Do you mean to murder me also?" cried Monima. "Worse than death shall be your portion" (p. 411).

2. *The History of Albert and Eliza. To which is prefixed, The Cruel Father.* Founded on Fact. Compiled by Russell Ladd. In reality "The Cruel Father" follows (pp. 55-88) "Albert and Eliza" (pp. 3-53). The authenticity of "Albert and Eliza" is stressed in an introductory remark (p. 3) and in the conclusion (pp. 52-53). There is a reference to "The Cruel Father" in a footnote, above, "Cruel Parents," pp. 208-9 n.43.

3. Killing one's adversary in a duel is a minor offense if the challenge is justified. Now, Palmer has amply merited chastisement for his insulting behavior toward Eliza; and according to the code of honor underlying the custom of dueling, Blake deserves praise rather than blame. Legally, of course, the matter is not quite so simple; Palmer's body is therefore quickly disposed of.

4. E.g., the Long Island families; the loving couple destined to be married; the heroine watching the boat leave with her lover on board; the latter's reappearance just as she is to be married to someone else.

5. The chief positive support for the attribution of *The Power of Sympathy* to Brown is a statement made by a relative of his in 1893. But it still remains easier to dismiss the earlier theory that Mrs. Morton wrote the book (in which a scandal in her own family is aired) than to offer additional evidence in favor of Brown's authorship. See below, in the context of the discussion of Brown's *Ira and Isabella*, for other suggestions. For the question of the authorship of *The Power of Sympathy*, see Arthur W. Brayley, "The Real Author of *The Power of Sympathy*," *Bostonian* 1(1894):224-33; Walter Littlefield's reprint of *The Power of Sympathy;* Emily Pendleton and Milton Ellis, *Philenia: The Life and Works of Sarah Wentworth Morton*, reviewed by Tremaine McDowell, *AL* 4(April, 1932):68; Milton Ellis, "The Author of the First American Novel," *AL* 4(January, 1933):359-68, and his introduction to the Facsimile Text Society edition of the novel (1937); Tremaine McDowell, "The First American Novel," *American Review* 2(November, 1933):73-81; Quinn, *Fiction*, p. 7 n.; and A. H. Quinn (ed.), *The Literature of the American People* (Appleton-Century-Crofts, 1951), p. 196.

6. Mr. Harrington is worried by the growing affection of Harriot and his son and tries to prohibit the match; he then witnesses Harriot's decline and death; this is followed by his vision of hell.

7. Ophelia is seduced by her brother-in-law Martin, gives birth to a child, and poisons herself (letters 21-23). Henry jumps into the river after Fidelia has disappeared with Williams on the eve of their wedding (letters 27-28). All references are to the 1789 edition.

8. The didactic ponderousness of *The Power of Sympathy* is reflected in some judgments on the novel. See, e.g., Cowie, *The American Novel*, p. 11; Fiedler, *Love and Death*, p. 97. Fiedler also mentions its "fundamental seriousness," and to him it remains, despite the "thinness of realization throughout," "more a psychological, even a metaphysical essay than a lurid story told to shock and amuse" (pp. 104, 102); a contrary view is that of Mary S. Benson, *Women*, p. 190.

9. It appears from Harrington's attitude that all men will seduce girls who are without a properly strengthened moral sense; Harriot, e.g., quickly transforms Harrington, who finds himself unable to propose to her that she should become his mistress (p. 23). See also Maria's reflections (2:41); other educational topics are discussed in letters 11 and 12.

10. This charge might have helped, along with the arguments of neighborly good will, to persuade Brown to withdraw the book from circulation. McDowell has pointed out, though, that advertising for *The Power of Sympathy* in the *Massachusetts Magazine* continued for eight months (*AL* 4[1932]:68). A sort of indirect advertising occurred in Hitchcock's *Memoirs of the Bloomsgrove Family*, where the quatrain of the title page of *The Power of Sympathy* is quoted with a minor alteration (2:22). The "first American novel" later furnished moral copy for the *New York Magazine* 5, no. 11(1795):687-88.

11. There is a reference to the affair in an anonymous play, *The Fatal Effects of Seduction* (1789), which focuses on the girl's suicide, and in the satirical *Occurrences of the Day* (1789), dealing among other things with the attempt at suppressing *The Power of Sympathy*. See Richard Walser, "The Fatal Effects of Seduction," *MLN* 69(1954):574-76, and "More about the First American Novelist," *AL* 24(1952):352-57.

12. Cf. 2:90-91, 113-14; and 2:151, from a letter written quite some time after Harriot's death.

13. See her wish, perhaps not entirely innocent, to help Harrington overcome

his timidity (1:19), and her cool remark about Mrs. Francis, who "like the rest of the world, bears the misfortunes of her friends with a most christian fortitude" (1:113).

14. Cf. his apostrophes to sensibility (2:32-33) and the god of love (2:10-11).

15. He begins by rationalizing his desire for his own benefit and Worthy's, arguing that in setting up Harriot as his mistress he would free her from her dependence on Mrs. Francis—an argument of a type popular with the seducers.

16. Like Werther, Harrington is heard walking about his room during his last night, when he composes a long and frequently interrupted letter before shooting himself. A copy of *Werther* is found on his table after his death. His first intimation of suicide occurs even before Harriot's death, incidentally (2:94).

17. The characters apparently were not meant to be that simple; see e.g., Harrington's half-serious self-analysis (1:8); Worthy's opinion of his friend (2:155); and Mrs. Holmes's praise of the beauties of nature and its endorsement in the Sterne quotation appended (1:27-28). Admittedly, the term "sensibility" must be used loosely to accommodate its various representatives: the cowardly feebleness embodied in Mr. Harrington, Myra's gushing sentimentalism (she swoons when she finds out why Harrington must not marry Harriot), the extreme sensibility cultivated by the hero, and the various sensitive characters of the subplots. Martin, on the contrary, is apparently impervious to any feeling at all.

18. Ophelia loses her parents' love; her father assumes for her the features of a stern judge. She then commits suicide; so does Henry, when there is no one about to help him. Insanity is Fidelia's form of alienation. Maria and her daughter Harriot die of a broken heart, the immediate or ultimate consequence of seduction. Harrington, increasingly isolated from his fellow beings, also kills himself.

19. See Harrington's "The Court of Vice" (letter 25).

20. Herbert Ross Brown has called *The Power of Sympathy* "one of the very worst" of American novels. See his introduction to the 1961 edition of the novel (Boston: New Frontiers Press), p. iii.

21. *AL* 4:359-68.

22. *The Power of Sympathy*, pp. v-vi, and *Ira and Isabella* (Boston, 1807), pp. xi-xii.

23. The list also includes the name of William Dodd, whose best claim to literary fame would seem to be his forgery (among other frauds) of the signature of Lord Chesterfield. Fielding and Goldsmith are not listed. A thoughtful reader of the copy of *Ira and Isabella* in the Boston Athenaeum in a penciled note gave a total of 14½ points to Brown, whose own marks to Dr. Johnson add up to 122.

24. These remarks and others of a similar nature occur in the context of observations addressed to "gentlemen who edify the world by writing novels," also called "these rulers of nature," and ending with Savage's comment: "I would not willingly make one remark inimical to good morals, but as I am not a professed dealer in literature, I may be allowed to speak the truth" (p. 116).

25. Fiedler, *Love and Death* (p. 105), calls the novel a "howling travesty" and adds: "One hopes the burlesque is deliberate, but it is hard to be sure." Terence Martin suggests that Brown may have felt the need to make up "for his insistence on tragic effects of seduction in *The Power of Sympathy*" and points to an ambiguity which may account for the reader's difficulties in accepting

[255]

wholeheartedly the burlesque theory: "Capable of irony, capable of toying with some of the most basic assumptions of his culture, he at once questions and employs the conventions of writing sentimental fiction" (*The Instructed Vision,* pp. 134, 132).

26. It is worth noting that Lucinda not only achieves her ends with several gentlemen but also succeeds in securing her retreat and maintaining her reputation and marries "an honest, industrious husband" (p. 116). The average victim of seduction has no such luck; the famous Elizabeth Whitman, for example, was disappointed even in her attempt to marry a substitute husband before the birth of her illegitimate child.

27. The discovery of a close relationship can also be a pleasant surprise. In the "Margaretta" story in *The Gleaner,* the heroine worries over her husband's interest in Serafina, whom he has known since they were children, and is relieved to find out that the girl is an illegitimate child of her husband's father. "Augustus and Aurelia," by John Blair Linn (*Miscellaneous Works,* pp. 201-16), seems to be verging on tragedy when Augustus finds his Aurelia, who has been fondly encouraging him, embraced by another young man; but the latter turns round and stands revealed as Aurelia's brother and Augustus's friend.

28. The combination of a mind "susceptible of cultivation" and a heart "feeling by nature" with an attractive appearance and an expressive face indicating "a soul, which broke out at the eyes" (pp. 18-19) is one which Ira knows how to appreciate; another might be less pleased with it: "What must be his disappointment, who thought himself fascinated by beauty, when he finds he has unknowingly been charmed by reason and virtue!" (*The Power of Sympathy,* 2:88).

Chapter Twelve

SEDUCTION

THE LUCINDA of *Ira and Isabella* startlingly reverses a conventional pattern. She is not a passive seducee yielding to a single-mindedly active seducer but a somewhat amoral girl who cheerfully cooperates in several affairs and knows how to exercise a mild form of blackmail on gentlemen with a sensitive conscience. To blame both partners for the actual seduction, and to blame them equally, as a rule did not occur to the novelists of the period here discussed.[1] Especially in the tales introducing seduction in a subordinate function[2] there is a simplified moralistic pattern, according to which the seducer must bear all the blame for what is presented as a brutal crime perpetrated on helpless innocence.[3] In the novels built round a seduction story, however, the seduced girls are frequently made out to have been betrayed by their own weakness as much as by their partners' deceitfulness; what interest these novels have may indeed be owing to an essentially fair-minded outlook qualifying the relative perfections or imperfections of their characters.

To begin with a strictly conventional seduction story, *Lucinda, the Fair Mountain Mourner* (1807), by Mrs. P. D. Manvill, purports to be a veracious account of the fate of Lucinda Manvill.[4] The letter-form and the diction give the report a suspicious novel-like appearance. Mrs. Manvill, Lucinda's stepmother, proves kind-hearted and charitable toward the girl; at any rate, there is no mention that she ever reproached Lucinda with her false step. On the other hand, Mrs. Manvill is full of anger at Lucinda's seducer, "her loved assassin" (p. 107), one Brown. She grimly passes on to the reader of her letters (nominally addressed to her sister) Lucinda's suggestion that she may have been taken by force rather than seduced (letter 25)[5] and her own interpretation of Brown's motive: vengeful spite at having first been repulsed by Lucinda (letter 15). The final letter, added in the second edition, which relates Brown's decline into poverty, must have been a soothing bit of poetic justice at least to one person. Mrs. Manvill takes herself so seriously, not merely in her compassion or sternness but in voicing all her views and sensations concerning Lucinda's fate, that the poor girl—in spite of the inclusion of some of her letters—materializes as a mere projection of her stepmother's opinions and feelings.[6] She is dead at the end of the story, but she is also given a martyr's apotheosis by the intensity of Mrs. Manvill's emotions: "That sweet smile with which, thro' all her distresses she had met every friend, was now indelibly stamped by the seal of death. Nor had the grim messenger left any trace of his unrivalled power behind, save the lily's mantle. Indeed, Nancy, such was the beauteous corpse, that I could have contemplated it for hours, with celestial delight!" (p. 153).[7]

To proceed from the flatness of the characters of *Lucinda* to the comparatively complex major figures of *The Coquette; or, The History of Eliza Wharton* (1797), by Mrs. Hannah Webster Foster (1759-1840), brings a welcome and invigorating change. It is hardly fair, indeed, to compare the near-tract about Lucinda to Mrs. Foster's novel, for in the few decades of American fiction treated here, there are not many novels that reach its level.[8] This is a compliment which we pay Mrs. Foster. It is at the same time another comment on the average crudity of the fiction written by her American contemporaries.[9] The trustful nature of Lucinda makes Brown's task easy, once he has determined to punish her for refusing him. But for Major Sanford to become Eliza Wharton's clandestine lover requires the combined operation of a number of motives and circumstances; to reveal this process in a novel demanded from the writer more skill and sophistication than the author of *Lucinda* possessed. Mrs. Foster knew *Clarissa:* that is obvious even without her reference to Sanford as "a second Lovelace" (p. 55). Neither the villain, though, nor Eliza, his antagonist and victim, can stand comparison with Lovelace and Clarissa, whom Richardson managed patiently and subtly to render convincing in the roles assigned to them.

Still, in spite of awkwardness about Eliza's, and especially Sanford's, exit, the final pieces of the plot fit neatly enough. Mrs.
Foster, too, succeeded in keeping her characters consistent with
her original conception of them.[10]

Brown, in *Lucinda,* appears to the reader in one character,
that of a villain, and a dull one at that. Whatever real or imaginary attributes made him lovable in the eyes of Lucinda have
long since vanished; Brown must have become a different man
when his admiration for the girl turned into hatred. Sanford, by
contrast, seems a creature of "mixed feelings" at war against one
another, except for some brief periods of respite when he succeeds in deliberately subduing one of the conflicting factions.
Even then we suspect him of failing to control unconscious ra-
diations still emanating from what he wishes to ignore. He is
attracted to Eliza by her fame as a local belle and coquette,
which makes her a coveted individual prize and also, since Sanford has declared war on all flirts, just one girl among others
whom it is his self-imposed duty to seduce (pp. 25, 26). And yet
Sanford cannot keep himself immune from the effects of Eliza's
personal charms.[11] To the reader he is on the one hand the professional ladies' man (pp. 32, 140, 188-89) and fortune-hunter
(pp. 49, 33), as well as an impersonal agent in the campaign
against the coquettes (pp. 104, 241-42); on the other hand, we
see him as a potential husband and a being with undeniable
roots in the moral order.[12]

A Sanford constantly practices conscious and unconscious
self-deceit; on the contrary, a rival like Boyer is likely to appear
almost entirely free from inner contradictions. This is evident
from Boyer's two letters to Eliza (5, 47), which emphasize his
ability to reach decisions. The second in particular stresses his
coolness, to a degree that might seriously endanger the reader's
sympathy with him, were it not for the fact that Boyer does
appear vulnerable at times.[13] His firmness derives from a solid
structure of conventions, established on basic moral and social
values. This structure lends strength to his indictment of Sanford
(p. 23). It also speaks through others: it underlies Lucy's condemnation of the seducer[14] and, significantly, Sanford's own view
that there *are* women unassailable even to such a seasoned cam-

paigner as he is (p. 213). Julia is no less explicit than Lucy (pp. 164, 251), yet she is not watchful at all times (p. 176). Nor is Mrs. Richman, who should have been the first to give Eliza an unequivocal warning against Sanford instead of only a vague qualified hint.[15] It is this sort of noncommittal judgment, compounded of naïveté, charitable making of allowances, and willful overlooking of potential dangers, that make the seducer's work easier. He knows how to concentrate all his resources in the pursuit of the one success dearest to him.

It is part of the coquette's character that she delays committing herself, or at least refuses to admit that she has made up her mind, regarding her admirers.[16] With Eliza, who early introduces the term "coquettish" herself (p. 9), the prevaricating technique clearly is just one aspect of her distaste for making as well as accepting binding decisions, particularly in situations which require quick and unambiguous resolves. She is eager for amusements, not responsibilities (pp. 9, 12), and therefore tends to ignore or adapt what she recognizes as reasonable demands made on her (p. 39). She is deaf to Mrs. Richman's opinion of Sanford after the first ball; with no apparent reason for distrusting her friend's information, she chooses to dwell on her own pleasant impressions of the hours spent in the major's company, of his handsome person, elegant manners, and presumable wealth (pp. 76-77).[17] She finds it possible to emphasize his assets, and minimize his liabilities; but since the contrasting figure of Boyer constantly reminds her of Sanford's imperfections (p. 147), Eliza cannot quite forget them. From the start she has had some misgivings about the tempting major, and her conscience refuses to be silenced: "My heart did not approve his sentiments, but my ear was charmed with his rhetoric, and my fancy captivated by his address" (p. 52).

If it were left to her conscience to warn Eliza, she might respond to it. But it is echoed by, or appears as a manifestation of, the consensus of her surroundings; and Eliza is very sensitive to interference on the part of the world. She resents the efforts made on Boyer's behalf (p. 17) and to prevent her from seeing the major (pp. 130, 186). More generally, she rebels against her background. A clergyman's daughter, she first agreed to marry a colleague of her father's, Mr. Haly, though she did not love him.[18] After his death, she is seriously courted by another clergyman, Boyer, and in a letter to her mother expresses her uneasiness at the prospect of her future station should she marry him (p. 56). In addition, she frets at the fact that she is obviously expected not to aim any higher, socially speaking (p. 38); and the superior wealth she attributes to Sanford therefore renders his suit more attractive still (p. 77). Lucy, however, informs her that Sanford is not rich at all and advises her not to overrate her ability to reform a rake;[19] she finally insists upon the necessity for Eliza to break with Sanford (p. 85). By her insistence, she unwittingly contributes to Eliza's indecision; this in turn favors Sanford.

In the face of the pressures brought to bear on her from various quarters, Eliza is inclined to look for the easiest way out. She is never so vulnerable to Sanford's appeal as when the advice from Mrs. Richman and Lucy joins forces with Boyer's expressions of impatient love and jealousy and the voices of common sense and her conscience, to try and make up her mind. Instead of meeting Boyer in the parlor to give him her reply to his proposal, she goes out into the garden and there joins Sanford, in spite of having earlier banned him from her presence. Their meeting is the immediate cause of Boyer's renouncing her, which event Eliza is later to look upon as the turning point in her career (p. 221). She has now confirmed that contact with the corrupting character which is to work inward and corrode her resolution. The parallel with the fate of Clarissa is indicated by a remark of Mrs. Richman (p. 55). By comparison with Eliza's present state as diagnosed by Julia (p. 199), her former habit of putting off difficult decisions was a rather playful and controlled attitude. Eliza is utterly convinced of Boyer's worth and integrity, yet cannot master her wounded vanity when he refuses her apology and her offer to become his wife. She is fascinated by Sanford even though she sees through him;[20] she is aware that he lies to her (letter 60), and she has long known all about his past (letter 19). When she writes, "My hopes and fears alternately prevail, and my resolution is extremely fluctuating" (p. 147), she is thinking not just of her emotions toward Boyer, to whom she is about to write her apology, but of Sanford as well. She may exclaim that she no longer fears Sanford's arts (p. 170), but when he calls some time after, her firmness is all gone; and she must ask her friends what she is to do (pp. 175-76). She finally yields to the major, presumably glad that the struggle is over and that she must not make that one decision any more.[21] The resolution finally to run away is not really an act of her own choosing but one imposed on her, for she has abdicated her will.

The stages of Eliza's downfall shed light on her seducer's confused state of mind. As was suggested before, Sanford wavers between a personal and an impersonal attitude toward the girl. The latter attitude is dominant when they meet and remains influential long after Sanford has begun to feel for Eliza something that in another character might be called love (pp. 81-82). It is at least an acknowledgement of qualities that distinguish Eliza from Sanford's earlier conquests, including his wife and the Miss Laurence whom he wooed at one time. These two have to him only one attractive feature: they are heiresses to considerable fortunes. He may have spoken of love to them; but the term does not occur with reference to either in his letters to Deighton, whereas Sanford often writes of his love for Eliza, the fortuneless girl. The reader cannot help remaining suspicious of his sincerity: one assertion of his love is awkwardly placed (p. 103) between outbursts of vindictive feelings (pp. 93, 140); another is made just after he has married Nancy (pp. 172-73). He later speaks of the completion of Eliza's seduction as having "arrived to the utmost bounds of my wishes; the full possession of my adorable Eliza!" (p. 211). This seems more important to him than the thought uttered later, that he cannot bear the idea of parting from her (p. 241). When Sanford introduces the notion of divorce, he sensibly qualifies the nature of the sacrifice he is willing to make in Eliza's favor:

...My wife may be provoked, I imagine, to sue for a divorce. If she should, she would find no difficulty in obtaining it; and then I would take Eliza in her stead. Though I confess that the idea of being thus connected with a woman whom I have been able to dishonor would be rather hard to surmount. It would hurt even my delicacy, little as you may think me to possess, to have a wife whom I know to be seducible. (pp. 241-42)

Soon the question of sacrifice is no longer relevant. Sanford is moved by Eliza's plight when he is conveying her from her home but he finds the situation unpleasant. He seems to have a conscience after all (p. 246). It becomes clamorous after he has been told the news of Eliza's death (p. 255).

Mrs. Foster succeeded with considerable discretion in steering clear of the numerous opportunities to preach which her plot afforded;[22] but she appears to have yielded to the necessity of making her moral points at the conclusion of *The Coquette*. The horror and remorse which she attributed to Sanford, culminating in his advice to Deighton to prove wiser than he, make one part of her lesson plain enough; the other is governed by the notion of *de mortuis nil nisi bonum:* Eliza's epitaph expresses a willingness to "let candor throw a veil over her frailties, for great was her charity to others" (p. 261). There is, of course, never any lack of clarity about Mrs. Foster's message; that it is not conveyed too explicitly is one of the merits of her book. Refraining from comments on the action, she could let her characters reveal themselves through their several actions as they related them. She handled the epistolary form well; in refusing to withhold information for the benefit of temporary suspense, she promoted the general interest of her story. She kept the letters short: they are simply means to keep the recipients[23] and the reader posted, not vehicles of moral instruction. Only in the second half of the novel do the letters grow longer: when the dejected Eliza has become less active and when she is more secretive because of her affair with Sanford, they occasionally offer a contribution to a discussion of the case rather than an account of its progress. Reserved in voicing her own opinions, Mrs. Foster showed discretion, too, in the use of stylistic embellishments; if the result was a rather dry manner of writing, it compares favorably with most novels by contemporary Ameriauthors.

Eliza Wharton, related through her vanity to Lucy Franklin,[24] is guiltier than Lucinda Manvill when she yields to her lover.

[263]

She is guiltier, too, than the heroine of *Amelia, or the Faithless Briton* (1798).[25] Amelia, just like Lucinda, is too willing to judge her lover by her own standards of honesty; she refuses to accept the fact of Doliscus's duplicity, a deceitfulness aptly illustrated by the fake wedding ceremony he devises. If Lucinda is partly the victim of social circumstances, since she must seek employment far from her father's home, Amelia becomes indirectly one of the political situation, which brings about her meeting with the wounded army officer. The same state of affairs makes for separation and distance, and thus also serves to call forth a characteristic quality of the girl. Seduced novel-heroines share the cumulative perfections of Amelia,[26] but in a crisis they are often helpless and meekly resign themselves to their fate. Not so Amelia. She acts in an attempt to redress her wrongs and follows Doliscus to New York and London, "wiping the useless tears from her cheek" (p. 16). Yet her courage avails her little; she suffers despair, is tempted to commit suicide, and finally becomes insane. After death has released her from her bitter troubles, the reader is invited to share the consolation offered her father, Blyfield, "this assurance, that whatever may be the suffering of virtue HERE, its portion must be happiness HEREAFTER" (p. 36).

The political scene creates a possibility of a meeting of the protagonists, of rapid changes of settings, and also of a contrast between love and war. This furthers the quick dramatic action, which itself reflects the high emotional content of the story. Not the least important part, as patriarch, tutor, and merciful judge, is given to Blyfield. He reverses the voyage across the Atlantic to be made by the father of Charlotte Temple; and like him, having found his daughter just before she dies, he wisely omits to reproach her for her lack of confidence in him, who could have offered guidance (p. 25). It is in keeping with the theme of *Amelia* and its melodramatic treatment that the style of the book is rather florid and hackneyed.[27] As in the case of *Lucinda,* this artificial aspect clashes with the assertion of the basic authenticity of the events related (p. 2).

Amelia or Lucinda is taken advantage of, under conditions in part created by themselves, by weak or villainous seducers. Unlike them, the heroine of *Laura* (1809), by Mrs. Leonora

Sansay,[28] is not won under false pretenses, nor does she blind herself to the nature of her act when she becomes Belfield's mistress. Among other couples in the novels of seduction, one partner inflicts his selfish will upon the other, who may however seem to be asking for it; but Belfield and Laura, both equally the victims of circumstance, share in their deliberate decision to become lovers. They seem to take for granted that they will get married sooner rather than later. They apparently feel, or perhaps wish to prove to themselves, that they do not live together merely to anticipate the physical pleasures of marriage; and a union of minds, vaguely modeled after the Pygmalion myth, completes tangibly the union prompted by their instincts and emotions.[29] Laura's literary education by Belfield is contrasted with the connection of the young man with Eliza, which is grounded on physical attraction alone (pp. 90-91) and therefore doomed quickly to dissolve. It is suggested that in his affair with Eliza, Belfield was governed mainly by the ill-disciplined impulses of an immature young male thoughtlessly following some pattern of sophisticated behavior (p. 129). He does not seem to have become much steadier by the time of his acquaintance with Laura. It does not occur to him that his brother might consider a mistress as damaging a liability as marriage with no proper means of support. His choice of a brothel as a temporary dwelling for his love is ill-advised, to put it mildly,[30] and his conduct on the eve of his wedding hardly consistent with his efforts to keep his love a secret from his brother.

Laura meets Belfield when she is still mourning her mother; she is perhaps burdened by what she may know of her mother's past. She faces the prospect of a loveless marriage, too, as her stepfather wishes to see her settled before he dies. All this is highly unwelcome to one so eagerly awaiting love and life:

She was at that perilous stage of female existence when the glowing heart expands to every new impression; when the lustre of the melting eye bespeaks the tender disposition of the soul; when the throbbing bosom beats with undefinable sensations, and the elastic, bounding step betrays an exuberance of life, and health and fire, which frequently bewilders its unguarded possessor. At the same time her heart was desolated by grief,

[265]

a situation in which more than in any other it is susceptible of tender impressions, and under such circumstances Belfield presented himself, as a heaven-sent messenger of peace. (p. 31)

The courage Laura displays in her search for Belfield during the yellow-fever epidemic is an unusual feature in a novel-heroine; her willingness to forgive her lover is more typical.[31] The reputation which gradually attaches to Laura is the result of superficial information and prejudice. She is accused of having led Belfield astray from a steady application to his studies, and the one glimpse of her at the brothel convinces Melwood that she must be a prostitute, though her behavior might reasonably make him doubt his conclusion. Melwood's consequent innuendoes cause the duel fatal to Belfield. The custom of the duel itself derives from man's exaggerated regard for the mere appearance of virtues such as honor and courage. Something similar holds true of the crime of passive seduction: according to our author, it is condemned because less regard is paid by society to genuine virtue, whether secret or visible, than to its reputed absence (pp. 89-90). Laura, then, is a victim above all of the world's shallow values and hypocritical customs. Yet in her final estimate, the author tried to minimize the malicious effect of these customs and values. Laura also experiences compensating gestures, as for example the protection she is given at Belfield's request after his death. In a detached view the prejudices of her fellow beings are not personally hostile but rather instruments of the punishment which Laura's fault must bring down on her.[32]

Thus *Laura* ends, like other novels, with an explicit and conformist moral tacked on to the narrative. This is not the only inspiration which Mrs. Sansay derived from the fiction in vogue in her day. If the brothel scene may seem descended from *Clarissa*, the yellow-fever passages recall Brockden Brown's *Ormond* and especially *Arthur Mervyn*. There is a Gothic flavor to these scenes, which is more pronounced in Laura's nightmarish search for a shelter, ending in the churchyard where her mother lies buried. Another form of interest is more general: it is the suspense of the struggle between the possibility of a charitable, happy ending and a stern insistence on justice: are Belfield and Laura to be given another chance, or must the law be enforced that retribution visits the children for their parents' sin and Laura made to pay for her mother's weakness as well as her own? A readable book and no more,[33] *Laura* uses a tone expressive of sensibility, on occasion emphatically so; we must expect the two chief characters to be keenly aware of all that quickens remorse and misgivings, or joyful acquiescence and communion. The sympathies evoked in Laura as Belfield reads Pope's "Eloisa to Abelard" to her offer an instance of her susceptibility:

> ...It would be vain to attempt describing the effect produced on her ardent imagination by Pope's letter of Eloisa to Abelard. In every passage she discovered sentiments of which she felt herself susceptible, and to experience, even during a short interval, the tenderness, the passion, the transports of Eloisa, she thought would be cheaply purchased by a life of torture.
>
> Fatal illusion! which was still more fatally augmented when she heard the eloquent, the pathetic voice of Belfield, repeat the tenderest, the most impassioned lines of that dangerous poem. (p. 40)[34]

Belfield is shown in a lengthy passage, the mood of which reverberates through the following pages, to be highly sensitive to Laura's charms, her particular state of mind, and the romantic Schuylkill setting where they first met (p. 26).[35]

Feelings too indulgently encouraged also cause trouble for the protagonists of *Infidelity, or the Victims of Sentiment* (1797), by Samuel Relf (1776-1823), especially as their effects combine with the consequence of unfortunate parental interference. The first letters of this epistolary novel, addressed by Caroline Franks to her sister Maria, immediately introduce the subject of strong susceptibility to, above all, melancholy emotions. Caroline writes that she has met Fanny Alfred and sympathizes with Fanny's unhappy love and her predilection for evening walks, another romantic feature. After a detailed description of a walk in common, she reports an outburst of grief on the part of Fanny.[36] From the two ladies' interest in natural beauties we thereupon move to Caroline's "benevolent" curiosity about Fanny's sadness (p. 26). Fanny has had to renounce her lover, their fathers being opposed to the match. Caroline herself is unhappy too: she has lost a baby, and she is married, in accordance to her father's wishes, to a man she does not love and who apparently does not much care for her. She confesses to dreaming of a man she could truly love (p. 18), and she can be expected to help Fanny to imagine the happiness which ought to belong to the latter and her Wellsford. The participants' and the reader's sympathies having been thus appealed to, another stimulant is added: the music overheard by Caroline on her way through a romantic landscape. Caroline's interpretation of the event is characteristic: "Who knows, my sister, but that this secluded musician, remote from the scenes of anguish and disappointed love, here and thus seeks to drown the recollection of woe, in the united music of his pipe and the responsive echo of the vale!—While he played, nature was hushed to listen to his lamentation; and even the stubborn oak moved not a leaf to interrupt the sacred sadness of the song" (p. 29).

The basic melancholy of her view is characteristic and prophetic too: she is to have few hours of happiness but many struggles. Should she yield to the love of Fanny's brother, Charles Alfred, or respect the moral order, defended by reason and discipline, which her sister's advice uncompromisingly represents? Her conflict is caused by her weakness and instability, of which she is as much aware as her sister and Fanny, who repeatedly deplore it.[37] She aggravates it by her defiance of certain conventions and of any advice she may be offered. She does not think her sister is in a position to understand and counsel her, since Maria and her husband married for love (letter 2); when she does ask for her guidance, she is unable to apply it to her case after all (letter 46). She maintains her right to disregard the views commonly held about love and friendship (letter 13). As time passes, her conflict wears her down. If she attempts to recover her self-discipline, she only lapses into greater weakness afterwards.[38] Significantly, letter 29 (out of a total of forty-five), is the last one she writes. After Alfred's absence and return, she uses up all her energy in intense feeling: her love, her sympathy with the fate of Fanny and Wellsford, and her self-accusation and maddened anguish after her husband's suicide prevent any act of hers and consume her strength. After her brother Courtney has cursed her, "Charlotte [sic], acquainted of the cause of his fury, with a single groan, followed her Charles into the regions of futurity" (p. 190).

In refusing to fire at his challenger, Alfred is presumably saying he has done enough mischief; he wishes to avoid corrupting yet more the innocence that began deteriorating when he fell in love with an unknown beauty—a married woman, as he was shocked to find out soon after. He tries to project this innocence of his initial love and so to rationalize his later relations with Caroline: "Before I knew the obligations of her heart to another, I admired, esteemed, and loved her; if there be heinousness in this, my least defence will be, that 'I could not help it ' " (p. 47). This line of argument leads to the apology in his prayer just before meeting his challenger: "If, oh heaven,. . .I have erred, impute it not to the vileness of my heart; but to the weakness of my head;—to the seeds thou hast planted in my nature!" (p. 189). Alfred shifts the responsibility for his acts onto someone else throughout, except when he fails to acknowledge the idea of responsibility at all. In one respect his view is sanctioned by others: when he denounces Caroline's parents for having imposed upon her "an early forced marriage, (a palliating term for prostitution)" (p. 76), he is supported by his friend and even by the rational Maria, as well as by the author's "Advertisement." Relf made his disapprobation of parental interference in matters of the heart an important theme, which links the Caroline-Alfred affair with the case of Fanny.[39] Such a view may account for the indignation expressed by a reader of *Infidelity,* who underscored the words reading, "excite an oppressed child to the defence of nature," and added his or her own comment: "What deliberate villainy!"[40] A further remark at the end of the book elaborates on this; the anonymous reader apparently felt so strongly about this that the sorry ending of the adventure for the lovers did not temper his or her resentment.

Courtney, involved in the apology of rebellion against marriages of reason, seems to escape punishment. But if in the final stages of the novel he assumes the part of a vindicator,[41] one inevitably feels that his rage is directed at himself, too, and not only at the partners in the adultery;[42] and he will obviously have to live with his memories of the part which he played in their affair. Courtney's role is more ambiguous than that of the two lovers. He lacks their plausible (though not defensible) impulse for equivocation. Maria, who is Caroline's mentor, is willing to admit her disapproval of the marriage of Caroline and Franks; yet she leaves no doubt as to what she thinks her sister should do. Unlike her words of advice, Courtney's waver between two standards is a very lax fashion. His very first letter to Alfred gives an indication of his characteristically noncommittal manner. On the one hand he parodies the sublimity of the lover's feelings and brings them down within reach of rational argumentation (p. 34), but on the other hand, he pronounces love to have its own, nonrational, laws (p. 35). His next letter starts from the premise that true love can be neither cured nor forgotten, and yet must respect the existing institutions. He then encourages Alfred to ask himself what he would rather face: the conventional status quo—that is, his beloved faithful to her husband—or the violence of a cuckolded Franks (letter 9, p. 51). Courtney later openly advises Alfred to brave the opinion of the world and make Caroline his, and explicitly tells him to confirm through physical consummation the love which has brought them together. To be sure, he qualifies this "reasoning in Alfred's behalf" by emphasizing that his friend's case is exceptional (pp. 113-14, 136). This lessens the villainy of his role; otherwise, he might have been compared to the plotters against virtue in *Les Liaisons dangereuses,* who also mutually suggest and excite action at a distance. He is, however, unwilling to confess his share of the guilt when it is revealed that it is his own sister whom he has indirectly been encouraging to take a lover. Instead he turns on his friend; and Alfred, for a change, has a grievous responsibility returned to him. Courtney writes an accusing letter, clearly a prelude to a duel: "While your infernal lust boiled in your blood, your tongue profaning the name of friend, you knew that the seduced Caroline Franks, was the sister of Courtney. But this idea, could not weaken or repel your diabolical design: By a perfidious encroachment on my understanding, you artfully angled, until you drew me into an approbation of the infernal deed!" (p. 187).

Alfred and Caroline die soon after the unfortunate Franks has shot himself. Fanny sees in his suicide a consequence of the man's gloomy isolation. He has indeed led a loveless existence. Yet his is not an unemotional nature. He needs someone to turn to; and the person he finds most understanding is one of the three malicious spinsters living nearby in a decaying house. They have similar views on infidelity and jealousy (letter 28), and he writes Harriot Hayward about his jealousy and his remorse at having been the first cause of his wife's estrangement. There seems to be a sympathy of sorts among those too selfish to adjust to their surroundings; for Harriot Hayward, described by Caroline as one of those who "murder the sanctity of character with delightful enthusiasm; and exult while wallowing in the guiltless blood of injured reputation" (p. 70), offers to become Frank's compassionate friend. This offer he tacitly accepts in his letter introducing the mention of suicide: "Can you, Harriot, unsex yourself, and be the friendly accomplice of my voluntary destruction?" (p. 156), a question which suggests ghoulish visions to his correspondent (p. 164).

The news of Franks's suicide and Caroline's madness are reported immediately after some letters on the topics of love and happiness. This type of strong contrast is one of the devices favored by Relf.[43] Such contrasts, however, may not be as effective as intended in a book where the highly emotional is constantly emphasized. Typical passages from the early stages of Caroline's friendship with Fanny have been referred to. In Courtney's letters the feelings are rhetorically heightened, too, just as in Maria's relation of the story of Louisa and Henry, especially of its climax (p. 107). Where literary references occur, they belong to the order of sensibility.[44] The hothouse temperature of the author's style suits the sensational aspect of the catastrophe, and in its manner the novel achieves a certain unity of effect. But there remain other defects not to be ignored: sensationalism as such, moral ambiguities, and the implausibility of one basic feature, the fact that Caroline's identity is not established earlier.[45]

The seduction theme could also be treated in a less portentous mood. *The Life and Adventures of Obadiah Benjamin Franklin Bloomfield, M.D.* (1818)[46] has on its title page, after two Shakespearean quotations, a motto signed Obadiah: "Neither Vice nor Folly shall escape me." But Bloomfield clearly did not want to take himself, or to be taken, too seriously. He waxes more or less satirical over the Methodists (chaps. 4-10) and the Quakers (chaps. 27, 32, 48), the Yankees (p. 110) and the Irish (p. 187), and one individual physician (p. 50).[47] His emphasis on the subject of seduction and adultery, in which he sounds as serious as he seems willing to become, more than any other ingredient dominates his story[48] without, however, making any commitment on the part of the writer or the reader inescapable. Yet the chief villains are emphatically punished: Mrs. Cole commits suicide; Maria is brought low both by her own excesses and Mrs. Cole's machinations, and the fact that she is physically repulsive at the end must be thought as appropriate a punishment as the castration of Blackheart and his consequent death. No one, however, is quite innocent in this sexual comedy, with the single exception of Sophia;[49] small wonder if she is particularly horrified when she thinks that she has unwittingly committed bigamy and that her child is illegitimate. She is soon cleared, and the test turns out to have been intended rather for a final punishment of Bloomfield himself, though he has paid for his youthful errors by his trials during his second marriage and has often manifested his generosity.

Most of the sinners do repent and atone for their wrongdoings. Only Mrs. Cole and Blackheart are not given an opportunity or time to mend their ways. But if the others occupy a middle ground of relative waywardness or innocence, which reflects a tolerance strikingly different from the black-and-white pictures of many contemporary writers, there is perhaps more shallowness and indifference at the root of this attitude of laissez-faire than a positive conviction. This seems to be borne out by what is revealed in other aspects of *Bloomfield*. The narrator is ironical about the Yankee's eye for the main chance, but apparently quite unconscious of his own interested pride in his parents' seventy thousand pounds and his own inherited three hundred thousand dollars. When he remarks on the difficulty of becoming wealthy as a physician while remaining scrupulously honest (chap. 38), he has himself not impressed the reader as one who will remain entirely honest. When he is tempted to trust to his own impression of himself, he perhaps had better bear in mind what his experience has taught him: we are easily taken in by appearances. He should remember Maria, who managed to deceive her brother by her air of innocence, and the clergyman among his acquaintance who had a career of crime behind him; he might also think of his wife's failure to recognize him when he called on her in gentleman's dress instead of wearing his Methodist preacher's garb or of his own inability to declare the second Maria an impostor, even though he had been present at the first Maria's death.

But the author of *Bloomfield* was not interested in the serious implications of his themes. If he followed some fashions in the novel of the day and concocted a plot with a goodly number of seductions and adulteries and a vengeful schemer in the background,[50] he was perhaps more concerned with the Sternean manner with which he meant to grace this matter.[51] In this he was not especially subtle and clever, either. His capacities appear to have been mediocre; and his didactic passages, satirical remarks, parodies, his straightforward narratives, his gallery of slightly sketched protagonists and peripheral figures, all are equally undistinguished.

1. The idea occurs, in a more sober and more conventional mood than Brown's in *Ira and Isabella*, in a story entitled "Florio" (*A Collection of Moral and Entertaining Stories*, pp. 10-18): "...In an ill fated hour they were both ruined, though it is hard to tell which was the seducer, or which the seduced" (p. 15).

2. Seduction may be used, for example, as one of the various topics chosen as a pretext for an author's moralizing, or simply as one among several items demonstrating the villain's wickedness, as in *The Gamesters* or in "The Fatal Effects of Gaming": of a character we are told, "Gambling was his business, and to seduction of females he was no stranger" (*The American Bee*, pp. 93-97).

3. This view is of course basically conditioned by the traditional attribution of activeness to the male and passiveness to the female, the former being ideally combined with chivalrous protectiveness, the latter with virtue. The uncompromising tone of the judgment on seducers is easily accounted for. On the level of the narrative, and by moral and sentimental elaboration, the victim of seduction is often shown in heart-wringing physical and spiritual

punishment; ostracized and victimized by all and sundry, if she does not die in childbirth she may render her fall comparatively less grievous by committing a more unpardonable sin, that of suicide. On the level of social criticism, many (female) authors felt impelled to crusade against the seducer because they considered that he could escape scot free, whereas his victim must irremediably suffer at the hands of "a censorious and misjudging world" (*Lucinda*, 2d ed., p. 45).

4. The author of *Lucinda* is otherwise unidentified. The introductory "To the Reader" of the first edition states that it is a true story. The second edition prefixes twelve pages "To the Public," which begin with a solemn endorsement, signed by eleven gentlemen, and then offer an account by two of these, charged to inquire into the Lucinda affair; this report is dated July 31, 1810, but refers to measures taken in May 1806. The first letter is dated July 20, 1806, the final one (not in the 1807 edition) December 31, 1806. There are loopholes in the guarantee of authenticity: phrases like "according to the best information" and "some of us are thoroughly acquainted with many of the circumstances" (*Lucinda*, 2d ed., p. iii; all references are to this edition).

5. In such delicate matters many authors tended to become evasive. Mrs. Manvill renders as follows the scene in which she elicits the confirmation that Lucinda is pregnant: " 'Tell me then—it is a cruel question, and I trust your goodness will pardon my suggestions if groundless—tell me my child—is not your situation peculiarly wretched?' She burst into tears—I was answered!" (pp. 39-40).

6. Among these appears an emphatic recommendation for young girls to study physiognomy: "Would each one of our sex, my Nancy, instead of contemplating in their mirrors, real or imaginary beauties, devote a small proportion of the inestimable moments of time, to the general study of physiognomy, we should not, I presume, so often see the victims of perjury, sinking to their untimely graves" (pp. 62-63). Helen W. Papashvily's view that after *Lucinda* the "fallen girls" disappear from American literature (*All the Happy Endings*, p. 32) must be qualified: they tend to be relegated to the subplots.

7. At times Mrs. Manvill is so overwhelmed by her feelings that even in retrospect, when writing to her sister, she cannot bear them (see pp. 113, 149-50).

8. W. P. Trent, *A History of American Literature* (Appleton, 1903), seems to have first ranked *The Coquette* above *Charlotte* (p. 196 n.); this opinion has since been echoed. Herbert Ross Brown writes in his introduction to the Facsimile Text Society ed. of *The Coquette* (1939): "It is surpassed in narrative power by only one early American novel, Hugh Henry Brackenridge's *Modern Chivalry*" (p. v). Cf. also Wagenknecht, *Cavalcade*, p. 5. According to Mott, *Multitudes*, "Appendix," *The Coquette* and *Charlotte* were the only American fiction best-sellers of the decade 1790-99. In view of the high rating of *The Coquette* one is curious about a novel that has not been traced, *Matilda Berkley*, described as "about upon a level with the Massachusetts novel of the Coquette" ("Literature of North Carolina," *Monthly Anthology* 3(1806):355-57.

9. Walter F. Taylor, *The Story of American Letters* (Chicago: Regnery, 1956), judges that *The Coquette* represents the "customary level," "effeminate and sentimental," of the early American novel (p. 93). It was called a "mournful tale" and listed among novels contrasted with the original and humorous *Modern Chivalry* in the *Monthly Anthology* 5(1808):499.

10. The story of Eliza Wharton obviously was modeled upon the Elizabeth Whitman affair. Mrs. Foster, incidentally, through her husband was distantly

related to the Whitmans. It is probably true, though, that the novel was "less inspired by facts than by the spirit of Richardson" (Brown, *The Sentimental Novel*, p. 51). The sentimental novelists usually "saw in nature what art [i.e., the Richardsonian tradition] had assured them would be there" (Van Doren, *American Novel*, p. 7). Caroline Dall deplored Mrs. Foster's use of the facts and asserted that "the influence of Richardson's story [*Clarissa*] may be seen wherever the author departs from the facts" (*The Romance of the Association; or, One Last Glimpse of Charlotte Temple and Eliza Wharton, A Curiosity of Life* [Cambridge, Mass., 1875], p. 70). Mrs. Dall had an axe to grind: it was her hypothesis that Elizabeth Whitman "married some foreigner, of rank and distinction" who for reasons of his own could not publicly acknowledge the fact (p. 111). She also believed that Elizabeth's mother and Charlotte Stanley, prototype of Charlotte Temple, were near cousins (p. 13), a theory which, in the words of Carl Van Doren (p. 9), results from a saga-like interaction of the actual and invented. See also James Woodress, *A Yankee's Odyssey: The Life of Joel Barlow*, pp. 60-64; Elizabeth Whitman was in love with Barlow. Woodress's judgment of *The Coquette* is severe (p. 64).

11. "I have not yet determined to seduce her....At present, I wish innocently to enjoy her society; it is a luxury which I never tasted before" (pp. 81-82).

12. See his plea for indulgence (p. 53), his view of his life and the retribution that is to follow (p. 255).

13. See Boyer's first letter, pp. 13 and 14 especially; cf. also, though the comment is Eliza's, p. 102.

14. "...To the disgrace of humanity and virtue, the assassin of honor; the wretch, who breaks the peace of families, who robs virgin innocence of its charms, who triumphs over the ill placed confidence of the inexperienced, unsuspecting, and too credulous fair, is received, and caressed..." (p. 91).

15. P. 19. Mrs. Richman soon regrets not having been quite frank about Sanford (see Boyer's letter to Selby, pp. 21-24) and tries to make up for it on the following day (p. 28).

16. "While, therefore, I receive your visits, and cultivate towards you sentiments of friendship and esteem, I would not have you consider me as confined to your society, or obligated to a future connection" (Eliza to Boyer, p. 41). Cf. pp. 17, 102, and see Eliza's remark on the "light breeze of discord" needed if love is not to "stagnate" (p. 45).

17. Edw. Wagenknecht (p. 5) stresses that her willful, pleasure-loving character, and not just conventional female weakness, is the origin of her fall. See also C. K. Bolton's view of her as a coquette led into evil ways, just like Miss Whitman (*The Elizabeth Whitman Mystery* [Peabody, Mass., 1912]). L. D. Loshe (p. 14) praised Mrs. Foster for not giving a black-and-white distribution of blame and praise. The obituary notices stressed that Miss Whitman owed many of her misfortunes to the biased view of life she had acquired from reading romances. This was also adduced in support of Holmes's theory on the dangers of fiction, in *The Power of Sympathy;* the footnote recalling the fate of Miss Whitman was written, possibly on the basis of obituary notices, immediately after the girl's death in July, 1788 (*The Power of Sympathy* appeared in January, 1789). In *The Coquette* there is, understandably enough, barely any reference to the dangers of novel-reading. But when dejected, Eliza asks for undemanding reading, "plays and novels" (p. 162), and she *does* pine for an ideal husband uniting, in the manner of fiction's perfect heroes, the best qualities of Boyer and Sanford (p. 31). In *The Boarding School* (1798) Mrs. Foster said some unfavorable things about novels; see

above, "Pernicious Fiction," and the brief discussion of *The Boarding School* in "Mentoria," Chapter 4, part 2.

18. She felt for him the "friendship and esteem" (p. 6) which she later promises to cultivate for Boyer (p. 41). Later still, she offers Boyer "esteem and love" (p. 147).

19. This is in answer to Eliza's query: "Is it not an adage generally received, that 'a reformed rake makes the best husband?'" (p. 76; cf. William Hill Brown's tale, "Harriot," *Massachusetts Magazine* 1[1789], no. 1: especially p. 4), Brackenridge offered a characteristic comment on this view: "...Make her think you would rather debauch her than marry her. Bring to this suspicion, and I warrant you, her whole study will be to entrap you into matrimony" (*Modern Chivalry*, p. 65). Incidentally, Brackenridge, too, inserted a sentimental seduction story into his quixotic pattern; see pp. 107-13.

20. "I am afraid you have hit his character exactly," is Eliza's reply to Julia's view of Sanford as a "Chesterfieldian" (p. 164).

21. She is not so fortunate as Charlotte Temple, who mercifully faints when she could still run away from Montraville. Perhaps she is past the swooning age: she is about twenty years older than Charlotte when she dies (i.e. 36). It is not clear at what point Sanford becomes her lover; he first refers to it when Eliza is pregnant already. Has the affair lasted for years? Eliza is described as young, gay, and volatile, and as having been the toast of the country for two years, in the early stages of the novel; there is no indication of a long break in the narrative except for the year or so of Sanford's absence.

22. See, however, her remarks on dissipation (p. 18), disposition (p. 59), learning from mistakes (p. 159), and theaters managed by ladies (p. 187). By contrast, *The Boarding School* is entirely didactic.

23. There are seventeen of these, who receive a total of 74 letters from seven different correspondents. Two of these provide most of the letters: Eliza (32) and Sanford (8); variety thus does not become dispersion.

24. See above, "Bildungsromane," Chapter 4, part 3.

25. *Amelia* was printed in the *Columbian Magazine* (1787), the *Massachusetts Magazine* (1789), and the *New York Magazine* (1795).

26. "Amelia had then attained her seventeenth year. The delicacy of her form was in unison with the mildness of her aspect, and the exquisite harmony of her soul, was responsive to the symmetry of her person. The pride of parental attachment had graced her with every accomplishment that depends upon tuition; and it was the singular fortune of Amelia, to be at once the admiration of our sex, and the favourite of her own" (*Amelia, or the Faithless Briton*, p. 4).

27. "The agitation of her mind, indeed, had hitherto rendered her insensible to the weakness of her frame; but exhausted nature, at length produced the symptoms of an approaching fever..." (p. 30). Cf. the outline of Doliscus's character (p. 6), the effect of tears (p. 10), Amelia's fainting (p. 15).

28. There seems to be no reliable biographical information about the author of *Laura;* but see the remarks made with reference to the discussion of her first novel, *Secret History,* below, in "Strands of History," Chapter 16. According to Samuel H. Wandell, *Aaron Burr in Literature* (London: Kegan Paul, 1936), p. 224, Rich attributed *Laura* to Miss Hassall, and Wandell suggests this may have been the maiden name of a Mme D'Auvergne; this lady is referred to in the *Correspondence of Burr and his Daughter Theodosia,* ed. Mark Van Doren, p. 300.

29. "...He was often delighted with the charms of her imagination. He had

himself enriched it, yet dazzled by its brilliant coruscations, he bowed involuntarily before the work of his own hands" (*Laura*, p. 45).

30. He later subtly distinguishes between "a house of doubtful character" and "a den of infamy" (p. 130).

31. His inconsiderateness has exposed her to the sordidness of a brothel, the scorn of a woman to whom Rosina had given help, and has forced her to spend one night on her mother's grave.

32. "...Her life was an exemplification of this truth:—'that perpetual uneasiness, disquietude, and irreversible misery, are the certain consquences of fatal misconduct in a woman; however gifted, or however reclaimed'" (p. 181).

33. The *Port-Folio* rather unaccountably twice offered its columns to an enthusiastic reviewer of *Laura*, in January and March, 1809. This review is illuminating in its listing of the defects of the average novel, "in an age when writers, from want of superior abilities, seem reduced to seek in eccentricity and deviation from nature the means of awakening interest; when most of the fashionable novels disgust by a bombastical assemblage of unmeaning words, appearing themselves astonished how they came together, and are rendered only somewhat less obnoxious by being crammed with the spoils of better times..." (3d ser., 1, no. 1: 69-70). The critic pronounced the style of *Laura* "superior to the crowd of novels daily issuing from the presses of Europe" (1:274).

34. See also her view of Belfield (p. 25). Laura herself appears as an angel to Eliza (p. 93).

35. Though he feels deeply, Belfield later finds it difficult to express his feelings (p. 128).

36. "I stood awhile almost petrified; and beholding the fair Miss Alfred's eyes deluged in tears of anguish, and the sympathetic currents from the rock, which at this time seemed to flow more rapidly, I involuntarily joined in the distressful concert" (*Infidelity*, p. 23).

37. "I am weak of mind, and even criminally susceptible!—Sentiment will finally destroy me!" (p. 83); cf. p. 99. See also Maria's letter 19, and p. 100 (from a letter from Fanny).

38. Her resolve to "war against feeling and check the advances of this generous lad" (p. 86) does not sound too promising; it follows soon after her admission of her weakness, quoted in note 37, above. Nothing comes of her request to Alfred to speak to her of friendship, and no longer of love. She suffers grief, not relief, when he leaves for Philadelphia (letter 23), and joy on his return (letter 29), though she says that she feels guilty about it.

39. See also letter 25, with the story of Louisa and Henry.

40. Harvard College Library copy, "Advertisement," p. 11.

41. He could not be numbered among divinely appointed instruments of retribution such as those who appear on the title page of Parson Weems's pamphlet *God's Revenge against Adultery*.

42. It is irrelevant whether the adultery is physically consummated or not. Letter 45 leads us to think the relation platonic, but the hero's own words might lend support to a contrary interpretation, even if allowing for the confused rhetoric of sentimental intensity, if not incandescence (p. 153). Cf. Fanny's view, p. 127.

43. See, e.g., in letter 1, the happiness of having a baby and the grief of losing it; in letter 43 the juxtaposition of the recollected scene of Wellsford's

[277]

parting from Fanny and the present reunion of the lovers, as Eugenius turns into Wellsford (pp. 166, 168).

44. Alfred likens Caroline to Werther's Charlotte (p. 76), though he would rather not be called a Werther. He also mentions the precedent of Yorick's courting a married lady (p. 91). "Eloisa to Abelard" is introduced as an appeal to sensibility (letter 13). There is also the Sternean story of Alfred's charity, interpreted by Courtney as an example of the ennobling power of love (letters 30, 34-35).

45. Richard B. Davis ranks Relf among the second-string minor writers of the decades before the publication of *Swallow Barn* (*Jefferson's Virginia*, p. 299).

46. The narrator (perhaps Edward Franklin) furnishes us with biographical information that is not necessarily truthful: the date of his birth, January 1, 1770 (chap. 2); he is a godchild of Franklin (p. 23); in 1818 he is on a European tour (title page); he has had a play applauded at Drury Lane but damned by the critics (Preface). His book appeared in Philadelphia in 1818.

47. See also his remarks on dueling, gambling, and on education.

48. At least eight of the personages introduced have affairs, and of these five are involved in several. See also the digressions about "dark houses," incest, and bundling (chap. 23), and Bloomfield's diatribe against flattery (p. 103).

49. Sophia calls forth a poem in praise of woman (chap. 31). Her plea for the false Maria procures a more lenient sentence for the latter.

50. Interpolated stories include the preacher's (chap. 3), sailor Jack's (8), Richard's (chaps. 27, 32, 39, 44, 48), and M'Donald's (chaps. 36, 37, 40).

51. For the Sternean style, see pp. iii, 3, 25, 54.

IV. THE NOVEL
OF ADVENTURE

T HE PRELIMINARY REMARKS of the preceding chapter apply to the present one as well. This study frequently approaches its subject through striking features of the novel-plots. Precedence is thus given to one aspect of the plot, yet the element singled out often may not appear to sustain the reader's interest exclusively or even predominantly. Among the novels classified as love stories, for example, there are many in which the element of the adventuresome is an essential ingredient. Conversely, the theme of romantic love suggests numerous plot elements in the novels of adventure to be introduced next. Nevertheless, in the narratives discussed in the preceding pages, the adventurous element does not truly rival the primary focusing on the issue of the love story; it is subordinated to it, being itself conditioned by the lovers' efforts toward reunion or, more commonly, their enemies' attempts at keeping them apart. On the other hand, the true novel of adventure as often as not strikes one as the work of a writer who seems to have kept on spinning adventures for the sake of enjoying and taxing his powers of invention; such fashioning of tales does not limit itself to devising tests for some lovers' steadfastness. Novels of adventure introduce situations whose immediate outcome is more important to the reader than the final conclusion toward which the story is moving. The question whether the heroine can escape the villain blots out the sad fact that her lover is still pining for her to return to him. In reading a love story, one does not forget the mutual love of the hero and heroine, though they may be worlds apart and quite estranged, perhaps even unfaithful, in appearance; and while the girl is strenuously busy preserving her virtue, she remains aware that among her motives for doing so is her wish to be worthy of her lover. But the lovers in an adventure story, as for instance Constantius and to some extent

Pulchera, occasionally do lose sight of that which gives some meaning to their incredible adventures—that is, the fact that they have a love to live for—so completely are they absorbed in extricating their lives from immediate perils.

Chapter Thirteen

"FORTUNE'S FOOT-BALL"

THERE are twenty-two chapters in *Ferdinand and Elmira: A Russian Story* (1804), by Mrs. Sarah Wood (1759-1855); of these only ten contribute to the action proper, whereas the other twelve serve to explain the genesis of the situation in which the hero and heroine find themselves.[1] This dependence on past occurrences and off-stage happenings is a typical and unsatisfactory feature of a first group of novels of adventure. For a general heading the title of one of them, "Fortune's Foot-ball," seems rather suitable. Their heroes' and heroines' lives are governed by an unpredictable fate whose instruments may be natural cataclysms, the caprices of superiors, or the disproportionately consequential effects of events long past and only sketchily related. The protagonists themselves are therefore placed in situations from which they cannot escape by their own efforts. Neither a proper understanding of the causes out of which their predicaments arose, nor fighting the figures of authority on whose whims they depend will help. They necessarily learn to roll with the punches or resign themselves to making gestures of resistance which they know to be no more than symbolic.

Ferdinand and Elmira are handicapped by exceptional circumstances which forbid them to use all of their knowledge and the influence that by rights is theirs. Ferdinand's actions are dictated throughout by honor and idealistic beliefs reflecting the nobility of his blood and indicating what position he should occupy. The young man remains nonetheless at the mercy of a man clearly inferior to him but favored by outward rank and by chance. It takes a *deus ex machina* in the person of a general to save Ferdinand. The general's intervention is a stroke of fate, too, just like the hostile acts that have nearly led to Ferdinand's death; but it must be understood in terms of providence not chance. Brunsdel may outrank Anstorm, but what is really decisive is that he is a good man overcoming a villain. As such he is among the instruments of providential guidance which operate together, even though with characteristic *ritardandi*, to restore the fortunes of the houses of Ferdinand and Elmira.[2]

The historical background to the young lovers' adventures is the Seven Years' War. The chaos of wartime destruction, the more or less accidental alliance of powers that may change sides as opportunity offers—such elements provide a fit environment for the selfish impulses relying on the codes of monarchical or military hierarchy to achieve their ends. Against such totalitarianism the individual, however honorable, does not stand the least chance unless helped by luck. To be sure, at the end of *Ferdinand and Elmira* virtue and honor do emerge victorious, but the margin of their success provides little comfort to the believer in the possibility of contributing to the direction of one's destiny. The insistence upon providential guidance can be looked upon as expressing Mrs. Wood's orthodox New England views, and it may be argued that the modern novel-reader's interest in character, developing and asserting itself in the face of the events, is quite irrelevant to it. On the other hand it is perhaps more to the point to assume that the author was guided above all by her knowledge of the current plot devices of her day. There was a substantial novel-tradition by the end of the eighteenth century, and it suggested numerous elements that could satisfy the expectations of the readers of novels of suspense and that probably conditioned certain weaknesses of *Ferdinand and Elmira:* its unsatisfactory structure, already referred to; its all too intricate patterning of events, and especially its dependence upon coincidence (meetings opportune or barely prevented); and its reliance upon clichés of romantic situations and an artificially elaborate diction.[3] Before long, a theatrical Gothicism is used, but the vigorous opening of the novel might have been a prelude to better things:

> Though she shut the door as easily as possible, yet the light, which she held in her hand, was extinguished by the draught of

[284]

air, and she was left in absolute darkness. She looked around: not a ray of light penetrated the gloom, or cheered her harassed spirits. She would willingly have returned to the apartment she had left, but all her exertions to open the door were ineffectual. (p. 5)[4]

Adventures of Alonso was published anonymously in London in 1775, and only in 1941 was its attribution to Thomas Atwood Digges (ca. 1741-ca. 1821) given substantial and plausible support.[5] The correctness of the attribution granted, there still remains the fact that the book appeared outside America, and the difficulty of Digges's nationality: born in America he seems to have spent the better part of his life in Portugal[6] and England. He apparently returned to America just before the turn of the century; this deliberate choice, or gesture, would seem to entitle Digges to be acknowledged in a survey of American fiction.

It would of course be reassuring to find *Alonso* rendered more positively North American by its setting and characters, but they belong to other countries. Our hero does visit the New World but never gets further north than Panama. The background required for his adventures is one of quickened mutability, emphasizing the irresponsibility of Alonso's break with the security offered by his surroundings. The advantages of an excellent education are thrown to the wind when he devotes himself to Eugenia. Alonso at first does not know that the young lady is married, but this fact is quickly rendered insignificant anyway by the couple's passion; and the reader is informed only through a kind of codicil that Eugenia is not free to love and be loved (1:19-20). The couple's flight from Lisbon is the first of Alonso's restless moves in search of a happiness that is to elude him to the end. The lovers transgress the moral precepts of their world, and their later life is governed by the retribution inseparably linked with this initial wrong decision. This seems as consistent and just as Ferdinand and Elmira's trials appear arbitrary: one couple is responsible for their errors while the other is not. In the case of Mrs. Wood's protagonists, the providential omnipotence which finally rewards them seems so remote that they can hardly be expected to believe either in its effectiveness or in their own acts under its auspices, and the reader finds it hard to sympathize with them. But Alonso, however often frustrated in his undertakings, is not a Ferdinand: he is more than a figurehead for certain virtues. This is due in part to his manly willingness to face his difficulties and perhaps also to share the blame for offending against the codes of allegiance and conduct—though he does not seem to be very much aware of the imperatives of transcendent justice, but certainly clearly realizes the immediate necessity of proving his endurance and resourcefulness. Alonso is also a more real character than Ferdinand because he occasionally forgets his personal concerns and comments on human affairs in the parts of the world with which he is acquainted, expressing liberal views about democratic principles of government[7] and the economic policies of colonial powers.

Most of the discussions of topical matters in which Alonso joins, center around aspects of Pombal's administration of Portugal. This one central subject counterbalances the narrative flights about Alonso's adventures in Spain, South America, on the seas, and during his period of slavery,[8] and reflects his attachment to his country, his father, and the moral order which is part of their character. After Eugenia's return to Lisbon, she is largely a silent partner in Alonso's experiences,[9] but the focusing on Portuguese affairs obliquely reminds the reader of her existence: we remember the couple's passion, and our forebodings as to its issue. Eugenia's decision to become a nun at a time when she is free to marry Alonso is her way of atoning for their common transgression (2:109-10). Perhaps Alonso's many hardships might be said to be the price he must pay for their love; but as he appears to have quite enjoyed many of his adventures, some of which were none too ethical at that,[10] their penitential value is doubtful. Alonso is punished more harshly by Eugenia's withdrawal; he returns alone to an existence of sobriety, which is to be permanently colored with the sad memories of his mistress (2:128). The sensibility which he betrayed in the earlier stages of his love (1:46, 53) has not left him and is likely to be still intensifying his grief while he tries to comfort his father; whether he can keep his youthful optimism (1:139) is questionable. The balance of the diversity of fortunes, and the conversational topics that reemerge, are reflected in Digges's style; from the breathless relating of adventures, or touching scenes of woe and parting, it easily recovers a sober straightforwardness in the discussions in which the hero joins. Digges refrained from any self-conscious literariness and thus preserved for his book a certain freshness; in other novels the violent to-and-fro between extremes often seems to call for an artificially heightened expression.

A case in point is *Fortune's Foot-ball: or, the Adventures of Mercutio* (1797-98) by James Butler (ca.1755-1842),[11] a novel which crowds an incredible number of adventures and people into its closely printed 380 pages. The reader at first follows the author willingly enough, for Butler attacked his narrative with gusto and managed to convey a lively movement to it. But very soon our attention begins to flag, the ups and downs of the hero's adventures following in too rapid succession. Another limitation quickly reveals itself: the fact that some situations have to be reestablished through rather artificial means for the story to be given a new impetus,[12] and the related fact of the near relations and alliances among most of the characters. Mercutio's opportunity to save Lucinda from drowning in the Hyde Park Serpentine, in the first pages of the book, connects him enduringly with her family, particularly with her brother Charles. At her death his grief drives him to seek diversion in traveling. His near-marriage to Lucinda, frustrated by the girl's death, is then paralleled by his runaway match with the Doge's daughter, a young lady who suggests a nocturnal assignation in the course of which Mercutio "found his heart powerfully assailed on all sides, by the charms of Leonora, whose movements were so rapid, that he had not time to collect his forces" (1:47); but just after having made an honest woman of Leonora he loses her and their son when pirates attack their ship. Mercutio's second marriage is more fortunate, though it also forces him to resume his travels rather abruptly and involves him in a series of further mishaps.[13] Before his chance meeting with Isabella, his second wife, Mercutio has just as opportunely happened to meet with Charles. He comes across George Wright in Italy after a shipwreck; is introduced to the Wilcoxes, the family of Wright's wife; and almost inevitably, on different occasions and in different places, is later thrown together with a son and daughter of the family. While a slave, Mercutio once meets Charles, as well as the latter's brother-in-law. Small wonder if at the close of the novel there are almost as many weddings as there are deaths in the final scene of *Tom Thumb:* they seem designed to ratify the communion and the elective affinities that have been established among the *dramatis personae* through their remarkable ubiquity.[14]

It is needless to say more about the range of inventiveness of our author. The reader is baffled at the rapid changes of settings and personnel which it brings about and may also be irritated by Butler's brusqueness in managing them.[15] Though one is at first grateful for such digressions as the reports offered by Mercutio's new acquaintances and old friends reencountered, the repetitiveness of this material and the uniformity of the narrative tone and speed soon grow tiresome; with more truth than Butler realized, one of his narrators says at the beginning of his tale that it "will afford neither pleasure nor amusement" (1:186). Another kind of variety one learns positively to dread is the attempt at subtle phrasing combined with an emphatic appeal to the reader's emotional susceptibility, in passages like this early one: "... No sooner did Lucinda, (the young lady) expand her beauteous eyes, than love, like the electrical fire, diffus'd itself through each avenue of our hero's heart, which being tender and susceptible, retained this first impression so firmly, that it was never eradicated until the lovely orbs, by which it was communicated, were quench'd in death" (1:10).[16] Such writing becomes less frequent as the story progresses, but reemerges when the characters are finally all reunited (2:176).

Fortune's Foot-ball is an appropriate title if ever there was one, and suggests an idea which need not have been in the author's mind when he picked it. The entire novel is something in the nature of an account of a contest between "fortune" and "providence." We have noted the inscrutability of providential intervention in *Ferdinand and Elmira*. In Butler's novel it is more explicitly an excuse for the author to go on writing, and Mercutio's adventures lead him back to his starting-point, as it were, every time to begin afresh: "But alas! Fortune, that fickle Goddess, had raised her foot with a design to give him another kick" (1:72).[17] This sounds promising from the point of view of the writer grateful for new sources and material. Since our author, however, was careful to distinguish between two functions of the providential plan, on other occasions the perspective appears changed. Man is then seen not at the mercy of a wanton fate but consciously depending and relying on God's wisdom and justice; these he must learn to acknowledge as gratefully as does Mercutio's father, after he has been rescued: " 'Miracles! Miracles all!' exclaimed his father, 'all bounteous Providence! Unsearchable are thy ways, gracious God! But a few hours past, my life was exposed to the greedy swords of assassins—suspended by a single hair over the dreary gulph of death!' " (2:184).[18] The God of Creation can turn His storms into instruments of chastisement (1:63-64); He singles out an individual offender for punishment (2:76), while granting His support to the cause of a wronged people, such as the Americans (1:92-93, 71).

It takes more than historical references of this kind or naval encounters described in a vein of realism (1:94) to persuade the reader that Butler could sincerely "with confidence vouch for the authenticity of the narrative" (1:iii). One puts down Butler's book regretting that his facility of invention did not leave him leisure to create more imaginatively, and to conceive, instead of footballs with human names, characters capable of thinking and feeling, and gifted among other things with a sense of humor.[19]

Early American fiction was not conspicuous for its humor, a fact of which even contemporary readers were aware. In the *Monthly Anthology* praise was awarded to *Modern Chivalry* for its comic gusto, and this novel was contrasted favorably with the sentimental fiction of Mrs. Rowson, Mrs. Foster, and some others. Most of the fun of *Modern Chivalry* was satirical and burlesque; so was the humorous content, slight though it was, of the American novels of the age, quite generally. With this in mind and taking *Modern Chivalry*—or better still—*Female Quixotism*—as examples of the tendency, it does indeed seem possible that *The History of Constantius and Pulchera; or Constancy rewarded* (1794) might have been conceived in a spirit of parody, as some critics have suggested.[20] It is impossible to take either the preposterous plot or the diction seriously, and only a quotation can do this incredible tale justice. Valorus-Pulchera must die to provide food for her starving fellow outcasts, and writes a final letter to her cruel father, informing him that after having been "the sport of fortune" she is about to enter "a state of changeless retribution":

> Valorus had just finished the letter, and delivered it, when one of his woeful partners took up the fatal gun, well loaded, and had got it to his face, and was just pulling the trigger in order to lodge its contents in his head, when he chanced to raise his eye a little, and discovered a bear wallowing in the snow, at about twenty yards distance—He exclaimed, "Valorus! Thank God, you may yet live!" and discharged his piece at the bear, lodging two balls in his head, of which he died instantly. (pp. 25-26)

By contrast with the fantastic versatility of Constantius and his Pulchera, *The Life of Alexander Smith* (1819)[21] is a sober book; yet its characters, too, are time and again called upon to prove their adaptability to the unforeseen. Smith is identified as "captain of the Island of Pitcairn; one of the mutineers on board His Majesty's Ship Bounty."[22] There is no doubt that the book draws heavily on the material of the mutiny case, though perhaps less on the facts than on some of their fictional and imaginative potential. Clearly, too, *Robinson Crusoe* or some imitation of it seems to have influenced the author, especially in the first part of *Alexander Smith;* for the second part he may have had another model.[23] That central section, an intermezzo between Smith's years on a desert island and the social experiment of Pitcairn, is much the weakest part of the book. It shows signs of hasty composition and writing, crowds too many incidents into a narrow compass, and ends unexpectedly on a didactic note of self-rebuke (p. 115); fortunately this section is comparatively brief.

The author of *Alexander Smith* insisted on his intention of offering his readers instruction of various sorts. But the Pitcairn section is rather too loosely utopian, where additions are made to the basic *Bounty* material, to quite succeed in this didactic aim. The seriousness of the Pitcairners' political organization may be evident, as is also that of Fletcher Christian's insistence on the faith they must preserve (p. 168).[24] Yet what is most memorable about the episode is the first flush of excitement as the mutineers start on their voyage to Pitcairn and the sense of threat haunting them until they can send off the male natives among their group. Though the descriptive style of the age is often painfully overblown, here the reader is likely to regret that little background painting is attempted. It might have made the mutineers' experience and choice more real. In the opening section of *Alexander Smith,* its most lively and successful part, the author managed to achieve a certain verisimilitude. The narrator's account of his years[25] on an island in the Indian Ocean sets forth the ways and means of his keeping alive and rendering his existence a little more comfortable; indeed, the narrator makes a point of praising the practical education his parents have given him (pp. 69-70). We share in the outcast's work, and though there is no wealth of details building up a picture as complete as that of *Robinson Crusoe,* enough material is visualized for us to accept the reality of the man's experience. Smith's rather flat and pedestrian manner here proves an advantage rather than a drawback. The story is sufficiently varied, especially with the introduction of the boat-building scheme, and mercifully short. But by the standards of this beginning, one regrets that two more sections had to be added, perhaps to make a full-size volume.

Mr. Penrose: The Journal of Penrose, Seaman is the latest contestant for the title of the first American novel, "that much argued and ever elusive phenomenon."[26] The English painter William Williams may have written this story during his thirty years' stay in Philadelphia and New York, or soon after his return to London, that is, in the late 1770s. What is beyond question is that the book has substantial merits. Williams's tale, which incorporates some of his own adventurous experiences, is about Llewellyn Penrose, a sailor accidentally abandoned off the Nicaraguan coast. After some years in complete isolation he makes friends with two natives, a young man Harry and his sister Luta. The latter bears Penrose two children but dies after the second birth, and the widower takes another Indian girl for his wife. Meanwhile, some more natives join Penrose, as well as a Dutchman Somer and a Scotsman Bell. Penrose resigns himself contentedly enough to his fate, though he sporadically fears detection by the Spaniards, and suffers many hardships and bereavements. After his death, in the twenty-eighth year of his exile, his manuscript diary finds its way to England.

Mr. Penrose makes its first impression upon the reader as a straightforward narrative free from any literary self-consciousness, using throughout a simple, often colloquially figurative vocabulary.[27] Its spontaneity shows, for example, in the author's description of natural, particularly zoological, phenomena, which seems to derive from a personal interest in such matters rather than from an acquired compulsion to combine the narrative with some instruction. The lifelike effect of the account, supported by the narrator's use of detail closely observed, wins over the reader to accepting the reality of what he is invited to share in; from the comforting impression that nobody would take the trouble of inventing so much plausible detail,[28] one moves to appreciate the essentially familiar nature of many strands woven into the pattern of Penrose's adventures in unfamiliar surroundings.

A closer look reveals that *Mr. Penrose* has more to recommend it than its seemingly unsophisticated reporting of observation.[29] Awesome elemental powers, exotic fauna, welcome discoveries and fearful shocks, meetings and partings, births and deaths, comic incidents and solemn meditation, colorful characters,

Indian oratory, Scotch and Irish speech—this variety of ingredients reflects a sense of the diversity to be found in any life investigated closely enough and also prevents any inappropriate insistence on single topics. The narrator does repeatedly draw an edifying lesson from his adventures,[30] but he keeps this relatively unobtrusive among his many accounts of the social development around him; and his frequent passages of zoological description are short and embedded among humorous episodes and sober narrative advances.

Robinson Crusoe is an obvious archetypal model with which to compare *Mr. Penrose*. In the two books (as also in the opening section of *The Life of Alexander Smith*), an outcast reenacts courageously man's attempt at asserting his rule over his natural environment—proceeding from mere name-giving to a true understanding of the essence of the strange new world. In the case of Crusoe's exile on an island, there are connotations of man's fall from grace and of a redemptive experience; his story is grimmer in tone and more committed to the exemplary than Penrose's. Crusoe has an initial advantage which Penrose must do without—the equipment salvaged from the wreck. Yet his assumption of command over his territory is slow and lacks confidence. Crusoe remains preoccupied with himself, looking inward whenever his life-preserving activities permit; revolving his sense of guilt from the moment he acknowledges that it is there for him to cope with, he weighs it against his hope of survival and rescue and concludes he is not fit for them yet.

Now, though Penrose starts out in miserable destitution and though his later providential finds are less generous than Crusoe's, he is soon granted the more than compensating gift of human fellowship: after having domesticated a hawk and a fawn, in his fourth year of exile he receives Harry and Luta on his territory. Thereafter, he is to be spared any obsessive concern with a confused self. His thought can turn to practical social issues,[31] and from then on he comes to the consideration of his individual anxieties by way of a remedy for them, a rewarding community of affections. To say this is at once to lay bare a distinctive feature of *Mr. Penrose*. Friday, though liked by

[293]

Crusoe, can never by the white man's equal; indeed, one of the troubles of Defoe's book is that his hero, even when apparently sobered, retains a hint of arrogance in his dealings with others, just as his legitimate longing for a life among his countrymen is also a pathetic illustration of his never quite humble acceptance of the fate he affirms having deserved. Penrose, however, knows how to treat others as his partners, even while his rule over the mixed settlement growing around him remains unquestioned. Both Penrose's firmness and his closeness to his European and American associates reflect a commonsensical approach to any problem confronting him. It is at all times important to reach decisions quickly and to insure a cooperative execution of such necessary measures, whether practical or institutional.

The fact that Penrose and his companions form a family rather than a political unit depends on his religious and philosophical outlook, an outlook as enlightened, in the sense of the mid-eighteenth century, as Defoe's was conditioned by late-seventeenth-century Dissenting values. Penrose and his friends represent the family of man, in which the white man's claim to superiority, supported by his technical and organizational experience, is invalidated by his moral frailty. This lesson is brought home in two ways: by contrasting the white man's cruelty and selfishness with both the Indian's and the Negro's essential innocence[32] and by stressing the individual white outcast's dependence on the moves of providence.[33] The reader may feel encouraged to see in the chance connections by which Penrose's diary is finally conveyed to England less a conventional guarantee of the truth of the story than a conclusive demonstration of God's patient guidance.

The moral and practical instruction which *Alexander Smith* and *Mr. Penrose* tried to impart is discreet when compared to the insistence on exemplary human sensibility that is distinctive of *Humanity in Algiers: or, The Story of Azem,* a tale published anonymously in 1801. It was designed to illustrate the hardships endured by slaves, whether Americans in Algiers or Negroes in the United States.[34] While his emancipation is delayed, Azem remains true to his innate noble qualities, which he can fall back on when the freedom he at length obtains brings home to him a simple truth: beyond one's immediate goal, there is always another thing to be desired. The difficulties which he encounters in his quest for love reflect on the cruelty and iniquities of slavery, that is, they are not just the result of the caprice of fortune but are related to the very theme of Azem's whole existence. It is a theme that can conveniently be served by plot devices of the novels of love and of adventure—for example, the rescue of a lady; arbitrary separation from one's beloved; helping his mother before discovering her identity; the hero's love for a girl who turns out to be his sister; his fight with brigands; outwitting those about to settle his fate; his late-revealed high rank; his reward in the guise of a happy, though short-lived, marriage.

For all his generous nature and the variety of his experiences, Azem does not come to life. His qualities are mere words, just as the place-names convey nothing except the outlandishness of the setting. The narrative purports to come from the pen of a former American slave, but the author has not visualized the world he is trying to make us believe in. It has been noted that the same thing is true of another slave narrative, the second half of *The Algerine Captive; or, The Life and Adventures of Doctor Updike Underhill*, by Royall Tyler (1757-1826). Yet if this second volume is inferior to the first, it is still superior to *Humanity in Algiers*.[35] Underhill's comments on the history of Algiers and the clashing policies in the Mediterranean are digressions;[36] they do offer, however, just such observations as might have been made by the naïve American physician he is. There is here a variety of adventures and settings seen through the watchful eyes of a recognizable individual, the doctor, and colored with his peculiar satirical temper. Not too many passages of any length in the second volume of *The Algerine Captive* sustain their interest, plausibility, and concreteness;[37] the few, to be met with at intervals, that do, reaffirm the stamp of the hero's wide-awake receptivity and wry detachment.

This is an achievement prepared in the first volume of Tyler's novel. Owing to his education and his early experiences in teaching and in the medical profession in America, Underhill forms a rather unflattering opinion of mankind. Though the hero's voice remains satirically tolerant, this view is further darkened by sinister and depressing implications during his journey to the southern states, where he witnesses the institution and practice of slavery. He nevertheless signs up as a surgeon with a slave trader bound for Africa. As a doctor he has a share in the process of capturing and transporting the African slaves, and only then does he fully realize the inhumanity of the treatment of the blacks. And at the close of the first volume, just after reaching this lowest point in his general estimate of mankind and of slavery, he is made a slave himself. The vicissitudes of the second volume thus begin at the end of a steady process of disillusionment and sensitizing: Underhill emerges from the test which they provide without hoping any longer for the realization of his ideals. He is soberly aware of how much is yet to be done for the practical cause of liberty and equality, for even the slightest progress in that cause can be achieved only if man summons up all his frail good will and limited resources. The conclusion of the story is therefore an explicit plea confirming the flattering hints about the United States dropped here and there in the two volumes, after the second volume has been redirecting the satirical touches of the first, American, volume.[38] Whether this is the most convincing and memorable part of the book is doubtful, though the sincerity of Tyler's patriotism need not be questioned.

The lively story of young Updike Underhill's experiences has quite a few things in common with that of Brackenridge's Captain Farrago.[39] His range of observation, however, is wider than the captain's, whose main concern it is to assess and to further his countrymen's preparedness for the forms and practices of democracy. But there is an obvious parallel between the lack of enlightened information concerning their science among Underhill's fellow practitioners of medicine[40] and that of Farrago's fellow citizens, those rash or recalcitrant democrats. Here again, selfish ambitions tend to crowd out the idea of public service. Neither hero finds much appreciation of classical learning among his countrymen. Underhill seems to consider this a reflection not only on those who fail to see any value in the old languages and literatures but also on the true uses of Greek and Latin (1: chap. 7, especially p. 74). Greek demonstrably does not help him in his schoolteaching and distracts him while farming, for "poring so intensely on Homer and Virgil had so completely filled my brain with the heathen mythology, that I imagined a Hamadryade in every sapling, a Naiad in every puddle; and expected to hear the sobbings of the infant Fauns, as I turned the furrow" (1:65). Nor does his knowledge of Greek better his chances with the ladies; on the contrary, a literary allusion of his leads to a challenge to a duel. Underhill naïvely agrees to meet his challenger, this is thought to show great courage, and a sheriff is mobilized to prevent the encounter. The instinct of self-preservation thus sensibly prevails, as in *Modern Chivalry* (1: chap. 12).[41]

The best parts of *The Algerine Captive* derive from Tyler's satirical inspiration. The parodying bent of the whole design, indicated in his preface,[42] as well as individual touches of mockery, provides the novel with another continuity apart from that of the hero's development. The mock-heroic dream of his mother, in which his head serves as a football to a group of Indians, is characteristic (1: chap. 4); so are the late quick summary of the plot (2: 239-40) and Underhill's daydreaming during his captivity, nourished from memories of novels once read and reflecting the hero's experience of ideals and sober actuality:

I fancied my future master's head gardener, taking me one side, professing the warmest friendship, and telling me in confidence that he was a Spanish Don with forty noble names; that he had fallen in love with my master's fair daughter, whose mother was a christian slave; that the young lady was equally charmed with him; that she was to rob her father of a rich casket of jewels, there being no dishonour in stealing from an infidel; jump into his arms in boy's clothes that very night, and escape by a vessel, already provided, to his native country. I saw in my imagination all this accomplished. I saw the lady descend the rope ladder; heard the old man and his servants pursue; saw the lady carried off breathless in the arms of her knight; arrive safe in Spain; was present at the lady's baptism into the catholic church, and at her marriage with her noble deliverer. I was myself almost stifled with the caresses of the noble family, for the part I had borne in this perilous adventure; and in fine married to Donna some body, the Don's beautiful sister; returned into my own country, loaded with beauty and riches; and perhaps was aroused from my reverie by a poor fellow slave, whose extreme ignorance had almost blunted the sensibility of his own wretchedness. (2:28-29)

The anonymous novel *Adventures of Jonathan Corncob, Loyal American Refugee,* published in London in 1787, is in a number of ways a close relative of *The Algerine Captive.* For its hero, too, a New-Englander like Underhill, there is an early ominous prophecy, communicated to his mother, and, much later, a glance back at a very chequered career:

Obliged to fly my country for the first little mistake I ever made in bundling; flogged by the first captain of the navy I ever saw; and p-xed by the first woman I ever intended to make my wife: surely, said I, no man was ever so ill-treated by his evil genius as I am. I have since been beat at Barbadoes; almost choked with the reed end of a clarinet; blown naked out of bed in a hurricane; p-ssed upon by the guard of a prison-ship; and to crown all, here I am with my legs and wings pinned down like a trussed pullet's.[43]

Corncob also makes fun of the reading habits of strict Presbyterians (chap. 2). His picture of a Rhode Island lady is similar to Tabitha Tenney's portrait of her heroine Dorcasina: they both dispense markedly with the conventional superlatives of sentimental novel-writers (pp. 89-90). The entire book is a catchall, sprung from the author's robust if not coarse sense of comedy and his mocking turn of mind. It combines in a lively manner the varied adventures of the Old World *picaro* with the New World setting, especially features on which satirical wit may be exercised. Corncob's experiences reveal to him the rascally intentions and inclinations apparently prevalent among mankind, and he adapts himself good-humoredly to them. Indeed, so readily does he do this that he must be suspected of letting his own bias color the view he takes of his fellow beings. Although none too scrupulous in his observance of the codes of honesty and gallantry, he occasionally forgets to extend his tolerance to others. But no one will quarrel with him when his intolerance is applied to the abuses of slavery or matters of discipline on board a British man-of-war. The author's rough talents were consistently devoted to a rendering of Corncob's adventures on land and sea, his love affairs, fights, and the quick turns of his fate, all of which are told in a straightforward and uninhibited manner. Having begun his narrative in reply to a question from a fellow traveler in an English stage coach, and perhaps to fight off the effects of the cheerless morning, Corncob pursues it with little care for the rules of composition[44] and concludes it with a vague hint that there might be more to come. Any number of picaresque experiences and satirical thrusts could easily have been tacked on to the body of the book; they would have provided a more suitable ending than the author's final reflection on the precarious values of works scientific or "serious" in intent (pp. 212-13).

Jonathan Corncob purports to have been written by a Loyalist refugee, and there are indication that seem to support the author's American origin; but his loyalty is to himself rather than to any country or institution. Certainly there is no bitterness in his satire of New England strictness,[45] nor does it reflect on the causes or nature of the Colonial revolution. The whimsical fate that pursues Jonathan has no political or regional prejudices. The author seems rather sympathetic toward his American background; one is reminded of pages in Samuel Peters's *General History of Connecticut,* where personal animosity yields momentarily to an affectionate amusement revealing the author's divided loyalties and his remaining attachment to the country he left in anger. The author of *Jonathan Corncob* seems to have been definitely less committed than Peters to any of the disputed issues of political and proprietary rights. He could transcend in humorous writing the painful aspect of the rupture between the colonies and Britain. Out of his familiarity with the American setting and his sympathy with some of its cultural implications, the author created in his hero a worthy precursor of later Jonathans;[46] his manner has nothing to do with the average didactic motivations and pretenses of fiction but is frankly, though crudely, devoted to imaginative creation.

The author of *Jonathan Corncob* seems to have carelessly selected a number of episodes and joined them to produce an entertaining narrative sequence. Mrs. Tabitha Tenney (1762-1837) announced that her *Female Quixotism* (1801) was written to instruct her readers.[47] Her didactic aim imposed a measure of discipline on her use of the story material available to her and suggested a pattern for the narrative. Mrs. Tenney meant to expose the follies to which her heroine Dorcasina Sheldon was driven when trying to fashion her sentimental life after the plots of her favorite novels. She therefore devised a series of situations similar in the sense that they all encourage Dorcasina's romantic dreams of love; but these situations are increasingly absurd, too, given Dorcasina's aging, and are increasingly cruel. The reader, witnessing the tragicomedy of the heroine's successive disillusionments, has been taken into the author's confidence from the very beginning, rather like a spectator who shares a playwright's knowledge while this knowledge is wholly or partly withheld from individual characters on stage. Mrs. Tenney's explicit intention is early illustrated quite plainly through the Lysander episode, in which a serious and deserving suitor is rejected by the heroine because his courtship offends against the practices of novel-heroes. The sense of this discrepancy between real nature and artificial forms is maintained in the sequel by the presence of Dorcasina's commonsensical, if coarse, servant Betty. Meanwhile the knowledge of Dorcasina's unreasonable expectations encourages the men who mean to profit by her fantastic naïveté, the pranksters who amuse themselves at her expense, and the friends who attempt to shame her by ridicule into a sober view of her genuine qualities and her confused standards.

Mrs. Tenney's literary precedents are not far to seek, and her particular indebtedness to Mrs. Charlotte Lennox's novel *The*

Female Quixote (1752) is obvious.[48] Yet she introduced a greater variety into her book through her inventive episodes, and the differences between the chief partners and antagonists of the heroine. She also used a coarser tone, to which various considerations inevitably led: the very importance of the gap between Dorcasina's artificial ideals and the down-to-earth standards of her surroundings; the crude back-country setting; the measures of deceit and disillusionment employed against her; and the character of the people playing up to her, many of whom are lower-class characters, while others deliberately cast off their gentle nature and politeness. Particular mention should perhaps be made of the part played in parts of the comedy of misleading and misunderstanding by Dorcasina's servant Scipio, apparently the first Negro character given a distinct role in an American work of fiction.[49] The obviousness of the whole design of *Female Quixotism* has its advantages; there is a lively pace to the story, rapid changes of mood, yet with a continuous reverberation of contrasting responses. The burlesque nature of the situations and of specific elements of the vocabulary, especially that of the heroine, quite effectively support the concept of ridiculous exaggeration which governs Mrs. Tenney's novel.

1. The foreground action is advanced in chapters 1-3, 13, 17-22. Chapters 4-12 paint the past experiences of the elder generation; chapters 14-16 give an account of Ferdinand's military career and his difficulties with Colonel Anstorm. References are to *Ferdinand and Elmira* (1804).

2. An accident initiates the process of their rehabilitation. A Russian officer loses his way near Warsaw, where he finds shelter with Elmira's parents, exiled by the vindictive Czarina Elizabeth. After the latter's death the exiles can therefore be sent for without delay and given back their former position and wealth. Yet their joy seems premature: a rumor reaches them of Ferdinand's forthcoming execution, and Mrs. Oldham faints. At this very moment Ferdinand, Elmira, and Oldham arrive at the Russian court, and without further transition sorrow yields to supreme happiness.

3. Oldham "would have thought that day lost, which was not marked in the calendar of humanity with some deed of kindness and philanthropy" (p. 41). Love is described as "the arch destroyer of tranquillity" that finds "its way into the bosoms" of young people (p. 146). We are poetically informed that the hero has reached manhood: "the blossoms of maturity had exposed his chin to the razor" (p. 149).

4. A note of grimness prevails in the relation of Mrs. Oldham's sentence (pp. 63-64) and her father's reaction to it (p. 85), and of her despair in finding her husband's house deserted (p. 112). For all this misery full com-

pensation is granted in the promising happiness at the end of the story which mentions "a lovely family of infants, who were heirs to the various virtues and charms of their parents" (p. 308).

5. See Robert H. Elias, "The First American Novel," *AL* 12 (January, 1941):419-34, an article which provides the introduction to the edition of the novel by the Reverend Thomas J. McMahon, for the United States Catholic Historical Society (1943), pp. x-xxviii; it is also included in an abbreviated form in D. V. Erdman and Ephim G. Fogel, eds., *Evidence for Authorship* (Ithaca, N.Y.: Cornell University Press, 1966), pp. 419-28. The New York Public Library copy of *Alonso* has a penciled note on its title page: "By Mr. Digges of Warburton in Maryland." The book appeared in a German translation as early as 1787; see L. M. Price, *The Reception of U.S. Literature in Germany* (Chapel Hill: University of North Carolina Press, 1966).

6. His stay in Portugal did not influence his northern view of the impulsive southern temper and "a climate where the passions between the two sexes are so easily inflamed" (1:20). Nor did his Maryland origin and possible Catholic upbringing make him uncritical of Roman Catholicism; see the intolerance of Alonso's mother (chap. 1), and a Franciscan's rebuke of Alonso: "you reason too much to be a good catholick" (1:140). References are to the original edition of *Adventures of Alonso*.

7. His remarks about the contempt for the people evidenced by some British ministers and by the readiness with which Parliament lends itself to their maneuvers might indeed have been well received in the American Colonies (1:125-27).

8. He once repulses the advances of his master, "who, being palled with the enjoyment of women, sought for pleasure in the abandoned prostitution of his own sex" (2:77); perhaps a surprising passage in view of the fact that the novels of the age were meant for a largely female, genteel, reading public. In Brockden Brown's "Stephen Calvert," Clelia claims that she left her husband because of his homosexuality (see Dunlap, *Brown*, 2:401).

9. The couple, "drowned in tears and embraces," last lay eyes on one another at the close of the first third of the novel (1:88).

10. E.g., he tries to smuggle past the official control a diamond obtained very cheaply from a Negro who had to get rid of it at once.

11. The *Oxford Companion to American Literature*, ed. James D. Hart, calls Butler an "English author resident in Pennsylvania" (4th ed., New York: Oxford University Press, 1965, p. 122). Butler has some un-English things to say about American independence (1:71) and British tyranny (1:92-93). These remarks suggest that he is possibly identical with the author of *American Bravery Displayed*, which awards praise to the Americans and charges the British with burnings, rapes, robberies, murders, treachery, brutality, inhumanity. References are to *Fortune's Foot-ball* (1797-98).

12. L. D. Loshe has noted how easily one love lost by the hero is succeeded by another "even more desirable" (p. 24).

13. Charles and Wright are also unlucky in their first marriages: the former's wife proves unfaithful; Wright's is carried off by an epidemic. Eugenio's match is similar to Mercutio's with Leonora but more fortunate.

14. They never proceed to the United States, though, as has been pointed out by A. H. Quinn (*Fiction*, p. 13). A writer following the established paths of storytelling found it easier to use the more romantically remote conventional settings than to attempt to convey local color.

15. For an illustration of the rapid to-and-fro between the various groups of travelers, see 2:158, 163, 167. The absence of chapter divisions makes the changes of setting and characters seem even more abrupt.

16. Isabella's falling in love with Mercutio is described in truly sentimental fashion (1:117). For a contrast, see the sober comment on Lucinda's death: "This was a severe stroke to the afflicted Mercutio! Yet well calculated to teach him resignation to the will of the Almighty" (1:31).

17. A similar passage is found later (2:5).

18. Cf. also 2:59-60; 1:91.

19. One conscious attempt at fun, emphasized by the typography, occurs in the oratory of a lieutenant addressing some impressed sailors: "Come, my brave mess mates, now is the time to EXTINGUISH yourselves in OFFENCE of your king and country" (1:73).

20. See P. H. Boynton, *Literature and American Life* (Boston: Ginn & Co., 1936), pp. 195-96, and Cowie, *Rise*, p. 30. Perhaps a sense of the burlesque also prompted the plagiarized version, *History of Lorenzo and Virginia, or Virtue Rewarded* (Concord, N.H., 1834). In this almost verbatim copy, the most important changes occur on the title page where the original didactic motto is replaced by one promising Gothic thrills; the dedication stresses the entertainment value rather than the instructiveness of the story. References are to the third edition of *Constantius and Pulchera*. (The original edition appeared in Boston in 1794.)

21. *Alexander Smith* is attributed to Charles Lenox Sargent. The preface, in an elaborate "authenticity guarantee," asserts that the manuscript, written by Smith, was first obtained by a Spanish sailor, then by an American. One of the latter's fits of madness occurred as the "editor" was passing by: the manuscript was sold to him after the madman had died.

22. Alexander Smith was the name used on board the historical *Bounty* by an American sailor named John Adams. When the Topaz reached Pitcairn in 1808, he was the only survivor of the mutineers there. In the novel he tells the story of his fellow exiles' mutual extinction (an actual event) as a subterfuge to discourage further pursuit.

23. E.g., it could have been *Narrative of the Adventures and Sufferings of John R. Jewitt*, reprinted in New York in 1815.

24. Smith keeps his pride in his American origins, too, and proudly reports, upon the arrival of the *Topaz* from Boston, that Christian "had no idea that the Americans had arrived at so much perfection in ship building and seamanship; and was sorry to say his own country's merchant vessels suffered much in the comparison" (p. 215).

25. There is some confusion in the dates and count of the years. The approximate date of Smith's casting off from his desert island is early June 1788, and he enlists on the *Bounty* in London after a series of adventures; but Bligh sailed from England in October 1787.

26. *Mr. Penrose: The Journal of Penrose, Seaman. By William Williams, 1727-1791.* With introduction and notes by David Howard Dickason (Bloomington and London: Indiana University Press, 1969), p. 13. This is the first edition to give the full text of Williams's manuscript, whereas the London editions of 1815 and 1825 are marred by abridgement and "correction." Professor Dickason provides information about Williams and a good assessment of Williams's literary abilities, as well as listing some motifs which *Mr. Penrose* shares with later American fiction. His conjecture is that the book was written

while Williams was in America, but the evidence which he submits only makes clear that the manuscript seems to have been complete by the early 1780s.

27. See, e.g., the references to "Sot's Bay" (pp. 40-41), the pithy estimate of an Irish captain's skill (p. 47) and of Penrose's musical ability (p. 254), the homely phrase "in dolefull dumps" (p. 54), the image introducing the mention of the flamingoes (p. 64), the metaphor of "an Old House" (p. 131), the proverbial saving one's breath (p. 298), the pun on "draw" (p. 330), the variants of speech and jargon (pp. 171 f., 212 f., 282 f.).

28. Penrose himself makes the point that he would be unlikely to invent details of his adventures (pp. 134, 259, 267).

29. Some obviously "arranging" hand may seem to have timed the arrival of Bell just before Somer's death and to have provided Penrose with paper and books. It is a gratifying coincidence that Penrose finds the lass meant for Toby "the finest Indian girl" (p. 145) he has seen, since he is to marry her later. Composition operates occasionally in a pictorial sense in *Mr. Penrose*, as might be expected from a professional painter (e.g., 178 f.).

30. See, e.g., pp. 71, 121 f., 218 f., 221 and 225 f., 302.

31. The prisoners' regulations (p. 45) anticipate Penrose's political sense.

32. See, e.g., pp. 90, 94 f., 117, 129 f., 139, 348-54, 358 f.

33. See, e.g., pp. 61, 64, 82, 254, 256, 258, 316.

34. The topic of slavery, often combined with that of the war with the North African states, was often used; e.g., the novels of Digges and Butler, and cf. Mrs. Rowson's musical comedy of sorts, *The Slaves of Algiers* (1794), or William Ray, *The American Tars*, an autobiographical account with fictional ingredients. *The Interesting Narrative of the Life of Olauda Equiano, or Gustavus Vassa* (1789) was probably known in America and may have influenced *Humanity in Algiers*. For the historical background, see the recent study by H. G. Barnby, *The Prisoners of Algiers*.

35. With this disproportion in mind, W. P. Trent wrote, "our clever American author is not even artist enough to master a simple form of narrative" (*A History of American Literature*, p. 205). Teut Riese credits the second half with one advantage: Tyler achieved a perspective transcending the picaresquely accidental of the first volume and could thus offer a relative view of the merits of America and her democratic principles (*Das englische Erbe in der amerikanischen Literatur*). G. Thomas Tanselle's excellent *Royall Tyler* contains a lengthy discussion of *The Algerine Captive*. Tanselle finds it advisable to treat the two volumes as two different books; if the first is related to *Modern Chivalry*, the second is related to the Indian captivities. Tyler's novel was the first American novel to have an English edition (1802); the *Monthly Review*, which, like the *Monthly Magazine*, praised the novel guardedly, qualified its praise by comparing the book with *Crusoe* and *Gulliver*, and hinting at "transatlantic peculiarities" (42[September, 1803]:93). In America, *The Algerine Captive* was comparatively well treated in the context of a gloomy survey of American fiction, in the *Monthly Anthology* (5[1808]: 499). Cooper pronounced the novel distinctly superior to most American fiction (*Early Critical Essays*, p. 97).

36. Vol. 2, chaps. 15, 25. There is some resemblance here with the technique of *Alonso*. The chapters about the relative merits of the Christian and Muslim faith, which were thought too lukewarm a defense of Christianism (*Monthly Review*, p. 93), indeed only confront terminologies (2: chaps. 5-7, 22-24). See also Tanselle, p. 172.

37. Frederick Tupper, "Royall Tyler, Man of Law and Man of Letters," *Proceedings of the Vermont Historical Society* (1926-28), pp. 65-101, thought that *The Algerine Captive* could well stand comparison with *Robinson Crusoe* in matters of probability and style.

38. See the conclusion, 2:240-41; and the references to Franklin (1:154), Yankee humanity (1:201), American prosperity (2:193). The treachery of Adonah's son is another, oblique, compliment to American integrity (2: chap. 36). Other kinds of references to America include the satire on the speculators (1:47) and the mention of regional rivalries (1: chap. 25).

39. Though *The Algerine Captive* is not so important a book as *Modern Chivalry*, the latter provides a more valid test for its qualities than the majority of the contemporary American novels.

40. Underhill is not determined in his choice of a profession by the example of famous American physicians but by the attractive bindings of some books on medicine (1: chap. 8).

41. The discussion of the duel matter is strikingly similar in tone to Brackenridge's, in *Modern Chivalry* (1792).

42. See especially pp. v-x, referred to occasionally in the first and third chapters of this study. Tyler's preface is echoed in Dennie's letter to him (August 30, 1797); see L. G. Pedder, ed., *The Letters of Joseph Dennie* (Orono, Me., 1936), p. 165.

43. *Adventures of Jonathan Corncob*, p. 164.

44. There is, however, a clever contrasting device in chaps. 12 and 13: Corncob first praises Barbados, but at regular intervals deplores the frequency of hurricanes there; and then, after the abuses of slavery have been brought to his notice, he inserts with the same regularity remarks about the just retributive function of the hurricanes.

45. The boy openly rejoices when an irascible aunt of his dies, and is rebuked for this, but Jonathan's parents forget almost as promptly as he that a decorous show of grief is required: "All the neighbours crowded to our house to condole with us, and as they unanimously said my aunt was in heaven, the whole family was soon consoled, and the next day we were all as merry as ever" (pp. 13-14).

46. While Robert B. Heilman (p. 72) called *Jonathan Corncob* "the first novel with a strikingly original American character and with an unmistakable American background," R.W.G. Vail more specifically stressed its pioneering use of "the character of Jonathan to typify the Yankee personality with its shrewd, dry wit, its inquisitiveness and ability to look out for Number One" (*PBSA* 50[1956]:101-14) Tyler's *The Contrast* introduced Jonathan to the stage in 1787 too; the play appeared in print in 1790.

47. See above, "Pernicious Fiction," pp. 46-59.

48. In the Philadelphia reissue (1802) of a London compilation, *The Female Mentor* (1793), the readers were urged to read Mrs. Lennox's book but to avoid *Sir Charles Grandison*, with its unrealistic painting of virtuous perfection (2:87-89). For Mrs. Lennox, see Miriam R. Small, *Charlotte Ramsay Lennox* (New Haven: Yale University Press, 1935); and Gustavus H. Maynadier, *The First American Novelist?* (Cambridge, Mass.: Harvard University Press, 1940). It has been pointed out that in *The Female Quixote* Mrs. Lennox was following the model of Marivaux rather than Cervantes; see James R. Foster, *History of the Pre-romantic Novel in England*, p. 80.

49. John Herbert Nelson (*The Negro Character in American Literature*, Vol. 4, no. 1 [Lawrence: University of Kansas, Dept. of Journalism Press,

1926]) mentions Cockloft's servant Caesar, in *Salmagundi*, as the earliest instance of a Negro character. He draws attention to the fact that liberal comments on slavery appear early, e.g., in *Modern Chivalry* (there are some in Vol. 2, vi, chaps. 1-2, published in 1792); some remarks indeed appear in *The Power of Sympathy* (1789), and frequently later (e.g., *Julia*, 1800, and *The Prisoners of Niagara*, 1810).

Chapter Fourteen

MYSTERY AND TERROR

THE HEROES and heroines assigned a passive role, perhaps that of a mere "fortune's football," demonstrate a
dependence on fate and providence that seems to reduce
their personal responsibility to a minimum. They may in theory
believe in freedom of the will, yet practically they are paralyzed
in an inability to act, and to act for the good and true. Their
best policy is to wait for lapses in the control exerted over them
by hostile forces: then only can such heroes and heroines begin
to fulfill their promise. In this limitation of their initiative, they
resemble the figures of an earlier chapter fighting overwhelming
odds. These, too, accept the fact of a decisive handicap re-
moving their enemies quite beyond their reach. But at least
they are resisting somebody with an identity, a name (even when,
because of some writer's lack of skill, the name is no more than
a label). They are not, as is the case with "fortune's footballs,"
confronted by an arbitrary, supernatural, alliance of individual
events or personal whims.

There is yet another group of stories whose heroes or heroines
are at a very unfair disadvantage, with heavy odds favoring their
antagonists. On two levels, however, differences exist between
their plight and that of the former figures. For one thing, the
enmity is not exclusively or mainly in the field of love; for
another, it creates an atmosphere of fear rather than of malice.
These heroes move in a fictional world characterized by the
devices of the novel of terror as developed in England from
Walpole to Mrs. Radcliffe and Monk Lewis. Thus the heroes
see through the motives of their enemies and are given ample
warning of their evil determination. This knowledge might be
sufficient to strike them with anxiety and terror; but they seem
even more impressed by the air of mystery that may accompany

[307]

the manifestations of their antagonists' hatred, for it appears to imply a command of supernatural powers.

The short tale *Adventures in a Castle* (1806) is a good illustration of this type of story. It rapidly creates on ominous mood of suspicion through some facts: a family quarrel, and the specific threat embodied in an impoverished relative; and Louis's and Henry's comparative unprotectedness and dependence on a guardian. The latter knows about the past and therefore about potential tensions. This material works as a sounding board when Henry mysteriously disappears from a locked room, an occurrence which coincides with the attack of a group of bandits against his brother. There follow, in the setting of a decaying castle, sinister intimations of murder and an intervention only partly successful on the part of Louis. This young man disappears, then unexpectedly returns to his guardian, but as he keeps silent about what happened to his brother and himself, the mystery is only increased. The confrontation with Vauban at the Duke of Alençon's at last starts a process clarifying the issues; as the enmities and grounds for discord stand revealed, Louis and his friend regain confidence. Vauban proves vulnerable: he is involved not just in the family feud, which is now intensified by jealousy over the Duke's daughter, but in a movement representing a threat to the community. This danger necessitates calling in the King's troops, and the defeat of Vauban and his bandits is quickly consummated. The rest of the mystery dissolves in the light of the blaze destroying the outlaws' castle. Henry's reemergence out of the darkness of his prison aptly illustrates the final solution. Reason and order are reestablished, usurping chaos and irrationality vanquished. A quotation may exemplify the type of irrational forces of aggression Henry suddenly finds himself attacked by; in the context of his experience he is bound to rely on reason and common decency to try to understand what lies behind the hostility he encounters, but so long as he does so its depth and complexity must remain unfathomable:

> Having alighted from the carriage, I was immediately conducted to the dreary dudgeon [sic] from whence the magnanimity of

my beloved brother released me. When I was secured by chains in that horrible place, my guide condescended to open his lips, and inform me, that here the remainder of my days was to be spent, that here I was to drag out in misery, the remnant of a life, which till then had been spent in a course of uninterrupted felicity, except when the death of my father, for a time, cast a shade over my happiness. I then repeated my request to know by whom, and for what motive, I was thus severely punished, but I could obtain no answer from the monster, and I thought I could perceive a horrible smile of satisfaction, gleam across his countenance, at having thus doomed a fellow creature to be miserable, as long as life remained.[1]

The theme of *Adventures in a Castle* is essentially a very simple one, that of a family quarrel over property. Its chief interest is obviously expected to derive from the villainous means and mysterious appearances employed by Vauban to help his luck. The plot is further complicated when the motive of jealousy joins that of greed, and still more because Vauban also has a share in the schemes of organized bandits. A similar pattern underlies *Julia, and the Illuminated Baron* (1800), by Mrs. Sarah Wood (1759-1855): a family rivalry over a large estate, the motive of lust, and de Launa's active membership among the Illuminati. If we were to take Mrs. Wood's sentiments at their face value, the last-mentioned circumstance should prove by far the most serious of de Launa's crimes.[2] Yet in the portrait which she drew of him (pp. 67-68) and in the sequence of actions for which he bears the responsibility, her explicit criticism is only vaguely borne out. De Launa emerges not as the representative of a formidable subversive movement but as something more familiar: a conventional villain of the Radcliffean variety. He has been consistently brought up as an Illuminatus, to be sure; but this education merely fosters ugly inclinations such as any novel-villain tends to possess and develop.[3] As we follow him through the narrative, he is above all obsessed with the idea of making Julia his mistress. He proves a would-be seducer with little patience in the formal approach, and because he lacks the confidence of a Montraville or a Sanford in his powers of seduction, he soon resorts to the use of violence. There is no indication that he has any time and energy left to devote to the purposes of the Illuminati, once he is in pursuit of Julia and trying to avenge himself on Colwort. We may assume that, having made over part of his estate to the movement, he is content to enjoy their principles for the simple sake of rationalizing to himself his own enjoyments.[4]

With this view of the villain, the problem of the Illuminati fails to function as a spiritual or ideological test; it is just another device for the creation of a sense of mystery and horror. This has something to do, of course, with the New England–Federalist conception of the Illuminati. Not that Mrs. Wood's indignation at the principles and goals attributed to them was not at least as genuine as Jedidiah Morse's when he preached a sermon against them;[5] but we must consider that to Mrs. Wood and Morse, the existence of the Illuminati provided a scapegoat, an embodiment of dangerously enlightened religious views and political radicalism. As such, they were a conveniently crass illustration of the potential corruption lurking in the Jefferson-ianism they abhorred, hence the insistence on the connection between Illuminatism and the violence of the French Revolution (pp. 284-88). The notion of Illuminatism was better left vague, suggestive rather than descriptive.

As a device in the service of the sinisterly mysterious, the phenomenon of Illuminatism is linked with the chief element of complexity in the plot of *Julia*: this story of a struggle between innocence and lust is also a twisted tale of mistaken and hidden identities in which the villain is endowed, with no gain to his reality as a character, with certain powers of an agent of fate, and therefore with some of the awe that fate calls forth. He plays a part in the manner of an evil destiny, from the day of Julia's birth all through her career of misfortune. He has her mother poisoned, which leads to Julia's removal from the de Launa castle and her being brought up in obscurity. Out of the latter circumstance arises the threat of an incestuous connection, since de Launa does not know that Julia, whose virtue he is trying to subdue, is his half-sister.[6]

The narrative proper, which begins when the Countess befriends Julia, introduces in the girl's account of her abandoned state, the element of mystery that is to characterize many of her adventures. She mentions the hints given her by Isabella concerning her future rank, and the circumstance of Isabella's abrupt disappearance (chap. 1). While Julia is tested by normal occurrences, such as falling in love, parting from her fiancé, and becoming seriously ill (chaps. 4, 5, 15), the strangeness of her origin is referred to again in remarks on her resemblance to some relative of the Countess. Gradually the consciousness of some hidden relationship and the elements of the strange and exceptional coalesce and dominate the narrative. Since de Launa has early been depicted as wicked (pp. 25, 26) and is obviously irritated at failing to impress Julia, the girl's abduction to Spain is likely to be attributed to him. It is soon shown that Julia has been the victim of an error, but the formerly vague distrust of de Launa remains more definitely with the reader and prepares him for the villain's later actions. After Julia's imprisonment, her adversities are unhesitatingly traced to him; meanwhile it appears that de Launa may also be mixed up with Julia's earlier history.

The girl grows more familiar with man's wicked ways through listening to the stories of the Countess, Mademoiselle de Gyron, and Leonora (chaps. 2, 12, 17), and experiencing de Launa's menace to her honor. She seems to feel the fascination of the forces of darkness, of the unknown, the potentially fearful, and proves her curiosity and fortitude in the visit to Leonora's grave; at the end of this visit she wishes to cut off a lock of her mother's hair: ". . . She had just touched the hair, when the stillness that pervaded the gloomy mansion was interrupted by a deep sigh; and Julia started, touched the face, to her horror it sunk into ashes, and mouldered into dust; not a feature remained; it was all an horrid chasm, for the affrighted imagination to fill up" (p. 192).[7] This is the culmination of the supernaturally horrible; further harassing experiences follow, but these are too obviously caused by de Launa's machinations. The death of the villain, as the result of an apothecary's error, ironically and finally disposes of all appearances of supernatural powers. Julia, to judge from her behavior in two thirds of the book, should at all times easily be de Launa's match. It is difficult to reconcile her fearlessness when a prisoner with her later meek acceptance of the loss of the Countess's esteem. In this change, however, our heroine conforms to the pattern of innocent sufferers of slander: they accept being abandoned by their former friends as quickly as the latter lend an ear to their calumniators. Significantly, in the final part of her story, Julia must rely on the help of fortuitous happenings. There is, for example, that chain of events acquainting her through Roswell with Madame de Shong a short time before a fire destroys this lady's dwelling; its former inhabitants eventually seek shelter at an inn just in time for a revealing reunion with the Countess (chap. 24), which is itself a prelude to the discovery that Julia is the Marquis's daughter (p. 263). Overhearing a conversation which sheds light on Colwort's origins is another helpful accident arranged by a destiny kindly preparing Julia's happiness (p. 288).

The anticlimactic features in the characterization of de Launa and Julia, and the transparent device of Julia's and Colwort's identities,[8] are typical of the weaknesses of the novel. The story is needlessly burdened with the episodes of Mademoiselle de Gyron's revenge, Leonora's elopement from the convent, Olivia's becoming de Launa's mistress, and the succession of deaths among Madame de Shong's relatives. There is repetitiveness in the parallel fates of Julia and Colwort-Ormond, both before and after their meeting with de Launa and in details of the accounts given of the villain. The style of *Julia* is undistinguished: it does perhaps tend less toward extremes of sententiousness or sentimentality than that of other writers. Mrs. Wood, mentioning in her "Dedication" her wish to write a moral tale, apologized for her European setting;[9] she clearly wished her patriotism not to be questioned and went out of her way to praise her country (p. 47) and Washington (pp. 131-35), and her female colleagues "Philenia" and "Constantia" (chap. 8).

From the latter, Mrs. Wood borrowed two mottoes and used them as chapter headings in her novel *Amelia; or, The Influence of Virtue* (1802), in which she extended her distrust of the

Illuminati not just to all French revolutionaries but to their country as a whole. By comparison the British became a nation as nearly exempt from faults as the Americans,[10] and she gave her French heroine an English mother and grandmother as well as an English education. Amelia must hold her own against two different types of villains. The difficulties which she encounters in the first two-thirds of the novel belong to the familiar elements of the novel of domestic victimization. There is the difference, however, that the emphasis of the narrative lies less on the sufferings of the heroine—as, for instance, in *The Hapless Orphan* or *Constantia Neville*—than on her exertions to manifest the influence of virtue which is at her command. This may not make her any more lifelike than her all too submissive fellow heroines, but it as least provides a welcome relief from the manifestations of Harriot's evil spell and the trials to the heroine's sensibility.[11]

It also, of course, suggests the idea of Amelia's perfection. Her only sign of weakness is her pique at Sir William's delay in consummating their marriage (chap. 6). She ranks first in the moral hierarchy of the characters, whereas Volpoon just as surely is at the other end of the scale. Young Barrymore really is no less accomplished than Amelia, for his one error apparently is his Roman Catholicism, of which he eventually rids himself. Lady Stanly, too, is near-perfect, except in too rashly assuming that her son and Amelia must marry. Sir William at least, though he has substantial virtues (p. 104), is of a frailer substance, and only an Amelia can be so patient with his slavish submission to Harriot. This girl, repeatedly in explicit contrast with Amelia,[12] is not deliberately evil but rather selfishly and impulsively weak and partly a victim, like De Everet, of those who spoiled her in her education. Clearly she is far from being a villain of the Volpoon caliber:

Alas, unfortunate man! he had never enjoyed one social comfort, or one solid pleasure: guilt corroded all his joys, and impressed discontent and despair upon his gloomy countenance: he had never known a dear domestic joy, nor one smiling comfort. He had not wiped the tear from the widow's cheek, or raised the

[313]

drooping heart of the fatherless; he had never given comfort to the friendless, or cheered the afflicted. He was a stranger to the god-like pleasure of doing good: he received no satisfaction from reflection; avarice had prompted guilt that he feared to remember; and to accumulate riches, he had waded through sighs, tears, and blood: this one passion had absorbed every other; and to the gratification of it, he had sacrificed his conscience, peace, and happiness, and left not one soul behind him, that regretted his death, or would have recalled him by a wish.[13]

The reader early realizes that Amelia is far superior to Harriot and must sympathize as the heroine's sensitivity is tested severely and cruelly by her rival's unscrupulousness. Amelia has suffered quite enough when the author appears to promise the imminence of her reward, Sir William's return to a sense of her shining Christian virtues. The concluding part of *Amelia,* however, inaugurates a new persecution. The heroine is carried to corrupt France and held captive in a deserted and decaying house; at length Volpoon's intention to murder her is made plain. Her earlier domestic and sentimental trials at this point assume the aspect of a mere anticipation of these freshly accumulated sufferings. It is as though Amelia's sensibility first has had to be heightened simply to make her more vulnerable to the quick changes of her destiny, from unhappiness to the promise of fulfillment and back again into desperate misery. Inevitably there is, in the ups and downs of her existence in England, a gradual blunting of the effects of her individual experiences; but this does not compensate an increasing sense of insecurity which results from the fact that her troubles proceed from different sources: apart from Harriot's agency, there have been some simple unfortunate coincidences[14] and the quite unrelated spiritual crisis caused by Barrymore's proposal.[15] On the other hand her vicissitudes from the time of her abduction are intensified by being entirely dominated by the mysterious purpose of one man rendered the more awe-inspiring because he remains in the background. He exerts his evil influence through the agency of a scoundrel whom he can blackmail into almost any crime. In France, therefore, Amelia lives in a sinister atmosphere long unrelieved by glimpses of human compassion such as she earlier

[314]

witnessed and supplied. There is only a temporary, and limited, luxury granted her: she can share with Henrietta the pleasure of scorning Volpoon and hearing that one at least escaped him alive: his sister-in-law, Amelia's mother. De Everet then summons up enough energy to rebel against Volpoon's orders, but apparently only to plunge Amelia into a new order of difficulties, the hardships of a snowstorm.

With Amelia recaptured in sight of the convent door, Mrs. Wood permitted herself a particularly flagrant piece of artificial suspense: she concluded one chapter with the scene in which Volpoon's servant raises his dagger over Amelia and began the following chapter with a ten-page account of the reasons for Volpoon's persecutions of the girl, and the stages of Sir William's efforts to rescue her (chaps. 17-18). We return to Amelia with the dagger still in midair; but its owner is by now half-convinced that he would be wrong in using it. Amelia recovers her liberty, is reunited with her husband and, just as the Terror of Robespierre begins, they leave France for peaceful England. In a mood of moral serenity, they reap the rewards of Amelia's goodness, while Harriot, doomed to an early death, at last profits from the chance to repent.[16]

Mrs. Wood described the story of Amelia as a "useful lesson"[17] and declared having recorded it for the benefit of her readers, as she heard it from the lips of Mr. Harley, an English visitor to America and admirer of the Federalist leaders. In other words, she claimed to be telling not fiction but a true story, warranted by Harley's worthy and judiciary character (pp. 75, 218). The Englishman is the actual narrator, in the first person; yet most of what he tells, and especially all of Amelia's adventures, he has learned secondhand, and Mrs. Wood gained nothing from using him as a narrator. Nor is *Amelia* superior to *Julia,* in either character-drawing or style. The author was satisfied in the later novel, too, with ready-made superlatives and phrases, whether introducing and grouping her figures, appealing to the reader's compassion, or attempting to convey the horror of Amelia's situation when she is at the mercy of Volpoon and his henchmen.[18] There is, however, in the whole of the design and execution of *Amelia* a certain energy and purposefulness which *Julia* was too overburdened with digressions to achieve; and *Amelia* is perhaps easier to read—or at any rate, less dull—than the majority of the contemporary American novels of sentiment and Gothic adventure.[19]

The most sustained effects of *The Asylum; or, Alonzo and Melissa* (1811),[20] by Isaac Mitchell (ca. 1759-1812), spring from the same sort of Radcliffean inspiration as the prison episodes in *Julia* and *Amelia*. Mitchell has been ridiculed for introducing a Gothic castle into his American setting.[21] His Connecticut fortress (2:58-59)[22] certainly does not seriously take hold of our imagination. But it is only one part of his Gothic theatricals; the author *was* briefly able to achieve the true touch of the novel of terror. This occurs when the heroine, a prisoner in the "castle," is in a desolate situation which makes her particularly receptive to the sinister quality of her surroundings without as yet plunging her into helpless fright. In twenty pages of *crescendi*, the smugglers' masquerade and the raging storm combine with Melissa's heightened but still rational sensitivity to cast a spell on the reader's imagination. The climax of the passage is reached in the following lines:

> . . . She was about to unbar the door, when she was alarmed by a deep hollow sigh; she looked around, and saw stretched on one side of the hall the same ghastly form which had so recently appeared standing by her bed-side. . . . Groping to find the stairs, as she came near their foot, a black object, apparently in human shape, stood before her, with eyes which resembled glowing coals, and red flames issuing from its mouth. As she stood fixed in inexpressible trepidation, a large ball of fire rolled slowly along the extended hall, and burst with an explosion which seemed to rock the building in its deepest foundations. Melissa closed her eyes and fell senseless to the floor; she revived, and reached her chamber, she hardly knew how; locked her door, lighted another candle, and after again searching the room sank into a chair in a state of mind which almost deprived her of reason. (2:85-86)

Isolating such a passage, of course, robs it of the tension which it has inherited from the pages preceding it, and consequently

stresses its melodramatic staginess.²³ Yet even this may be seen
to be of a different texture than Mitchell's rather mechanical
description of the coming of dawn and dusk by degrees, as
contrived as the gradual turning on and off of stage-lights. Two
parallel passages within the Gothic stretch of *The Asylum* show
Melissa witnessing these transitions:

> Melissa seated herself at a western window and watched the
> slow declining sun as it leisurely sank behind lofty groves.
> Pensive twilight spread her dusky mantle over the landscape;
> deepening glooms advanced; the last beam of day faded, and
> the world was enveloped in night. The owl hooted solemnly in
> the forest, and the whipperwill sung cheerfully in the garden.
> Innumerous stars glittered in the firmament, intermingling their
> quivering lustre with the pale splendours of the milky-way.
> (2:79)²⁴

The properties used in the concluding lines point to the strict
conventionality and imitativeness of Mitchell's manner. This
must lead us to expect touches of sentimental and genteel writing; in the case of Mitchell such features are the more irritating
as, from the author's preface, we might have thought he knew
how to avoid the weaknesses of minor novel-writers. Rereading
his introductory "Short Dissertation on Novel," with its admittedly loose terminology, we find that at any rate he did not run
against its positive requirements. He was undoubtedly influenced
by his admiration of Mrs. Radcliffe (1:xviii) and may have
profited from reading *The Gleaner*²⁵ and *Constantius and Pulchera.*²⁶ Curiously there are some parallels with *The Gamesters,*
a book which appeared after the first publication of *The Asylum*
and was praised in Mitchell's 1811 preface.²⁷

If other parallels with contemporary works of fiction, whether
of plot, emotional attitude, or style, are not likely to prove an
asset, neither is the repeated use of individual devices, such as
the pair of prophetic dreams, one gloomy and one rosy, which
both the hero and heroine dream.²⁸ The rawest bit of the story
is the "joke" played on Melissa's father: he is given to understand that the girl is dead when a cousin of hers, conveniently
a namesake living at a great distance, dies of consumption.

This is intended to shield Melissa from further persecutions, but indirectly also to punish her father for his mercenary violation of his promise that Melissa and Alonzo should marry. Mr. Bloomfield repents, but the reader wonders all the more at the use of such a method because of Mitchell's reference to a similar trick that backfired cruelly, the story of Balcombe (2:chap. 13). The treatment inflicted on Melissa's father reflects the emotional instability of some of the characters, who are liable to be overwhelmed by their feelings. Alonzo offers an extreme illustration of this: witness his transports of grief at the news of Melissa's death.[29] In view of Melissa's remarkable self-possession amidst Gothic terrors, we need not fear that she might go to such lengths. Her sensibility is of a calmer, lyrical kind, responsive to the soothing melancholy echoes of nature[30] or to the pastoral promise of the Avernum of which she dreams with Alonzo (1:263-64), and which she realizes at long last after they have emerged from their nightmare of imprisonment and separation (2:277). It is fitting, if we consider these instances of the importance of feeling, that the harshest portrayals should be those of the soberly unromantic fathers (1:69, 2:36) and the shallow ladies' man (1:251-52); not that such sketches really carry any more punch than the hackneyed composition of the hero's and heroine's pictures (1:209, 37).

The landscapes are particularly "sublime"[31] in the subsidiary, European episode. It would seem that such painting is in the nature of an ornament, whereas Mitchell was personally committed to a view of America as a paradise within reach of those willing to emigrate from the Old World. Into the story of the Berghers, refugees from European corruption in an America about to become independent, the following piece of propaganda therefore found its way quite as naturally as did Imlay's propagandistic descriptions into his books:

The new land is the poor man's Canaan; to him it is a land flowing with milk and honey. He there finds not only a plentiful supply for himself, but independence and affluence for his children. The forest affords abundant provender for his cattle, and in no small degree comforts for his family; it abounds with a

variety of fruits, nuts, herbs and roots, some of which possess
in an eminent degree a nutricious, others a medicinal quality;
acorns which fall from the oak in autumn completely fatten his
swine, and they require no other feeding; then the maple is
itself a treasure; from its trunk you extract a liquid which by
various processes is transformed into spirituous or fermented
liquor, vinegar, molasses, and the richest of sugars. The birch
tree affords a similar fluid, though much inferior in quality. In
clearing the land, we obtain materials for building, firewood for
the winter, and even the ashes produced by burning the useless wood and timber on the grounds, are valuable for the
potash-works. The earth being fertile needs little tillage and
yields copiously. (1:77-78)[32]

Yet the new world is not free from moral corruption and sources
of fear, and an innocent imagination can respond to them, as
the case of Melissa proves, as strongly in America as in the
France of Henry and Louis, Julia and Amelia.

Similar to Melissa and her Alonzo, the hero of *Glencarn; or,
The Disappointments of Youth* (1810), by George Watterston
(1783-1854), is endowed with an impressible sensitivity. He
therefore experiences terrors whose effects are increased by their
sheer number and quick succession. The novel is a tale of victimization with a male protagonist. This made it possible for the
author to stress not just Glencarn's heroic patience and sublime
virtue[33] but his physical prowess as well. The hero can act in
situations in which a heroine's resistance must be passive, and
even in the midst of difficulties is called upon to prove his
chivalrous gallantry.[34] The highly developed sensibility which
Glencarn literally enjoys[35] is, to begin with, a positive and
commendable disposition. Thus he is governed by, and unreservedly acknowledges, his gratitude and admiration toward Mr.
Richardson. His love for Amelia might be in part an expression
of his reverence for her father. He appreciates her characteristic
qualities because Richardson has taught him the importance of
virtue. Correspondingly he must become painfully aware of the
scorn of the second Mrs. Richardson and her son Rodolpho for
his benefactor. By making Richardson's virtues his ideal, he
becomes a rival heir who is all the more detestable. One specific
difference between him and Rodolpho is the preference they

habitually give to nature and solitude and to the more frivolous aspects of social enjoyments, respectively. Apart from contributing to the moral portrait of Glencarn, his love of nature and refinement serves in the narrative to introduce elements as diverse as his courageous fight with a bear[36] and his first meeting with the stranger later identified as his father. This event is related very early (1:24), and in conjunction with the circumstance of Glencarn being a foundling, establishes, in a manner reminiscent of Mrs. Wood's in *Julia,* a strong undercurrent of mystery, a chord that is struck again repeatedly while the hero is involved in one set of adversities after another (1:chaps. 6, 13, 19; 2:chaps. 1, 12).

Indeed, Glencarn's enemies prove so numerous, so implacable and therefore so unpredictably resourceful and ubiquitous, that our hero occasionally sinks into a state of despairing frustration. Whatever he does is misinterpreted, from his saving Rodolpho's life to his killing the scoundrel in self-defense (1:chap. 3, and 2:chaps. 11-15). His adversaries' slander costs him the esteem of all but a very few friends; even Amelia is temporarily alienated from him by the crafty Gray (1:chaps. 11-12).[37] When Glencarn follows the last piece of advice given by Richardson and starts on a journey to the western territories, he leaves his foes behind but soon acquires new ones. The adventures which now begin for him are of a new kind and can be said to mark a decisive turn in his career, in two ways in particular. For one thing the balance between friends and foes is reestablished at least as a possibility: out of the entirely hostile world with which he meets at first among the bandits, there emerges the contrast between, on the one hand, Montalbert and Reynolds, the persistently evil ones, and on the other, the old nurse Phebe and Wilson himself, who stand for man's ability to resist wickedness or to reform from it. Furthermore, the persons of Phebe and Wilson connect Glencarn again with his own mysterious past; and though our hero presently has once more to face the enemies in league against him, a great step has been taken toward clearing up the obscurity of his origins.

The episode of Wilson's bandits stands out in the narrative

of Glencarn's vicissitudes as something quite alien. There is in the persecutions which he suffers the common denominator of a struggle between merit and envy, unselfishness and base interest, sensibility and unscrupulousness. The same situation is repeated again and again: Glencarn's behavior can be used against him because its appearances are misleading enough to prepossess against him a gullible public. But in his encounter with the outlaws and in Wilson's story, Glencarn is faced with adversity on a different scale, a menace not just to the individual but to the whole country, with roots in a long tradition of corruption and mistaken values. Thus the promise of the New World is implicitly contrasted with the fundamental liability to decay and abuse inherent in man's social and moral institutions. This is the main significance of the outlandishness of Wilson's band, hiding-place, and practices, which at first sight strikes one rather as a mere reflection of literary indebtedness, comparable to the castle in The Asylum.[38] Wilson attributes his crimes to the spoiling which he enjoyed as a child in the place of a sound education. This corruption he brought to America caused Montjoy's jealousy and violence and prevented his own reform; only recently has he learnt to feel remorse (2:146). Glencarn, on the other hand, though the son of English parents, owes his high standards to the education received through the American-born Richardson. They enable him to weather the "disappointments of youth" which Wilson was unable to cope with, and to survive the terrors of his clash with Wilson's world of corruption (2: 117).

Although some of the plot elements of Glencarn may be traced to Fielding and more to Brockden Brown,[39] the author relied heavily, both in individual episodes and style, on a highly colored variety of the sentimental tale. Its surface didacticism and moralizing[40] is no less unoriginal than the preference for descriptions composed of ready-made parts[41] or the effusively superlative.[42] Amelia's conscious social satire (1:31-32) sounds as artificial as Rodolpho's unconsciously ironical self-portrait as a "fellow of fashion" (1:75-76). Watterston seems to have taken some pains to build a structure around the mystery of Glencarn's birth, but he loaded that flimsy structure with so many hack-neyed and melodramatic effects of the quirks of fate, and with such a variety of narrative devices and individual stylistic exer-cises, that the result was a preposterous book.[43]

The hero of his first novel *The Lawyer, or Man as he ought not to be* (1808)[44] responds to the potential terrors of his situation not through ignorance of the limits of man's capacity for evil, as does the innocent Glencarn, but because he knows all too well what mischief man is capable of. Morcell himself has been a criminal for years; the story which he offers is the con-fession of one who has committed seduction and attempted murder, who has inflicted poverty and had a share in the re-sponsibility for some people's death. When he hears himself threatened by a man he cannot remember ever having met or harmed and whom he never sees except at a distance and in the dark, his experience of his own corruption starts his imagination working. His early training and his career as a crooked lawyer suddenly prove unavailing, and he finds himself helpless in the face of a menace that is terrible because indefinite and inexplic-able. A natural desire for survival further intensifies Morcell's anticipation of the fate that may befall him; it tends to exaggerate the danger he thinks himself exposed to in order to justify what-ever measure of self-defense he may be prompted to adopt. More-over, Morcell knows full well that he has deserved punishment. He feels guilty; the sense of his troubled conscience is alive in spite of what he has been taught because it has been kept alert by his contact with the upright Ansley (pp. 32, 79-80, 212). This example proves the more effectual as Morcell all too eagerly, and perhaps implausibly, allows himself to believe Ansley a hypocrite (chaps. 5, 15): he must therefore be shown instances of Ansley's behavior that will reconvince him of his integrity.

The reader is certainly not taken in by what he must consider mere superficial tricks in the service of the author's technique of Gothic suspense (chap. 6, *passim*; p. 167), even though they are given a particular weight through the nature of Morcell's receptivity. The actual accounting for the apparitions in the narrator's bedroom and in front of his house are to be looked upon as means of opening the villain's eyes to the magnifying and scarifying which his guilty predisposition has effected. The concept of a troubled conscience exaggerating worries and fears into shapes apparently beyond the reach of rational means of defense (p. 47) would have been worthy of a treatment less clumsy. Watterston's intial error was the stress which he gave to the didactic aim of *The Lawyer* (pp. v, vii, 50, 56), to the extent of slighting any claim to literary distinction, and even to correctness. At first sight the book seems to present a black-and-white picture of man in the contrast between Morcell and Ansley. On looking closer, though, we find that Ansley himself has his weaknesses, whereas Morcell's eventual conversion endorses the author's belief in education and in the perfectibility of man, which may be reasserted even after a corrupt education has led a child and youth astray. Watterston's picture of mankind is made up not of blocks of black and white but of various mixtures of the two. Enlightenment is a progress from a darker to a lighter shade, from ignorance or neglect of the good to a shining practice of love and charity. The case of Morcell's rehabilitation illustrates such an evolution. His settling down to a life of benevolence shows how radically he has changed, for he used to be restless, in consequence of his moral shiftiness and pursuit of dissipation as well as his moves to escape punishment for his misdeeds. Significantly scenes of and in darkness abound in *The Lawyer*, such as the seduced Matilda's wanderings in the storm (pp. 29-30), the apparitions in Morcell's room (chaps. 5, 17), or the attempted murder of Ansley (chap. 16). These dark scenes echo the element of violence beyond the control of reason in Morcell, in the vindictive Edwards, and in the passionate Ansley too.

Watterston had to rely on the very crudity of the impact of such somber violence because he lacked the skill and discipline better to express it. All too readily, he employed well-worn clichés, and his own diction easily turned into stiltedness and artificiality.[45] To use the terms which he introduced in his praise of Burns, he may consciously have aimed at the "pathetic" style, but he clearly was not aware of the power of "the most simple" language (p. 150).

A Journey to Philadelphia: or Memoirs of Charles Coleman Saunders (1804), by a writer using the pseudonym of Adelio, is like *The Lawyer* a confession narrative. Its hero, Saunders, only appears to be a criminal, however. He has been sentenced to death on the strength of circumstantial evidence and while in jail relates his story to Adelio. On his return from a voyage to Europe, the latter to his surprise runs across Saunders, who then tells him of his *in extremis* escape. The misleading evidence of his guilt resulted from persecution by a villain and a number of unfortunate coincidences. These misunderstandings are of the "mistaken identity" kind so much used in the "fortune's football" novels, among the adverse elements over which a hero can exert no control. The persecution, on the other hand, originates in the jealousy of a rival. There develops in *A Journey to Philadelphia* (as, for example, in *The Hapless Orphan*) a disproportion between the initial cause of jealousy and the rival's implacability, not because the cause might not fester so corrodingly, but because the persecutor is not given any tangible substance by the narrative. The tale is comparatively little affected by this lack of bodily presence, for Saunders's tendency to brood over what happens to him makes a plausible and adequate sense of mystery result simply from the combination of consistent hostility and accidental discredit.

Saunders is ordinary enough as far as the circumstances of his early life are concerned: one can believe his dissatisfaction with them and his desire for a change. Exceptional events then precipitate his decision to leave for Philadelphia; they also stimulate his reflective turn of mind, an inclination which has struck his neighbors as eccentric. This inclination therefore becomes a pronounced indulgence in reflection at a time when Saunders might be expected to act rapidly in order to protect himself. It is a feature which recalls Brockden Brown's heroes, and more particularly Arthur Mervyn, though the latter is far better realized than Saunders, perhaps partly because *A Journey to Philadelphia* is too short for the creation of a complete

[324]

character. Mervyn, too, is an alien among his neighbors and prefers solitary entertainment to social pleasures. He and Saunders have similar reasons for preferring Philadelphia to their rural background. Mervyn's curiosity is, however, a stronger incentive than the rather vague longings of Saunders, a mere feature of fictional characterization.[46] Mervyn and Saunders further resemble each other in their typical and at times devious honesty, and in their sympathy with their fellow beings and unselfish readiness to help, in their need for a wife more mature than themselves. Above all, they sound alike, so closely are they related in their manner of pursuing chains of reflections. Here is Saunders wondering about the meaning of Carnell's appearance in Philadelphia:

> ...This man I was convinced, had sought to destroy me, and now again haunted me for the same dreadful purpose. Yet, how could he have discovered my residence? I had imparted no hints of the place of my destination on quitting my spot, to any human being; yet he was here; causes with which I was wholly unconnected, might have induced him to visit Philadelphia; pleasure, business, for aught I knew, this city might be his home, yet I still labored under the conviction that I, and I alone, was the object of his journey, to gratify his revenge, to embrue his hands in the blood of an innocent man. And was his vengeance to be gratified only by my destruction? Was there no method of warding off the impending danger? Could I not cause him to be apprehended? I had seen him in my chamber, armed with the instruments of death, at the hour of midnight; but I was the only one; my voice alone would not condemn him, and if it would, dare I charge him with meditating a deed, of which he perhaps never formed an idea? (pp. 29-30)

Some other details might be named to indicate Brown's influence on Adelio: Susan's attempted suicide and change of mind, which recall Welbeck's jumping into the Schuylkill and eventually reaching the New Jersey shore; the appearance of a sleepwalker, as in *Edgar Huntly*; the use of a double (though not a twin brother), as in "Stephen Calvert." But *A Journey to Philadelphia* lacks the intensity of Brown's narratives, deriving from their heroes' stubborn inquisitiveness and their suscepti-

[325]

bility to development. That is why we are given Huntly's and Mervyn's painstaking attempts at conveying every minute groping toward an accurate or at least a plausible understanding of their situations, of the significance of their lives and the values they believe in. When brought into contact with a Welbeck, Mervyn cannot help acquiring new features and tapping new resources. Saunders, on the other hand, cannot develop in such a manner, since Carnell, his antagonist, is a mere backround replica of the conventional novel-villain, and part of that corpus of novel lore that Brown generally ignored. Adelio was probably well acquainted with Brown's work, but also knew another allegiance: this may be seen in his use of the typical diction of the imitative novel of terror, in a passage that otherwise contains echoes of Brown's method of rendering thinking processes:

> ...I asked myself who could be the person that fired, it was evident it was an enemy; every concurrent circumstance, the hour, the place, seemed to impress this belief; but who could it be? I had injured no being on earth, I was almost a stranger (owing to my romantic notions) even to my nearest neighbors; I soon recovered the slight injury I had sustained; the circumstance no longer caused any anxiety, and I again ventured to revisit my favorite retreat; returning home one night, as I passed through my brother's chamber to gain my own, I saw by the light of the moon, the figure of a man standing near the bed of my brother, armed with a dagger; I stood almost petrified with fear and astonishment; I had imbibed from our rustic neighbors, some superstitious ideas, it was near "the noon of night," that solemn hour, when the dead forsake their graves, and wander forth to revisit scenes once dear to them; I believed I saw a spectre; I made no alarm, my tongue clave to the roof of my mouth, horror almost froze the blood in my veins, and my limbs scarcely supported my tottering frame! The figure moved towards me,—I made a desperate effort, reached my chamber, and locked the door; the silence of death reigned in the house,— not a sound reached my ear.... (pp. 13-14)

The character of Saunders and the plot of *A Journey to Philadelphia* are also reminiscent of Watterston's *Glencarn*, another book by an admirer of Brown. Yet the passage above shows that Adelio at least avoided the wildness and incoherence that frequently make Watterston's two novels pretentious and ridiculous.

1. *Adventures in a Castle,* p. 61.

2. *Julia,* title-page motto, and pp. iv-v, viii-ix.

3. One does not have to be an Illuminatus to behave badly; this is demonstrated in *Julia* by the elder Ormond in his dealings with his brother, Camilla, and with their son, and by the behavior of Don Gasperd and Lord B— toward Miss Gyron and Leonora, respectively.

4. See de Launa's arguments when he tries to convince Julia that she may reasonably yield to him (p. 203). If he was inspired by Brockden Brown's *Ormond,* he is a far cruder representative of the enlightened atheist. The story of Olivia incorporates a naïve account of the precepts and some practices of the Illuminati (p. 243).

5. *A Sermon, exhibiting the present dangers, and consequent duties of the citizens of the U.S.A.,* delivered at Charlestown, April 25, 1799. Cf. also Timothy Dwight, "The Duty of Americans at the Present Crisis" (1798), reprinted in H. R. Warfel, R. Gabriel, and S. T. Williams, eds., *The American Mind,* rev. ed. (American Book Co., 1947), p. 220, which gives a succinct list of the principles of the Illuminati; Benjamin Trumbull, *A Century Sermon,* p. 8; Seth Payson, *Proofs of the Real Existence and Dangerous Tendency of Illuminatism* (Charlestown, 1801), a summary of Robison and Barruel on the subject of the Illuminati; the review of Payson's compilation in the *American Review and Literary Journal* 2, no. 1(1802):57-67. Vernon Stauffer, *New England and the Bavarian Illuminati* (New York: Columbia University Press, 1918), is a comprehensive study of the subject.

6. They are both children of the Marquis Alvada: De Launa by his first wife, Julia by his second, Lavinia. De Launa lusts first after his stepmother, later after his half-sister. Among plot elements of the same order, there are the Countess's unwitting bigamy and the crudity of Ormond's offer to marry her officially, just after he has dispatched her husband in a duel.

7. Julia is perhaps more impressed later, when she supposes that it must have been Colwort's ghost she saw and heard in the vault (chap. 20); it turns out that it was Colwort himself.

8. Both carry miniatures that can serve as a clue to or a proof of their identity (chaps. 5, 24).

9. The European setting was obviously a necessity if Mrs. Wood chose to use the theme of Illuminatism. The choice itself, however, was perhaps dictated by convenience and topicality rather than necessity. It is worth remembering that, of her four novels, only *Dorval* has an American setting. See below, Chapter 15, pp. 331-35, and (for *Ferdinand and Elmira*) above, Chapter 13.

10. The endings of *Amelia, Julia,* and *Ferdinand and Elmira* are similar: the heroes settle in England; it seems safer to leave the Continent "While France her huge limbs bathes recumbent in blood,/And Society's base threats with wide dissolution" (Robert Treat Paine, Jr., "Ode: Adams and Liberty," 1798).

11. See Mrs. Selbeth's view of Amelia's sensibility: *Amelia* (Portsmouth, N.H., 1802), p. 121.

12. See pp. 10-11, 21-22, 28-30, 77, 143-44, 157-58, 241-42.

13. P. 225; cf. also pp. 133, 195, 204, 220.

14. There is, for example, Sir William's delayed return from the Continent

and the timing of his homecoming and Lady Stanly's death (chaps. 4-5); in this context the fact that Lady Stanly overhears two revealing conversations between Harriot and Amelia (pp. 12-13, 28-29) must be remembered, since it renders her insistent in the question of marriage between Sir William and Amelia.

15. The heroine's attitude in this crisis is influenced by Morcan's story, which thus acquires a significance rather grater than that of a pretext for Amelia's benevolence.

16. Her repentance is one of the features recalling the example of Mrs. Rowson's *Charlotte* (specifically, Mlle La Rue). *Julia* is more in the line of Mrs. Radcliffe or Charlotte Smith.

17. Among obvious didactic features of the novel, there are reflections on domestic education (p. 12), self-discipline (p. 177), "Man proposes but God disposes" (p. 76), the unpredictable turns of destiny (p. 209), and the "retribution of Providence" (p. 233).

18. See, e.g., the descriptions of Amelia's voice (p. 6), Barrymore (p. 41), Sir William (p. 104), "a truly lovely woman" (p. 146); the parting from the Barrymores (p. 20), tantalizing and elusive sleep (pp. 55, 172), rewarding Shakespeare reading (p. 174); the scenes of Gothic foreboding and suspense: solitude (p. 168), dreariness (p. 170), waiting for dawn (p. 191), a hostile wind (p. 199), approaching footsteps (p. 211).

19. There are two stories in Mrs. Wood's *Tales of the Night*: "Storms and Sunshine; or, The House on the Hill" (74 pp.), and "The Hermitage; or Rise of Fortune" (90 pp.). They are made up of conventional ingredients of the romantic tale; since they are short, and crowded with incidents, there is no room left for explicit and prolonged passages of moralizing and didacticism.

20. Published under the title "Alonzo and Melissa" in weekly installments in the Poughkeepsie *Political Barometer* (June 5-Oct. 30, 1804) (see Milton W. Hamilton, *The Country Printer 1785-1830* [Columbia University Press, 1936], p. 152). This was plagiarized in 1811 by Daniel Jackson, Jr., whose version was to become a bestseller. Mitchell republished his novel in book form, with an additional preface as *The Asylum;* references are to this edition.

21. Cowie speaks of "papier-maché scenery" and "bogus Gothic effects" (*Novel*, pp. 107-8). He also mentions the stumbling dialogue; this is at its worst in a conversation between Melissa and Alonzo on the shores of Long Island Sound (1:219-21).

22. Mitchell inserted a remark vouching for the authenticity of his castle and describing how it was destroyed after the Revolution (2:78). He has more than one footnote on plants and birds native to America, perhaps striving to underscore the realism of his story and to prevent the Gothic machinery from becoming too dominant; see 2:59, 88-89, and cf. his emphasis on his American setting, p. xxvii.

23. Some of the events of the nights before: noise of people trampling below, dark forms passing swiftly in the yard; hum of voices, quick shutting of a door, sharp sound, footsteps and voices, "a hand, cold as the icy fingers of death, grasped her arm"; loud whisper: "away! away!"; a shot; a sulphurous smell; a flash like lightning; a loud and deep roar; hollow, horrible groans dwindling into a faint, dying murmur, a tall white form gliding by; the slamming of doors; violent noises; clamorous voices, boisterous menaces; a cry of "Murder!"; a shot, groans, apparently in death-agony; an expiring gasp; a hoarse peal of laughter; a gruesomely wounded man, bleeding copiously; a bloody dagger; the command "Begone!" With the exception of the whole sequence of Melissa's

castle experiences, individual Gothic passages and details of plot machinery
are mere "mechanical imitations" resulting from the writer's lack of discipline
(O. S. Coad, "The Gothic Element").

24. A matching passage on dawn is found in 2:74.

25. See, e.g., the Courtland episode in "Margaretta."

26. The journey to France and the meeting with Franklin suggest this comparison.

27. Parallels include the figures of the villain who contrives to accompany
the heroine on her flight, and of the honest tar.

28. Melissa (chap. 9) dreams first of happiness, then of misery, but with
Alonzo it is the other way round (chap. 12). This is perhaps an alteration
meant to be prophetic.

29. "Ah! where is she? Oh! reflection insupportable! insufferable consideration! Must that heavenly frame putrify, moulder, and crumble into dust! Must
the loathsome spider nestle on her snowy bosom! the odious reptile riot on her
delicate limbs! the worm revel amid the roses of her cheek, fatten on her
temples, and bask in the lustre of her eyes!" (2:133). These weird broodings
are followed by a vociferous prayer proclaiming Alonzo's resignation. His
complaints on Melissa's grave, much later, are more Sternean (2:200).

30. See 1:45-46, 213 (and cf. Mrs. Bergher's predilections, 1:63). Melissa is
not proof against emotional storms, but she recovers comparatively quickly
(2:36).

31. Here is a description of Radcliffean sublimity: "By a long, gradual
ascent, hedged on each side with impenetrable shrubbery, we reached the
top: from its craggy summit, which arrested the course of careering clouds,
the eye extended over an immeasurable space of wilderness and cultivation,
picturesque and romantic in the extreme. As we passed along our ears were
frequently stunned by the piercing screeches of the cormorant, as it pounced
upon its prey in an adjoining lake; the harsh croakings of the raven, winging
to his nightly covert, or the sonorous voice of the solitary eagle, soaring high
above our heads, or hovering among the loftiest cliffs" (1:129).

32. The Bergher story is given complete, and not in installments liable to
distract from the main plot (see p. xxvi). Its early insertion (1:62-207) gives
it the function of a warning for Melissa, an anticipation of her difficulties; see
her reflections (1:206).

33. Glencarn is chaste, too, and in this he is conspicuously different from
Tom Jones, with whom he has much in common, especially as regards his
childhood and education, and his harassing confrontations with his foil
(Rodolpho).

34. See his rescue of Mary (2:chap. 5), and his withdrawal when he realizes
that Sophia is in love with him (2:chap. 4). References are to *Glencarn* (1810).

35. But Sophia represents "that sickly sensibility that preys upon itself, and
destroys every pleasure of life" (2:160).

36. "...We struggled in the water for several minutes, I found my strength
decreasing, and determined to make one desperate effort to conquer my
opponent. With great difficulty, I liberated my other arm from his grasp, and
thrusting it down his throat as far as I could reach, kept his head under water
until he expired..." (1:45).

37. Here Amelia is the typically credulous heroine; but Glencarn is as
easily duped and believes that Amelia has become a prostitute (2:chap. 11).

38. An episode akin to the Wilson material occurs in the story of the Berghers

(*The Asylum*, 1:chap. 5): a Venetian nobleman, hurt in his pride, leads a band of robbers, but (like Robin Hood) stops only the wealthy travelers. In *The Robber* (1816), a 2,000-word tale of the same type with an unreal Bohemia setting, the chief of the "Sons of Night" is the victim of an unfeeling, ambitious father and his own passions, but is at least trying to keep his men from committing murder. Peter Irving translated Charles Nodier's first (anonymous) edition of *Jean Sbogar* (1818); his *Giovanni Sbogarro* (1820) is in the *Abaellino* and *Rinaldo Rinaldini* tradition, with a Trieste and Venice setting and a hero leading a double life, as a bandit chief with a reputation for cruelty and superhuman courage, and a nobleman well liked in Venetian society and admired for his generosity and justice by the people. Irving said that he had made "great alterations" to the original, but *Sbogarro* is really a fairly close, and a good, translation, with embellishments here and there. Cf. also the tale, "The Adventures of Sociviza," *The American Bee*, pp. 3-29.

39. There is the parallel between Huntly's encounter with the cougar and Glencarn's fight with the bear; Huntly's Indians and Glencarn's bandits; the pathological manifestations in Wieland, Clithero, and Wilson; the naïve Mervyn, Stephen Calvert, and Glencarn; the exemplary role (in the eyes of the heroes) of Clelia Neville, Achsa Fielding, Clara Howard, and Amelia Richardson; Glencarn's first interview with the stranger and Mervyn's meeting with Welbeck; the ventriloquism of Carwin and Glencarn; the dawning of a sense of love in Glencarn and Calvert (toward Clelia).

40. See Watterston's remarks on the relation between innate attributes and education (1:3, 12, 67), and the rewards and punishments of the final chapter.

41. E.g., the description of Richardson's house (pp. 1:9-10), Glencarn's bower (1:23-24), a romantic wilderness (2:155).

42. See the portrait of Richardson (1:6-7, 15), and the contrasting one of his wife (1:8); their respective adoration of Amelia (1:11) and Rodolpho (1:12); the portraits of Amelia (1:28-29, 30-31) and Sophia (2:158); Glencarn's emotions after he has saved Rodolpho's life (1:20), and his despair at losing Amelia (1:70); the memorable first kiss of Glencarn and Amelia (1:52-53).

43. "*Glencarn* may serve as an example of the American novel at a very low ebb" (Cowie, *Novel*, p. 108).

44. There is in the title an allusion to Robert Bage's *Hermsprong, or Man as he is not*. Hermsprong's virtues—sincerity, simplicity, strength, both moral and physical—are attributed to his having been brought up among the North American Indians; i.e., far from the corruption of an unjust social order and the city. The narrator of *Hermsprong* is called Glen. References are to the first edition of *The Lawyer*.

45. See the portraits of Matilda (pp. 22-23) and Maria (pp. 145-46), and a typical landscape: "The moon shone with the most magnificent brilliancy; a number of lombardy poplars, planted near the house, waved to and fro by the cool refreshing gale, and sent forth a solemn and melancholy sound; while at a small distance below, flowed a murmuring stream, on whose dimpled surface the moon-beams sweetly played" (pp. 65-66). Morcell is "completely lessened in his estimation" by Ansley's glance (p. 32); he watches a man burning to death until "the relentless element had evaporated the fountain of vitality" (p. 63). Watterston's mannerisms are no less artificial than the affectations which he satirically invents for Rattle (pp. 133-34).

46. Appropriately, a conventional style of sentiment is used in the account of Saunders's parting visit to a favorite spot of his (*A Journey to Philadelphia*, pp. 19-20).

Chapter Fifteen

LOFTY CRIME

WHEREAS the very mystery surrounding the enemy of Saunders or Morcell feeds their terror and should affect the reader, Julia and Amelia are victims of persecutors whose evil character is early analyzed; the thrills, if any, of *Julia* and *Amelia* depend more on the horror of the exceptional events and less on their source, though naturally the unpredictability of the villains' next move helps to condition the heroines' sensitivity. Aurelia, the heroine of Mrs. Wood's American novel *Dorval; or the Speculator* (1801), is also harassed both directly and obliquely by a cunning and violent villain. The novel ends with a chapter denouncing the Georgia land sales as well as the avidity and gullibility of those who let themselves be swindled.[1] Morely, with remarkable confidence, buys a great many war veterans' securities at their face value; and he is rewarded, for the prosperity of the United States allows the government to redeem them in full.[2] But this successful transaction also renders Morely vulnerable to the illusory promises of the promoters of the Georgia scheme. His readiness to speculate is, from Aurelia's point of view, a form of betrayal: she expects protection from him, and has learned to count on his integrity.

Similar shocks are yet in store for her: the apparent desertion of her best friend, Elizabeth Dunbar, and of her fiancé, Burlington, "the dupe of a villain, and the victim of his own credulity" (p. 173). Every loss to the heroine is a gain to Dorval; when he marries the widowed Mrs. Morely, he deprives the girl of her last grown-up friend, while securing for himself the remnant of the Morelys' fortune. But Aurelia's apparent unprotectedness turns into an advantage when it is revealed that she is not really a Morely at all. Dorval can no longer claim to govern

[331]

her conduct, since she is not his stepdaughter. By keeping at a distance, Aurelia seems to acquire a less awe-inspiring view of the villain and independently recovers a few friends. Meanwhile, some of Dorval's villainies become known, and the criminal resolves to attempt at least an act of revenge: if he cannot possess Aurelia, he will kill her. Soon after Dorval has been introduced to the Morelys, a sketch of his life informs the reader of his depravity. Mrs. Wood was careful to handicap Dorval from the start by an illegitimate birth and parents from the lowest social class, as well as by a misguided education. It is no wonder that he can secure his advancement only by means of flattery and cruelty, and later by seduction and murder. A confidence man and forger, he commits bigamy and appropriates his wife's money. After his downfall, caused by bad luck in gambling and a clumsy forgery, he completes the list of his crimes by committing suicide.[3] Dorval is clearly a "complicated villain": "Dorval, the plunderer of their property, the murderer of her father, the defamer of her lover, and the destroyer of her happiness, was presented before her as the husband of her mother" (p. 188).[4] Aurelia faces, like many other novel-heroines, an enemy obviously vulnerable who yet cannot be brought to justice;[5] while Dorval is alive, he seems to paralyze all the actions that might lead to her happiness. Significantly, after his death, no less than five marriages can be arranged and celebrated and two fortunes enjoyed; seven chapters are required to tie up the loose ends.

Such mopping up is typical of the sentimental and didactic impulse[6] of writers like Mrs. Wood, who felt they had to punish and reward uncompromisingly. Other features connect *Dorval* with the sub-genre of the novel of suspense; also, being reminiscent of elements in the rest of Mrs. Wood's work, they reveal how narrowly limited her scope and talents were.[7] Aurelia has much in common with contemporary fellow heroines.[8] She possesses a wisdom that makes her foresee consequences to which her parents are blind; but at the same time her innocence renders her an easy prey for Dorval's subterfuges (chaps. 16, 18). She proves eminently attractive and collects at least four proposals; she is resilient and resourceful, yet at the most critical moments she is overcome by her feelings and depends on the intervention of others.[9] The motif of a concealed identity to be revealed on a certain date, and proved by surviving witnesses, is no more unusual than the figure of the heroine; neither is the fortune made in the East, or the kind-hearted sailor protecting young girls. The topical themes which Mrs. Wood touched upon are those of all her books: the shameless Mary Wollstonecraft (pp. 46-47), ladies who gamble and the question of friendship between the sexes (chap. 6), American literature and Mrs. Murray (chap. 14). She deserves praise for her choice of an American theme and a contemporary setting,[10] as well as for her ability to restrain her style. It is recognizably the manner of popular novelists of the age,[11] but it seems freer from clichés in rendering picturesque and pathetic scenes and occasionally achieves a straightforward, if pedestrian, almost Johnsonian movement.

The weaknesses of Charles Brockden Brown (1771-1810) are very much those of the average American novelist, like Mrs. Wood: an imitative variety of events, particularly in his concentrated subplots and in the past, European adventures of some of his protagonists;[12] a predilection for some few motifs and plot elements;[13] the structural unwieldiness of his tales, with their digressions and disproportions.[14] The charges are familiar, and so is the praise for Brown's distinctive merits, which outweigh his deficiencies and account for the rank he occupies among the early American novelists.[15] They can be described under two heads: the originality of his subject matter and the appropriateness of the means which he used in its treatment. In his novels, which are stories of intellectual crises and mental disturbances,[16] deceptively fragmentary appearances generally both condition and are conditioned by the crises and disturbance. The novels profit by Brown's reliance on American settings, not necessarily because the settings are clearly visualized, but because the characters are felt to be at home in them.[17] As for Brown's method, his use of gradual characterization to further his plot is of prime importance. The steps and turns of the action result only in part from individual gestures and acts, severally shedding light on a character observed from the outside; they are above all phases in the process of a character's self-discovery, into which process the step-by-step acquaintance with other figures may be incorporated together with the newly realized significance of experiences and ideas.[18]

A certain parallelism in the figures of Dorval and Welbeck, the villain in Brown's *Arthur Mervyn; or, Memoirs of the Year 1793* (1799-1800) may serve for a transitional clarifying of these general remarks. The two resemble each other in the texture of their criminal past;[19] they establish themselves in their American surroundings by a shrewd manipulation of their business partners and acquaintances, who lay themselves open to deception by trusting to the villains' appearance of poise and financial know-how. They become careless, overreach themselves, and are abruptly eclipsed by the rising stars of Aurelia and Arthur Mervyn, respectively. Yet the manner of this eclipse reveals essential differences between the two novels. Mrs. Wood's characters are two-dimensional creations moving in a moral landscape with no depth; what passes for a meeting between such characters is a distant confrontation. When Dorval is eclipsed by Aurelia, the reader is no more convinced of the girl's superiority than the villain himself; he is simply faced with the fact that Aurelia and her world outlive Dorval. The villain has just so many tricks up his sleeve, and once he has used them all up he evaporates; good then automatically succeeds evil. In spite of Dorval's proposal to her, Aurelia does not seeem to have meant more to him than the personification of chastity, the concretization of a legal impediment that frustrates his plan to get hold of the Morely fortune. Conversely she has not bothered to look beyond his function as a herald of misfortune. With Brown the encounter between Welbeck, the protagonist of the forces of darkness, and the basically innocent Mervyn is not merely negative. There is a close contact between the two, for they experience a reciprocal attraction and repulsion, a mutual sympathy aroused by their more or less conscious acknowledgement of a real element of affinity between them. To Mervyn, his patron and foe is a fascinating mixture of the humane and monstrous, of the admirable and detestable. Such a view Aurelia could not comprehend; we feel that she has no conception of the closeness of the association of good and evil, but rather imagines clear and permanent distinctions between their manifestations and representatives. The very fact that Mervyn feels strongly about Welbeck commits him to the association with the villain and, since he is Mervyn, to the innocent task of reforming him. That is why Welbeck's disappearance, halfway through the second volume of *Arthur Mervyn,* is a serious weakness of the novel. Mervyn's survival is as inevitable as Aurelia's: it is part of an entirely impersonal moral message.

Yet, on closer examination, the superfical parallelism of the plot movement, as well as the moral content of *Dorval* and *Arthur Mervyn,* assumes a different aspect. The shift of focus from Welbeck to Mervyn does not merely reflect the lifting of a shadow temporarily cast on potential good: it is part of the process by which the hero is revealed to have been affected by his contact with the villain.[20] Mervyn is essentially altered—he is enriched—by his concern with Welbeck's person and misdeeds. He obtains a startling insight into his own character, something unthinkable in the case of Aurelia simply because she is perfect from the beginning and cannot really gain from her dealings with Dorval. The very nature of the girl can have no other effect than to emphasize how irrecoverably Dorval is lost to a world of ethical and social responsibility. Mervyn, on the contrary, stirs the dulled moral sense of Welbeck, however sluggishly and sporadically it may make itself felt afterwards. At any rate, Welbeck seems seriously to look upon Mervyn as still uncorrupted; when he confesses to the young man, he apparently thinks that this narrative may discourage Mervyn from any further involvement in his dishonest schemes.[21] Hence his show of feelings at hearing that Mervyn has informed Stevens about his past:

And hast thou then betrayed me? Hast thou shut every avenue to my return to honor? Am I known to be a seducer and assassin? To have meditated all crimes, and to have perpetrated the worst?

Infamy and death are my portion. I know they are reserved for me; but I did not think to receive them at thy hands, that under that innocent guise there lurked a heart treacherous and cruel. (p. 247)[22]

This is something else than a Gothic villain's expression of impotent rage: it springs from a genuine feeling of betrayal, to which Welbeck is acutely sensitive, given his respect for reputation and the appearance of wealth and influence.[23]

His first impact on Mervyn doubtless owes much to the very impression of power and richness which the youth registers (pp. 43-44, 48-49). Mervyn's naïveté and daydreaming, possibly stimulated by his reading,[24] quickly respond to the features of the fairy tale as he is taken up by Welbeck. No wonder that, installed in a position which appears to correspond to that of his idol Clavering, he should imagine himself married to Clemenza and enjoying the fortune to which she must be heiress (pp. 51-54). He is unwilling to reflect at what cost he may be offered an easy rise to prosperity; yet having just emerged from the consequences of Wallace's mystification, he might well pause and consider that Welbeck is providing him with more than an evening meal and that he, Mervyn, could therefore be expected to pay a greater price than the fear of passing for a burglar. Some first intimation of this comes to him when the abstract principle of secrecy to which he has pledged himself is unexpectedly put to the test. As the discovery of Clavering's miniature at Mrs. Wentworth's is followed by the lady's questions about it, Mervyn becomes aware of a possible gap between his innocent willingness to forget his country origins and the motive that has prompted Welbeck's advice: "He answered that my silence might extend to every thing anterior to my arrival in the city" (p. 58). What Mervyn has looked upon as a happy coincidence of wishes might in effect mean a subjection of his will to the schemes of his mysterious protector. That there may be a discrepancy between appearance and reality is brought home to him clearly as he witnesses Welbeck's change of manner when calling on Wortley (p. 68).[25]

The mystery surrounding Welbeck is, however, not only disturbing but, more importantly, also fascinating. It emanates from the foreign aspects of his household as well as from his person. Struck with the outlandishness of Clemenza's appearance and language and with the beauty of her person and her piano-playing, Mervyn is at first content simply to gaze and listen (pp. 49-50). It takes some time for him to wonder whether he understood Welbeck properly: is Clemenza really Welbeck's daughter? When he realizes that the two are lovers and that Clemenza is pregnant, he is so confused as to hesitate over whether he would prefer their relationship to be simply sinful or, more specifically, incestuous (pp. 71-72). What with his characteristic curiosity and submerged misgivings, by that time he has reached a state of mind that will make him a willing listener to Welbeck's confession: "I was now confused, embarrassed, ardently inquisitive as to the nature of the scene" (p.80).[26] Having heard Welbeck out, he proceeds from an uneasy sense of duplicity to a consciousness of complicity. From this time on Welbeck and Mervyn are partners and equal. To make the balance complete, it is now Mervyn who has wisdom to impart: "Welbeck had ceased to be dreaded or revered. That awe which was once created by his superiority of age, refinement of manners and dignity of garb, had vanished. I was a boy in years, an indigent and uneducated rustic, but I was able to discern the illusions of power and riches" (p. 192). Mervyn's wisdom is not worldly but moral, and may assume the negative form of refraining from evil, or express itself in the positive demand that Welbeck should try and reform (p. 184).[27] If their relationship becomes meaningful to both of them, this is due to more than their guilty partnership in the matter of Watson's death and burial and their tense rivalry over the Lodi inheritance. Welbeck's confession really does serve to clarify the issues for Mervyn and to reestablish his moral standards. This is to determine his refusal to shield Welbeck any longer, in spite of his promises. Strengthened by the Stevenses' confidence he begins to obey the rules of an order of values socially rather than individually binding; hence his eagerness to follow the doctor's suggestion that he should become a physician himself (pp. 213, 206).

Part II of *Arthur Mervyn* takes up the story at this point. This second half of the novel may have appeared logically necessary to Brown, but from a literary point of view it turned out unfortunately. Having discovered to what extent he has shared in Welbeck's activities, Mervyn starts out to deal with the consequences of his duplicity and complicity. There is Welbeck's reform to be promoted; he must inquire into the fate of the Hadwins and Wallace; Clemenza has to be provided for. Brown's original program for Part II is contained in a letter to his brother James:

> The character of Wallace is discovered to have been defective. Marriage with this youth is proved to be highly dangerous to the happiness of Susan. To prevent this union, and to ascertain the condition of this family, he speeds, at length, after the removal of various impediments, to Hadwin's residence, where he discovers the catastrophe of Wallace and his uncle, and by his presence and succour, relieves the two helpless females from their sorrows and their fears. Marriage with the youngest; the death of the elder by consumption and grief, leaves him in possession of competence and the rewards of virtue.[28]

Things became more complicated for two reasons, the first legitimate enough, but the second far less defensible: Stevens's investigations and Mervyn's sentimental confusions. When he returns to the country and Eliza depends upon him, Mervyn reconsiders the reasons that earlier made him reject the idea of marrying her—that is, his inability to support her and the fact of his not being a Quaker like her. They might now live on the Hadwin farm, and Eliza's desertion of her Quaker faith would no longer hurt anyone. But there is a new objection: Mervyn wonders whether they are not too young to marry, after all. Had they not better wait some more years, until they know their own minds? His arguments resemble those of a father or elder brother (pp. 277-81); and they fail to satisfy Eliza, who is something of a feminist and ready to disregard time-honored appearances and decorum (pp. 283-84). Soon after, Mervyn meets Achsa Fielding, quickly asks for her advice concerning

Eliza, and persuades her to receive the girl into her home. This is a prelude to an embarrassingly protracted discovery that he and Achsa are in love.[29]

The first part of *Arthur Mervyn* is, for all practical purposes, Mervyn's answer to the questions raised in Stevens's mind by Wortley's accusations. Offering the young man a chance to become his apprentice, after listening to his narrative, is a proof of Stevens's trust. Yet the fair-minded doctor is still inclined to try and obtain corroborating testimonies of Mervyn's reliability. What he discovers is far from reassuring, and though he can extricate from the conjectures of Wortley and Mrs. Wentworth, and Mrs. Althorpe's evidence, the fundamental core of truth beneath plausible distortions and misunderstandings, his mind, and the reader's, is not quite set at rest until Mervyn explains that Mrs. Althorpe's charges resulted from deceptive appearances and well-meaning righteousness (pp. 325-30). Again, Stevens believes the young man's words, preferring the inside story to an account based on fragmentary observation by an outsider. Mervyn's truthfulness could be questioned because of his shielding of Welbeck and because he has so frankly revealed a certain tendency toward casuistry and a rather indiscreet curiosity (pp. 59, 76-77, 113-14). But by going over his adventures for the benefit of Stevens, the youth seems himself to have found out the truth about his conduct; his activities in the second part of the novel speak for his newly born sense of responsibility and constitute a process of rehabilitation which is sanctioned by Stevens's acceptance of his explanations.[30]

When sure of himself, Mervyn acts with cold-bloodedness;[31] but when his convictions are shaky or his conscience guilty, he is far from keeping such control of himself. His imagination runs wild in the Gothic scenes of the cellar burial of Watson and of the approach of "Colvill" (pp. 103-4, 182-83). Before proposing to Achsa he dreams that Fielding has murdered him, and that dream appears to follow immediately upon a fit of sleepwalking (2: chap. 25). Yet throughout, Mervyn remains curious —about people, above all—and a good observer. The yellow fever episodes have unanimously been praised,[32] and indeed, they cast a spell on the reader. This brilliant piece of descriptive realism[33] owes perhaps more than has been realized to the scenes that have gone before, and in which Brown achieved a remarkable psychological realism.[34] The suspense of the episode of Thetford's bedroom closet, for example, is created through the minuteness of detail in rendering the thought process of the bewildered captive as it feeds upon general ideas, conjectures, and fresh observations. The same is true of the inner conflict experienced by Mervyn during and after his first visit at Mrs. Wentworth's.[35] But the very style which proves an asset in these scenes strikes one as too formal and mannered in passages of lesser tension, where greater lightness would be required.[36]

Ormond; or the Secret Witness (1799), which preceded *Arthur Mervyn,* is another story with a Philadelphia setting and yellow-fever scenes, and again one whose protagonists are truly a match for each other.[37] Both Ormond and the heroine, Constantia, are different from the usual leading characters of contemporary fiction. Ormond, the "new" villain,[38] is not a mere schemer against the individual virtue and wealth of his acquaintances and enemies; he aims at no less than the establishment of a new society.[39] The secret organization to which he belongs is planning to build, in a remote corner of the world, a model state according to the laws of reason; the practices which will prove most successful in their experimental structure are to take the place of the abstract and ineffectual virtues of the Christian view of religion and morals,[40] at the same time bringing about a disruption of the traditional social hierarchy.

There are two flaws in the scheme to which Ormond subscribes. It does not take into account that the realization of rational concepts is illusory as long as there are attributes which rebel against any more than temporary discipline through rational principles. Ormond, to be specific, fails to consider that no process of enlightenment can be completed in his terms within a time span short enough to maintain a firm control over his impatience at imperfection. Consequently he deludes himself about the practicable purpose of the revolution he dreams of:

[340]

instead of replacing an unsatisfactory order by a satisfactory one it will at best place power over others in the hands of different people (p. 147). They are people who, like himself, wish to be compensated by the free use of power for their having so far accommodated themselves to principles and institutions they find inhibiting. The second mistake of Ormond's revolutionary plan is his view that woman is unable to assume a part among the leaders of the new order. This error proves more immediately unsettling than the former one. Ormond can rationalize his self-delusion about the necessity of abolishing the old system, but he must gradually admit having been wrong in his estimate of woman's intellectual power. This very acknowledgement involves him in doubts about the entire scheme of revolution, suggesting the degree of hypocrisy which it incorporates.

Constantia's mind, he discovers, is disciplined and penetrating like his own, well-informed and clearly susceptible of further expansion. To his surprise at finding a woman attractive not just to his sexual appetite but to his intellect, there is added another: he comes to see that Constantia's belief in disinterestedness is genuine and in no way indicates a diminished mental capacity. It is possible, then, to combine intellectual clarity with the consistent practice of the traditional virtues. Constantia's loveliness and brains together arouse a feeling which, according to his notions, should be kept in check by considerations of expediency. He may indeed ask the girl to become his mistress; but he knows that she is unlikely to listen to him, since she still believes in chastity. Now his reliance on reason should be so unqualified that he should believe Constantia's conversion to his views, considering her intelligence, to be merely a question of time; he should simply be patient a little longer. But he refuses to be patient any more when he finds that Constantia is about to leave for Europe and makes up his mind to take her by force. This determination reduces him to the dimensions of the common villain, a Dorval or de Noix.

This change occurs at the very time when Constantia herself loses something of the status of the extraordinary independent heroine by acknowledging her allegiance to the religious beliefs

[341]

preached by Sophia. She has been entirely adequate and admirable even before her meeting with Sophia has opened her eyes to the merits of a definite religious system and moral order.[41] Given from birth the advantages of a pretty face and lively mind, Constantia has been shaped into a remarkable young woman through a twofold process of education—her father's principles providing for the cultivation of her mind, and her resourcefulness being trained by practical experiences within a normal household and, later, under the strain of poverty and illness. Stephen Dudley has thought proper to keep his daughter from the fashionable and superficial education of a young lady meant to be charmingly conversant on belles-lettres and the arts:

> The education of Constantia had been regulated by the peculiar views of her father, who sought to make her, not alluring and voluptuous, but eloquent and wise. He therefore limited her studies to Latin and English. Instead of familiarizing her with the amorous effusions of Petrarcha and Racine, he made her thoroughly conversant with Tacitus and Milton. Instead of making her a practical musician or pencilist, he conducted her to the school of Newton and Hartley, unveiled to her the mathematical properties of light and sound, taught her, as a metaphysician and anatomist, the structure and power of the senses, and discussed with her the principles and progress of human society. (pp. 27-28)

Dudley has further preferred not to bring up his daughter to any denomination, relying on her instinctive ability to discover the principles of religion. The visible outcome of his educational concept seems satisfactory enough: Constantia manages to support her father and herself, and holds her own in discussing with Ormond his behavior toward Helena. Her actions doubtless prove her possessed of the qualities with which she is credited: her thirst for knowledge, rational nature, clear perceptions, independence of mind,[42] as well as her practical turn (pp. 19-20, 46).[43]

In one sphere above all has Constantia asserted her right to make her own decisions: in the question of marriage. She does not want to find herself the wife of any man simply because, by the standards of public opinion, he is eligible. There is a minimum age to be considered too (pp. 18-19); in this she is like Mervyn, who finds Eliza and himself so inexperienced that they necessarily lack any standards of selection and comparison among possible choices. Her rejection of Balfour exemplifies another consideration. She disregards the benefits her father and she would gain if she married this prosperous and decent gentleman, a marriage which custom would judge more than a fair chance for her, because she firmly believes that her mental superiority and greater moral delicacy can by no means be balanced by Balfour's material offerings (pp. 68-70). As to Ormond himself, Constantia is aware that in many ways she would be better suited to him than is Helena, but she respects his moral engagement to her friend (pp. 138, 114, 120). She later judges that she is too sketchily acquainted with his character, and, as there are still some years to go until she will be "of age" (according to her own conditions), she feels she can well afford waiting to get to know him better (pp. 150, 175). Her knowledge of Ormond indeed gradually improves, not by facts newly related but by a different way of judging him, suggested by the experience of Sophia. This is the latter's view of her too innocent friend:

> She had lived at a distance from scenes where principles are hourly put to the test of experiment; where all extremes of fortitude and pusillanimity are accustomed to meet; where recluse virtue and speculative heroism give place, as if by magic, to the last excesses of debauchery and wickedness; where pillage and murder are engrafted on systems of all-embracing and self-oblivious benevolence, and the good of mankind is professed to be pursued with bonds of association and covenants of secrecy. Hence, my friend had decided without the sanction of experience, had allowed herself to wander into untried paths, and had hearkened to positions pregnant with destruction and ignominy. (p. 209)[44]

To complete Constantia's formation, as it were, Ormond metamorphoses into a sex maniac, oblivious of any ambitious plans and narrowly intent upon selfish gratifications.[45] The test

[343]

he provokes shifts the conflict between him and the heroine from the philosophical or ideological to the physical. In the confusion of her last clash with Ormond, Constantia quickly weighs the alternatives open to her. Should she yield to her pursuer, she would be left with the memory of her dishonor,[46] but Ormond could boast of an individual virtue overcome and, as well, of woman's inferiority of will; but she could also kill herself immediately, so as not to suffer a "fate worse than death." Suicide is what she seems to resign herself to, for to use her knife against her aggressor has appeared impracticable to her. When the test comes, however, Constantia does stab Ormond (p. 240). Here, too, as in earlier instances (pp. 130, 136, 146), the girl has possibly deceived herself and not really meant to take her own life.[47]

Ormond has been completely straightforward with Constantia, judging that she can be addressed as a rational creature. In words and manners, he generally speaks to his fellow beings in terms of what they expect and are able to grasp. That is to say he does not adhere to his code of uncompromising frankness. His frankness is deceptive because it is partial, and though he expresses his scorn for the dishonest formalities of social life, he habitually practices hypocrisy and imposture himself. He is a typical Brown villain in his ability to assume the personality of another through imitating his voice or adopting a disguise (pp. 95-96, 111; 230, 212-15), and thus makes himself a "secret witness" of the true character or the intimate conversations of others. If this implies a suspicious attitude, which Ormond accounts for by his experience of duplicity, it is also one aspect of an arrogant nature holding itself superior to the rest of mankind. This again lends additional strength to his prejudiced and limited view of woman. His treatment of Helena is revealing: women have a mere entertainment value to him, and one that is beautiful, like Helena, and bright enough, too, is a better buy than another. Ormond has no appreciation of Helena's genuine qualities, her faithfulness, her kindness of heart, or even her admiration of what in him is admirable. He can therefore, like Dorian Gray, with one gesture blot out the memory of her as

[344]

he is faced with the implications of her parting letter and suicide. His conduct here is as callous and as consistent with his peculiar view of the really estimable human attributes, as in the affair of the Tartar girl (p. 218).[48]

While Helena represents one type of woman far removed from the model of excellence set up by Constantia, she nevertheless emerges as innocent; a born follower, she is dramatically opposed to Martinette. Ormond's sister is too much of a replica of the villain and at the same time too little related to the main narrative to require further discussion. But she is obviously some sort of an example of the lengths to which the emancipation of woman may lead.[49] A cosmopolitan of extraordinary intelligence, she lacks not simply any notion of religion[50] but any sense of conventional morality. Her fierce courage appears to have blotted out other praiseworthy values and, in particular, the sort of sensibility which makes for a sociable existence. Constantia, after having admired her as a star of the first magnitude, is chilled by her cold brilliance. Martinette's exceptional fate is too clearly outlined to retain that suggestion of mystery which is part of the reader's impression of Ormond. Sophia, as has been suggested before, is a moral *dea ex machina* designed to support Constantia's resistance to Ormond's spell. Her sentimental or homosexual[51] attachment to Constantia is less important to the story than her account of the detective work she has been doing to find Constantia again. It fills most of her autobiographical section, which is introduced, in the manner of the novelists of suspense, after individual acts of violence have raised the temperature and dramatic interest of the main plot, and just as an important revelation is about to be made.[52] The first part of the novel, before the appearance of Ormond, is a tale of vicissitudes distinguished from many others only through the yellow-fever episodes and the conclusions drawn from them, and through the gratifyingly definite outlines of such figures as Dudley, Craig, and Constantia. Brown followed this up with the intellectual and moral tests carried into Constantia's life by Ormond, before embarking upon the more strictly Gothic manifestations of the villain's purposes.[53] The whole is a narration made by Sophia in

[345]

reply to inquiries of one I. E. Rosenberg, unidentified beyond his name. Outwardly, the form adopted for the narrative makes for surface resemblances to Mervyn's, or Clara Wieland's and Huntly's, but the use of the third person robs it of that element of immediacy and gradual self-revelation so characteristic of the other novels.

The utopian schemes of Ormond are also those of Ludloe in "Memoirs of Carwin, the Biloquist,"[54] and they prove rather appealing to some notions formed by the America-conscious mind of the confessor-narrator, Frank Carwin (pp. 311-12). In the fragment, anything like the realization of the ideas of Ludloe's secret organization is still far distant, and our interest concentrates instead on Carwin's experiences of the actual. His story, after all, is meant to explain his irresponsible compulsion as manifest in *Wieland*. It recalls, not unexpectedly, quite a number of features with which *Ormond* and *Arthur Mervyn* have familiarized us. There is the general similarity between Ormond and Ludloe, and their specific role as a secret witness.[55] There is the hero-villain's characteristic assumption of another personality.[56] Carwin's gradual addiction to the fascinating faculty of ventriloquism (shown to its full extent in *Wieland*) is reminiscent of Craig's acquired habit of crookedness: his manner of reasoning sounds much like Welbeck's or Mervyn's rationalizations (pp. 296-97, 341-42). Like Mervyn, Carwin finds himself unexpectedly dispossessed, after having earlier borne the unpleasantness of an unsympathetic family. When prompting Carwin not to be hurried into any commitment, Ludloe speaks like Mervyn or Constantia weighing the question of marriage; and Carwin himself uses familiar arguments about the importance of an adequate marriage partner (p. 327). Ludloe guides Carwin's curiosity as Ormond directs Constantia's, skillfully leaving it only half-satisfied. Certain remarks about the unpredictable consequences and appropriateness of some of our actions could be spoken by Mervyn, or with respect to Mervyn's insistent meddling (p. 334). Mrs. Benington, like Achsa or Clara Howard, seems more mature than the hero courting her. This use of many familiar elements is particularly striking in a short, incomplete work. What is more important about the fragment, considered as a comment on Carwin's character and behavior in *Wieland,* is the conclusion we are led to draw by the contrast between Ludloe and Carwin. Together they illustrate the illusory nature of the concepts of a perfectible man and a radical renewal of the whole of society: there may be a few like Ludloe, who might live up to noble ideas, even though liable to self-delusion about their aims; but beyond question there are many Carwins, carried away by their particular talents, who turn out to be not revolutionaries but mere mischief-makers.

In *Wieland; or the Transformation* (1798)[57] the importance of the "principal person"[58] is not that of a fully rounded character: Carwin's function is above all dramatic. What happens in the set of relationships between Wieland, Clara, and Pleyel is triggered by the mischief-making which Carwin indulges in.[59] He has trained himself so well in the use of ventriloquism that it has become two things for him, an instinctive means of defense and a form of entertainment.[60] He is on the run from the outset;[61] and because of the precariousness of his situation, his first indiscretion at the pavilion is potentially so damaging that he practices his deception on Wieland. The effective use of it, which Carwin considers legitimate only in self-defense, makes it available again for less honorable purposes. A technique of camouflage is made to serve the curiosity, the experiments, of a practical jokester, and it is these later uses which determine the consequences of Carwin's ventriloquism for the Wielands.[62] That Carwin's success depends on the intellectual material upon which he practices is obvious, but it also owes something to the man's intelligence—the knowledgeable experience of one widely traveled.[63] These are advantages that give Carwin self-assurance and to some extent allow him to anticipate the results of his experiments or imagine some of their possible effects. The fascination of his appearance and voice, as felt by Clara, seems to imply that a remarkable personality has made his appearance among the Wieland circle:

I cannot pretend to communicate the impression that was made upon me by these accents, or to depict the degree in which

[347]

force and sweetness were blended in them. They were articulated with a distinctness that was unexampled in my experience. But this was not all. The voice was not only mellifluent and clear, but the emphasis was so just, and the modulation so impassioned, that it seemed as if an heart of stone could not fail of being moved by it. It imparted to me an emotion altogether involuntary and uncontroulable. (p. 59)[64]

Pleyel is presented as a soberly rational being, one not easily brought to believe the unheard-of.[65] He is therefore skeptical concerning Wieland's first experience of the mysterious voice; and though he later hears it opposing the project of Wieland's journey to Europe, and announcing the death of Theresa, it really takes the testimony of the passenger from Hamburg to convince him that the voice was right and that Theresa must be dead. When he chooses to believe that Clara has yielded to Carwin,[66] we must suppose him influenced by the shock of his earlier encounter with the extraordinary, and consider the turmoil affecting his heart and mind (pp. 44, 50-55, 140-55). All the same, the scene in which Clara confronts Pleyel's horrified suspicions with the sincerity of her account and fails to make him weigh the evidence more judiciously is an awkward one.[67]

Wieland responds more characteristically to Carwin's tricks, since they obviously appeal to a hypersensitive, irrational aspect of his mind.[68] His is a "thrilling melancholy" which we later learn to associate with his quest for significance and for religious meaningfulness in particular (pp. 25-26, 185-86). From his father and his maternal grandfather, he has inherited a tendency to a brooding type of speculation; both have left him with the twofold idea of their guilty neglect of duty toward their God, and that God's revengeful wrath (pp. 10, 14, 201-2). He wishes to avoid their error and intensely desires to know the will of God. From this flows his fatal willingness to accept as God's will whatever is communicated by means which suggest or appear to express a supernatural source, an all too easy readiness to invest the unusual with the validity of the divine. This mind is brought to fermentation by the experiments of Carwin. Wieland is the very first to hear the mysterious voice—near the former temple of his father, at that. When soon after it addresses

Pleyel as well as him, enjoining them not to go to Europe, Wieland interprets this as an indication that his duty lies in America, and by this vague hint he is apparently precipitated into a career of intensified self-questioning. Now the voice he has heard seems supernatural, and Wieland is likely to attribute it to the supreme being whose will he has been trying to fathom. The voice, to him, confirms both the existence of God and the fact that God speaks to man and utters his will. This manifestation, at first reassuring and exalting enough, in turn provokes more precise expectations; and, with a pressing wish for individual enlightenment, we must suppose in Wieland a correspondingly augmented susceptibility to signs of its imminence. The consequent strain gradually develops into the insanity which, breaking out, assumes the form of multiple sacrificial homicide among those Wieland loves best: for duty must be accomplished at the cost of something important if it is to deserve its name and a reward (pp. 195, 213, 251).

The workings of Wieland's mind cannot be followed at close range because of Wieland's almost total eclipse between his discussion of the European journey with Pleyel and his reappearance in Clara's house after he has killed his family.[69] Meanwhile, the reader's attention is deflected from the portrayal of religious mania, intrinsically a promising subject, to the sensational, pseudo-Gothic effects of Carwin's actions. Only once is Wieland introduced at some length during this interval, when he and Clara try to understand Pleyel's behavior toward the girl. There is nothing in their coversation to indicate the beginning of Wieland's insanity. It is above all Wieland's own statement at his trial that belatedly sheds some light on the processes that have caused his crisis; another contribution toward clarifying them is made by the narrator, Clara Wieland.

For Clara, without realizing it, has shared some of Wieland's observations and conclusions. The girl, whose religious education has been similar to Wieland's, is conscious of an exceptionally close affinity between them. Her first sketches of her brother and herself, nonetheless, reveal an important difference in their tempers, for she considers herself gay, whereas Wieland tends

[349]

toward melancholy. Yet if Wieland cannot be happy because of his speculative ponderings, Clara's lightness of heart must not be taken for granted. Thus it is soon threatened by her love for Pleyel.[70] Her feelings create such a confusion that she considers declaring herself to Pleyel, a notion of the most revolting and humiliating sort for the proper eighteenth-century girl that she is.[71] Successively, she is troubled, too, by Wieland's and Pleyel's experiences of Catharine's disembodied voice and by the extremely vivid first impression made on her by Carwin's appearance and voice. This is followed by the sinister threats uttered in her closet, which send her seeking shelter at her brother's house; as she loses consciousness, a voice is heard, rousing the Wielands' household, so that she can immediately be taken care of. In this case already, Clara identifies the voice with a spirit of protective benevolence. Her dreaming and waking experiences at the summerhouse strengthen her belief that she is being watched over by some divinely appointed guardian, and this guides her interpretation of the former instances when the voice was heard.

Wieland and Clara thus both consider the mysterious voice a manifestation of a superior power. Clara's situation, however, presently becomes more complex than her brother's. Wieland is apparently by then committed to the narrow path that will end in homicidal aberration, a goal toward which he is hurried by his introspective habits. Meanwhile, pledged to secrecy after the summerhouse encounter, Clara finds herself nearly assaulted by Carwin. She reasons that the danger foretold has now come to pass, and to her the mysterious voice seems definitely sanctioned as that of heaven, or a guardian angel, and Carwin must be an agent of evil.[72] Before the girl can quite adjust to the situation, she is attacked from an unexpected quarter: Pleyel accuses her of being Carwin's mistress. Clara rationally defends herself, yet is confronted by a blank wall of disbelief. In her misery and bafflement she is ready even to brave Carwin once more, alone, at night. She must make sure that she has not missed any clue that might undeceive Pleyel. She desperately longs to retrieve the notion that Carwin is indubitably black and

Wieland, Pleyel, and Catharine are spotlessly white. But the last props are knocked away from under her faith. Pleyel's hurried departure seems to render his damning judgment of her final, and within a few hours Wieland assumes the aspect of an insane murderer. Clara now remembers that in the summer-house she dreamt of Wieland trying to make her fall into an abyss. Her dream has a new significance, revealing some unconscious knowledge on her part of the violence lurking in her brother's character (pp. 71, 98-99). And what is so frightening to Clara as she comes to her senses again, after twice being mad rather than delirious,[73] is that if she assumes that Wieland's insanity was latent before the murders, she must fear that she might go mad herself:

> I wondered at the change which a moment had affected in my brother's condition. Now was I stupified with tenfold wonder in contemplating myself. Was I not likewise transformed from rational and human into a creature of nameless and fearful attributes? Was I not transported to the brink of the same abyss? Ere a new day should come, my hands might be embrued in blood, and my remaining life be consigned to a dungeon and chains. (pp. 202-3)[74]

The idea of suicide then suggests itself to Clara, and it is only the fortuitous meeting with Carwin that prevents her from killing herself. For Carwin's confession makes plain that there have been two sources to Wieland's actions: his predisposition, which fostered its own visions, and the accidental and ill-timed use of Carwin's ventriloquism. Whatever doubts are left in Clara's mind are dispersed by Wieland's words when he deliberately tries to ignore the full meaning of Carwin's confession:

> For a time, I was guilty of thy error, and deduced from his incoherent confessions that I had been made the victim of human malice. He left us at my bidding, and I put up a prayer that my doubts should be removed. Thy eyes were shut, and thy ears sealed to the vision that answered my prayer.
> I was indeed deceived. The form thou hast seen was the incarnation of a daemon. The visage and voice which urged me

to the sacrifice of my family, were his. Now he personates a human form: then he was invironed with the lustre of heaven. (p. 253)

Carwin and his perculiar gift are now exorcized.[75] But the knowledge of her brother's turn of mind keeps alive for Clara the fearful possibility of her going the same way. It is only in the course of her last meeting with Wieland that the intimate connection between them is neutralized: before Wieland kills himself, Clara has resolved to stab him, if necessary. She seems instinctively to recognize then what presently Wieland's response to Carwin's final intervention is to substantiate: there is in the delusion of Wieland a dimension alien to the nature of Clara.

Two centers of interest alternately and cumulatively make demands on the attention of the reader of *Wieland:* on the one hand, the mystery and human weakness which are the distinctive features of Carwin's role; and on the other, the horror and tragedy marking Wieland's development. In these alternate and cumulative effects lies the clue to the weakness and the strength of Brockden Brown's first novel. The balance between the sensible consequences of Carwin's intellectual irresponsibility and the insensible effects of Wieland's pseudo-religious sub-mersion of reason is imperfectly preserved. We lose sight of the inner drama because of the spectacular Gothic distraction of Carwin and his peculiar gift are now exorcized.[75] But the dove-tailing of the plot; and the whole barely fails to crumble into a series of successive stories (about the elder Wielands, the Conways-Stuarts, Pleyel in Europe) and statements (by Pleyel, Wieland, Carwin), until it ends with a sort of postscript.[76] But there is a redeeming element of continuity, which is not the insistence on the moral meaning of the tale[77] but the unifying role of Clara as a narrator deeply involved in the story. Carwin's conduct and Wieland's character jointly and cumulatively spark off the suspense to which Clara's sensitive but, on the whole, rational mind is subjected. The various sub-plots become ingredients of her intellectual and emotional fabric, as it develops under the stress of her adventures.[78] It is her gullible nature or mental instability that provides for a plausible misreading of all that is reported to her and experienced by her, and the continued tension between erroneous conclusions and the possibility of, and hope for, a refutation of them. Here for the first time, as later in analyzing the thinking of Mervyn and Constantia, Brown secured his best effects by the minuteness of his rendering. An agonizing pace and nightmarish inevitability is what the events experienced share in the registering faculties of his heroes and heroines.[79]

The narrator of *Edgar Huntly; or, Memoirs of a Sleep-Walker* (1799) is also particularly susceptible to the ebb and flow of clarity, sanity, and hope characterizing his tale. Huntly himself is, like Clara Wieland, the hero and also the sufferer of adventures in the darkness of night and insanity. His narrative has not quite the same tone of anguished immediacy as *Wieland*, though.[80] His experiences have been varied and upsetting enough, to be sure; but he has been spared Clara's intimate involvement, placed as she was between a beloved brother, a secretly adored friend, and a fascinating villain. Brown could best show her predicament through a succession of slow-motion scenes in which she is groping toward an understanding of new mysteries and complexities. In *Edgar Huntly* there is an alternation of slow and rapid phases in which the hero either pursues a chain of thoughts and emotions to some temporary conclusion or quickly weighs alternatives to decide on his next move.

Huntly is subjected to two kinds of terror. The first he can more or less cope with, thanks to his courage and the physical resources he commands.[81] This terror is inspired by the condition of the country he inhabits: it is wild, desolate, unapproachable, and hostile to man's encroachments. The nature of these surroundings is vividly illustrated by encounters and experiences which we are told to look upon as characteristic rather than exceptional:[82] wild animals, a tumultuous river, a maze of caverns, pits, and rocks. Huntly's country is a frontier region, too, still haunted by Indians; and these are familiar with the tracts so unapproachable to the white settlers. Thus the wilderness proves an ally to the Indians, and they are representative of its general hostility. The association of wild country and wild people generates a cumulative fearfulness, which the cavern scene aptly demonstrates. Huntly's imprisonment in the dark is all the more agonizing because he does not know how he was made a captive; but when he discovers the Indians, the vague and passive threat of his predicament turns into the possibility of imminent aggression.

The other sort of terror has a delayed effect on Huntly, an effect felt only when he sets down the full story of his adventures; for in so doing he clearly sees that he has been skirting, and underrating, the danger lurking in Clithero.[83] The effect of the wilderness is terrible; so is the knowledge of man's liability to perilously irrational behavior, and the latent hostility between the settlers and the Indians is a reminder of it. As Old Deb's claims and treacherous instigations show, the dispossessed owners of the soil are revengeful; there is a corresponding resolution and stubborn righteousness among the dispossessors, who are as liable to individual acts of violence.[84] The necessity to kill may therefore suddenly be imposed on one utterly convinced of its moral wrongness:

> How otherwise could I act? The danger that impended aimed at nothing less than my life. To take the life of another was the only method of averting it. The means were in my hands, and they were used....Never before had I taken the life of an human creature. On this head, I had, indeed, entertained somewhat of religious scruples. These scruples did not forbid me to defend myself, but they made me cautious and reluctant to decide. Though they could not withhold my hand, when urged by a necessity like this, they were sufficient to make me look back upon the deed with remorse and dismay. (pp. 188-89)[85]

A recognizable motive underlies the animosity between the Indians and the settlers, and their murderous violence can be explained. Clithero's behavior, however, is not to be accounted for so simply, and it is only after a series of misinterpretations that its cause is unequivocally diagnosed as a form of insanity. To Huntly, Clithero is not a psychopathological case but a moral issue. He first approaches him amidst his own preoccupations about the Waldegrave murder and sees him only in the light of

his suspicions. These are by no means allayed by Clithero's
story of his life, but the fascination of this story as such successfully rivals the interest of Huntly's original quest. It also appeals
to Huntly's sense of justice and to his belief that he can personally
do something to make the truth known to his fellow beings
(p. 12). A prime condition is, of course, his ability to fully
sympathize with Clithero. This is encouraged by the favorable
impression made by Clithero among his acquaintances: "He was
a pattern of sobriety and gentleness. His mind was superior to his
situation. His natural endowments were strong, and had enjoyed
all the advantage of cultivation. His demeanour was grave, and
thoughtful, and compassionate. He appeared not untinctured
with religion" (p. 11). As Huntly progresses from the mystery
of Clithero's sleepwalking to sharing the wonder and horror of
his confession, he quickly learns to believe that Clithero is telling
the truth. He sticks to this view until his proposed cure of the
Irishman has a contrary effect: informing him that Mrs. Lorimer
is alive convinces Clithero not that he is innocent of killing her
but that he still has to accomplish the task of murdering her.

   Huntly is led astray by his generous estimate of Clithero to
disregard the possibility of another interpretation of Clithero's
account of his past. Because of the extraordinary, yet to him
plausible, story of the Irishman, he makes him a cause in his
self-imposed quest for justice, trying to the end to rehabilitate
the man who has convicted himself of a murder that was never
committed. Huntly's attitude is due not only to the immaturity
of a naïve, inexperienced young man, perhaps inclined to take
himself too seriously, but also to his peculiar affinity to Clithero.
They share, if not insanity, at least that type of excitability that
makes sleepwalkers out of both of them.[86] His case is a comment
on that of Clithero: somnambulism is not quite so exceptional
and may be just one aspect of some individual's confusion.[87]
In addition we may look upon Huntly's experience as an
example of self-suggestion, the result of an exaggerated preoccupation with one problem; specifically, the overriding concern
is Huntly's wish to see justice done. When the two affairs in
which he is mixed up mutually prevent one another from being

cleared up, they cause his successive fits of sleepwalking.

In the gradual unfolding of the truth the reader must follow Huntly, since no other information is offered. He accepts the fact of Clithero's sleepwalking, early observed by the narrator, and later may be as slow as Huntly himself in detecting that the narrator, too, walks in his sleep.[88] The general mood of ominous mystery of the opening chapters and Huntly's discovery that Clithero apparently does his digging in his sleep are meant to create a suspension of disbelief from which the Irishman's story is to profit. If that suspension of disbelief is effective with the narrator, it is not surprising that the reader should share his credulity and judge Clithero to be sane. In spite of the latter's ominous preliminary remarks and one show of excessive feelings, he does not appear unbalanced, and the manner in which he refers to transitory fits of madness during that critical last night in Dublin[89] seems to prove that he has now full control over himself. Moreover, his painting of Wiatte's depravity speaks for his moral soundness.[90] It can only serve to confirm our belief, if in one point Huntly qualifies his trust in Clithero: he is willing to accept the Irishman's story of his earlier years but not to consider it as proof of his innocence in the Waldegrave murder.[91]

When Sarsefield finds out that Clithero has impressed his young friend so favorably, he strenuously attempts to convince Huntly that he is making a dangerous error. Yet he fails in this; for his denunciations are violent but vague. On the contrary, it is Sarsefield who is swayed to believe what Huntly believes:

> During this recital, I fixed my eyes upon the countenance of Sarsefield, and watched every emotion as it arose or declined. With the progress of my tale, his indignation and his fury grew less, and at length gave place to horror and compassion.…
>
> When the tale was done, some time elapsed in mutual and profound silence. My friend's thoughts were involved in a mournful and undefinable reverie. From this he at length recovered and spoke:
>
> "It is true. A tale like this could never be the fruit of invention, or be invented to deceive." (p. 288)

The unfortunate man's version fits the facts as Sarsefield knows them, so why should it not be true? It *is* extraordinary, but so is Huntly's narrative of his own recent adventures, which itself corresponds to Sarsefield's partial knowledge, as he has wonderingly admitted (p. 259). Huntly, then, believes Clithero's self-portrait as a repentant near-criminal; Sarsefield seems to feel that his former conjectures may have been wrong and that Clithero has spoken the truth. After this has gradually been established as a fact in the mind of the reader, the sudden reversal which proves Sarsefield to have been right and Huntly wrong inevitably comes as a shock. There is a surface resemblance here between the sudden revelation of Wieland's madness and Clithero's: they are made after a comparatively long absence of the two men from the narratives. But Wieland's insanity is then analyzed, and retrospectively some light is shed on details of the former pages; this renews our interest in all of their implications. The first mad scene itself and Wieland's defense at his trial are impressively handled and represent a climax. Compared with this, the conclusion of *Edgar Huntly* is sadly anticlimactic; the knowledge of Clithero's true state of mind and of the dangers that have surrounded the hero in dealing with the Irishman are of no more use to the tale as a whole than the perfunctory report on Clithero's final off-stage deeds of violence.

Apart from the psychologically inadequate preparation of the abrupt ending, there are two reasons why this part of the plot sounds flat. One is the unsatisfactory overall characterization. The second is that it must compete with the Indian episodes, which are really the novel's chief merit. There is no need to say much more about Huntly or Sarsefield. The latter, introduced at a late stage, does not come up to the expectations we have been induced to build up. For an omnipresent narrator, Huntly appears curiously incomplete. We may regret that his schemes to rehabilitate Clithero and to bring to justice the murderer of Waldegrave prove inconclusive.[92] More seriously, he does not become quite real to us. His desire to know the truth and his curiosity are clearly genuine; he is sincere, well-meaning, and extraordinarily courageous. But he allows himself to be ridden by one fixed idea, to be deaf to well-meant advice;

if in addition his sleepwalking is an index to his emotional instability, it is difficult to visualize him in a life of normal experiences and demands.[93] He stands in a social vacuum, as it were, undefined by any comment that would be implied in another person's sustained view of the events and characters introduced in the narrative. In a community which, as a matter of course, acts in unison against the Indian marauders, Huntly chooses to watch and search for Waldegrave's murderer all by himself. Nor is there anyone with whom he might discuss, for example, the religious topics mentioned in connection with Waldegrave's letters.[94] We are the more inclined to carp at the poverty of Huntly's characterization because in *Wieland,* which has a similar structure and technique, the character of the narrator-sufferer Clara emerges as a full portrait.

As for Clithero, he seems more tangible because we know at least what image he created for his own benefit and that of his surroundings. He has appeared worthy of Mrs. Lorimer's protection for years, and she has even promoted his engagement with Clarice; then, unaccountably, he adopted the ways of a murderer. The mere diagnosis of his trouble as insanity does not satisfy the reader as it does the bitterly unsympathetic Sarsefield, and we therefore turn back to Clithero's own description of the stages of his obsession. Clearly, it is impossible to assess with any accuracy the measure of self-delusion that enters into his report. We are quickly rendered uneasy by his dodging the responsibility for his actions.[95] Clithero's narrative nonetheless provides fascinating reading. The long passage tracing the multiple transitions and shifts in his mind, from the relief at the fact of Wiatte's death to the decision to attempt to kill Mrs. Lorimer, has a compelling intensity which is as remarkable as the suspense of Huntly's adventures in the cave, among the Indians, and on his flight.

The self-sustaining interest of these events (chaps. 16-25) and the place of their insertion tend to establish too great a distance between the reader and Clithero,[96] practically obliterating the sleepwalker from the consciousness of the reader as well as of the hero. They constitute a closely knit narrative structure, in

[358]

length more than one-third of the novel; by comparison, owing to the shifting motives of the hero, the first half of *Edgar Huntly* and its final chapters are far less unified. All the same there remains a unity of mood underlying these various parts of the novel. The beginning of the cavern scene has a nightmarish quality which continues a characteristic of the preceding Clithero episodes:

> I have said that I slept. My memory assures me of this: it informs me of the previous circumstances of my laying aside my clothes, of placing the light upon a chair within reach of my pillow, of throwing myself upon the bed, and of gazing on the rays of the moon reflected on the wall and almost obscured by those of the candle. I remember my occasional relapses into fits of incoherent fancies, the harbingers of sleep. I remember, as it were, the instant when my thoughts ceased to flow and my senses were arrested by the leaden wand of forgetfulness.
> My return to sensation and consciousness took place in no such tranquil scene. I emerged from oblivion by degrees so slow and so faint, that their succession cannot be marked. When enabled at length to attend to the information which my senses afforded, I was conscious for a time of nothing but existence. It was unaccompanied with lassitude or pain, but I felt disinclined to stretch my limbs or raise my eyelids. My thoughts were wildering and mazy, and, though consciousness was present, it was disconnected with the locomotive or voluntary power.
> ...I attempted to open my eyes. The weight that oppressed them was too great for a slight exertion to remove. The exertion which I made cost me a pang more acute than any which I ever experienced. My eyes, however, were opened; but the darkness that environed me was as intense as before. (pp. 166-67)

We may legitimately see in Brown a precursor of the Poe of "The Pit and the Pendulum" or "The Premature Burial";[97] if so, we should also be fully aware of the distance Brown had already traveled from the pseudo-medieval dungeons of contemporary literature, which were still to be echoed in the work of Mrs. Wood, Isaac Mitchell, and Watterston. This becomes the more evident as we read on and discover the nightmarish experience to be no mere trick of suspense but one continued naturally in breathtaking scenes of near-realism.

A comparison between Brown's and Cooper's Indians must, in the present context, be limited to underscoring the radical difference in the conception they reveal and the function they fulfill. Huntly's view is that of the settlers' child who has lost his parents by the hand of the natives, and Brown's Indians serve as one element among many in a generally hostile and terrifying world which acts upon irrational and amoral responses. Twenty years later, Cooper could identify the redskin with a form of nature and with ways of life suddenly subjected to uncongenial conditions, both economic and moral. These conditions had been transplanted from another world with insufficient regard for their immediate practicability. Cooper's prejudiced white settlers damned each and every Indian; but the more judicious observer found it fairer to match Indian against Indian and then to decide for the good in Chingachgook and against the bad in Magua, while still making allowance for their common difference from the white man's views.[98]

1. C. Peter Magrath, *Yazoo: Law and Politics in the New Republic* (Providence, R.I., 1966), gives a revealing impression of the moral mood of the times. See also Thomas P. Abernethy, *The South in the New Nation, 1789-1819* (Baton Rouge: Louisiana State University Press, 1961), pp. 136-68.

2. The flourishing state of America is enthusiastically described, *Dorval*, p. 17.

3. Dorval, who "boldly declared his mind unhampered by any religious sentiments, acknowledged he did not believe in a future state, and had many doubts respecting the being of a God" (p. 61), apparently shoots himself in frustration when prevented from killing Aurelia. Another suicide is Dunbar, Jr., who cannot bear the thought of inflicting poverty on his fiancée; his family thinks that "his disappointment and sudden arrest must have deranged his intellect, and urged him to the perpetration of a deed, which, in his rational moments, he would have viewed with horror" (p. 128).

4. See also the list of the multiple consequences of gambling and speculation, which applies to Dorval as to many others (p. 284).

5. The very first portrait which Aurelia gives of Dorval reveals that she is suspicious of the man (p. 36).

6. Burlington's and Dorval's way to wealth, Dunbar's and Dorval's suicides, are didactic oppositions; so are the bigamies of Seymore and Dorval, the one innocent, the other deliberate. We are given to understand that good actions, like Burlington's saving of a life, provide friends and riches, whereas complicity in wickedness fosters quarrels, as between Dorval and his fellow-schemers.

7. Both in *Julia* and *Dorval,* for example, we find accidental bigamists, fortune-tellers, and fiancés who die just before their wedding day.

8. "Possessed of a happy, even temper," Aurelia finds idleness "almost torture" (p. 20). She genteelly insists that she "will never love unsolicited" (p. 48);

she also holds that a girl may be friends with a man without having to marry him (pp. 49-50). She is beautiful (pp. 143-44), her taste remarkable (p. 145), and, "a convincing proof of a pure and innocent mind" (p. 269), she knows how to appreciate the beauty of nature. She has had a sensible education, too, and can consider suporting herself.

9. Perhaps all this does not quite add up to a "fair" picture of an American woman (Benson, *Women*, p. 194), but Aurelia is more sensible and lifelike than especially Mrs. Wood's own Amelia and Elmira.

10. The authenticity of this "Novel, founded on recent facts" (title page) is emphasized in a footnote (p. 62). The subject of *Dorval* was also treated by Royall Tyler in his comedy *The Georgia Spec* (1797); there is a reference to it in *The Algerine Captive* too (1:47).

11. See, e.g., Aurelia's state of shock after Burlington has disappeared (p. 104), Morely's dejection in prison (p. 148), the reunion of Aurelia and Seymore (p. 261), or this prelude to a proposal: "The moon was at the full, and its beams played upon a sheet of water, that was at the bottom of the garden. A soft western breeze fluttered among the leaves of the trees, and wafted the fresh air in at the window, perfumed by the various shrubs and flowers, with which the garden was filled.—Here, the mind was fitted for contemplations, and the heart for love" (p. 166).

12. E.g., the lives of Sophia, Martinette (*Ormond*), Welbeck, Achsa (*Arthur Mervyn*), Clelia, and the forebears of the hero ("Stephen Calvert").

13. E.g., the tense relationships between brothers and sisters: the Wielands, Mrs. Lorimer and Wiatte, Jessica and Harry (in "Jessica"), Mary Selwyn and her brother ("A Lesson on Concealment"), Jane Talbot and Frank; the patron-hero relationship: in *Arthur Mervyn, Edgar Huntly, Clara Howard*, "Carwin"; the similar episodes concerning Weymouth (*Edgar Huntly*) and Morton (*Clara Howard*); the resemblance motif: Mervyn-Lodi-Clavering (*Arthur Mervyn*), the twin brothers of "Stephen Calvert"; ventriloquism (*Wieland*, "Carwin"; *Ormond;* in *Arthur Mervyn* Welbeck imitates Colvill's voice).

14. Various narratives are intricately interwoven in *Arthur Mervyn*, Part I: the tale of the Lodis is inserted in Welbeck's confession, which is contained in Mervyn's story, itself communicated to the reader by Stevens. Part II of the novel is rather disjointed; the stories of Martinette, Sophia, Whiston, and Baxter are inadequately integrated into the structure of *Ormond*. The reader never learns what Mervyn saw in Welbeck's attic, what finally happened to Eliza Hadwin, or (in *Edgar Huntly*) what stranger called on Clithero or who the drunk man was whom Huntly saw during his night of flight.

15. Brown was early singled out as deserving particular attention among American writers. See, e.g., the *American Review and Literary Journal* 1, no. 3(1801):333-39, and 2, no. 1(1802):28-38; Samuel Miller, *A Brief Retrospect,* 2:390; *Port-Folio* 5, no. 16(April, 1805):125-26; 3d ser., 1, no. 1(January, 1809):21; 6, no. 1(July, 1811):30-35; 4th ser., 3, no. 6(June, 1814):570-73; *Monthly Anthology* 5(1808):499; Mitchell, *The Asylum*, p. xix; *NAR* 9(1819): 58-77, 15(1822):281-82; Paulding, *Salmagundi* (New York, 1835), 2:271-72, in Spiller, *Literary Revolution*, p. 386; Henry Wheaton, *An Address, pronounced at the opening of the New-York Athenaeum*, p. 8(1824); John Neal, *American Writers* (1824-25), pp. 56-68; [N. P. Willis], "Literature of the Nineteenth Century: America," *Athenaeum* (London, January 3, 1835), p. 9, where we read that "his novels are too well known to require more than a passing mention." For British views, see the aggressive voice of the *Anti-Jacobin Review* 6(1800):451, and the rather unfriendly opinion of Hazlitt (1829), *The Com-*

plete Works of William Hazlitt, ed. P. P. Howe, 16:319; earlier Hazlitt seems to have held a more favorable view; see Keats's letter of September 21, 1819, to Richard Woodhouse. The majority of British critics were willing to treat Brown with respect, e.g., *Blackwood's* 6(1820):554-61 (on Brown and Irving); *New Monthly Magazine* 14(1820):609-17; *Gentleman's Magazine* 92(1822):622; *Retrospective Review* 9(1824):304-26. Thomas Hood knew enough of *Edgar Huntly* to use its hero in "The Fall," a poem about a man who dreams that he is falling down Niagara and wakens to hear the cry, "It's Edgar Huntley in his cap and nightgown, I declares!/He's been a-walking in his sleep, and pitch'd all down the stairs!"

16. "His heroes, on the whole, are rather ordinary beings, whom some accident suddenly plunges into difficulties and perplexities, that awaken all their faculties, while they baffle their comprehension" (*New Monthly Magazine* 14:611). Cf. *Whittier*, p. 28 (from a review of *The Wept of Wish-ton-Wish* [1830]); Henry T. Tuckerman, "The Supernaturalist: Charles Brockden Brown," *Mental Portraits* (London, 1853), pp. 271-86, especially pp. 280-81. Edith Birkhead feels that Brown's "characters leave so faint an impression on our minds that we are not deeply concerned in their fates," and adds that "he is interested rather in conveying states of mind than in portraying character" (*The Tale of Terror*, p. 200); this is perhaps true of Wieland and Clithero, rather than of Clara or Mervyn. (Margaret Fuller, *Papers on Literature and Art*, p. 149, and Richard Chase, *The American Novel and its Tradition*, p. 30, contain statements which require the same qualification.)

17. We trust the characters to keep a memory of these settings, which we cannot do with, say, Caroline in *The Hapless Orphan*, Aurelia in *Dorval*, Alonzo and Melissa in *The Asylum*.

18. See Lulu R. Wiley, *The Sources and Influence of the Novels of C. B. Brown* (Vantage Press, 1950), p. 31; Warner Berthoff, "The Literary Career of C. B. Brown" (Ph.D. dissertation, Harvard University, 1954), p. 99; Teut Riese, *Das englische Erbe in der amerikanischen Literatur*, p. 132.

19. The plot outline in "Walstein's School of History" is the story of *Arthur Mervyn*, I; this is followed by a critique that may be interpreted as Brown's ideal conception of the novel, "a tale, in which are powerful displays of fortitude and magnanimity; a work whose influence must be endlessly varied by varieties of character and situation of the reader, but, from which, it is not possible for any one to rise without some degree of moral benefit, and much of that pleasure which always attends the emotions of curiosity and sympathy" (*The Rhapsodist*, ed. H. R. Warfel, pp. 155-56). Brown proclaimed himself a "story-telling moralist" ("Sky-Walk"), a "moral painter" (*Edgar Huntly*) who could "illustrate the moral structure of man" (*Wieland*). In "A Lesson on Concealment" Haywood's career parallels that of Welbeck, and Henry has some of the features of Mervyn (*Monthly Magazine* 2[1800]:174-207).

20. In the words of R. W. B. Lewis, *Arthur Mervyn* focuses less on lofty crimes than on "the modifying effect of such wickedness upon an honest and foolish character. It is the American theme" (*The American Adam*, p. 95).

21. *Arthur Mervyn*, ed. Warner Berthoff, p. 80. The more generally accessible twentieth-century editions of Brown's major novels have been used here rather than the collected editions of the nineteenth century. It is reassuring to hear that scholarly editions of Brown's fiction and letters are being prepared. Two useful tools have been provided, "A Census of the Works" (S. J. Krause and Jane Nieset, *Serif* 3[1966]:27-57), and "A Check List of Biography and Criticism" (Robert Hemenway and D. H. Keller, *PBSA* 60[1966]:349-62).

22. Cf. also p. 280.

23. "The esteem of mankind was the spring of all my activity, the parent of all my virtue and all my vice" (p. 84); see also pp. 97, 323, and D. L. Clark, *C. B. Brown—Pioneer Voice of America*, p. 179. Mervyn (p. 191) and Watson (p. 100) are well aware of Welbeck's weakness. He is at his most Gothic when he fears that his true character might be exposed (pp. 179, 183-84, 197-98).

24. See Mervyn's self-portrait, pp. 7-9, and Part II, chap. 14. Rather surprisingly, he feels competent to judge Clemenza's piano-playing (p. 50).

25. Mervyn may be surprised at this play-acting, but he has ambiguous ways of his own. They are evident during his visit to Mrs. Wentworth's and when he reports on it to Welbeck (chaps. 7-8).

26. See also pp. 55, 59, 68. Part II, chap. 14, is devoted to countering, among other charges, the idea that he was "incurious, destitute of knowledge, and of all thirst of knowledge" (p. 325-26).

27. See also Mervyn's view of the necessity "to regard the wicked with no emotion but pity, to be active in reclaiming them, in controlling their malevolence, and preventing or repairing the ills which they produce" (p. 181).

28. Letter of February 15, 1799, quoted in Dunlap, *Brown*, 2:98.

29. Mervyn wavers between Eliza and Achsa as does Stephen Calvert between Louisa and Clelia; the attractiveness of Clelia's and Achsa's European sophistication and the stabilizing influence which these ladies, who have been married before, might exert on the two heroes are not easily assimilated. "Memoirs of Stephen Calvert" appeared in the *Monthly Magazine and American Review*, June, 1799-June, 1800, and was reprinted in Dunlap, *Brown*, 2:274-472. It is, like *Arthur Mervyn*, a story of confession and explanation. Calvert resembles Mervyn in his naïveté and impulsiveness; both warmly imagine a lover's bliss but can be very diffident toward the ladies. They resent a distrustful watcher's interference. Calvert's delusions seem less unconscious than Mervyn's, as appears from his dealings with Louisa and Clelia; and because he is really afflicted with a double standard, the use of his twin to account for all misunderstandings is an all-too-easy solution of the existing part of the narrative (described by Brown as the first of five "acts"). The plot: Calvert imagines his cousin Louisa to be immensely attractive and is disappointed when he first meets her. Later he proposes and is accepted, but his friend Sidney advises the girl not to commit herself yet. Meanwhile, Calvert has saved Clelia Neville from a fire; he frequently visits her. He believes that she has left a wicked husband, but Sidney tells him that she deserted her husband after having had a love affair. Sidney considers Calvert quite as dishonest as Clelia. At length, however, many apparent lies of Calvert are explained by the existence of a twin brother of his.

30. Warner Berthoff (in his introduction) and Donald Ringe (*C. B. Brown*, especially pp. 80-85) judge Mervyn rather unfavorably. Yet this innocent young man's "dishonesty" seems to flow from his lack of assurance, which prevents him from quickly and clearly saying "yes" or "no". This is a disturbing uncertainty, but it is cured by his confession to a sane man (Stevens) with standards that may safely be accepted by the reader. For though the Stevenses seem inclined to trust Mervyn even before he begins his story (pp. 13, 14), the doctor later carefully weighs all the evidence. See also Kenneth Bernard, *"Arthur Mervyn: The Ordeal of Innocence," Texas Studies in Literature and Language* 6(1965):441-59.

31. Mervyn ventures into plague-ridden Philadelphia (especially p. 132), braves Welbeck's wrath in the deserted house (pp. 183-86, 193-98), buries Susan

(pp. 268-69), confronts Philip Hadwin (pp. 289-96), and keeps superhumanly calm even when shot at (pp. 315-16).

32. Even Prescott, who wrote Brown's "Life" unwillingly (see *The Literary Memoranda of W. H. Prescott*, ed. C. H. Gardiner, 2 vols. [Norman: Univ. of Oklahoma Press, 1961], 1:164) and only grudgingly acknowledged his merits, admired the art of selection practiced in the yellow-fever scenes ("Life of C. B. Brown," *The Library of American Biography*, ed. J. Sparks [Boston, 1834], 1:151). According to Eleanore Sickels, Shelley knew Brown's work when he wrote *Zastrozzi* and *St. Irvyne*, and may have been influenced by *Arthur Mervyn* in writing Cantos x-xii of "Laon and Cythna" ("Shelley and Charles Brockden Brown," *PMLA* 45(1930):1116-28). Various writers, among them Quinn (*Fiction*, p. 29), and Ringe (*Brown*, p. 67), have pointed out the symbolic meaning of the yellow-fever scenes, and especially the connection which exists in Mervyn's mind between the corruption of the city (as opposed to the salubrity of the country) and the disease. Since Mervyn is not immune to either the moral or the physical contagion of the Philadelphia he experiences, Stevens may be said to effect a double cure, as a physician and as a confessor. Incidentally, his actual presence in the narrative gives *Arthur Mervyn* an advantage over Brown's other major novels, which are addressed to distant confessor-correspondents. There are interesting parallels, especially in the "methods" of prevention and the ways of conducting a hospital, between *Arthur Mervyn* and Mathew Carey, *A Short Account of the Malignant Fever* (Philadelphia, 1793).

33. Vol. 1, chaps. 15-19. Other examples of close observation carefully rendered: a room in Mrs. Villars's house (p. 301), Mervyn's fellow passengers on the stagecoach to Baltimore (pp. 354-55). The hearse drivers' talk (pp. 133-34) and Mervyn's conversation with a Philadelphia youth (pp. 55-56) are not unskilfully caught; but when the English actor John Bernard was asked to criticize a play which Brown had written, the quality of the dialogue apparently did not impress him, and he discouraged Brown from continuing work on his play (*Retrospections of America, 1797-1811* [New York, 1887], pp. 254-55).

34. A. H. Quinn speaks of "realistic supernaturalism," and says that Brown's method "is to retail a series of minute facts or sentiments until the number and the logical sequence of them paralyze the reader's capacity for doubt" ("Some Phases of the Supernatural in American Literature," *PMLA* 25[1910]: 114-33). Cf. also E. A. Baker, *History of the English Novel* (London: Witherby, 1934), 5:215; Baker devotes six pages to Brown, who "contributed something to the development of fiction in English."

35. See also Mervyn's reasoning about the Lodi notes (pp. 175-76).

36. See Mervyn's bathing at night (pp. 68-69), Welbeck's recollection of the Lodi manuscript (p. 189), or an encumbered sentence like the following: "The old man being reminded, by a variety of circumstances, of the incident of that eventful period, was, at length, enabled to relate that he had been present at the meeting which took place between Watson and his son Walter, when certain packets were delivered by the former, relative, as he quickly understood, to the condemnation of a ship in which Thomas Thetford had gone supercargo" (p. 235). In particular Brown's use of the passive weighs his sentences down and at the same time creates an impersonal distance between the scene or observation related, the observer, and the reader: "At length, however, a visible change took place in her manners. A scornful affectation and awkward dignity began to be assumed. A greater attention was paid to dress, which was of gayer hues and more fashionable texture. I rallied her

on these tokens of a sweetheart, and amused myself with expatiating to her on the qualifications of her lover. A clownish fellow was frequently her visitant. His attentions did not appear to be discouraged. He therefore was readily supposed to be the man. When pointed out as the favourite, great resentment was expressed, and obscure insinuations were made that her aim was not quite so low as that" (p. 17). Cf. pp. 101, 137, 184, 186. If rather stiff and pompous, Brown's style is pleasantly sober by comparison with that of the sentimental novelists, who made one attempt after another to phrase what they were simply too awkward or cliché-addicted to express. See Harold C. Martin on Brown, Cooper, and Neal, in "The Development of Style in 19th-Century American Fiction," *Style in Prose Fiction*, pp. 114-41.

37. *Ormond* was translated into German before it appeared in a London edition. See L. M. Price, *The Reception of U.S. Literature in Germany* (Chapel Hill: University of North Carolina Press, 1966), and W. B. Cairns, "British Republication of American Writings, 1783-1833," *PMLA* 43(1928):303-10.

38. Craig, on the contrary, is a villain of the conventional type.

39. Ormond does have something of the aristocratic arrogance of Godwin's Falkland, but his attitude reflects a radical view of society, not a conservative one like that of Falkland (see David B. Davis, *Homicide in American Fiction*, pp. 51-52). L. D. Loshe (p. 41) noted another difference: "Falkland becomes a criminal in a moment of passion, and thereafter the principles which have guided his life honorably are made to lead him to infamy. But Ormond...[has] been led into evil ways while seeking a good end." Cf. Mary S. Benson, *Women*, p. 200. There is a Wisconsin dissertation (1965) by Jane T. Flanders on "C.B. Brown and William Godwin: Parallels and Divergences." No doubt Brown knew Godwin's *Political Justice*, and was impressed by his analysis of the patron-villain and the hero-victim of *Caleb Williams*. There is a resemblance between his gifts and Godwin's twofold talents for building "abstract card-houses, lofty but ephemeral," and for writing "criminal or alchemical fiction" (Oliver Elton, *A Survey of English Literature, 1780-1830*, 2 vols. [London: Edward Arnold, 1920], 1:210). F. H. Deen has demonstrated a filiation between *Caleb Williams* and a later American novel, Simms's *Martin Faber*, apparently with no influence from Brockden Brown ("The Genesis of *Martin Faber* in *Caleb Williams*," *MLN* 59(1944):315-17.

40. *Ormond*, ed. Ernest Marchand (1937) (repr. New York and London: Hafner, 1962, pp. 208-9). For Ormond's notion of happiness and destiny, see pp. 92-93, 138, 210, and his rationalizing of the murder of Dudley: "My happiness and yours depended on your concurrence with my wishes. You father's life was an obstacle to your concurrence. For killing him, therefore, I may claim your gratitude" (p. 231).

41. See Ringe, *Brown*, pp. 59-60. Rather aimlessly, perhaps, but quite consistently, Constantia has been conforming to the moral precepts of orthodox Christianity.

42. See the impression which Constantia makes on Mrs. Melbourne (pp. 90-91), her request for an interview with Ormond (pp. 120-21), and cf. also pp. 17, 24, 26.

43. Constantia has the presence of mind to keep a copy of the impromptu letter she sends to Craig, and can later conveniently produce it (p. 88). She is a good observer, a physiognomist (p. 63), though with Craig this proves of little value (p. 82). In her essay "Shelley and Charles Brockden Brown" Eleanore Sickels comments on the poet's identification of Constantia with

Claire Clairmont, to whom the poems "To Constantia" and "To Constantia Singing" may have been addressed.

44. There are allusions to Illuminatism here, though they are less definite than Mrs. Wood's in *Julia;* see above, "Mystery and Terror," pp. 309-10, and L. D. Loshe, *Novel,* pp. 41-43.

45. See pp. 214, 227, 233-35. Ormond announces that he is about to rape Constantia and adds, in scornful reply to the girl's threat to kill herself, "Living or dead, the prize that I have in view shall be mine" (p. 235).

46. Constantia has, of course, rejected the way out suggested by Ormond's reasoning, i.e., that no one will know about their affair, and that her reputation will therefore be secure.

47. There is in *Political Justice* a passage on the hidden workings of the mind which incidentally may illustrate the stylistic affinity between Godwin and Brown: "The human mind is incredibly subtle in inventing an apology for that to which its inclination leads. Nothing is so rare as pure and unmingled hypocrisy. There is no action of our lives which we are not ready at the time of adopting it to justify, unless so far as we were prevented by mere indolence and unconcern. There is scarcely any justification which we endeavour to pass upon others, which we do not with tolerable success pass upon ourselves" (*An Enquiry Concerning Political Justice,* 2 vols. [London, 1793], 1:98-99).

48. During a campaign against the Turks, Ormond kills a friend who disputes his possession of a Turkish girl, makes love to her, then stabs her and kills five enemies to expiate his first crime.

49. "Die romantische Abenteurerin ist die übersteigerte und pervertierte Verkörperung desselben stolzen Frauentyps, der in Constantia in reiner Tugend erscheint" (Riese, *Erbe,* p. 129).

50. This is no worse a fault than the type of religious self-delusion shown by Lady D'Arcy, in Martinette's story, or by Sophia's mother.

51. See Warfel, *Brown,* pp. 133, 135, and L. A. Fiedler, *Love and Death,* p. 79.

52. Constantia faints at hearing Sophia's voice in the next room (p. 184). There follows Sophia's story of her life, concluding with the sounds of confusion she hears from a neighboring room and the discovery, there, of Constantia, still unconscious (p. 207).

53. The climax of mystery is reached on pp. 222-26. Anticipatory Gothic touches include the Baxter-Miss Monrose episode (published separately in the *Weekly Magazine,* March 3, 1798).

54. *Wieland, or the Transformation, together with Memoirs of Carwin, the Biloquist,* ed. F. L. Pattee (1926), pp. 275-351; all references are to this edition. "Carwin" originally was printed in the *Literary Magazine and American Register,* in 10 installments, from November 1803 to March 1805.

55. See Ludloe's discussion of the idea of gratitude (pp. 298-99) and his profession of sincerity (p. 307). His knowledge of the affair of the Spanish lady (pp. 349-51) is so unexpected that one uneasily suspects Ludloe must know all about each of Carwin's uses of ventriloquism.

56. This is the basis of his schemes against his father (pp. 284-86) and Dorothy (pp. 296-97). His gift is also made use of disinterestedly in the case of the Spanish lady (p. 310) and when he assists Mrs. Benington (p. 323).

57. Among Brown's novels, *Wieland* has generally been accorded highest marks. The *American Review and Literary Journal* honored it with a long re-

view (1, no. 3 [1801]: 333-39, and 2, no. 1 [1802]: 28-38). Watterston praised it in *Glencarn* (p. 92), and it was the only American novel mentioned by James Ogilvie in his classification of fiction (*Philosophical Essays*, p. 246). Cooper's *Notions of the Americans* referred to it as a memorable novel (letter 23). In London, however, the *Gentleman's Magazine* condemned it (81[1811]:364). *Wieland* appears to have been the first American novel translated into French (1808); see Durand Echeverria, *Mirage in the West* (Princeton, 1957), p. 233.

58. These are Brown's words to define Carwin's role (*Wieland*, ed. Pattee, p. 3). They are inaccurate, the more so as Brown's first readers did not have the advantage, which is here made use of, of building on the information communicated by the "Carwin" fragment.

59. In addition some coincidences multiply their troubles. Carwin's improvised statement that Theresa is dead (pp. 50, 226) coincides with the actual news of her death and burial (p. 55), and his "hold! hold!" is heard just as Clara dreams that she is about to fall into the pit (pp. 71, 230).

60. See his justification of the deceptions used on Wieland (p. 225) and Pleyel (p. 236).

61. See pp. 149, 238, 224. His feeling of being hunted presumably conditions the troubling airs of secrecy and ambiguity which Pleyel and the Wielands notice about him; see p. 83, and pp. 80, 87, where Clara remarks on "the uncertainty whether his fellowship tended to good or evil."

62. Carwin sees himself as a sorcerer's apprentice: "...Had I not rashly set in motion a machine, over whose progress I had no controul...?" (p. 242; cf. p. 223). This passage may have been the origin of Mary Shelley's *Frankenstein*, as was suggested by F. C. Prescott (*"Wieland* and *Frankenstein,"* *AL* 2[1930]:172-73). The reviewer of the *American Review* (1802, p. 34) doubted whether ventriloquism could be so skillfully used, anticipating W. H. Prescott's dissatisfaction with this element of *Wieland* ("Life of C. B. Brown," pp. 145-46). Prescott was answered by *The American Review: A Whig Journal*, which stated, in an article on "Charles Brockden Brown," that Carwin and ventriloquism must not be overrated, for "the whole destiny of the Wielands is made to rest upon the character of Wieland himself" (New Series, no. 3 [March, 1848], p. 269). Peacock, after stating that Brown's novels "carry the principle of terror to its utmost limits," added: "What can be more appalling than his *Wieland?* It is one of the few tales in which the final explanation of the apparently supernatural does not destroy or diminish the original effect" (*Gryll Grange*, 1860 [Harmondsworth: Penguin, 1947], p. 238).

63. He fits easily into the Wieland group; see pp. 83, 84, 86, 140-41.

64. But see the whole passage of Carwin's first appearance at Mettingen, pp. 57-62.

65. See pp. 38, 50-51, 85, 126, 150. Pleyel is also given to making fun of what others may take seriously (p. 27). His spirit is akin to Cambridge's (pp. 21, 267-68), and to Brown's, which is most palpably revealed in his own footnotes.

66. In this Pleyel conforms to the pattern of the sentimental novel, according to which a lover may rashly believe himself betrayed and forgotten; but his disposition leads one to expect a more discerning reaction, perhaps in the manner of Ormond, who intelligently analyzes the letters allegedly sent to Craig by Constantia (*Ormond*, pp. 82, 124).

67. The miraculous news of Theresa's arrival in Boston reaches Pleyel just

then and probably offers him a welcome opportunity to run away from his mental anguish, as it were.

68. This is unconsciously anticipated by Clara, who writes after the first manifestation of the voice, while still skeptical of its genuineness: "All that was desirable was, that it should be regarded by him with indifference. The worst effect that could flow was not indeed very formidable. Yet I could not bear to think that his senses should be the victims of such delusion. It argued a diseased condition of his frame, which might show itself hereafter in more dangerous symptoms" (p. 39). Wieland's multiple murder may owe something to real events; see Pattee's Introduction, pp. xxxiv-xxxv; and James C. Hendrickson, "A Note on *Wieland*," *AL* 8(1936):305-6. The analysis of Wieland's character was probably influenced by Cajetan Tschink's *Der Geisterseher* and Schiller's tale bearing the same title, which both appeared in the New York *Weekly Magazine*, Tschink's as "The Victim of Magical Delusion" (1796-97), Schiller's as "The Apparitionist" (1795-96; in book form: *The Ghostseer* [New York, 1796]). For discussions of Brown's interest in the psychology of his times, see L. Ziff, "A Reading of *Wieland*," *PMLA* 77(1962):51-57, and Ringe, *Brown*, chap. 2. Ventriloquism was discussed in the New York *Weekly Magazine*, e.g., in "An Instance of Ventriloquism, Related by Adrianus Turnelius," and "An Account of Haskins, a Late English Ventriloquist" (June and July, 1798). Mrs. Bonhote's novel *Bungay Castle* (1797) has a ventriloquist, too.

69. Wieland is virtually absent from the pages of the novel between chaps. 5 and 17 (pp. 55 and 172).

70. After Pleyel has been shaken by the news of Theresa's death, Clara reflects that she "is able and willing to console him for her loss" (p. 52). She very much resents the idea that Pleyel might laugh at her for being in love with Carwin, while it is Pleyel himself who occupies her thoughts (p. 80).

71. Her uncertainties (pp. 89-93) culminate in the following conclusion: "I saw with the utmost clearness that a confession like that would be the most remediless and unpardonable outrage upon the dignity of my sex, and utterly unworthy of that passion which controuled me" (p. 93). Pleyel is soon to accuse her of quite another outrage—her supposed affair with Carwin.

72. "The agent was not good, but evil" (p. 200). Cf. pp. 179, 203-4, where Carwin is given monstrous features, owing to his pretended design to rape Clara.

73. She loses her reason when she discovers the bodies of Catharine and the children (pp. 179-80), and when she is told that Wieland, not Carwin, is their murderer (p. 197).

74. Cf. p. 221. William M. Manly, "The Importance of Point of View in Brockden Brown's *Wieland*" (*AL* 35[1963]:311-21), underscores the importance of Clara, "a rational being with emotional upswellings," as the central figure of the novel. Henry T. Tuckerman put it more generally: "One reason that Brockden Brown succeeded was that a self-possessed intelligence, a reflective process goes on simultaneously before the reader's mind, with the scene of mystery or horror enacting; he cannot despise as weak the spectator or the victim that can so admirably portray his state of feeling and the current of his thoughts at such a crisis of fate..." (*Mental Portraits*, pp. 271-86, esp. pp. 282-83). The intensity of Clara's experience is characteristic of Brown's narratives; see above, note 16, and cf. Neal's remarks on Brown's sincerity (*American Writers*, p. 56). His sincerity and intensity were emphasized in the *Edinburgh Review* in 1889, though in an article ("American Fiction," pp. 515-53)

which numbered Brown among those who wrote "novels in America, not American novels" (p. 518). But to W. B. Blake, Brown was "a man scarcely ever intense in his feelings, or overpoweringly in earnest" (*SR* 18[1910]:431-43).

75. The exorcizing begins quite early, when Carwin appears as a mere potential rapist (p. 104) after having seemed a mysterious but also an intelligent and cultured gentleman; the process is continued by the information on Carwin which Pleyel collects from the paper and Mr. Hallet (pp. 146-49), and completed by Carwin's confession (pp. 223-42).

76. Chap. 27, written at Montpellier, in France, three years after the main events. There are similar disruptions at the end of *Arthur Mervyn*, when the hero takes over as narrator, and *Edgar Huntly*, with the three letters exchanged between Huntly and Sarsefield grafted onto Huntly's narrative.

77. The importance of the story is either explicitly announced or implied in the heroine's reiterations of the exceptional nature of her experience and the efforts it costs her to live through it again in her retelling; see pp. 5, 273 (cf. Carwin's statements, pp. 234, 238), 6, 24, 30, 56, 96-97, 166, 248, 256, 263-64.

78. It is clear that the love story of Clara and Pleyel, the latter's character, and his involvement with Theresa (pp. 43-44, 206-7, 266-67), are less relevant to our understanding of the heroine than the view which she takes of Carwin and Wieland. Pleyel is more important in the abstract, as one type of character tested by the appearance of the supernatural.

79. See especially chaps. 15-16. In this connection the importance of darkness and twilight may be noted: most of the events occur in the evening and at night. On the other hand Brown's solid background descriptions keep the tale on firm ground; see esp. Clara's description of her house (p. 63), and cf. pp. 13, 70.

80. But see the opening remarks, in which Huntly states that at long last he has recovered from fears and wonder sufficiently to begin his account (*Edgar Huntly*, ed. D. L. Clark, p. 1; all references are to this edition), and also his preamble to the Indian episodes (p. 165).

81. Some of Huntly's feats are very nearly incredible, e.g., his tomahawking the panther in the dark (p. 174) and his jumping out of the river to clutch at a saving branch (pp. 235-36).

82. The author promised in his address "To the Public" "to exhibit a series of adventures, growing out of the condition of our country" (p. xxiii). Brown's promise to dispense with "puerile superstitions and exploded manners, Gothic castles and chimeras" was echoed by John Davis, the British traveler and writer: "...The reader must not look for haunted forests, or enchanted castles" ("Advertisement," *The Farmer of New-Jersey* [New York, 1800]).

83. This reminds one of Mervyn's awareness of the contagion of Welbeck's example as he is unfolding his story to Stevens, and of Clara's realization that insanity may be latent in her as it was in her brother.

84. "...A long course of injuries and encroachments had lately exasperated the Indian tribes..." (p. 182). Cf. *Wieland*, p. 12.

85. Cf. *The Female Review*, whose heroine must also kill an Indian in self-defense; *The Champions of Freedom*, in which Judge Brown, a Quaker, becomes General Brown in the American army during the War of 1812, a case of patriotic self-defense; and the better-known example of *The Deerslayer*, when Natty Bumppo must kill a man for the first time.

86. Huntly's madness seems almost taken for granted throughout Donald

Ringe's interpretation of *Edgar Huntly,* yet his final summary uses other terms: "Huntly's friendship with Waldegrave and his desire to avenge his friend's death disqualify him as an objective seeker of truth in trying to determine the identity of the murderer; and his abnormal mental condition, parallelling that of the mad Clithero, makes him an unsuitable judge of that unfortunate man" (*Brown,* p. 103).

87. See Huntly's reflections on discovering the manuscript which Clithero has buried (p. 125).

88. A contemporary anecdote of sleepwalking was "The History of Cyrillo Padovano," which was reprinted in the *Massachusetts Magazine* in January, 1790, and in the New York *Weekly Magazine* in June, 1798. Since Padovano finally violates tombs, his story may have played a part in the genesis of Poe's "Berenice."

89. "The moment of insanity had gone by, and I was once more myself" (p. 87); cf. pp. 68, 78, 83.

90. Wiatte is no lofty criminal, no blend of the admirable and the monstrous, but an unmitigatedly vicious criminal; see pp. 44, 62.

91. Huntly apparently never reverses the proposition to extend his suspicion of Clithero in the Waldegrave affair to the veracity of the man in general.

92. It is discovered by accident that Waldegrave was killed by an Indian, a solution to the puzzle of his death which inexplicably no one seems to have considered.

93. Such demands are going to be made on him, for he has his sisters to look after and he is to marry Mary Waldegrave.

94. Waldegrave was afraid that his tendency "to deify necessity and universalize matter; to destroy the popular distinctions beween soul and body, and to dissolve the supposed connection between the moral condition of man anterior and subsequent to death" (pp. 136-37) might have affected Huntly. But Huntly's behavior seems to be inspired by an orthodox Christian spirit; see also his reflections on a providential power "that called him from the sleep of death just in time" to kill the last of the Indian marauders (p. 213).

95. Clithero thinks himself the victim on the one hand of "the schemes of some infernal agent" (p. 34) and "accursed machinations" (p. 68), his "Daemon" and "evil genius" (p. 85); and on the other hand, of conventions and prejudices, his "condition" (p. 37) and the "barrier" (p. 52) separating the classes. He stresses that he may have committed a crime, but that he was conscious only of acting out of gratitude and was afraid of being thought ungrateful (pp. 51, 84, 126).

96. Clithero disappears at the end of Chapter 8, after announcing his intention to kill himself, is briefly seen alive, in Chapters 10 and 12, then pushed into the background by Huntly's worries over the Weymouth business and the Waldegrave letters. This pattern resembles that of *Wieland,* with the relative prominence and insignificance of the Carwin and Wieland plots.

97. See Boyd Carter, "Poe's Debt to Charles Brockden Brown," *The Prairie Schooner* 27(1953):190-96. Robert T. Kerlin's *"Wieland* and 'The Raven'" (*MLN* 31[1916]:503-5) is hardly a valid contribution to the discussion of Brown's influence on Poe.

98. For appreciations of Brown's use of the Indians, see the *NAR* review of *The Red Rover,* which pronounces his Indians to be superior to Cooper's (27[1828]:144); L. D. Loshe, *Novel,* p. 73; Albert Keiser, *The Indian in American Literature,* pp. 33-37; Mabel Morris, "C. B. Brown and the American Indian," *AL* 18(1946):244-47. For remarks on the Indian in American literature, see below, "Strands of History," pp. 372-76, 388 n.3-391 n.15.

Chapter Sixteen

STRANDS OF HISTORY

T HE ACHIEVEMENT of Charles Brockden Brown may be qualified in various ways, but his work is still distinctive and stands out among the imitative efforts of most of his American contemporaries. Only Brackenridge and Irving detach themselves with equal clarity from the background of the limited and stylized current fiction. With Irving, the present and actual are mixed with the past and the fantastic; he gave his narrative materials a translucent coloring of humorous nostalgia, the suggestive effect of which was to dissolve the dividing line between the real and the imaginary. Brackenridge, deliberately addressing his country's consciousness and the conscience of his fellow citizens, used for his purposes a satirical heightening of the civic and social realities that impressed themselves upon his acutely registering critical and sympathetic mind. As for Brown, he was taking first steps in psychological realism within a more or less distracting Gothic framework, and in a number of haunting passages he re-created genuine experience.

The very raw material of these three authors is potential subject matter for the writer of historical romances, but it did not appeal to them through this aspect. Among the minor writings of Brockden Brown, there are such historical reconstructions as his "Death of Cicero" and the not unimpressive "Thessalonica." He was quite aware of the steps to be taken to transform a historical event into a fictional creation, as his remarks in "Walstein's School of History"[1] make plain; yet in his novels he made little use of historical subject matter. Irving was clearly responsive to the historical; but his processes of transformation avoided, as too definite, the core of realism that governs the historical romance. It therefore remained for Cooper after 1820 to lay bare the historical subject matter of America and to make use of it; his pages contain the first integrated romantic evocation of the spirit of the War of Independence and, above all, of the frontier, with its twin processes of advance and settlement, conquest and social unrest.[2]

In pre-Cooperian fiction the possibilities of the historical generally affected little except superficial intimations and associations. Thus a historical setting served to start the plot of *Amelia, or the Faithless Briton* and *The Fortunate Discovery* and conditioned episodic links in the action of *Constantius and Pulchera, The Gambler,* and *The Asylum.* The mere mention of the mood of war, in particular, could dramatically intensify the incidents of any romantic plot. Mrs. Rowson exploited this skillfully in *Charlotte.* Her *Reuben and Rachel,* on the other hand, was a kind of chronicle of the colonization of America as it affected the life and loves of a succession of generations vaguely descended from Columbus. (The latter's history, incidentally, as early as 1774 inspired Freneau's curious sequence, "The Pictures of Columbus, the Genoese.") Brockden Brown's "Stephen Calvert" and *Ormond,* as well as his "Sketches," capitalized on the mysterious repercussions of Old World history and schemes of change or revolution, whereas the Indian and frontier scenes of *Edgar Huntly* derived from the fact of a brutal American past. The character of the American historical material could easily be obscured; this was caused in *The Emigrants* by Imlay's glamorizing of the Mississippi territories and the valor of his hero, and in *The Hapless Orphan* by the remoteness of the off-stage campaign against the Indians.[3] Nor could the nature of the frontier past assert itself in those chapters of Neal's *Keep Cool* in which Sydney recovers firmness and self-reliance by living among an Indian tribe.[4]

The Indian presence, with its potential threat, was still a reality in the first decades of the nineteenth century. It was kept alive indirectly as well, in at least two ways: (1) through the discussion of the "noble savage" concept, which brought with it the related indictment of the white settlers' inordinate greed and ruthlessness, the source of overt and violent as well as hypocritically corrupting means to overcome the Indians;[5] and (2), in literature, in the numerous "captivities" handed down from the late seventeenth and eighteenth centuries. These "captivities" were written by settlers who had experienced at first hand or had been witnesses to, and transmitters of, the hardships undergone by people taken and carried off by Indian bands.[6]

The History of Maria Kittle,[7] by Mrs. Ann Eliza Bleecker (1752-1783), is best approached through the literary tradition of the "captivity," which clearly gave it its final shape.[8] But it is essential to realize, too, that Mrs. Bleecker's urge to write, or to unburden herself, must have been originally quite independent of any such formal model. For about five years, at least, her life in a remote New York settlement was made precarious by the presence of Indians and British soldiers, and the men were frequently absent from their homes. Twice she fled from Tomhanick; and she lost a little daughter, her mother, and a sister in consequence of these hardships. Her husband was captured by Indians; and though they were intercepted before crossing over into Canada, Mrs. Bleecker's anxiety apparently proved too much for her, and she did not recover from the shock. Such a contemporary story as that of Miss McCrea[9] must have been familiar in the frontier regions infested by the Indians and have called to mind a number of related experiences among the Bleeckers' neighbors and visiting friends, who in turn revived the narratives of earlier sufferers at the hands of the Indians. A pattern could thus develop and become serviceable for a fictional account of a captivity when it was suggested by Mrs. Bleecker's story or that of some neighbor.[10]

But a mere retelling of the captivity ordeal, without any extraneous elements would not do in 1780 as it had done in the days of Mary Rowlandson.[11] There are a number of obvious parallels, though, between the latter's account and that of Mrs. Bleecker. Both the actual Mrs. Rowlandson and the fictional Mrs. Kittle have no husband to protect them when the Indians attack their homes. Rowlandson and Kittle, on returning from a mission to obtain help, find their houses in ashes. The babies

of Mrs. Rowlandson and Mrs. Kittle are among the victims of
the attacks: the former, wounded at the very first, dies within
a week; the latter is disposed of by an Indian as an unnecessary
burden. Mrs. Rowlandson's baby is injured in her arms; so is
Mrs. Bratt's baby in a supporting episode of *Maria Kittle*.[12]
The meeting with King Philip in the "capitivity" is paralleled
with that of Mrs. Kittle with the French governor at Montreal,
where Mrs. Bleecker, as though refuting Mrs. Rowlandson, has
her heroine condemn the anti-French prejudice of the colonists,[13]
which was a reflection of the new attitude at the time of the
Franco-American alliance.

Though the two accounts not unexpectedly express strong
feelings about the Indians, there is yet in this a difference
between the genuine "captivity" and the fictional one. Mrs.
Rowlandson was trying to be factual; and her vindication of
Providence was buttressed by objectivity in her relation of her
adventures and her captors, whose customs she described briefly
in passing.[14] She expressed her horror and disgust at their
cruelty and their barbarity, and she deplored that the hard-
earned property of the settlers should be so quickly and
senselessly dissipated by the Indians. She noted their proneness
to lying and boasting; but on the other hand, she emphasized
that she hardly met one drunkard among them and that they
did not molest their female captives. If she had her reservations
about the praying Indians, she may have also had them about
the Puritans, who in some respects proved as frail as the red-
skins.[15] In keeping with her moderate tone, her language remained simple;[16] and even when she was outraged by the
bloodshed, she only briefly yielded to employing the condemna-
tory rhetoric of pulpit eloquence: "It is a solemn sight to see
so many Christians lying in their blood, some here, and some
there, like a company of Sheep torn by Wolves. All of them
stript naked by a company of hell-hounds, roaring, singing,
ranting and insulting, as if they would have torn our very
hearts out. . ." (p. 5).

The rhetoric of Mrs. Bleecker's characters in similar situations is much louder and more artificial: ". . . In the unutter-

able anguish of her soul, she fell prostrate, and rending away her hair, she roared out her sorrows with a voice louder than natural, and rendered awfully hollow by too great an exertion. 'O barbarians!' she exclaimed, 'surpassing devils in wickedness! so may a tenfold night of misery enwrap your black souls, as you have deprived the babe of my bosom, the comfort of my cares, my blessed cherub, of light and life ...'" (p. 38).[17] The emotional content of Mrs. Bleecker's language is much higher than Mrs. Rowlandson's, and though she is dry enough in her brief observations about Indian habits (pp. 42, 54, 61), it is evident that she welcomed the sentimental formulas of the contemporary novel.[18] Soon after the exposition, which is mainly factual, a character's forebodings introduce a note of heightened sensibility into her story (p. 27), and this dark shade is recurrently brought into relief to enforce some appeal to sympathy. After the melodrama of the writer's apostrophe to Mr. Kittle (p. 44) and his wife's moralizing about the animals' blessed insensibility and amorality (p. 53), there is finally an implicit admission of an occasionally selfish indulgence in emotions for their own sake.[19] In the emotional state reached at length, the feelings are over-violent to the point of swinging over to their opposite pole: "...They wept aloud; and the house of joy seemed to be the house of lamentation" (p. 83). Some of the cumulative effect of the emotional tensions may have been deliberate. It evidently runs parallel with the crude building up of suspense by focusing the reader's attention now on one, now on the other, of the Kittles, in transitions palpably engineered.[20] Both Kittle and Maria go through a period of illness that might conceivably prove fatal; and Maria, to whom we are returned on one occasion to be offered a contrast between the beauties of the setting and her misery (p. 49), is led back through a series of expectations and disappointments to the communion of gossip, sympathy, and love.[21] Yet though such a tentative patterning can be detected,[22] the best points of *Maria Kittle* derive not from its innovations but from the tradition of the "captivity," with its purposeful chronicling of events and its sound realistic backbone. How

[375]

much Mrs. Bleecker owed to it can perhaps also be shown by comparing *Maria Kittle* to her other story, built along the lines of the tale of romantic love, which quickly sinks into the sentimentalism so tempting to many writers of fiction.[23]

Maria Kittle is a late representative, as it were, of a dying narrative tradition based on a fading historical situation. By contrast, a group of novels seem to celebrate the advent of a new age, paying their compliments to the American republic and proclaiming its promise. Of these, *Secret History; or, The Horrors of St. Domingo* (1808),[24] attributed to Leonora Sansay,[25] assumes the epistolary form, like Mrs. Bleecker's "captivity." It also has a practical purpose: whereas Mrs. Bleecker was publicizing the dangers of life in wartime in a frontier settlement, the letters of *Secret History*, "written by a lady at Cape François to Colonel Burr," may have been meant as a declaration of loyalty when Burr was in disgrace.

The adventures of Maria Kittle were conceived in a historical frame of mind, in the consciousness shared by Mrs. Bleecker and her readers of the bloody border warfare during the French and Indian Wars and the War of Independence. *Secret History*, too, has a background familiar enough to the public; what it lacked in local immediacy, it balanced with the closeness in time and the significance of some of its implications as to the relationship between the white and black population. The historical events related took place between 1802 and 1804;[26] they begin with, and culminate in, an uprising of the Negroes (letters 1, 20, 22, 25). The anecdotes of the brutalities committed by the former slaves (letters 9, 22) could, of course, be taken as a prophetic warning for the slave-owning states.[27] If they were so meant, they lose some of their point because of the unfavorable picture given of the French military regime and especially the French commander Rochambeau: for the white colonists, there seems to be little to choose between the terror of their former slaves and exploitation by the French officers and soldiers (letters 3, 4).

The background of unrest combines with another conditioning element of the heroine's sentimental misadventures. From the

[376]

first the narrator stresses the sensual and voluptuous attributes of the exotic setting and, above all, of the Creole ladies;[28] and a burden of her book is the charge of moral decadence brought against the inhabitants of the Caribbean islands.[29] Newcomers find it more or less easy to conform to the local customs, according to their disposition: thus the ways of the country apparently do not displease General Leclerc's wife (p. 10) nor, possibly, the bereaved mistress of General Mayart (p. 68); and they seem to suit Clara, the narrator's sister and the unfortunate heroine of *Secret History,* only too well for the peace of her husband's mind. Mary admittedly gives a partial account of Clara's experiences;[30] she mentions as an important extenuating circumstance the fact of her unfortunate marriage (pp. 6, 42, 223). Though Clara early displays coquettish features, she yet retains an (American) sense of decency and scorns the moral laxity of Santo Domingo society: "How often has she assured me that she would prefer the most extreme poverty to her present existence, but to abandon her husband was not to be thought of. Yet to have abandoned him, and to have been presented as the declared mistress of General Rochambeau would not have been thought a crime nor have excluded her from the best society!" (p. 61). Clara is described as very attractive, but her intelligence and sensibility are praised as well.[31] Her idealism, however, strikes her sister as too liable to disappointment. Clara is very much aware of her physical charms: her husband's threat to disfigure her effects on the spot what all her former trials have not caused—she runs away from him (p. 188).

At this point *Secret History* assumes even more definitely than before its multiple character. It is a romantic narrative, introducing a clear picture of an actual historical episode with some of its real protagonists; it is also a sort of tourist guide to the beauties and sights of the Caribbean islands. The comments on the moral outlook of their inhabitants are part of it, and so are the remarks of the Edenic nature of pre-Toussaint L'Ouverture Santo Domingo. The description of Madame Leclerc's dressing room (p. 51) and of Cape François (letter 10) are further contributions to it. A characteristic combination of the elements of the picturesque, the martial, and the romantic is found in many passages:

> A few days ago we went to Picolet, to see the fort. The road to it winds along the sea-shore at the foot of the mountain. The rocks are covered with the Arabian jessamin, which grows here in the greatest profusion. Its flexible branches form among the cliffs moving festoons and fantastic ornaments, and its flowers whiter than snow, fill the air with intoxicating fragrance. After having visited the fort we were preparing to return, when we saw a troop of horsemen descending the mountain. They came full speed. We soon discovered they were the general and his suite; and as they followed the windings of the road, with their uniform à la mameluc, and their long sabres, they appeared like a horde of Arabs. (p. 93)

Clara's account of her removal into the country concentrates on the peculiar and picturesque, the appeal of which she cannot resist even though she is fleeing from her husband (p. 190).[32]

The book closes on the announcement that Mary and Clara are about to leave Jamaica for Philadelphia, which to Mary is a sheltering home, apparently owing to the protection which Burr has given her and may possibly be willing to extend to her sister (pp. 39, 225). She has early expressed a wish to return to the United States, and the note of nostalgic praise for them has been implicit in her critical comments on the morals of the French and Spanish possessions in the Caribbean; a healthy view of married love, in particular, has been underscored as distinctively American and relevant even to that restless American, Clara (pp. 79-80; 77, 6, 17).

This sort of praise need not be too obtrusive if it is conveyed by a writer competent to deal, without boring his reader, with the manifold aspects of his account; and Mrs. Sansay was such a writer. America is also praised obliquely, rather than directly, in much of the anonymous novel The Irish Emigrant (1817).[33] Only its preface, a dedication of the book to Ireland and the Irish literary great, paints America as a haven where the natural rights of man are respected (1:iv). The parallelism between the fight for freedom against British rule in America after 1775 and in Ireland before the turn of the century is pointed out by our author's Irish heroine, Emma O'Niall:

> In modern times, she had the example of a Washington presented to her view, whose unwearied perseverance in the cause of his country, and exalted patriotism for the love of liberty, had at length been favored by Heaven with the pleasure of beholding that his efforts were crowned with success. The American Republic she viewed with all the philanthropic zeal that Heaven could implant in the human breast, as a glorious and transcendant example to the world of justice, liberty, equality and patriotism unparalleled. She contemplated with delight on the heroes and sages that country had produced, at a time when it was looked upon by other countries with the most supercelious [sic] contempt. Her Franklin then wielded the lightnings of Heaven, her Washington then wielded the virtues of earth. (1:127-28)

There is also the symbolic presence in Dublin's Newgate of an American prisoner, Warren, brought there by British perfidy (1:169, 2:60-110). When Warren returns to Philadelphia, Emma and Owen M'Dermott, her husband, go with him quite as a matter of course: their revolution having failed, the Irish patriots bide their time in a country exemplary of, and sympathetic with, their aspirations. Meanwhile, the Irish emigrant M'Dermott's story may be told.

The neighborly alliance of Warren and the M'Dermotts reminds one of the conclusions of many novels of sentimental love and adventure, whose heroes remove with their parents and friends to some hospitable district.[34] The nature of *The Irish Emigrant* is indeed determined rather more by the protagonists' love affairs than by the relation of historical events. The latter are introduced in the first thirty pages and dealt with at considerable length, but they are gradually not so much overlaid as permeated and tinctured with the conventional texturing and coloring of the love-and-trials story. The love intrigues, secret though pure or furtive because unhallowed, shape the chronicle of the political drama, until the closing pages, fittingly, record four marriages. Of these, three are rewards and promise well, and the last, which unites two villains, at any rate spares other possible partners.³⁵ A simplified handling of the moral issues is also evident in the punishment decreed for the captain who caused Warren's arrest and the barbarous jailor who tried to terrorize Emma. We must not, in such a context, expect any significant characterization. Emma is a compound of patriotism, republicanism, courage, benevolence, and patient love, whose example confirms and inspires afresh M'Dermott's dedication to his country (1:94-95). All of the true patriots—such as M'Dermott, Fitzgerald, O'Connor, Coigley, O'Connell—are noble by birth or precepts; among their adversaries we find Major S—, the ruthlessly ambitious upstart; Sir Phelim O'Niall, a hypocritical plotter; Butler and Sophia, selfish seekers of gratification; Miss Robison and Bonsel, two traitorous intriguers; and the brutal Barbour, who "had all the ferocity of the tyger, all the fawning submission of the dog, all the venom of the rattle-snake," and who, as executioner and Emma's jailor, "would frequently enter her apartment, and present to her his blood stained hands which were still reeking with human gore (from a fresh victim immolated on the altar of despotism)" (2: 141, 148). The only exception to the general rule is the English general Nugent, "a republican at heart," who is finally rewarded with the hand of Athanasia Ormond, a noble Irish girl. The potential interest of the Romeo-and-Juliet situation of Emma and M'Dermott is stifled by their unreality as characters, as well as by the bias inevitably felt toward the family feud in such a setting of black and white.³⁶

Though itself a slight production, *Secret History* is considerably subtler in the handling of its characters and, by comparison, rather successful in the rendering of its setting; with *The Irish Emigrant* we are given little more than names and a style with no distinctive qualities. The balance achieved in the former novel between its various ingredients may have been fortuitous rather than deliberate, but it *is* an element that lifts the book above the average run of contemporary fiction; in *The Irish Emigrant* we find an example of a more common disproportion of overemphasizing the sentimental at the cost of the rational and the sensibly lifelike.

A similar lack of balance rather unexpectedly mars the compilation, *The Female Review: or, Memoirs of an American Young Lady* (1797), by Herman Mann (1772-1833). Ostensibly prompted by gratitude for God's providence[37] and by patriotism and sympathetic admiration for Deborah Sampson, Mann seemed to build around her person a chronicle of the successful final phases of the War of Independence; the result, however, is an ill-ordered account not of American devotion and endurance but of a disguised girl's anxieties over the possible discovery of her sex. The very premise of Deborah's concealed identity creates an interest not unlike that aroused by the question, Will the heroine remain virtuous?, in the novels written after the pattern of *Pamela*. Her story occasionally reveals a more ambiguous tendency which raises misgivings about Mann's boast that his book ought to prove beneficial to his female readers. He professed to be a firm believer in the potential qualities of the novel; and he hoped that his account, which included "a series of moral reflections" and "some literary and historical information" (p. ix), might be found "agreeably entertaining and useful" (p. xiii), rather like a good novel. He was careful to endow his heroine with a respectable ancestry (her mother is descended from Governor William Bradford)[38] and with common sense and sound principles (pp. 27, 50, 99-100) before launching her into the world. Yet he was vague about her motives for disguising herself, though he did mention her curiosity about her country, the fact that a lady could not travel unprotected, and, finally, Deborah's notion of doing something for the Colonies in their fight against the British (p. 114). He seemed to avoid making her exceptional in her ways and views, and yet he referred to her prophetic dream, four days before Lexington, as if she were another Joan of Arc.

Perhaps Deborah's troubles (and Mann's) really begin when the girl whom the soldiers know as "the blooming boy" and whom Mann calls "our blooming soldier," "our distinguished Fair," and "our Gallantress" (pp. 146, 162, 173) provokes the jealousy of a fellow soldier by capturing his girl friend's heart.[39] A later episode of the same kind is protracted because the heroine keeps her secret even though insistently wooed by a lady from Baltimore. All this has little to do with the portrait of the "historical" Deborah and jars with the author's professed respect for delicacy, as expounded in his preface and practiced heavy-handedly in a number of passages.[40] The appendix of *The Female Review* reveals Mann's own concern about possible misconstructions of his literary effort, or, in other words, about the difficulty of keeping history and fiction apart, and keeping fiction within the bounds of reason and decency. It lists documents testifying to the authenticity of his heroine's experience and tells, among other things, the story of Fatima and Philander. This story contains a scene that might have been written expressly to illustrate those talents of the writer held in restraint in order to observe the rules of the "agreeably entertaining and useful." Ironically, the passage opens with the statement "It is needless to paint the scenes that succeeded," and proclaims at the end that "Heaven was a recording witness to their criminal pleasures" (pp. 245-46). It is as though the author, refusing any further responsibility, was in a hurry to return his reader to the moral context of the scene.

Though allegedly written in a didactic spirit and deliberately charged with meaning, the passage in question was obviously also inconsistent with Mann's determination to "yield the palm of style to the rapturous and melting expressions of the novelist."[41] It was by no means the only time that he was betrayed into a luxuriant manner. His apology for the love of the Baltimore lady is a related example.[42] Another topic in the treatment of which he let himself go is that of the patriotically significant, especially addressed to his female readers (pp. 136, 173-174; 73). This sort of writing manages almost to eclipse episodes such as Deborah's brief journey to the frontier; and it is difficult to reconcile with the report of Deborah's childhood and youth, the blunt fact of her seasickness (p. 145), and the etymological footnote on the word "yankee."[43] Yet it is passages such as the last mentioned or the description of the British attack on Bunker's Hill[44] that are appropriate for the stabilizing function which might be fulfilled by the historical background of actuality; it would seem that Mrs. Bleecker and Mrs. Sansay understood that function better than Mann.

The Prisoners of Niagara, or Errors of Education (1810), by Jesse Lynch Holman (1784-1842),[45] is another novel with a background of revolution and patriotism which leans heavily on the conventions of the tale of adventure and love. The main narrative is inserted in a frame whose setting is Fort Niagara in late 1782, and deals mostly with events of the years 1775 to 1782, concluding with the hero's marriage, which coincides with the peace treaty ratifying American independence. Within this historical scaffolding, the theme developed by Holman is that of his alternate title. Errors of education prove to be the main source of Evermont's sentimental lapses as well as the cause of the antagonisms and misunderstandings which make life difficult for him and those he loves.[46] Holman apparently felt that he could not rely on the setting in history alone to render his theme interesting, and he concocted an intricate story motivated alternately by his hero's vulnerable flesh and by his restless sense of guilt and expiation. Evermont oscillates between the poles of pastoral innocence, embodied in Zerelda, his true love, and of corruption, represented by the city and Mrs. Willford, in particular. The lovers are Americans, of course; part of their trials must be traced to British perfidy and oppression.[47]

Zerelda is the quintessence of female purity and love-inspiring sensibility.[48] Though her unpleasant experiences include being carried off by an unwelcome suitor (a British officer, too), we may assume that her most painful anxieties are caused by her mixed feelings and divided loyalties about Evermont, "Holbert," and "Bridford." She felt certain of her love for Evermont, so how can she help being puzzled when she feels herself falling in love with the two strangers, under whose disguise Evermont remains undetected even by her loving eye.[49] She is all forgiveness except once, when she even asks Evermont to return the medal she has given him; but it is his complying with her request that really wounds her, and so she is quite happy when she discovers that he has kept the original and sent her only a copy. Evermont also fails to recognize the disguised Zerelda. If this is pardonable

[383]

in the darkness of his prison, it is less understandable later when they escape from Fort Niagara. In another sense Evermont fails Zerelda when he believes the rumor that the angel-like being who visits the American prisoners (Zerelda in disguise) is really the mistress of the British commanding officer. Evermont is so much steeped in despair at the time that such a disillusionment is perhaps inevitable. There are so many things that contribute to his dejection: the memories of his misconduct with Armilda, whom he believes to be his half-sister, with Emerald and someone impersonating Susan; the facts of his apparent blood-relationship with Mrs. Willford and his illegitimate birth; and the idea that he may have killed his own father. And then Zerelda is lost to him; not only is she married to Barville but, what is much worse, he is not worthy of her, and he has therefore determined to keep her free from any association with his opprobrious blood (p. 280). The satisfaction of having served Zerelda well[50] no longer balances his various betrayals of virtue and of her love.

Holman took pains to explain his hero's character, ascribing to him an impulsive nature which could be swayed by any dominant influence (pp. 109, 240, 300-301).[51] Plausible or not, Evermont's inconsistent behavior does much to encourage a varied use of narrative material and elaborate mechanisms of complication.[52] So does the presence in the novel of a ubiquitous villain, Mrs. Willford: she has played a part in Evermont's earliest years *and* been connected with Zerelda's father, and can therefore conveniently turn up again as the main stumbling block in the progress of the young lovers' happiness. An adept at illicit relationships, procuring, imposture, blackmail and murder plots, she is the stock type of the versatile evil character finally caught in her own trap. Her world is the world of darkness and secrecy into which Evermont strays through his dalliance with Armilda and Emerald, and his gambling. Since the hero is sensitive, he increasingly broods over his corruption and unworthiness:

> What had I been! but what! Oh what! tremendous judge! what am I now!—A paracide [sic]! Awful—Awful thought—A paracide!!!

The pangs of eternal agony rolled in a horrible chaos upon my feelings!—I felt the indignant denunciations of heaven hovering over my head, and involuntarily raised my eyes to behold the blazing bolt of lightning descend, with the thunder of divine malediction, to blast my guilty soul into perdition—A whirlwind of desperation burst in my mind, and hurled the shattered fragments of reflection, into terrible consternation—I grasped a pistol with the infernal purpose of ending a dreadful existence!! But I was yet incapable of the diabolical deed—I started affrighted at my daring assumption of the sovereignty of omnipotence—The pistol fell—life was struck dumb in awful petrefaction—My hair stood upright in horror!!! (pp. 292-93)[53]

If such is his state of mind when he feels depressed, the nightmarish melodrama of the first chapter is really appropriate to it; its opening paragraph, a possible reminiscence of *Edgar Huntly*, certainly reflects Holman's familiarity with Gothic effects.[54] The horrors of reality contrast strongly with the prisoner's sentimental fancies or with such aspects of the actual which he hardly dares to believe true: thus his vision of Carmont's murder is embedded between the miraculous apparitions of the compassionate lady.

Holman favored the technique of abrupt changes of mood.[55] This is consistent with the instability of the hero, and it enhances, too, the feeling of insecurity which Evermont must be felt to experience. It also serves, even though crudely, to create suspense. Artificial ritardandi are frequently used for that purpose, from the Sternean chapter ending (p. 70) to the series of circumstances that delay Evermont's discovery of the identity of the "lady with the lamp."[56] Before his own identity can be ascertained, he conjectures that he might be related to the Evermont who found him and gave him his name, then believes that he is the son of Valindon and Mrs. Willford, or Huron and Mrs. Willford. Evermont would not have gained much if Huron had completed his revelation at their first meeting, since Huron himself finds out the whole truth about his wicked wife only later; but the time-honored method of interrupting a revelation is typical of Holman's level of achievement. So is the scene in which Evermont listens for sounds that may betray Zerelda's ravisher (p. 181). Characteristically, at the end Evermont's individual dejection yields to general sentimental rejoicing as the various severed couples reunite. The hero's ability to indulge his feelings thoroughly has been demonstrated before; it also manifests itself in confrontations with settings of natural loveliness or grandeur[57] and when he imagines, or can sympathetically share in, someone else's emotions.[58] His success with Zerelda owes much to their common sensibility, properly fostered in childhood.[59] Their cousin Emerine, though, who has benefited from the same education, has retained more sprightliness and detachment, possibly a feature meant to differentiate between Zerelda and herself.[60]

George Washington Willoughby, the hero of *The Champions of Freedom, or the Mysterious Chief* (1816), by Samuel Woodworth (1785-1842), is frail like Evermont, but his frailty is treated as a more serious offense. In spite of the coincidence of Evermont's adventures with the course of—or at any rate, the beginning and end of—the War of Independence, they are for the most part unrelated to the historical events. In fact Evermont, disapproving of war, reluctantly and at a late date takes an active part in the hostilities. His troubles arise from his involvement in, and his offenses against, the code of chastity and from his encounter with a malevolent schemer. He remains throughout an advocate of his own concerns, even when acting on behalf of Zerelda; and extenuating circumstances are advanced to reduce his misdemeanor to pardonable lapses in the eyes of both his friends and the reader. But in Woodworth's celebration of American valor during the War of 1812,[61] the hero is early taught to see matters of a private nature (such as love), and of national significance in the light of their respective importance: national concerns are of primary importance and take precedence over all others. Willoughby becomes grievously culpable when, anxious over the fate of his Catharine, he allows himself temporarily (and uselessly, too) to place his personal claims to happiness above the cause of his country. His dilemma, unlike Evermont's, could appear with sufficient clarity only if it was shown in close association with the progress of the war.

[386]

Woodworth therefore saw to it that the various encounters and campaigns in which his hero took part were incorporated in the narrative complex made up of his own chronicling of events and the letters and journals written by his part-narrators, Major Willoughby and O'Hara.

Apparently this was not enough, and Woodworth emphasized Willoughby's conflict and guilt in a far more striking manner: he introduced, rather in the manner of early chronicle plays, an allegorical figure appearing to his hero when necessary, in order to forewarn him of impending tasks or rebuke him for neglecting his patriotic duties.[62] Under the guise of an Indian chief, this embodiment of the "spirit of Washington" at length seems to invest the young man with the high seriousness of the American example; he raises him to the status of personified patriotism, as it were, and decrees that patriotism is one of the first virtues to be inculcated in American children (2:335-36). So much for the essential program underlying the story of Willoughby at home, at Harvard, and on various fronts during the war. This program loses much of its high-sounding ambitiousness when it is linked with Willoughby's sentimental biography; whatever serious nobility may have been meant for the "Mysterious Chief" becomes mere ludicrousness as the plots of love, jealousy, envy, and revenge spread their melodramatic coloring to it. The idea that Sandford might succeed in seducing Catharine is of sufficient interest without any additional implications; but we are made to feel that his success would be a kind of providential punishment for Willoughby's dereliction of duty.[63] A conflict between love and allegorical patriotism, however, is liable to appear too academic when at the same time the struggle of a good woman and a wicked one over the man they love lays claim to the reader's interest.

The Champions of Freedom strikes one as an unsatisfactory combination of a pronouncedly chauvinistic chronicle[64] and a conventional tale of love and faithfulness.[65] The hero of the novel is active on its two levels; but the conflict he was meant to experience in that position fails to achieve even the minimum of urgency which we at least sympathetically sense in his trials as

[387]

a lover guilty of betraying his true love. The year 1816 was perhaps too close to the events of the war for their successful assimilation into fiction, in the first place; at any rate, the force of literary patterns and conventions easily prevailed with Woodworth and smothered what might have become his original contribution to the development of the American historical romance. The philosophical disquisitions about the necessity of war (2:26, 32) or the sententious remarks about providence,[66] do as little to ensure the relevance of this American chronicle as the appearance in its pages of genuine historical characters or references to verifiable news items.[67] The historical scaffolding collapses into an accumulation of names (of men, places, ships) and a jumble of individual scenes, under the pressure of compulsive narrative and stylistic habits: the stereotype characterization of the hero (1:17), mannerisms such as a sailor's speech (2:27), heroic superlatives,[68] the pastoral or domestic mood (1:20-21), the rhetoric of moral indignation[69] or selfish revenge,[70] the didactic pictures of dangerous sensuality (1:95-96; 2:154-55)—all these ingredients are employed as a matter of course. Woodworth's preface seemed to promise better things, but it is soon suspected of being above all an apology revealing the author's uneasiness about his creation.[71] It could be used to prove that a writer may know his faults and yet be unable to mend them.[72]

1. "Death of Cicero" is appended to the second issue of the first edition of *Edgar Huntly*, Vol. 3; "Thessalonica" appeared in the *Monthly Magazine* 1(1799):99-117 and was reprinted in Dunlap's *Life*, 2:170-99; "Walstein's School of History," first published in the *Monthly Magazine* 1(1799):335-38, 407-11, is included in *The Rhapsodist*.

2. Cooper's novels apparently met a real need. See G. H. Orians, "The Romance Ferment after *Waverley*," *AL* 3(1932):408-31. Harvey Wish (p. 300) notes that half a million copies of Scott's books were printed in America from 1814 to 1823.

3. In Mrs. Tenney's *Female Quixotism*, too, there is a wounded officer returning from the Indian wars; his appearance at the Sheldons' home proves a powerful stimulant to Dorcasina's fiction-fostered imaginings. Emily Thompson, in *The Soldier's Orphan*, and Willoughby, in *The Champions of Freedom*, are born and lose their mothers on the day their fathers suffer for their country: Thompson falls at Quebec (December 31, 1775) and Willoughby, Sr., is wounded at the battle of Fallen Timbers (August 20, 1794).

4. There is an earlier anticipation in American fiction of the motif developed by Cooper in *The Wept of Wish-ton-Wish*: Mrs. Rowson had two ancestors

of Reuben and Rachel carried away and brought up by Indians (*Reuben and Rachel*, 1: chaps. 16, 18, 19). Mrs. Sarah Wentworth Morton's *Quâbi*, a narrative poem derived from a story published in the *American Museum* (September, 1789), is in part about a fugitive from Europe, adopted at his request by an Indian tribe. See also the long narrative poem *Yamoyden*, by James W. Eastburn and Robert C. Sands (1820).

5. Mrs. Rowson (*Reuben and Rachel*, 1:160), William Wirt (*Letters of the British Spy*, pp. 38-39), Irving (*A History of New York*, pp. 51-63), Paulding (*Koningsmarke*, 1:196-97, 2:113): these are some of the writers in whose fiction we find expressions of blame for the white settlers of America for their dispossessing and actively corrupting the Indians as well as their failure to set unequivocal standards of moral behavior. On the other hand, a writer in the *Columbian Magazine* ("An Account of the Vices Peculiar to the Savages of North America," September, 1786), and Silliman (*Letters of Shahcoolen*, letters 13-14) held that the Indians were savage and cruel long before the Whites settled in America, and did not profit by the good example of the Christians. This was also the view of Silliman's Yale colleague Timothy Dwight (*Travels*, 3:19-22). Henry M. Brackenridge wondered whether the Missouri Indians he met in 1811 exemplified natural barbarism, or corruption by Western civilization (see "The Indians of the Upper Missouri," in Warren S. Tryon, ed., *A Mirror for Americans*, 3:492).

6. The English traveler and writer John Davis (1775-1854), who thought (in sentimental sympathy, rather like Freneau's) that the Indians were civilizable, may be mentioned in passing here, since according to him his "literary birth" took place in the United States. He proclaimed his British loyalty (*Travels of Four Years and a Half in the U.S.A.*, p. 4), but resided in America about sixteen years, including two at Richmond from 1812 to 1814. After 1816 and to his death he lived in England. He would rate a longer discussion here if his fiction had been more original and verifiably influential in America, but it is poor even by the standards of the contemporary American novel. His books are clearly very hastily devised and written, and frequently repetitive in phrasing. Jay B. Hubbell, "The Smith-Pocahontas Literary Legend," in *South and Southwest: Literary Essays and Reminiscences*, pp. 175-204, calls Davis an initiator but also reminds us that the Smith-Pocahontas material was already somewhat assimilated in America when Davis wrote his versions of it. We may list the accounts of Smith and/or Pocahontas in: the *Columbian Magazine* (July, 1787, August-December, 1788); the *American Magazine* (December, 1787, March, 1788); Belknap's *American Biography* (1:240-308); Wirt's *Letters of the British Spy* (1803), letter 4; Marshall's *Life of George Washington* (1: chap. 2). Davis first summarized the Pocahontas material in *The Farmer of New-Jersey* (New York, 1800), p. 11, treated it more extensively in his *Travels*, pp. 259-95, and *Captain Smith and the Princess Pocahontas* (Philadelphia, 1805); it was further elaborated in *The First Settlers of Virginia* (New York, 1805). He followed Smith's 1624 account, expanding and embellishing it in the manner of the sentimental novelists, perhaps following the example of Wirt in the expression of his feeling for the place and persons. The reviews of Davis's early novels were extremely discouraging; see the *American Review and Literary Journal* (1[1801]:83, 427-30) and the *Port-Folio* (1, no. 38[1801]:303). Davis's Indian novels do not seem to have been noticed. For Davis, see Thelma Louise Kellogg, *The Life and Works of John Davis;* Philip Young, "The Mother of Us All: Pocahontas Reconsidered," *KR* 24(1962):391-415; and Davis, *Jefferson's Virginia*, pp. 300-302). *The Female American, or the Extraordinary Adventures of Unca Winkfield, compiled*

by herself (London, 1767), uses an adaptation of the Smith-Pocahontas material in its opening chapters, of the Crusoe story later, and of accounts of missionaries at the end. The Indian setting in the main part of the book is South American rather than North American; in the Virginia chapters the execution of the white prisoners is considered a punishment for their greed. An American edition of the novel appeared in Newburyport, Mass., 1800 [?]; it is doubtful whether the alleged authoress was really writing her autobiography, and whether she was an American at all (but see Tremaine McDowell, "An American Robinson Crusoe," *AL* 1[1929]:307-9). A later echo of the legendary material is to be found in *The Christian Indian; or, Times of the First Settlers* (New York, 1825), a novel which introduces a number of very noble savages indeed.

7. The story (or "letter" to Mrs. Bleecker's friend Susan Ten Eyck) was apparently begun in Dec., 1779, and perhaps completed in 1781. It was published in the *New York Magazine,* in five installments, from September, 1790, to January, 1791, and included in *The Posthumous Works of Ann Eliza Bleecker;* references are to this edition.

8. See Albert Keiser, *The Indian in American Literature,* p. 33.

9. Michel René Hilliard d'Auberteuil, *Mis Mac Rea* (1784); see the Scholars' Facsimiles and Reprints edition, Introd. by Lewis Leary (Gainesville, Fla., 1958), and cf. James Austin Holden, "The Influence of the Death of Jane McCrea on the Burgoyne Campaign," *Proceedings of the New York State Historical Association* 12(1913):249-310. See also the references to the affair in Marshall, *Life of Washington,* 3:272, and Lydia H. Sigourney, *Sketch of Connecticut, Forty Years Since* (Hartford, Conn., 1824), pp. 119-34. Another French work of fiction written in, or inspired by, America is *L'Héroïne du Texas* (1819); see Edwin P. Gaston, Jr., *The Early Novel of the Southwest* (Albuquerque: University of New Mexico Press, 1961).

10. Mrs. Bleecker herself was never a captive of the Indians, yet her experience was spectacular enough for the Duyckincks to refer only to her life, not to her pioneer work in American fiction, in their *Cyclopaedia of American Literature,* 1:365-67.

11. Mary Rowlandson, *The Soveraignty & Goodness of God, together with the Faithfulness of his Promises Displayed; being a Narrative of the Captivity and Restauration of Mrs. Mary Rowlandson.* References are to the second edition, the earliest extant (Cambridge, Mass., 1682). According to Frank Luther Mott, this was the first American prose best seller. (*Multitudes,* p. 20). The "captivity" remained long popular: two collections appeared as late as 1841, Joseph Pritts, *Incidents of Border Life* (Lancaster, Pa.), and Samuel Gardner Drake, *Tragedies of the Wilderness* (Boston). The "captivities" were perhaps rejuvenated by accounts of prisoners of the English or Algerines; see above, the chapters "John Bull and Brother Jonathan" (esp. pp. 91-92), and "Fortune's Football" (esp. pp. 286-98). See also Phillips D. Carleton, "The Indian Captivity," *AL* 15(1943):169-80; Roy H. Pearce, "The Significance of the Captivity Narrative," *AL* 19(1947):1-20, and the same author's *The Savages of America.*

12. There is also a reversal of the situation: Mrs. Rowlandson's brother-in-law buried his own wife with the other victims of the fire laid by the Indians, though he was unaware of it, whereas Kittle, who cannot find his wife's body, assumes it must have been consumed when their house burnt down.

13. Mrs. Rowlandson wrote of her son that "it might have been worse with him, had he been sold to the French, than it proved to be in his remaining

with the Indians" (p. 36). Mrs. Kittle is made to say: "From my infancy have I been taught that the French were a cruel, perfidious enemy, but I have found them quite the reverse" (p. 73).

14. So did other writers of "captivities". See, e.g., *Jonathan Dickinson's Journal or God's Protecting Providence* (1699), ed. E. A. and C. M. Andrews, repr. (New Haven: Yale University Press, 1961).

15. See her remarks on smoking (p. 24) and on her inability to sympathize with an Indian mother (p. 39). William Bartram was another writer who tried to give a fair picture of the Indians; see his *Travels through North and South Carolina, Georgia, East and West Florida*...(1791), ed. Mark Van Doren, pp. 182-84, 44-45.

16. "...The Indians shot so thick that the bullets rattled against the house, as if one had taken an handfull of stones and threw them" (p. 3); cf. the phrase, "haveing my burden more on my back than my spirit" (p. 42).

17. Cf. Kittle's despair, pp. 45-46. A similar spirit of violence found expression in "Kintair and Seaton; or the Unfortunate Sisters," *The American Bee*, pp. 158-69.

18. "Maria smiled benignly through a crystal atmosphere of tears" (p. 66); for other situations of sensibility, see pp. 80-81, 82-83. Roy H. Pearce calls *Maria Kittle* "simply a captivity narrative turned novel of sensibility" (*The Savages of America*, p. 198).

19. Mrs. Willis is invited to tell her sad tale, one lady saying, by way of enticement, "my heart is now sweetly tuned to melancholy." Later "the ladies severally embracing her, expressed their acknowledgement for the painful task she had complied with to oblige their curiosity" (pp. 74, 81); cf. the phrases "pleasing melancholy" and "indulged herself in the luxury of sorrow" (pp. 69, 56).

20. "But doubtless, my dear, your generous sensibility is alarmed at my silence about Mrs. Kittle; I think we left her reposing under a tree" (p. 49); see also p. 42.

21. She is disappointed by the Indian women's pitilessness, then overwhelmed by the compassion of an English lady (pp. 59-60, 64); when she has given up the hope of seeing her husband again, they suddenly meet (pp. 81-82).

22. The pattern is also supported by parallelisms in the main story and the subsidiary episodes, told by Mrs. Brattle and Mrs. Willis.

23. "The Story of Henry and Anne" (*Posthumous Works*, pp. 89-114). Henry wishes to be released from army service, and his commanding officer answers "in a softened tone, 'I know what love is—my Henry can be happy, I only great;...I know you deserve to be happier than I am!'"

24. There is only one edition printed in Philadelphia in 1808. The vaguely commendatory review of the novel in the *Monthly Anthology* 5(1808):384-87, above all celebrates the rich associations of Santo Domingo for all Americans since the days of Columbus.

25. There are references which possibly apply to the author of *Secret History* in James Parton, *The Life and Times of Aaron Burr;* see especially, in a letter written on the eve of Burr's duel with Hamilton: "...I would suggest that Madame—, too well known under the name of Leonora, has claims on my recollection. She is now with her husband at St. Iago, of Cuba" (12th ed. [New York, 1859], p. 352). See above, "Seduction," for a discussion of another novel by the same author, *Laura* (in particular note 28).

26. Rochambeau's capture (chap. 21), occurred in November, 1803.

27. One Negro uprising in the States seems to have been inspired by the example of Toussaint L'Ouverture, that of Gabriel, the slave of a Richmond landowner. See Wish, *Society*, p. 229.

28. Mary envies "the Creole ladies whose time was divided between the bath, the table, the toilette and the lover" (p. 25); see also pp. 18, 20.

29. According to Mary seduction is rare but adultery commonplace, in Santo Domingo (p. 77). "Every girl sighs to be married to escape the restraint in which she is held while single, and to enjoy the unbounded liberty she so often sees abused by her mother" (p. 80). The Cubans seem to be a race of thiefs (p. 122), while the descendants of the Spaniards have retained only their characteristic jealousy (p. 141).

30. See especially pp. 180, 221. Mary is perhaps something of a flirt herself: see her appreciation of Major B— (p. 67), the American consul (p. 136), and Don Carlos (p. 176).

31. See pp. 31, 223; and letter 5, pp. 180, 221, 223.

32. There are also the descriptions of a shrine (pp. 195-96), and of a nocturnal land-crab exodus (pp. 201-3).

33. The copyright notice of the only edition of the novel mentions the names of John T. Sharrocks and Adam Douglass. The latter may have been the author; Sharrocks appears on the title page as publisher of the novel.

34. See, e.g., Mrs. Wood's *Julia, Amelia*, and *Ferdinand and Elmira;* Mrs. Botsford's *Adelaide;* Mrs. Rowson's *Reuben and Rachel;* Butler's *Fortune's Foot-ball;* the anonymous *The Fortunate Discovery.*

35. "Sophia was a compound of vice, malignity, of the most vindictive malice, jealous of the perfections of others, hypocritical, and overbearing, all of which passions operated on her by turns, so that she was always accompanied by one of those deamons [sic] at least and the reader may conjecture, when all her forces were combined, they were not the least formidable array, that has been seen" (1:144). Butler's portrait is given in 1:137.

36. More memorable "Irish emigrants" occur in Brackenridge's *Modern Chivalry*, whose Teague O'Regan is partly an elaboration of Father Bombo, a creation of Brackenridge and Freneau; in Mrs. Tenney's *Female Quixotism* (the scoundrel O'Connor); in Brown's *Edgar Huntly* (Clithero) and "Carwin" (Ludloe). The Irish revolution of 1798 was to be used by James McHenry in *O'Halloran* (1824) with better success.

37. See the Dedication and Preface. All references are to *The Female Review* (1797).

38. In all likelihood there must have been some truth about the person and the basic situation of the "female soldier" Deborah Sampson, alias Robert Shurtliffe. It is the treatment and elaboration of the material, apparently devised to bring the story into conformity with current patterns of fiction, that raise misgivings in the minds of the readers (see Quinn, *Fiction*, p. 23, and the factual corrections suggested by John Adams Vinton in his edition of *The Female Review* [Boston, 1866]). To some contemporary or near-contemporary readers, the example of the Deborah publicized by Mann or other reports of her career was real and stimulating enough. This is evidenced, e.g., by the confession story published (in part anonymously) by Lucy Brewer West. Its second installment is entitled, *An Affecting Narrative of Louisa Baker*, "a native of Massachusetts, who, in early life having been shamefully seduced, deserted her parents, and enlisted in disguise, on board an American frigate as a marine, where, in two or three engagements, she displayed the most heroic fortitude, and was honourably discharged therefrom, a few months since, with-

out a discovery of her sex being made" (3d ed., Boston, 1816). There are explicit statements that Louisa was encouraged by the example of Deborah, and that she copied some of the measures of her model to secure an effective disguise. Lucy West could of course have been inspired by other models, e.g., the New York reprint (1807) of *The Female Shipwright*, about Mary Lacy, who was a sailor for four years and a dockyard worker for another seven years, or the "Account of Frances Scanagatti," another young lady who distinguished herself in the army (see the *Literary Magazine and American Register* 8(1807):183-89. A later related story is Cordelia Stark, *Female Wanderer* (1829).

39. We are informed that Deborah's conquest "bordered on subjects that might have enraptured the other sex" (p. 179).

40. When Deborah's section are ordered to bathe in the Hudson River, the girl finds a spot "thickly enclosed with the aspen and alder. Thither she unnoticed retired. And whilst the Hudson swelled with the multitude of masculine bodies, a beautiful rivulet answered every purpose of bathing a more delicate form" (p. 189).

41. P. xiii. The clichés of situation and phrasing also proved irresistible to Lucy West (see note 38), e.g., Part II, pp. 5, 10, Part III (*The Awful Beacon* [Boston, 1816]), p. 11. If Parson Weems can be called "a novelist or poet manqué" (Weems, *The Life of Washington*, ed. Marcus Cunliffe, Introduction, pp. lv, lvi, and cf. xxiv, xxviii), this could be said, as a flattery, of Herman Mann, too. The pretentiousness of *The Female Review* is shown up by such a straightforward contemporary account as John Plumb Martin's *Private Yankee Doodle*, ed. George F. Scheer (Boston: Little, Brown, 1962).

42. "O love! how powerful is your influence! how unlimited your domain! The gallant Solomon could not have composed three thousand proverbs and his madrigals to his love, without much of your conviviality. The illuminations of Venus were known in those days. And it was by her rays, the Preacher of love so often strolled with his Egyptian belles in his vineyard, when the flowers appeared on the earth, the mandrakes gave a good smell, and the time of the singing of birds had come; when they reciprocated their love amidst the dews of dawn.

Sufficient it is, that this love is preserved, and that it will remain incontrovertible. And happy it is, that it is not only enjoyed by the prince of the inner pavillion. It leaps upon the mountains; and, under the shadow of the apple-tree, it is sweet to the taste. From the moss-covered cottage, it is pursued, even amidst the thunders of war and the distraction of elements. And the nymph of Maryland was as much entitled to it, as the mistress of him, who had the caressing of a thousand" (pp. 195-97).

43. "The derivation of this word is from farmer Jonathan Hastings of Cambridge about 1713. He used it to express a *good quality*. Thus, a *yankee horse* and *yankee cider* were an *excellent horse* and *excellent cider.*—The British used it wrongly, as a word of contempt to the Americans" (p. 153n.).

44. This has been praised by Quinn, *Fiction*, p. 23.

45. Perry F. Kendig has published a sound description of this novel (Charlottesville: University of Virginia Press, 1953). He describes a copy not listed in Wright's *American Fiction*. The copy is in the Bittle Memorial Library, Roanoke College, Salem, Va. There seems to be only one edition of the novel, Frankfort, Ky., 1810. Israel George Blake records that "some of the best scholars of his day have expressed the belief that the moral tone of the novel was at least as elevated as the better class of fiction of the early part of

the century" (*The Holmans of Veraestau* [Oxford, Ohio: The Mississippi Valley Press, 1943], p. 5). Holman apparently did not in later years share this flattering opinion of the "piece of over-florid, dramatic writing, indiscreetly committed to paper by him in his youth" (R. E. Banta, *Indiana Authors and their Books, 1816-1916* [Crawfordsville, Ind., 1949], pp. 151-52).

46. Evermont himself has no one to advise him in Richmond and falls into vicious city ways. Armilda knows no other example than her mother's wickedness. Whitford grows up in the brutal atmosphere of his parents' home. Emerald's parents have no time for her, her mother is a "votary of high life," her father a busy merchant, just like Zerelda's father and grandfather; but then Zerelda is brought up far from her father's home, by her wise aunt.

47. Barville is a British officer, Fort Niagara a British prison where Zerelda and Evermont are detained against their will, and where Whitford believes he can safely use violence against Amacette.

48. Even when she is disguised and comes to Evermont in the obscurity of the jail, the hero is characteristically responsive to her charms (e.g., pp. 19-20).

49. Evermont becomes "Holbert" in chap. 9, "Bridford" in chaps. 14-15 (see esp. pp. 142-46, 193).

50. He has saved her from drowning and murderous Indians, rescued her from captivity, prevented her rape, shot a leopard about to attack her, led her out of a desert where she could have died of thirst and hunger, or been devoured by wolves, and finally kept Mrs. Willford at bay as long as possible.

51. Evermont is frequently led into temptation simply because he is invincibly attractive to the girls he meets; in this he is like many novel-heroines, who have their hosts of admirers. His popularity also causes him to be pardoned perhaps a trifle too quickly (e.g., pp. 342-43).

52. Holman was not content with the usual device of the "double level" of one or more concealed or mistaken identities but cumulated its effects by using disguises. Evermont passes himself off for "Holbert" and "Bridford", Emerald impersonates Susan, Amacette wears the uniform of a soldier, Evermont and Carmont play the part of British soldiers, Mrs. Willford disguises herself as a man, and Zerelda becomes in succession the "lady with the lamp" and the servant Bourbon.

53. See also his reflections in chaps. 8, 11, 15, 17, 18, 23.

54. Later Gothic touches include the appearance of Anderville's "ghost" (pp. 304-5), the circumstances in which Huron is led to begin, and interrupt, his revelations (chaps. 20, 27), and Evermont's sensations as he loses his way while Zerelda remains unprotected in the forest, and at night, too (chap. 15).

55. There are, e.g., the quick transitions from Evermont's sorrow over the death of Haylard (pp. 105-6) to his joy at an assignation (p. 109) and the moralizing farewell note he sends his supposed girl-friend (p. 117). Occasionally there is a didactic intent rather than a melodramatic one behind such changes, as when real and pretended values among the Indians and the Whites are contrasted.

56. Evermont's lamp breaks as he is about to read the manuscript, then he is distracted by Anderville's "ghost" and the opportunity to escape; the manuscript is mislaid during his flight, but miraculously found again after Evermont has given it up for lost.

57. "I rambled to the banks of Jackson's River, and throwing myself on a rock, listened with frantic earnestness, to the screaming river birds, and the wild yellings of the owls, which, by fits, were reverberated through the dark-

ness, from an hundred echoing hills. Successive volumes of frowning clouds, rushed up the west, and overran the heavens, their magazines of embosomed fire, would burst and stream through the atmosphere in sheets of flame. Rumbling thunder followed them with a deep muttering sound; and all would be silent, threatening, blackness. In an instant, the Heavens would again burst, with an hundred daring torrents of keen, forked blaze; and fiercer peals of conflicting thunder roll in tremendous reverberations over the quaking hills. This awful clash of contending elements, long continued to swell its stupendous grandeur, on the dark bosom of night; but I still remained unmoved among the wild rocks that hung lowering around the stream" (p. 288). Cf. the view from Fort Niagara (p. 24), a Potomac landscape (p. 71), Zerelda's "grotto" (pp. 125-27), the emancipation of the slaves (p. 353).

58. See, e.g., the following passages: the first appearance of the lady among the prisoners (p. 14); Evermont watching Zerelda unseen (p. 132); remarks on the poetry and experience of unrestrained sensibility (p. 151); a parting scene (pp. 260-61) and a reunion (p. 330).

59. Here is a sample of Zerelda's sensibility: "I saw a tear fall from his eye, and light on a rose that bloomed a little below the mark of the ball. His agitation increased, and he bowed, bid us a good evening and departed. I flew to the rose that caught his tear—The little inestimable sparkler hung on its bosom with a smile—I raised it to my lips, and drank it with rapture; then kissed the flower a thousand times and opening my handkerchief, pressed it to my bosom" (p. 152).

60. Their relation is similar to that of Adelaide and Morgiana in Mrs. Botsford's *Adelaide*.

61. Among other celebrations we may mention William Dunlap's *Yankee Chronology* (New York, 1812), on the *Constitution-Guerriere* encounter; the biographies of heroes contributed by Irving to the *Analectic Magazine* (1813-14); and James Butler, *American Bravery Displayed, in the Capture of Fourteen Hundred Vessels of War and Commerce, since the Declaration of War*.

62. See 1:143, 228-29, chap. 29; and 2:293. The first time Willoughby meets his spiritual mentor, he is just beginning to take an interest in a gypsy at a masquerade; the apparition, of course, immediately drives away all thoughts of dalliance. In retrospect this appears the more significant as the gypsy is Sophia, who will later seduce the hero when there is no one to assist him. Woodworth's preface reveals that he was aware that "probably the book would have been better without" the Mysterious Chief (see William Alfred Bryan, *George Washington in American Literature* [New York: Columbia University Press, 1952], p. 195).

63. Such a punishment would not be easy to reconcile with Woodworth's simple "philosophy of history": "Woman ever has been, still is, and always will be, the main spring, the 'primum mobile' of every masculine achievement, from the hero to the clown—from the man to the stripling; and whether she fire a Troy, or excite emulation in a game at marbles; whether she influence a court or rule in a dairy, the end, cause, and effect, are still the same. We may talk of Patriotism—we may prate of Fame; but who could feel the one, or seek the other, but for the sake of woman?" (2:99).

64. The Americans are patriotic and victorious (1:249; 2:92, 302, 335-36), but the British are accused of brutality and cruelty, and of encouraging the Indians to harass their enemies.

65. See Bryan, *Washington*, p. 194, and Cyrille Arnavon, *Histoire littéraire des Etats-Unis* (Paris: Hachette, 1953), p. 95.

66. See Willoughby's outburst when he escapes from the arms of a prostitute (1:95), his final resolve to devote himself to the American cause (2:294).

67. Our hero meets personally a great number of men destined to distinguish themselves in various encounters. The mention of a storm calls for an explanatory footnote: "The destructive storm which occurred on Tuesday morning, November 24, 1812, is probably well remembered. Many vessels were shipwrecked in the Sound, and a church-steeple in Orange county was blown down" (2:49n.).

68. At the Richmond theater fire, Willoughby rescues two ladies who have fainted: "...He took one in each arm, leaped into the pit, and bore his insensible burdens, through the thick smoke and scorching flames, until he gained in safety the semi-circular avenue which led him to the door of the theatre" (1:169).

69. See the hero's rebuke of Sandford (1:107) and self-reproach (2:173).

70. Sandford wants to seduce Catharine to make Willoughby suffer (1:183-84; 2:296), and Sophia drastically describes the change of her feelings: "You have driven an angel from my bosom, and a devil has usurped its seat!...My brain's on fire! You have trampled on my heart, and converted the nectar of love to wormwood. I hate you more than I ever loved you—I risked the loss of Heaven for my love—I would willingly incur certain damnation, to make you feel my hate. Willingly would I plunge into the burning centre of hell, could I drag you thither with me" (2:165).

71. Woodworth promised to write short paragraphs and chapters, for the convenience of his readers, and to observe variations of tempo in the different parts of his narrative. There is an apologetic tone to his patriotic appeal, his emphasis on the fact that the book is by an American and offers American subject matter.

72. There was a good measure of truth in the words which the author put in the mouth of a friend criticizing his novel: "...The plot is unnatural, the incidents absurd, and the language inelegant. But the greatest monster of all is your Mysterious Chief" (p. iii). Perhaps the novel is so poor because "the author was often compelled to deliver his unrevised manuscript to the waiting compositor—*a dozen lines at a time!*" ("Biographical Sketch of Samuel Woodworth," in *The Poems, Odes, Songs, and other Metrical Effusions, of Samuel Woodworth*, p. x). See also the devastating review in the *Port-Folio*, new ser., 3(1817):165-67.

Conclusion

IF WE ASSUME the average size of the early American works of fiction to have been about 220 pages, one-sixth of these books are definitely subnormal in length, and as many have more than four hundred pages. One-third are first person narratives; half that number have a frame introducing the narrative proper. This frame is likely to have often been not an artistic necessity but a device of camouflage to conceal the author's identity, and simultaneously perhaps guarantee the authenticity and intrinsic interest of the story that was thus introduced. If the epistolary form was employed in one out of every four works of fiction, this is not due to a survival of the novel in letters but to the convenience of the device of the fictitious traveler who finds much to write home about. Such imaginary correspondents were generally created by men, who made more frequent use of fictional forms for non-novelistic purposes than their female colleagues, while they were about equally responsible for the production of the novels, in the strict sense. A small number of books went beyond a first edition within the period discussed; yet half of the authors discussed tried their luck as writers of fiction more than once.

If we limit our view to the novel, we cannot help concluding that the novels published in America to the end of 1820 are marked, above all, by the limited range of their authors. Their plots at first sight strike one as inventive, even wildly so; but it soon becomes evident that they merely achieve new combinations of old and familiar elements. Perhaps this is true of all fiction. It applies in a particularly crippling sense to the early American novel because of the nature of the material then at hand. The unfolding of its plots hinges on coincidences and misunderstandings; cases of mistaken identities, frequently combined with apparent infringements of the social barriers and conventions, puzzle the protagonists and the reader of, for example, *Margaretta,* until a more or less fortuitous and spectacular revelation restores their certainties. The underlying patterns—lovers' trials, young girls' vicissitudes, young men's adventures—depend on and reveal the heroes' and heroines' passivity; the actively conditioning elements on the other hand are unsympathetic parents, jealous rivals, petty surroundings, agents of pure evil, and providential interventions which appear deterministic more often than not. The characters themselves are subordinated to the events; individually they tend to remain undeveloped and static, and differentiation between them is attempted only in the moralistic opposition of good and bad characters. The writers' limited range also shows in their preference for only a few moods and tones. Their emphasis lies in the didactic confrontation of good and evil, which they strive to render more dramatic by a pronounced reliance on the pathetic, especially the helplessness and alienation of some victims of villainy, as in Mrs. Read's *Monima;* conversely the horrifying may also have a similar effect, some persecutor or form of persecution assuming monstrous proportions. In other cases horror and terror seem to suggest the presence of the inexplicable in our existence, but are at length explained away as an irrational response to some phenomena inaccurately perceived and imperfectly understood. The authors' limited range of style, finally, derives from these conventional plot situations and moods that impose upon the writer a certain vocabulary, which is in many instances language worn down to clichés. While some of the writers were content to work within this narrow framework, others tried to shake off or offset the imitativeness threatening them by an exaggerated attempt at originality. They gave their heroes and villains superlative features and, in particular, overexerted themselves in the cumulative descriptions of their settings, which were probably meant to convey a sense of place or, more generally, to heighten the mood of fear or grief associated with their narrative. Mrs. Botsford's *Adelaide* is a typical product of constant straining for effect.

Generally speaking, innovations were few and far between. The use of American settings, topographical as well as historical, was attempted, but this went little further than a listing of place names or the names of historical figures and events. Such topics as democracy and slavery appeared early; but they were introduced, at best, as elements of exposition and discussion that had no valid connection with the narrative as such or its characters. A notable exception, of course, is *Modern Chivalry.* In view of what the next decade was to bring, the introduction of the American Indian into fiction was perhaps, on the whole, the most successful elaboration of an element still comparatively fresh. Here, too, a distinction must be made: the Indian could be used as one picturesque ingredient among others which vary the adventures and responses of the protagonists, as in Mrs. Rowson's *Reuben and Rachel;* or he could be treated as a part of the American experience rendered by the author, as in *Maria Kittle.*

The poverty of early American fiction (and early American literature generally) argues for a dearth of individual talents, as well as the powerful influence of the models from which the authors were trying to learn. Yet what they wanted to create was an American literature, that is, a literature independent of, but equal to, any European—and especially English—models. They strove to fulfill the nationalistic program voiced in many solemn statements: literature by Americans and for Americans, using American settings and characters, themselves the (possibly propagandistic) expression of the principles underlying the new country and its institutions—church, government, education. But though they were suspicious of their Old World models, the ambitious American writers were beginners and had yet much to learn; could they do this without imitation of these very models? Lewis Leary has aptly described the achievement of a typical writer of the period, John Blair Linn: "Accepting him as he is, he represents with John Dennie in criticism, William Dunlap in the drama, and Brockden Brown in the novel, more certainly than any other poet of his immediate generation the struggle of American men of letters to catch up all at one jump with the literature of England, to create by imitation a literature which would be at once full-blown and distinctively American." The American authors needed models, but it was their duty to imitate them selectively, that is, without following corrupting examples; this meant that the problem could become a moral, rather than an esthetic, literary issue. The field of the novel could perhaps be looked upon as more promising than other departments of literature. The novel was a new genre, for which as yet no formidable prescriptive canon existed; above all, the novel was popular, and the novelist could hope to find an immediate response among the existing novel-reading public, which was a consideration that might encourage a writer's nationalistic as well as personal ambitions. Yet if there was no canon for the novel, this also meant that no helpful rules were provided. The beginning novelist was therefore most likely to be guided by the demands of a comparatively inexperienced reading public which seemed to prefer the familiar to the new. This raised a further difficulty: the popularity of the novel and its recurrent elements were suspected of being in direct ratio to its immorality. This again returned the writer to the need for morally selective imitation.

The pull of such forces of habit, prejudice, and criticism—some encouraging, some hostile—made for an uncertainty which could hardly be expected to foster strong individual talents and ideas. In spite of its reputed dangers, it was the European novel —and naturally the English novel, first of all—that served as an example for most American novelists of the day; but this had fallen away considerably from the level of Richardson's and Fielding's achievements. American authors generally sidestepped controversial sociopolitical topics and employed the patterns of the conventional story of love, adventure, and mystery, though with circumspection. The motif of seduction, for example, was wrapped up, as *The Power of Sympathy* demonstrates, in explicit warnings and lessons and counterbalanced by serious contemplations on death and a moral existence. Such contrived and extraneous checks and balances frequently proved, however, insufficient to change the essentially worldly character of the human concerns and weaknesses that fundamentally determine the plots and the characters' actions and reactions of any novel.

Within the strictly conventional forms and uses of the customary motifs of fiction, there are only perhaps three novels which emerge slightly above the contemporary average: Mrs. Foster's *The Coquette,* Miss Rush's *Kelroy,* and John Neal's *Keep Cool.* But the best American fiction of the age used the fashionable models as a starting point rather than as a norm, and it took a decisive personal element, in addition to specific American materials, to give their work distinction. The robust inventiveness of Mrs. Tenney and the satirical detachment of Royall Tyler perhaps took them beyond the established forms of the burlesque or the picaresque purpose novel. Brackenridge's scope and learning, literary sophistication, and humor joined forces with his serious concern over the possibilities and pitfalls of democratic practices. Less vigorous than Brackenridge, Irving possessed more wit, more charm, and above all a stronger determination to do his literary gifts justice (above and beyond the necessity to live by them). Brockden Brown brought to his work as a writer an absolute intensity which accounts for his insight into his characters' confused intellects and emotions, and the implications of the settings and conflicts of his novels, but also perhaps for their structural incompleteness. Brackenridge, Irving, and Brown clearly are not unrelated to English and Continental traditions. They apparently did not find them inhibiting: the literary precedents were to them an indication of where expansion was possible, and their individual talents together with their sense of literary openings made them the active pioneers (among a larger group of passive ones) of American fiction.

Appendix: Synopses

I N ADDITION to the synopses of the novels treated in this study,
the appendix contains summaries of such works discussed in
chapters four and five as offer a more or less continuous narrative, so far as they do not appear to have been adequately outlined in
the account of their didactic or satirical content. If a title does not
appear here, this means that a synopsis would not further facilitate its
appreciation. It has been thought advisable in most cases to give indications of chapters and pages, that is, indirectly, of proportions and
structural patterns. The titles are listed in alphabetical order.

Adelaide.—At V*** near Philadelphia, Emilia Delmont watches
as her daughter Adelaide and the son of some friends of hers, Mandeville Clifford, fall in love; the Cliffords, on Barbados, are kept informed and express their approval (letters 1-8, 10-12, 14-18, 20-23).
But affairs take an unpromising turn when Delmont unexpectedly
turns up with a suitor for Adelaide—the Marchese di Vironaldi (24).
Years ago, Delmont had married Emilia knowing that she loved
Ormond Pembrooke. After killing his rival in a fit of jealousy, he
fled to Europe, taking his son Edgar with him but leaving Emilia and
Adelaide behind (letter 13, 1:53-135). Adelaide resigns herself to
her fate, and Clifford returns after a while to his parents. Alternately
we hear news from Barbados and V***, where Adelaide is comforted by independent-minded Morgiana, a cousin of Clifford who
has so far been teasing her favorite admirer, Clayton (letters 25-43).
Clifford travels to Europe with his friend Montwilbert, who is much
taken with a young lady they meet near Paris. Meanwhile, Adelaide
is led to the altar but faints before the marriage ceremony is completed; Vironaldi is challenged as he leaves the church. Severely
injured, he dies soon afterwards; Delmont does not survive him long
(44-81). Everyone seems to gravitate to V***: Wellingham, a friend
of the Cliffords, has been there for some time; his daughter Olivia,

who was seduced by Vironaldi (9), has found him there shortly
before the Marchese's death. Now Montwilbert, back from Europe,
recognizes her as the lady from France. Clayton has found out that
he is really Edgar Delmont and a very wealthy man (82-93). Four
weddings are celebrated. One interpolated story is that of Cazelli,
Vironaldi's successful challenger, who wanted to vindicate the honor
of his sister and his wife (71).

Adventures in a Castle.—Henry and Louis Boileau, two young
men watched over by a conscientious guardian named Dupont, have
an uncle, the Count of Vauban, who bears them a grudge: he had
quarreled with their father, and he would like to obtain the fortune
which they are to inherit. One night Henry mysteriously vanishes
from his room (found locked in the morning), and soon after Louis
must fight off a gang of bandits. He and Dupont some time later
overhear a conversation about a murder to be committed; Louis
pursues the plotters, discovers Henry in an old castle, and kills the
man about to dispatch him. Caught himself, together with his brother,
Louis reappears at his guardian's home with the news that Henry has
been killed. He saves the Duke of Alençon's life when he is waylaid;
at the Duke's castle he meets the Duke's daughter Antoinette, who
is being courted, though unsuccessfully, by Vauban. Alençon's son,
charged by Vauban and his outlaws to murder the Duke, fails to do
so and is himself killed. The King's troops are called in to stop the
bandits' activities. As their stronghold is set on fire, Vauban rushes
out but is killed; and from a prison emerges Henry, who has after all
survived. A suitable wife is found for him, too, when Louis and
Antoinette marry.

Adventures of Alonso.—Alonso is the son of the Lisbon merchant
Alvares. He falls in love with young Donna Eugenia, who is married
to sixty-year-old Don Pedro; and they elope to Madrid, then move
on to France and back to Spain. They hear that their elopement has
caused the death of Alonso's mother and a young man who was
mistakenly challenged by Don Pedro (chaps. 1-4). The lovers go
back to Lisbon, and Eugenia enters a convent while a friend of
Alvares procures Alonso some employment in Brazil (5-8). Alonso
wins the confidence of the exceptionally honest governor of Brazil
but betrays it when he attempts to smuggle a diamond out of the
country. He is detected just before reaching Rio. The officer in

charge, however, runs away with his prize, and Alonso escapes (9-16). He next joins a British sea captain in contraband operations; and when his vessel is shipwrecked in the Caribbean, he escapes his Spanish pursuers by crossing the Isthmus to Panama (17-18). Alonso embarks for Spain, only to be intercepted by Algerines. Sold into slavery, he repulses his master's advances, is tried for this act of rebellion, but saved from punishment by the testimony of a Christian turned Muslim. This is none other than the officer who took Alonso's diamond from him and who has since been made a slave, then freed; he is now married to his first master's widow (19-22). When Alonso is at last back in Lisbon, Don Pedro is dead; but Eugenia, who has taken her final vows, dies soon after his return. The hero carries on his father's business (23-25). The conversations during Alonso's voyages (6-7, 9-13, 19-20) touch upon Pombal's despotism, as well as Portuguese economic policies, monopolies, etc.

Adventures of Jonathan Corncob.—Traveling by coach from London to Salisbury, Corncob fights off boredom by telling his story (chap. 1). This son of strict Presbyterians, after bundling with Desire Slawbunk, chooses neither to marry the girl nor to pay a fine when she becomes pregnant, runs away. He witnesses a tarring and feathering in Boston, takes a ride on a deer's back, fights on board an American privateer, plunders a Dutch vessel, serves on a British man-of-war, then joins with a band of Loyalist plunderers (2-5). After a love affair with a virtuous-looking landlady's daughter, he must place himself under medical care. Nearly arrested after a brawl, he again serves on a British vessel (6-8). In New York he meets Desire, who is now married to a Scots captain. He also meets his father, who has left rebellious New England (9-11). He takes a trip to Barbados which he enjoys until he comes to understand the abuses of slavery there (12-14). Sailing back with a British ship under cowardly Captain Quid lands him in a prison ship in Boston harbor. Desire, now living with an Irish deserter who has killed her husband, spends some nights with Corncob, others with the jailer, whose wife our hero then consoles (15-17). The story ends after Quid's trial, with words of praise for entertaining fiction (18).

Alcuin.—(1) Alcuin is a schoolmaster who is dissatisfied with his profession, rather awkward in society, and therefore often lonely. He joins the *salon* of Mrs. Carter, a widow who keeps house for her brother, a physician, and whose interesting personality has gradually converted a number of her brother's callers into a circle of habitual visitors. With the young man she discusses various topics related to the question of the rights of woman. To prevent women from being accorded an education equal to that of a man is an offense against human nature and a handicap imposed on human potentialities generally. Why shouldn't women be lawyers or doctors and play a part in public life? It is no wonder that women question the practicability of the American Constitution with its provisions for equality, and cannot be genuinely interested in the distinction between Federalists and Republicans. (2) In the fragment of *Alcuin* printed in Dunlap's *Life of Brown,* the dialogue is resumed after a week's interruption. Alcuin describes a utopian country he claims to have visited where many of the superficial differentiations between man and woman have been abolished. The conversation finally turns to the subject of marriage and divorce. Mrs. Carter maintains the necessity of the former institution but is also in favor of the latter, since there are many cases where marriage is entered into for the wrong reasons (Dunlap, 1:75-105).

The Algerine Captive.—Updike Underhill, the hero of the novel, makes his appearance after introductory chapters concerning his ancestor, Captain John Underhill (1:chaps.1-3). Born in 1762, Updike prepares to enter college in 1780; the project fails, but he at least acquires respect for Latin and Greek (4-6). He tries schoolteaching, then decides to become a physician (7-10). He also tries courting; but his poetic compliments are misconstrued, and he is sent a challenge. This he accepts, much to the surprise of his opponent; but the police are notified and interfere before any damage is done (11-12). By 1785 Underhill has completed his training, yet still has to learn how to make his living from his practice without becoming a quack. He starts traveling, and first visits Boston and the empty science museum at Harvard (13-19). He meets various types of doctors in the North, then tries his luck in the South, where he sees little except slavery and superstition (20-23). As a ship's surgeon bound for Africa, he visits London on the way and mocks the English liberties and Tom Paine (24-29). Underhill is appalled by the manner of capturing and treating the African slaves; soon he is made a slave himself by the Algerines (30-32). He comments, generally with

[406]

exaggerations, on the Dey of Algiers and his court, the slave market, the efforts made to convert him, the language of the inhabitants, and their history and present government (2:1-2, 4-7, 15-25, 27). He also joins a pilgrimage to Mecca (31-34). Underhill briefly dreams of escaping but is deterred by the fear of being caught and punished (3, 9-10). Sent to a hospital, he becomes a member of the staff (12-14). He is befriended by a Jew and starts saving in order to pay his own ransom; but when his friend dies, he cannot recover his savings. He is also exploited by his friend's son (30, 35-36). It takes a coincidence to make Underhill a free man again, and he returns to America after an absence of seven years (37).

Amelia, or the Faithless Briton.—During the War of Independence, the British officer Doliscus is wounded near Blyfield's house on Long Island and nursed back to health by Blyfield's daughter Amelia. She falls in love with him, and he takes advantage of her feelings. He insists on a secret marriage and arranges for a fake marriage ceremony. After he has returned to New York, his letters become scarce and cool; he leaves for England when Amelia tells him that she is pregnant, but the girl follows him there. Repudiated by Doliscus, Amelia gives birth prematurely to a baby who lives only a few days. Blyfield discovers her whereabouts just as she is about to kill herself. She later goes mad and dies. Meanwhile, Blyfield's son Horatio has challenged Doliscus and wounded him fatally; Horatio falls at the battle of Monmouth.

Amelia, or the Influence of Virtue.—Amelia's story is told by Harley, an Englishman on a visit to America. At the age of nine, the heroine is entrusted to Lady Stanly, whose affection she gradually conquers, partly because she compares very favorably with Harriot, an orphan girl adopted by Lady Stanly. The latter wants her son Sir William to marry Amelia. Harley advises against it because he feels that Sir William may be attracted to Harriot. Lord Barrymore, from a strictly Roman Catholic family, proposes to Protestant Amelia but must give her up as she cannot be converted to Catholicism. He is sent to Paris where he is tricked into marrying Harriot. Stanly and Amelia marry when Lady Stanly, who is dying, expresses her wish. Once his mother is dead, Stanly explains to Amelia why he has not yet consummated their marriage: he is in love with Harriot. Amelia, who loves her husband, refuses the divorce and generous settlement which he offers (chaps. 1-6). When the Barrymores settle in London, Stanly and Harriot become lovers. Barrymore divorces his wife, but Amelia refuses to follow suit; her arguments convert Barrymore to Protestantism. Among other charitable acts, Amelia brings up the baby of Stanly and Harriot. When Stanly discovers the presence of his child under his own roof, he is overwhelmed; and a full reconciliation between Amelia and himself seems imminent (7-11). At the instigation of a sinister Frenchman named Volpoon, Amelia is abducted by De Everet and held a prisoner in a deserted house in France. She meets a fellow-prisoner, Volpoon's wife Henrietta, who is in love with Barrymore. De Everet determines to defy Volpoon and save Amelia, but the heroine falls into the hands of another murderer commissioned by Volpoon. While she is pleading with him, Volpoon and De Everet kill each other, and Stanly and Barrymore at long last find Amelia's prison. Stanly and his wife now begin their life together, and Barrymore marries Henrietta. Harriot is comforted by Amelia during the final miserable weeks of her existence (12-21). Volpoon's father, who first married a wicked woman, had one son by her, Volpoon. He married a second time, and his English wife gave him a worthy son, Maximilian. The two young men later courted wealthy Rosalind, who married Maximilian. Volpoon presumably poisoned his rival and had Rosalind imprisoned and her baby (Amelia) exposed. But the latter was brought up in England, first by a Mrs. Benloe, later by Lady Stanly (18). The story of Morcan, a case of a religious vow broken (pp. 33-41), is apparently told in anticipation of Amelia's conflict over Barrymore and the question of her faith.

Arthur Mervyn.—During the 1793 yellow-fever epidemic in Philadelphia, Dr. Stevens receives in his home a young man named Arthur Mervyn, who has fallen ill. After his recovery Mervyn tells him his story in order to defend himself against accusations of Stevens's friend Wortley. A farmer's boy, Mervyn has been spared hard work and allowed much freedom by his mother, who died young. When his father marries again, Mervyn leaves for Philadelphia. He is swindled at roadside inns, loses his clothes and a miniature of his friend Clavering, and is locked in Thetford's bedroom by a practical jokester who is later identified as Wallace. Determined to return to the country, Mervyn comes across Welbeck; they impress one another, and Mervyn becomes Welbeck's secretary. But his promise not to tell people where he comes from soon causes trouble, esepcially with Mrs. Wentworth, who appears to have been connected with Clavering. Mervyn discovers that Clemenza, who lives with Welbeck, is not his daughter but his mistress. Once more he is about to leave Philadelphia; but he happens to witness Welbeck's shooting of Watson, helps him bury the body, and rows his employer across the Schuylkill. Welbeck, however, jumps into the river and disappears (chaps. 1-9, 12). Mervyn goes to work on the Hadwins' farm, falls in love with the youngest daughter Eliza, and returns to Philadelphia in search of Wallace, the fiancé of Susan, the eldest. He finds that Wallace is recovering from the yellow fever and has him taken to the Hadwins' farm. He then returns to Welbeck's house in order to dispose of $20,000 which his former master is keeping from their rightful owner, and there meets Welbeck, who is himself looking for the money. Welbeck convinces him that the notes in question are forged, whereupon Mervyn burns them instead of handing them over to him. At that moment people enter the house, Welbeck vanishes and Mervyn hides in the attic (13-23). Welbeck's past is presented in chapters 9-10: Welbeck fled from an unhappy marriage in England and followed his American friend Watson to Charleston. There he had an affair with Watson's sister, and after running off once more, he appropriated for himself half the fortune left to Clemenza. He has risen to some importance in Philadelphia but has become involved in a risky swindling scheme with Thetford. He shot Watson when the latter challenged him. Stevens is told disturbing things about Mervyn while the young man is absent from Philadelphia (2:1-5). Upon his return Mervyn reports that Wallace has disappeared and that Hadwin and Susan are dead. He has placed Eliza with some friendly neighbors. He has also confronted her suspicious and bullying uncle, as well as the Villars women, at whose house of ill-repute Clemenza has been living. Back in Philadelphia Mervyn finds Welbeck dying in the debtors' prison and satisfies Stevens's curiosity with respect to the new charges brought against himself (6-15). He travels to Baltimore to restore to their owners papers and money found on Watson and learns that his father is dead. Mervyn reestablishes himself in the confidence of Mrs. Wentworth. Though he finds Eliza less and less congenial, he obtains for her the protection of Achsa Fielding (16-20). During his apprenticeship with Stevens, he very slowly finds out that he is in love with Achsa; when he proposes, he is immediately accepted (21-25). Achsa has experienced many misfortunes—her husband's infidelity and desertion, her father's bankruptcy, the loss of her child (23).

The Asylum.—Melissa Bloomfield resists her father's efforts to marry her to Bowman, and remains faithful to Alonzo, who once saved her life (chaps. 1, 7-9). She is taken to a remote part of Connecticut where her great-grandfather had a castle built (10). Though frightened by nocturnal noises and apparitions, the girl is determined to be true to Alonzo (11). He discovers her prison; but when he returns to rescue her, she has vanished (12). Some time later he hears that she has died; he leaves America, witnesses the death of Bowman in a London jail for American prisoners, and is comforted by Franklin in Paris (13-14). Shipwrecked near Charleston, he reaches the shore with one other survivor; at Charleston he is miraculously reunited with Melissa, who has been conveyed there from Connecticut to escape further persecutions. She has been staying with an uncle of hers, the father of the Melissa whose death was reported to Alonzo (15-16). It takes an elaborate masquerade of a wedding to reconcile the lovers with Melissa's father. The lovers then settle in a village they have long since chosen for their residence (8, 17), far from the smugglers' doings which used to scare Melissa in her prison. Another story is inserted early (2-6), as an anticipation of Melissa's troubles: Selina prefers Colonel Bergher to Count Hubert, of royal Austrian blood. Her decision causes an elopement, fatal fights and duels, imprisonment and escapes, and instances of treachery and fidelity. The Berghers, unwilling to return to their native Vienna and feeling insecure in Paris, London, and Boston, choose a backwoods existence in Connecticut.

The Boarding School.—Mrs. Williams, a clergyman's widow, establishes a boarding school for girls. She tries to prepare the girls for their various duties in life, both during their stay with her (in groups of seven) and, by correspondence, after they have returned to their families. The pupils themselves exchange letters which prove that all of them have profited by her teaching.

The Champions of Freedom.—George Washington Willoughby's mother dies while his father is being wounded at the battle of Fallen Timbers. He and his sister are brought up in the secluded home which Major Willoughby has built near Lake Erie. Willoughby falls

in love with Catharine Fleming but must part from her when he is
sent to Harvard. There he innocently makes one enemy, Thomas
Sandford (chaps. 1-14). At a masquerade he is addressed by an
Indian figure, that of a Mysterious Chief first met by Major Willoughby at Fallen Timbers. The Mysterious Chief tells Willoughby to
prepare for war, and at the very same hour also appears, with the
same message, to the major. At Washington an ensign's commission
is obtained for Willoughby. He saves two ladies from the Richmond
theater fire (Catharine is one of them), and a little later intercepts
a message addressed to the British governor in Canada, announcing
the imminent outbreak of the War of 1812 (15-17). After a further
visit from the Mysterious Chief, Willoughby tastes his first battles;
twice made a prisoner, he is delivered the first time and later exchanged. He is wooed in vain by Sophia, whom he met while at
Harvard and who has since married. But Sophia disguises herself as
a servant calling herself Reuben. Willoughby employs this supposed
young man. On a warm summer evening she seduces him. About the
same time, after yet another appearance of the Mysterious Chief, the
homes of the Willoughbys and the Flemings are destroyed; and
Catharine is sent to relatives at Ithaca (28-55). Willoughby breaks
with Sophia, who vows revenge. She is seen talking to British officers,
then becomes the mistress of Sandford, who is suspected of having
betrayed Fort Niagara to the enemy. The two villains desert to the
British, then lure Catharine to New York and convey her by force
on board a ship. But their luck turns: the vessel is captured by
Lafitte's pirates, and Sandford is killed with the crew. Catharine, a
prisoner, is later rescued from Lafitte's hideout on Lake Barrataria.
Our hero, sternly rebuked by the Mysterious Chief for deserting his
post to try to see Catharine, distinguishes himself at New Orleans.
When the war is over, he settles with Catharine on his father's estate.
Sophia dies with curses on her lips some time later (56-66). Some
of the ups and downs of the war are reported by Major Willoughby
and by William O'Hara, a sailor (Catharine's uncle).

Charlotte.—Shortly before embarking for America in 1774, Lieutenant Montraville meets Charlotte Temple and soon thinks he is in
love with her; the fifteen-year-old girl is swept off her feet. Assisted
by Mademoiselle La Rue, a French teacher with an unsavory past
who is occupying a post at Charlotte's boarding school, Montraville
persuades the girl to sail with him to America. Torn between love

[411]

and duty, Charlotte faints at the critical moment when she might still change her mind and is then carried away by Montraville. Mlle La Rue embarks as the presumptive bride of Montraville's friend Belcour (chaps. 1-12). She is soon after bigger game, though, and becomes a Colonel's wife when they reach New York. Montraville is by now sorry for having betrayed Charlotte, but does not consider marrying her since that would mean forfeiting his father's favor and support—a sacrifice which he, unlike Charlotte's father a generation earlier, is unwilling to make. His mind is made up for him when he falls in love with Julia Franklin, a lovely and wealthy girl whom he has met in dramatic and romantic circumstances (13-22). Meanwhile, Belcour manages to render Montraville suspicious of Charlotte; his end is accomplished when he is found in bed with the innocently sleeping girl. Montraville breaks with Charlotte, though he knows that she is expecting his child, and asks Belcour to look after her. To render Charlotte entirely dependent upon himself, the villain withholds the money entrusted to him, but, as her misery and pregnancy make her less and less attractive, he deserts her (23-28). Chased from her house by her landlady, Charlotte sets out for New York in a snowstorm; but her only friend, Mrs. Beauchamp, is away, and the former Mlle La Rue cruelly repulses her. Charlotte gives birth to a girl and dies just after her father has discovered her, having come to America to take her back to England. Montraville kills Belcour in a duel. Temple refuses to proceed against the seducer, judging that Montraville will be amply punished by remorse to the end of his life. About ten years later Mlle La Rue applies for assistance to the Temples; she is given help, but soon after dies in pain and misery, the consequence of her sinful life (29-35).

Charlotte's Daughter.—Lucy Blakeney lives with one of her guardians, the Reverend Mr. Matthews, together with two fellow orphans, the vain Mary Lumly and the kind Aura Melville. On several occasions she displays her charity and sensible benevolence. When Lucy is twenty, the three girls are taken to Brighton. Lucy and Lieutenant Franklin there fall in love with each other. A sergeant, a veteran of the American wars, at the sight of them is reminded of former acquaintances of his and begins telling their story, but is not allowed to finish it. Franklin, called to his dying father's bedside, shows him Lucy's picture and is told that the girl is his half-sister, the illegitimate daughter of Montraville (who later has adopted the name of his wife's family) and Charlotte Temple. Lucy herself bears the name of her godfather. When Montraville dies, Franklin leaves for India; he later fights and falls in Spain. Lucy, after a long illness, dedicates herself to schoolteaching and charity. Her two friends fare differently. While Aura is rewarded with the worthy love of Edward Ainslie, Mary runs away to Scotland with Sir Stephen Haynes, who promptly deserts her; after a period of madness, the girl repents and reforms.

Clara Howard.—Philip Stanley, after enjoying the protection of Mr. Howard, is apprenticed to a Philadelphia watchmaker. He is on friendly terms with Mary Wilmot, a few years older than himself, who falls in love with him. But she takes herself out of his life when Howard and his daughter Clara, now twenty-three, return to Philadelphia, for she does not want to stand in the way of Stanley's marriage to Clara. Yet she might use his help, because a mysterious legacy left her by her brother, recently dead, is claimed by one Morton (letters 2, 13). Clara judges that Stanley must make sure whether he is not dutybound to marry Mary. When he at last finds her, after a two months' search, Mary seems to be happy in the love of Sedley, whom she has always respected. She advises Stanley to go back to Clara, but the young man feels that he has lost Clara as well as Mary. He must be summoned back from a journey across America: Clara reminds Stanley that he must fulfill his duty to his sisters (29). A flashback (20-21) tells the story of Mary's parents: her father was a German who was expected to marry his employer's daughter at Boulogne, but had an affair with a Bristol girl and married her when she became pregnant.

Constantia Neville.—Constantia must shift for herself after the death of her parents, for her brother Montagu is unreliable. She stays in London with her friend Amelia Rochford until Amelia's husband contracts a passion for her. Her acquaintances strike her as affected and vain, and the one person whom she feels she could trust, De Eresby, has a bad reputation (Vol. 1, chaps. 1-12). Constantia's next hosts, the Mansells, accuse her of stealing Sir Charles Lumley away from their daughter Eliza; they quite fail to see that he is after a wealthy widow. One Connolly behaves too familiarly toward Constantia, then Rochford pursues her again, while Montagu dissipates her fortune and absconds to Barbados. De Eresby, however, impresses her more and more favorably (2:13-22). Constantia delays accepting his proposal because he appears to have been neglecting his studies and also because there have been unfounded rumors about an affair between the gentleman and her, which a marriage might seem to confirm! She goes to an aunt of hers at Chesterfield, but the aunt's son begins to take too proprietary an interest in her. A fortunate encounter with an old nun who turns out to be De Eresby's mother smoothes the way to a happy ending (3:23-34). The beginnings of Volumes 1 and 3 (pp. 23, 29-31), tell the story of Constantia's parents and the more complex one of De Eresby's family, whose background included bankruptcy, suicide, madness, and, in the case of De Eresby, years spent among the Indians of North America.

The Coquette.—In her first letters to her friend Lucy, Eliza Wharton describes her state of mind after mourning for Haly, the clergyman whom her parents wanted her to marry. She now enjoys the admiration of Boyer, another clergyman, and dashing Major Sanford (letters 1-3, 5-6). Boyer reveals to his friend Selby his love for Eliza and his concern over her acquaintance with the disreputable Sanford (4, 7). The latter tells his friend Deighton that he is determined to flirt with Eliza, whom he seems genuinely to admire (8, 11). Eliza cannot yet make up her mind to avoid Sanford and marry Boyer (9-16). The latter leaves to attend to his duties (17), the former admits that what he needs is a wealthy wife (18). He fails to convince Eliza that he is not so black as he has been painted; but his visits are still permitted, and Boyer is worried (19-27). Though Sanford is confident of yet winning Eliza and defeating his detractors, the girl pronounces his dismissal but continues to behave inconsistently; and Boyer finds her in the garden with the major when he calls to obtain her answer to his proposal (28-40). His withdrawal opens Eliza's eyes to his merits; too late she asks him to reconsider, for by then Boyer has become engaged to Selby's sister (41-47). Eliza's friend Julia finds her restless and suspects that Eliza is still infatuated with Sanford, in spite of the latter's recent marriage (48-53). Sanford, whose wife has brought him 5,000 pounds, seems really to love Eliza; his behavior as a married man is quite impossible (54-64). He triumphantly announces to Deighton that he has seduced Eliza (65) but appears moved by her distress when she runs away from home. The remorse and despair he experiences when he hears that she has died in childbirth are turned into a moralizing conclusion (66-74).

Dorval.—The Morelys, wealthy, tasteful, and patriotic, have one daughter, Aurelia, who is courted by Burlington. These two do not trust Dorval, the man who has induced Morely and Dunbar, the father of Aurelia's friend Elizabeth, to invest large sums in Georgia land purchases. One day Elizabeth and Burlington disappear, and Dorval insinuates that they have eloped together. He has however been presented by the author as a murderer and crook (chap. 11) and has posed as a fortune-teller to deceive Aurelia (1-18). Soon the Morelys and Dunbars are ruined; the latter leave for Europe with Charlotte, the fiancée of their son who has shot himself. Morely dies in jail after telling Aurelia not to trust Dorval. The girl has a few friends left; she even receives a proposal from Derbage but refuses, for she has not quite given up Burlington. (The author tells the reader how Burlington was fooled by Dorval, chap. 30.) Dorval also proposes to Aurelia, is rejected, and marries Mrs. Morely (19-33). On her twenty-first birthday Aurelia finds out that she is not a Morely but the daughter of a British major, Seymore, who thought his wife was dead. He married again before discovering that his first wife was still alive. Aurelia meets Addela, who is lawfully married to Dorval, and Elizabeth, who was tricked into eloping with Dorval; she has been insane but is now recovering. Mrs. Morely depends more and more on our heroine as Dorval appropriates her fortune; one morning she is found murdered. Aurelia is robbed of her last savings but saved from worse by a young man. Her luck now turns. Dorval, in jail at last, commits suicide after having tried to kill her. Her rescuer turns out to be Seymore's son, and Aurelia meets her father, now a wealthy man. Burlington returns with a fortune; the Dunbars, too, come back to America, and Charlotte marries their youngest son. Of course, Aurelia and Burlington marry, and there are three more weddings to end the book (34-54).

Edgar Huntly.—This novel is an account of Huntly's recent adventures, addressed to his fiancée Mary Waldegrave. He begins by trying to detect the murderer of Mary's brother, is led to suspect Clithero Edny, whom he discovers to be a sleepwalker, and speaks to him about it (chaps. 1-3). Clithero, the son of a farmer, has been brought up in Ireland by Mrs. Lorimer, then employed by her as her steward. He has fallen in love with her niece Clarice and, to his surprise, has been assured by his protectress that Clarice loves him too and that they may marry. Wiatte, Mrs. Lorimer's wicked brother, the instigator of her marriage and her separation from her true love, Sarsefield, returns to Ireland and one night attacks Clithero, who kills him in self-defense. Mrs. Lorimer has always believed that what happened to her brother must immediately affect her; Clithero therefore anticipates her grief at her brother's violent death, and by an intricate chain of reasoning concludes that it is his duty to kill her. He nearly stabs Clarice by mistake, tells Mrs. Lorimer that Wiatte is dead, and runs off when she faints because he believes her to be dying. He then emigrates to a remote part of Pennsylvania (4-8). Huntly remains preoccupied with Clithero and his possible crimes in the following days. He finds that Clithero is hiding in a wild tract of country and there barely escapes a "grey cougar." He has other worries, too—the disappearance of some letters of Waldegrave which he was to destroy and the claim of one Weymouth upon money left Mary at Waldegrave's death (9-15). Huntly then abruptly embarks upon a nightmarish experience. He awakens in the dark, feeling bruised and hungry. It takes him some time to discover that he is at the bottom of a pit. Climbing out of this brings on a succession of dangerous adventures: a fight with a panther, an encounter with a group of Indians, an escape with a girl the Indians had captured, and the crossing of a wild river. He then happens to meet Sarsefield, who has just arrived in America with his wife, the former Mrs. Lorimer. The Waldegrave letters are in Sarsefield's hands; Huntly seems to have been hiding them in his sleep: he must be a sleepwalker like Clithero (16-25). They discuss the latter. Sarsefield thinks that Clithero is dangerously mad; Huntly holds that he may be cured by being told that Mrs. Lorimer is not dead. He tries this, and Clithero immediately sets out for New York in order to kill the lady but is intercepted. Clithero then succeeds in escaping his guards and drowns himself. Meanwhile the shock of his reappearance has caused Mrs. Sarsefield to lose the baby she was expecting (26-27, and three final letters exchanged between Huntly and Sarsefield).

The Emigrants.—Caroline T—n and Captain Arl—ton fall in love at first sight when the captain overtakes the T—n family on their journey from Philadelphia to Pittsburgh (letters 4, 5, 11), and cannot long hide their feelings from one another (13). Caroline's sister Maria, however, interferes, causing misunderstandings between the lovers (17-18). Arl—ton runs off to Louisville (21) and, in spite of his friend Il—ray's reproaches and comfort (34, 42), to Lexington (46). When he and Caroline meet again, Maria makes trouble for them once more (49-50). Caroline is carried off by a group of Indians; Arl—ton comes across them and rescues their captive without at first realizing who she is (56, 59). They marry with the approval of Caroline's parents and her uncle P. P., whom they have found in America. P.'s story is that of his love for Lady B—, whom he compromised through the schemes of her villainous husband; P. P. and Lady B— marry, share persecutions, and emigrate to America, where Indians kill the lady and the couple's seven children. P. P. expounds the injustice of the English divorce laws too (19, 22-23, 25-26, 28-30). His views are confirmed by the experience of Caroline's sister who is unhappily married to a Mr. Fitzgerald (35, 62, 69-72). While the T—n parents and Maria return to Europe, the others settle in the promising new country. Arl—ton and Caroline marry, so do Il—ray and the widowed Mrs. Fitzgerald. A further wedding is announced, that of Caroline's brother George, a wastrel reformed by American frugality (5, 8, 32, 38-39, 43, 62), and Mrs. S—, who was first tricked into marrying the rascally S— (6, 15-16, 32-33, 61).

Emily Hamilton.—This novel consists of seventy letters exchanged by three girls over a period of four years. The heroine Emily Hamilton is wooed by Lambert (13), who turns out to be a scoundrel (20-22, 27, 39) literally born to be hanged (64). More serious trials begin when Emily is saved from drowning by Belmont, with whom she quickly falls in love (19, 25). Unmarried at the time of the rescue, and though he too loves Emily, Belmont obeys his father and marries Clara Belknap, who is in love with Le Fabre (40, 70). Belmont settles in the neighborhood of the Hamiltons (35) but does not speak of love to Eliza. Even after his wife has died (48) he waits another four months before he calls on the girl (52). Eliza herself insists at that time upon formally acknowledging her engagement (53) to her considerate friend Devas (5); a month later the news of Devas's accidental death reaches her, and the date for the wedding of Emily and Belmont can now be fixed. Eliza's friends get married, too. The orphaned Mary Carter (1) escapes a tedious suitor (3, 12, 16) and consoles Gray over the loss of his beloved Sophia (3, 4, 7, 8). Eliza Anderson's first admirer, Cutler, deserts her for the wealthy Miss Willson (34); she refuses to be depressed over this and accepts the proposal of Selwyn (22), who has long been in love with her (38).

The Factory Girl.—Mary Burnham, alone in the world except for her grandmother, takes a job in a factory when she is eighteen. She maintains her habits of virtue and religion but is found stand-offish and is ridiculed by her fellow-workers. Her only friend, Nancy Raymond, has a brother named William who appears to conform to Mary's standards; but when Mary expects him to propose to her, she is told that he has become engaged to some other girl. Our heroine finds consolation as a Sunday school teacher, and in selflessly nursing a number of relatives. In the end she marries a widower and proves to be an excellent stepmother.

The Farmer's Friend.—Charles Worthy is an orphan, poor and at the mercy of a relative who mistreats him. He becomes a soldier, fights the Indians, saves an officer's life, and later marries the officer's sister. The two settle on the frontier, work hard and grow prosperous; but there is a cruel test in store for them—the loss of their eldest son. Church and educational issues are faced and solved; the Worthy children grow up according to their parents' precepts; and suitable matches are arranged at the end of the story.

The Female Review.—Deborah Sampson is entrusted to various families from the age of five onwards. She learns to practice observation and reflection to make up for the deficiencies of her education. Four days before the battle of Lexington, she dreams of fighting a serpent and an ox. Her curiosity about her own country suggests to her the idea of disguising herself as a man in order to travel freely. Her plan is realized in an altered form when she enlists as a soldier in the Continental army. Her sex remains undetected though she is twice wounded; but when she falls ill, a doctor finds out her secret. He later sees to it that Deborah obtains an honorable discharge. The female soldier's other experiences include being courted by two young ladies and an encounter in which she must kill an Indian and rescue a white captive.

[418]

Female Quixotism.—Brought up by her father after her mother's death, Dorcas Sheldon is allowed to read novels until she becomes a regular addict, deriving her idea of real life from them. At the age of twenty she refuses the sensible Lysander because she finds him too unromantic (1: chaps. 1-2); her reputation as an avid novel-reader scares away other potential suitors. Dorcasina, as our heroine calls herself, is past thirty when the Irish adventurer O'Connor wins her heart. He adopts the manner of romantic lovers in fiction and almost obtains her father's consent; but Sheldon kicks him out of the house when he hears of O'Connor's past as a thief and gambler. Later Dorcasina attends the public whipping of O'Connor; this, at last, destroys her belief in the Irishman's innocence (1:3-13, 18). The local schoolmaster, a practical jokester, then writes love letters to Dorcasina and persuades the village barber to court her. The two men arrange for her to be carried off and to make her escape (1:14-18). Some years later Dorcasina imagines that an officer, young enough to be her son, must be in love with her while staying at Sheldon's house. For a while Captain Barry humors her; he even suggests a plan of elopement. This is later carried out (without his knowledge) by his servant; an accident reveals the latter's identity, and Dorcasina returns home (2:1-5). Sheldon then tries to marry his daughter to a respectable widower, but Dorcasina refuses the match. Once more, her maid and confidant Betty gets involved—as is usual with her (2:6-7). After Sheldon's death, Dorcasina fancies her servant John Brown to be a gentleman in disguise. Brown is flattered by her attentions but scared out of his pretensions by his fellow servants' pranks and a rival's threats. This rival, a "Captain Montague," is Harriet Stanly, a neighbor's daughter trying to cure Dorcasina of her illusions (2:10-15). It takes an enforced confinement on Stanly's farm to prepare the heroine for facing the truth. A Mr. Seymore, who has left his wife and children, is attracted by Dorcasina's small fortune; he pretends being a widower, touched at finding Dorcasina strikingly like his former wife. But his bluff is called, and he tells Dorcasina that no man in his right senses would marry her, old and ugly as she is (2:17-18). Dorcasina settles down to a life of charitable activities. But Barry and Harriet, who have married, experience sorrow and illness and lose their youthful inclination to have their fun at the expense of others.

Ferdinand and Elmira.—The two daughters of the Russian Count Lapochin fall in love with foreigners—the eldest with Oldham, an

Englishman, and the youngest with the Polish Count Peletre. The Czarina Elizabeth has made advances to Peletre. She now has the Lapochins and Peletre accused of treason, and they flee to Poland; but Mrs. Oldham is left behind and sent to Siberia. When she is free again, she searches for her husband and her son Ferdinand in England. By chance she finds Peletre and her sister near Warsaw with their daughter Elmira and Ferdinand. The latter becomes an officer and serves with distinction under Frederick the Great and General Brunsdel (chaps. 4-10, 12). In the opening chapters Elmira finds herself imprisoned in a castle, for she has been mistaken for a runaway daughter. Set free again, she leaves in the company of a mysterious "man in the gown" (1-3). They come across Ferdinand, just back from the army, who has found their house empty and his mother and Elmira's parents gone (13). When the three travelers reach a nearby military camp, Ferdinand reveals to Elmira that he is to be shot: he has interfered with his colonel's attempt to seduce Maria, the fiancée of his best friend who is an American named Laurence (14-18). The "man in the gown" is discovered to be Oldham, who is a good friend of Brunsdel. He obtains the latter's intervention as Ferdinand is facing his executioners. Brunsdel endows Laurence and Maria, his illegitimate daughter, with a fortune; and they leave for America. Meanwhile the Peletres and Mrs. Oldham have been taken to Russia to be rehabilitated by the new Czar Peter. It is there that Ferdinand and Elmira and Oldham find them. They all then settle on the Oldham estate in England (19-22). There is an inserted story about Count Sterit, who lost his bride and his post because he disapproved of dueling, then challenged his rival, after all, and killed him. After that he lived in retirement, exchanging letters with his former love for another twelve years (11).

Fidelity Rewarded.—This story, told in letters exchanged between Polly Granville and Sophia Danielson, begins with the demand made by Polly's father that she should break with Danford, her acknowledged suitor, and take wealthy Stapleton instead. The lovers are denied further communication, and Polly is even confined to her room and forced to see Stapleton. With the girl's approval Danford leaves for China (letters 1-9). Polly convinces her father that she cannot marry Stapleton and is permitted to leave Boston and stay with her sympathetic Uncle Finter in Philadelphia for a while (10-15). Granville is in trouble soon after, for some of his ships

[420]

fail to make port and his son-in-law Murfee refuses to help him
(16-17). Granville repents his former behavior and turns to religion
again. Danford returns from a successful voyage, and with the support of Finter the date for the wedding can be settled (18-23). Danford pays off Granville's debts and engages in partnership with him;
even Murfee reforms. Polly's first child is christened William Granville Danford (24-29). Meanwhile Stapleton has found a suitable
partner and is, therefore, unhappily married.

Filial Affection.—Phebe Unwin, whose father has died, lives with
her mother in her grandfather's home. She learns early to think of
others first and herself last. Phebe gives up her projected trip to
Washington in order to take Unwin's maid home to her dying
mother. This voyage to Maine also leads Phebe to an island where
she hears sentimental stories of misfortune due to the neglect of religious duties. She meets an attractive clergyman, Mervin, and a
religious skeptic. Some time later she accepts the proposal of Edward
Stewart, but the young man dies before they can be married. Phebe
also loses her mother and grandmother, and refuses to become Mervin's wife, judging that her duty is to look after her grandfather.
After Unwin's death she devotes the rest of her life to charity.

The Fille de Chambre.—Rebecca Littleton applies for help to
Lady Mary, the mother of the Littletons' landlord, Sir George Worthy. Lady Mary is much taken with her, and Rebecca becomes her
companion. Lady Mary tells her that her son is to marry his cousin,
Lady Eleanor, whereupon Rebecca pledges herself not to listen to
any talk of love on his part. Littleton and Lady Mary die, so that
foolish and peevish Mrs. Littleton is the only relative left to Rebecca
(chaps. 1-10). Humiliated by Lady Mary's daughter, Lady Ossiter,
and pursued by her husband, Rebecca refuses to accept Worthy's
generous offers of help. The young man leaves for the Continent,
while Rebecca accompanies a young lady, Miss Abthorpe, to America. They survive a rough crossing and a shipwreck, and undergo
many trials when the Abthorpes refuse to join the cause of the
American colonies (11-26). Back in England, Rebecca is suspected
of furthering Lady Winterton's affair with Mr. Savage, and the
miserly and suspicious Mrs. Penure stops her husband's financial
aid to her. Rebecca shares the misery and illness of her mother, who
is now chastened but a beggar after a rash second marriage. When

she tries to sell her last valuables to a jeweler, Rebecca attracts the notice of a lady and is asked to call at her house (28-33). The jeweler's words lead her to believe that the lady is Worthy's wife, so that she fails to keep her appointment. She is at last discovered by chance when Savage mentions her case to Lady Eleanor as she is distributing her bounty to the poor (33, 36). Lady Eleanor is truly married to Sir George, but he is not the young man Rebecca is in love with: he is a foundling brought up with Eleanor, whereas Rebecca's faithful admirer is her own cousin, whom she can finally marry (34, 35, 37). George's father had secretly married his employer's daughter; this was discovered during his absence from England, and the poor girl turned out of doors. She died after the birth of her son and just when her husband had found her again (27). We are also told the story of Jenny, tricked into a fake marriage by a bigamous nobleman, then married properly in order to have a protector for herself and her son. When her repentant seducer pays her a visit, Jenny is overcome by emotion; her husband refuses to keep her, and she follows her former lover, only to experience poverty after his death and to end her life as a prostitute (19-20).

The Fortunate Discovery.—During the War of Independence a British officer, Henry Hargrave, falls in love with Eliza Sommers in New York (pp. 47-52). A succession of discoveries reveal that he is the son of the Villars, and his parents' story is then told. Mrs. Villars had been cast off by her father, Lord Beauclair, for marrying a commoner (65-78). Beauclair even had the couple jailed with their children (79-90). After some years they were allowed to leave for America, but during this voyage Henry's nurse fell overboard with the boy. The two were picked up and taken to England, where Hargrave was brought up as Beauclair's heir. Married to Eliza (146-48), Hargrave returns to England where he can help his friend Bellmore. The latter, wounded in America, had been nursed by Louisa Villars; and they had fallen in love (1-16). Encouraged by Hargrave, Bellmore declared his love, though he knew his father would object to his choice (16-27). Gossips were already discussing the two lovers (27-37) when Bellmore sailed for England. There he is told that his father has picked a wife for him, Miss Lovemore. Hargrave's skillful handling of the situation makes this lady declare that she will never have Bellmore for her husband. The latter then marries Louisa, and Miss Lovemore is "rewarded" when a former lover of hers returns from India a wealthy man (150-80).

Fortune's Foot-ball.—Mercutio saves Lucinda from drowning in the London Hyde Park; he is to marry the girl, but she dies on the day appointed for their wedding. Mercutio leaves for Venice with his friend Wright, who is now married to Amelia after overcoming the opposition of their parents (pp. 1-40). In Venice the Doge's daughter Leonora falls in love with Mercutio. They flee to Naples where Leonora gives birth to a son. But soon after, their ship sailing from Naples is attacked by pirates, and Leonora and her son are killed. Sold into slavery, Mercutio is ransomed by Wright; yet hardly has he returned to England that he is captured by a press gang. Luckily he serves under Charles, Lucinda's brother, who has become an officer after a fight with Howard, his wife's lover (40-80). During a battle Mercutio is taken prisoner by the Spanish but is soon set free in Spain. He suffers an accident and is carried to a castle where he falls in love with Isabella, his host's daughter. Assisted by the girl's mother and brother, he runs off with Isabella to Marseilles. The couple survive a storm and land in Leghorn. They are taken up by Wilcox and discover that he is Wright's new father-in-law, for Amelia has died. Wright and his wife Eliza invite Mercutio and Isabella to their home near San Marino (80-144). The party there comes across Eugenio, a young Englishman who has secretly married Terentia, the daughter of the governor of San Marino. The three couples embark on Wilcox's ship, bound for Holland (145-92). Their vessel barely escapes capture by pirates, but Mercutio falls overboard and is picked up by their pursuers. Once more a slave, he finds among his fellow-captives Charles, his brother-in-law Davenport, and Eliza's brother. Mercutio and his friends make their escape; and Wilcox journeys to Russia, while the others travel to Ispahan. They save the life of the Sophi's son, whose tutor Mercutio now becomes; Charles and Davenport are made instructors in the Persian army (2:3-62). Meanwhile Wilcox, Sr.; the Wrights; the Eugenios; and Isabella have been captured too and taken to Constantinople. There Isabella is acquired by an Ispahan merchant. Mercutio and his friends happen to pass the latter's house as Isabella is calling for help, and they rescue her. They help to quell an uprising; and the Sophi, delivered through their efforts, expresses his gratitude by setting free his thirty-seven harem wives (2:62-127). Among these are a Miss Sydney and a sister of Eliza, whose fiancé Cameron recovers his liberty at about the same time with the entire Constantinople group. Mercutio travels from Ispahan to Moscow, where he briefly meets Howard, who settled there after getting tired of Charles's wife and killing her; Howard will presently be executed for treason. The various groups of travelers gather in Amsterdam and sail to Liverpool. Near London Mercutio rescues two ladies and a gentleman: his parents and Davenport's wife. There are numerous weddings at the end of these adventures (2:127-91).

Fragments of the History of Bawlfredonia.—Though discovered by Fredonius, Bawlfredonia, a country southwest of Botany Bay, derives its name from the leader of a group of adventurers who followed Fredonius to the newly discovered country and called him an impostor. Part of the country is later settled by Christians (in Asylum Harbour and its surroundings), whose heterodoxy is tolerated by their king in the home country as long as he profits from their trade. Another part of the country is called Blackmoreland, which proves a receptive soil when Tom Anguish spreads his views. Under General George Fredonius, Asylumonia and Blackmoreland rebel against their king and secure their country's independence. But inner dissensions begin between the Asylumonians and the Bacchesians, the supporters of the former mother country and of the Saltatoreans.

The Gambler.—On a visit to the King's Bench prison in London, the narrator hears two confession stories. The fifty-page tale, "The Gambler," stresses that its protagonist was spoiled as a child since his father, an officer, was rarely at home. The Gambler serves with the British troops in America during the War of Independence, and there takes up gambling. His father tries to help him by paying some of his debts and making him his aide-de-camp; fatally injured, his father asks the Gambler to look after his family. Soon after the Gambler marries the daughter of the lieutenant-governor. After three years of good behavior he is tempted to gamble with the last installment of his debts. His decline begins. Some years later his wife is forced to sell her family estate. His sister cannot marry and dies of a broken heart because he has lost her dowry; his mother is turned out of her house, and he leads his firm into ruinous speculations. Finally, his mother having died, he fails to meet his creditors' demands and is jailed. The narrator has him released and provides for his wife and children, but the Gambler has only three days left to live. "The Prodigal" (36-74) lives beyond his means while at Eton and Cambridge because his guardian does not tell him what his financial expectations are, and he later proves unable to shake off his spendthrift ways. His guardian agrees to help him only if his wife undertakes to look after their affairs. At the guardian's death, the Prodigal and his wife inherit a considerable fortune.

The Gamesters.—Leander Anderson is entrusted to his uncle Herbert after the death of his parents (chaps. 1-2), completes his college education, and enters the law office of Mr. Granville (11). He meets and falls in love with Amelia Stanhope (4-6), and they become engaged. But his envious companion Edward Somerton, who is trying to seduce Herbert's daughter Eliza (3, 12, 14), employs his associate Ebbert to insinuate that Leander is courting another lady (15-16). Ebbert manages to carry Amelia off but is forced to release her, and Leander is cleared of all suspicion of duplicity (17-21). Ebbert also fails in his attempt to involve Leander in a duel (24). Leander makes such a good impression that he is given control of his estate before he has reached his majority, and he marries Amelia (22-23). Soon after, he yields to Somerton's solicitations and begins to gamble, but breaks the habit at the birth of his son Alonzo (26-28). His reform is short-lived, however; he loses his own fortune, gambles away his wife's jewels, takes to drink, and commits suicide (30-36). Somerton, meanwhile, not only marries a wealthy girl, but also seduces Eliza (32), who has a baby, goes mad, and mercifully dies (35, 37). A hasty concluding chapter shows Ebbert and Somerton plagued by remorse; the former gives Amelia some money to provide for the bringing-up of Alonzo (37). A subsidiary story relates how Ebbert seduced Celestia Williamson, who then committed suicide and caused lasting grief to her father (7-8, 10, 29); another episode concerns a young man absurdly hurried into fighting a duel (28).

Glencarn.—Glencarn is brought up in the country under the supervision of his adoptive father, Richardson. He is hated and slandered by the latter's second wife, her son Rodolpho, and their tutor, Johnson, but finds compensation in the love of Amelia, Richardson's daughter by his first wife, and in the beauty of nature. In his solitary bower he meets a stranger who appears struck with his appearance (1:chaps. 1-9). Richardson sends Glencarn to William and Mary College. The young man saves the life of Gray, but the latter repays him by slandering him to Amelia. The rivals then meet in a duel, and Gray is wounded. Amelia is won back by Glencarn, but he must remove to Pittsburgh because of the duel. Yet there, too, he is pursued by the calumnies of Mrs. Richardson, finds only false friends (such as one Jones), and is even fined and jailed (9-18). In some wild Ohio district our hero is made a captive by a gang of bandits headed by Wilson; this Englishman is plagued by memories of the jealousy he caused between his friends, the Montjoys. Glencarn saves Wilson's life when some subordinates rebel against him, and is allowed to go free. Wounded by Montalbert, one of the rebels, he is looked after by Sophia McWilliams until he discovers that she has fallen in love with him; he then discreetly sets out for home (1:18-21; 2:1-4). He finds that Richardson has died and that he has more enemies than ever; he can however save Mary Baldwin from seduction by Jones and earn the gratitude of Mary's father. He also defeats Jones in a political campaign. He travels to Philadelphia and next to Washington where one night he is attacked: he wounds one of his aggressors (who turns out to be Rodolpho), then escapes his pursuers, using ventriloquism to throw them off the scent. Deeply upset at hearing that Amelia has become a courtesan, he is temporarily distracted from this grief by a new acquaintance: he has saved a lady whose horses were running away with her; and she asks questions about a miniature he was given by the stranger, then offers to adopt him (5-14). Rodolpho dies, and Glencarn is arrested. At the trial Gray gives false evidence but is unmasked by the testimony of the stranger. It is revealed that Mrs. Richardson has poisoned her husband, and she hangs herself. The stranger is Montjoy; Glencarn is his son and that of the lady who has adopted him. Our hero can now buy Richardson's estate, and he can marry Amelia (who, of course, has remained chaste and true). Meanwhile, Wilson has been killed by Montalbert, and the latter has been hanged; this is to be Gray's fate, too (15-18).

The Hapless Orphan.—Caroline Francis's 118 letters to her friend Maria B— first tell the story of her early years when she was entrusted to two different aunts. At Princeton she attracts the attention of several students and of Clarimont, who is to marry Eliza, though he does not love her. The young man shoots himself, and Eliza vows revenge (1-3), while Caroline becomes engaged to Captain Evremont (3, 8-9). She goes to stay in Virginia with her friend Lucy, who has just married Wilkins. Jealous without a cause, Wilkins one day vanishes, after which Lucy is dangerously ill (16-17, 20-21, 23). She dies before Wilkins relents; her father then shoots Wilkins and commits suicide (24-31). Meanwhile, Caroline has met the Gardners, especially young Fanny and her married brother, Frederick, who hopes in vain for financial aid from their cold-hearted brother Charles (14-16). The Gardners and a Captain Clark console Caroline; the latter, a friend of Evremont, leaves for the Indian front with Frederick (32, 36, 43). Caroline will be furnished with military reports at regular intervals (49, 57, 62, 67, 71). When the expedition ends in defeat, all three officers are reported dead. Again and again there is evidence that Eliza is still plotting against Caroline and that she is constantly informed of the latter's moves (6-7, 12, 21, 43, 55, 69). She has successfully slandered her to Evremont (77) but she long fails to lay hands on the persecuted heroine. Eventually, however, Eliza manages to have Caroline carried off (119, the first of three letters sent by Maria B— to her sister) during the absence of her protector Mr. Helen (74-76, 78, 93-94, 99, 104). Helen later finds Caroline's body about to be dissected by medical students; she has died of a broken heart (120-21). Meanwhile, Fanny has been shot by Ashely, whom she persistently refused and who, influenced by too much reading of *Werther,* has then committed suicide (108-15). Among digressions more loosely connected with Caroline's fate, there is the story of the seduction of Harriot by Lee, complete with a mock wedding and priest, and a stay in a brothel (52-54). Laura Gleason marries the elderly Gibbins, who goes bankrupt and becomes an invalid soon after; and her mother nearly marries her late husband's illegitimate son (63-64, 89-90, 102, 111).

Henry and Julietta.—Lord Clareville, only son of the Earl of Clarendon, stays overnight at Mr. Granville's cottage in Cumberland and promptly falls in love with his host's daughter Julietta. He is soon given an opportunity to save her life and a few days later escorts her home after she has lost her way. But, at the same time, he introduces the Duke of Monmouth to her; and the latter presently carries her off. Julietta is rescued by an officer; when he takes her back to her parents, he is discovered to be their son Henry, who had been entrusted to Mrs. Granville's brother Lord Ormond and who then disappeared. Henry is to inherit the Ormond title and fortune, so that his sister now appears eligible to marry Clarendon (chaps. 1-5). Monmouth succeeds once more in abducting Julietta; this time it is

Clareville who can free the girl (7). Meanwhile, Henry has met the accomplished Rosabella and saved her from drowning. They fall in love; and the young man rapidly obtains the consent of Rosabella's father, General Dermot, though the girl, far less spoiled than her sister, Lady Wentworth, is the old man's favorite (6, 8-10).

The History of Albert and Eliza.—Albert and Eliza, the children of two Long Island families, are to marry as soon as the young man returns from a business trip to England. In New York Eliza is courted by Palmer and by the governor's nephew, Blake. When Palmer behaves rudely toward her, Blake challenges him. But after Palmer's death he discovers that Albert is a far more formidable rival. Eliza's fiancé, however, fails to reach America long after he has announced his departure from England; it is rumored that he has married an heiress. A gentleman just home from England confirms this rumor, and Blake obtains Eliza's consent to marry him. The marriage ceremony has just begun when Eliza discovers Albert among those present and faints away. It was a cousin and namesake of his who got married in England. Albert himself has been made a slave by the Algerines. Miss Smith, who used to be seen in Blake's company and who has tried to drown Eliza, now reveals that Blake is her half brother and her husband too: they married years ago before he knew that she was an illegitimate child of his father. She also had a brother, who is none other than Palmer: Blake has thus killed his half brother. Horrified by these revelations, Blake rushes to his room and shoots himself.

The History of Constantius and Pulchera.—Pulchera is promised to Constantius, but her father suddenly decides that she must marry the Frenchman Le Monte. Constantius delivers her from the room where she is kept a prisoner but is caught by a British press gang near Philadelphia. The lovers meet again when the French vessel taking Pulchera across the Atlantic is intercepted by the British: the sympathetic English captain notices the glances exchanged between the girl and his American sailor and sets them free; Le Monte is willing to give up the girl. A storm once more separates the lovers. Pulchera is picked up, after some days on a desolate coast, by an American vessel, which is soon pursued by British ships. Pulchera disguises herself as Lieutenant Valorus before the Americans are captured. Another storm wrecks the ship on which she is sailing.

[428]

There follows a period of hunger on a desert island, at the end of which Valorus is picked to be eaten by the other outcasts. Food, in the shape of a bear, is discovered just in time. After a cruel winter there is another American ship to rescue Valorus, a successful attack on a British vessel, and another reversal: Valorus, prize master on the captured boat, is taken to Halifax. She escapes, is caught again, and set free once her captors have reached London. Valorus then travels on to Lisbon and Bordeaux, and as she is making inquiries there about departures for America, she accidentally meets Constantius. He believes her dead and is about to marry Le Monte's sister. Valorus tests him incognito and finds that he still loves his Pulchera; and the faithful couple are eventually united.

The History of Maria Kittle.—The Kittles live in Tomhanick near Albany; they have a daughter and a baby boy. While tension mounts in the frontier region, Kittle's brothers leave Fort Edward and join the family at Tomhanick. One of them, Peter, is killed by Indians soon after; and Kittle goes to a neighboring village to find help. During his absence the Indians attack Tomhanick, a number of the inhabitants are killed, including the children of the Kittles; and Maria and her brother-in-law are carried off (pp. 19-42). On his return Kittle finds Tomhanick destroyed and is seriously ill for a while; once again in good health, he joins the English to take revenge on the Indians (42-49). The Indians journey with their captives to Lake Champlain and across, then on to their villages. Maria, who has found them relatively friendly and considerate, is disappointed with their unsympathetic womenfolk. At Montreal, however, her story moves the governor, and the English lady with whom she lodges (49-68). Other ladies, Mrs. Bratt and Mrs. Willis, tell similar stories of Indian attacks. One day Maria meets her husband in the street. Kittle, convinced that she had been burned in their house, has been looking not for her any more, but for his brother (69-87).

Humanity in Algiers.—Azem, a captive, is given to Selictor and his wife Sequida and brought up with their children. Before he dies Selictor decides to sell Azem to Testador, for he is certain that Azem would find it hard to obey his children (chaps. 1-2). Azem contemplates suicide, then runs away from Testador. But he follows wise Omri's advice that he should return and resign himself to his fate (3). He is to work toward his emancipation by remaining for one

[429]

year with each of the surviving members of Selictor's family. At the end of two years, he rescues his mistress from an Arab and is given his freedom (4-5). Next Azem tries to obtain the slave Alzina for his wife, but her master refuses to give her up (6-12). Azem leaves Algiers and travels to Senegal, where by a coincidence he can set his mother free. On their return to Algiers they discover that Alzina (whose story has been sketched in Chapter 9) must be Azem's sister (13-16). Azem spends the next years educating himself. He becomes a successful merchant in Gambia, where he witnesses the brutal warfare of the natives. Captured by some Spaniards, he gets control of their ship, yet refuses to sell his prisoners into slavery (17-19). He then marries a wealthy young widow, Shelimah, but she dies, together with their son and Alzina, during the plague. Azem bequeathes half his fortune to the poor, the other half to set free one deserving slave every year (20); the narrator, "an American, late a Slave in Algiers," is later to profit from this institution.

Infidelity.—Four letters from Caroline Franks to her sister Maria Hartley serve as an exposition in this epistolary novel. Caroline has been forced to marry Franks by her parents; she has had and lost one child. She is now living near Philadelphia and has as neighbors three spinsters who live in a decaying house—the Misses Hayward— and a Mrs. Alfred with her son and daughter. The latter, Fanny, is much given to evening walks and solitude. Young Charles Alfred confesses to his friend William Courtney that he has fallen in love and receives a flippant reply (5-6). After Caroline's account of Fanny's unfortunate love for Henry Wellsford, another pair of letters (8-9) return to the topic of Alfred's love: he has found out that his beloved (whose name he never mentions) is a married woman. It appears that Caroline is not unattracted to Alfred; the latter does not consider his love hopeless, and Courtney judges that the lady's loveless marriage allows Alfred to pursue the affair (10-14). A visit from the Hayward sisters shows Franks behaving gallantly (15), while Caroline is clearly pleased with the idea of Alfred's love (16, 18). Maria, however, is disturbed over this (19). Caroline and Alfred then agree not to mention love anymore (20-21); but when the young man goes to Philadelphia on business, Caroline reveals how much she loves him (23, 24, 26). Courtney encourages Alfred to make Caroline his mistress. Meanwhile Franks writes to the sympathetic Harriot Hayward that he is jealous of Alfred; he complains about his wife's indifference and yet admits that he is partly responsible for it. In spite of her sister's warnings, Caroline now no longer objects to Alfred's talk of love (33, 40). The two of them accompany Fanny to an appointment with an unknown Eugenius (36-38), who turns out to be Wellsford (43) and identical with Tallman (45), a young man Courtney has been mentioning (17, 27, 39). Courtney learns from Wellsford's letters that the lady whom Alfred has been courting is Courtney's sister Caroline. Franks writes to Harriot that he is about to kill himself and is actually found dead, whereupon Caroline goes mad (41-42, 46). Courtney accuses Alfred of having maliciously enticed him to promote his love affair and challenges him. Alfred, appalled at hearing that Caroline is Courtney's sister, accepts, but shoots in the air when they meet and is killed by his opponent. Courtney disappears after cursing his sister, and Caroline dies on the spot when she discovers the cause of her brother's rage (47-48). Two additional episodes illustrate (1) the disastrous effects of countering true love for material reasons (Henry and Louisa, letter 25), and (2) the contagious effect of love, which renders a lover generally sympathetic and sensitive (30, 34-35).

The Inquisitor.—The main character of this book wishes to be invisible at will, so as to make sure that he cannot be imposed upon by impostors and villains in his readiness to offer assistance and sympathy. When his wish is granted, he witnesses many instances of deceit and some of true goodness. He can accordingly help, punish, and derive moral lessons. In the end, the Inquisitor loses the magic ring which conveys invisibility just as he is watching a budding intrigue between an heiress and an officer he suspects of being a fortune hunter.

Ira and Isabella.—In his preface the author ironically deplores his lack of inventiveness in an age looking to the novel for elements of the sublime, the picturesque, or the fearful. He also insists on the necessity of creating a style that will accommodate the various characters (pp. iii-xiv). The orphan Isabella is a companion of Mrs. Savage, who is to complete her education. Ira makes her acquaintance and gradually falls in love with her. Though his friend Lorenzo ridicules him, he declares his love to Isabella, who accepts him without reluctance. The girl's old nurse warns against marriage, because men cannot be trusted; but Isabella is indifferent to her arguments. She is sent to her guardian, Dr. Joseph, who now admits that Isabella is his illegitimate daughter; he earnestly urges her to stay unmarried. Joseph dies soon after, and the lovers decide to marry; the ceremony has just been completed when the nurse declares that she suspects Ira of being another illegitimate offspring of Joseph. The young couple is shocked by this revelation, but under Isabella's guidance they rationally map out their future conduct. Belatedly Mr. Savage then confesses that he is Ira's real father; he relates how he was seduced by Lucinda while he thought he was seducing her and how he was shielded by Joseph, who suggested that Isabella's nurse should also look after Ira (pp. 15-118).

The Irish Emigrant.—In 1798 the Irish are divided between the pro-Irish and pro-English factions. M'Dermott, an Irish patriot, is nearly dispossessed by an opportunist, Major S—, while his neighbor, Sir Phelim O'Niall, remains suspiciously indifferent (pp. 1:5-55). M'Dermott's son Owen meets his friend Fitzgerald, and they swear to fight the British rule. During Owen's absence S— attacks the M'Dermott estate; Owen's father and sister are killed, and the house is burned down. Owen starts on a journey through Ireland to sound out the people's feelings. He discovers that he shares strong republican and revolutionary convictions with O'Niall's daughter Emma. The girl, who has proved her courage in a haunted castle, plans to free Fitzgerald, now a prisoner in Dublin's Newgate (55-153). She obtains admission there, disguised as a blind harper; and Fitzgerald escapes wearing her clothes. M'Dermott, leading the patriots in the North, kills S— and his traitorous assistant Bonsel in battle. On the side of his enemies, too, O'Niall behaves disgracefully (153-200). A gallant soldier and gentleman, M'Dermott saves Fitzgerald's sister Eliza from a would-be seducer, Lord Butler. But he cannot stop the doings of the "Orange Men", who undermine the patriots' confidence. Fitzgerald falls, and the death of O'Niall is only a meager consolation. The patriots abandon this attempt to obtain their independence. Emma is tried for her part in the deliverance of Fitzgerald and triumphantly acquitted (Vol. 2). Among digressions of Volume 2 is the story of Butler's attempts to seduce Eliza and his masquerading as an Irish patriot (1-49). Eliza finally marries Arthur O'Connor, the rightful heir to the Irish throne, while Butler takes the wicked Sophia Ormond for his wife. Another story introduced (62-144) is that of Warren, a Virginian kidnapped by a British captain and held a prisoner in Dublin for two years. When

Warren, tried and acquitted at the same time as Emma, returns to America, Owen and Emma M'Dermott sail with him.

Jane Talbot.—Jane early loses her mother. Her elder brother Frank gradually spends the family fortune, then absconds to France, where he is to become successful and allied to a good family. Jane's cousin Risberg, who was to marry her, has preferred a wealthy European girl (letters 2-6). According to the wishes of her father and her adviser, Mrs. Fielder, Jane marries Talbot, though since becoming engaged to him she has fallen in love with Henry Colden (9). Talbot, however, soon dies. Jane's relations with Colden keep worrying Mrs. Fielder (10, 15-17). When the girl asks her why she disapproves of Colden (11-12, 14), Mrs. Fielder accuses her of hypocrisy (13), then proceeds to indict Colden as a dangerous radical and a follower of Godwin, and intimates that he has seduced Jane (15-17). Jane thinks that she must have been slandered (21). She appears willing to break with Colden (19-20) but reconsiders after remonstrances on his part (22, 24, 25). Neither Frank's sinister appearance on the scene (31-33) nor Jane's brooding over her reputation and her dealings with Mrs. Fielder (34, 36) improves the couple's prospects. When Jane hears that Colden's father means to repudiate his son because of her, she decides to sacrifice her happiness by rejecting Colden (37, 39). She is soon to waver again (44). Colden now wonders who has calumniated Jane. He finds out that a Miss Jessup, who loved Talbot, has been causing the trouble and on one occasion forged an incriminating letter (43, 46-48). Mrs. Fielder, however, believes that Jane has been planning to run away with Colden; the girl once more makes an effort to give up her love (55, 59). The conclusion of the novel, beginning about a year after these events and covering a period of three years, shows Jane struggling to abandon the hope of seeing Colden alive again; he has, however, returned from extended voyages (56-58, 60, 62). She is now being courted by Cartwright (62-65); it is the latter who informs Colden that Jane is not married yet. Colden returns to Jane, no longer an agnostic but a Christian, whose conversion Jane initiated many years earlier (69-70).

A Journey to Philadelphia.—Charles Coleman Saunders lives on his father's farm near the Susquehannah. He does not share his father's fondness for the secluded spot nor his contentment with his

routine work. Saunders weighs his chances in a military and a political career, but rejects both as uncongenial, and determines to use
his gifts as a mechanic in Philadelphia. His departure is dramatically
hastened: he has happened to interfere with an attempt at carrying
off a young lady without, however, identifying either the girl or her
attacker; and since then he has been shot at and threatened with a
dagger in his house. On the eve of his journey (secretly prepared
for), Saunders pays a farewell visit to a favorite spot of his on the
banks of the Susquehannah, where he is just a little too slow to stop
a girl from jumping into the river. In Philadelphia he presents himself before a watchmaker; the man has not yet made up his mind
to make Saunders his apprentice when his daughter walks into the
shop: she is the girl saved from abduction by Saunders. The young
man works with the watchmaker and courts his daughter, the beautiful Emilia. But Carnell now shows up in Philadelphia: he is Emilia's
would-be ravisher and, presumably, the man who has tried to kill
Saunders. One day the latter is arrested and charged with the murder
of one Susan Warfield. He finds that he has aroused suspicion by
his precipitate departure from his father's farm and by using the
name of Coleman. At the trial some witnesses testify to having heard
him swear he would kill Susan; others think that they saw him push
a woman into the river about the time of Susan's disappearance.
Saunders is sentenced to death but saved on the place of execution
when Susan reappears. After jumping into the Susquehannah to
drown herself, she changed her mind, reached the river-bank, and
sought refuge in Maryland; the man heard vowing he would kill her,
Carson, has since married her. (He looks very much like Saunders.) Entirely rehabilitated and informed that Carnell is dead, Saunders can now marry Emilia.

Julia.—Count de Launa and Marquis Alvada, two French noblemen, each have one son and one daughter, and they decide to marry
these children to one another. Young Alvada loses his wife, however, when she gives birth to a son, and remarries years later: by
Lavinia he has a daughter. But Lavinia dies too, and the baby vanishes. Meanwhile, his sister, who should have married young de
Launa, falls in love with Henry Ormond, and they marry secretly.
Ormond is called back to England when his wife is pregnant, and
is reported dead some time later. His brother William offers to bring
up his son. Ormond's widow marries de Launa after all; but Henry

Ormond is then discovered to be still alive. Challenged by de Launa, he kills him. He had been the dupe of his family, who had led him to believe that his wife was dead because they were opposed to his marriage to a Roman Catholic. To make matters more complicated, Alvada's son inherits de Launa's title (chap. 2). The eighteen-year-old Julia, alone in the world after the disappearance of her mother Isabella two years earlier and the recent death of her grandfather, is befriended by a countess. Soon Julia conquers a gentleman's heart, that of Francis Colwort, introduced into her life when he saves the countess's life. After Julia and Colwort have become engaged, the young man leaves for America on family affairs (1, 3-5). Julia wins the welcome sympathy of the Marquis Alvada, the countess's brother, and attracts the obnoxious attentions of Alvada's son de Launa. When she is carried off to Spain, one suspects de Launa to have had a hand in the scheme; but it is only later that he has her held up on the road to Paris and taken to his castle (6-7, 9-12, 14-15). There she hears some fragments of the de Launa history, is pestered by her lustful pursuer, visits a grave and thinks that she has seen a ghost, and is rescued by Colwort, also imprisoned in the castle (16-20). The lovers are parted once more, and Julia, trying to rejoin the countess, is denied access to her. She is assisted by an Englishman, Roswell, and Madame de Shong. When the latter's house burns down, she is driven to seek shelter at an inn. There she accidentally meets the countess and Alvada again; a miniature which she is trying to sell triggers off the revelation that she is Alvada's daughter by Lavinia (who was poisoned by de Launa because she refused to become his mistress) (21, 23-24). De Launa himself dies, confessing his misdeeds. Colwort turns out to be the son of the countess and Ormond. Julia and Colwort are married, so are a few others, among them Isabella, a former servant of the Alvadas, who brought up Julia after Lavinia's death, but was captured by de Launa's associates (1, 25). Subsidiary episodes include one which involved Julia in the schemes of Mademoiselle Gyron: this lady, deserted by Don Gasperd with their illegitimate son, manages to get hold of Gasperd's niece, an heiress, and to marry her to her son (12). There are also cases of seduction, that of Leonora, who eloped from a convent (17), and Olivia, who scorned an honest lover to become de Launa's mistress (23).

Keep Cool.—Laura St. Vincent intrigues and fascinates by turns James Earnest and Charles Percy, but is felt by the reader and by her New York friends to be mysteriously linked to the former British officer Sydney (chaps. 2, 8, 14, 15). Earnest proposes, is refused, and leaves America for Scotland (14), where he is to console himself with an old girl friend (21). Sydney and Laura invariably meet at social gatherings that do not allow for private conversation and revelations; it is evident that Laura likes to flirt, while Sydney has had a checkered past which gives him a Byronic aura (11, 18). Two more characters, Mrs. Granville (4, 13) and the eccentric and contradictory poet Echo, are introduced and explained. The latter challenges Sydney, because of some inconsiderate words; but an opportunity offers to rationally discuss the question of dueling (18-19); and the two men part good friends. Public opinion takes a dim view of this peaceful solution, and Sydney is accused of cowardice. He breaks his determination not to fight duels: Percy, himself a suitor of Laura, is wounded by Sydney and dies after a long illness (28). Sydney temporarily loses his reason; his gradual recovery is paralleled by a series of discoveries. Mrs. Granville turns out to be his sister Elizabeth (21); and Echo is, in reality, Eustace St. Pierre, to whom she was engaged years earlier and who was believed to have died (25). Sydney, whose real name appears to be Henry Moreland, leaves New York (23), in order to punish himself by renouncing all the ties dear to him—his sister's affection, the love of Julia (Percy's sister), and his own love for Louisa. He returns from his wanderings, having experienced disappointments even among the Indians with whom he used to be friends (29). Finally Laura and Sydney are reconciled after the story of their mutual deceptions has been elucidated (30-32). *Keep Cool* begins with a fictitious review by Neal of his own book; its opening chapter is a discussion about an old man's plan of writing a novel. Humorous episodes, such as a practical joke in the spirit of frontier humor (5) and a hunting episode (16), are inserted.

Kelroy.—Seventeen-year-old Emily Hammond meets Kelroy, a poet, in Philadelphia and falls in love with him (chaps. 5-6). This love threatens to upset the plans of her mother, a widow who has lived in retirement to hide the fact of her comparative poverty and to save enough money to last her until her two daughters are married to wealthy husbands (1-2). Lucy, who resembles her calculating mother, wins the love of Lord Walsingham (3, 6). Six weeks after their wedding, Mrs. Hammond begins to sponsor the repulsive Mar-

ney's suit for Emily (8). Walsingham, who is Kelroy's friend, blackmails Mrs. Hammond into agreeing to the engagement between
Emily and Kelroy (9-10). Emily's mother, whose money has been
dwindling faster than expected, loses her possessions when her house
burns down (which gives Kelroy an opportunity to save his fiancée),
but miraculously recovers her prosperity thanks to a lottery ticket
(11-12). Kelroy leaves on a voyage to China in order to secure a
fortune before marrying Emily. The latter finds a new admirer in
the person of Dunlevy, who obtains Emily's hand after a letter from
Kelroy has informed the girl that he has changed his mind about her
(13-15). Soon after Emily's wedding Mrs. Hammond dies; among
her papers are found copies of the letter purportedly written by
Kelroy and of a similar one from Emily to Kelroy. Emily pines away
and dies. Her friend Helen tells Kelroy on his return to Philadelphia
of Emily's faithful love and Mrs. Hammond's treachery. Kelroy,
whose reason seems threatened, embarks on a ship that sinks off the
American coast (conclusion). There are figures providing comic
relief and social satire, such as Mrs. Hammond's friend Mrs. Cathcart (1, 6, 12), the newly-rich Gurnets (14), and Helen's stubborn
admirer Dr. Blake (3, 7).

Laura.—Laura is the daughter of Rosina, who eloped from a
convent in Lisbon, was widowed soon after settling in Philadelphia, and has married again for the sake of her child; when Laura
is about fifteen, Rosina dies (p. 15). The orphan is consoled by
Belfield, a medical student whom she trusts completely. After the
death of her stepfather, she dismisses the man whom he wished her
to marry. Belfield and Laura now live together outside Philadelphia,
and the young man undertakes to give his companion a literary
education (p. 45). During a yellow fever epidemic Belfield one day
fails to return from town; Laura seeks him out and nurses him back
to health (p. 65). Belfield finds her temporary lodgings in Philadelphia; but Laura discovers that she is in a brothel. She meets a
young prostitute who thinks that she has claims on Belfield, is asked
to entertain a customer named Melwood, and runs away before
Belfield returns for her (p. 90). Laura undergoes a series of harrowing experiences, once having to spend a night in a churchyard
on her mother's grave (p. 130). The lovers are reconciled; Belfield
is about to complete his studies, and the day for the wedding is fixed
upon. He has stopped seeing his more or less dissolute friends but

[437]

accepts one final invitation on the eve of his wedding day. He quarrels with Melwood, who challenges and fatally wounds him. Belfield dies in Laura's arms, with her name on his lips. The girl goes mad, but recovers, and is offered protection by a respectable gentleman to whom Belfield has recommended her (p. 181).

The Lawyer.—Morcell, whose mother has died, is brought up in a Maryland town by his father and a corrupt lawyer named Dorsey; he is to adopt Dorsey's profession. He seduces Matilda Ansley, who dies soon after giving birth to a boy. Morcell proves unfeeling toward debtors, and he gambles; but he also fears Matilda's brother Edward and an unknown person who has been threatening him (chaps. 1-7). A conversation overheard reveals that one Rattle has seduced Morcell's sister; blows are exchanged. Morcell anticipates a challenge and runs off to Baltimore. He is successful as a lawyer but wastes his inheritance and gambles again. He suspects Ansley of having attempted to kill him, is jealous when Rattle's sister Maria visibly admires Ansley, and decides to kill him; but the man whom he stabs in the dark turns out to be Rattle (8-18). On the run once more because he has been taking bribes, Morcell practices law with the idea of getting rich quickly, i.e., before he is found out. He overhears Ansley telling his story to Rattle, and so learns that it is Ansley who has repeatedly given him assistance. Finally he is sent for by a man named Edwards, who wishes to confess that he has tried to murder Morcell because he held him responsible for the death of his father and sister. The son of Morcell and Matilda has died; Morcell's sister has ended her days in a brothel. Ansley and Maria marry, while Morcell lives a retired life and distributes charities (19-25).

The Life and Adventures of Obadiah Benjamin Franklin Bloomfield.—The son of an honest workingman, Bloomfield first tries to make good his father's ambitions: he receives a thorough schooling in the ancient languages and Hebrew and is taught in the school of Methodist preaching. But, though his father has the pleasure of once listening to a sermon of his, Bloomfield soon changes over to his own vocation, medicine (chaps. 1-6). After a casual affair with a country girl, he falls in love with Louisa, with whom he stays during her dissipated husband's absence. They marry after the man's death, but Louisa dies in childbirth (7, 9-15). Bloomfield's second wife, Maria, betrays him with Blackheart, is caught *in flagranti,* and sent home. She convinces her brother Henry that she has been wronged; yet, after he has challenged Bloomfield and been wounded, she insists on living with Blackheart. Blackheart is whipped by Henry and later castrated by an angry husband, an operation which causes a fatal infection. Maria works in a brothel, starts drinking, and dies (17-24). Bloomfield next falls in love with a pretty eighteen-year-old widow and marries her, though at first her family do not approve of him; they soon have a son. But Maria reappears; it takes a trial to show that she is really Maria's half-sister, an illegitimate child of Maria's father and Sophia's aunt, Mrs. Cole. The latter felt she had been badly treated by her family and wanted to avenge herself; she commits suicide when she hears that her plan with the pseudo-Maria has failed (25, 26, 28-34, 41-43, 44-47, 49). There is an inserted story about young Richard, who gambles his fortune away in spite of the advice of two Quakers and though he loves Ruth Steady, the daughter of one of them. He finally reforms, after attempting suicide (27, 32, 39, 44, 48). Col. M'Donald, a Scotsman, who fought for the Americans during the War of Independence, is nearly killed by a nephew of his who feels that M'Donald has betrayed his country (36-37, 40, 43). Jack, a sailor, sells his hat to two Jews who have been led to think it can work wonders and provide free accommodation for them (8).

The Life and Reflections of Charles Observator.—The hero, brought up by his father Charles Wise in the only right manner (unlike those adopted by his neighbors Slack and Indulgence), also profits from the guidance of Barton, the local pastor, and the example of schoolmaster Studious. When he is twenty-two, he leaves his father's farm to see the world. Charles is troubled by the fact that a boy is killed by lightning in a peaceful village, but reconciled to the fact of this death by the sermon preached at the burial of the boy. He joins an elderly gentleman named Americus, and he meets proud and prejudiced Mrs. Aristocrat and Christian and efficient Mrs. Demo, as well as a couple who have been married against their will because their union meant mutual profit to their parents. In Boston Charles is welcomed by his father's friend Philanthropos, and feels strongly attracted to his eldest daughter Prudentia, who is exactly like the perfect wife as depicted by Wise, even bearing the name of that imaginary ideal. The conversations in Philanthropos's house touch upon many domestic subjects. Certain aspects of Boston life strike Charles rather unpleasantly, as, for example, insolent children, indecent fashions, prostitutes, and an undignified Fourth of July celebration. He and Prudentia very sensibly discuss their views of life and marriage; and accordingly, once married, they are entirely happy.

The Life of Alexander Smith.—Smith informs the reader that he was born in 1760. He becomes a fisherman in Gloucester, Massachusetts, then follows British recruiting agents to Halifax. Military drill, however, does not suit him; and he sails on board an American ship to Europe and India. In April, 1784, he is left alone on an island between Madagascar and Ceylon. Living on cocoanut milk and turtles, he builds himself a hut, then learns to obtain fire and to fashion clothes out of seal skins. The presence of rats on the island suggests to him that a ship may have been wrecked on its shores, and he does discover it. The wreck provides him with material for tools, which he uses to build a boat. In July, 1788, he sets out on a voyage that ends in the Dutch colony of Cochin in India (pp. 9-82). Smith then joins a seal hunting expedition in the Falklands, is temporarily stranded on a rocky island with one other survivor, and parts with his comrades again at Port Cox. Together with an Englishman, he there builds a boat ordered by an Indian chief who believes in the coming of a deluge. The two boat builders do not trust the chief and escape; they finally land at Luconia in the South Pacific, sell the boat, and separate. By the time Smith reaches London the firm transferring his share of the Luconia gains has gone bankrupt (82-115). Smith next finds himself a member of the crew of the *Bounty*. He remains neutral when the crew mutinies. After Capt. Bligh and his men have been sent off, Fletcher Christian tries to overcome the dissensions among the twenty-five mutineers but finally agrees to a suggestion made by Smith: a select number sail with their Otaheite women to Pitcairn. They organize expeditions into the interior, make sure that they can establish positions of defense against possible aggressors, then establish democratic institutions, and keep a register of marriages and births. They are uneasy over the presence of native men among them and are glad when they can put them on a boat and send them away (115-86). Having devised a constitution, they build a council house. Occasionally ships are sighted (in 1795, 1796, 1799); when in 1808 the *Topaz*, from Boston, casts anchor in a bay of the island, Smith is there to receive her captain. He pretends that

[440]

he is the only survivor of the mutineers, that Christian is dead, and that the whites and the natives have exterminated one another. In 1810 a first wedding of Pitcairn children is celebrated. Four years later a young couple vanish but return after another year and explain what has happened: the girl's mother, Mrs. Christian, refused to consider the young man's proposal, so they have been secretly married by Christian, Jr., and have since lived on an island off the Pitcairn coast (240).

Lucinda.—Mrs. Manvill is Lucinda's stepmother and tells the girl's story in letters addressed to her sister. They live in Greenfield, N.Y.; the place is a retreat for Lucinda when she returns from stays at Marcellus and Troy, where she has been courted by one Brown. Mrs. Manvill discovers that Lucinda is pregnant (1-6, 8), and the girl confesses her fall in two letters (9, 11); a hint that Brown used force is given later (25). The Manvills and their relatives try to persuade Brown to assume his responsibilities toward Lucinda (7, 12-14), but it is soon clear that he does not intend to marry her (15, 16). A delegation from the parish calls upon the Manvills: they do not want Lucinda to become a burden to the parish (17-18). The girl has clearly not much longer to live (19-20). She gives birth to a girl, writes Brown a last letter in which she asks for the forgiveness of God for both of them, and dies (21-27). Some more letters mention the Manvills' joy at keeping Lucinda's little Polly. In the second edition an additional letter states that Brown has come down in the world (31).

Margaretta.—The breakdown of a coach in a Maryland village introduces Margaretta Wilmot to three travelers: Miss Stewart, young Will de Burling, and Waller, a sea-captain, who detects in her a resemblance to someone he used to know. Soon the girl is courted by de Burling and Waller; her simplicity makes de Burling forget the West Indian heiress he is to marry. Waller proposes and is accepted, but as it transpires that Margaretta was forced to say yes by her unsympathetic father, he gives her up and vows to remain her protector (letters 1-15, pp. 1-68). De Burling's acquaintance Archibald Custon unsuccessfully attempts to carry Margaretta off and in revenge hints to de Burling's fiancée Arabella Roulant that she is about to be jilted. Under an assumed name, Arabella takes Margaretta along with her to Santo Domingo; she pretends that she wants to protect her from the disingenuous de Burling. The latter, certain that he loves Margaretta, announces his rupture with Arabella. Roulant thereupon severs his partnership with the elder de Burling, who goes bankrupt (16-29, pp. 68-159). At Cape François Margaretta attracts the attention first of Welton, then of Montanan, but also of Roulant. Arabella's father has her carried to another estate of his. Temporarily protected by Vernon, who escorts her to Fort Dauphin, Margaretta is told by Custon that de Burling and Arabella have married. A Mr. Howard's attentions toward Margaretta cause bad blood in the Duchamp family with whom she lodges, and she is glad to find a disinterested friend, Louisa Barton, a consumptive. She now hears that Arabella is in fact married to Custon; there is a rumor that de Burling has found a wife in Philadelphia. Montanan is found to be really named Edward Warren, and to have been married to Louisa's aunt, Lady Matilda (30-47, pp. 159-288). In a last effort to cure Louisa, Montanan and Margaretta take her to England. There Margaretta meets Sir Henry Barton and his sister, Lady Montraville. While Louisa is slowly dying, Margaretta is suspected of living in sin with Montanan, who has really asked her to marry him. She is about to accept his proposal when a ring given her by Louisa leads to two discoveries: Lady Montraville is Lady Matilda, and Margaretta her daughter and Montanan's. Believing that the latter was dead, Lady Matilda has married again; her second husband has died, however. We learn that the nurse employed by Lady Matilda in America substituted her daughter for Margaretta and entrusted the latter to Mrs. Wilmot, when Lady Matilda returned to England. Sir Henry refuses to believe Margaretta's identity and innocence, and carries her off; but she is rescued by Lord Orman (48-59, pp. 288-367). At this time, de Burling arrives in England with the faithful Waller; he has heard that Margaretta is Montanan's mistress, but finds her in the company of Orman. The girl still believes him married; and when the truth dawns on her that he is yet to be had, another obstacle arises: de Burling thinks he is socially unworthy of her, for her father is now a lord. Orman is then revealed to have behaved badly toward a clergyman's daughter, he makes amends, Margaretta is free, and de Burling proposes and is accepted (60-73, pp. 367-419).

Memoirs of Carwin, the Biloquist.—Living with a father and brother unsympathetic to his thirst for knowledge, Frank Carwin is eager to stay with his aunt in Philadelphia, who is willing to give

him a sound education. He discovers that he is a ventriloquist and
wants to use this gift to induce his father to send him to Philadelphia,
when unexpectedly his father gives him permission to go. At his
aunt's death Carwin is disappointed because her will does not mention him; he intends to use ventriloquism to work on the superstitious fears of Dorothy, the beneficiary of the will. Before he can
carry his plan into execution, he is befriended by Ludloe and follows
him to Europe (pp. 275-98). Ludloe, after some time spent at his
Irish home, sends Carwin to Spain. On the young man's return he
hints that Carwin could join a secret movement of which he is a
member. Carwin must however first tell him the story of his life
without omitting any detail. Carwin has not revealed to Ludloe that
he is a ventriloquist; to his dismay he realizes that Ludloe knows
details about his stay in Spain which he thought no one could have
detected. What if Ludloe should also be aware of his secret gift?
Meanwhile, he has saved the life of Mrs. Benington: when her car-
riage was stopped by highwaymen, he imitated several voices, as of
a group of people approaching, and the attackers took to their heels.
Ludloe appears to favor a match between Lady Benington and
Carwin (pp. 299-351).

Mentoria.—The orphan Helena, brought up by Lady Winworth,
informs her mistress that she is being courted by her son, whereupon
young Winworth is sent traveling on the Continent. Helena resists
his last-minute plea to marry him secretly; he returns to England
with a bride. Helena marries a friend of his but is soon widowed.
She then becomes the governess of Winworth's daughters. After
young Lady Winworth dies, the girls return to their father; this
separation from Helena serves as a pretext for *Mentoria.* Helena's
letters to her young charges are didactic stories offered as warnings
and examples, but without any close connection with the girls' own
experience except once, when they object to their father's plan to
marry again. He does take a second wife, however, and his daughters
follow Helena's advice and try not to render their stepmother's task
too difficult.

Modern Chivalry.—Captain Farrago leaves his farm to see how
America is making out in its newly-won independence and its experiment in democracy. He soon discovers, thanks to the behavior
of his Irish servant Teague Oregan and the apparent affinity between

[443]

Teague and the people, that there is as yet only a limited awareness in America of the workings of democracy and of the individual self-control required to develop reliable institutions in a democratic government. Teague nearly becomes a member of the state parliament (p. 15) and of a philosophical society (23), a preacher (38), and a fake Indian chief (55), before actually becoming an actor (132). His tendency to make love to every female he meets leads him and others into scrapes, and puts an end to his stage career. Meanwhile, Farrago discusses the nonsense of dueling (45) and the rights and wrongs of slavery (134). He is also appalled at the way in which lobbying interests interfere with the work of Congress (123). Teague is impervious to fashionable manners (205), but not unsuccessful with the Washington ladies (238). Appointed an excise officer (254), Teague soon quarrels with Duncan Ferguson, Farrago's new servant, who is a Scotsman and a strict Presbyterian. He fails miserably to invest his governmental functions with authority and effectiveness. After he has been tarred and feathered (304) by the people of his excise district, Farrago and Duncan think it prudent to withdraw, though they do not escape the suspicion of having helped the rebels against Federal authority (325). Studied by the philosophical society, Teague is sent on loan to a similar body in France. On his return to the States, he witnesses with Farrago a campaign of slander between two newspaper editors. Soon they are involved in various reform activities, aimed at the church, schools, lawyers, democratic institutions. Teague is a would-be editor (342), a memorialist, the unauthorized auctioneer of an apothecary's wares (373), a Fourth of July orator (402). When it is proposed that he should become a judge (457), someone suggests he might as well be made a devil; a number of coincidences convince the Irishman that he has actually turned into a devil (493), and he disappears. Farrago leaves with a few others to form a new settlement on the frontier (510). On their way they pass through the towns of Lack-Learning and of the Madcaps. The captain becomes governor of the new state (555), while Teague, who has failed as a judge (546), provokes admiration when his cowardice is mistaken for heroism (596). Farrago reestablishes laws and a regular constitution (635), but cannot prevent a number of amendments being proposed, such as extending the suffrage to animals (646) and making them eligible for the legislature (661). A plan to educate the animals is dropped after some fruitless attempts (759); other plans are stopped by Farrago's strongly worded protests (788). At the end he is respected by the citizens and still served, more or less reliably, by Teague.

Monima.—At the beginning of the novel, Monima has just lost her mother and sister through the yellow fever. To support her father and herself, she applies for needlework to Madame Sonnetton (or Sontine), who, however, refuses to give her any. She is apparently afraid that her husband might meet Monima and has the girl taken to the workhouse (chaps. 1-3). After Monima has been released through Sonnetton's agency, both the girl and her father are made prisoners in Sonnetton's country house; they make their way back to town weeks later after suspicion has been aroused and Sonnetton has started investigating (5-9). Sonnetton again helps Monima, though, as previously, without realizing that she is the daughter of Fontanbleu, an old acquaintance of his; nor does he know that his wife is jealous of the girl. Another evil agent has meanwhile appeared: he is called de Noix, and he stimulates Mrs. Sonnetton's jealousy (25); difficulties accumulate for Monima and Fontanbleu. They are made to suffer by society for the very circumstance of their poverty; this prejudice repeatedly draws accusations of theft on Monima (24, 34). She is also once taken to a lunatic asylum (27); released, she is shocked at finding out that the gentleman who has frequently helped her is the husband of her enemy (28). De Noix arranges for Mrs. Sonnetton to find Monima and her husband together (29). In her rage the jealous wife blurts out the whole truth about her schemings against Monima, and even reveals that she and de Noix have been lovers; she dies soon after this. Monima is now pursued by de Noix. Left unprotected after Sonnetton has been made to believe that she is the villain's mistress, she is saved from de Noix by Greenway, who promptly proposes to her (but in vain). De Noix again attempts her virtue, this time she shoots at him. But now she falls ill (33). At long last Sonnetton discovers who she is, and de Noix's machinations are revealed. Monima and Sonnetton marry about the time of the girl's brothers' return (they were thought to have been massacred on Santo Domingo). Chapters 11-23 relate what happened in France between the Fontanbleus and de Noix: Monima's brother Ferdinand won the love of Julia Frenton; jealous de Noix pretended to have thwarted Ferdinand's plan to elope with the girl. Ferdinand was tortured and tried, Julia escaped from de Noix's clutches, and her testimony exonerated

[445]

Ferdinand; but she died soon after the trial, and de Noix killed Ferdinand in a duel. Fontanbleu, also accused of a crime he did not commit, was acquitted only after much suffering.

Moreland Vale.—Eliza Vernon and her father's ward, Henry Walgrove, fall in love. But the present Mrs. Vernon, Eliza's stepmother, makes advances to the young man, who rejects them. The lovers are separated when Walgrove leaves on a West India voyage; Mrs. Vernon is very friendly toward Lovemore. At the death of Vernon, his widow inherits his entire fortune, and within six months she marries Lovemore. The penniless Eliza runs away because Lovemore tries to seduce her, finds shelter with a farmer couple, and next meets the Stanlys, who suspect that Vernon's will must have been a forgery; this belief is shared by another close friend of Vernon, General Preston (pp. 1-60). Lovemore succeeds in carrying Eliza off but is intercepted by Walgrove and his servant Patrick, just back from their voyage (85-102). A witness, O'Needy, confesses that Vernon's will was forged. Lovemore and his wife escape arrest but meet their death in a shipwreck (122-43). Walgrove was tricked by Lovemore on board an East Indiaman and robbed of his passage money. On his voyage to Canton he made friends with Captain Manly and was recommended by the latter to the American merchant Harvey. He next came across a wealthy uncle of his who had treated Walgrove's mother harshly because he did not approve of her husband. After his uncle's death Walgrove returned to New York with the Harveys, whose eldest daughter, Lavinia, was in love with him (29-32, 102-22). When Eliza and Walgrove marry, Lavinia accepts a former suitor of Eliza; they all settle in the same neighborhood as Manly and his wife (164-84). An inserted tale is that of Julius and Juliana. The girl's father, a proud Scotsman, made her believe that her suitor, the Frenchman Julius, was dead. She retired to a convent, but her father confessed his treachery; and she married Julius after all. They settled in a remote mountainous district of Switzerland (143-64).

The Mother-in-Law.—Glorvina De Bowdoin, the granddaughter of a French emigrant who settled in England after the revocation of the Edict of Nantes, marries Francis De Morville, also a member of a French Protestant family. De Morville, vicar of Keswick, has been married before; he divorced his wife, and took their four children with him (chaps. 1-3). His eldest daughter, Nanette, believes that he has treated his first wife badly; without consulting either him or her stepmother, she marries Alonzo, an officer. She sails for Boston with her husband and her mother, who is accompanied by a sergeant, after fraudulently obtaining a portion of De Morville's bank deposit (4-7). De Morville's second daughter, Angelica, becomes Mrs. Charles Granby, whose husband takes up farming near Keswick (7-8). Nanette cruelly suffers as her mother leads a disgraceful life in the army camps before dying of a loathsome disease; and both her husband and the sergeant fall soon after the outbreak of the War of Independence. She expresses her repentance in letters and a diary, then dies in childbirth (9-13). The De Morvilles and Granbys live a harmonious and contented life (14-16); but Glorvina's health makes it necessary for her to travel to France, Switzerland, Germany, and Holland (17-18). She returns just in time to prevent Juliette, De Morville's third daughter, from taking a false step. Glorvina marries her to a brother of Granby, while another takes Harriet, the last of her stepdaughters, for his wife. Glorvina and De Morville have three children of their own. The eldest, Adeline, marries a physician, whose sister later becomes young Francis's wife and whose cousin, a clergyman, marries Laura, the youngest De Morville (19-21). After the vicar's death (20), Glorvina survives for another thirteen years, doing work of charity among French refugees. She is particularly attentive to a lady who is to complete the story of her life and experiences as a mother-in-law. This lady's niece takes the manuscript along when she goes to America, and there the editor obtains possession of it (p. 6, chaps. 22-23).

Ormond.—Stephen Dudley, trained as a painter, reluctantly takes over his father's apothecary business in Philadelphia. He is swindled by Craig, whom he has befriended, loses his wife, becomes a drunkard, and loses his sight. His daughter Constantia tries to make ends meet and contrives to support her father and herself during the crisis of the yellow fever; she must sell her father's lute and a miniature portrait of her friend Sophia Westwyn. But when the honorable Balfour, who has frequently helped the Dudleys, proposes to her, she cannot bring herself to accept him. She hears that Craig is in town and tries to see him; he pacifies her with a fifty-dollar note which turns out to be forged. But this proves a blessing in disguise, for when Constantia appears before Melbourne, J.P., she can convince him that she is innocent of the forgery; and he arranges for some relief for the Dudleys (chaps. 1-11). At this point Constantia meets Ormond, and this gentleman begins to take an interest in her, although Craig has told him that the girl has been seduced by Craig's brother, almost his twin in resemblance (all of which is a fabrication). Ormond finds Constantia better suited to him than Helena, his present mistress. They discuss the moral issue of his seduction of Helena, as well as the whole question of the traditional social and moral institutions, which Ormond dreams of replacing according to the rationalistic schemes of a secret society. Helena, weary of her lot and aware of Ormond's preference for Constantia, takes her own life. The latter, thrown together with a fascinating and mysterious lady, Martinette de Beauvais, is both moved and frightened by her new acquaintance's intrepid and rational conduct. Much disturbed, too, by Ormond, she is planning to go to Europe with her father when Dudley is murdered (12-22). Constantia is now discovered by Sophia, who has come to America in search of her. Sophia assumes the role of her protectress, warning her against the irreligious Ormond. This gentleman surprises Constantia in the lonely house to which she has moved, scares her by confronting her with the corpse of Craig, then announces that he is about to rape her; in self-defense, Constantia kills him (26-29). Chapters 5 and 7 contain stories which illustrate the strange events of plague times, Chapter 20 presents the autobiography of Martinette, whose checkered career has been conditioned by her education, her loves, and her revolutionary views; she has fought in battles like a man. In chapters 23-25 we find the story of Sophia, especially the trials deriving from the various changes of denomination which she has witnessed and been subjected to.

The Power of Sympathy.—This epistolary novel opens with letters exchanged between Harrington and Worthy: the former is planning to seduce Harriot; his friend tries to dissuade him (1-3). Myra, Harrington's sister, is about to marry Worthy and hears from Harriot that the latter is aware of her brother's admiration (4-5). Harrington finds Harriot's virtue too much for him, and Worthy expresses his joy at his friend's conversion to true love (6, 8). Meanwhile, Mrs. Holmes has been introduced; her enthusiastic views about nature are echoed by Worthy when he visits her country home, Belleview (7, 10). The next few letters contain some character sketches from Mrs. Holmes's pen (11-13). Harrington finds his father reluc-

tant to agree to his proposed marriage with Harriot but is still happy
(14-16, 19-20). His sympathies develop; he discusses social rank
and slavery (17-18). Writing to Myra, Mrs. Holmes offers guidance
in matters of education (29-30) and intimates that a match between
Harrington and Harriot may be ill-advised. She insists on this point
(33), is asked to be more explicit (35), and reveals that Harriot is
the half-sister of Myra and Harrington (37). Harrington has been
showing signs of uneasiness and deplored his sensibility (32, 36).
The story of Maria Fawcet is now related: seduced by Mr. Harrington, she died after Harriot's birth; the stress in this account lies
on Mr. Harrington's fear of facing the truth and on Maria's exemplary death (39-40). Harrington, Sr., feels incapable of telling his
son the truth about Harriot (42-43), and Harrington is very much
looking forward to his wedding day when an anonymous letter informs him of Harriot's origin (41, 44). Harriot falls ill (45, 47);
Harrington is baffled and despairing (46, 48) and, after Harriot's
parting letter and death (50-51), increasingly passive, while his
thoughts turn to suicide (48, 50-57). His father dreams of hell, where
he sees himself among the seducers and his son among the suicides
(49). Worthy offers his friend some advice and comfort (58-62).
Letter 63 reports that Harrington has killed himself; his parting letter
(64) expresses his grief over Harriot's death; a concluding letter is
an apology for sensibility (65). Letters 21-25 deal with the seduction
of Ophelia by her brother-in-law Martin, who, however, denies the
affair. Ophelia poisons herself because she feels that she could not
stand the confrontation with Martin on which her father insists. In
two letters (27-28) we are told the story of Fidelia and Henry. Fidelia having been led astray by a friend of his, Henry drowns himself. The girl, restored to the circle of her friends, goes mad when
she hears that Henry is dead.

Precaution.—Two events cause excitement among the family of
Sir Edward Moseley: the arrival of their new neighbors, the Jarvises
(chap. 2), accompanied by Colonel Egerton, and the death of a
traveler, sixty-year old George Denbigh (5). Egerton soon courts
Jane Moseley (6); young Denbigh appears to love her younger sister,
Emily (9). Meanwhile, the eldest, Clara, marries Francis Ives, a
clergyman (8); and her brother John is attracted to Grace Chatterton. Lady Moseley and Lady Chatterton are too eager to get Egerton
and John to propose (17). In the case of Jane the delay is really all

[449]

to the good, for Egerton is suspected of gambling (24); and he proves himself a fortune hunter when he elopes with Mary Jarvis (25). Denbigh's behavior toward Emily and others has been rather peculiar, however (11–12); the girl's aunt, Mrs. Wilson, advises her to refuse his proposal (2:chap. 3). Not long after Emily's suitor has taken his leave, news reaches the Moseleys of the marriage of George Denbigh (2:6). After being introduced to some Denbigh ladies at Bath (2:8) Mrs. Wilson and Emily pay a visit to Chatterton, a former lover of Emily's (1:14), who has married Lady Harriet Denbigh (2:14). There they learn the complex facts about the Denbigh family (2:16-20): there are two George Denbighs, and Emily's is a lord (Pendennyss) who has chosen to use his family name and appear as a commoner, so as to avoid becoming a target for title hunters among young ladies and their mothers. Pendennyss is all the more acceptable to Emily as he has earlier earned the gratitude of Mrs. Wilson without their having ever met. Egerton, known by Denbigh-Pendennyss to have behaved badly toward Mrs. Fitzgerald (2:1), falls at Waterloo (2:23). The heroine can be married to her love, so can John and Grace Chatterton.

The Prisoners of Niagara.—Evermont awakes one morning in the darkness of a prison, that of Fort Niagara. He witnesses the death of his fellow prisoners Anderville and Carmont, and the visits of a lady, rumored to be the mistress of the British commanding officer. She takes a particular interest in Evermont and asks him to write the story of his life for her (1-2). Evermont is eighteen months old when he is found among Indians and entrusted by the finder (whose name he is given) to the Whitfords. At five he runs away, rescues two-year-old Zerelda, and is brought up with her and her cousin Emerine by the latter's parents, the Haylards. At thirteen, about the time of the battle of Lexington, Evermont is sent to Richmond, where he attends college; but he also begins to gamble. He is too intimate with Armilda Willford and with a merchant's daughter named Emerald. He helps Whitford but must interfere when the latter tries to run away with a girl called Amacette. On a visit to the Haylards, he saves Zerelda and Emerine from a group of Indians (3-7). Dismissed by Zerelda, who has been informed of his behavior at Richmond, he twice spends a few days in her company, in two different disguises. She pardons him when he rescues her from a party of Indians and escorts her back to her father's home, fighting off wolves, a panther, thirst, and hunger along the way. He has meanwhile been told the story of Sir William Valindon, and from this has concluded that he must be the illegitimate son of Sir William and Mrs. Willford, Armilda's mother (8-16). Zerelda's father insists that she accept Barville for her fiancé; the girl tries to resist, and his new housekeeper, Mrs. Willford, makes her a prisoner. Evermont is twice challenged for crimes he has not committed; a rumor that he has been killed in a duel reaches Zerelda, and she declares herself willing to marry Barville. Evermont rushes to her to show that he is still alive, but cannot make her retract her promise. He witnesses the beginning of her wedding, then leaves and is seriously ill for a few months. He reads a letter left for him by Huron, a highwayman whom he has wounded, and learns that he must be the son of Huron and Mrs. Willford. In despair, Evermont fights at Yorktown, then joins Carmont who is searching for Amacette; they find and free her, but are made prisoners themselves, and taken to Fort Niagara (17-24). Evermont delivers his manuscript to the lady and receives one in exchange, but cannot read it because unexpectedly he escapes from Fort Niagara. He flees with Evermont, the man who left him with the Whitfords and who has served as a physician at the fort, and an American wearing the uniform of the commanding officer. At Bedford, Pennsylvania, Evermont finds that the lady's manuscript is in the handwriting of Zerelda: carried off from home by Barville (after the latter had broken their engagement and promised to marry Armilda), she has been taken to Fort Niagara, where Barville was in command; she has remained chaste but at the time of writing she has been expecting Barville to try to take her by force. Evermont is close to despair again, but Zerelda turns up: it is she who has been using Barville's uniform as a disguise. A final revelation is made by Huron: he has killed Mrs. Willford in self-defense and has extracted from her, in extremis, the confession that Evermont is the legitimate son of Valindon and his wife Emerine, an aunt of Zerelda's. Many marriages are celebrated at the end of this novel; Evermont and his wife Zerelda emancipate their slaves and outline an educational program for their newborn son (25-27).

Reuben and Rachel.—Don Ferdinando, the son of Columbus and his wife Beatina, marries the South American princess Orrabella. Their surviving daughter Isabella falls in love at first sight, in Madrid, with Sir Thomas Arundel and marries him, in spite of the family prohibition (he is a Protestant). Soon, however, she is widowed when her husband is accused of plotting against Edward VI and executed (1: chaps. 3-9). About 1550, Sir Egbert Gorges, pursued by Bloody Mary, hides in Isabella's castle on the Welsh border and falls in love with her daughter Columbia. Their union is delayed until after the fall of Mary through the wiles of another admirer of Columbia, Sir James Howard. Of the five children of Sir Egbert and Columbia, Elizabeth marries Henry Dudley, the son of Lady Jane Grey, and Beatina marries a Penn (1-2, 10-14). Elizabeth's son, another Henry Dudley, marries his cousin Isabella, daughter of Sir Egbert's eldest son, Sir Ferdinando, but is killed by the jealous grandson of Howard. Isabella's son Edward marries in 1644 and emigrates with his wife Arabella, née Ruthven, to New Hampshire. In 1661 their fifteen-year old son William and their two-year-old daughter Rachel are taken prisoner by Indians. William enjoys the favor of Chief Otooganoo, marries his daughter Oberea and after the chief's death rules his tribe. During an attack on Edward Dudley's settlement William is killed while trying to save his father's life. His son Reuben is then entrusted to Edward's family, who returns to England about 1680. There Reuben marries Cassiah Penn, a distant cousin descended from Beatina Penn, and becomes a Quaker. Ten years later, their two children are born, the twins Reuben and Rachel, but Cassiah dies (15-19). At the age of eighteen the twins are parted. Rachel, unprotected and poor, falls in love with Major Hamden Auberry. They marry secretly, so as not to forfeit the favor of Auberry's aunt, Lady Anne, who has other plans for her nephew. Rachel's unsophisticated and kind behavior, and the envy of some of her acquaintances, cause an estrangement from Auberry, who is led to think her unfaithful. Coincidences keep them apart, but they sail to America at about the same time. When the ship carrying Rachel and her friend Jessy (who loves Reuben) is shipwrecked on the Delaware, Reuben is among those who save the passengers. The young man has come to America to claim the estate held there by his father and a former protégé of his, Jacob Holmes. Finding it impossible to prove that Holmes has appropriated what belongs to Reuben's family, Reuben has fought against the Indians, been taken prisoner, but saved by the half-breed Eumea, and made his way back to Philadelphia. Holmes's widow is now only too glad to restore to Reuben what her late husband has been withholding from him.

Reuben marries Jessy; Rachel and Auberry are reconciled, but Eumea, who was in love with Reuben, drowns herself (2:1-16).

Rosa.—Just after first seeing Rosa, fifty-year-old Mrs. Charmion adopts the little girl under mysterious circumstances: Rosa's house burns down at night; but the girl, gagged and tied to a mattress, is found at some distance, thanks to a flaming arrow shot to the spot. These happenings are later revealed as a device employed in the hope that Mrs. Charmion would behave generously toward the girl. The fire has attracted a journalist, whose erratic behavior causes confusion (chaps. 2, 3, 6). Mrs. Charmion shines to advantage at a dinner party where others are shown in a satirical light; she is the widow of a gentleman who separated from her on the very eve of his death, during the British attack on St. Leonard, Maryland, in 1775. Her daughter was lost to her at that time and was taken to England (1, 4). The following chapter (5) is devoted to Richard Orvaine, a fifteen-year-old youth protected by Mr. Derwent (1). Richard gambles, loses Derwent's money, and runs away. Tricked into paying a bill and nearly blackmailed into forgery, he is rescued by a generous Quaker, then saves a would-be suicide. An employee with a friend of his father in Boston, he reestablishes his reputation for honesty and is sent to England on confidential business. Orvaine returns to Baltimore and wins Rosa's love, thereby thwarting self-assured Belmain as well as Peerwell, a bashful suitor. It then appears that Rosa is the daughter of Sol, a Peruvian who used to serve the Charmions and who took her to England with the missing daughter. This daughter also reappears, married to Longpee; but the latter is none other than Derwent's son, taken away by Mrs. Derwent when she eloped with Longpee, Sr. The affair turned out unhappily; and Mrs. Derwent, after a period of insanity, sought shelter in a French convent (6).

Rosalvo Delmonmort.—Delmonmort is the illegitimate son of Ceceline Monmortency, a clergyman's daughter seduced and abandoned by Henry Fitzalban. Brought up by his Uncle Horatio, Delmonmort causes the latter to lose his stipend by rescuing Eliza Clonton from Lord Elform, for this would-be seducer is the son of the lord on whom Horatio depends (pp. 26-65). In London Delmonmort makes friends with the three children of Lord Bonville, Eugenio, Frances, and Lucinda; and when he is taken in by the rumor that

Eliza has run away with Lord Bellerton, he decides to marry Lucinda (73-138). Actually Eliza has been carried off by Bellerton; but he and Elform are rivals, which causes a confusion that allows Eliza to escape. She is then protected by Eugenio; since there also occurs a mistaken abduction of Eugenio's love, Miss Maretleon, misunderstandings arise between Delmonmort and Eugenio. They are only aggravated after Eliza and Delmonmort have become reconciled, for the young man naturally forgets Lucinda (138-59). A concluding section, however, leads to a general reconciliation and reform, with three weddings: between Delmonmort and Eliza, Eugenio and Angelina (or Miss Maretleon), Bellerton (who is identical with Fitzalban) and Lucinda. Two digressions shed light on the past of Eliza's mother and of Angelina. The former made the mistake of marrying the ambitious and rapacious Charles Napier instead of the sensible, while socially less polished, Eliphalet Waldron (65-73). Angelina, adopted by an Italian family as a child (5-25), is much later discovered to be the daughter of the Count of Roxillion; she was taken away from her family by the evil Mandoni, who also caused jealousy between the count and his wife and attempted to have the countess's brother sentenced to death for the alleged murder of the count. Mandoni at least succeeded in having him exiled to Italy, after administering a slow-working poison to the unfortunate man. When Angelina sees her uncle on his dying bed, she recognizes him as the "man in black" who had intrigued her and her foster parents in Italy (159-75).

St. Herbert.—St. Herbert and Louisa Howard fall in love at first sight. The girl is the ward of Maurisson, who is bitterly hostile to St. Herbert's father because the latter won his love away from him. When Louisa is about to be married to an unloved suitor, she elopes with St. Herbert. The couple lives on the frontier in New York State. Maurisson finds them and asserts that they have been married by a mock clergyman; he then turns St. Herbert out of the house. This proves too much for Louisa, who dies after she has given birth to a daughter, another Louisa. Many years later this girl and Julius Cuthbert fall in love. Julius refrains from proposing because he feels he cannot yet support a wife, and after he has left, Louisa pines away. There are rumors of Julius's engagement to a Southern heiress; and though Louisa finds out that they are not true, she can no longer be saved. Julius shoots himself on her grave. St. Herbert learns to bear all his sufferings stoically from the example of an

Indian who has told him his own humiliations and their beneficial results. The story of St. Herbert is framed by a related tale: The parents of Albudor and Caroline approve of their mutual love without letting them see this. Caroline runs away when her father tells her that she is soon to meet her future husband, since she does not guess that he is talking about Albudor. Her lover finally finds her again near St. Herbert's house where she has taken refuge with St. Herbert's sister, who was formerly married to a Catholic Canadian, for which she was repudiated by her family.

St. Hubert.—This story, told in a spirit of true repentance, is the confession of Father Nicholas. Dying, he looks back on a life that has brought misery and death to his wife and child. His mother was responsible for his education but was rather indulgent with him. St. Hubert goes to Paris and there comes under the influence of an envious companion, Delaserre, who lives a dissipated life. St. Hubert's susceptibility to all that is good and honorable reasserts itself, however, when he meets and marries Emilia de Santonges. They first live in the country, then move to Paris. There St. Hubert unfortunately meets Delaserre again and resumes his former habits. Madame de Treuville, who takes part in the gambling, becomes St. Hubert's mistress. She advances him money, but when pressed herself, causes him to sell his estate. Ruined, St. Hubert deserts his wife and child, who presently die. He falls ill and is comforted and converted by a monk, assuming the name of Father Nicholas for the rest of his life.

Sarah.—The main body of this epistolary novel covers the years between 1775 and 1780 in the lives of Sarah and her husband Darnley (letters 1-33, pp. 3-242). Sarah has agreed to marry Darnley though she does not love him. Darnley knows this but he is sure that his wife will gradually learn to love him. He, however, soon resumes an affair with Jessey, who has just returned from the convent to which her husband (now dead) had sent her. Jessey does all she can to stir up trouble between Sarah and Darnley; when Darnley finds himself in jail because of his improvidence, he is ready to blame his wife for this. They separate, and Sarah tries to earn a living in Ireland, only to find herself exposed to the cruelty of wicked and unscrupulous women and the ambiguous attentions of a gentleman. Reconciled, Sarah and Darnley settle on a Warwickshire farm, thanks to the intervention of Sarah's Irish admirer, who also provides a job for

Darnley. The final pages (letters 34-38, pp. 242-69) relate Darnley's short-lived reform and the final sufferings of Sarah until she is relieved by death at the end of 1793. Retribution hits the wicked: one of the O'Donnell women who made life difficult for Sarah in Ireland leads a sinful life and dies young; and Jessey and Darnley marry, to their predictable mutual wretchedness. Included in the first part of the novel are a flashback of the beginning of the Jessey-Darnley affair (letters 8-12, pp. 39-68) and a narration of Sarah's early years: her unhappiness at her mother's death, the irresponsibility of her father, her separation from her adopted brother, the hard-heartedness of her relatives, and her exhaustion through over-conscientious school-teaching—these are some of her experiences (letters 2-7, pp. 8-39).

Secret History.—The narrator, Mary, writes from Santo Domingo in 1802, touching chiefly upon four topics: the latent and active violence of the black population; the fears of the white inhabitants and their dissatisfaction with the French troops supposed to protect them; the intrigues between officers and ladies; and the general character of the town and of the Creole ladies. Orphaned at an early age, Mary was separated from her sister Clara. After the death of her fiancé, she had the good fortune of being assisted by Aaron Burr. She is now staying with Clara, who is married to St. Louis, a Frenchman with an irascible temper. Clara is a coquette, and is happiest when receiving the attentions of several gentlemen. General Rochambeau's pursuit of her, which greatly angers St. Louis, is, however, too insistent. Clara agrees to being speedily shipped off to Cuba, but Rochambeau temporarily stops all outgoing shipping (letters 1-14, pp. 1-104). When the sisters are allowed to leave, their ship is promptly intercepted by British vessels. Mary and Clara are taken to Barracoa, a Spanish possession, and from there sent to St. Iago, Cuba, where St. Louis joins them. His jealousy is soon fired again, and Mary feels that she cannot blame Clara for finally running away from her husband (letters 15-24, pp. 105-63). Mary moves on to Kingston, Jamaica, where she is rather impressed by Don Carlos, who needs consolation after having given up his love to a viceroy. Clara writes that she left St. Louis after he had threatened to disfigure her; she has been hiding from her husband, but a Spanish admirer has found her hiding place. She is about to leave for Portici, from where she is to sail for Kingston. The final letter mentions Clara's safe arrival and the sisters' plan to leave for Philadelphia, where they will place themselves under Burr's protection (letters 25-32, pp. 164-225).

The Soldier's Orphan.—On the day she is born, Emily Thompson loses both her mother and her father, who is killed in the battle of Quebec (December 31, 1775) (chap. 1). She lives with her mother's sister, the wife of Morris the sea captain, and receives an excellent education. She is never made to feel her dependence on the Morrises nor allowed to forget her parents (2-4). When she is of an age to attract men, her thoroughly moral education, as well as the careful selection of her friends by her aunt, keep away any undesirable suitors. She feels happy in the company of two of her Boston cousins, Robert Center and Augustus Robinson (4-6). Mrs. Morris's misgivings before her husband's last voyage prove justified, for she is dead by the time he returns. Center and Morris have been captured by Algerians but are quickly rescued from their slavery (9-13). Morris recovers from the shock of his wife's death and advises Emily to marry Center; the story ends on a gesture of reverence toward Emily's parents (14-16). A defense of marriage (7-8) and a disquisition on the foolishness of contemporary fashions (10) are among the topics introduced during the course of Emily's education.

The Spiritual Voyage.—The *Convert* weathers storms, loses and replaces part of her crew, overcomes various enemy vessels, keeps away from some others whose crews are not equally convinced of the Christian precepts she has made her own, and finally reaches the haven of Felicity, after stops at Point Comfort, Ordinance, Securehope, and Perseverance.

The Step-Mother.—Caroline Williams, a clergyman's daughter, loses her mother at the age of twelve, but is befriended some time later by Lady Glanvile. At seventeen she is entrusted with the education of the two Glanvile girls, Lucy and Maria (chaps. 1-3). There is some unpleasantness over the dismissal of their former governess, Mrs. Wilson; but Caroline is more seriously worried about the declarations of love from young Edward Glanvile (4). Though she loves him, she refuses to encourage him because of her humble social rank. Edward leaves for the Continent, while the heroine moves to Liverpool to live with a cousin, Mrs. Belton (5). She rejects the unwelcome proposal of the recently widowed Mr. Brummell, forces herself again to refuse Edward, and, in order to protect herself, becomes the wife of Wentworth, a sea-captain and widower with four daughters (10, 12). Edward dies; his last letters are brought to Caroline by Dr. Belton, her cousin's nephew who has inherited Mrs. Belton's fortune (13, 14). Belton is later to be an unsuccessful candidate for Caroline's hand (21) after Wentworth has been drowned (15); he is Caroline's steadfast friend throughout and finally becomes her son-in-law (35). Caroline's elder stepdaughters cause her no trouble, but the younger two are persuaded by the devious Miss Hartley and their guardian Caldwall to leave their mother's home in the country and go to London (25). Theirs is however a harmless escapade into the dangerous city world, and they soon learn to repent having listened to Miss Hartley, who had herself been influenced by Mrs. Wilson (28). They eventually marry Campbell and Montgomery, respectively (35). The various gentlemen who become Caroline's sons-in-law have had distressful experiences. Thus Campbell, believing that Belton had been having an affair with his sister, Mrs. Malcolm (33), challenged him; they wounded each other seriously, which gave them time for reflection. Mrs. Malcolm's adultery (with a cousin, not Belton) can be explained by the unhappy marriage imposed upon her during the absence of her faithful lover, Montgomery (21, 22, 29). Mrs. Malcolm died when she heard about the duel (34), and her calculating mother survived her only a short time (35).

Symzonia.—Captain Seaborn starts out on August 1, 1817, on a voyage to the South Pole. His vessel stops at the Falkland Islands before crossing the ice belt in latitude 78° S. Part of the crew is left on the continent found further south (chap. 4), while Seaborn proceeds with the intention "of sailing into the globe at the south pole, and of returning by way of the north pole, if no land intervened to obstruct the passage." Inside the earth, whose inner surface reflects the sunbeams like the moon, Seaborn and his companions discover land, which they call Symzonia (7). The Symzonians are lighter in complexion than the inhabitants of the earth. They are morally superior beings, whose values actually govern their actions and whose technical skills are applied only to what is truly profitable and beneficial to everyone. They find much that is despicable and base in the humans' habits and pursuits, and Seaborn and his crew are therefore sent back with the distinct understanding that they are not to return to the interior of the globe (15). Seaborn tries to raise himself and his compatriots in the Symzonians' estimation by casting aspersions on the character of other nations (chiefly the British) and hopes to establish commercial relations between his country and the inner world; but he is nevertheless ordered to sail from Symzonia on August 13, 1818. He picks up the rest of his crew, crosses the ice-belt, and, on his way to Canton, makes his fellow passengers promise to keep their discoveries a secret (18). A providential storm kills Slim, the only member of the crew who would not keep quiet about Symzonia, but also causes the loss of all the evidence of their discoveries. Finally the captain is swindled out of his profits by his agent, Mr. Slippery (whom he had ill-advisedly preferred to Mr. Worthy), and publishes *Symzonia* to earn some money (20).

Trials of the Human Heart.—Meriel leaves her convent school to be present during the last days of her godmother's life and remains with her family after Mrs. Mirvan's death. Her brother Richard envies her because of the few thousand pounds she has inherited from Mrs. Mirvan. Her father is having an affair with Mrs. Talbot, but Meriel's innocence and purity convince Mrs. Talbot that she must leave. Meriel is introduced to the world of romances; she behaves according to the pattern of these books when she thinks that she is in love, and her mother is angry about it. Her father tries to make love to her, and Meriel runs away. She is found again; and thereafter, her mother treats her with suspicion, and her father is harsh (letters 1-9, Apr. 20-Sept. 9, 1775). Howard is ruined and takes his family to London, where his sister is living with her husband, Mossop, and their two daughters. One of these, Hester, feels jealous when Frederic Rainsforth proposes to Meriel. Various circumstances delay the wedding; while Meriel is awaiting Rainsforth's coming eighteen months later, she hears through a friend of Hester that he has married an heiress named Kingly (10-25, December 19, 1775-May 17, 1778). Howard's debts land him in jail with his wife and daughter; soon after, Meriel's parents die. The girl is protected by Welldon; then works with a milliner, Mrs. Lacour; but is accused of having an affair with Lacour. She fares well with a milliner's shop of her own until she is swindled by her friend Mrs. Moreton. Fortunately, she can renew her friendship with Amelia Sidney and meet Mr. and Mrs. Kingly, her former lover and his wife, who have assumed the heiress's surname. They seem surprised to find Meriel unmarried; the girl pretends to be frivolous, so as not to cause

Kingly any regrets, but also informs his wife of the love she still feels for Kingly (26-38, May 29, 1778-March 3, 1781). A companion to Mrs. Rooksby, Meriel decides to marry her son Clement Rooksby in order to save the lady from worrying about him and, at the same time, to separate him from his mistress, a married woman named Clara who has been neglecting her three children. After they have been married for some time, her husband meets Clara, poor and ill. Meriel seeks her out to help her and finds that Clara is none other than Mrs. Moreton (39-45, March, 1781-June 10, 1783). Rooksby and Clara resume their affair; the latter travels with the Rooksbys to France, where they are to attend the wedding of Amelia and Rooksby's nephew. A storm during the crossing gives Kingly an opportunity to save Meriel's life, while Rooksby looks only after Clara. Mrs. Kingly dies, and Rooksby suddenly becomes violently jealous of Kingly, wounds him in a duel, and flees to Italy. Meriel returns to Glamorganshire alone, while Kingly slowly recovers and then leaves for America (46-57, June 10, 1783-Aug. 29, 1784). Meriel sees her husband again when he is ill and in prison. Their daughter Clementina dies; but even in her utmost misery, Meriel resists the temptation of leaving Rooksby. She meets Mrs. Harcourt and is suddenly restored to ease and comfort, for she is Mrs. Harcourt's daughter, and not a Howard. Richard finds out that the Miss Alton he has been vainly courting is his own half sister, the daughter of Howard and Mrs. Talbot. Rooksby then dies, and Meriel marries Kingly; but Clara and the Mossops must confess their various misdeeds (58-70, Dec. 13, 1788-Sept. 29, 1791). Clara's story (as told by herself) is a romantic tissue of lies, in which she appears as a victimized girl (46). Another pathetic story is that of Harriet Venables, who elopes from a convent with Rooksby when he is married to Meriel and carrying on with Clara; she is left alone when he runs off to Italy (62). The Harcourts married secretly; their child Meriel was brought up in the place of Mrs. Howard's child who had just died. Harcourt, sent off to India by his suspicious family, was re-united to his wife years later in Constantinople, where she had been kept in the Sultan's seraglio (77).

The Unfortunate Lovers and Cruel Parents.—The New England merchant Beaumont goes bankrupt and sends his son Samuel to Europe to try and retrieve their fortune. Samuel is shipwrecked, and a nobleman's daughter falls in love with him. He remains true

[460]

to Nancy Gauze, though Nancy's father has broken off their engagement after the Beaumonts' bankruptcy; and the nobleman's daughter dies of a broken heart, bequeathing all her wealth to Samuel. The young man returns to America on the eve of Nancy's wedding, devised by Gauze, but he is able to run away with the girl, and they are married.

The Vain Cottager.—Lucy Franklin is frequently complimented on her pretty face and later given the castoff dresses of a lady to wear. She does well at school and flirts a little; yet she honestly loves Ned Symmonds and is about to become engaged to him when she is apprenticed to a milliner. The pretty clothes turn her head; she wears the latest fashions, attracts attention, is seduced, and then deserted with her baby. By hard work Lucy gradually regains the respect of her fellow citizens; but Ned has, in the meantime, married her sister.

Wieland.—The elder Wieland, descended from a Saxon family, is apprenticed to a London merchant. He accidentally discovers, as a form of distraction, the reading of the Bible, which he learns to interpret along narrow, sectarian lines. Intending to become a missionary, he emigrates to America; later in his life he is obsessed with the idea that he has not accomplished his task adequately. Wieland cultivates a brooding sort of religion, often retiring to a pavillion; it is there that he is found one night, his body covered with burns. He dies soon after, apparently the victim of spontaneous combustion. His son Theodore has a rather gloomy disposition, which also affects his religious views; but he can be as sociable as his sister Clara. When Wieland marries Catharine Pleyel, Clara moves to a house near the Wieland home. She and her brother's family often meet at the pavillion, together with Catharine's brother Henry and Louisa. This girl, brought up with the Wielands, is discovered to be the daughter of a Major Stuart, whose wife ran away with her because she felt that the attentions of one Maxwell had quite alienated her from her husband (chaps. 1-4). Maxwell is later presumably responsible for the murder of Stuart (27). Once when alone and once when together with Pleyel, Wieland hears a mysterious voice dissuading him from some project. A few days later Clara is frightened by the voices of men apparently discussing her murder; she runs to Wieland's house, where she faints on the doorstep. A voice then calls on the inhabitants of the house to look after her. Not long after, as Clara is in her summer house, a voice shouting "Hold! Hold!" cuts into her nightmare, in which Wieland threatens her; and a disembodied voice advises her to stay away from the summer house and to keep silent about her experiences with the voice. The same voice tries to dissuade her from entering a room, from which Carwin presently emerges. Carwin, whose first appearance at the Wielands' has made a disturbing impression on Clara, states that he has been planning to rape her, then vanishes; the girl is afraid to open her door when someone knocks some time later (4-10). On the following morning she is accused by Pleyel of having an affair with Carwin, who, it is now learned, is being sought because of crimes he has committed in Europe. Now, Clara is in love with Pleyel, though the young man is engaged to a German baroness named Theresa; she denies Pleyel's charges, but he replies that he overheard a revealing conversation between her and Carwin on the night before and that he had begun even before to suspect her of being in love (11-14). Carwin offers to explain his conduct, and Clara agrees to meet him at her house that same evening. Once again a voice warns her not to enter her room, but she disregards it and discovers the body of Catharine there. Wieland soon joins her and talks rather confusedly about superior commands; he disappears when people are heard approaching. Clara is seriously ill for a while; and when she recovers, she learns that it is Wieland (and not Carwin) who murdered Catharine, as well as his children and Louisa: he thought himself ordered to express with a sacrifice his gratitude to the Supreme Being who had put an end to his doubts and given him a strong faith instead. Wieland has since been placed in a lunatic asylum (15-20). Carwin next tells Clara his story. He possesses the gift of ventriloquism, but has tried not to use it; at the Wielands' home, however, he had to make use of it, so as not to be found at the pavillion, where he had no business to be. Later he employed the "mysterious voice" for selfish purposes: he wanted to scare Clara away from the summer house because he used to meet her servant Judith there, whereas the conversation overheard by Pleyel was devised as a test of Pleyel's rational conceptions. As Carwin completes his confession, Wieland appears; Clara tells him that he has mistaken Carwin's tricks for manifestations of a Superior Being. But Wieland is completely convinced of this only when Carwin tells him of instances of his interference; he realizes that he has been the prey of inner delusions as well as of Carwin's spurious supernaturalism, and he kills himself. Carwin disappears, and Clara is taken to Europe (21-26). At Montpellier, three years later, she seems about to marry Pleyel, now a widower (27).

Bibliography

THIS bibliography is, of course, selective. In one respect only
has completeness been attempted: all the American works of
fiction discussed in this study are listed in Section One, together with other works by the authors of fiction which may be considered useful background reading. Section Two is a sampling of
complementary sources which may contribute to a better understanding of the contemporary American literary and cultural scene,
"contemporary" being stretched to embrace a generation or so after
1820. These titles have been chosen for the information they offer
or the manner they use. Thus Dwight's writings have much to say
about current issues of the day, and their strongly-worded opinions
suggest clashes with opponents as dogmatic as Dwight, while Allen's
Narrative or the Burrs' correspondence illustrate, above all, modes of
literary expression which were characteristic of the age. Section
Three lists book and articles that have been generally serviceable.
It naturally includes certain literary histories frequently referred to,
but also books and articles devoted to individual writers and aspects
which have been useful, beyond the discussion of their immediate
subject, through their suggestive effect—perhaps a comparison or the
outline of a general background. Otherwise, this bibliography has
tried to avoid duplication of material found elsewhere in the present
study. Books and articles with a specific relevance to individual
authors and issues are mentioned only in the footnotes, and "obvious"
books have been omitted (especially handbooks and reference works).
Some items published after 1967 have been added for the sake of
completeness.

An (R) marks the editions referred to in the text where more
than one edition of any given work is listed here. Unless stated
otherwise, the titles published through 1820 are first editions.

Section One

Adelio [pseud.] *A Journey to Philadelphia; or, Memoirs of Charles Coleman Saunders.* Hartford, Conn., 1804.
Adventures in a Castle. Harrisburg, Pa., 1806.
Adventures of Jonathan Corncob, Loyal American Refugee. London, 1787.
Amelia; or, The Faithless Briton. Boston, 1798.
American Bee, The; a Collection of Entertaining Stories. Leominster, Mass., 1797.
[Belknap, Jeremy.] *The Foresters, an American Tale.* Boston, 1792. 2d ed., revised and considerably enlarged. Boston, 1796 (R).
———. *American Biography.* 2 vols. Boston, 1794-98.
[Bigelow, Jacob, and Nathan Hale.] *The War of the Gulls.* New York, 1812.
Bleecker, Ann Eliza. *The Posthumous Works of Ann Eliza Bleecker, in Prose and Verse.* New York, 1793. (This contains "The History of Maria Kittle," pp. 19-87, and "The Story of Henry and Anne," pp. 89-114.
Bloomfield, Obadiah Benjamin Franklin; *see* Franklin, Edward.
Botsford, Edmund. *The Spiritual Voyage.* Philadelphia, 1819.
[Botsford, Margaret.] *Adelaide.* 2 vols. Philadelphia, 1816.
Brackenridge, Hugh Henry. *Modern Chivalry.* Part I: Vol. 1, Philadelphia, 1792; Vol. 2, Philadelphia, 1793; Vol. 3, Pittsburgh, 1793; Vol. 4, Philadelphia, 1797. Part II: Vols. 1-2, Carlisle, Pa., 1804-5; Vol. 4 [sic], Philadelphia, 1815. Subsequent editions: Edited with introduction, chronology, and bibliography by Claude M. Newlin (1937). Reprint. New York: Hafner Publishing Co., 1962 (R); Edited for the Modern Reader by Lewis Leary, New Haven, Conn.: College and University Press, 1965.
———. *Gazette Publications.* Carlisle, Pa., 1806.
Bradford, Ebenezer. *The Art of Courting.* Newburyport, Mass., 1795.
[Brown, Charles Brockden.] *Alcuin; a dialogue.* New York, 1798 (R). Subsequent editions: A Type-Facsimile Reprint of the first edition...with an introduction by LeRoy Elwood Kimball. New Haven: Carl and Margaret Rollins, 1935, under the title of *Alcuin.*
———. *Arthur Mervyn; or, Memoirs of the Year 1793.* Philadelphia, 1799; second part, New York, 1800. Subsequent edition:

[466]

Edited with an introduction by Warner Berthoff. New York: Holt, Rinehart & Winston, 1962 (R).

——. *Clara Howard.* Philadelphia, 1801.

——. *Edgar Huntly; or, Memoirs of a Sleep-Walker.* 3 vols. Philadelphia, 1799. Subsequent edition: Edited with an introduction by David Lee Clark. New York: Macmillan, 1928 (R).

——. *Jane Talbot.* Philadelphia, 1801.

——. *Ormond; or, The Secret Witness.* New York, 1799. Subsequent edition: Edited with an introduction, chronology, and bibliography by Ernest Marchand (1937). Reprint. New York: Hafner Publishing Co., 1962 (R).

Brown, Charles Brockden. *The Rhapsodist and Other Uncollected Writings.* Edited by Harry R. Warfel. New York: Scholars' Facsimiles and Reprints, 1943.

[Brown, Charles Brockden.] *Wieland; or, The Transformation.* New York, 1798.

——. *Wieland or the Transformation. Together with Memoirs of Carwin the Biloquist.* Edited with an introduction by Fred Lewis Pattee, 1926. Reprint. New York: Hafner Publishing Co., 1960 (R).

Brown, Charles Brockden; *see* Dunlap, William.

[Brown, William Hill.] "Harriot; or, The Domestic Reconciliation," *Massachusetts Magazine* 1, no. 1 (1789):3-7.

Brown, William Hill. *Ira and Isabella; or the Natural Children.* Boston, 1807.

[Brown, William Hill.] *The Power of Sympathy; or, The Triumph of Nature.* 2 vols. Boston, 1789 (R). Subsequent editions: Edited by Walter Littlefield. Boston, 1894; edited by Milton Ellis. New York: Facsimile Text Society, 1937; with an introduction by Herbert Brown. Boston: New Frontiers Press, 1961; definitive edition edited by William S. Kable. Columbus: Ohio State University Press, 1969.

Butler, James. *Fortune's Foot-ball: or, the Adventures of Mercutio.* 2 vols. Harrisburgh, Pa., 1797-98.

Celadon [pseud.] *The Golden Age: or, Future Glory of North-America...Vision I.* 1785.

[Clopper, Jonas.] *Fragments of the History of Bawlfredonia...By Herman Thwackius.* 1819.

Collection of Moral and Entertaining Stories, A. Northampton, Mass., 1798.

[Cooper, James Fenimore.] *Precaution.* 2 vols. New York, 1820.
Cooper, James Fenimore. *Early Critical Essays (1820-22).* Facsimile
Reproductions, with an introduction by James F. Beard, Jr.
Gainesville, Fla.: Scholars' Facsimiles and Reprints, 1955.
————. *A Letter to His Countrymen.* New York, 1834.
————. *The Letters and Journals of James Fenimore Cooper.*
Edited by James Franklin Beard. 6 vols. Cambridge, Mass.:
Harvard University Press, 1960-68.
————. *Notions of the Americans.* 2 vols. Philadelphia, 1828.
[Dennie, Joseph.] *The Lay Preacher; or Short Sermons, for Idle
Readers.* Walpole, N.H., 1796 (R). Subsequent edition:
Edited with an introduction and bibliographical note by Milton
Ellis. New York: Scholars' Facsimiles and Reprints, 1943.
(Contains the 1796 and 1817 collections of Lay Preacher
essays.)
————. *The Spirit of the Farmer's Museum, and Lay Preacher's
Gazette.* Walpole, N.H., 1801.
[Digges, Thomas Atwood.] *Adventures of Alonso...By a Native
of Maryland. . .* 2 vols. London, 1775. Subsequent edition: In
Facsimile, edited by Thomas J. MacMahon. New York: U. S.
Catholic Historical Society, 1943 (including the article "The
First American Novel," by Robert H. Elias) (R).
[Douglass, Adam?] *The Irish Emigrant.* 2 vols. Winchester, Va.,
1817.
Eugenius and Selima: or, The Fatal Effects of Parental Tyranny.
West Springfield, Mass., 1798.
Fidelity Rewarded; or The History of Polly Granville. Boston, 1796.
Fidfaddy, Frederick Augustus, Esq. [pseud.] *The Adventures of
Uncle Sam, in Search after His Lost Honor.* Middleton, Conn.,
1816.
[Finch, John?] *The Soldier's Orphan.* New York, 1812.
Fortunate Discovery, The. Or, The History of Henry Villars [by
the author of *Moreland Vale*]. New York, 1798.
[Foster, Hannah Webster.] *The Boarding School; or, Lessons of a
Preceptress to her Pupils.* Boston, 1798.
————. *The Coquette; or, the History of Eliza Wharton.* Boston,
1797 (R). Subsequent edition: Edited by Herbert Ross Brown.
New York: Facsimile Text Society, 1939.
Fowler, George. *A Flight to the Moon; or, The Vision of Randalthus.*
Baltimore, 1813.

———. *The Wandering Philanthropist; or Lettres* [sic] *from a Chinese*. Philadelphia, 1810.

[Franklin, Edward?] *The Life and Adventures of Obadiah Benjamin Franklin Bloomfield*. Philadelphia, 1818.

Freneau, Philip. "Father Bombo's Pilgrimage." Edited by Lewis Leary. *PMHB* 66(1942):459-78.

[Freneau, Philip.] *Letters on Various Interesting and Important Subjects...By Robert Slender*. Philadelphia, 1799. Subsequent edition: Edited by H. H. Clark. New York: Scholars' Facsimiles and Reprints, 1943.

Freneau, Philip. *The Miscellaneous Works of Mr. Philip Freneau*. Philadelphia, 1788.

———. *The Prose of Philip Freneau*. Selected and edited by Philip M. Marsh. New Brunswick, N.J.: Scarecrow Press, 1955.

———. *The Poems of Philip Freneau*. Edited by F. L. Pattee. 3 vols. Princeton, N.J.: Princeton University Press, 1902-7.

———. *The Last Poems of Philip Freneau*. Edited by Lewis Leary. New Brunswick, N.J.: Rutgers University Press, 1945.

Gambler, The, or Memoirs of a British Officer. 2d ed. Washington City, 1802.

Hapless Orphan, The; or, Innocent Victim of Revenge. 2 vols. Boston, 1793.

History of Constantius and Pulchera, The; or Constancy Rewarded. 3d ed. Norwich, Conn., 1796.

Hitchcock, Enos. *The Farmer's Friend, or the History of Mr. Charles Worthy*. Boston, 1793.

———. *Memoirs of the Bloomsgrove Family*. 2 vols. Boston, 1790.

———. *A Discourse on Education*. Providence, R.I., n.d.

[Holman, Jessee L.] *The Prisoners of Niagara, or Errors of Education*. Frankfort, Ky., 1810.

Hopkinson, Francis. *The Miscellaneous Essays and Occasional Writings*. 3 vols. Philadelphia, 1792. (Contains a revised version of "A Pretty Story.")

[Hopkinson, Francis.] *A Pretty Story: Written in the Year of Our Lord 2774, by Peter Grievous, Esq., A.B.C.D.E. [pseud.]*. Philadelphia, 1774. In *American Prose (1607-1865)*. Edited by Walter C. Bronson. Chicago: University of Chicago Press, 1916. Pp. 183-97.

Humanity in Algiers: or, The Story of Azem. Troy, N.Y., 1801.

Imlay, Gilbert. *The Emigrants, &c. or The History of an Expatriated*

[469]

Family. 3 vols. London, 1793 (R). Subsequent edition: *The Emigrants. Traditionally ascribed to G. I., but, more probably, by Mary Wollstonecraft.* Facsimile reproduction of the Dublin edition of 1794 with an introduction by Robert H. Hare. Gainesville, Fla.: Scholars' Facsimiles & Reprints, 1964.

―――. *A Topographical Description of the Western Territory of North America.* London, 1792.

[Ingersoll, Charles Jared.] *Inchiquin, the Jesuit's Letters.* New York, 1810.

Ingersoll, Charles Jared. *A Discours[e] concerning the Influence of America on the Mind.* Philadelphia, 1823.

Irish Emigrant, The; see Douglass, Adam.

[Irving, Peter.] *Giovanni Sbogarro. A Venetian Tale.* "Taken from the French. By Percival G―." 2 vols. New York, 1820.

[Irving, Washington.] *A History of New York...By Diedrich Knickerbocker.* 2 vols. New York, 1809 (R). 2d ed. New York, 1812. Subsequent editions: *Diedrich Knickerbocker's A History of New York.* Edited by S. T. Williams and Tremaine McDowell. New York: Harcourt, Brace, 1927; edited for the Modern Reader by Edwin T. Bowden. New York: Twayne, 1964.

[Irving, Washington.] *Letters of Jonathan Oldstyle, Gent.* New York, 1824 (R). Subsequent edition (which includes a letter not reproduced in the 1824 edition): Edited by S. T. Williams. New York: Facsimile Text Society, 1941.

Irving, Washington. *Letters of Washington Irving to Henry Brevoort.* Edited by George S. Hellman. New York: G. P. Putnam's Sons, 1918.

―――. *Notes while Preparing Sketch Book &c. (1817).* Edited by S. T. Williams (with a critical introduction). New Haven, Conn.: Yale University Press, 1927.

[Irving, Washington.] *The Sketch Book of Geoffrey Crayon, Gent.* New York, 1819-20.

Irving, Washington. *Washington Irving's Contributions to "The Corrector".* With an introduction and attribution by Martin Roth. Minneapolis: University of Minnesota Press, 1968.

[Irving, Washington, William Irving, and James Kirke Paulding.] *Salmagundi; or, The Whim-Whams and Opinions of Launcelot Langstaff, Esq. and Others.* 2 vols. New York, 1807-8.

[Jenks, William.] *Memoir of the Northern Kingdom, Written, A.D.*

1872, by the Late Rev. Williamson Jahnsenykes. "Quebeck, A.D. 1901" [Boston, 1808] (R). Reprinted in *The Magazine of History with Notes and Queries* 39, no. 2, Extra No. 154. Tarrytown, N.Y.: William Abbatt, 1929.

[Knapp, Samuel Lorenzo.] *Extracts from a Journal of Travels in North America...By Ali Bey.* Boston, 1818.

———. *Extracts from the Journals of Marshal Soult.* Newburyport, Mass., 1817.

Knapp, Samuel Lorenzo. *American Cultural History, 1607-1829.* A facsimile reproduction of *Lectures on American Literature* (1829). With an introduction and index by R. B. Davis and Ben H. McClary. Gainesville, Fla.: Scholars' Facsimiles & Reprints, 1961.

Ladd, Russell, comp. *The History of Albert and Eliza.* Philadelphia, 1812.

Life and Times of Father Quipes, The; see McFarland, John.

Life of Alexander Smith, The; see Sargent, Charles.

[McFarland, John?] *The Life and Times of Father Quipes, otherwise Dominick O'Blarney. Written by Himself.* Carlisle, Pa., 1820.

[Mann, Herman.] *The Female Review: or, Memoirs of an American Young Lady.* Dedham, Mass., 1797 (R).

Mann, Herman. *Life of Deborah Sampson, the Female Soldier in the War of the Revolution.* Introduction and notes by John Adams Vinton. Boston, 1866.

Mannering, Guy [pseud.] *Rosalvo Delmonmort.* Boston, 1818.

Manvill, Mrs. P. D. *Lucinda, or the Mountain Mourner.* Johnstown, N.Y., 1807. 2d ed. (with additions). Ballston Spa, N.Y., 1810 (R).

Margaretta; or, the Intricacies of the Heart. Philadelphia, 1807.

[Markoe, Peter.] *The Algerine Spy in Pennsylvania.* Philadelphia, 1787.

Mitchell, Isaac. *The Asylum; or, Alonzo and Melissa.* 2 vols. Poughkeepsie, N.Y., 1811.

Moreland Vale; or the Fair Fugitive [by the author of *The Fortunate Discovery*]. New York, 1801.

[Morgan, Joseph.] *The History of the Kingdom of Basaruah.* Boston, 1715.

Morgan, Joseph. *The History of the Kingdom of Basaruah, and Three Unpublished Letters. By Joseph Morgan.* Edited (with an introduction) by Richard Schlatter. Cambridge, Mass.: Harvard University Press, 1946 (R).

Murphy, Francis, comp. *Tales of an Evening*. Norristown, Pa., 1815.

Murray, Judith Sargent. *The Gleaner: A Miscellaneous Production by Constantia* [*pseud.*] 3 vols. Boston, 1798.

[Neal, John.] *Keep Cool.* 2 vols. Baltimore, 1817.

Neal, John. *American Writers.* A series of papers contributed to *Blackwood's Magazine* (1824-25). Edited (with notes and bibliography) by F. L. Pattee. Durham, N.C.: Duke University Press, 1937.

Patterson, Mrs. *The Unfortunate Lovers, and Cruel Parents....The Seventeenth Edition.* Random[?], 1797.

[Paulding, James Kirke.] *The Diverting History of John Bull and Brother Jonathan. By Hector Bull-us.* New York, 1812.

――――. *Letters from the South.* 2 vols. New York, 1817.

――――. *Salmagundi. Second Series. By Launcelot Langstaff, Esq.* 2 vols. New York, 1819-20. (Quotations from the *Salmagundi* article "American Literature" are from Spiller, ed., *Literary Revolution.*)

――――. *John Bull in America; or, the New Munchausen.* New York, 1825.

――――. *Koningsmarke, the Long Finne.* 2 vols. New York, 1823.

Paulding, James Kirke. *The Letters of James Kirke Paulding.* Edited by Ralph M. Aderman. Madison: University of Wisconsin Press, 1962.

[Paulding, James Kirke.] *Sketch of Old England, by a New-England Man.* 2 vols. New York, 1822.

――――. *The United States and England.* New York, 1815.

[Peters, Samuel.] *A General History of Connecticut...By a Gentleman of the Province.* London, 1781 (R).

――――. *The Works of Samuel Peters of Hebron, Conn....(1735-1826).* Edited by Kenneth W. Cameron. Hartford, Conn.: Transcendental Books, 1967.

[Pope, Eliza.] *Henry and Julietta, or Virtue Rewarded.* New York, 1818.

[Read, Martha.] *Monima; or, the Beggar Girl.* 2d ed. New York, 1803.

[Relf, Samuel.] *Infidelity, or the Victims of Sentiment.* Philadelphia, 1797.

Robber, The, or Sons of Night. Weathersfield, Conn., 1816.

Rosa; or, American Genius and Education. New York, 1810.

Rowson, Susanna Haswell. *Charlotte. A Tale of Truth.* 2 vols. Philadelphia, 1794 (R). Subsequent editions: Edited by Francis W. Halsey. New York, London: Funk & Wagnalls, 1905; edited for the Modern Reader by Clara M. and Rudolf Kirk. New York: Twayne, 1964.

————. *Charlotte's Daughter: or, The Three Orphans.* Boston, 1828.

————. *The Fille de Chambre.* Philadelphia, 1794.

————. *The Inquisitor; or, Invisible Rambler.* 3 vols. Philadelphia, 1793.

————. *Mentoria; or the Young Lady's Friend.* 2 vols. Philadelphia, 1794.

————. *Reuben and Rachel; or, Tales of Old Times.* Boston, 1798.

————. *Sarah, or the Exemplary Wife.* Boston, 1813.

————. *Trials of the Human Heart.* 4 vols. Philadelphia, 1795.

————. *A Present for Young Ladies; Containing Poems, Dialogues, Addresses, &c. as Recited by the Pupils of Mrs. Rowson's Academy.* Boston, 1811.

————. *The Slaves of Algiers.* Philadelphia, 1794.

[Rush, Rebecca.] *Kelroy, a Novel.* Philadelphia, 1812.

Sabin, Elijah R. *The Life and Reflections of Charles Observator.* Boston, 1816.

St. Herbert, a Tale. Windsor, Conn., 1813.

St. Hubert; or, Mistaken Friendship. District of Columbia, 1800.

[Sansay, Leonora?] *Laura.* Philadelphia, 1809.

————. *Secret History; or, The Horrors of St. Domingo.* Philadelphia, 1808.

[Sargent, Charles Lenox.] *The Life of Alexander Smith, Captain of the Island of Pitcairn,* Boston, 1819.

[Savage, Sarah.] *The Factory Girl.* Boston, 1814.

————. *Filial Affection, or the Clergyman's Granddaughter.* Boston, 1820.

Seaborn, Captain Adam [pseud.] *Symzonia: A Voyage of Discovery.* New York, 1820. Subsequent edition: Edited by J. O. Bailey. Gainesville, Fla.: Scholars' Facsimiles & Reprints, 1965 (R).

Sherburne, Henry. *The Oriental Philanthropist, or True Republican.* Portsmouth, N.H., 1800.

[Silliman, Benjamin.] *Letters of Shahcoolen, a Hindu Philosopher, Residing in Philadelphia.* Boston, 1802. Subsequent edition: A facsimile reproduction with an introduction by Ben H. Mc-

Clary. Gainesville, Fla.: Scholars' Facsimiles & Reprints, 1962 (R).

——. *A Sketch of the Life and Character of President Dwight.* New Haven, Conn., 1817.

Soldier's Orphan, The; see Finch, John.

[Spafford, Horatio Gates.] *The Mother-in-Law: or Memoirs of Madam De Morville. By Maria Ann Burlingham.* Boston, 1817.

[Tenney, Tabitha.] *Female Quixotism: Exhibited in the Romantic Opinions and Extravagant Adventures of Dorcasina Sheldon.* 2 vols. Boston, 1801.

[Tucker, George.] *Letters from Virginia, Translated from the French.* Baltimore, 1816.

——. *Essays on Various Subjects of Taste, Morals, and National Policy.* Georgetown, D.C., 1822.

Tucker, George. "Discourse on American Literature," *Southern Literary Messenger* 4(1838): 81-88.

[Tyler, Royall.] *The Algerine Captive; or, The Life and Adventures of Doctor Updike Underhill.* 2 vols. Walpole, N.H., 1797 (R). Subsequent edition: With an introduction by Jack B. Moore. Gainesville, Fla.: Scholars' Facsimiles & Reprints, 1967.

——. *The Verse of Royall Tyler.* Edited (with an introduction) by Marius B. Péladeau. Charlottesville: University Press of Virginia, 1968.

——. *The Yankey in London.* Vol. 1 [no more published]. New York, 1809.

Vain Cottager, The: or, The History of Lucy Franklin. New Haven, Conn., 1807.

[Vickery, Sukey.] *Emily Hamilton, a Novel.* Worcester, Mass., 1803.

[Waln, Robert.] *The Hermit in America on a Visit to Philadelphia.* ...*Edited by Peter Atall, Esq.* Philadelphia, 1819.

——. *American Bards. A Satire.* Philadelphia, 1820.

[Warren, Caroline Matilda.] *The Gamesters; or, Ruins of Innocence.* Boston, 1805.

[Waterhouse, Benjamin, ed.?] *A Journal of a Young Man of Massachusetts.* Boston, 1816 (R). Reprinted in *Magazine of History* 5, extra no. 18. New York: William Abbatt, 1911.

Watterston, George. *Glencarn; or, The Disappointment of Youth.* 2 vols. in 1. Alexandria, Pa., 1810.

[Watterston, George.] *The Lawyer, or Man as he ought not to be.* Pittsburgh, 1808.

Watterston, George. *The Child of Feeling. A Comedy.* George Town, D.C., 1809.

[Watterston, George.] *The L... Family at Washington; or, A Winter in the Metropolis.* Washington, 1822.

———. *Letters from Washington...By a Foreigner.* Washington, 1818.

Wells, Helena. *Constantia Neville; or, The West Indian.* 3 vols. 2d ed., London, 1800.

———. *The Step-Mother; a Domestic Tale, from Real Life. By Helena Wells, of Charles Town, South-Carolina.* 2 vols. 2d ed. London, 1799.

Williams, William. *Mr. Penrose: The Journal of Penrose, Seaman. By William Williams, 1727-91.* With an introduction and notes by David Howard Dickason. Bloomington and London: Indiana University Press, 1969.

[Wirt, William.] *The Letters of the British Spy.* 2d ed. Richmond, Va., 1803.

———. *The Old Bachelor.* Richmond, Va., 1814.

Wollstonecraft, Mary; see Imlay, Gilbert.

[Wood, Sarah.] *Amelia; or, The Influence of Virtue.* Portsmouth, N.H., 1802.

———. *Dorval, or the Speculator.* Portsmouth, N.H., 1801.

———. *Ferdinand and Elmira: A Russian Story.* Baltimore, 1804.

———. *Julia, and the Illuminated Baron.* Portsmouth, N.H., 1800.

———. *Tales of the Night.* Portland, N.H., 1827.

———. "War, the Parent of Domestic Calamity: A Tale of the Revolution," *A Handful of Spice: Essays in Maine History and Literature.* Edited by Richard S. Sprague. Orono: University of Maine Press, 1968. Pp. 53-105. (This tale is introduced by an article by Hilda M. Fife, "An Unpublished MS. by Madam Wood," pp. 41-51.)

Woodworth, Samuel. *The Champions of Freedom, or the Mysterious Chief.* 2 vols. New York, 1816.

———. *The Poems, Odes, Songs, and other Metrical Effusions.* New York, 1818.

Yankee Traveller, The; or the Adventures of Hector Wigler. Concord, Mass., 1817.

For the periodicals of the age, consult the footnotes.

Section Two

Allen, Ethan. *The Narrative of Colonel Ethan Allen.* 1779. Introduction by Brooke Hindle. New York: Corinth Books, 1961.

American Spectator, The, or Matrimonial Preceptor. Boston, 1797.

Austin, William. *Letters from London.* Boston, 1804.

Barlow, Joel. *The Political Writings of Joel Barlow.* A new edition, corrected. New York, 1796.

Bartram, William. *Travels through North and South Carolina, Georgia, East and West Florida....* 1791. Edited by Mark Van Doren. New York: Dover Publications, 1928.

Bentley, William. *The Diary of William Bentley.* 4 vols. Salem, Mass.: The Essex Institute, 1905.

Bernard, John. *Retrospections of America, 1797-1811.* New York, 1887.

Bowne, Eliza Southgate. *A Girl's Life Eighty Years Ago: Selections from the Letters of Eliza Southgate Bowne.* Introduction by Clarence Cook. New York, 1887.

Breck, Samuel. *Recollections of Samuel Breck.* Edited by H. E. Scudder. Philadelphia, 1877.

Bristed, John. *The Resources of the U.S.A.* New York, 1818.

Brown, Solyman. *An Essay on American Poetry.* New Haven, Conn., 1818.

Buckingham, Joseph Tinker. *Personal Memoirs and Recollections of Editorial Life.* 2 vols. Boston, 1852.

Burr, Aaron. *Correspondence of Aaron Burr and his Daughter Theodosia.* Edited by Mark Van Doren (with a preface). New York: Covici-Friede, 1929.

Butler, James. *American Bravery Displayed.* Carlisle, Pa., 1816.

Cady, Edwin H., ed. *Literature of the Early Republic.* New York: Rinehart, 1950.

Channing, William Ellery. "Remarks on National Literature," *Christian Examiner* 7(1830):269-80.

Cobbett, William. *Porcupine's Works.* 12 vols. London, 1801.

Cooper, Thomas. *Some Information Respecting America.* London, 1794.

Cooper, William. *A Guide in the Wilderness.* Dublin, Ireland, 1810.

Cowles, Julia. *The Diaries of Julia Cowles: A Connecticut Record, 1797-1803.* Edited by Laura Hadley Moseley. New Haven, Conn.: Yale University Press, 1931.

Crafts, William. *Address Delivered before the New-England Society of South Carolina.* Charleston, 1820.

Crèvecoeur, Hector St. John de. *Letters from an American Farmer.* 1782. Introduction and notes by W. B. Blake. Everyman's Library. London: Dent; New York: Dutton, 1945.

Dana, Richard Henry. *Poems and Prose Writings.* 2 vols. New York, 1851.

Davis, John. *Travels of Four Years and a Half in the U.S.A.* London, 1803.

Drayton, John. *Letters Written during a Tour through the Northern and Eastern States of America.* Charleston, S.C., 1794.

Dunlap, William. *Diary of William Dunlap.* 3 vols. New York Historical Society, 1930.

————. *A History of the American Theatre.* New York, 1832.

————. *The Life of Charles Brockden Brown.* 2 vols. Philadelphia, 1815. (This work contains reprints of some of Brown's writings: "Alcuin [2d dialogue]," 1:75-105; "Jessica," 1:108-69; "Memoirs of Stephen Calvert," 2:274-472; "Sketches of a History of Carsol," 1:170-258; "Sketches of a History of the Carrils and Ormes," 1:262-396; "Thessalonica," 2:170-99.)

Dwight, Timothy. *A Discourse on Some Events of the Last Century.* New Haven, Conn., 1801.

————. *An Essay on the Stage.* Middletown, Conn., 1824.

————. *The Folly, Guilt, and Mischiefs of Duelling.* Hartford, Conn., 1805.

————. *Remarks on the Review of Inchiquin's Letters.* Boston, 1815.

————. *Travels in New-England and New-York.* 1821-22. 4 vols. London, 1823.

Fay, Joseph Dewey. *Essays of Howard: Or, Tales of the Prison.* New York, 1811.

Flint, Timothy. "Sketches of the Literature of the U.S.A.," *The Athenaeum,* July 4–Nov. 7, 1835, pp. 511-12, 526-27, 584-86, 624-25, 666-68, 696-98, 714-16, 782-83, 802-3, 817-19, 831-32.

Fuller, Margaret. *Papers on Literature and Art.* New York, 1846.

Goodrich, Samuel Griswold. *Recollections of a Lifetime.* 2 vols. New York, 1856.

Hall, Sarah. *Selections from the Writings of Mrs. Sarah Hall.* Philadelphia, 1833.

Hamilton, Alexander. *Gentleman's Progress: The Itinerarium of Dr.*

Alexander Hamilton. 1744. Edited by Carl Bridenbaugh (with an introduction). Chapel Hill: University of North Carolina Press, 1948.

Harris, Thaddeus Mason. *The Journal of a Tour into the Territory Northwest of the Alleghany Mountains*. Boston, 1805.

Hazlitt, William. "W. E. Channing, Sermons and Tracts," review in the *Edinburgh Review* (Oct., 1829), contained in *The Complete Works of William Hazlitt*. Edited by P. P. Howe. 21 vols. London: Dent, 1930-34. 16:318-38.

Heckewelder, John. *Thirty Thousand Miles with John Heckewelder*. Edited by Paul A. W. Wallace. Pittsburgh: University of Pittsburgh Press, 1958.

Hilliard d'Auberteuil, Michel René. *Miss McCrea: A Novel of the American Revolution*. 1784. A facsimile reproduction together with a translation from the French by Eric LaGuardia. Introduction by Lewis Leary. Gainesville, Fla.: Scholars' Facsimiles & Reprints, 1958.

Holmes, Abiel. *American Annals*. 2 vols. Cambridge, Mass., 1805.

Hubbell, Jay B., ed. *American Life in Literature*. Rev. ed. 2 vols. New York: Harper & Row, 1949.

Hyde, Nancy Maria. *The Writings of Nancy Maria Hyde of Norwich, Conn. Connected with a Sketch of her Life* (The "Sketch" by Lydia Huntley Sigourney). Norwich, Conn., 1816.

Janson, Charles William. *The Stranger in America, 1793-1806*. 1807. Introduction and notes by Carl S. Driver. New York: Wilson-Erickson, 1935.

Kendall, Edward Augustus. *Travels through the Northern Parts of the U.S.* 3 vols. New York, 1809.

Kinloch, Francis. *Letters from Geneva and France...Addressed to a Lady in Virginia. By her Father*. 2 vols. Boston, 1819.

Ladd, Joseph Brown. *The Literary Remains of Joseph Brown Ladd ...To which Is Prefixed a Sketch of the Author's Life*. New York, 1832.

Lambert, John. *Travels through Lower Canada, and the U.S. of North America*. 3 vols. London, 1810.

Lewis, Meriwether, and William Clark. *The Journals of Lewis and Clark*. A new selection with an introduction by John Bakeless. New York: The New American Library, 1964.

Linn, John Blair. *Miscellaneous Works, Prose and Poetical, By a Young Gentleman of New York*. New York, 1795.

————. *The Powers of Genius.* 2d ed., corrected and enlarged. Philadelphia, 1802.

Marshall, John. *The Life of George Washington.* 5 vols. Philadelphia, 1804-7.

Melish, John. *Travels in the U.S.A.* 2 vols. Philadelphia, 1812.

Miller, Samuel. *A Brief Retrospect of the Eighteenth Century.* 1803. Part the First, 3 vols. London, 1805.

————. "Sermon on the Burning of the Theatre at Richmond," in *A Serious Inquiry into the Nature and Effects of the Stage,* by John Witherspoon. New York, 1812.

Morton, Sarah Wentworth. *Beacon Hill: A Local Poem, Historic and Descriptive.* Book I. Boston, 1797.

————. *Ouâbi: or the Virtues of Nature, an Indian Tale in Four Cantos.* Boston, 1790.

Nott, Eliphalet. *The Addresses, Delivered...at the Anniversary Commencement in Union College.* Schenectady, N.Y., 1814.

————. *Miscellaneous Works.* Schenectady, N.Y., 1810.

Ogilvie, James. "On the Modern Abuse of Moral Fiction, in the Shape of Novels," *Philosophical Essays.* Philadelphia, 1816. Pp. 148-266.

Parkinson, Richard. *A Tour in America.* 2 vols. London, 1805.

Priest, William. *Travels in the U.S.A.* London, 1802.

Ramsay, David. *The Life of George Washington.* New York, 1807.

Ray, William. *The American Tars in Tripolitan Slavery.* Troy, N.Y., 1808. Reprinted in the *Magazine of History,* extra no. 14. New York: William Abbatt, 1911 (R).

————. *Poems, on Various Subjects, Religious, Moral, Sentimental and Humorous.* Auburn, N.Y., 1821.

Rush, Benjamin. *Essays, Literary, Moral and Philosophical.* Philadelphia, 1798.

————. *Letters of Benjamin Rush.* Edited by L. H. Butterfield. 2 vols. Princeton, N.J.: Princeton University Press, 1951.

Sampson, Ezra. *The Brief Remarker on the Ways of Man.* Hudson, N.Y., 1818.

Sands, Robert Charles. *The Writings of Robert Charles Sands, in Prose and Verse. With a Memoir of the Author.* 2 vols. 2d ed., New York, 1835.

Sanford, Charles L., ed. *Quest for America, 1810-1824.* Garden City, N.Y.: Doubleday, 1964.

Sigourney, Lydia Huntley. *Moral Pieces, in Prose and Verse*. Hartford, Conn., 1815.

Simms, William Gilmore. *Views and Reviews in American Literature, History and Fiction*. First series. New York, 1845. Subsequent edition: Edited by C. Hugh Holman. Cambridge, Mass.: Harvard University Press, 1962 (R).

Simpson, Lewis P., ed. *The Federalist Literary Mind: Selections from the "Monthly Anthology and Boston Review," 1803-1811*. Baton Rouge: Louisiana State University Press, 1962.

Spiller, Robert E., ed. *The American Literary Revolution, 1783-1837*. Garden City, N.Y.: Doubleday, and New York University Press, 1967.

Spiller, Robert E., and Harold Blodgett, eds. *The Roots of National Culture*. Rev. ed. New York: Macmillan, 1949.

Sutcliff, Robert. *Travels in Some Parts of North America*. York, England, 1811.

Taft, Kendall B., ed. *Minor Knickerbockers*. American Writers Series. New York: American Book Co., 1947.

Thomas, Isaiah. *The History of Printing in America*. 2 vols. 2d ed. Transactions and Collections of the American Antiquarian Society. Vols. 5 & 6. Albany, New York, 1874.

Trumbull, Benjamin. *A Century Sermon, or Sketches of the History of the Eighteenth Century*. New Haven, Conn., 1801.

Trumbull, John. *The Autobiography of Col. John Trumbull, Patriot-Artist, 1756-1843*. Edited by Theodore Sizer. New Haven, Conn.: Yale University Press, 1953.

Tryon, Warren S., ed. *A Mirror for Americans*. 3 vols. Chicago: University of Chicago Press, 1952. (Abr. ed., *My Native Land*. Chicago: University of Chicago Press, 1961.)

Tudor, William. *Letters on the Eastern States*. New York, 1820.

Verplanck, Gulian Crommelin. *Ceremony of the Installation of David Hosack...as President of the New-York Historical Society*. New York, 1820.

———. *A Fable for Statesmen and Politicians of all Parties and Descriptions. By Abimelech Coody, Esq.* New York, 1815.

———. *The State Triumvirate, A Political Tale, and the Epistles of Brevet Major Puff*. New York, 1819.

Warren, Mercy Otis. *History of the Rise, Progress and Termination of the American Revolution*. 3 vols. Boston, 1805.

Webster, Noah. *A Collection of Essays and Fugitiv* [sic] *Writings.* Boston, 1790.

————. *A Collection of Papers on Political, Literary and Moral Subjects.* New York, 1843.

————. *Dissertations on the English Language.* Boston, 1789.

————. *Letters of Noah Webster.* Edited by H. R. Warfel (with an introduction). New York: Library Publishers, 1953.

————. *An Oration Pronounced before the Citizens of New-Haven ...July 4th, 1798.* New Haven, Conn., 1798.

————. *The Prompter; or a Commentary on Common Sayings and Subjects.* Hartford, Conn., 1791.

————. *The Revolution in France, Considered in Respect to its Progress and Effects.* New York, 1794.

Weems, Mason Locke. *God's Revenge against Adultery.* 2d ed. Philadelphia, 1816.

————. *God's Revenge against Gambling.* 4th ed. Philadelphia, 1822.

————. *A History of the Life and Death, Virtues and Exploits, of General George Washington.* 3d ed. Philadelphia [1800?].

————. *The Life of Washington.* 9th ed. Philadelphia, 1809. Subsequent edition: Edited by Marcus Cunliffe. Cambridge, Mass.: Harvard University Press, 1962.

Whittier, John Greenleaf. *Whittier on Writers and Writing: The Uncollected Critical Writings of John Greenleaf Whittier.* Edited by E. H. Cady and H. H. Clark. Syracuse, N.Y.: Syracuse University Press, 1950.

Willis, Nathaniel Parker. "Literature of the 19th Century: America," *The Athenaeum,* Jan. 3-Feb. 21, 1835, pp. 9-13, 52-55, 105-7, 147-50.

Section Three

Adkins, Nelson. *Philip Freneau and the Cosmic Enigma.* New York: New York University Press, 1949.

Almy, Robert Forbes. "The Role of the Club in American Literary History: 1700-1812." Ph.D. dissertation. Harvard University, 1935.

Angoff, Charles. *A Literary History of the American People* [to 1815]. 2 vols. New York: Knopf, 1931.

Axelrad, Jacob. *Philip Freneau, Champion of Democracy.* Austin: University of Texas Press, 1967.

Bailey, Marcia Edgerton. *A Lesser Hartford Wit, Dr. Elihu Hubbard Smith, 1771-1798.* University of Maine Studies, 2d series, no. 11. Orono, 1928.

Barnby, H. G. *The Prisoners of Algiers: An Account of the Forgotten American Algerian War.* New York: Oxford University Press, 1966.

Benson, Mary Sumner. *Women in Eighteenth-Century America.* New York: Columbia University Press, 1935.

Birkhead, Edith. *The Tale of Terror.* London: Constable, 1921.

Black, Frank Gees. *The Epistolary Novel in the Late Eighteenth Century.* Eugene: University of Oregon Press, 1940.

Bohner, Charles H. *John Pendleton Kennedy: Gentleman from Baltimore.* Baltimore: Johns Hopkins Press, 1961.

———. "*The Red Book*, 1819-1821: A Satire on Baltimore Society," *Maryland Historical Magazine* 51 (September, 1956): 175-87.

Bolwell, Robert Whitney. "Concerning the Study of Nationalism in American Literature," *AL* 10(1939):405-16.

Bowden, Edwin T. *The Dungeon of the Heart: Human Isolation and the American Novel.* New York: Macmillan, 1961.

Bradsher, Earl L. "Americanism in Literature," *SR* 35(1927):94-102.

———. *Mathew Carey, Editor, Author, and Publisher.* New York: Columbia University Press, 1912.

———. "Some Aspects of the Early American Novel," *Texas Review* 3(1918):241-58.

Brooks, Van Wyck. *The World of Washington Irving.* New York: World, 1944.

Brown, Clarence Arthur, ed. *The Achievement of American Criticism.* New York: Ronald Press, 1954.

Brown, Herbert Ross. "Elements of Sensibility in *The Massachusetts Magazine*," *AL* 1(November, 1929):286-96.

———. *The Sentimental Novel in America, 1789-1860.* Durham, N.C.: Duke University Press, 1940.

Bryan, William Alfred. *George Washington in American Literature, 1775-1865.* New York: Columbia University Press, 1952.

Cairns, William B. *British Criticisms of American Writings, 1783-1833.* University of Wisconsin Studies in Language and Literature, nos. 1 & 14. Madison, 1918-22.

Calder, Isabel M. *Colonial Captivities, Marches and Journeys.* New York: Macmillan, 1935.

Calhoun, Arthur W. *A Social History of the American Family.* 1918. Reprint. 3 vols. New York: Barnes & Noble, 1960.

Callow, James T. *Kindred Spirits: Knickerbocker Writers and American Artists, 1807-1855.* Chapel Hill: University of North Carolina Press, 1967.

Carleton, Phillips D. "The Indian Captivity," *AL* 15(May, 1943): 169-80.

Charvat, William. *Literary Publishing in America, 1790-1850.* Philadelphia: University of Pennsylvania Press, 1959.

———. *The Origins of American Critical Thought, 1810-1835.* 1936. Reprint. New York: A. S. Barnes, 1961.

———. *The Profession of Authorship in America, 1800-1870: The Papers of William Charvat.* Edited by Matthew J. Bruccoli. Columbus: Ohio State University Press, 1968.

Chase, Richard. *The American Novel and its Tradition.* Garden City, N.Y.: Doubleday, 1957.

Christadler, Martin. *Der amerikanische Essay 1720-1820.* Heidelberg: Carl Winter, 1968.

———. "Politische Diskussion and literarische Form in der amerikanischen Literatur der Revolutionszeit," *JA* 13(1968):13-33.

Clark, David Lee. *Charles Brockden Brown—Pioneer Voice of America.* Durham, N.C.: Duke University Press, 1952.

Clark, Harry Hayden. "The Influence of Science on American Ideas from 1775 to 1809," *Trans. Wisc.* 35(1943):305-49.

———. "Nationalism in American Literature," *UTQ* 2(1933):492-519.

———. "What Made Freneau the Father of American Prose?" *Trans. Wisc.* 25(1930):35-50.

———, ed. *Transitions in American Literary History.* Durham, N.C.: Duke University Press, 1953.

Coad, Oral Sumner. "The Gothic Element in American Literature before 1835," *JEGP* 24(January, 1925):72-93.

———. *William Dunlap.* New York: The Dunlap Society, 1917.

Cole, Charles W. "Jeremy Belknap: Pioneer Nationalist," *NEQ* 10(1937):743-51.

Cowie, Alexander. *The Rise of the American Novel.* New York: American Book Co., 1948.

Cronin, James E. "Elihu Hubbard Smith and the New York Friendly Club, 1795-1798," *PMLA* 64(1949):471-79.

Cunliffe, Marcus. *The Nation Takes Shape, 1789-1837*. Chicago: University of Chicago Press, 1959.

Curti, Merle. *The Growth of American Thought*. 3d ed. New York: Harper & Row, 1964.

Davidson, Marshall B. *Life in America*. 2 vols. Boston: Houghton, Mifflin, 1951.

Davis, David Brion. *Homicide in American Fiction, 1789-1860*. Ithaca, N.Y.: Cornell University Press, 1957.

Davis, Richard Beale. *Intellectual Life in Jefferson's Virginia, 1790-1830*. Chapel Hill: University of North Carolina Press, 1964.

―――. "The Virginia Novel before *Swallow Barn*," *VMHB* 71(1963): 278-93.

Dickinson, A. T., Jr. *American Historical Fiction*. 2d ed. New York: The Scarecrow Press, 1963.

Diebels, M. Chrysostom. *Peter Markoe (1752?-1792): A Philadelphia Writer*. Washington, D.C.: The Catholic University of America Press, 1944.

Ellis, (Harold) Milton. *Joseph Dennie and his Circle*. Austin: University of Texas Press, 1915.

Feidelson, Charles, Jr. *Symbolism and American Literature*. Chicago: University of Chicago Press, 1953.

Fiedler, Leslie A. *Love and Death in the American Novel*. New York: Criterion Books, 1960. Rev. ed. New York: Stein & Day, 1966.

Field, Vena Bernadette. *Constantia: A Study of the Life and Works of Judith Sargent Murray, 1751-1820*. University of Maine Studies, 2d series, no 17. Orono, 1931.

Fishwick, Marshall W. "*The Portico* and Literary Nationalism after the War of 1812," *WMQ* 3d series, 8(1951):238-45.

Folsom, James K. *Timothy Flint*. New York: Twayne, 1965.

Foster, James R. *History of the Pre-Romantic Novel in England*. New York: MLA; London: Oxford University Press, 1949.

Free, William. *The "Columbian Magazine" and American Literary Nationalism*. The Hague: Mouton, 1968.

―――. "A Lost American Critical Document," *EALN* 1(Winter, 1966-67): 8-10. *See also* Goldberg, J. Philip.

Gabriel, Ralph Henry. *The Course of American Democratic Thought*. 2d ed. New York: Ronald Press, 1956.

Goldberg, J. Philip. "Some Conjecture upon John Shippen's 'Ob-

servations on Novel Reading,'" *EALN* 2(Spring, 1967):6-11.
See also Free, William.

Granger, Bruce I. "From Silence Dogood to Launcelot Langstaff,"
EALN 3(Spring, 1968):11-16.

―――. *Political Satire in the American Revolution, 1763-1783.*
Ithaca, N.Y.: Cornell University Press, 1960.

Greene, Sue N. "The Contribution of the *Monthly Anthology and
Boston Review* to the Development of the Golden Age of
American Letters." Ph.D. dissertation. Michigan State University, 1965.

Haight, Gordon S. *Mrs. Sigourney, the Sweet Singer of Hartford.*
New Haven, Conn.: Yale University Press, 1930.

Harrington, Richard P. "The *Monthly Anthology and Boston Review, 1803-1811*: Literary Excellence as Interpreted by 'A Society of Gentlemen.'" Ph.D. dissertation, University of Texas,
1965.

Hart, James D. *The Popular Book: A History of America's Literary
Taste.* New York: Oxford University Press, 1950.

Hastings, George E. "How Cooper Became a Novelist," *AL* 12
(March, 1940): 20-51.

―――. "John Bull and his American Descendants," *AL* 1(March,
1929):40-68.

Hazard, Lucy Lockwood. *The Frontier in American Literature.* New
York: Crowell, 1927.

Hedges, William L. *Washington Irving: An American Study, 1802-
1832.* Baltimore: The Johns Hopkins Press, 1965.

Heidler, Joseph B. *The History, from 1700 to 1800, of English Criticism of Prose Fiction.* University of Illinois Studies in Language
and Literature, Vol. 13, no. 2. Urbana, 1928.

Heilman, Robert B. *America in English Fiction, 1760-1800.* Baton
Rouge: Louisiana State University Press, 1937.

Hemenway, Robert. "Fiction in the Age of Jefferson: The Early
American Novel as Intellectual Document," *Midcontinent
American Studies Journal* 9(Spring, 1968):91-102.

Herron, Ima Honaker. *The Small Town in American Literature.*
Durham, N.C.: Duke University Press, 1939.

Hoffman, Daniel G. *Form and Fable in American Fiction.* New
York: Oxford University Press, 1961.

Holt, Charles C. "Short Fiction in American Periodicals: 1775-1820."
Ph.D. dissertation. Auburn University, 1968.

Hornberger, Theodore. "A Note on Eighteenth-Century American Prose Style," *AL* 10(March, 1938):77-78.

Horner, Joyce M. *The English Women Novelists and their Connection with the Feminist Movement (1688-1797).* Smith College Studies in Modern Languages, Vol. 11, nos. 1-3. Northampton, Mass., 1929-30.

Horton, Rod W., and Herbert W. Edwards. *Backgrounds of American Literary Thought.* 1952. Reprint. New York: Appleton-Century-Crofts, 1967.

Hubbell, Jay B. *The South in American Literature, 1607-1900.* Durham, N.C.: Duke University Press, 1954.

———. *South and Southwest: Literary Essays and Reminiscences.* Durham, N.C.: Duke University Press, 1965.

Isani, Mukhtar A. "The Oriental Tale in America through 1865: A Study in American Fiction." Ph.D. dissertation. Princeton University, 1962.

Jones, Howard Mumford. *America and French Culture, 1750-1848.* Chapel Hill: University of North Carolina Press, 1927.

———. *Ideas in America.* Cambridge, Mass.: Harvard University Press, 1945.

———. *Jeffersonianism and the American Novel.* New York: Teachers College Press, 1966.

———. *The Theory of American Literature.* Ithaca, N.Y.: Cornell University Press, 1948.

Keiser, Albert. *The Indian in American Literature.* New York: Oxford University Press, 1933.

Kellogg, Thelma Louise. *The Life and Works of John Davis, 1774-1853.* University of Maine Studies, 2d series, no. 1. Orono, 1924.

Kennedy, Julia A. *George Watterston, Novelist, "Metropolitan Author," and Critic.* Washington, D.C.: Catholic University of America, 1933.

Knight, Grant C. *The Novel in English.* New York: Richard R. Smith, 1931.

Koskimies, R. *Theorie des Romans.* Annales Academiae Scientarum Fennicae, B, 35(1), Helsinki, 1935.

Kraus, Michael. *The Atlantic Civilization: Eighteenth-Century Beginnings.* Ithaca, N.Y.: Cornell University Press, 1949.

Krout, John Allen, and Dixon Ryan Fox. *The Completion of Independence, 1790-1830.* A History of American Life. Edited by

A. M. Schlesinger and D. R. Fox. Vol. 5. New York: Macmillan, 1944.

Lange, Viktor, "Erzählformen im Roman des 18. Jahrhunderts," *Anglia* 76(1958):129-44.

Leary, Lewis. "John Blair Linn, 1777-1805," *WMQ*, 3d series, 4(April, 1947):148-76.

————. *That Rascal Freneau.* 1941. Reprint. New York: Octagon Books, 1964.

Lehmann-Haupt, Hellmut, in collaboration with Lawrence C. Wroth and Rollo G. Silver. *The Book in America.* New York: R. R. Bowker Co., 1951.

Leisy, Ernest E. *The American Historical Novel.* Norman: University of Oklahoma Press, 1950.

Lewis, R. W. B. *The American Adam: Innocence, Tragedy, and Tradition in the Nineteenth Century.* Chicago: University of Chicago Press, 1955.

Loshe, Lillie Deming. *The Early American Novel.* New York: Columbia University Press, 1907. 2d ed., 1930. Reprint. New York: Frederick Ungar, 1958.

Lüdeke, Henry. *Geschichte der amerikanischen Literatur.* 2d ed. Bern: Francke Verlag, 1963.

McClosky, J. C. "The Campaign of Periodicals after the War of 1812 for a National American Literature," *PMLA* 50(1935): 262-73.

McDowell, Tremaine. "Sensibility in the Eighteenth-Century American Novel," *SP* 24(1927):383-402.

Macy, John. *The Spirit of American Literature.* New York: Doubleday, Page, 1913.

Male, Roy R. "The Story of the Mysterious Stranger in American Fiction," *Criticism* 3(1961):281-94.

Marchand, Ernest. "The Literary Opinions of Charles Brockden Brown," *SP* 31(1934):541-66.

Marovitz, Sanford E. "Frontier Conflicts: Villains, Outlaws, and Indians in Selected 'Western' Fiction: 1799-1860." Ph.D. dissertation. Duke University, 1968.

Marsh, Philip M. *Philip Freneau, Poet and Journalist.* Minneapolis: Dillon, 1967.

Martin, Harold C. "The Development of Style in 19th-Century American Fiction," *Style in Prose Fiction.* English Institute

Essays, 1958. Edited by H. C. Martin. New York: Columbia
University Press, 1959. Pp. 114-41.
Martin, Terence. "Social Institutions in the Early American Novel,"
AQ 9(Spring, 1957):72-84.
————. *The Instructed Vision: Scottish Common Sense Philosophy
and the Origins of American Fiction.* Bloomington: Indiana
University Press, 1961.
Mott, Frank Luther. *Golden Multitudes: The Story of Best Sellers
in the U.S.* New York: Macmillan, 1947.
————. *A History of American Magazines.* 5 vols., especially Vol.
1, 1741-1850. Reprint. Cambridge, Mass.: Harvard Univer-
sity Press, 1957.
Nelson, Arnold Gerhard. "Class and Status in the American Novel,
1789-1850." Master's thesis. University of Minnesota, 1952.
Newlin, Claude M. *The Life and Writings of Hugh Henry Bracken-
ridge.* Princeton, N.J.: Princeton University Press, 1932.
Nye, Russel Blaine. *The Cultural Life of the New Nation, 1776-1830.*
1960. Reprint. New York: Harper & Row, 1963.
Orians, G. Harrison. "Censure of Fiction in American Romances
and Magazines, 1789-1810," *PMLA* 52(1937):195-214.
————. "The Romance Ferment after *Waverley*," *AL* 3(1932):
408-31.
Osborne, William S. "The 'Swiss Traveller' Essays: Earliest Literary
Writings of John Pendleton Kennedy," *AL* 30(1958):228-33.
Paine, Gregory. "American Literature a Hundred and Fifty Years
Ago," *SP* 42(1945):383-402.
Papashvily, Helen Waite. *All the Happy Endings.* New York: Har-
per, 1956.
Parrington, Vernon Louis. *Main Currents in American Thought.* 3
vols. New York: Harcourt, Brace, 1927-30.
Parrington, Vernon Louis, Jr. *American Dreams: A Study of Ameri-
can Utopias.* Providence, R.I.: Brown University, 1947.
Pattee, Fred Lewis. *The First Century of American Literature, 1770-
1870.* New York: Appleton-Century, 1935.
Pearce, Roy Harvey. *The Savages of America: A Study of the Indian
and the Idea of Civilization.* Baltimore: The Johns Hopkins
Press, 1953. Rev. ed., 1965.
Peckham, Howard H. *Captured by Indians.* New Brunswick, N.J.:
Rutgers University Press, 1954.
Pendleton, Emily, and Milton Ellis. *Philenia: The Life and Works*

of Sarah Wentworth Morton, 1759-1846. University of Maine Studies, 2d series, no. 20. Orono, 1931.

Pochman, Henry A. *German Culture in America.* Madison: University of Wisconsin Press, 1957.

Pretzer, Wallace L. "18th-Century Literary Conventions in the Fictional Style of John Pendleton Kennedy." Ph.D. dissertation. University of Michigan, 1963.

Quinn, Arthur Hobson. *American Fiction.* New York: Appleton-Century, 1936.

————. "Some Phases of the Supernatural in American Literature," *PMLA* 25(1910):114-33.

Raddin, George Gates, Jr. *An Early New York Library of Fiction.* New York: H. W. Wilson, 1940.

Redden, Sr. M. Mauritia. *The Gothic Fiction in the American Magazines (1765-1800).* Washington D.C.: Catholic University of America, 1939.

Redekop, Ernest. "The Redmen: Some Representations of Indians in American Literature Before the Civil War," *CAAS Bul.* 3(Winter, 1968):1-44.

Richards, Irving Trefethen. "The Life and Works of John Neal." 4 vols. Ph.D. dissertation. Harvard University, 1932.

Riese, Teut. *Das englische Erbe in der amerikanischen Literatur.* Beiträge zur englischen Philologie, 39. Heft. Bochum-Langendreer: Verlag Heinrich Pöppinghaus, 1958.

Ringe, Donald A. *Charles Brockden Brown.* New York: Twayne, 1966.

Rothwell, Kenneth S. "Another View of *The Fredoniad*: A Plea for Method," *AL* 33(1961):373-78. (This is a reply to Squier, below.)

Rourke, Constance. *The Roots of American Culture and other Essays.* Edited by Van Wyck Brooks. New York: Harcourt Brace, 1942.

Rubin, Louis D., Jr., and John R. Moore, eds. *The Idea of an American Novel.* New York: Crowell, 1961.

Ryder, Frank G., ed. *George Ticknor's The Sorrows of Young Werter.* With an introduction and critical analysis. University of North Carolina Studies in Comparative Literature, no. 4. 1952. Reprint. New York: Johnson Reprint Co., 1966.

Sanford, Charles L. *The Quest for Paradise: Europe and the Ameri-*

can Moral Imagination. Urbana: University of Illinois Press, 1961.

Scudder, Horace H. "What Mr. Cooper Read to His Wife," *SR* 36(1928):177-94.

Shipton, Clifford K. *Isaiah Thomas, Printer, Patriot, and Philanthropist, 1749-1831*. Rochester, N.Y., 1948.

Shoemaker, Erwin C. *Noah Webster*. New York: Columbia University Press, 1936.

Silver, Rollo G. *The American Printer, 1787-1825*. Charlottesville: University of Virginia Press, 1967.

Simpson, Lewis P. "Federalism and the Crisis of Literary Order," *AL* 32(1960):253-66.

Singer, Godfrey Frank. *The Epistolary Novel*. Philadelphia: University of Pennsylvania, 1933.

Snell, George. *The Shapers of American Fiction, 1798-1947*. New York: Dutton, 1947.

Spencer, Benjamin T. *The Quest for Nationality*. Syracuse, N.Y.: Syracuse University Press, 1957.

Spiller, Robert E. "Critical Standards in the American Romantic Movement," *CE* 8(1947):344-52.

———. "The Verdict of Sydney Smith," *AL* 1(March, 1929):3-13.

Spingarn, Lawrence P. "The Yankee in Early American Fiction," *NEQ* 31(1958):484-95.

Spurlin, Paul M. "Rousseau in America, 1760-1809," *The French-American Review* 1(1948):8-16.

Squier, Charles L. "Dulness in America: A Study in Epic Badness: *The Fredoniad*," *AL* 32(1961):446-54. *See also* Rothwell, Kenneth.

Stanzel, Franz. *Die typischen Erzählsituationen im Roman*. Wiener Beiträge zur englischen Philologie, 63. Band. Wien, Stuttgart: Wilhelm Braumüller, 1955.

Stein, Roger B. "Royall Tyler and the Question of Our Speech," *NEQ* 38(1965):454-74.

Strozier, Robert. "*Wieland* and Other Romances: Horror in Parentheses," *Emerson Soc. Quart.* 50(1st quarter, 1968):sup. 24-29.

Sweet, William Warren. *Religion in the Development of American Culture, 1765-1840*. New York: Scribner's, 1952.

Tanselle, G. Thomas, ed. "Author and Publisher in 1800: Letters of Royall Tyler and Joseph Nancrede," *HLB* 15(1967):129-39.

————. *Royall Tyler*. Cambridge, Mass: Harvard University Press, 1967.

Taylor, John Tinnon. *Early Opposition to the English Novel*. New York: King's Crown Press, 1943.

Tompkins, J. M. S. *The Polite Marriage*. Cambridge: Cambridge University Press, 1938.

————. *The Popular Novel in England 1770-1800*. 1932. Reprint. Lincoln: University of Nebraska Press, 1961.

Tyler, Moses Coit. *The Literary History of the American Revolution, 1763-1783*. 2 vols. New York, 1897. Reprint. New York: Barnes & Noble, 1940.

Vail, R. W. G. *The Voice of the Old Frontier*. Philadelphia: University of Pennsylvania Press, 1949.

Van Doren, Carl. *The American Novel, 1789-1939*. Revised and enlarged edition. New York: Macmillan, 1940.

Wagenknecht, Edward. *Cavalcade of the American Novel*. New York: Holt, 1952.

————. *Washington Irving: Moderation Displayed*. New York: Oxford University Press, 1962.

Warfel, Harry R. *Charles Brockden Brown, American Gothic Novelist*. Gainesville: University of Florida Press, 1949.

Whipple, Edwin P. "A Century of American Literature," *The First Century of the Republic: A Review of American Progress*. New York, 1876. Pp. 349-98.

Williams, Stanley T. *The Life of Washington Irving*. 2 vols. New York: Oxford University Press, 1935.

Winston, George Parsons. "Washington Allston as a Man of Letters." Ph.D. dissertation. Syracuse University, 1955.

Wish, Harvey. *Society and Thought in Early America: A Social and Intellectual History of the American People through 1865*. 1950. Reprint. New York: David McKay, 1962.

Woodall, Guy R. "The Relationship of Robert Walsh, Jr., to the *Port-Folio* and the Dennie Circle, 1801-1812," *PMHB* 92 (1968): 195-219.

Woodress, James. *A Yankee's Odyssey: The Life of Joel Barlow*. Philadelphia: Lippincott, 1958.

Wright, Lyle H. *American Fiction, 1774-1850*. Rev. ed. San Marino, California: Huntington Library, 1948.

————. "A Statistical Survey of American Fiction, 1774-1850," *HLQ* 2 (1939): 309-18.

Wright, Walter Francis. *Sensibility in English Prose Fiction, 1760-1814.* Illinois Studies in Language and Literature, Vol. 22, nos. 3-4. Urbana, 1937.

Index

Addison, Joseph: in *The Spectator*, 114, 115, 116, 121
Adelaide. *See* Botsford, Margaret
Adelio. *See Journey to Philadelphia, A*
Adventures in a Castle, 308–9, 319, 404
Adventures of Alonso. *See* Digges, Thomas Atwood
Adventures of Jonathan Corncob, x, 157 n.51, 289–300, 405
Adventures of Uncle Sam, The (Frederick Augustus Fidfaddy), 99–101
Alcuin. *See* Brown, Charles Brockden
Allen, Ethan, 154 n.15, 465
Algerine Captive, The. *See* Tyler, Royall
Algerine Spy in Pennsylvania, The. *See* Markoe, Peter
Amelia, or the Faithless Briton, 206 n.6, 209 n.43, 264, 276 n.25, 372, 407
Amelia; or The Influence of Virtue. *See* Wood, Sarah
American Bee, The, 20 n.51, 154 n.18, 273 n.2, 330 n.38, 391 n.17
American Bravery Displayed, 303 n. 11, 395 n.61
Arbuthnot, John, 87, 88, 91, 99, 153 n.4
Arthur Mervyn. *See* Brown, Charles Brockden
Art of Courting, The. *See* Bradford, Ebenezer
Asylum, The. *See* Mitchell, Isaac
Austen, Jane, 29, 174, 184 n.18
Austin, William, 13, 155 n.22

Bage, Robert: *Hermsprong*, 207 n.20, 330 n.44
Bancroft, Edward, 221 n.28
Barlow, Joel: in *The Columbiad*, 94
Belknap, Jeremy, 87, 99, 389 n.6; *The Foresters*, 87–88, 90, 153 n.3
Bigelow, Jacob, and Nathan Hale, Jr., 101; *The War of the Gulls*, 101
Blair, Hugh, 18 n.34, 81 n.1
Bleecker, Ann Eliza, 35, 373, 376, 383; *History of Maria Kittle*, 35, 373–76, 390 n.7, 399, 429; "The Story of Henry and Anne," 391 n.23
Bloomfield, Obadiah Benjamin Franklin. *See* Franklin, Edward
Boarding School, The. *See* Foster, Hannah Webster
Botsford, Edmund, 81; *The Spiritual Voyage*, 66, 457
Botsford, Margaret, 196, 207 n.26; *Adelaide*, 196–99, 229 n.13, 392 n.34, 395 n.60, 399, 403–4
Brackenridge, Hugh Henry, 17 n.17, 20 n.63, 126, 141, 145, 147, 151, 152, 158 n.57, 161 n.96, 371, 389 n.5, 401; *Modern Chivalry*, 104, 109, 126–36, 161 n.93, 276 n.19, 289–90, 296–97, 305 n.39, n.41, 306 n.49, 392 n.36, 399, 443–45
Bradford, Ebenezer, 70; *The Art of Courting*, 70–71, 81, 83 n.12, 229 n.9
Brown, Charles Brockden, xii, 6, 16, 16 n.1, 17 n.12, 20 n.54, 69, 152, 160 n.77, 177, 182 n.1, 193, 194, 201, 233, 321, 325, 330 n.39, 333–34, 359, 361 n.15, 362 n.16, n.19, 364 n.33, n.36, 367 n.65, 368 n.74, 371, 372, 399, 401–2

[493]